AN INTRODUCTION TO

BIBLICAL
ETHICS

AN INTRODUCTION TO
BIBLICAL
ETHICS

ROBERTSON McQUILKIN

COLUMBIA
BIBLE COLLEGE AND SEMINARY

Tyndale House Publishers, Inc.
Wheaton, Illinois

The *"NIV"* and *"New
International Version"*
trademarks are registered in
the United States Patent and
Trademark Office by
International Bible Society.

Scripture quotations, unless
otherwise noted, are from the
Revised Standard Version,
copyright 1946, 1952, 1971 by
Division of Christian Education
of the National Council of
Churches of Christ in the
United States of America.

Quotations marked NIV are from
The Holy Bible, New
International Version, copyright
1973, 1978, 1984 by
International Bible Society.
Used by permission of
Zondervan Publishing House.
All rights reserved.

Quotations marked NEB are
from *The New English Bible*,
copyright 1961, 1970 by the
Delegates of the Oxford
University Press and the
Syndics of the Cambridge
University Press.

Quotations marked Phillips are
from *The New Testament in
Modern English,* translated by
J. B. Phillips; copyright 1958,
1959, 1960, 1972 by J. B.
Phillips.

Quotations marked NASB are
from the *New American
Standard Bible,* copyright
1960, 1962, 1963, 1968, 1971,
1972, 1973, 1975, 1977 by The
Lockman Foundation. Used by
permission.

Library of Congress Catalog
Card Number 88-50247
ISBN 0-8423-1619-1

Printed in the United States of
America

96 95 94 93 92
9   8   7   6   5   4

To

MURIEL

in whom the words
of this book have become
flesh to my eternal benefit

CONTENTS

Ethics might be called a system of

moral values and duties. It has to do with ideal human character, actions, and ends. What ought a person do or refrain from doing? What attitudes and behavior should be viewed as good? and *why* should they be considered good? What is the highest good, "the chief end of man," the purpose of human existence? These are the questions the study of ethics seeks to answer.

There are many approaches to discover answers to these questions, but the approach of this book is turning to Scripture and examining all texts that deal with each ethical question. We do this because of the conviction that the Bible is a revelation by God of his will for human behavior, and because of the confidence that it is fully trustworthy. Though we may utilize other sources for assistance in understanding and applying biblical truth, we shall treat the Bible as our final authority. And we will seek to apply biblical principles as well as direct mandates, but we will attempt to go only as far as Scripture itself goes and maintain the emphases of the Bible itself. So we call our study *Biblical Ethics*.

"An Introduction," as part of the title, implies that the study of any given ethical issue will not be exhaustive. Nevertheless, we will attempt to be comprehensive in two ways. First, we will accurately note all essential elements so that the student may expand his understanding through additional study with the confidence that his introductory foundation is reliable. Select and annotated bibliographies are provided on major issues. Second, we will attempt to survey all essential ethical issues, classical and contemporary, personal and social. Though some divide personal ethics from social ethics, we will seek to integrate them in the conviction that few issues are exclusively personal and that social problems will only be solved by individual people taking responsible action.

Before noting our methodology, it might prove helpful to

pause and note how ethics relates to other disciplines—philosophy, psychology, sociology, political science, and religion—and what the major approaches to ethics have been.

Since *philosophy* seeks the meaning of all things, ethics has traditionally been considered a part of philosophy. Christian ethics, then, would be part of Christian philosophy, or what we call systematic theology.

When a new ethical problem arises in society, such as euthanasia or homosexuality, newspaper reporters frequently consult a local professor of *psychology*. It would make just as much sense—if not more—to consult the local bartender. Psychology is descriptive and can only tell us, with greater or lesser precision, what the average person does and what may result if averages hold. It lacks any authority to speak of what human behavior *ought* to be. Since it lacks this authority, and since it should hold tentatively any conclusions it reaches, it is properly relativistic in its approach. Many psychologists, however, impose relativity outside their sphere in the field of ethics and reject all norms. For example, psychology may help us understand what produces conflict, but whether we use this information to produce conflict or to allay it will depend on our values. As a matter of historic fact, psychological insights are used by some to create conflict. And this is an ethical problem, not a psychological one. Psychology helps people understand why they do what they do and how they may change; ethics tells them what they *ought* to do.

Other behavioral sciences such as *sociology* and *cultural anthropology* are similar to psychology. If these disciplines would stick to descriptive science and tell us how societies and cultures function and what seems to result from particular behavior and social arrangements, they would be very useful to politicians and ordinary citizens in understanding themselves and how they might prove more successful in changing the way things are done. But these sciences have become increasingly prescriptive, imposing moral (cultural) relativity or, more recently, certain humanistic values. Of course, the behavioral scientist has every right to sort out and advocate his own values. But he lacks any authority deriving from his discipline to speak to ethical issues.

Political science, on the other hand, should combine many disciplines including the insights of the behavioral sciences and, above all, ethics. The world suffers because so many politicians choose goals—and the pragmatics of how to accomplish those goals—without ethical controls. Above all, the leader of people should specialize in ethics. The first question should be, What is right? not, What is in my best interest? or, What is the current pressure in my constituency? or, What is possible? The pragmatic is properly the sphere of the politician, and the behavioral sciences will certainly help him answer questions about how a given goal may best be achieved. But the control in choosing which goal to pursue must be the ethical.

Finally, how does ethics relate to *religion?* That may depend on one's definition of religion. Is religion that which deals with the supernatural, the belief in and service of a god? If so, classical Confucianism can hardly be called a religion as it was purely an ethical system. On the other hand, is ethics an essential part of religion? If so, Japan's Shintoism would not qualify, since it is an amoral set of rituals. The definition of religion is elusive to both scholars and lawmakers. But to the common man, religion ought to have a primary concern with moral conduct, with setting norms for behavior. If this common intuition is correct, then religion, though comprised of philosophy and ritual and other elements, ought also to speak to questions of ethics. Most people consider their own religion, at least, to be highly ethical, answering with authority the fundamental questions of what a person ought to be and do and why he exists at all. If there is any common ground at all among religions, it is in the area of ethics.

We will not analyze the major ethical systems, but a brief overview will help those who wish to identify our approach as it relates to other systems. Traditionally, ethics has been divided into naturalistic and transcendental ethics.

Naturalistic ethics, ruling out any realm of the spiritual or religious, has been divided into humanistic and egoistic (individualistic). *Humanistic ethics* has faith in the supreme value and self-perfectibility of human personality; moral good is seeking the welfare of mankind. Some humanists have moral codes created exclusively by their own reason, whereas others reject any absolute norm of human behavior. The other naturalistic stream of ethics, *egoistic or individualistic ethics*, does not think in terms of all mankind and its welfare, but rather bases ethical decisions on personal benefit. Historic Greek individualistic ethics divided into the Stoics and the hedonists. The Stoic was willingly submissive to natural law and all events, whereas the hedonist considered pleasure the sole or chief good in life. Moral duty is fulfilled by gratification.

Transcendental ethics is often divided between the philosophical idealists like Immanuel Kant, William James, and Ralph Waldo Emerson on the one hand, and theological ethicists on the other. Both assert the primacy of the spiritual or superindividual as against the material and empirical in settling ethical issues. The ethical system of most religions could be called "theological ethics."

There are many approaches within specifically Christian theological ethics, but in order to identify our own position, we will risk oversimplification by clustering them into two categories: antinomian (literally "against law") and absolutist.

Those who oppose law do so for varying reasons and in various degrees. For example, *situation ethics* is antinomian in the sense that it rejects all laws but the law of love. Many liberal ethicists and left-wing evangelicals have been so influenced by radical biblical criticism and, of late, behavioral scientific presuppositions, that biblical authority no longer controls ethical thinking. Some reject all ethical authority in Scripture, using it as a casebook of past religious experiences if at all, whereas others are selective in recognizing some biblical standards as universally normative. Both tend toward an "absolute" or, more accurately, a "relative" relativism. Finally, there are dispensational conservatives who reject all law as a requirement for the Christian believer. This extreme form of dispensationalism, though recognizing the authority of Scripture in principle, is properly called antinomian because, in the interest of advocating "absolute grace," they reject all law as *law* and view scriptural standards as merely helpful instruction, not binding the conscience.

Among *absolutists* there are *conflicting absolutists* and *nonconflicting absolutists*. Both agree that the universal laws of Scripture are absolute in their demand for obedience of all people of all time. The problem is that there are situations in which it seems one must break one law to obey another. For example, a child is given contradictory commands by his father and mother. Which one does he obey? The conflicting absolutist would say such situations present a tragic moral choice, and the faithful believer must choose the lesser of two evils and ask God for forgiveness for his sin. The nonconflicting absolutist, on the other hand, says that there can be no conflict in the will of God and that what may seem to be a choice between two wrongs, when properly understood from a biblical perspective, is not such a choice. It is the choice between right and wrong, and the believer does right in choosing the option which under other circumstances might have been wrong. For example, the disciples, in choosing to obey God rather than the civil authorities (Acts 5), did not choose the lesser of two evils but rather did the right thing and gained God's approval for the choice.

Though we will adhere to the biblical model of practical realism rather than reasoning abstractly about various ethical theories, it may prove helpful to state at the outset the perspective of this text. Our approach is that universal biblical norms are absolute and that these absolute norms, properly understood, will not conflict one with another. Technically stated, then, the position of this book is nonconflicting absolutist, transcendental, theological ethics. Though we will not analyze the various theological systems, the position will be indicated when the difference in viewpoint brings conflict in deciding an ethical issue.

We will seek to let the Bible set its own agenda rather than imposing a logically deduced system of ethics on the biblical data. So we begin with what the Scripture spotlights as the foundation of all ethics: love. Next we will analyze God's standard for human behavior—law—and then that major theme of Scripture which deals in great detail with the violation of law—sin. After these fundamental biblical doctrines are established, we will pause to look at the most conspicuous current alternative—situation ethics. Then the bulk of the text will be devoted to examining specific ethical standards of Scripture under the categories of the Ten Commandments. This will be followed by a consideration of three matters which do not easily fit under the Ten Commandments: the Christian and society, an approach to handling ethical issues on which Christians differ, and finding the will of God in nonethical matters.

Our basic presupposition in interpreting Scripture is that only Scripture is the final authority in ethical matters and that every ethical teaching of Scripture is normative for us unless Scripture itself limits the audience to others or modifies the teaching. This means that in some things the position espoused here will be less demanding than contemporary evangelical views, and in others it will be more demanding. Ancient cultural forms will be used for clarifying the meaning of the biblical author but will not be used to modify or set aside the teaching. Historical passages may be used to reinforce the teaching of Scripture, but the mere recording of an event without a biblical judgment as to its ethics will not be used to establish standards of behavior. The exception to this general rule for handling historical passages is that any act attributed to God or his Son is taken as sufficient evidence that the act was moral. I have dealt in detail with these and other principles of interpretation that are followed in our study of ethics in the text *Understanding and Applying the Bible* (Moody Press, 1983). I have defended in greater detail the more crucial presuppositions concerning the use of culture in interpretation in several articles: "Limits of Cultural Interpretation" (*Journal of the Evangelical Theological Society,* June 1980), "Problems of Normativeness in Scripture: Cultural Versus Permanent" (chapter 4, *Hermeneutics, Inerrancy and the Bible* [Zondervan, 1984]).

What study could be more important for the Christian than the will of God for his life? We turn now to the exciting study of God's standard for Christian behavior. This study will not reveal how we are to obey this standard, how we are to grow in our likeness to Jesus Christ. That is another subject, the doctrine of sanctification. Ethics does not answer the question, How? But before the how of Christian growth comes the what of biblical ethics. And the what, or goal of life for the Christian, is nothing less than the image of God restored. Let us turn now to consider carefully what kind of people we will be in our thinking and in our behavior as we become more and more like him.

PART I

FOUNDATIONAL CONSIDERATIONS

CHAPTER ONE

LOVE

Poets and lovers—and some theologians—tell us that love is the greatest thing. But what is love? Human language seems unable to capture a passion they say inflames the imagination beyond telling, a standard that pricks the conscience beyond bearing. Love is so difficult to define that the biblical idea of love cannot be found in the vocabulary of any language—not even ancient Greek, chosen to communicate God's revelation of truth.

Ancient Greek had four different words for love, but even in combination they could not capture the biblical idea. The Jewish scholars charged with translating the Old Testament Hebrew into Greek (the translation known as the Septuagint) chose the word *agape* to express the Hebrew word for love, *aheb,* probably because it had the volitional, or "choice," element that the other Greek words lacked. But *agape* was a cold, intellectual concept of relationships, little used in classical Greek. The Bible itself had to fill it with deeper meaning.

English has its problems also. The translators of the Authorized (King James) Version of the Bible spurned the simple Anglo-Saxon word *love* and chose the Latin-based word *charity.* And look what has happened to that word! But even after centuries of influence by the widespread use of Scripture, our English is still inadequate:

"I love hot dogs and milkshakes."
"Love me, love my dog."
"Raw love."
"John loves Mary."
"For God so loved the world."

Whether among the Kpelle of Liberia or the Siriono, hidden away in the jungles of the upper Amazon, translators have wrestled with how to translate *agape.* Perhaps the biblical idea of love is so difficult to express because it has been so little lived and thus never assigned a name. When the translator was seeking to put into the Siriono language, "Beloved, if God so loved us, we also ought to love one another" (1 John 4:11), he uncovered the root of the universal human problem.

"The Siriono will never do that," Echobe, his Christian informant, said.

"No, by yourselves you can't. But God is the one who causes us to love each other."

Echobe answered, "We Siriono say, 'That's just the way we are,' and keep right on fussing, fighting, and ignoring God's Word. Even if God helps us, it's not probable that we will love each other." No wonder the word is missing in every tongue!

And yet, God's entire will for what people should be and do hangs on this command, "You shall love." What, then, does God expect of us?

THE BIBLICAL DEFINITION OF LOVE

There are both internal and external elements in the biblical concept of love. *Love* is a noun which may indicate a particular kind of feeling, but it is also a verb which emphasizes how we should behave. The internal aspect focuses on emotion, disposition, motive. The external aspect focuses on volition, choices, actions, a way of life.

THE INTERNAL ASPECTS OF LOVE

In the Old Testament, love speaks of a spontaneous feeling which impels to self-giving.[1] This was true both for God and man. When man "loved" God, it was to have pleasure in God, striving impulsively after him, seeking God for his own sake. From God's side, the warm, strong feeling of affection which characterizes a healthy parent-child relationship is taken as a picture of how God the Father relates to Israel, his son. Love is the foundation of the covenant relationship. If the legal, covenantal aspect of the relationship is strong in the father-son analogy, the passionate loving-kindness of a good marriage is strong in the picture of God the husband and Israel the wife. The climactic revelation of this love relationship is seen in the

[1]*agapao*, in *Theological Dictionary of the New Testament* (TDNT), vol. 1, ed. Gerhard Kittel, trans. Geoffrey W. Bromiley (Grand Rapids: Eerdmans, 1964), 45.

prophet Hosea and his well-loved harlot-wife. The same analogy
of father-son, bridegroom-bride continues in the New
Testament, focusing on the warm affection and unfailing bonds
between two who love each other deeply.

But the internal aspect of love is more than a feeling. It is a
characteristic of life, a disposition. Old Testament scholars seem
to have a problem in translating another Hebrew word, *chesded*.
Some translations speak of *loving-kindness* (KJV), some of
steadfast love (ASV, RSV), some of *constant love* (TEV). Indeed, the
love of God is steadfast, unfailing—a basic disposition which
never changes and controls all that he does. This has to do with
commitment. God's kind of love is not a sometime thing,
tentative and sporadic. It does not run out. His covenantal love
is from youth to old age, from generation to generation, from
age to age, from eternity to eternity. This unending love is
faithful through all kinds of circumstances, even rejection.
Biblical love, then, is not a passing emotion but a way of life, a
disposition, a relationship of permanent commitment to the
welfare of another.

There is yet another element in the internal aspect of biblical
love: loving feelings motivate. In fact, it is not too much to say
that love is the only motive. At the root of every choice, every
action a person takes, lies love. It may be purely from love of self
that a person takes action, or it may be other-love. But always
love is the dynamic that propels, the catalyst that transforms
thought into action.

Some speak of the glory of God as a motive. But strictly
speaking, glory is not a motive. If I seek my wife's glory, for
example, my motive may be my own glory. If she is highly
thought of, I will be more praiseworthy for having caught her
and kept her. Of course, I may seek to put her in the best light
before others because I love her, not me. But the *motive* is not
her glory. The motive is *my* love, one way or the other. In the
same way, the Great Commission is said to be a motive. But I
may obey any command of God because I love me—it is the
smart thing to do. A pastor may work himself into an ulcer to
build his own reputation on earth or in heaven. I may give
generously for the impression it will make on others or witness
for fear of the consequences if I do not. Thus, I may seek my
own glory because I love me. Or I may be totally indifferent to

how people think of me. I may prefer pleasure. Or money. But money, pleasure, honor do not motivate; they are the means by which I may seek my own fulfillment. The same is true of seeking God's fulfillment, or my neighbor's. The basic drive, the mainspring, the motive of all human action is love.

Later we shall see how the Bible treats self-love and other-love and how conflict between them may be resolved. But at this point it is important to identify how biblical love is a feeling, a disposition, and a motive.

Our focus on the internal aspects of love is immediately shifted to the external by the term *motive*. Motivated to what? To act. So we now turn from love as an inner response to love as a description of how a love-motivated person behaves.

THE EXTERNAL ASPECTS OF LOVE

The Bible emphasizes what love does more than how love feels. This is no doubt why those who translated the Hebrew Old Testament into Greek chose the colorless *agape* over the strong, vibrant *eros* and the warm, affectionate *philia*. *Agape* had this going for it: It emphasized choice, action. The others did not. *Eros* (not to be restricted to contemporary definitions of erotic or sexually-oriented affections) was so passionate as to be compared with intoxication. There was no choice, no will, no freedom for the man seized by the tyrannical omnipotence of *eros*.[2] But *agape* referred to a free and decisive act determined by the subject himself, not by the drawing power of the object, as in the case of passionate *eros* or warm, but duty-bound *philia*. The primary characteristic of biblical love is action.

In the New Testament, as in the Old, loving is often linked with obeying—the outward response of an inward condition of love. We are *commanded* to love. "You shall love the LORD your God. . . . You shall love your neighbor as yourself" (Deut. 6:5; Lev. 19:18; Matt. 22:37-39). "If you love me, you will keep my commandments" (John 14:15). "For this is the love of God, that we keep his commandments" (1 John 5:3; 2 John 6). The first question Scripture asks is not, How do you feel about this person? but, rather, What choices must you make concerning this person?

[2]*agapao*, in TDNT, vol. 1, 45.

Of course, a human being is a whole and cannot be divided, for example, into knowledge, will, and emotions. However, since a whole person does function both volitionally and emotionally, it is proper for us to say that the will "controlled" one action and the emotions "controlled" another. One can will to act contrary to the impulse of his emotions. Jesus did this when his heart (emotions) cried out, "Father, let this cup pass from me." Yet he chose the Father's will, contrary to what he wanted, or how he felt. From the Bible's viewpoint, the choice to act lovingly, not the intensity of the feeling, is the test and ultimate proof of love. The concept of volitional love overriding affectional love is of paramount importance, for one may not be able to control his emotional response. But by the grace of God he can choose to act lovingly, no matter how he feels.

Some contend that this is dishonest. One must act in conformity with his feeling, it is said; otherwise he is attempting to deceive the other person into thinking that he feels a way he does not. But this line of reasoning emasculates a person, cutting away from him all his functions but one. Not only am I a person with feelings, I am also a person of choice—not to mention intelligence, commitments, and many other facets of my whole self. To be honest to myself I must be honest to my whole self; I must choose to act in conformity to my total being. Above all I must be honest to God, to act in conformity with his will and my commitment to him. This is indeed a liberating truth—I can choose to act for the welfare of another no matter how I feel about him or about the action God desires of me. For example, honesty does not demand that a son tell his father of his hostility—or of any other unworthy feeling. And love will not permit it. Loving obedience to God will spare his father until the grace of God has healed the hateful spirit. It will do more—it will choose to act consistently in loving ways. The loving act does not cancel the guilt of unloving feelings, but it is a start in the right direction.

To say that acting lovingly takes precedence over the emotion of love does not mean that biblical love is exhausted by acting lovingly. Without the emotion, love can be authentic, but it is not complete. If we act in love, ordinarily the affection will follow. Thus one can love in a biblical, active sense, without liking. In fact, it is required that we act lovingly no matter how we feel.

Love-in-action has both a negative and a positive aspect. The so-called Silver Rule speaks of refraining from harming—that is, do no harm, or "Do not do to others what you do not want others to do to you." The great Chinese master, Confucius, and the great Jewish master, Hillel, taught this. It is true, of course—that is how love behaves. But this is only a faint shadow of the Golden Rule, that we should do to others as we would have them do to us (Matt. 7:12). Biblical love is positive and active—constantly planning and acting for the welfare of others. To refrain from killing one's enemy is a loving thing, but to give one's life for an enemy is the ultimate act of love.

In fact, the Silver Rule can easily become the very opposite of biblical love. This is highlighted in a culture where the Silver Rule has been dominant. A Japanese philosopher, Kitamori, tells us that the Silver Rule lies at the base of a strong Japanese characteristic: disentanglement. To refrain from harming another is best achieved by staying clear of him. So the Japanese characteristic is to assume incredible obligations for those with whom one is inevitably related (family, work) but to remain adamantly aloof, disentangled from all other responsibility. But love deliberately entangles itself. Biblical love does so whatever the cost.

An emerging definition of love, then, is an affection, or a desire for the welfare of another that moves to a commitment to act in his behalf. Ordinarily, this is the way love moves, from attitude to action. But when the internal aspects are missing, one can begin with loving action, the external, and leave the feeling to tag along as it will. And this is not an aberration, an undesirable last resort. No, *acting lovingly without the feeling of love can be of the very essence of biblical love*—that which causes it to stand out in bold contrast to ordinary human love, sacrificial love. Thus love may flow either direction—joyfully from affection to action or painfully across the bridge of the cross—"nevertheless," no matter how I long for some other way, "not my will but thine be done."

If the internal aspects (love as affection and as motive) lead to a disposition that is characterized by a consistently loving attitude, the external aspects (love as choice and action) will lead to a loving way of life. But this way of life, by definition, cannot be expressed in isolation. Love demands a second party. We have concentrated thus far on the one loving, rather than on the one loved. How do the two relate? Ideally, of course, love is mutual. Affection is met with affection; loving acts are reciprocated.

RECIPROCAL LOVE AND NONRECIPROCAL LOVE

Some disparage reciprocal love, calling it "need-love" or even "swap-love." They say it is unworthy to expect or even to desire a return on one's investment of love in another. But it is easy to become more "spiritual" than the Bible. C. S. Lewis speaks to this:

We must be cautious about calling Need-love "mere selfishness." *Mere* is always a dangerous word. No doubt Need-love, like all our impulses, can be selfishly indulged. A tyrannous and gluttonous demand for affection can be a horrible thing. But in ordinary life no one calls a child selfish because it turns for comfort to its mother. . . . Since we do in reality need one another ("it is not good for man to be alone") . . . the illusory feeling that it *is* good for us to be alone . . . is a bad spiritual symptom; just as lack of appetite is a bad medical symptom because men do really need food. . . . Every Christian would agree that a man's spiritual health is exactly proportional to his love for God. But man's love for God, from the very nature of the case, must always be very largely, and most often be entirely, a Need-love. This is obvious when we implore forgiveness for our sins or support in our tribulations. . . . It would be a bold and silly creature that came before its Creator with the boast, "I'm no beggar. I love you disinterestedly."[3]

Indeed, God himself expects a "return on his investment." He longs and desires to be loved (Hosea; Matt. 22:37; John 4:23; Rev. 3:20). But the difference is this: he does not demand it. He does not make a loving response the condition for giving love (Rom. 5:6-8). And, humanly, we always do. *Eros* to the ancient Greek, and to the modern man as well, is passionate love that desires the other *for itself*. We continue to give only so long as we receive—or so long as we hope to receive. But God's kind of love is not preoccupied with the question, How well am I loved? but rather, How well do I love?

Thus the focus of biblical love is on the quality of the subject, the loving character of the one loving, not on the quality of the object, its worthiness of love, its desirability, its lovableness.

[3]C. S. Lewis, *The Four Loves* (London: Collins-Fontana, 1960), 8-9.

Jesus spells this out in great detail with many examples (Luke 6:27-35). He teaches that to love those who love us is nothing great. It is when we choose deliberately to love those who do not deserve it that we have reflected divine love.

And yet the ideal is reciprocal love, each finding in the other abundant reason to appreciate, to feel drawn to, to be overwhelmed by the desire to give. We give because we want to, not because we have to—we delight in the loved one. Then we rejoice in receiving from the one loved. But when the object is not lovable, or the emotion is not present, it is then that the character of the giving lover shines in greatest splendor.

Biblical love, then, is an affectionate disposition that motivates the lover to consistently act for the welfare of another, whether or not the other deserves it or reciprocates.

We have tried to define love. But the length and breadth and depth and height of it (Eph. 3:18-19) stretch far beyond our reach. In fact, such love reaches all the way to "the fullness of God." What shall we do? Often, to understand an abstract idea or a large concept it is necessary to define by description or demonstration. How good that God has given us both.

LOVE DEFINED BY DESCRIPTION

The most well-known description of love was penned by Paul (1 Cor. 13). Notice that he gives examples of the internal but also the external; love's attitude and disposition, but also love's activity. On the one hand love does not boast, is not proud or self-seeking, keeps no record of wrongs, does not delight in evil but rejoices with the truth, always trusts and hopes. On the other hand, love takes action: it is patient and kind, is not rude and quick-tempered, always protects, and always perseveres.

Scripture is filled with many other descriptions of love. Love is without hypocrisy (Rom. 12:9; 2 Cor. 6:6; 1 Pet. 1:22), works no ill for others (Rom. 13:10), will lay down its life for another (John 15:13), takes the servant's role (Gal. 5:13), is brotherly (Rom. 12:16; 1 Thess. 4:9; Heb. 13:1).

Though direct descriptions of love are plentiful enough to challenge for a lifetime, the indirect descriptions seem all but exhaustless. Consider the teachings on what have been called the "reciprocal verbs" of the New Testament. Not only are we told to love one another thirteen times (John 13:34-35; 15:12, 17; Rom. 13:8; Gal. 5:13; 1 Thess. 3:12; 4:9; 1 Pet. 1:22; 1 John 3:11, 23; 4:7, 11-12; 2 John 5), we are commanded to have the same care one for another (1 Cor. 12:25), to receive one another (Rom. 15:7), to be affectionate to one another (Rom. 12:10), to greet one another with a holy kiss (Rom. 16:16; 1 Cor. 16:20; 2 Cor. 13:12; 1 Pet. 5:14), to wait for one another (1 Cor. 11:33), to be kind one to another (Eph. 4:32), to prefer one another (Rom. 12:10), to forbear one another in love (Eph. 4:2; Col. 3:13), to forgive one another (Eph. 4:32; Col. 3:13). Furthermore, we are not to judge one another (Rom. 14:13), speak evil of one another (James 4:11), lie to one another (Col. 3:9), "bite" one another (Gal. 5:15), provoke one another (Gal. 5:26), or complain against one another (James 5:9).

But this is only part of it. Love also will submit one to another (Eph. 5:21; 1 Pet. 5:5); everyone is actually a member one of another (Rom. 12:5; Eph. 4:25); we are to live in harmony one with another (Rom. 12:16; Rom. 15:5); we are to edify one another (1 Thess. 5:11), exhort one another (Heb. 3:13; 1 Thess. 5:11), admonish one another (Rom. 15:14; Col. 3:16), sing to one another (Col. 3:16; Eph. 5:19), encourage one another (1 Thess. 4:18; 1 Thess. 5:11), confess sins to one another (James 5:16), serve one another (Gal. 5:13; 1 Pet. 4:10), wash one another's feet (John 13:14), use hospitality toward one another (1 Pet. 4:9), stimulate one another to love and good works (Heb. 10:24), pray for one another (James 5:16), and bear one another's burdens (Gal. 6:2). Incredible as this listing may be, it is only one of any number of teachings in Scripture that describe the attitudes and behavior of love.

Perhaps the most extensive descriptions of love are the commands of Scripture. Our next chapter will deal extensively with the relationship between law and love, but at this point, let us agree that the commands of Scripture reveal God's will for those to whom they are addressed and that his ultimate will is that we be like him in moral character. Since "God is love" it should come as no surprise that the entire Old Testament revelation of God's will for man hangs on the law of love (Matt. 22:37-40). After stating the Golden Rule, Jesus concluded, "For this is [the essence of] the law and the prophets" (Matt. 7:12). Paul repeats the thought: "For the whole law is fulfilled in one word, 'You shall love your neighbor as yourself'" (Gal. 5:14). Again he says that this law of love sums up the Ten Commandments (Rom. 13:8-9). This basic fact about the relationship of love to the commandments of Scripture means that every command applicable to Christians is a description of how love will behave. In other words, the instructions for life in Scripture give substance and definition to the basic law of love.

And yet, a description can be a lifeless code of ethics, an intimidating statement that lays a heavy hand of condemnation on me, confuses by its complexity, numbs by its impossible demands, blurs my perception by its distance from my own experience. God knows we need an example. We need to have love demonstrated, and this task he took upon himself at infinite cost.

LOVE DEFINED BY DEMONSTRATION

"God is love," says John (1 John 4:8, 16). This is the basic difference between the biblical concept of love and our concept of love. The Bible defines love by the nature of God. We tend to define love by the nature of man.

To say that God is love does not mean that God *equals* love. Love does not describe God exhaustively. He has other qualities, such as wisdom and strength. But this does not mean that those characteristics in God's nature violate love. And God always acts lovingly, even in judgment.

Again, "God is love" does not mean that *love equals God*. Love is not an entity, having existence as an object, let alone having personality. To say that love and God are equivalent would deify love and make it some absolute concept to which God himself is subject and by which he could be judged. Both situation ethics and Christian Science would tend to do this. Rather, love gains whatever stature it has because God is that way. He forms the concept by his nature. He is the source of all true love (1 John 4:7, 19). Since God himself defines love, true human love is godlikeness (1 John 4:16).

God was not obliged to love by some external "ought."

Loving is the way he is. This is one of the greatest evidences for the Trinity. God the Father loves God the Son and God the Holy Spirit from all eternity. God the Son loves the Father and the Spirit; and the Spirit loves the Son and the Father. Thus by love they are bound, and only out of love for others was that unity broken at the cross when, by the power of the Spirit, the Son assumed our guilt, and the Father turned away in judicial rejection from part of his very being.

The loving nature of God is the basis for his creative and redeeming activity. He created man because he is love and desired a being designed on his own pattern so that he could love that creature and be freely loved in return. When man rejected this loving approach of God, breaking that relationship, God continued loving because God is love by nature. And so we have the story of redemption. Love became incarnate. Thus all of life finds meaning in being loved by God and loving him.

By his life, Jesus demonstrated flawlessly how godlike love behaves, and in his death he demonstrated the ultimate proof of love. He was our model—we can now *see* how we are to "walk in love, as Christ loved us and gave himself up for us, a fragrant offering and sacrifice to God" (Eph. 5:1-2). We now can *see* what it means to have the kind of mind-set that was his who "being in very nature God, did not consider equality with God something to be grasped, but made himself nothing, taking the very nature of a servant, being made in human likeness. And being found in appearance as a man, he humbled himself and became obedient to death—even death on a cross!" (Phil. 2:6-8, NIV). "By this we know love, that he laid down his life for us; and we ought to lay down our lives for the brethren" (1 John 3:16). Throughout the New Testament Christ's love is given as our model: "This is my commandment, that you love one another as I have loved you" (John 15:12).

All of Christ's life puts on display God's loving character, but the cross of Christ demonstrates the love of God more clearly than any other act of any other person in all history.

Christ himself is the perfect, living model of God's character. But God graciously recreates that character in other people who, in turn, demonstrate true love. In fact, "By this all men will know that you are my disciples, if you have love for one another" (John 13:35).

Pastor Son was . . . a mild, little man—less than five feet tall—whose two great joys in life were his two sons, Tong-In and Tong-Sin. During the war Tong-In, like his father, had refused to worship at the Shinto shrines and had been thrown out of school by the Japanese. After the war, at twenty-four years of age, he went back to high school. . . . In October 1948, a wild Communist uprising swept through his part of South Korea and Communist youths seized the school in a reign of terror. A nineteen-year-old Communist leveled a pistol at Tong-In and ordered him to renounce his Christian faith. But Tong-In only pleaded with him to turn Christian himself and try the Christian way of love. Tong-Sin, the younger brother, rushed up to save him. "Shoot me," he shouted, "and let my brother live." "No," cried Tong-In, "I am the elder. I am the one who should die. Shoot me." The Communist shot them both. . . . Two days later the uprising was smashed and the murderer of the two boys was caught and brought to trial. Pastor Son found him with his hands tied behind his back, about to be condemned to death. He went to the military commander. "No amount of punishment will bring back my two sons," he said, "so what is to be gained by this? Let me, instead, take the boy and make a Christian of him so that he can do the work in the world that Tong-In and Tong-Sin left undone." Stunned at first by the proposal, the authorities reluctantly consented to release the young man into the custody of the father of the boys he had killed, and Pastor Son took him home.[4]

God graciously demonstrates his loving character not only in his eternal Son but in other sons and daughters in every land, in every time.

In summary, love is a warm affection, suffusing a disposition till it concentrates on others whether or not they are worthy of the gifts of love. Is that too theoretical? Then consider the attitudes and activities the Bible describes as godlike and the commands revealing God's will—they describe the loving way of life. Is that overwhelming, perhaps confusing by its multifaceted complexity? Then look at Jesus. He is the complete demonstration, the full incarnation of love. But perhaps you need someone you can see and touch? Then choose an authentic Christian and watch him. Not too critically, of course, remembering that someone may be watching you, too. Consider these things and you will discover that God's kind of love moves beyond feeling to take the initiative and acts to promote the welfare of another.

BIBLICAL OBJECTS OF LOVE

All the infinite variety of potential loves can be divided into four groups: love for God, love for others, love for self, and love for

[4]Samuel Moffett, *The Christians of Korea* (New York: Friendship, 1960), 120-121.

things. It is quite possible to love many people and even many things at once without any sense of competition or conflict. But often there is conflict among the "loves" and nothing can be more painful and destructive. First let us identify the objects of love and then turn to the biblical way for resolving the conflict.

LOVE FOR GOD

Christ tells us that this is the supreme objective: "Love the Lord your God with all your heart" (Matt. 22:37). This is the first command, first in importance, and the greatest, superseding all others as the controlling authority of life. Thus the Old Testament command (Deut. 6:5) identified by the teachers of Israel as the ultimate, comprehensive summary of God's will for man was affirmed by Jesus the Messiah as the most important commandment of all.

But how does a mere human being love the infinite God? By the loving adoration of worship, by unceasing thanksgiving, by a life of steadfast obedience, by sharing his companionship and exulting in the endless profusion of his gifts. This is the goal of creation and redemption, to love God. Not so much to find my fulfillment, but to find his, to bring him joy, to seek his purposes, to do his will.

Indeed, to love God is the first and great commandment, but it is not the only commandment. The "law and the prophets" do not depend on this alone. There is another commandment. And, in truth, one cannot obey the first without obeying the second (Matt. 22:34-40; 1 John 3:11-18; 4:19–5:1).

LOVE FOR OTHERS

Jesus identified two commandments on which all else depends, and the second, he says, is very like the first: "Love your neighbor as yourself" (Matt. 22:39; cf. Lev. 19:18). Both Jesus himself and John the well-loved took pains to spell out in great detail that other-love is the indispensable evidence of love for God. But the demands of other-love are not equal for all people. Consider the various levels of responsibility.

When God created the male, he judged that he was incomplete. He had God in daily companionship, yet still God said, "It is not good that the man should be alone" (Gen. 2:18), so God created a partner to complement him. Thus the primary horizontal or human relationship-in-love was God's wonderful idea of a man and woman united as one in marriage. So important is this relationship that the husband is charged with loving to the level of that high-water mark of love: as Christ loved the church and gave himself for it (Eph. 5:25). And wives, in turn, are to love their husbands (Titus 2:4).

Then comes love for one's own family: parents, children, brothers, sisters. So important is this relationship that one who does not care for his own family is worse than an unbeliever (1 Tim. 5:4, 8).

But there is brotherhood beyond one's human family. The Old Testament focus of responsibility was on love for fellow countrymen, and the apostolic guiding principle was love for the brethren. For example, in the most exhaustive treatment of the theme of love in the Bible (1 John 3–5), John consistently speaks of love for *the brothers*. Paul concurs: "Let us do good to all men"—yes—"and especially to those who are of the household of faith" (Gal. 6:10). And this is the New Testament pattern (John 15:12, 17; 1 Pet. 1:22; 2:17; 3:8). It draws the altogether startling picture of a group of people, the church, that is, a true family bound together by closer blood ties than human blood relations, the blood ties of Calvary. It is the picture of a people bound by love in interdependent responsibility for one another in every facet of life: spiritual, physical, emotional, material. Such is New Testament "love of the brethren."[5] But biblical love does not end there.

The Old Testament theme of "neighbor love" was never restricted in Scripture to fellow Israelites. The foreigner was included (Lev. 19:33). But Jewish people, being human, wanted to restrict the application of the sweeping demands of love. So the lawyer, who demonstrated that he knew the summary command of love well enough, wanted to justify his unloving behavior and asked: "And who is my neighbor?" (Luke 10:29). Jesus turned his question upside down (or right side up) with the story of the half-breed Samaritan who understood love better than the credentialed religious leaders and became a neighbor to the one who needed him. So neighbor-love reaches beyond brother-love to anyone at all who

[5]R. E. O. White, *Christian Ethics* (Atlanta: John Knox, 1980), 18-25.

is in need. Almost. "Neighbor" does not really mean "anyone" or "everyone." It is so easy to love mankind in the mass and neglect or even despise the one nearby.

Love is not mere tolerance, a warm feeling for everyone "out there" or even special indignation for the oppressed in some distant place. It must be for one's neighbor—the person within reach. Anyone within reach, to be sure. But love as action must be for someone who needs what I have and can give (Gal. 6:10). Neighbor-love extends to a wider circle than love of the brotherhood, just as love of the brotherhood extends beyond family love. And it is not restricted to worthy neighbors. It includes even one's enemy.

Love for one's enemy was taught in the Jewish law (Exod. 23:5; Job 31:29-30; Prov. 24:17; 25:21) but no one took it very seriously. In fact, Jesus says that tradition held it was all right to hate your enemy (Matt. 5:43). But he taught love of enemy with a force and consistency that startled the Jewish world. He startled the world of Roman law and Greek philosophy as well. This was unique: Love your enemy. And if you cannot *feel* all that warm about him, you can *choose* to act lovingly: pray for him, do good to him, speak well of him (Matt. 5:43-48; Luke 6:27-38). But the world-shattering message was not that he *taught* this way of life—incredible as that is—but that he loved his own enemies just that way: "But God shows his love for us in that while we were yet sinners Christ died for us" (Rom. 5:8). And we are to love our enemies just that way.

Those are the two commandments on which all else depends. Love God. Yes, and love your neighbor, too. Not three, just two. Some contend there is a third, that we are commanded to love self. But the sentence structure will not bear such an interpretation. Love for self is assumed, not commanded, in both Matthew 22:39 and Ephesians 5:28-29. If it is assumed, it is not condemned, so let us consider love for self.

LOVE FOR SELF

Paul Vitz, professor at New York University, has documented in a convincing manner that contemporary psychology, in seeking to make people whole, is committed to the "cult of self-worship."[6] Apparently in accommodation to this pervasive atmosphere, there is a tidal wave of Christian promotion of self-love as the biblical norm, so that self-discovery, self-affirmation, self-assertion, self-fulfillment, self-actualization, self-worth, self-esteem, self-importance are all advocated as worthy objectives for the Christian. In fact, we are told, we cannot be whole without them. How does this fit with the Bible's injunctions to self-sacrifice, self-crucifixion—indeed, with the command to hate oneself? (See Luke 14:26.) Part of the problem is in the definition of "self-love," and part is a basic ideological difference.

The term *self-love* can be used to mean either "self-centered-ness" or "self-acceptance," as John R. Stott has pointed out in his incisive critique of the contemporary fascination with loving oneself as the foundation of all other love.[7] If we have in mind self-centeredness, no Christian would advocate it; if we have in mind self-acceptance, there is something to discuss. Since the term is ambiguous, Stott suggests we avoid it. But the problem is not just a matter of semantics. There is a basic ideological difference that is pointed up clearly by Professor John Piper:

The proponents of this interpretation put the two assumptions together like this: a person's first task in obedience to Jesus is to develop a high self-esteem so that he can fulfill the second half of the command, to love others as he now loves himself.

After a very thorough exposition of the passage and of the issues, Piper concludes:

As I see it, the meaning of the command "You shall love your neighbor as yourself" is this: Our Lord is aiming to call into being loving, compassionate, merciful men and women whose hearts summon them irresistibly into action when there is suffering within their reach. And to that end, he demands that they again and again ask themselves this question: Am I desiring and seeking the temporal and eternal good of my neighbor with the same zeal, ingenuity, and perseverance with which I seek my own?[8]

No, we are not commanded to love ourselves—we are built that way. Yet some are so strong on self-sacrifice that they hold self-love to be wrong. Is not self-love a mark of the utter decadence of the end times (2 Tim. 3:2)? Did not Christ himself

[6]Paul Vitz, *Psychology as Religion* (Grand Rapids: Eerdmans, 1977).
[7]John Stott, "Must I Really Love Myself?" *Christianity Today*, 5 May 1978, 34-35.
[8]John Piper, "Is Self-Love Biblical?" *Christianity Today*, 12 August 1977, 8-9.

say that a person should hate himself? However, the same passage says that we are to hate our parents (Luke 14:26).

We are dealing here with a special Hebrew use of the terms love and hate. The idea of emotion is not intended. God did not feel animosity of such intensity that he "hated" Esau. No, a judicial decision is the point—he chose to reject Esau and to affirm Jacob as the line through which the Messiah would come. To "hate" in this sense is to reject; to "love" is to accept, affirm. It could thus be said that, for our sake, the Father "hated" the Son—took the judicial position of forsaking, condemning him. So when the time comes that love for parents and love for God come into conflict, we must decide one way or the other. In the same way, we are called upon to deny self or to deliberately choose to reject self-interest in favor of God's interests or even those of another person. The one who "loves" his own life (his own self) is the one who affirms his own rights and self-interest at all costs. By doing so, he rejects God's claims. Also, in the final analysis, he loses his own life—the very thing for which he was grasping.

The contemporary notion is that wholeness begins with self-affirmation and ends with self-fulfillment, whereas Scripture teaches that wholeness begins with self-denial and ends with God's fulfillment. If one begins with self-affirmation and makes self-fulfillment the primary goal of life, neither he nor God will find fulfillment in his life. But if he makes the fulfillment of God's purposes in this world his goal, God will be satisfied and glorified, and he will find, as a by-product, the fulfillment of the purpose for which God created and redeemed him. And that is true self-fulfillment.

If a person actually hates himself emotionally, dislikes himself, he is abnormal. And nonacceptance of self is indeed a great problem. Many psychologists seek to solve this problem by convincing a person that he is truly worthy or that he is not guilty. His failure is the fault of his environment or his inherited characteristics, for which he has no responsibility. Self-worth psychology dominates evangelical counseling theory and practice, as psychologist Jay Adams documents so thoroughly in *The Biblical View of Self-Esteem, Self-Love, Self-Image*.[9] The self-worth approach identifies a nonbiblical source of the human

[9]Eugene, Ore.: Harvest House, 1986.

problem, external to the person's own moral choices. According to this view, others have imposed a low view of self on a person and thus diminished his potential, and possibly crippled him. Since the root problem is inaccurately identified, a false solution also is provided. Building a high view of oneself is never given in Scripture as a solution to any problem. Such a "solution" only compounds the problem, for sooner or later the hurting person will discover that he really is not all that important in the eyes of others and that he truly is guilty.

The biblical solution to this problem is very different. It is the assurance that God forgives and accepts us. We are responsible for what we do and what we have become; we really are guilty. But the guilt has been done away with. And if God accepts us, we can certainly accept ourselves. Furthermore, Scripture teaches that we are created in the image of God and that we were created and saved *on purpose*. Though we may not be important or significant to anyone else, we are important to God. What a self-image: created in God's likeness, redeemed at infinite cost, and invested with a unique purpose in life by God himself!

This great self-discovery of who I am in Christ then frees me and makes me strong to hate and exterminate the evil in myself and to sacrifice (self-denial) my own rights and even my own welfare for others. Now I can gratefully accept what I am—and what I am becoming—as God's loving gifts.

From this comes a biblical concept of self-image. A "strong" self-image is that perception of self which is true, which is most nearly aligned with the facts, including all the weakness and corruption that is mine by nature and all the glory that is mine by grace.

Self-love, then, properly defined, is recognized by Scripture as the way God made us. To treat self in this way is to be in alignment with reality and thus to promote wholeness.

Are there other loves? I believe the Bible makes room—just a little—for one other reality: love for things.

LOVE FOR THINGS

It is possible to have an appreciation for some object so intense as to be called "love." This can be either demonic, as in covetousness, or it can be legitimate, as in the admiration of something beautiful. Such love can be seen most clearly in the love for a great idea or a cause. The Bible does not speak directly to the question of love for inanimate objects, other than to condemn such affection when it becomes idolatrous. But Scripture does speak of kindness for animals (Mosaic laws; Prov. 12:10), and certainly human experience is replete with examples of love for some animal friend.

God, others, self, things: one may love all so long as they do not conflict. But what if love for someone else conflicts with the love due God? What if my best interests and those of my neighbor's cannot coexist? How do we handle the conflict of loves?

CONFLICT OF LOVES

Most people choose and act from the motive of self-interest. The highest loyalty for unredeemed man is to self. Even in the most altruistic of humanistic ethics, the top priority is mankind, not God. But in biblical love the ultimate, controlling love, the integrating factor of life, the pivotal relationship, is love for God. How can I tell if I love God supremely?

It is futile to try to decide whether we have as warm an affection for God as we do for a parent or child, a wife or husband, but there is a way to tell which love is paramount. The controlling love becomes quite evident when a confrontation comes. When the best interest of another or ourselves and the best interest of God come into conflict, love must make a choice.

Ordinary human love gives for another to a point. But when the cost of acting lovingly gets too high, loving behavior ends. God's kind of love is different. How can I tell if I truly love my neighbor as Christ would have me love? Ask the key question: Does my love for self limit the expression of my love for the other person, or does my love for the other limit the expression of my love for myself? Love is not measured by the intensity of its feeling but by the sacrifice it stands ready to make.

Jesus indicated this when he said, "Greater love has no man than this, that a man lay down his life for his friends" (John 15:13). Often love is present without sacrifice, but so long as there is a return benefit, there is no *proof* that the love is truly other-love rather than self-love. No matter what our emotional response, if we choose to sacrifice what we perceive to be our own interests for the welfare of another, we have loved as God loves. Sacrifice. That is God's way of loving. And the world finds it beyond comprehension.

Natural man does not ordinarily want to get involved for someone else's benefit. Above all, he does not want to suffer loss for someone else. When Kitty Genovese was brutally stabbed to death in front of her apartment in New York in March 1964, thirty-eight people watched from behind darkened windows. No one did anything to help her, though she cried for help for thirty minutes. Why? The police investigator said, "The word we kept hearing from the witnesses later was *involved*. People told us they just did not want to get involved. They do not want to be questioned or have to go to court." Her case was celebrated because of nationwide coverage, but the story is repeated daily. No one wants to be involved. But godlike love is precisely the opposite: It chooses to get involved, no matter what the cost.

And yet the sacrifices we shrink from are not usually life-threatening: the sacrifice of a parent to allow the child to be childish when he is young and to let him grow free when he is older, the sacrifice of a child to allow his parent to "smother 'im with motherin'," the sacrifice by a spouse of his right to be right—all the small irritations of the daily routine. For the conflict of interests to be resolved, someone must be sacrificed. Who will it be? Will I take up my cross or nail him to his? It depends on whom I love the more.

Shirai was a young Japanese wife whose husband was the traditional lord of the house. When she came to faith in Christ he was furious. If she ever went to that Christian meeting again, he warned, she would be locked out. Sunday night Shirai came home to a darkened, locked home. She slept on the doorstep till morning, and when her husband opened the door, she smiled sweetly and hurried to prepare the best possible breakfast of bean soup, rice, and raw fish. Every Sunday and every Wednesday the story was the same. Winter came, and with it the rain and cold. Shirai huddled in the darkness as her wet cotton-padded jacket froze about her. Week after week for six months she forgave, freely and fully. No recriminations, no sulking.

It was costly—she bore his sin. But her poor husband finally could stand it no longer. Love finally won out. When I met him, he was a pillar in the church, learning to walk the thorny path of sacrificial love. Shirai's example shatters my own complacency with a sharp, clear picture of what it means to deny oneself, take up one's cross daily, and follow Jesus.

"That a man should always be ready to forgive has been called Jesus' most striking innovation in morality."[10] Perhaps one of the most painful sacrifices that love makes is forgiveness. To forgive is costly, for someone must pay the price of wrong. If I choose to treat the person as if the wrong had never been done (forgive), then I may have to pay for it. It is not just the sacrifice of ego—that seems to be painful enough. But if I forgive—truly forgive—the smashed fender, then I pay for it. And I do not make the guilty party pay for it in installments through petty insinuations. When President Ford forgave Richard Nixon, he paid for it, they tell us, in the next election. Even when the relationship is such that discipline is necessary, as with a parent and child, forgiveness means full restoration without the haunting specter of subtle reminders. And sometimes it's not forgiveness at all, but a joint assumption of guilt that is needed. In some cases, "I'm sorry I came home drunk last night" may call for the Christian wife to respond, "Please forgive me for making life so miserable." A self-righteous "I forgive you" at that point may be another nail in his cross, not hers.

On the other hand, some people have the knack for making an accusation under the guise of apologetic words. I may say, "I'm sorry to have been so dumb as to say that and tee you off. Please forgive me." The not-so-hidden implication: "I forgot how you are so unreasonably touchy. Too bad you had to sin again with your insensitive tongue." The net result of such an "apology" is a double wound, one for your badness and a second for my own implied innocence. An honest response might have been, "I wonder if you know how you sound?" Or, better, "Here we are miscommunicating. What should we do next?" The best response, of course, may well be silence and a cheerful moving ahead with the next topic or the business at hand. Painful, this not pressing ahead to vindication? Yes, the painful

[10]L. H. Marshall, quoted by Carl F. H. Henry, *Christian Personal Ethics* (Grand Rapids: Eerdmans, 1957), 483.

way of the cross, as true forgiveness accepts the expense incurred by the other's sin.

Must I forgive if the other person does not repent, does not ask forgiveness? Jesus said, "If your brother sins, rebuke him, and if he repents, forgive him" (Luke 17:3). So we *must* forgive the one who indicates regret for sin against us. That is when God forgives. But Christ and Stephen both prayed that God would not hold accountable those who sinned against them, even though the murderers had not asked forgiveness. So it is all right to forgive anyway. And since we are not godlike in our knowledge of the other person's thoughts, it may be the best thing to forgive anyway. Usually the other person does not view the circumstances from my perspective and does not sense a need to repent or ask forgiveness. In any event, an attempt at reconciliation is always my responsibility, no matter who the chief wrongdoer was. Besides, unforgiveness is a cancer that eats away at the spirit of the one who fails to forgive, so there is great therapeutic value in forgiveness as a way of life, no matter how the offenders in one's life behave.

THE IMPORTANCE OF LOVE

CHARACTER OF GOD

Agape-love is said to be "the centre of Christianity, the Christian fundamental motif *par excellence*."[11] Is this statement claiming too much for love? I believe Augustine was nearer the truth when he said that the supreme good is nothing other than God himself. Surely the center of Christianity is Christ himself. And yet, what kind of god is God? And what is the character of Jesus Christ? As we have seen, God is loving. Indeed, God *is* love. The supreme importance of love is seen in this: love is the way God is.

Great and sharp has been the contention over whether righteousness or love is paramount in God's character. And how do his justice and holy wrath against sin fit with his love? Some hold that righteousness is the comprehensive description and that love is an element of what is right or true. Others hold that love is the comprehensive category and that righteousness is one

[11]Anders Nygren, *Agape and Eros,* trans. Philip S. Watson (Philadelphia: Westminster, 1953), 48.

facet of love. Perhaps we can do no better than rejoice with the psalmist that "steadfast love and faithfulness will meet; righteousness and peace will kiss each other" (Ps. 85:10). This they did at Golgotha when God's righteous indignation against sin fell on his own beloved Son because of love for you and me. Certainly it is true that God's kind of right cannot exist without love, and God's kind of love cannot exist without righteousness. Love is of supreme importance because that is the way God is.

GOD'S IMAGE IN MAN

Love is not only a primary characteristic of God, it is the imprint of his likeness in human beings, the indispensable family characteristic without which no one can claim membership in the family of God (1 John 4:7-8). Love binds the Trinity into one, and from the overflow of that love came the creation of a being that is not the "highest of the animals" but a "little less than God" (Ps. 8:5), capable of companionship and loving unity with God himself. Not only is this loving unity the central fact about God and the purpose of creation, it is also the purpose of redemption in restoring the image man marred. He did not restore man merely to prove his powers and defeat Satan. He was out to fulfill the original purpose—nothing less than loving union with himself.

True love is so deep, so broad, so high it is beyond understanding (Eph. 3:18-19). In fact, somehow it is related to "all the fulness of God" (v. 19). But if Christ indeed lives in us through faith, we can be so established in the experience of love that *we* have the power to comprehend this greatest of all qualities (vv. 17-18).

SOURCE AND SUMMARY OF ALL VIRTUE

Not only is love so important because it is characteristic of God and suffuses the origin and destiny of man, it is the foundation of all ethics, God's revelation of what he wills us to be and do.

Not only is love the source of all the other virtues, in itself it is the comprehensive summary statement.

Augustine saw this clearly:

Augustine's ethics centered completely in this love. The cardinal virtues were subsumed under love. Virtue consists in nothing else but in loving what is worthy of love; it is prudence to choose this, fortitude to be turned from it by no obstacles, temperance to be enticed by no allurements, justice to be diverted by no price.[12]

INCOMPARABLE RESULTS OF LOVE

Finally, the results of loving attitudes and behavior underscore the supreme importance of our theme. God's love for us provided life and salvation and now provides all that we need. "Who shall separate us from the love of Christ? . . . Neither death, nor life, nor angels, nor principalities, nor things present, nor things to come, nor powers, nor height, nor depth, nor anything else in all creation, will be able to separate us from the love of God in Christ Jesus our Lord" (Rom. 8:35-39). How great the results of God's love for us! But what of our love for God?

When we love God with all our affections (heart), with every choice (soul), and with the concentration of all our mental powers (mind) (Matt. 22:37), we not only prove to be his and please him, but we validate all the other loves. Love for God makes love for others and even for ourselves operate at the level he designed. If I fail to hold love for God as the ultimate, I may do more than damage love for others or diminish the worth I have as a person in Christ. I may even invalidate the other loves altogether. For example, when parents put a child on the highest throne of affection and sacrifice responsibilities to God and obedience to his will for that child, the relationship to the child himself becomes warped and grotesque.

I enjoyed visiting the Nakamuras. God had rescued them from a miserable life at the brink of divorce and brought them into the family of God's people. Their six-year-old son, Hideyaki, was a great playmate for our youngest. One day I asked if they had any pictures of him. Did they! The first album, to my amazement, brought me only through the first six months of Hideyaki's life—pages and pages at his birth, pages for the first month "birthday," and then more pages for the first hundred days. The whole closet was full of albums almost exclusively of Hideyaki. What affection for an only son!

[12]George W. Forell, *History of Christian Ethics,* vol. 1 (Minneapolis: Augsburg, 1979), 167.

Gradually the affection crowded out God's place and, inevitably, began to erode the affection of the couple for one another.

But perhaps Hideyaki at least would benefit? The last I heard, he had broken the hearts of those adoring parents, falling deeper and deeper into a life of drugs and crime. The idolatrous affection not only destroyed the relationship with God and other relationships, it participated in the destruction of the very object of supreme devotion itself.

But love for God, when enthroned above all other loves, has the power to anchor the other loves, to give them direction and power, to fill them with meaning, discipline them, and lift them to their highest and best.

Above all other results, the person who lives in love actually lives in God (1 John 4:16), the ultimate goal of all our existence.

SUGGESTED ADDITIONAL READING

Adams, Jay. *The Biblical View of Self-Esteem, Self-Love, Self-Image*. Eugene, Ore.: Harvest House, 1986.

Bilheimer, Paul E. *Love Covers*. Fort Washington, Penn.: Christian Literature Crusade, 1981.

Brunner, Emil. *The Divine Imperative*. Trans. Olive Wyon. Philadelphia: Westminster, 1937.

Burnaby, J. *Amor Dei*. London: Hodder, 1938.

D'Arcy, M. J. *The Mind and Heart of Love*. New York: World, 1945.

Geisler, Norman L. *The Christian Ethic of Love*. Grand Rapids: Zondervan, 1973.

Henry, Carl F. H. *Christian Personal Ethics*. Grand Rapids: Eerdmans, 1957.

Kagawa, Toyohiko. *Love, The Law of Life*. Chicago: Winston, 1929.

Kierkegaard, Søren. *Works of Love*. Trans. Howard and Edna Hong. New York: Harper, 1962.

Lewis, C. S. *The Four Loves*. London: Collins-Fontana, 1960.

Moffatt, James. *Love in the New Testament*. London: Hodder, 1929.

Niebuhr, Reinhold. *Love and Justice: Selections from the Shorter Writings of Reinhold Niebuhr*. Ed. D. B. Robertson. New York: World, 1957.

Quell, G., and E. Stauffer. *Agapao*. In vol. 1 of *Theological Dictionary of the New Testament*. Ed. Gerhard Kittel; trans. Geoffrey W. Bromiley. Grand Rapids: Eerdmans, 1964.

Smedes, Lewis B. *Forgive and Forget*. San Francisco: Harper and Row, 1984.

Sweeting, George. *Love Is the Greatest*. Chicago: Moody, 1974.

CHAPTER TWO

LAW

Why is law to some a hobgoblin of incarnate evil to be exorcised from life, while to others it is the only hope of salvation? What is law's purpose and how can it be known?

A law is any rule or injunction that must be obeyed. In religion, these rules normally make requirements of a ceremonial or ritual kind and of an ethical or moral kind. In fact, these laws are so prominent in most religions as to be considered the substance of that religion. This was true of the Jewish religious leaders in Christ's day, and it is true in much of Christendom today. Is this the biblical point of view? Certainly there are many laws in the Bible—more than six hundred Mosaic command-ments and more than six hundred direct commandments in the New Testament. Are they rules that must be obeyed? *Can* they be obeyed? If not, for what purpose were they given? Before these and other vital questions can be answered it is important to permit the Bible itself to define the term.

DEFINITION OF LAW

The Bible uses the *law* term in several ways, and often these meanings are not differentiated precisely. In some passages of the New Testament a more specific meaning is clearly seen. Some say there are as many as twelve distinct uses of the term.[1] Here are some of them.

LAW AS THE EXPRESSED WILL OF GOD THAT PEOPLE BE LIKE HIM MORALLY

God created man in his own image morally. There are, no doubt, other elements in man's likeness to God, but a morally right character is primary. It is the basis of shared love and

[1] Robert C. McQuilkin, *God's Law and God's Grace* (Grand Rapids: Eerdmans, 1958), 13-17.

Our call is to be: 1) Holy ⟍ to manifest
2) Perfect ⟋ God's character!

46 ■ BIBLICAL ETHICS

To be Holy/Perfect is an obligation! not advise or an option!

fellowship; it is indispensable to demonstrating in human life the glory (glorious character) of God. Mankind has ever neglected this aspect of God's image and worked to attain likeness to God in his attributes of knowledge and power. This was Satan's temptation to Eve: "You will be like God." How? She was already like God in his moral nature. She rejected this likeness in order to reach for God's infinities and from the outset lost both. All her descendants, save one, have followed in her steps. But God's purpose remained the same: he wanted people to be like himself.

This is the purpose of the sovereign Lord, commanded through Moses at the beginning of the Old Covenant and through Jesus Christ at the beginning of the New Covenant: You must be holy *as I am holy* (Lev. 19:2; 1 Pet. 1:16), you must be perfect *as the heavenly Father is perfect* (Matt. 5:48). It is not optional. Since it is a divine imperative, we properly call this will of God *law*.

It is wrong not to be like God morally. This wrong is not just a weakness or unfortunate deviation from the norm. The Bible calls it sin. To be holy is to be separated from sin; to be right is to be in alignment with God's character. This is the holiness required of men. It is an obligation, not mere instruction or advice. Without it no one will see God (Heb. 12:14). As Calvin said, "The law not only teaches, but also imperiously demands."[2]

This most important use of the word *law* is often called the "moral law," God's expressed will concerning what constitutes likeness to God. Does the New Testament use the term in this way?

When Paul speaks of the work of the law being written in the hearts of those who do not have the written law (Rom. 2:14-15), he is speaking of God's moral law. When he says, "Through the law comes knowledge of sin" (Rom. 3:20), he is referring to the moral law, or the commandments of God which deal with human behavior. (See also Rom. 4:15; 7:2, 5, 7-9, 12, 16, 22; 8:3-4, 7; 13:8-10; 1 Cor. 7:19; Gal. 3:13; 5:14; 6:2; and 1 Tim. 1:8.) The author of the Letter to the Hebrews sometimes uses the term *law* in the same way: "I will put my

The Law:
1) Teaches +
2) Demands

[2]John Calvin, *Institutes of the Christian Religion,* trans. John Allen, vol. 1 (London: James Clark, 1949), 310.

laws into their minds, and write them on their hearts" (Heb. 8:10ff.; 10:16). This is especially significant since the Letter to the Hebrews usually uses *law* to mean the ceremonial system. Of course one would expect James to use *law* in reference to the right behavior God demands of his people, and he does (James 1:25; 4:11).

This, then, is a common use of the concept of law in the New Testament as well as the Old: God's expressed will that we be like him, commonly called the "moral law."

LAW AS THE MOSAIC LEGAL SYSTEM

A second major use of the term *law* in the New Testament, especially in the writings of Paul, refers to the entire network of regulations given by God to Israel for the era beginning with Moses and ending with Jesus Christ, who came to fulfill the law. John also uses the term in this way when he says, "For the law was given through Moses; grace and truth came through Jesus Christ" (John 1:17). The statements "sin indeed was in the world before the law was given" (Rom. 5:13) and "law came in, to increase the trespass " (Rom. 5:20) are typical of Paul's use referring to the Mosaic system of law. When Paul writes to the Galatians he often uses *law* to mean the whole system of the "old covenant" from which Christ has freed, so that the Christian is not required to live under all the demands of the system under which Israel lived (see Gal. 3:17, 19, 21). John Murray finds this meaning in some cases in the expression "under the law" (1 Cor. 9:20; Gal. 3:23; 4:4-5, 21).[3]

LAW AS OBEDIENCE TO THE LAW

Sometimes the term *law* is used figuratively to refer to a person's obedient response to the law. When Paul says, "If justification were through the law" (Gal. 2:21), he obviously is not speaking of the commandments themselves, but rather of the idea that a person can achieve acceptance as righteous through obeying the law. The same thought is found in his reference to the "works of the law" (Rom. 3:20) and the recurring teaching that "no man

[3]"Law," in *The New Bible Dictionary*, J. D. Douglas et al, eds., rev. ed. (Wheaton, Ill.: Tyndale, 1982), 687.

NO ONE is JUSTIFIED BY "Obedience" TO The LAW!

is justified before God by the law" (Gal. 3:11). He meant no one is justified by *obedience* to the law.

This idea was the chief object of Paul's attack. It was the error of the Pharisees to believe that a person could earn God's acceptance by obedience to the law, and it was the error of the Judaizers in the early church, at least in part. Since Paul does not stop to define *law* every time he uses it, some interpreters have confused the use of *law* referring to the Mosaic system and *law* referring to the false idea that righteousness could be attained by obedience to that law. Paul was very clear that no one—"under Moses" or "in Christ"—could ever be justified through his own efforts to obey the law. "By the works of the law shall no flesh be justified" (Gal. 2:6; see also Gal. 3:2, 5, 10, 18; Rom. 4:14; 6:4, 15; Phil. 3:9).

There are other distinct meanings of *law* in the New Testament, but these first three meanings are of primary importance, and not simply because they have been a theological battleground from biblical times. For anyone who wants to know and do God's will, it is of utmost importance to discover what that will is. Since both Jesus Christ and the apostles taught that some change had taken place in the relationship of God's people to "the law," we must be careful to discover exactly what that law is and what that change is.

All would agree that a change was long overdue from the damning idea that a person can gain acceptance with God through his own efforts. At least some elements of the Mosaic system of law were done away in Christ's sacrificial death and the institution of the church. But here agreement ends. Some hold that Paul makes no distinctions among laws and that the Christian is not obligated to any of the Mosaic law, including the moral law.

[The Scriptures of the New Testament] both assume and directly teach that the law is done away. Consequently, it is not in force in the present age in any sense whatsoever. . . . The Old Testament system of law is absolutely superseded by the new system under grace. Christians are not under law either for justification or for sanctification.[4]

We will examine this position more carefully later, but at this point it is important to emphasize that the New Testament uses the term *law* to refer to the moral requirements of God, the

[4]Lewis Sperry Chafer, *Grace* (Grand Rapids: Zondervan, 1922), 215, 239.

Mosaic system of regulations, and the figurative use of the *law* referring to obedience to it.

LAW AS THE OLD TESTAMENT

Since Moses, the great lawgiver, recorded the law in his writings, the Pentateuch (the first five books of the Bible) was commonly called "the law" (Gal. 4:21). The Hebrew Bible was divided into three sections, commonly called the Law, the Prophets, and the Writings (or the first of that section, the Psalms). Thus Christ spoke of "my words which I spoke unto you, while I was still with you, that everything written about me in the law of Moses, and the prophets, and the psalms must be fulfilled" (Luke 24:44). Here the "law of Moses" clearly refers to the first division of the Hebrew Old Testament, the Pentateuch.

Sometimes the Old Testament was simply referred to by two divisions, the Law and the Prophets (Matt. 11:13; Luke 16:16; Rom. 3:21).

Again, since "the law" was the first section of the Old Testament, it was often used of the Old Testament as a whole. This can be seen when quotations made from "the prophets" or from "the psalms" are attributed to "the law" (see 1 Cor. 14:21; Rom. 3:19; see also Matt. 5:18; Luke 16:17; John 8:17; 10:34; 15:25). Thus "the law" often refers to the Old Testament as a whole or to some part of it.

A) LAW OF CHRIST. "THE LAW"
B) ROYAL LAW > OF LOVE

LAW AS SPECIFIC LAWS

Sometimes the term *law* actually refers to specific commandments such as the Ten Commandments (Rom. 2:20ff.; 7:7; 13:8ff.). "We have a law" (John 19:7) is another example of a specific law in mind. When Paul speaks of fulfilling the law of Christ in Galatians 6:2 and when James speaks of the royal law (James 2:8), the reference is to the specific law of love. Again, when James speaks of keeping the whole law (James 2:10), he is speaking of specific laws, probably the Decalogue, or Ten Commandments.

LAW AS AN OPERATING PRINCIPLE

Sometimes the New Testament uses the term *law* to mean a principle much as we would say the "law of gravity." "The law

of my mind" and "the law of sin" (Rom. 7:23, 25), "the law of
the Spirit of life" (Rom. 8:2), and "the principle of faith" (Rom.
3:27) are all examples of the term *law* being used as a synonym
for "principle."

Because *law* is used in many different ways and often with
several meanings overlapping, it is important to be sure from the
context what meaning was intended by the author. Otherwise
we shall be applying a teaching concerning the law that does not
actually apply. For example, if we speak of being free from the
law and use this to refer to the moral law of God when in fact
Scripture is referring to the condemnation resulting from the
law (Rom. 8:1-2) or the Old Testament system of sacrifices, we
are making a great error. For the time being, we will use the
term *law* in its primary meaning: law as the expressed will of
God that people be like him morally.

This ultimate standard for the Christian is not merely a code
of ethics or system of doctrine or a subjective feel for what is
right. The standard for the Christian is God himself (Matt.
5:48; Rom. 8:29; 2 Cor. 3:18; Eph. 4:13; Col. 3:10; 1 Pet.
1:15-16).

This is exciting. It means that the foundation of our moral
standard is not man, his wisdom, his fallen nature, his desires,
his values, his traditions, nor his culture. These may be the
foundation of man-made law, but not of the Christian standard
of life. Since God himself is our standard, our standard is not
relative, changing with each age or society. God's law is *absolute*,
perfect, unchanging, and eternal.

Since God himself is our standard, the standard is *universal*.
The moral character of God as a standard applies to all men of all
ages.

This standard is *personal*, living, and visible rather than a dead
code. It is not something that God imposes on us arbitrarily. It
derives from his own nature.

This truth also means that God's character is not derived from
the moral structure of the universe. Some would hold that God
behaves rightly and lovingly because he is obliged to do so by
ultimate "natural" law. Rather, we say that righteousness and
love are good because that is the way God is. We do not, as
some theologians, derive our ethical standard from nature,
setting up great cosmic moral hoops through which God must

[handwritten top margin: WE WERE → CREATED INTO GOD'S MORAL IMAGE/likeness. → Reflecting His glorious CHARACTER.]

jump. Rather, we see these standards flowing out of the nature of our infinite, ultimate, personal God.

Thus, God's will for man is that we be like him. We were created in his moral likeness, reflecting the glory of his character. His purpose in redemption is to restore that image that has been marred. *(The Fall)*

But why does God want us to be like him?

PURPOSE OF THE LAW

[handwritten: Political → Spiritual (Didactic)]

The law of God is often likened in Scripture to light (e.g., Ps. 119:105). Like the streetlight, God's law restrains evil (1 Tim. 1:9-10). God's law does not control evil men, but it is a retarding influence to the forces of evil in the world. Some call this the *political* use of the law. By moral standards a society is held together. When moral standards loosen, a community or nation begins to come apart.

[handwritten left margin: Restrain Sin! reveal sin! Manifest the character of man!]

Like the light in the washroom, God's law reveals man's moral defilement (Rom. 3:20; 7:7). By the law comes the knowledge of sin. If I do not believe I am dirty, I will not seek cleansing. If I do not think I am lost, I will not welcome a rescuer. But if I know that I am polluted and incapable of doing that which I wish to do, I will seek a savior and welcome him. This is the "custodian" work of the law that brings us to Christ (Gal. 3:24). The law in Paul's sense here is not, strictly speaking, a teacher ("schoolmaster"). Rather, the law for the sinner is the school bus driver or even the truant officer to bring the sinner to Christ. For the sinner, the law makes sin very plain, "sinful beyond measure" (Rom. 7:13). Thus the terrifying law condemns us and is designed to make men seek a way of escape. This is the *evangelistic* use of the law. If he does not flee to the cross, the law becomes the basis for his judgment in the last day, and law will have failed in its evangelistic purpose (Rom. 3:19).

[handwritten left margin: Show man that: He is Lost! Dirty! Point to Christ! Kill you! To Condemn! Cannot justify! Make you Flee!]

For the Christian, the law has an entirely different function. Like the headlights on an automobile, the law for the Christian shows the way he must go if he is to reach the destination of being like Jesus.

God is light and in him is no darkness at all. If we say we have fellowship with him while we walk in darkness, we lie and do not live according to the truth;

but if we walk in the light, as he is in the light, we have fellowship with one another, and the blood of Jesus his Son cleanses us from all sin. (1 John 1:5-7)

This standard is the goal of our Christian life. This has been called the *spiritual* use of the law, or the *instructional* (didactic) use of the law.

Thus God's purpose in giving the law is for our good, for our fulfillment, whether we are unsaved or saved.

And now, Israel, what does the LORD your God require of you, but to fear the LORD your God, to walk in all his ways, to love him, to serve the LORD your God with all your heart and with all your soul, and to keep the commandments and statutes of the LORD, which I command you this day for your good? (Deut. 10:12-13)

Legalists forever want to turn it around and recreate people for the sake of the law, whereas Jesus insisted that the law (of the Sabbath) was made for man and not man for the law (Mark 2:27). "He puts that law into practice and he wins true happiness" (James 1:25, Phillips).

Man's welfare, happiness, fulfillment is ever the purpose of a loving God. The more like him we become the more we are fulfilled. This is the way of freedom, not restriction and bondage. James calls this the "law of liberty" (James 2:12). The tragedy of the lawless person is that he is forever diverted from the true and right trajectory. Righteousness is alignment with reality, and the one who is out of alignment with reality will finally destroy himself. But to be true and right, in alignment with ultimate reality, will make a person free, fulfill the purpose of his existence.

The person who abides by the rules of the game is the one who enjoys the game and the only one who is qualified to win. The owner who follows the instruction manual of the manufacturer is the one who finds satisfaction with the product. And so it is with traffic laws or criminal law—each is for our good. It is not simply that God rewards good behavior and punishes evil behavior, true as that may be. Sin brings its own punishment, righteousness its own reward: "The iniquities of the wicked ensnare him, and he is caught in the toils of his sin" (Prov. 5:22).

This common theme of Scripture (Num. 32:23; Ps. 7:15;

The LAW WAS NEVER Intended TO: 1)MAKE US Righteous!
But RATHER TO:- Give us knowledge of sin! 2) JUSTify US!
- Point us to Christ Jesus! 3) Sanctify US!
4)Empower US!

9:15; 40:12; Prov. 1:31; 11:1-31) does not mean merely the obvious, that the drunkard may get hurt, will have a hangover, and often ruins his own life as well as others. It is even deeper than the truth that "the measure you give will be the measure you get" (Mark 4:24). The sin itself warps and ultimately destroys the person. Covetousness eats like cancer, taking away peace and joy, binding and demeaning the spirit—even if it does not lead to some other grosser behavior. In adultery a person sins against himself, depriving himself of the very things that make life worthwhile: love, security, belonging, fidelity, peace, integrity, the ecstasy of full oneness. Indeed, there is inherent punishment in sin (2 Pet. 2:13).

On the other hand, "Great peace have those who love thy law; nothing can make them stumble" (Ps. 119:165). "And I shall walk at liberty, for I have sought thy precepts" (v. 45). "Moving within the bounds of law, yet finding them to be no restraint" was not only Jesus' experience.[5] The law is the birthright of all who are his. No wonder the longest chapter in the Bible is devoted to extolling the glorious wonders of the law of God (Ps. 119).

Note carefully that the purpose of God's law is different from the purpose of regulations and laws in other religions. The law was never intended to make us righteous. There are passages in the Old Testament that sound as if the law had this purpose, and a few in the New Testament as well. (See Lev. 18:5; Matt. 19:17; Luke 10:28.) But Paul repeatedly emphasizes that no one—under the Old Covenant or under the New—has ever been or ever will be justified by obedience to the law: "For no human being will be justified in his sight by works of the law" (Rom. 3:20; Gal. 2:16). Paul insists that this theme was taught in the Old Testament, from the days of Abraham (Rom. 4:1-3) through David (vv. 4-8) to the age of the prophets (Gal. 3:11). Jesus himself clearly taught that none was good (Matt. 19:17), that even the best of men must be born from above (John 3:1-7) and are saved by grace through faith (vv. 14-16). It is not the would-be keeper of the law, he taught, but the penitent sinner that is justified (Luke 18:14).

This biblical theme of man's inability to save himself is reinforced by another theme—man's utter sinfulness and failure.

[5]Patrick Fairbairn, *The Revelation of Law in Scripture* (New York: Carter, 1869), 245.

Beginning in the earliest writings, man is seen as wicked (Gen. 6:5, 12; Job 9:20; 25:4). Centuries later, David cries out, "There is none that does good, no, not one" (Ps. 14:3; 53:1-3) and "For no man living is righteous before thee" (Ps. 143:2). David's son Solomon joins the theme: "Who can say, 'I have made my heart clean; I am pure from my sin'?" (Prov. 20:9). "Surely there is not a righteous man on earth who does good and never sins" (Eccles. 7:20). The prophets agree in this testimony: "All we like sheep have gone astray; we have turned every one to his own way" (Isa. 53:6).

This truth of man's depravity does not mean, of course, that every person is as wicked as possible, that no one ever does anything good. The uniform testimony of Scripture is that God's image is marred, not totally effaced. God took note of Cornelius's good works, reflecting his faith (Acts 10:1-2). God always recognizes and welcomes obedience, goodness. But all people sin and fall short of God's glorious character (Rom. 3:23). No man is good enough to merit acceptance with God. No one is pure enough to be united with God. Like a bridge halfway across the chasm, the works of a good person are all the more poignant in their utter inability to save.

The law never was intended to make us righteous. The law simply shows us what we ought to be. For the lost sinner this is good news, for it leads him to the Savior. For the saved sinner this is good news, for it describes clearly what he is growing toward, what he longs to be in order to satisfy his Savior: likeness to Jesus Christ.

With such a glorious purpose, our minds and hearts are moved to run to this wonderful gift of grace, the law. But how does God reveal his will to us?

SOURCES OF KNOWING THE LAW

God reveals his will in many ways: through conscience, instruction, commandments, principles, and living demonstration.

The Roman Catholic church, following the theology of Thomas Aquinas (1224–1274), has built a great superstructure of morality based on "natural law." But Protestants hold that truth and goodness are defined by, and flow from, the nature of God. There is not some ultimate "way things are" that would seem to sit in judgment on God. There is no "nature of things" to which God must conform if he is to be good. No, he defines truth and goodness by being good and truthful. It is true that God reveals his existence and his power through creation (Rom. 1:18-20), but Protestants have held that the only sure guide for truth and goodness is the supernatural revelation of the written Word of God through prophets and apostles.

Having said this, however, we quickly admit that there is some knowledge of right and wrong, however dim and distorted, apart from the Bible, stamped somehow in the consciousness of human beings. This Paul teaches clearly (Rom. 2:14-15).

INNATE MORAL JUDGMENT

Although the Old Testament does not use the term *conscience,* the idea is there (1 Sam. 24:5; 2 Sam. 24:10; Jer. 31:33) and it is explicitly taught in the New Testament (Rom. 2:14-15; Acts 24:16; 2 Cor. 1:12; 1 Tim. 1:5; 2 Tim. 1:3; Heb. 10:2, 22).

Conscience is no more and no less than one's judgment in the moral realm. Naturally, this judgment is strongly conditioned, like all our judgments, by what we have learned from parents and society. Nevertheless, the Bible teaches that moral awareness is innate—everyone knows that there is right and wrong, though all do not agree on precisely what. Our moral judgment is distorted by our cultural environment and therefore is not an adequate moral light to follow.

Not only does environment condition our judgment, man's moral judgment is fallible, dimmed by his severe limitations of knowledge and wisdom. He doesn't have all the data needed to make the right judgment, and he doesn't have sufficient wisdom to evaluate the data he does have. Furthermore, his moral judgment is obscured by his separation from God, the source of moral light. His mind is inclined by sin to suppress the knowledge of the right, to distort the moral light he does have.

Thus, the human mind is like a computer of inadequate capacity, programmed with misinformation and short-circuited. Consequently, "Let your conscience be your guide" can be a dangerous maxim. Having said this, however, there is "the true light that enlightens every man . . . coming into the world" (John 1:9). And what a hell this world would be if God had not imprinted in man that moral likeness, however limited and blurred by sin.

A person's moral judgment is untrustworthy, but it can be renewed and become increasingly reliable. This mind renewal about which the apostles speak so insistently is intimately bound up in the idea of conscience or moral judgment. The regenerated mind, molded by study of the Word of God, obedient and sensitive to the Holy Spirit, and constantly asking for enlightenment, will become increasingly reliable.

The thought process of the Christian is the means by which God transforms him into the likeness of his Son. Often in the writings of Paul, when we might have used *heart* he used *mind*, and when we might have used *affections* he used *knowledge*. Of course, this is knowledge in the Hebrew sense, so it is not merely intellectual apprehension of truth, but personal experience and commitment. Nevertheless, it is the *mind* that God is after, the mind that bears the imprint of his likeness, the mind that must be renewed so that its moral judgments are increasingly reliable. Even that great experience of the heart and ultimate achievement of the moral good, love, has to do with the mind. Christ, in quoting the Old Testament law of love for God, deliberately added what was not said by Moses (Deut. 6:5), that we should love him with all the *mind* (Matt. 22:37). God's great mind renewal program reprograms our moral judgment so that it becomes increasingly reliable.

Nevertheless, apart from the written, revealed will of God, even the renewed and Spirit-sensitized conscience is not wholly reliable. Revelation is essential.

In Scripture God reveals his will through instruction in right thinking and right behavior, through direct commandments, through principles, and through the example of good and bad behavior. Instruction seemed to be the primary mode before the time of Moses and in the New Testament, whereas commandments seemed the prominent mode during the era of "the law." Examples of right and wrong conduct abound in the Old Testament, but the supreme model is found in Jesus Christ.

Principles, whether stated as such or derived from example and instruction, permeate the whole of Scripture.[6]

INSTRUCTION IN GOD'S STANDARD

At the very beginning some of God's will for man was revealed: he should have children and participate with the Creator in superintending the creation (Gen. 1:28). Those may or may not have been universal absolutes, but Adam also was not to eat a certain fruit (Gen. 2:17). Was that a moral issue? We continue to reproduce and attempt to superintend the part of creation we can get our hands on, but who can identify some forbidden fruit? Yet it was a moral issue; Adam and Eve both perceived this clearly. The moral issue was obedience. The test case was setting something desirable off limits.

We do not have a command about animal sacrifice recorded in the early chapters of Genesis, but from the beginning of sin, mankind knew God expected an atonement. Man knew that animal sacrifice would somehow allay God's wrath against sin. And sin was known, of course. How else could it "couch at the door" like some wild animal ready to pounce (Gen. 4:7)? The command to Abraham was clear enough: "Be perfect" (Gen. 17:2). But what is inherently moral about circumcision? It became a moral issue when God commanded it as the sign of the covenant. The Ten Commandments are moral, all would agree, but what about not eating pork? To love one's enemy is as high a moral standard as one could set, but in what way would baptism be a moral issue if Christ had not commanded it?

From the beginning God gave instruction about his will for mankind, but what *is moral law,* indicating characteristics of God that man also should have, and what *became a moral issue* only because God required it, seem to be interwoven. Christians freely violate many of the ancient laws (we eat pork and shellfish, for example) and carefully keep others, but on what basis do we separate what is God's sure will for us today from what may be safely ignored?

Some say that only requirements that are rooted in the nature of God should be considered binding. But who is to decide which teachings qualify? Does not that person become the real

[6]For guidelines on how to derive principles from Scripture, see Robert McQuilkin, *Understanding and Applying the Bible* (Chicago: Moody, 1983), chapters 18 and 19.

authority rather than Scripture? And where in the Bible is such a principle given? Others say that only what is repeated in the New Testament or only what is repeated in the epistles is binding for the Christian. But Jesus and the apostles seemed ignorant of such a principle. They both consistently quoted Scripture as the ultimate authority, and the Old Testament was all the Scripture they had. Furthermore, in the apostolic writings the teaching of Christ assumed ultimate authority. It would surely surprise them to have his words set aside in favor of theirs.

If Scripture is to be the final authority, sitting in judgment on all human opinion, not subject to evaluation and parceling out by some contemporary scholar, any teaching once given by inspiration of God must not be set aside except by subsequent divine revelation recorded in Scripture.[7] If this principle is accepted, what biblical instruction concerning God's will for man's obedience is still in force and what was subsequently set aside?

During the long period from the Fall to Sinai, not many specific commands were recorded. Nevertheless, it is evident throughout the record that God clearly revealed his moral requirements. Man was sinful, deliberately sinful, and he knew in what his sin consisted: lying, cheating, stealing, murder, adultery, idolatry. Then, from the depths of all this corruption, God chose by "the election of grace" a man and his descendants and gave him a promise and a command: "Be blameless" (Gen. 17:1). The Patriarchs knew the covenant—both the promise and their obligations as well. Since few of God's requirements are articulated in precise commandments recorded in Genesis, little controversy has divided Christians over what is applicable today.

Then came Moses, the lawgiver, and the law he gave from God combines moral and ritual law, health rules and civic ordinances for the nation Israel. Which are for us and which are not? Most hold that only the moral laws have continuing authority as a contemporary rule of life. But Moses made no such distinction. How may we? Even if we had the authority to do so, it would not be an easy task. Adultery is a moral issue

[7] J. R. McQuilkin, "Problems of Normativeness in Scripture: Cultural Versus Permanent," in *Hermeneutics, Inerrancy, and the Bible*, ed. Earl D. Radmacher and Robert D. Preus (Grand Rapids: Zondervan, 1984), 219.

(Deut. 22:22), all would agree, and so is failing to help someone in need (v. 1ff.). Even putting a railing around one's flat rooftop to prevent falls sounds moral enough (v. 8). But what about a woman wearing man's clothing (v. 5)? That rule is certainly not civic, hygienic, or even ceremonial. Is it moral? If so, what of sowing two kinds of seed in the same plot of land (v. 9) or putting fringes on the borders of one's clothing (v. 12)? Moses did not put God's laws into neat categories: "the following are for this era only" or, "these are moral laws with abiding authority." Therefore, *all* the requirements of the law under Moses were added to the covenantal requirements and promises given to Abraham, and all became binding on all of God's people. Then came the promised Messiah. Did he change the system? Did he set aside any of the law? Did he set aside all the law?

GOD'S WILL REVEALED IN JESUS CHRIST

The question of what Jesus thought of the law is not easily answered, for he seemed to say both yes and no to it. "Think not that I have come to abolish the law and the prophets," he said, "I have not come to abolish them, but to fulfill them" (Matt. 5:17). On the other hand, "You have heard that it was said, 'An eye for an eye and a tooth for a tooth.' But I say unto you . . ." (v. 38). Indeed, they had heard it said over and over: in Exodus (21:24), Leviticus (24:20), and in Deuteronomy (19:21)! And this was not a ceremonial or merely a civic law. This was moral.

In what sense, then, did he fulfill the law, and in what sense did he set it aside? *Fulfill* translates a rich word, used of fulfilling predictions, of completing or bringing to maturity or perfection, and of obeying.

1. *Jesus fulfilled the moral law by obeying it*. He obeyed the moral requirements of the law without fail (Luke 23:41; 2 Cor. 5:21). Thus he became the basic working model for Christian behavior.

God's will for man has ever been likeness to himself. But what is he like? For centuries God sent prophets to tell us. But in the end, he himself came to show us by living example. "He who has seen me has seen the Father" (John 14:9ff.). How blessed we are in the age of grace—we can see God in Jesus Christ. This does not mean that we can be right with God by imitating his Son. No, salvation is a free gift of his rightness to replace my wrongness. We are justified only by faith in Christ. But we were "created in Christ Jesus for good works" (Eph. 2:10), and he has clearly demonstrated that life since he came to do the will of the Father (John 4:34; 14:31; 15:10). True, we do not follow him in his obedience to Mosaic religious customs, which he himself was soon to abolish, nor do we imitate him in his unique ministry as the Son of God and Savior. But in his faithful reproduction of the character of the Father, he is our sure and certain example.

2. *Jesus fulfilled the law by fulfilling the prophecies contained in the law.* His birth, life, and ministry had been predicted in great detail, and these prophecies he fulfilled. Among them all, the great central event in history was his death, by which he simultaneously brought the law to completion and abolished it. He brought it to completion by becoming *the* sacrificial lamb to satisfy the demands of the law once for all. He "abolished" it by destroying the power of the law to condemn. By enacting the reality foreshadowed in the symbolism of the ceremonial laws, he brought them to an end (Heb. 7:26-28; 9:1, 9-10, 23-27).

Jesus Christ fulfilled the entire system of ceremonial laws and thus set them aside. This explanation of the meaning of Christ's death after he accomplished it fits perfectly with the pattern of his life and teaching. He consistently affirmed the authority of the "law," but his teaching was ever centered in the moral law. He never affirmed the ceremonial elements of the law.[8] In fact, he rather did the opposite on occasion. For example, he "declared all foods clean" (Mark 7:19) even before the cross, thus setting aside all the dietary regulations.

But his death was more than the fulfillment of the law in the sense of paying the penalty demanded by the law. It is also our example of supreme godlikeness. In fact, he put on display the highest form of love—complete sacrifice of self, even for one's enemy (Rom. 5:8). Never had the world even imagined such love. And it became the foundation for Christian behavior as well as the source of Christian life. The preaching of Christ and him crucified is the only enduring foundation for sound morality. "For God," Paul insists, "has not called us for

[8]*nomos,* in TDNT, vol. 4, 1062.

uncleanness, but in holiness" (1 Thess. 4:7). "And he died for all," he repeats, "that those who live might live no longer for themselves but for him which for their sake died and was raised" (2 Cor. 5:15). In this fact he finds the motive for holy living. That is why Paul never tires of relating the obligations of morality to the fact that Christ died for us. Is it a matter concerning domestic relationship? "Husbands, love your wives, as Christ loved the church and gave himself up for her" (Eph. 5:25). Is it a matter concerning the weaker brother? "Do not let what you eat cause the ruin of one for whom Christ died" (Rom. 14:15). Is it a matter of ambitious rivalry?

Have this mind among yourselves, which is yours in Christ Jesus, who, though he was in the form of God, did not count equality with God a thing to be grasped, but emptied himself, taking the form of a servant, being born in the likeness of men. And being found in human form he humbled himself and became obedient unto death, even death on a cross. (Phil. 2:5-8)

Is it a matter of daily living? "And walk in love, as Christ loved us and gave himself up for us, a fragrant offering and sacrifice to God" (Eph. 5:2). Is it a matter of sexual morality? "Do you not know that your body is a temple of the Holy Spirit . . . ? You are not your own; you were bought with a price. So glorify God in your body" (1 Cor. 6:19-20). The writers of the New Testament consistently appeal to the work of Calvary—to an accomplished redemption—as a ground and a motive of holy living.[9]

Christ fulfilled the law by fulfilling another prophecy: He sent the Holy Spirit as prophesied by the prophet Joel (Acts 2:17ff.). The day of Pentecost marked the birth of a new people of God, the church. This also seems to have been predicted, according to Paul (Rom. 9–11), though this is not as clear as other strains of prophecy. In any event, in establishing the church (Matt. 16:18) Jesus established a new way of administering God's people here on earth. The new dispensation of authority was no longer with political or military power. In fact, his Kingdom was no longer "of this world" (John 18:36). In setting up the church, Jesus set aside the administration of his purposes through the nation Israel. And by that setting aside, all

[9]Stuart Barton Babbage, "The Preacher's Task Today," *The Presbyterian Journal,* 2 September 1964, 7.

the regulations for that earthly Kingdom were rendered inoperative.

Christ fulfilled the law by obeying it and by fulfilling Old Testament prophecy, bringing the temporary elements to completion and setting them aside.

3. *Jesus fulfilled the law by affirming and explaining it.* He fulfilled the law by "completing it" in the sense of bringing out its perfect, ultimate meaning: murder is wrong, to be sure, but so is hatred (Matt. 5:21ff.). Adultery is sinful, but so is lust (v. 27). He gave the essence, the inner meaning of the law, he radicalized it, raising it to the highest. He gave the positive stimulus of love as well as the negative prohibitions. Throughout his ministry, he consistently affirmed the Old Testament as the authoritative Word of God (e.g., Matt. 5:17-19; 23:23). Furthermore, he used the Scripture's authority to reinforce his own teaching. His criticism of the law was primarily of the Pharasaic interpretations of the law (e.g., Matt. 5:20, 38) and the traditions added to the law (Matt. 15:1-9; chapter 23). Jesus' rejection of Pharisaical tradition was as sharp and clear as his identification with the law and the prophets.[10]

Jesus, then, catches up all the enduring truth about the character of God and his will for man revealed in the Old Testament and clarifies it, extends it, deepens it. The Sermon on the Mount (Matt. 5–7) is the most concentrated example of clarifying the law, but this approach permeated all his teaching. The law becomes *his* teaching ("*I* say unto you . . ."), which in turn becomes the standard for Christian behavior. In fact, in passing on the commandments of the Father he warns us repeatedly and clearly that we will be judged by that standard (e.g., John 12:47-50).

Furthermore, it is this whole body of teaching—all that he commanded—with which we are to disciple the nations (Matt. 28:18-20). Only those specific laws of the Old Testament or those categories of law (dietary, ceremonial, civil) that he set aside may we set aside on *his* authority.

4. *He fulfilled the law by being the real substance of which the law was only a shadow.* He accomplished what the law promised; he became the sacrifice which did what the law of animal sacrifice could never accomplish. In this he established the validity of the

[10]*nomos,* in TDNT, 1064.

ceremonial law, becoming what it pointed toward, but he also established the validity of the moral law. He demonstrated just how holy God really is, just how terrible sin really is in the sight of God. The cross of Christ is indeed the supreme fulfilling of the demands of the law. And by this he simultaneously proved the righteousness of God who long forgave sin before the sacrifice had been made (Rom. 3:21-31). Indeed, Jesus the Messiah came to fulfill the law!

GOD'S WILL REVEALED THROUGH THE APOSTLES

The apostles consistently appealed to the life and teaching of Jesus as having the highest authority. Christ's commission was clear: Go, disciple the nations and teach them everything I have commanded (Matt. 28:20).

No wonder the apostles made this teaching the touchstone of truth. For example, Paul exhorts Timothy,

If any one teaches otherwise and does not agree with the sound words of our Lord Jesus Christ . . . he is puffed up with conceit, he knows nothing. (1 Tim. 6:3-4)

Then with apostolic authority they added teaching they themselves received from God. This was in the form of commandments—hundreds of them—and in descriptions and explanations of the way Christians should think and live. For example, the description of love in 1 Corinthians 13 or of the fruit of the Spirit in Galatians 5 presents a standard of thrilling grandeur for Christian behavior. Negative descriptions also abound, as in Paul's description of the works of the flesh—fornication, uncleanness, lasciviousness, idolatry, sorcery, enmities, strife, jealousies, wraths, factions, divisions, parties, envyings, drunkenness, revellings, and such. Does he intend these as benevolent counsel or as law? He leaves no doubt: "I forewarn you that they who practice such things shall not inherit the Kingdom of God!" (Gal. 5:19-21). Happily, all shades of theological opinion affirm that the teaching of the apostles in the epistles is fully authoritative as a standard for Christian living.

But what about the law revealed in the Old Testament? Do the apostles join Jesus in affirming this law as authoritative for the era of the church? The apostolic answer, as in the case of Jesus Christ, seems to be a yes and a no (see 1 Cor. 9:19-23).

Are we under the law? Yes, say the apostles: Romans 7:12, 25; 8:7; 13:8-10; Galatians 5:13-14; Ephesians 6:1-3; Colossians 3:5-8; James 2:8; 1 Peter 1:16; 1 John 2:4-5; 3:7-8; 5:2-3; 2 John 5-6.

Are we under the law? No, say the apostles, especially Paul: Romans 6:14; 7:4, 6; 8:3-4; 10:4; 1 Corinthians 3:11; Galatians 3:19-25; 4:1-6; Ephesians 2:14-17; Colossians 3:14-23.

The words the apostles use seem clear enough: "He that saith, I know him, and keepeth not his commandments, is a liar, and the truth is not in him" (1 John 2:4-5). "So the law is holy, and the commandment is holy and just and good" (Rom. 7:12). "You are not under law but under grace" (Rom. 6:14). "But now we are discharged from the law" (Rom. 7:6).

How may these teachings be reconciled? Only a very small minority of Bible scholars have ever denied that the Old Testament law and the teachings of Christ prior to the Upper Room discourse (John 13–17) are addressed to Christians. Rather, the majority of theologians throughout church history have sought a resolution of this apparent conflict by making a clear distinction among the various uses of the term *law* and, on the basis of this, holding that the moral law is enduring and the ceremonial law has been done away with. But this is not easy to do. Neither Moses nor the prophets made this distinction, and it is not always apparent what is moral and what is merely ceremonial. Furthermore, though Jesus seemed to distinguish the two by his behavior and what he stressed, neither did he make this distinction explicitly. But the gravest problem with this interpretation is that Paul himself did not seem to make this distinction. He seemed often to lump together everything in the Mosaic economy as "the law" and teach that in Christ we have done with it. In Paul there is no distinction between the Decalogue and the rest of the law. The law is one, the revealed will of God.[11]

Thus the Mosaic dispensation seems to have been set aside. And yet the Mosaic law was clearly the undisputed authority, the divine Word, the final court of appeal for Christ and the

[11]*nomos*, in *Theological Dictionary of the New Testament*, 1069.

apostles.[12] Old Testament commands, promises, and principles of behavior reveal God's character and will for mankind. These instructions, filtered through the sieve of later revelation (the teaching of Christ and the apostles), are authoritative guides for faith and life. But what elements are screened out? Clearly the ceremonial system in its entirety was fulfilled in Christ, and the system of laws governing a nation has been replaced by another economy, the church. All would agree on that. But what of "moral" law?

In solving this dilemma of strategic importance, perhaps the common wisdom will lead us to the best solution. Throughout church history the Ten Commandments have been taken as the epitome of moral truth, a summary of what God expects of man.

The Ten Commandments seem to summarize what the descendants of the Patriarchs already understood. Did they understand solely because the laws were imprinted in their moral consciousness, or were those laws communicated by God in other ways unknown to us?

When the Decalogue was given, it seemed to be the focus of attention. It was the first part of the law God gave; it alone was inscribed in stone with his own finger. And that not once, but twice. Furthermore, it was this sacred law—not the scrolls of the entire Torah—which was placed in the holiest place, in the Ark of the Covenant. In other words, these ten "words," as they were called, seemed to be the basis of the Mosaic covenant—not given to a people to show them how to get right with God, but given to a people who long since had been chosen by God to instruct them how not to break covenant and be put out of the circle of grace.

When we come to the New Testament, it is to the Decalogue and to parts of it that both Jesus and the apostles constantly return as the basis of authority for what God expects of his people.

In the light of this clear focusing on the Decalogue, coupled with the ambiguity of the New Testament witness to the other elements of Old Testament law, the nearest we can come to a solution is this: The Mosaic economy indeed has been surpassed

[12]"More than ninety times Jesus and the New Testament writers affirm 'it is written,' citing the Old Testament as the authority for their teaching [as in] Matthew 4:4, 7, 10." Norman L. Geisler, *The Christian Ethic of Love* (Grand Rapids: Zondervan, 1973), 46.

by the incarnate Son of God (John 1:17; Luke 16:16), but the Decalogue is a touchstone to discern, among all the recorded Old Testament laws of all varieties, what is the enduring will of God for his people of all ages. Those laws or other teaching which derive from, interpret, or reinforce one of the Ten Commandments should thus be recognized as having enduring authority.

Note carefully that this selection from among the laws of the Old Testament is not made on the basis of what is repeated in the New Testament. That would be to impose on Scripture the judgment of the interpreter. The selection is made on the basis of what subsequent revelation—Scripture itself—sets aside of earlier revelation. Ceremonial and national elements of the law, along with some moral laws, are clearly set aside. Indeed, the entire dispensation seems to have been disallowed by Paul as having binding authority on Christian conscience. But the Ten Commandments and moral law as law are constantly reaffirmed. On this basis we apply Old Testament teaching to Christian life and doctrine.

God's will for us is thus revealed through innate moral consciousness, through written instruction, through Jesus Christ, and through the teaching of the apostles. There is one other way that is part of these ways already mentioned: example.

GOD'S WILL REVEALED THROUGH PEOPLE

The most obvious example we have already considered: Jesus himself perfectly modeled the will of God. The example next in importance is probably Paul, not only because we know so much more about him than others, but because six times we are instructed to follow his example (1 Cor. 4:6; 11:1; Phil. 3:17; 1 Thess. 1:6; 2 Thess. 3:7, 9). This does not mean Paul's example is perfect; he was a sinner just as we are. But his life is exemplary, even if not as infallible as his teachings.

Beyond these paramount models, however, Scripture is filled with examples of conduct and attitudes, both good and bad, revealing God's will for us. We cannot take the examples of the people of Scripture as our standard, of course, unless Scripture itself extols the conduct as good or condemns it as evil. But

when it does, this becomes another means of knowing God's
will.

In these ways, God in his loving grace has revealed clearly
what he wants us to be and do. God's purposes for giving the
law, however, will be fulfilled only when the law is used rightly.
If used wrongly, we will become more like the Devil, not more
like the Son. Christ and Paul both said yes and no to the law;
they were saying no to the wrong use of the law, yes to the right
use of the law. A major wrong use of the law is called "legalism."

LEGALISM

The law is good (Rom. 7:12), the law is spiritual (v. 14), the
law is continuing in effect (Matt. 5:17-19), but it is only good if
it is used lawfully, as it was intended (1 Tim. 1:8). How is it
possible to misuse the law? How can the law be used illegally or
unlawfully?

LEGALISM THE BIBLE OPPOSES

Obedience as a Way of Salvation. Relying on obedience to
moral law or observance of ceremonial law for salvation (Rom.
3:20, 28; Gal. 2:16; 3:11, 21) has been the historic theological
meaning of legalism. Much of what Paul wrote to the churches
in Rome and Galatia was to combat this deadly heresy. It was
not an innovation of the Pharisees who, through law, put Christ
to death, nor the Judaizers who dogged Paul's footsteps. It has
ever been man's method of attempted salvation.

This is the primary meaning of *legalism*—relying on
obedience to law for acceptance with God. But there are other
forms of legalism or, literally, lawism.

Obedience for Self-Glory. It is quite possible to teach salvation
by grace through faith alone and yet to be legalistic, misusing
the law by seeking to "save" oneself through obedience to the
law. When we let our light shine before men that they may see
our good works and glorify *us,* we are taking the credit that
belongs to God. This can be seen when a Christian measures his
own acceptability with God or the acceptability of other

Christians with himself on the basis of performance. The good feeling accompanying successful obedience to the law that gives self the credit rather than being filled with amazement and thanksgiving to a gracious, enabling Holy Spirit, is another evidence of legalism which God hates. Such will receive no reward at all (Matt. 6:1-18). This is the opposite of the way of faith: "How can you believe, who receive glory from one another and do not seek the glory that comes from the only God?" (John 5:44).

Obedience through Self-Effort. Closely related to the motive of obedience for self-glory is obedience through one's own strength. When we try to obey the law without relying on the enabling of the Holy Spirit, we, though saved by grace, are "saving" ourselves by works.

> Legalism is always the worst kind of corruption; or, in other words, the worst state of man is that in which he has complete confidence in himself. For this state of mind constitutes the source of all falsity, for it is the denial of the fact that the Good is always the Gift of God . . . that he cannot live on his own resources. . . .[13]

Unremitted Guilt. Another way to deny the sufficiency of God's provision in Christ is to bear the burden of guilt that the Savior has already borne. God "is faithful and just," not just merciful and kind (1 John 1:9). If the Father did not forgive our sins, he would be unfaithful and unjust, for he would be demanding of us a second payment for what has already been paid. He would be breaking contract with the Son. But where God is faithful and just, we are often unfaithful and unjust, bearing our own sense of guilt as if we ourselves by adequate remorse or additional good behavior could atone for it, as if Christ's work of atonement is not quite adequate. This is legalism of a terrible sort.

Obedience from the Motive of Fear. Though obedience for less than the highest motive is not necessarily sinful and, therefore, not legalism in the same way, it nevertheless reflects

[13]Emil Brunner, *The Divine Imperative,* trans. Olive Wyon (London: Lutterworth, 1937), 71.

an immaturity in relationships. If we obey the law out of fear of the consequences, rather than from love for the law-giver, we are, once again, coming under the condemnation of the law. To be sure, it is better to obey legalistically than to disobey illegalistically. And God appeals to his children to obey both from a hope of reward and a fear of loss (Ezek. 3:17-21; 33:7-9; Dan. 12:3; 1 Cor. 3:10-15). But the highest motive is love. Obedience out of gratitude for all the gifts of grace is the best antidote to the virus of legalism.

These are the abuses of the law which the Bible warns against. But the term *legalism* is applied by most people to attitudes and activities that are thoroughly biblical or at least legitimate.

LEGALISM THE BIBLE DOES NOT OPPOSE

Legalism Does Not Mean "Affirming Law as a Standard of Life." Most situational ethicists and some dispensationalists oppose law as law; they have no place for any externally imposed imperative. "We are not under law" means that we are not under obligation to any codified standard of behavior. For this position, love for the law is legalistic. "O how I love thy law" is sure evidence of the psalmist's legalism. We have attempted to point out the place of the law in human life from a biblical perspective, but this particular view of law will be dealt with in greater detail later (sections on "Law and Grace" and "Situation Ethics") since it is of such crucial importance and widespread influence.

Legalism Does Not Mean "The Bondage of Obligation as Opposed to Freedom." In the Bible freedom is not license to do what we please, but power to do what we ought. And what we ought is to obey the will of God. That will is revealed, among other ways, by the laws of God. The contemporary view that man is basically all right and restrictions make him bad has influenced the thinking of Christians so that law and freedom are set in opposition. But this is not the biblical view. To begin with, according to Scripture, freedom in any ultimate sense is an illusion. All we are really offered in human existence is the choice of masters: sin or righteousness, Satan or God.

The liberty of the God who would have his creatures free is in contest with the slavery of the creature who would cut his own stem from his root that he might call it his own and love it. . . . If he says, "At least I have it in my own way!" I answer, you do not know what is your way and what is not. You know nothing of whence your impulses, your desires, your tendencies, your likings come. They may spring now from some chance, as of nerves diseased; now from some roar of a wandering devil; now from some infant hate in your heart; now from the greed of lawlessness of some ancestor you would be ashamed of if you knew him; or it may be, now from some far-piercing chord of a heavenly orchestra: the moment comes up into your consciousness, you call it your own way, and glory in it.[14]

Not only is ultimate freedom an illusion, but in a sense law actually provides what true freedom there is. The locomotive is most free to fulfill its purpose when it runs freely on the confining tracks, most in bondage and condemned to failure in reaching its destination when it abandons those tracks for the pasture across the fence. So man is most free when he runs on the tracks of God's revealed will, most certain to miss the purpose of his humanity as he leaves those tracks for the "freedom" of his own way. It is a wrong use of the term *legalism* to set law in opposition to freedom. The opposite of freedom is bondage. And the ultimate bondage is bondage to sin, not to law.

Legalism Does Not Mean "Setting Specific Regulations."
Perhaps the most common misuse of the term *legalism* is to mean creating rules, especially many rules, more especially negative rules, and most especially minor rules or, as it is said, "picky little rules." Often people—and some scholars—say the Bible is not a shopping list of "dos" and "don'ts."

Some people look to the Bible for a set of one, two, three rules. We do not find that kind of printout from the Bible. What we do find are timeless guidelines that direct and lead us toward freedom in the Lord.[15]

I don't know what Bible he was reading. Moses is not the only one who set forth a list of don'ts. Paul gave many a list of don'ts and included some "picky little rules" having to do with hair styles and dress, among other things.

[14]*George Macdonald: An Anthology*, ed. C. S. Lewis (New York: Macmillan, 1947), 87.
[15]Robert L. Maddox, *Adult Bible Study* (Nashville: Baptist Sunday School Board, July 1981), 12.

The existence of a set of rules and regulations or a code of law does not constitute legalism (Gal. 6:2; 1 Tim. 3:2; Rom. 8:2). If on the basis of our spiritual blessing in Christ we are expected to walk worthy of our calling and obey the commands of God, then a desire to obey God does not constitute legalism (Eph. 1:3; 4:1; 5:8; Phil. 1:27). Having to do something is not legalism (1 Tim. 3:2; Eph. 5:28; 2 Thess. 1:3; Rom. 15:27). Paul spoke of owing, being indebted, obligated—having to do something. Having a list of don'ts is not legalism (Rom. 12:2; Col. 3:9; Gal. 6:9; Eph. 4:25–5:18; 1 John 2:13).[16]

It is not legitimate to call a society "legalistic" simply because it has many laws. If so, the Bible is indeed one of the most legalistic of all books.

Legalism Does Not Mean "Insisting on the Letter of the Law Rather Than the Spirit." One of the most common misunderstandings of legalism is to set the letter of the law ("legalism") over against the spirit of the law ("freedom"). In this view, conscientious conformity to the explicit commands of Scripture is held to be legalistic. "Conformity as the essence of Christian morality" is given as a definition of legalism, so that strict adherence, regular obedience to exactly what Scripture teaches, is held up as soul-destroying bondage. But is this a biblical understanding of legalism? Often those who say that "obeying the letter" is legalism mean that it's all right to ignore the law so long as you mean well, so long as you are loving in your spirit. This is sheer situationism, and those who take the authority of Scripture seriously are not likely to take this position.

But what does Paul mean in contrasting the "letter" and the "spirit"? He means exactly what he always means in attacking legalism: salvation by works. Paul is adamant against certain kinds of rules: those that would offer a substitute or supplement to Christ's atoning work on the cross.

Two passages in the New Testament contrast the letter and spirit (Rom. 7:6; 2 Cor. 3:6, NIV). "The letter kills, but the Spirit gives life." In both cases Paul uses "letter" as a synonym for law—the law that shuts us up to condemnation—and "Spirit," the Holy Spirit who gives life. In both cases Paul is

16Paul Wright, class notes on "Legalism," (Columbia, S.C.: Graduate School of Bible and Missions).

giving the same teaching against legalistic dependence on self-effort to earn our salvation.

Further, the Bible is very clear in condemning observance of the legal statement ("letter") as a cover for violation of the intent or spirit of the law. The Pharisees used the statement of the law to subvert the intent of the law while professing great loyalty to the law. They taught that if one swore by the altar, rather than by the offering on the altar, the oath was not binding. If a person made a contract in the name of the temple, rather than by the gold of the temple, that contract could be broken. If a possession of value was verbally "dedicated to God," one need not use it to assist his own parents who were in need (Matt. 23:17-18).

The Pharisees emphasized obeying the lesser, easier, visible, external "letter" while neglecting the heavy, more important thing, the "spirit" of the law. Their motive was to be seen of men (Matt. 23:5). They wished to receive credit for a level of godliness that was not true. They attempted to buy a good reputation at discount prices. And they were successful. "Pharisee" means "saint," and they were not called this in derision. People considered them the highest and best in moral uprightness. But Jesus condemned this.

You tithe mint and dill and cummin, and have neglected the weightier matters of the law, justice and mercy and faith; these you ought to have done, without neglecting the others. You blind guides, straining out a gnat and swallowing a camel! (Matt. 23:23-24)

Their problem was not legalism, strictly speaking, but hypocrisy. They were play actors. "They preach, but do not practice" (Matt. 23:3).

It is reported that some evangelical German SS troops in World War II would not dance or drink alcoholic beverages, although they executed thousands of Jews. "Bible-believing" young people have been known to refrain from going to movies and dancing in order to be approved by the church, but then "make out" in the backseat of a car. Many Christians religiously tithe but are thoroughly materialistic. How many zealous Christians are there who aggressively go after decisions for

Christ but whose daily life witnesses not to Christ, but to themselves, to their own self-centered thinking?

No, Christ's answer is clear: "These you ought to have done, without neglecting the others" (Matt. 23:23). "Practice and observe whatever they tell you, but not what they do; for they preach, but do not practice" (Matt. 23:3). He is not setting the letter against the spirit. Christ says that the letter is important, but above all the spirit of the law is important. The statement of the law will never violate the principle of the law, but we must above all guard the principle.

Legalism Is Not "Obedience to Man-made Laws." Some hold that obedience to God-made laws is truly Christian, but to require obedience to man-made rules is legalistic. But Scripture takes a stand squarely on the side of human authority. In fact, human authorities are ordained by God. Obedience to human authority is not optional. On the other hand, no human authority is absolute, for all human authority stands under the judgment of God, and each person must finally give an account of his ultimate allegiance to the Authority above all authorities.

1. Marriage: "Wives, be subject to your husbands, as to the Lord" (Eph. 5:22).

2. Home: "Children, obey your parents in the Lord, for this is right" (Eph. 6:1).

3. Government: "Let every person be subject to the governing authorities. For there is no authority except from God" (Rom. 13:1).

4. Employment: "Slaves, be obedient to those who are your earthly masters . . . as to Christ" (Eph. 6:5).

5. Church: "Obey your leaders and submit to them; for they are keeping watch over your souls, as men who will have to give account" (Heb. 13:17).

The genuineness of one's obedience to God is often tested at the point of human authority. Human authority is not given by God merely to police the Ten Commandments or to issue benevolent advice. Human authority is law-making and law-enforcing authority. Every person who is under a legitimate authority must obey that authority unless obedience would violate the revealed will of God (Acts 5:29).

Human authority should be exercised with justice, wisdom,

and love. It should be cheerfully obeyed. When it is not just or wise or loving, however, the one under authority is not thereby released from responsibility to obey (1 Pet. 2:18). It is quite legitimate for him to seek for change in biblical ways, but if he resents and resists the authority, the relationship becomes destructive. Some human relationships can be legitimately dissolved, others cannot. In our society a child ultimately leaves the home, a citizen can move to another nation, an employee can resign and seek other employment, a church member can move to another church. But the wife cannot leave her husband, the child cannot leave until he is of age. It is certainly not always the will of God for citizens, employees, or church members to flee the difficult situation, but often it is in the will of God. However, so long as the relationship is maintained, the authority is God's own, delegated to human administrators. Apparently God knows that it is better to have inadequate human government than to have no government at all.

Legalism Is Not "Law" in Opposition to "Love." Some hold that it is legalistic to be law-oriented, for by definition that means that one is not person-oriented. This way of setting law over against love is so widespread and so influential, we shall devote the last section of this chapter to the theme "Law and Love." As we saw in the earlier chapter on "Love," love is actually the fulfilling of the law. So far from being opposed, in a sense Scripture identifies the two.

LAW AND GRACE

What sweeter and more glorious word than *grace!* When a righteous God looks down on us today, he does not see his own image hopelessly distorted and polluted. He does not see weak, stumbling moral derelicts. He sees us as pure and innocent and right and strong as Jesus Christ. Because he sees us through the cross, we are clean.

Grace is not merely favor to one who does not deserve it. Grace is loving favor to one who deserves God's wrath. Reconciliation with God and eternal life cannot be earned. All the good I have is God's free gift (Rom. 3:21-31; Eph. 2:1-8).

But this is not a new thing. Men have always been saved by the grace of God alone. Then what of that terrifying word *law*? Is it not opposed to grace? Was it not done away in Christ?

All would agree that without law, grace would have no meaning. Without law there would be no sin (Rom. 7:7). Without sin there would be no need of forgiveness. The cross of Jesus not only brings forgiveness through grace, it proves the reality and the significance of the law. Breaking the law is so terrible that God would have to give his only Son to meet the law's demands and set aside the judgment due Adam's race. That is how real and how strong the law truly is. But once that purpose of the law is fulfilled, is it not done away?

No, as we have seen, the law is still holy and just and good. No longer does it stand scowling over me in judgment. It shines a bright, clear light on my roadway to glory. It spotlights my destination—the glorious character of God himself. And who could object to that? Two schools of thought, primarily.

The first and most influential in the church is the antinomian (against-the-law) stance of existential theologians. When they apply their basic touchstone to ethics, it is called situation ethics.

[What] Rudolf Bultmann expressed as early as 1930 has become generally accepted, namely, that any ethics that hopes to answer the question, "What must I do?" is based on a misunderstanding of the human situation. Discussing the "great commandment," he insisted that loving the neighbor does not tell you what to do but only how to do it. Bultmann's observation has become a cliche in Christian ethics. Christians allegedly know intuitively what to do if they stand under the power of love. . . . Similarly, Joseph Fletcher says, "No law or principle or value is good as such—not life or truth or chastity or property or marriage or anything but love. Only one thing is intrinsically good, namely, love: nothing else at all."[17]

This position is so widely held and so influential, even in erstwhile evangelical circles, that we will later devote a full chapter to it. But at this point, it will not be necessary to discuss their rejection of law because the view is not based on Scripture to begin with. The authority of Scripture does not figure in the discussion other than as a resource for notions that may reinforce the philosophical position already adopted for nonbiblical reasons. Many of the most influential people of the

[17]George W. Forell, *History of Christian Ethics*, vol. 1 (Minneapolis: Augsburg, 1979), 21.

movement, like Joseph Fletcher, do not even believe in a personal God.

But there is another school of thought that stands solidly within the evangelical mainstream of commitment to an authoritative revelation in the Bible. Many leading dispensationalists of the last quarter of the twentieth century have moved away from the position of the movement's most articulate systematizer, Lewis Sperry Chafer, but a host of popularizers hold with Chafer in seeing no place for law—not just Moses' law, but Jesus' teaching, as well.

It is evident that the law was never addressed to any outside the one nation Israel, and also that, since the death of Christ, no Jew, Gentile, or Christian is now under the law either for justification, or as a rule of life.[18]

There is a dangerous and entirely baseless sentiment abroad which assumes that every teaching of Christ must be binding during this age simply because Christ said it.[19]

Since law and grace are opposed to each other at every point, it is impossible for them to coexist, either as the ground of acceptance before God or as the rule of life. Of necessity, therefore, the Scriptures of the New Testament which present the facts and scope of grace, both assume and directly teach that the law is done away. Consequently, it is not in force in the present age in any sense whatsoever. This present nullification of the law applies not only to the legal code of the Mosaic system and the law of the Kingdom, but to every possible application of the principle of law.[20]

It is clear that, for Chafer, law as law has been done away with. Neither the Ten Commandments, the Sermon on the Mount, nor even the instructions in the apostolic letters are law for the Christian in the sense of a rule of life or as binding obligations that must be obeyed. But what do other theologians say?

Augustine: The law was given that grace might be sought; grace was given that the law might be fulfilled.[21]

Westminster Confession (Presbyterian): The moral law doth forever bind all, as well justified persons as others, to the obedience thereof . . . as a rule of life informing them of the will of God, and their duty, it directs and binds them to walk accordingly.[22]

Articles of Religion (Church of England): The Old Testament is not contrary to the New: for both in the Old and New Testament everlasting life is offered to Mankind by Christ, who is the only Mediator between God and

[18]Chafer, *Grace*, 99.
[19]Ibid., 179.
[20]Ibid., 215.
[21]*De Spiritu et Littera*, Sec. XIX.
[22]Westminster Confession, Chap. XIX.

Man, being both God and Man. . . . Although the Law given from God by Moses, as touching Ceremonies and Rites, do not bind Christian men, nor the Civil precepts thereof ought of necessity to be received in any commonwealth; yet notwithstanding, no Christian man whatsoever is free from the obedience of the Commandments which are called Moral.[23]

Formula of Concord (Lutheran): The law is the certain rule and norm for achieving a godly life and behavior in accord with God's eternal, immutable will.[24]

Institutes of the Christian Religion, John Calvin: There are not various rules of life, but one perpetual and inflexible rule; and, therefore, when David describes the righteous as spending their whole lives in meditation on the Law (Ps. 1:2) we must not confine to a single age, an employment which is most appropriate to all ages, even to the end of the world.[25]

Carl F. H. Henry, a Baptist and leading evangelical theologian: There is no depreciation of law, nor of the essential continuity of Old and New Testament ethics, in Augustine, Aquinas, Luther, Calvin, and Wesley.[26]

Many preachers and lay people continue to follow Chafer's stance on the law and even go beyond him in antinomian teaching, but few of the leading theologians of the dispensational movement go along with the earlier view. Increasingly, dispensational theologians have moved toward mainstream Christian teaching in affirming the moral law as God's requirement of Christians. For example, Charles Ryrie, a leading spokesman, writes:

The Sermon on the Mount does not present the way of salvation but the way of righteous living for those who are in God's family. . . . It was also an elaboration of the spirit of the law. For all of us it is a detailed revelation of the righteousness of God, and its principles are applicable to the children of God today.[27]

The author does not say that the commands themselves are binding, but he clearly affirms the spirit and principles of the law as authoritative for believers today.

With unanimous voice, the great streams of orthodox theological thinking have held that the law is for the believer. Yet it is true that the emphases of the Old Testament and the New are different. This is inherent in the necessary historical sequence of events. The loving grace of God revealed in its full splendor in the person of Christ could not in the nature of the

23Articles of Religion, VII.
24Formula of Concord, 4. See also Luther's *Large Catechism,* I, 311.9
25Calvin, *Institutes,* Book II, chap. VIII, 13.
26*Christian Personal Ethics* (Grand Rapids: Eerdmans, 1957), 259.
27*The Ryrie Study Bible* (Chicago: Moody, 1976), 12.

case be fully revealed before the Son of God appeared. Not only was the historical event of the incarnation necessary, it was also necessary that people be prepared through knowledge of a holy and righteous God. Otherwise, they would not even want a Savior. In a sense every person who comes to God comes through a sequence of divine revelation on the pattern of Holy Scripture. For until he understands the just requirement of the law, a person will not seek salvation. So long as there is no great problem, one is not concerned about a solution. Until the ears of the heart are opened by the thunders of Sinai, one does not truly hear the beautiful grace notes of Calvary.

Thus law and grace are two sides of the single coin of God's salvation. Without grace, law is a terrifying destroyer. Without law, grace is meaningless. Each is true only as the other is rightly understood. As Jesus said, those who set aside the least of God's laws will indeed be least in his realm (Matt. 5:18-19).

Thus it is that the Gospel secures liberty, and, at the same time, guards against licentiousness. To look only . . . or even principally, to the demands of law . . . constituted as human nature now is, cramps and deadens the energies of the soul, generates a spirit of bondage, which . . . ever vacillating between the fear of doing too little, and the desire of not doing more than is strictly required, can know nothing of the higher walks of excellence and worth. On the other hand, to look to the grace and liberty of the Gospel away from the law of eternal rectitude . . . with which they stand inseparably connected, is to give a perilous license to the desires and emotions of the heart . . . nurses a spirit of individualism, which, spurning the restraints of authority, is apt to become the victim of its own caprice, or the pliant slave of vanity and lust; for true liberty . . . in the spiritual as well as in the civil sphere, is a *regulated* freedom; it moves within the bonds of law, in a spirit of rational obedience; and the moment these are set aside, self-will rises to the ascendant, bringing with it the witchery and dominion of sin. It is only, therefore, the combined operation of the two which can secure the proper result; and with whom is that to be found except with those who have received the Spirit of life in Christ Jesus?[28]

Work, work the law demands
But gives us neither feet nor hands.
A sweeter sound the gospel brings:
It bids us fly and gives us wings.

If law and grace are not opposed to one another, what of law and love?

[28]Fairbairn, *Revelation of Law*, 283-284.

LAW AND LOVE

Well-meaning people who claim to believe the Bible join with well-meaning people who deny the authority of Scripture relegating to the outer darkness of unlove all law or all laws save the law of love. It would seem that one must choose between the hard virtues of righteousness and holiness or the supreme virtue of love.

Yet if love sums up the will of God for humankind, and righteousness is described as right or truth in the moral realm, even though we do not hold the two to be synonymous, certainly each is an essential element in the character of God. And both are essential elements in the will of God for us.

If God's righteous character and will for humankind is expressed, among other ways, in laws, the keeping of those laws is the outworking or practical expression of love, taken either as a comprehensive summary of the other laws or as motive. Apart from this loving obedience to law we do not know God, and our Christian profession is a lie (Matt. 28:20; John 14:15, 23, 31; 15:10, 14; Rom. 13:10; James 2:8; 1 John 2:4-6; 3:24; 4:8; 5:3; 2 John 6).

> The Christian is sometimes faced with a false dilemma; it is either the love of law or the law of love, we are told. Either one is concerned with the love of duty or the duty of love. This makes better poetry than morality. . . . The laws define the duty of love in each sphere of responsibility. . . . It is incredible to give a man a summary of a story he has never read and then ask him to write the whole story. . . . The fact that many of the commandments are negative in form does not mean they are negative in intent. It is much easier to name the few things which are not loving than the many things which are. . . . The law is love put into words.[29]
>
> Biblical ethics does not exhibit love and law or principles as mutually exclusive categories; the good life is the life of love, and sin is a lawlessness and the unprincipled life. To love God is to do the will of God or to keep his commandments. Every statement of the love of God, in terms either of Old Testament or of New Testament ethics, equates it with the fulfillment of specific commandments.[30]

So far from being at odds or merely incompatible, love is the essence of God's law, and other laws are the outworking of the law of love. As the ancient saying has it, "Love is the mother of all the virtues." By saying that love summarizes the law, neither

[29]Geisler, *The Christian Ethic of Love*, 43, 51-52.
[30]Henry, *Christian Personal Ethics*, 261.9

Christ, John, Paul, nor James meant that it was a substitute for the law.

If love does not substitute for the other commandments, neither does the law of love reduce the requirements of law. Rather, it extends them. Love radicalizes the law, showing the true extent and inner meaning of the specific (and, therefore, limited) and external commandments.

If love does not substitute for nor reduce the requirements of law, neither is it weaker than law. Love, if conceived of as motive, is not the full meaning of "the law of love." It is the law which goes beyond motivation or feeling and, indeed, sometimes bypasses love-as-emotion.

Must I do it?

Yes.

Must I do it whether I want to or not?

Yes.

Must I do it no matter what my motivation?

Yes. That is what law means. Of course, if love sets the spirit free, God's commands are no longer a grief (1 John 5:3). Then I will long to obey this law as my high privilege. Love, then, far from being an enemy or even a stranger to law, actually serves simultaneously to motivate obedience to law (love as a noun describing the emotion) and to summarize the requirements of the law (love as a verb describing righteous behavior).

In summary, the enemies of the law come in three varieties:

1. Those who are "friends" of the law, who assign it a role it was never designed to bear: a way to reconciliation with God;

2. Friend-enemies who recognize laws, but only certain kinds: law-as-principle, or the law of love, or God-made laws only; and

3. Enemies—the pure antinomians who relegate law to the past (and perhaps the future), who substitute freedom for law, or the work of the Spirit for law.

But as we have seen, none of these views is biblical. Law is limited—it cannot produce righteousness in sinner or saint, it cannot give life or overcome sin. And he is no true friend of law who treats it as if it could. But law does have a place. It is a gift of grace, no enemy of grace. Grace may not substitute for it. Law leads us to grace, and grace then, in turn, enables us to obey the law. And law is no enemy to freedom. True freedom is found only in the release of wholehearted submission to the will of God, much of which is revealed in his laws. Neither is the blessed Holy Spirit a substitute for law. A subjective reliance on his inner impulse was never God's intent as a substitute for the written revelation of his will. He is the author of the laws, and he is the enabler of law-keeping.

If law as such may not be set aside, neither may one aspect of law be substituted for the whole. Principles are indeed paramount in God's revelation of his will; they are, indeed, law. But they were never intended to substitute for other kinds of law. They are one variety of law, but they will never release from the obligations of other, specific commandments. Principles only extend them and help apply them to contemporary situations. Nor may God-made laws be the sole criterion of biblically right behavior. God has established human authority as part of his God-given requirements. Finally, the single law of love may not be substituted for all other laws. The law of love summarizes all the rest, traces the source, illumines the purpose, clarifies the motivation, but is no substitute for all its "children."

Is it true that "law is bondage"? "And I shall walk at liberty, for I have sought thy precepts" (Ps. 119:45).

Is it true, as Joseph Fletcher says, that "no twentieth-century man of even average training will turn his back on the anthropological and psychological evidence for relativity in morals. . . . There are no 'universal laws' held by all men everywhere at all times . . . no more tablets of stone"?[31] The Scripture says, "The sum of thy word is truth; and every one of thy righteous ordinances endures for ever" (Ps. 119:160).

Is it true that "each believer should seek the enlightenment of the Holy Spirit rather than adhering to rigid rules that disregard his individuality"?[32] "I had not known sin except through the law" (Rom. 7:7). "How can a young man keep his way pure? By guarding it according to thy word" (Ps. 119:9). "Thy word is a lamp to my feet and a light to my path" (v. 105).

Is it true that "law and grace are opposed to each other at every point? . . . Consequently, [the law] is not in force in the

31Joseph Fletcher, *Situation Ethics: The New Morality* (Philadelphia: Westminster, 1966), 76, 50.
32Carol A. Usher, "One Kind: Conformity or Liberty," *Christianity Today,* 28 March 1975, 10.

present age in any sense whatsoever. This present nullification of the law applies not only to the legal code of the Mosaic system and law of the kingdom [Christ's teaching], but to every possible application of the principle of law."[33] "Whoever then relaxes one of the least of these commandments and teaches men so, shall be called least in the kingdom of heaven" (Matt. 5:19). "If you love me, you will keep my commandments" (John 14:15). "And by this we may be sure that we know him, if we keep his commandments. He who says 'I know him' but disobeys his commandments is a liar, and the truth is not in him" (1 John 2:3-4).

Is the spirit of Christ truly represented in the senior theological student who testified publicly, and with great fervor, "I can't *stand* any system of law"? "Oh, how I love thy law! It is my meditation all the day" (Ps. 119:97). "How sweet are thy words to my taste, sweeter than honey to my mouth!" (v. 103). "Thy testimonies are my heritage for ever; yea, they are the joy of my heart" (v. 111). "My eyes are awake before the watches of the night, that I may meditate upon thy promise" (v. 148). "The law of thy mouth is better to me than thousands of gold and silver pieces" (v. 72). "Thy statutes have been my songs in the house of my pilgrimage" (v. 54).

SUGGESTED ADDITIONAL READING

Bolton, Samuel. *The True Bounds of Christian Freedom*. Carlisle, Penn.: Banner of Truth, 1978.

Brokke, H. J. *The Law Is Holy*. Minneapolis: Bethany Fellowship, 1963.

Brunner, Emil. *The Divine Imperative*. Translated by Olive Wyon. London: Lutterworth, 1937.

Chafer, Lewis Sperry. *Grace*. Grand Rapids: Zondervan, 1922.

Dodd, C. H. *Gospel and Law*. Irvington-on-Hudson, New York: Columbia University, 1953.

Durham, J. *The Law Unsealed*. Edinburgh: D. Schaw, 1802.

Eldersveld, P. H. *Of Law and Love*. Grand Rapids: Eerdmans, 1954.

Fairbairn, Patrick. *The Revelation of Law in Scripture*. New York: Carter, 1869.

Henry, Carl F. H. *Christian Personal Ethics*. Grand Rapids: Eerdmans, 1957.

Kaiser, W. C. *Toward Old Testament Ethics*. Grand Rapids: Zondervan, 1983.

Kevin, E. F. *The Evangelical Doctrine of Law*. London: Tyndale, 1964.

_____. *Keep His Commandments*. London: Tyndale, 1955.

Knight, G. A. F. *Law and Grace*. Naperville, Ill.: Allenson, 1962.

Lloyd-Jones, D. Martyn. *Romans*. London: Banner of Truth, 1973. See exposition of Romans 7:1–8:4.

Manson, T. W. *Ethics and the Gospel*. New York: Scribner's, 1960.

[33]Chafer, *Grace,* 215.

McQuilkin, R. C. *God's Law and God's Grace*. Grand Rapids: Eerdmans, 1958.

Murray, John. *Principles of Conduct*. Grand Rapids: Eerdmans, 1957. See chapter 8.

The entry *nomos*, in *Theological Dictionary of the New Testament*. Vol. 4. Edited by Gerhard Kittel; translated by Geoffrey W. Bromiley. Grand Rapids: Eerdmans, 1967.

Oestborn, G. *Torah in the Old Testament*. Lund, Sweden: Hakan Ohlssons, 1945.

Plumer, W. S. *The Law of God as Contained in the Ten Commandments*. Philadelphia: Presbyterian Board of Education, 1864.

Ridderbos, H. N. *The Coming of the Kingdom*. Nutley, N.J.: Presbyterian and Reformed, 1962.

————. *When the Time Had Fully Come*. Grand Rapids: Eerdmans, 1957.

Rushdoony, Rousas John. *Law and Society*. Vol. 2 of *The Institutes of Biblical Law*. Vallecito, Calif.: Ross House, 1982.

————. *The Institutes of Biblical Law*. Nutley, N.J.: Presbyterian and Reformed, 1973.

Ryrie, C. C. *Dispensationalism Today*. Chicago: Moody, 1965.

Smith, J. M. P. *The Origin and History of Hebrew Law*. Chicago: University of Chicago Press, 1931.

CHAPTER THREE

SIN

Sin is an unpopular word, but a very popular activity. Thought lightly of on earth by those who practice it, sin is considered the heaviest of all weights in heaven, where the cost of it was borne.

The nature of sin is little understood, the origin of it little known, and the results of it considered only too late. Yet sin is a major theme of Scripture, and without understanding it, the greater themes of righteousness and salvation can never be rightly known. Let us consider what the Word of God teaches concerning the nature of sin, its roots and fruits.

DEFINITION OF SIN

Sin is moral wrong. There is much wrong in the world that is not moral. Rust on my automobile fender is evil, and so is a bank failure, the weakness of old age, or an earthquake that destroys a city. Evil, indeed, but we do not hold anyone guilty for poor judgment, for the troubles and grief of our human condition, or for natural disasters. When the lion pounces on the antelope, the antelope, at least, considers it an evil. But we do not say the lion sinned. Why not? Because, unlike "wrong," "evil," "badness," or even "crime," sin introduces the idea of *God*. *Webster's Collegiate Dictionary* is altogether correct in giving only religious definitions of sin. Sin has to do with moral conditions and behavior relating to the righteous character of God and his will for creatures made in his moral likeness.

The Bible views sin as both active and volitional and also as dispositional.

SIN AS TRANSGRESSION

Sin is transgression against the law. In fact, where there is no law, there is no sin (Rom. 7:7). It can be volitional, a deliberate choice—and usually it is. The rebel deliberately violates the law. The sinner knows to do right, but doesn't do it. That is sin (James 4:17).

But sin is not the violation of just any law—laws of reason, laws of parents, laws of state. Sin is against the law of *God*. In fact, to violate the law of God is to violate God. The great problem is vertical, and from a wrong vertical relationship flow all the horizontal wrongs (Ps. 51:4; 1 Thess. 4:8; Gen. 39:9). When David said, "Against thee, thee only, have I sinned" he did not mean that he had not sinned grievously against Uriah and Bathsheba and, indeed, the whole nation. What he meant was that these responsibilities to fellowmen pale into insignificance compared with the terrible sin of violating God and his law. The biblical concept of sin "assumes the existence of a personal God of infinite perfection, and . . . assumes the responsibility of man."[1]

Some would say that deliberate violation of the known will of God is the only attitude or activity we may classify "sin."

Sin is the willful disobedience of God—the knowing transgression of his law, the conscious denial (in effect) of his absolute sovereignty in the universe.[2]

The Pelagian view of sin, which has been rejected by all branches of the Christian church, is: 1) That law can command only volitions. 2) That states of the soul can be commanded only insofar as they are the direct effect of previous volitions. 3) Hence sin consists simply in acts of volition. 4) That whatever a man has not plenary ability to do he is under no obligation to do. 5) That there is no such thing, therefore, as innate depravity.[3]

Wesley (in "Meth. Doc. Tracts," 294-312) distinguishes between "sin properly so called, i.e., voluntary transgression of known law, and sin improperly so called, i.e., involuntary transgression of law, known or unknown," and declares, "I believe there is no such perfection in this life as excludes these involuntary transgressions, which I apprehend to be naturally consequent upon the ignorance and mistakes in-separable from mortality."[4]

Does the Bible restrict its definition of sin to deliberate violation of the known will of God? Before considering passages of Scripture that deal directly with this question, note the mood of Scripture as indicated in the words chosen to convey God's idea of sin.

[1]Charles Hodge, *Systematic Theology*, vol. 2 (New York: Scribner's, 1871), 130.
[2]Calvin Linton, "Sin," in *Baker Dictionary of Christian Ethics*, ed. Carl F. H. Henry (Grand Rapids: Baker, 1973), 622.
[3]A. A. Hodge, *Outlines of Theology* (New York: Hodder and Stoughton, 1878), 320.
[4]Ibid., 321.

SIN AS FALLING SHORT

The primary word for sin in the Old Testament (*chata*) means to miss the point or to miss the mark. It was used of missing a target or losing one's way, as well as the moral meaning of missing God's standard of behavior or losing one's way spiritually. The translators of the Old Testament chose a word in Greek that had the same basic meaning (*hamartano*) and thus transformed it into a religious concept: missing God's mark, falling short of God's standard, straying from God's way. The final result of this process, across the years, was that New Testament writers transformed another form of the word (*hamartia*) into the idea of sin as the disposition of human nature. Sin in the singular, describing a mentality of alienation from God, came to predominate over the idea of sins or specific violations of various laws. Sin against the law rather than sins against laws became the focus of attention.

This Christian idea of sin was in sharp contrast to the Greek idea of man as mortal, encumbered with a finite body, subject to error through ignorance. For the Greeks the problem was not moral, defects did not bring guilt, the gods were not offended. But the Bible taught that man is essentially morally flawed in his nature and that he is guilty before God as a result. The biblical concept of sin, as an inner state for which a person is responsible, is seen in three basic teachings about sin: sinful nature, sinful thoughts, sins of omission.

Sinful Nature. Most people believe one becomes a sinner if and when he commits sinful acts. The Bible puts it the other way around. The Bible teaches that man is a sinner by nature (Eph. 2:3) and that he sins because he is a sinner. According to Scripture, the root problem is not a poor environment, and it certainly is not the responsibility of another person such as his parents (Ezek. 18). Man's heart is, from birth, inclined to evil. This does not mean that he is incapable of doing anything good (Rom. 2:14). It does not mean that everything an unconverted person does is wrong (Acts 10:31). It simply means that man is fallen and does wrong things inevitably because it is his nature to do wrong. Thus before a person chooses deliberately to transgress a specific commandment, he has already "missed the mark," fallen short in his inner being. It is from this polluted spring that flow streams of contaminated behavior. It is lack of conformity to the holy character of God that is the ultimate sin.

The Bible speaks of an evil heart (Heb. 3:12) that is deceitful above all things and desperately wicked (Jer. 17:9). Paul, in the most thorough analysis of sin, its origin, results, and cure (Rom. 1–8) identifies the root problem as a wrong heart. As the great Baptist theologian A. H. Strong said, "These representations of sin as a principle or state of the soul are incompatible with the definition of it as a mere act."[5]

2. **Sinful Thoughts.** Many believe that a person sins only if he commits sinful acts, but the Bible teaches that the inner thought is sinful as well (Matt. 15:18-19; Matt. 5:28ff.). Hatred is not wrong merely because it may lead to acts of violence. Hatred itself is sin. The underlying contention of Christian ethics is that every want of conformity to God is sinful and wicked. This includes both lack of conformity in action and in motive and affection.[6]

3. **Sins of Omission.** We sin also by failing to do what we ought. All have sinned, to be sure, but also all are continuously falling short of the glorious character of God (Rom. 3:23). "Whoever knows what is right to do and fails to do it, for him it is sin" (James 4:17). "For whatever does not proceed from faith is sin" (Rom. 14:23). Here Paul does not speak of a positive choice to think or do evil, but clearly teaches that failure to measure up to the right is sin. It is not only sinful to actively hate my neighbor; it is sinful to fail to love him as I ought. I am commanded to love as Christ loved; when I do not, I have not merely demonstrated a morally neutral personality weakness, I have sinned.

The sin offering for sins of ignorance (Lev. 5:14-15), the trespass offering for sins of omission (Lev. 5:5-6), and the burnt offering to expiate general sinfulness (Lev. 1:3; cf. Luke 2:22-24) all witness that sin is not confined to mere act.[7]

[5]A. H. Strong, *Systematic Theology,* vol. 3 (Philadelphia: Judson, 1907), 553.
[6]Carl F. H. Henry, *Christian Personal Ethics* (Grand Rapids: Eerdmans, 1957), 184.
[7]Strong, *Systematic Theology,* vol. 3, 554.

It is significant that the Westminster divines, in answering the catechism question, "What is sin?" began with sins of omission, rather than sins of transgression: "Sin is any want of conformity unto or transgression of the law of God."

Biblical sin, then, is not just sins against men but sin against God; not just sinful behavior but a sinful nature; not just sinful activity but sinful thoughts; not just sins of violation but sins of omission, falling short of likeness to God.

Who can stand before such a standard? "Wretched man that I am!" we cry with Paul. His picture of the titanic struggle with sin (Rom. 7) was surely not the battle to refrain from theft and murder. No, it was the warfare within, his total inability to measure up to God's standard, to "be perfect, as your heavenly Father is perfect" (Matt. 5:48). He stood condemned and guilty, though he testified of keeping the law perfectly (Phil. 3:6).

SIN AND GUILT

Sin in Scripture is almost indistinguishable from guilt. There was never a sharp distinction to the Hebrew between sin and guilt.[8] One is guilty of violating God's standard when he may not even know of it. The plea of ignorance does not excuse. The involuntary, unconscious moral deficiency of one's disposition brings guilt.

There are two elements of guilt: blameworthiness and obligation to suffer punishment. Christ assumed our obligation to suffer punishment and thus cleansed our guilty record. But he was never worthy of blame. In fact, his innocence is what qualified him to stand in place of the guilty. As a result, those who have been redeemed will never have to pay the penalty for sin (are guiltless in the legal sense), but are nevertheless guilty in the sense of being blameworthy. It is the glory of God's grace that we who are blameworthy, guilty sinners have the just results of our sinfulness set aside. God today does not see us as weak, failing, guilty sinners, but as pure and innocent and holy as the One who took our place. But to understand the glory of grace, we must first understand the wicked depth of iniquity in that corrupt nature on which God's grace has fallen. We are more

[8]*amartano*, in TDNT, vol. 1, 277.

guilty today than ever—we have sinned and are blameworthy. But we are guiltless today, free from any obligation whatsoever to pay for our sin. Jesus paid it all. Consider this testimony of one who understood God's view of sin:

> Often . . . I have had very affecting views of my own sinfulness and vileness, very frequently to such a degree as to hold me in a kind of loud weeping, sometimes for a considerable time together, so that I have been often obliged to shut myself up. I have had a vastly greater sense of my own wickedness and the badness of my heart than ever I had before my conversion. It has often appeared to me that if God should mark iniquity against me, I should appear the very worst of all mankind, of all that have been since the beginning of the world to this time; and that I should have by far the lowest place in hell. When others that have come to talk with me about their soul's concerns have expressed the sense they have had of their wickedness, by saying that it seemed to them they were as bad as the devil himself; I thought their expressions seemed exceeding faint and feeble to represent my wickedness.

What kind of degenerate criminal could honestly give such a testimony? None other than the saintly Jonathan Edwards, of whom A. H. Strong reports:

> Jonathan Edwards was not an ungodly man, but the holiest man of his time. He was not an enthusiast, but a man of acute, philosophic mind. He was not a man who indulged in exaggerated or random statements, for with his power of introspection and analysis he combined a faculty and habit of exact expression unsurpassed among the sons of men.[9]

To such a man, let us listen, as he continues:

> My wickedness, as I am in myself, has long appeared to me perfectly ineffable and swallowing up all thought and imagination—like an infinite deluge, or mountains over my head. I know not how to express better what my sins appear to me to be, than by heaping infinite on infinite and multiplying infinite by infinite. Very often for these many years, these expressions are in my mind and in my mouth: "Infinite upon infinite—infinite upon infinite!" When I look into my heart and take a view of my wickedness, it looks like an abyss infinitely deeper than hell. And it appears to me that were it not for free grace, exalted and raised up to the infinite height of all the fullness and glory of the great Jehovah, and the arm of his power and grace stretched forth in all the majesty of his power and in all the glory of his sovereignty, I should appear sunk down in my sins below hell itself, far beyond the sight of everything but the eye of sovereign grace that can pierce even down to such a depth. And yet it seems to me that my conviction of sin is exceeding small and faint; it is enough to amaze me that I have no more sense of my sin.

[9]Strong, *Systematic Theology*, vol. 3, 556.

Such is the response of one who came to understand the biblical view of sin. Where did this fatal moral illness come from?

ORIGIN OF SIN

Scripture clearly and repeatedly teaches that sinfulness had no part in mankind as originally designed by God, that sin entered the human race from the outside, and that the agent was Satan. But why Satan is morally evil is not so clearly revealed. Some within the Christian tradition have held to a Greek duality of existence—both good and evil, God and anti-God (Satan) are eternal. But this theory is based on speculation, not on biblical data, and has been rejected by all major branches of the church. From the scant data in Scripture on the subject of Satan's origin, plus a great deal of logical deduction from that data, Christian theologians have held that Satan is a created being, originally righteous and high-ranking among God's servants, who chose against God out of pride and self-interest. However accurately this brief statement on the ultimate origin of sin reflects historic (but unrevealed) reality, the origin of sin in the human race is very clear in Scripture. Through Satan's influence Adam and Eve chose to disobey God and thus became sinful (Gen. 3; 2 Cor. 11:3; 1 Tim. 2:14).

Satan persuaded Eve to doubt at least two things: that God's rule was in her best interests and that God's will is unconditionally binding. Satan provided the first "assertiveness training," and Eve embarked on the first "quest for personal fulfillment." Adam, the responsible head of the home, chose Eve's proposal above God's commandment, and thus sin polluted the clear stream of human innocence. This is clearly the origin of sin in the first two people. But how did that affect Adam's descendants? The fact that all Adam's descendants became sinners through Adam's moral fall is universally held by biblical theologians and churches, but, in the words of Charles Hodge, "The nature and extent of the evil thus entailed upon his race, and the ground or reason of the descendants of Adam being involved in the evil consequences of his transgression, have ever been matters of diversity and discussion."[10]

Protestants in general have held that sin was imputed, or legally counted, against all of Adam's descendants based on the covenantal relationship Adam had with God. Others have held that this sinful condition was passed on to his descendants through natural generation as other human characteristics are passed on from parents to children. There are many other theories, seeking to explain in biblical or logical terms how this natural inclination to sin is a universal part of human nature. But all are agreed that the Bible teaches all men are sinful in nature. The Bible states this repeatedly, assumes it consistently, and argues it clearly as the foundation of all its teaching concerning God and salvation. (1 Kings 8:46; Eccles. 7:20; Isa. 53:6; 64:6; Ps. 130:3; 143:2; Rom. 3:23; Gal. 3:22; 1 John 1:8, 10; 5:19)

The Bible was given to reveal God's salvation of sinners, so everywhere human sinfulness and inability to save one's self is assumed. Furthermore, Paul in writing to the Romans sets out in logical order the case for this universal malady of the human condition and the only way of cure (Rom. 1–8). Every person has inherited a disposition to think and act in the promotion of self-interest, whether or not this harms others. Every person is born estranged from God and resistant to his rule. All have an irremediable tendency to morally wrong thinking and behavior. On this the Bible and the record of history agree.

Not only are we born in such a condition, we consistently choose to sin and thus compound the evil condition we inherited. What results from this foul condition?

RESULTS OF SIN

DEPRAVITY

This condition of sinfulness theologians have called "total depravity." The Westminster Confession of Faith speaks of this original corruption as making all men "utterly indisposed, disabled, and made opposite to all good, and wholly inclined to all evil."

[10]Hodge, *Systematic Theology*, vol. 2, 192.

By total depravity is not meant that all men are equally wicked; nor that any man is as thoroughly corrupt as it is possible for a man to be; nor that men are destitute of all moral virtues. The Scriptures recognize the fact, which experience abundantly confirms, that men, to a greater or less degree, are honest in dealings, kind in their feelings, and beneficent in their conduct. Even the heathen, the Apostle teaches us, do by nature the things of the law.[11]

Total depravity does mean that the downward trend is irreversible by human effort and that every person is infected in every dimension of his life—his thinking, his affections, his body, his relationships and, above all, his will. He is incapable of consistently choosing the right.

JUDGMENT

Separation. God judges sin because of his own nature. Therefore, by nature he is incompatible with anything not morally right. The two cannot coexist. This is the meaning of holiness: God is separate from sin. Thus the judgment of sin is the inevitable result of the nature of God and the nature of sin—separation. Adam and Eve experienced this judgment as the immediate result of that first, fatal choice to reject God's way. They were not only driven from the Garden; their intimate companionship with God was ruptured. The independence for which they grasped was granted, which itself was the judgment—separation from God. Most people would not consider this a very terrible judgment, never having known union with God. But separation from God, the source of life, means separation from the gifts God would give, including, supremely, the gift of life. "The wages of sin is death" (Rom. 6:23).

This death works inexorably in every facet of a person's life. God in his grace gives man a probation period (his lifetime) to reverse the choice of Eve and during that time gives gifts in abundance. The goodness of God is designed to lead to repentance (Rom. 2:4). But if the rejection of God's grace continues till physical death, the judgment—separation from God—is complete. This is the essential characteristic of hell. Sin by definition is violation of the law of God, rejection of the will of God, and thus the judgment for sin—separation—is actually

[11]Ibid., 233.

chosen by the sinner. He chooses to distance himself from God and God allows him to do so. This is the awful outcome of sin.

The psalmist shows how the judgment of separation is the choice of the sinner: "My people did not listen to my words and Israel would have none of me; so I sent them off, stubborn as they were, to follow their own devices" (Ps. 81:11-12, NEB).

Paul reiterates the same truth in his terrible denunciations recorded in Romans 1: "God gave them up . . . God gave them up . . . God gave them up."

Unpardonable Sin. Both Jesus and John spoke of sin which is not pardonable:

> Every sin and blasphemy will be forgiven men, but the blasphemy against the Spirit will not be forgiven. And whoever says a word against the Son of man will be forgiven; but whoever speaks against the Holy Spirit will not be forgiven, either in this age or in the age to come. (Matt. 12:31-32)

> There is a sin which is mortal; I do not say that one is to pray for that. All wrongdoing is sin, but there is sin which is not mortal. (1 John 5:16-17)

What is the unpardonable sin? Theologians do not agree because neither Christ nor John explained their statements. John's is less troublesome because he seems to be speaking of physical death, and in any event final damnation cannot be proved from his warning. On the other hand, Christ's warning seems to clearly threaten eternal damnation and that for a particular verbal statement. This is especially troublesome because people have been so frightened by this warning as to feel irresistibly drawn by some psychological compulsion to speak those forbidden words. Devout Christians have come to me with just this dread upon them. But if salvation cannot be gained by stating a particular formula that does not represent the heart condition, how could damnation be so secured? For this reason, the church has always looked beyond the mere statement to see what heart condition would be unforgivable.

In the context, the Pharisees had ascribed the work of Christ to the power of demons, rejecting the authenticity of Christ's life and teaching. Thus some have held that the only unpardonable sin is to reject finally the work of the Holy Spirit—in the person of the Son, in the Spirit-inspired Word of God, and in his convicting work in the sinner's own heart. Thus if a person goes out of this life resisting the call of the Spirit, rejecting Jesus Christ, and the Bible as God's Word, there is no hope. He can never be forgiven.

Until that final judgment, however, anyone who truly repents of whatever sin will be forgiven. Because this is the clear teaching about salvation throughout Scripture, most Bible scholars have held that the only unpardonable sin is final rejection of God. The difficult passage under study is thus explained by the abundant light of many other passages.

But does this satisfy the text? Many hold that it does not, that there is a clear distinction *in this life* among the many sinners who are eligible for redemption and some who are not. Though we may not dogmatize about the specific nature of the sin, it certainly is sin against the Holy Spirit, and it certainly results in a permanent state of alienation from God. Perhaps the only statement that can be made with assurance is that there is a self-induced state of mind, a spirit that has so rejected the convicting work of the Holy Spirit that it is no longer salvable. Does this mean that the Holy Spirit abandons such a person, or that the person has so hardened himself as to be deaf to the continuing gracious voice of the Spirit? The effect is the same either way, and the warning is solemn. It is possible to sin away the day of grace.

"Have I committed this sin?" cries the tormented soul. I think not. Any soul that is tormented, that is, anyone who cries out to God for forgiveness, will be heard. The sure evidence that he has not committed the unpardonable sin is that he longs for pardon. But the God-rejecter who has no remorse is the one who is in mortal danger and who should seek a repentant spirit for himself before it is forever too late.

Inherent Punishment. Sin is often its own punishment. "The wicked are snared in the work of their own hands" (Ps. 9:16). "The iniquities of the wicked ensnare him, and he is caught in the toils of his sin" (Prov. 5:22). "Do not be deceived; God is not mocked, for whatever a man sows, that he will also reap" (Gal. 6:7). "They will quite certainly destroy themselves by their own work of destruction, and get their reward of evil for the evil that they do" (2 Pet. 2:12-13, Jerusalem Bible).

Though the Tempter will disguise sin so that it appears most desirable, it has within itself its own judgment. A bitter and critical spirit condemns its owner to a joyless, troubled existence. The unmerciful rarely experiences mercy, the self-centered person locks himself into the solitary confinement of his own narrow commitment. Sin itself kills the sinner by degrees. The wages of sin is death.

HARM TO OTHERS

Sin also results in harm for others. This is obvious for most sins: murder, theft, drunken driving. But some sins are said to be private, harming only the sinner himself. But we can question whether any sin is truly private. At the very least, the "private" sin helps form the character of the sinner. That person, with his sin, affects every person with whom he comes in contact. The father who practices the private sin of covetousness does not provide the model of generous contentment for his child. Furthermore, every sin keeps a person from becoming all he could be and thus from loving and serving as he should. So the loss, once again, is not merely his own.

HARM TO GOD

Above all, sin harms God. Were it not for sin, there need be no cross. And who can fathom the depths of pain in the Father and in the Son? The Son identifying with all that is his opposite— our sin and corruption. The inevitable result: separation—the incredible plan of God that the Father and Son should suffer our judgment, our just separation from a holy God. Until this result of sin is seen in sharp focus, the enormity of it, the vile iniquity of it, the stark horror of it can be but dimly understood. Many years passed after I knew my sins were forgiven before I shed a single tear over those sins. The result of sin in my own life was disturbing, the result of my sin in the lives of those I loved was a grief, but not till I began to sense what my sin had done to the Father and the Son did my heart break in deep contrition.

God has died! If this does not startle us, what will? The church must keep this astonishment alive. . . . The fact that man is no longer astonished by the news "the Son of God died on the cross" is most saddening. . . . Another wonder struck me when I read Heb. 2:10: "For it was *fitting* that he, for whom and by

whom all things exist, in bringing many sons to glory, should make the
pioneer of their salvation perfect through suffering." The word *eprepen*
thundered in my ears as though it would shake the universe. . . . With God sin
should never be forgiven. "Sin is the death of God. Die sin must, or God."
And yet this God forgives sin![12]

Sin would not only unthrone God, but un-God him. If the sinner could
help it, God would no longer be God. . . . "O man," says Augustine, "consider
the greatness of thy sin, by the greatness of the price paid for sin."[13]

Sin destroys the sinner, harms others, and hung the Son of
God in agony and shame in the dark shadow of his Father's
rejection. So terrible are the results of sin.

A ROOT SIN?

Many theologians hold there is a root sin from which all other
sins grow or a comprehensive sin that includes all others as
aspects of *the* sin. What that basic sin might be, however, is a
matter of strong disagreement. Since the great commandment is
to love, some have held that the violation of this or the opposite
of love must be the root sin. But what is the opposite of love? Is
it positive hatred, or is it simple indifference? Misdirected love is
a summary statement that might qualify as the root sin, but it is
so general that it conveys little precise meaning.

Strong held that the opposite of love is selfishness and that
this is the source from which all other evil flows.

By selfishness we mean not simply the exaggerated self-love which constitutes
the antithesis of benevolence, but that choice of self as the supreme end which
constitutes the antithesis of supreme love to God. Love to God is the essence
of all virtue. The opposite to this, the choice of self as the supreme end, must
therefore be the essence of sin.[14]

Charles Hodge took strong exception to this view.

It of course is not denied that selfishness in some of its forms includes a large
class of the sins of which men are guilty. What is objected to is the making
selfishness the essence of all sin, or the attempt to reduce all the manifestations
of moral evil to this one principle. This cannot be done. There is disinterested
sin as well as disinterested benevolence. A man may as truly and as deliberately

[12]Kazoh Kitamori, *Theology of the Pain of God* (Richmond: John Knox, 1958), 26,
119-120.
[13]Thomas Watson, *A Body of Divinity* (London: Banner of Truth, 1965), 134.
[14]Strong, *Systematic Theology*, vol. 3, 567.

sacrifice himself in sinning, as in doing good. Many parents have violated the law of God not for their own benefit, but for the benefit of their children. . . . There is no selfishness in malice, nor in enmity to God. These are far higher forms of evil than mere selfishness. The true nature of sin is alienation from God and opposition to his character and will. It is the opposite of holiness.[15]

Since pride is the idolatry that enthrones oneself in God's place, many, such as Augustine and Thomas Aquinas, have held that pride is the taproot of sin. Is not this the sin that brought down Lucifer?

On the other hand, since the right relationship to God is summarized in the great biblical concept of faith, it should come as no surprise that the Reformers Luther and Calvin held the root of all other sins to be unbelief.

Perhaps idolatry, refusing to allow God to be God in the kingdom of one's life, could be considered the sin that summarizes the other sins. For example, unbelief is failing to acknowledge and trust God as God. Selfishness is replacing God with self, and pride is the same. Again, to fail in love is to fail in a right relationship to God first of all.

Or perhaps we should conclude that sin is so unutterably evil and so grotesquely complex that we shall never sort out all its hidden twistings and turnings. Perhaps our very disagreement serves to underscore the awful, incomprehensible nature of sin.

Sin is so hideous and destructive a force in our lives and in our society it deserves our fullest hatred. But the sad thing is that none of us by nature hates sin. We may hate it in its final, gross manifestation. We may hate the results when they are painful or distasteful. We certainly may hate it in others. But we do not naturally hate sin in its beginning, enticing forms. And yet, we will never seek the cure until we see sin from the viewpoint of the Great Physician and abhor it.

VARIETIES OF SIN

LISTS OF SINS

The medieval church identified seven deadly sins: pride, covetousness, lust, anger, gluttony, envy, and sloth. Answering

[15]Hodge, *Systematic Theology*, vol. 2, 149.

to these, the church also developed the seven cardinal (chief) virtues. To Plato's four virtues of wisdom, courage, temperance, and justice were added the biblical qualities of faith, hope, and love. Nowhere does Scripture give a comprehensive list, and nowhere are we authorized to consider these lists of virtues and vices either exhaustive or comprehensive categories that include all other sins or virtues. But that they are indeed prominent in the teaching of Scripture is beyond dispute.

Carl F. H. Henry notes varieties of sin from another perspective:

The Apostle Paul presents seven lists of vices (Rom. 1:29ff.; 1 Cor. 5:11; 6:9; 2 Cor. 12:20; Gal. 5:19ff.; Eph. 4:31; 5:3; and Col. 3:5ff.). Lindsay Dewar has noted that the sin of fornication holds a prominent place in five of the lists, appearing first on numerous occasions. . . . Sexual sin includes fornication, adultery, uncleanness, lasciviousness, and effeminateness. Second in prominence is the sin of covetousness or greed. "Idolatry" in the Colossians passage probably refers to this sin. Extortion may be considered as an extension of it. The unusual evil caused by this sin is suggested by its appearance in five of the lists. . . . Also conspicuous is the sin of bad temper, sometimes designated wrath. Its appearance in four of the lists suggests the devastating effect upon the soul of uncontrolled outbursts of violence. Related to this evil are anger, passion, bitterness, railing, blaspheming, malice, and murder. Paul's lists include also the sins of the tongue, such as reviling, whispering, backbiting, insolence, boasting, shameful speaking, filthiness, foolish talking, jesting, clamor, and deceit. There are sins of quarreling, such as strife, jealousy, factions, divisions, heresies, swellings, and tumults. . . . Of these sins Paul listed, it is noteworthy that Jesus also condemned fornication, lasciviousness, covetousness, railing, clamor, and deceit.[16]

There is another way to put sins together in "affinity" groups or clusters. Scripture seems to identify certain basic sins of the spirit from which other sins flow.

BASIC SINS

Each of these is the distortion of a good desire that God has put within us. We are created with the desire to enjoy things, the desire to have things, and the desire to accomplish things. When we fulfill these desires in a God-pleasing way, we are satisfied and God is satisfied. However, when we fulfill these in the wrong way, they become sin, sin which God categorizes as lust (the lust of the flesh), covetousness (the lust of the eye), and pride (the pride of life) (1 John 2:16).

[16]Henry, *Christian Personal Ethics*, 183.

When do these desires become evil? Note that temptation is not a sin. Temptation to do wrong is inevitable in the morally polluted environment in which we live. Christ himself was tempted in every way we can be tempted (Heb. 4:15). We should not feel guilty because we are tempted to lust, covet, or to be proud. However, to yield to the thought is to sin. To entertain lustful thoughts, for example, is to "make provision for the flesh" and is wrong.

Again, to break God's laws in order to fulfill legitimate desires is wrong. For example, to lie in order to succeed or to cheat in order to possess is sinful.

Again, to fulfill legitimate desires in a wrong way, to go beyond God's design, is to sin. Being extremely overweight, unless glandular in origin, is a manifestation that one has eaten more than God intended. The person has given in to the sin of lust and has become gluttonous. Enjoying good food is not a sin, but fulfilling this legitimate desire beyond God's design is to sin.

Also, when the desire controls us, that desire has, in a sense, become our God. This, of course, is sin.

Some people seek the solution to temptation by refusing these God-given desires. The desire to enjoy things is denied through asceticism and celibacy. The desire to have things is controlled with vows of poverty. The desire to achieve or to "be something" is controlled through monasticism. However, these are not biblical ways of handling our God-given desires. The Roman Catholic church, Buddhism, and Greek dualism have held that asceticism is the highest and best way. Our human desires are evil and are to be reduced or eliminated. But the great good news of Christianity is that Jesus came eating and drinking, teaching a life-affirming doctrine. These basic human desires are God-given and good. They are not to be suppressed or denied, but enjoyed.

Having said this, however, we must point out the biblical truth that these desires sometimes should be denied in order to demonstrate our love for God and our love for others. This is why the teaching of self-denial in Scripture is so clear and strong. Not asceticism for its own sake but self-denial, when it is necessary to act in love for God or for others, is the biblical way. Self-denial is not a popular idea in our age or, in fact, in any age.

But the way of the cross is still the way of love. Nevertheless, in the normal flow of life, these basic drives are created by God to be fulfilled. They become sinful when abused or misused. And when this sin is repeated, it can become an habitual characteristic.

When one habitually gives in to the temptation to lust, he descends into a life-pattern of sensualism. When covetousness becomes a way of life, one becomes a materialist. When pride reigns unchecked, the character becomes egotistical.

Because these basic sins are so important for understanding the full scope of sin and for successfully overcoming sin, we shall consider each in some detail in the next chapter. Before we turn our attention to that, however, consider a vexing problem: are all sins equally sinful?

HIERARCHY OF SIN

Some have held that before God there is no difference among sins. All sins are equally vile and there is no legitimate gradation of guiltiness among sins. This curious notion probably originated in a misunderstanding of Christ's meaning in the Sermon on the Mount. Not only is murder wrong, he taught, but anger is wrong in itself, whether or not it leads to murder; it is in the same category of evil, in the same family of sins. Christ never intended to teach that the first beginning of sinful thought and its mature manifestation in action were equally heinous. The notion is a terrifying one. It is intended to reinforce the sinfulness of sin, but in actual fact it has the opposite effect. If it is as wrong to desire a woman as to take her by force, why not act on your impulses? You are no more guilty. The rest of mankind would plead with the one holding such a doctrine: if you covet my possessions, please keep it at that level and do not take them; if you hate me or fail to love me as Christ does, please keep it at that level and do not assault or kill me.

There is a biblical hierarchy of both virtue and sin. Love for God takes precedence over love for my neighbor. Those who sin without knowledge are to be punished on the judgment day with less severity than those who sin with knowledge (Luke 12:47-48). In the Old Testament where specific punishments were prescribed by God, there was a gradation from capital punishment down to a slight fine. There are "least commandments" (Matt. 5:19) and "weightier matters" (Matt. 23:23). Some insults, for example, are worse than others, and to speak in wrath is worse than merely feeling it (Matt. 5:22).

To hold that all sins are of equal gravity in the sight of God finds no confirmation in either the Old Testament or the New Testament. It is true that one who breaks the least commandment is guilty of the whole in the sense that he has become a lawbreaker (James 2:10). He is no longer an innocent person. It is also true that the least sin separates from a holy God. In this way, it could be said that all sins are equally sin. But it can never be said on biblical grounds that all sins are equally sinful.

Not all sinners will receive the same punishment. For example, those who have sinned deliberately for a lifetime against great light certainly will receive far greater condemnation than those who had no gospel light and died in childhood. Karl Marx and Adolf Hitler will give an account for their rejection of biblical truth they learned so well in their youth.

The notion that all sins are equally sinful does not tend to make guilt heavier on sins of the spirit, like selfishness, as much as it tends to make light the guilt of more heinous violations. Criminal law and church discipline must be based on the biblical view that there is a great difference among sins and that they should be punished accordingly.

To say there is a great difference in the weight of various sins does not mean that our view of that variation is accurate. In the nature of the subject—sin—we could almost assume in advance that fallen human evaluation will go astray. For example, in the sight of God, which would be the graver sin: a ghetto child who steals a loaf of bread to feed his crippled mother, or a university professor who delights in destroying the faith of hundreds of freshmen? Yet which would be punished in the courts of our land if found guilty of such activity? Sins against God are lightly thought of, even by Christians, but from God's point of view they are the most worthy of judgment. So it is that God alone may evaluate the level of guilt. But far be it from any just judge to assign to Anne Frank and Adolf Hitler the same level of punishment.

Having said all this, however, let us remember that the slightest falling short of God's glorious character brings separation from God, suffering, death, and hell. Let us remember that the least of all my sin would nail Jesus to the cross as the price of love to set me free. In contrast to murder, what is so terrible about eating a piece of fruit? And yet it was enough to rob heaven of its glory and damn the whole race.

As we have examined what Scripture has to say about the nature and results of sin, where it comes from and what it leads to, we may feel as if we have been sounding the depths of some vast and unfathomable cesspool. We have been probing the edges of some horror of impenetrable darkness. And why is the holy Word of God so full of this foul subject? In order to know God and become like him, it is not enough to love righteousness. We must hate sin. To induce this hatred, God strips sin of all its guises and fully reveals its hideous reality. But there is a prior reason for this grim revelation—against this dark background the splendor of his glorious grace stands revealed. Only when the hideous pollution of our corrupt nature is known will we seek cleansing. And only with this reality pressed upon us will we be willing to acknowledge how utterly hopeless and how helpless we are and run for refuge to the mighty Savior.

CHAPTER FOUR

ROOT SINS AND VIRTUES

Scripture identifies hundreds of sins and, with the application of biblical principles, the list could easily be extended to thousands. It would be a formidable task just to catalogue them, let alone keep them in mind for spiritual assault in an attempt to destroy them from one's life. The warfare against temptation to sin would be greatly assisted if a few easily identified sins led to all the rest.

Furthermore, if there are root sins buried inside—even below the level of consciousness—how important to identify that root in dealing with the fruit (the outward sinful activity). For example, a person may be convicted of being hostile toward another person or actually seeking his harm. He can ask for God's deliverance from this sinful attitude and activity and he should. But for final conquest, would it not be helpful to understand *why* he hates the person? It may be because the person has attacked him and his pride is hurt. But it could be because the person has something he wants. The root must be dealt with or the fruit will surely grow again. So it would be very useful, if not strategically necessary, to know whether there are indeed root or feeder sins and, if so, what they are.

Lust, covetousness, and pride were the three temptations Satan used in his successful seduction of Eve and also when he failed to seduce Jesus.

The fruit in the Garden seemed to be good for food (lust), it was a delight to the eyes (covetousness), and it was desired to make one wise—in fact, like God (pride), and Eve chose to reject God's way (Gen. 3:5-6). Satan tempted a hungry Jesus to make bread (lust), to display his powers for self-glory (pride), and to gain the world (covetousness) through compromise, and Jesus resisted (Matt. 4; Mark 1; Luke 4). He cut off sinful behavior at the roots, whereas his original human ancestor had allowed the enemy's seed of temptation to take root and bear the fruit of a terrible, life-destroying, race-infecting sinful choice and action.

But is there not other sin that comes from another root? What of unbelief? Certainly in Eve's case she sinned because she doubted God—that he knew best and was out for her welfare—and God's word, that God would punish her as he said. Jesus, on the other hand, resisted Satan's blandishments precisely because he believed God and his word. Did unbelief lead to lust, covetousness, and pride in Eve's heart, or did *they*, rather, lead to unbelief? However these roots were intertwined in Eve's case, it does seem quite possible to sin because of fear and unbelief without any lust, covetousness, or pride. The desire for plain self-preservation (a God-given quality) can be distorted into doubt and unbelief. Let us consider, then, these four roots of sin and the virtues that stand opposite each: lust, covetousness, pride, and unbelief.

LUST AND SELF-CONTROL

In the Hebrew Old Testament and in the Greek New Testament, several words are used to express strong desire. The words are used to express desire for good things as well as for evil things, though in the New Testament the chief words came to be used primarily for wrong desire. The essential point in *epithumia* (the chief New Testament word for "lust") is that it is desire as impulse, as a motion of the will. It is, in fact, lust, since the thought of satisfaction gives pleasure and that of nonsatisfaction, pain.[1]

Though there is an overlap in use for words expressing desire for the fulfillment of physical appetites and those expressing desire to possess things, certain words are used primarily to express the desire for pleasure, which can become lust, and

[1]*epithumia*, in TDNT, vol. 3, 171.

others to express the desire to own, which can become covetousness. We consider these separately because the ideas are distinct and the biblical authors treat them thus, even while occasionally using them in a synonymous sense.

Lust in the New Testament is often linked with the word *flesh*. In Scripture, natural bodily appetites that can become temptations to misuse include desire for sex, food, drink, and rest. When sought or satisfied in wrong ways, they become the sins of impurity, gluttony, drunkenness, and sloth.

IMPURITY

Although the other "sins of the flesh" are forbidden in Scripture, there is much emphasis on sexual sins. In the Old Testament, adultery and related sins were emphasized second only to idolatry. In the New Testament, the term *lust* came to be used in the epistles almost exclusively of illicit sexual desire, and even covetousness was commonly linked with sex. The emphasis is so strong and the teaching so thorough, we will consider this particular lust in greater detail in chapter 7, "Sex, Marriage, and the Family."

GLUTTONY

Overeating is identified as sin in both the Old Testament (Deut. 21:20; Prov. 23:21) and the New Testament (Luke 21:34). There is not much teaching on the subject, however, so that one wonders why it was included in the medieval church as one of the seven deadly sins. The reasons are adequate if not overwhelming. Gluttony and drunkenness are associated in the Bible and often in life, so that the medieval church subsumed drunkenness under the single sin gluttony, and the Bible does have a great deal to say about drunkenness. Both are sins of excessive intake. There may be a more basic reason. Even though the ancients did not have the present-day scientific evidence of the negative effects of being overweight, they were aware that the body is the temple of the Holy Spirit and that it does not belong to the Christian himself, so that to abuse it is sin against the rightful Owner and Resident.

Paul speaks of those whose god is their belly (Phil. 3:19), an apt description of multitudes in our affluent society. An added reason for discipline at the table is the presence in our world of hundreds of millions of people who do not have enough to eat; indeed, who starve while other millions of Christians glut. Some may be overweight because of glandular imbalance, of course, not because of overeating, and some may sin through gluttony who do not evidence it outwardly, but to eat intemperately is to violate the revealed will of God.

DRUNKENNESS

Drunkenness is condemned throughout Scripture (Deut. 21:20; 29:19; 1 Sam. 1:14; Prov. 23:20, 29-35; Isa. 5:11-12, 22; 28:1-8; 56:12; Hos. 4:11; 7:5; Joel 1:5; Amos 6:6; Hab. 2:15-16; Luke 21:34; Rom. 13:13; Gal. 5:20; Eph. 5:18; 1 Thess. 5:7-8); the judgment of it is severe. The severe church discipline of disfellowshiping is assigned to the drunkard (1 Cor. 5:11), and God assigns an even greater judgment: the drunkard shall not inherit the Kingdom of God (1 Cor. 6:9).

Today we speak of alcoholism as an illness whose victims are unfortunate, but this is not biblical terminology. It is true that alcohol brings many illnesses and is a habit with a viselike grip. Whether the dependence is purely psychological or partly physical—a genetic weakness toward addiction—the specialists may debate; but that the Bible calls it sin is beyond debate. The initiation of the so-called illness was certainly a deliberate choice, and the best cure is spiritual renewal. Repentance is not an appropriate response for illness, but without it the drunkard will never be delivered. In fact, the acknowledgment of one's condition and expressed desire for help and deliverance ("repentance") is considered by secular specialists the indispensable first step for rehabilitation. What is said in Scripture of the misuse of alcohol can be said with equal force concerning the misuse of drugs, the contemporary manifestation of a similar problem.

Not only does the Bible condemn drunkenness vigorously, it also speaks against the use of alcohol as a beverage: "Wine is a mocker, strong drink a brawler; and whoever is led astray by it is not wise" (Prov. 20:1). "It is not for kings, O Lemuel, it is not for kings to drink wine, or for rulers to desire strong drink; lest they drink and forget what has been decreed, and pervert the rights of all the afflicted" (Prov. 31:4-5).

Having said this, however, it is clear that Scripture does not teach total abstinence as God's requirement of all his people. Abstinence was a requirement for priests (Lev. 10:8-10), Nazarites (Num. 6:3-4), and John the Baptist (Luke 1:15). But Christ drank (Matt. 11:19; Luke 7:34), and nowhere does the Bible explicitly forbid drinking alcoholic beverages.

Why then do so many Christians take a strong stand for total abstinence? Is such a stand biblically permissible? I believe total abstinence is the most biblical position in twentieth-century America. The principle is one of giving up my rights for the welfare of others (Rom. 14; 1 Cor. 8, 10) in a situation that is radically different from Bible times. In the biblical culture where water was scarce and often polluted, wine was the simplest way of purifying drinking water and was the common mealtime beverage. It was mixed with water, up to two hundred parts water to one part wine. In fact, it was considered barbaric to drink wine that was only half-and-half.[2] Because of the common use of high-alcohol-content beverages today, we have problems the people of Bible days could not have imagined. In the United States half the population drinks, and 10 percent are alcoholics.

The result? Studies show that a third of those committing suicide in the U.S. each year have alcohol in their blood. About 10,000 murders occur each year in situations involving alcohol. Alcohol may be involved in 40 percent of accidental deaths (fires, falls, drownings) each year. In 1984 a third of the 44,000 traffic fatalities were the result of intoxication. About 30,000 Americans die each year of advanced cirrhosis of the liver, a disease often caused or aggravated by alcohol consumption. This is only one example of the numerous medical problems increased by alcohol use. One estimate, made in 1985, was that medical expenditures required by alcohol abuse ranged from $10 to $20 billion, and that would certainly be much higher now.[3] But the human loss to families and to the drinker himself—who can measure it?

The only certain way to avoid alcohol- or drug-influenced

[2]Robert H. Stein, "Wine Drinking in New Testament Times," *Christianity Today,* 20 June 1975, 9.
[3]Statistics quoted are from Steve Olson and Dean R. Gerstein, *Alcohol in America: Taking Action to Prevent Abuse* (Washington: National Academy Press, 1985), 14-17. Obviously the data change constantly, but most sources indicate that since *Alcohol in America* was published in 1985, alcohol use and abuse has increased.

thinking, speaking, and behavior, and to avoid addiction is not to take the first drink or the first dose of a drug. Though others may not reach the same conclusions from these data, I conclude that the production, sale, and use of beverage alcohol and addictive or mind-altering nonprescribed drugs are incompatible with biblical principles.

SLOTH

God not only gave the delights of sex and good food and drink to satisfy our bodily appetites, he made our bodies to require rest. But even the blessing of sleep and rest can be abused. The "Protestant work ethic" did not originate with Protestants. Solomon was the greatest denouncer of sloth and advocate of diligence, to be sure, but Paul reinforced Solomon's teaching in at least six of his letters. Consider the following sample:

Go to the ant, O sluggard; consider her ways, and be wise. . . . A little sleep, a little slumber, a little folding of the hands to rest, and poverty will come upon you like a vagabond, and want like an armed man. (Prov. 6:6-11)

A slack hand causes poverty, but the hand of the diligent makes rich. (Prov. 10:4)

Love not sleep, lest you come to poverty. . . . He who gathers little by little will increase it. . . . Whatever your hand finds to do, do it with your might. (Prov. 20:13; 13:11; Eccles. 9:10)

Whatever your task, work heartily, as serving the Lord and not men, knowing that from the Lord you will receive the inheritance as your reward; you are serving the Lord Christ. (Col. 3:23-24)

We gave you this command: If any one will not work, let him not eat. . . . Now such persons we command and exhort in the Lord Jesus Christ to do their work in quietness and to earn their own living. (2 Thess. 3:10-12)

Scripture is clear that slothfulness is indeed sin and hard work is pleasing to God. Notice that work is profitable, sloth unprofitable according to Solomon, but that Paul adds the other dimensions: work is serving God (Rom. 12:11; Eph. 6:6ff.; Col. 3:22ff.); makes one self-sufficient (2 Thess. 3:12; 1 Thess. 4:12); enables one to provide for his family (1 Tim. 5:8); is a good testimony to others (1 Thess. 4:12); enables one to give generously (Eph 4:28). Over Paul's teaching on work hovers a spirit of enthusiasm and joy. Work is not a curse to be avoided but part of God's original plan for man's good (Gen. 1:28ff.), part of the likeness man bears to God, the model Worker.

SELF-CONTROL

The term *self-control* is used in the Greek New Testament only four times, and in all four cases in lists of virtues that do not shed much light on its meaning (Acts 24:25; Gal. 5:23; Titus 1:8; 2 Pet. 1:6). The word means to have control of one's appetite. The word may not be common, but the teaching is. Job succeeded in keeping his eyes from looking on a virgin (31:1) whereas David sinned grievously through failing to keep his body under rigorous control (1 Cor. 9:27). Daniel purposed in his heart not to be defiled with the king's menu (Dan. 1:8). One who controls his spirit is more powerful than the military conqueror (Prov. 16:32). We are to make no provision for the flesh (Rom. 13:14) and to cut off the member that would lead us astray (Matt. 5:30). Self-denial is not one optional way of life, it is the *only* way of life (Matt. 16:24-26).

The axe for the root of lust is self-control. Bodily appetites are to be fulfilled in God-honoring ways. And those ways are spelled out in Scripture. Sex outside of marriage, overeating, drunkenness, laziness, or inordinate squandering of free time on self, must all be rejected through the deliberate control of one's desires. Only God can successfully control these strong, built-in drives. But through reliance on him, even a weak human being can live self-controlled. And this controlled life-style is not a bleak, joyless stoicism. Rather, it is a channeling of life forces into the greatest possible fulfillment.

COVETOUSNESS AND CONTENTMENT

Covetousness is a strange human characteristic. God views it as a terrible evil; man views it as the route to all kinds of personal fulfillment. God puts it in the Ten Commandments and lists it in the New Testament along with idolatry, adultery, homosexuality, and thievery; man considers it the least of human foibles. Why does God view covetousness so seriously?

COVETOUSNESS DEFINED

To covet is to seek for something, someone, some position, some recognition, or some pleasure not in the will of God. Notice that I used the word *seek* rather than *desire*. To covet is not merely wishing for more, but going after it, lusting for it, working to hold onto it. Although the terms used in Scripture for a covetous attitude speak of strong desire for any of the things already noted, the chief use of the term, especially in Paul's letters, refers to longing for and "going after" material things. Although the slightest desire to get something God does not intend is rightly called sin, the original word is strong: greedy, avaricious, insatiable.

In Scripture covetousness is so terrible a sin that it separates a person from God (Rom. 1:29, 32), destroys community (James 4:1-4), breaks fellowship in the church (2 Pet. 2:14ff.), is the just object of church discipline (1 Cor. 5:10-11), brings the wrath of God on mankind in this age (Col. 3:5-6), and the wrath of God on the covetous person in eternity (1 Cor. 6:9-10). It is a special temptation for the Christian minister and rightly debars him from service (1 Tim. 3:3; 1 Thess. 2:5; 2 Cor. 7:2). It is a form of idolatry, substituting things for the living God (Eph. 5:5; Col. 3:5).

Desire to have things is not evil in itself. It is the distortion of this God-given desire, aiming at what is not in the will of God for a person, that is such a terrible and destructive sin. According to Scripture, a covetous spirit becomes visible in those who steal, defame others, lust sexually, fight with a Christian brother to recover material losses, scheme and plot to make unjust gain, pursue recognition, are discontented, give sparingly or grudgingly.

No wonder the Bible treats covetousness so ruthlessly. And we American Christians domesticate this sin as a house pet. So far as the recorded words of Jesus indicate, he said more about a person's relationship to possessions than he did about heaven and hell. Why is the issue so important?

Covetousness is a root sin (1 Tim. 6:10) that leads to stealing, adultery, murder—almost any other sin.

The sin of covetousness is an especially gross form of idolatry. Paul speaks of the heinous character of sin which puts the created thing in place of the Creator (Rom. 1:23).

If the first and great commandment has to do with love, covetousness stands opposite the great commandment. Covetousness is interested in getting; love is interested in giving.

Covetousness is a sin against the one who covets. This sin

illustrates the basic principle that God's laws are for our good. A covetous person builds inner tension. In fact, covetousness often leads to emotional illness. Materialism is a very frustrating way of life because one can never be satisfied. The more you get, the more you want. John D. Rockefeller was asked how much money it takes to satisfy a man. The reply of one of the world's wealthiest men was, "A little more!" Of all the foolish and frustrating activities, to seek to fill the void of one's *spirit* with *things* must rank near the top.

THE CHRISTIAN AND THINGS

It is quite possible to covet not only what belongs to other people but to covet that which belongs to God. This is possible especially with that portion of his property that is in my keeping. In fact, Scripture seems to say that my relationship to material possessions is a key to understanding my relationship to God. Standing opposite covetousness are two Spirit-given qualities, one passive, one active: contentment and generosity. Consider first the active quality: a biblical pattern of giving. I suggest six levels of giving: infant, childhood, youth, adult, mature, and a special ability given by God.

Infant: No Giving. The infant level of giving is not giving. Did you ever see a generous infant? He is in the getting business. Like many in the church, he must be fed, entertained, cleaned up. He cries when he doesn't get what he wants. In fact, such infant Christians behave like the typical worldling (1 Cor. 3:3).

This level of spiritual nongrowth may be seen also in the popularity of the prosperity doctrine—"I'm a child of the King, so I go first-class." "Believe in Jesus and you will prosper materially." Nothing could be further from New Testament teaching on the Christian and money. But in an affluent society, the doctrine has great appeal. Another evidence is seen in those who insist on becoming wealthy on the gospel. The evangelical star system, amplified in print and television, means that famous musical performers, popular preachers, and best-selling authors can and often do demand large fees and live like royalty. The general public finds it difficult to discern any similarity with the one who did not have a home to lay his head. They have more kinship with Simon, it would seem, who thought the gospel was a way to make money (Acts 8:18ff.). God pronounces great judgment on those who consider religion a way of making money (1 Tim. 6:5ff.).

Childhood: Impulse Giving. Some move beyond the infant, self-oriented way of life to respond to generous impulses. Such Christians may give extravagantly, but only when there is a strong emotional appeal. A particularly skillful presentation of human need may evoke such giving. The prospect of seeing one's name in print or on some building would be a lesser motive, but often produces generous response. When group excitement or expectancy takes over and others are giving generously, such a person may be moved to participate. Impulse giving is not bad, necessarily. But the person who gives only in that way needs to grow beyond the impulsive childhood level of occasional impromptu giving to giving as a way of life.

Youth: Legalistic Giving. When a person grows in knowledge of the Word and obedience to it, he discovers that the Old Testament principle of giving the first 10 percent of one's income to God is affirmed by Jesus Christ in the New Testament. Some hold that this is legalistic giving. And it may be. But far better to give legalistically than not to give (Matt. 23:23; Luke 11:42). In fact, the growing Christian discovers that should he spend that 10 percent on himself, God considers him a thief (Mal. 3:8ff.). Many have stepped into this obedience with trembling, fearing the consequences, only to discover that God proves true to his promise—he secures his child's welfare and rewards him in time and eternity.

Adult: Management. When the Christian begins to obey God seriously, he discovers that the tithe was only a token of the fact that the child of God is not an owner at all but is simply a manager of another Person's property. This teaching is clear in the Old Testament, but even clearer in the New Testament. Luke 16 is a key passage on this basic Bible teaching on managership. Christ's disciples are foolish because they do not plan for the future by using money to store up treasure in heaven (v. 8). They are foolish because they see money from the world's viewpoint.

Notice five contrasts in attitudes toward money taught in the parable of the "Unrighteous Steward" or the Cheating Manager.

1. Little . . . much (v. 10). No matter how wealthy a person may be in earthly currency it is very little compared to heavenly treasure. So only a fool would live for "the little" of this life. Furthermore, a person does not need to have much to deposit riches in the heavenly vaults. All he needs is to be faithful with the little he has. By the same token, one can cheat with very little, using what he has for his own benefit instead of the Owner's.

2. Imitation . . . real (v. 11). The world considers earthly currency the real value, but Christians are fools if they do the same. Money is literally "deceitful," "counterfeit." Only a fool would live to accumulate the counterfeit, play money of this world when he could invest it in true riches at the end of his journey.

3. Manager . . . owner (v. 12). Here is the heart of the teaching: We are not owners at all. God is the owner, and we are given a stewardship, a trusteeship, the job of manager to use a certain portion of God's possessions to advance his program in the world. How many "managers" prove to be embezzlers, using God's possessions for themselves!

4. Money . . . God (v. 13). There are those who would try to manage things to benefit both the Owner and the manager—to build God's Kingdom and their own simultaneously. But Jesus said, "No servant can serve two masters; for either he will hate the one and love the other, or he will be devoted to the one and despise the other. You cannot serve God and mammon."

These teachings seemed foolish to the Pharisees, who believed that their abundance was direct proof that God was well-pleased with them (v. 14). They were charter members of the "prosperity cult." They scoffed at Jesus' teaching on money. They believed money was real, important, and their own. So Christ said this revealed their heart condition and that there would be heavy cost to them if ever they were to get into his Kingdom (vv. 15-16). But if they didn't, the cost would be infinitely greater.

5. Heaven . . . hell (vv. 19-31). We normally use the story of

the rich man and Lazarus for evangelistic purposes. But the story was given originally not so much to teach about hell as to teach about using money to prepare for heaven. It was to teach disciples how they should relate to things. We hear of a poor man who loved God and a rich man who lived for things. And you see the end of these choices: heaven and hell.

That the Christian is no more than a manager is taught throughout the New Testament, not just in Luke 16 (Matt. 6:19-34; 19:16-29; Mark 12:41-44; Luke 12:13; 17:7-10; 19:21-26; Acts 2:44-45; 4:32-37; 20:35; Rom. 14:8; 1 Cor. 6:19-20; 2 Cor. 8 and 9; Gal. 6:6-10; 1 Tim. 6:5-10, 17-19; Heb. 10:34; 13:5).

Managership is the level at which one's life-style begins to change. Managers live more simply than owners in this world. How difficult to live more simply than Jesus, the Owner, did! And yet, is the disciple greater than his master?

Managership is the level at which responsible choices must be made. Until now, the tither simply chose to obey his Lord and used a little arithmetic to honestly "pay up." Now he must look at the enterprise of God in the world and make hard decisions about where to invest most wisely to accomplish God's purposes and how much he may honestly invest in his own "traveling expenses" on the way to his eternal home. But there is a higher level of giving.

Mature: Sacrificial Giving. The spiritually mature are moved, at least in part, by the highest motivation: love. David refused to make an offering that cost him nothing (2 Sam. 24:24). Later David was to give what was doubtless the largest offering in human history, the fruit of twenty years of planning and a lifetime of heroic effort. The impoverished widow gave from her meager income "all the living that she had" (Luke 21:1-4). Does anyone question the motive of David or the widow? They stand out in stark contrast to a world of avid getters and grudging givers.

Do we feel we have an option about sacrifice? Is that level of giving for an elite? Christ taught that the first step of discipleship was to radically realign one's life-style: "Sell your possessions and give your money away to those in need . . . wherever your treasure is, you may be certain that there your heart is too" (Luke 12:33-34, Phillips). The principle works the other way too: Where your heart affection is, there you will invest sacrificially. Does anyone actually live that way? Christians in poor Macedonia did, even when those in prosperous Corinth did not.

We must tell you, friends, about the grace of generosity which God has imparted to our congregations in Macedonia. The troubles they have been through have tried them hard, yet in all this they have been so exuberantly happy that from the depths of their poverty they have shown themselves lavishly open-handed. Going to the limit of their resources, as I can testify, and even beyond that limit, they begged us most insistently, and on their own initiative, to be allowed to share in this generous service to their fellow-Christians. (2 Cor. 8:1-4, NEB)

In 2 Corinthians 8 and 9 Paul gives the most exhaustive teaching on Christian giving found in Scripture. The focus is on a group of believers who gave sacrificially out of deep love for God and for their brothers (8:7-8, 24). I do not read in Scripture that God loves a successful getter or a careful keeper. I do read that he loves a cheerful giver (9:7).

For a model of this sacrificial love we have Jesus, who deliberately divested himself of his wealth and chose to become poor so that we through his poverty might become spiritually and eternally rich (8:9).

Special Grace: Faith. Note that the levels of giving are not mutually exclusive. For example, a poor person would need to act in faith and sacrifice to give 10 percent. But in general, levels of advance in spiritual maturity are reflected in one's giving. The final level—faith—should characterize all giving. Actually, most giving is "sight" giving—looking at what is available and projecting on that basis what one should give, either as an honest tither, a wise manager, or a loving sacrificer. Faith moves beyond this to believe God to provide what cannot be given, even with sacrifice. This faith is a virtue to be pursued by all.

Yet the Bible speaks of the *gift* of faith (1 Cor. 12:9) which makes it clear that certain people are given a special ability to trust God in ways that others do not. Those who have the gift of faith in the area of finance move beyond managing wisely and giving sacrificially. They believe God for what they do not have and cannot get in order to accomplish some task for him.

What results from a life of generous giving? When we rightly handle money and other things, considering all of these a trust from the true Owner, and in gratitude and love seek to sacrificially invest these possessions as wisely as possible for his Kingdom, two wonderful promises are ours. First, the person who is a faithful manager has the guarantee that all his needs will be provided in full (Phil. 4:19; Matt. 6:19-34; 2 Cor. 9:8). This certainly is an incredible guarantee and simplifies all of life.

Second, God promises to reward the person (Luke 9:12-13, 16-26; 18:18-30; 2 Cor. 9:6; Gal. 6:6-10). He treats us as if these possessions were our own and we were doing something praiseworthy in investing in his purposes in the world.

We have looked in some detail at the opposite of covetousness—generosity with one's possessions. Yet it is possible to covet nonmaterial things, to be discontented in other areas of life and thus to violate the Tenth Commandment, "Thou shalt not covet."

COVETING NONMATERIAL THINGS

When we desire whatever is not ours in the will of God, we are coveting. It is possible to covet the abilities or position of another person. It is possible to covet the affection of another person. We call these sins "envy," a particularly pernicious and destructive form of coveting.

One form of coveting, as we have seen, is to covet one's own possessions, since these in reality are not our own, but God's. Another even more precious possession, normally considered our own, is time. But this also belongs to God. It is quite possible to covet time God has not given, or to use time entrusted to us in ways God does not desire.

For many Christians "time covetousness" is the greatest of temptations, discontent with one's time allotment, a destructive and demoralizing sin.

Coveting Time. Consider two presuppositions basic to successfully handling the problem of time covetousness. First is the conviction that God has a plan for each life committed to him (see chapter 10) and that he has time necessary to fulfill all he expects me to do according to his plan.

The second presupposition is that if the 168 hours each week seem inadequate, either I have missed the will of God for my life (I am doing something he never intended), or I am doing it inefficiently. There is a very beautiful passage concerning this basic presupposition: "Thy eyes beheld my unformed substance; in thy book were written, every one of them, the days that were formed for me, when as yet there was none of them" (Ps. 139:16).

The Gospels often speak of "the time" not yet having come. "Mine hour has not yet come." We would say in modern English, "The time is not right" or, "It's not time yet."

The Preacher in Ecclesiastes refers to this principle: "For everything there is a season, and a time for every matter under heaven: a time to be born, and a time to die; a time to plant, and a time to pluck up what is planted." And this poetic passage closes with a very wonderful word: "He has made everything beautiful in its time" (Eccles. 3:11). Everything is beautiful when it's on schedule. God has planned it, and when it comes according to God's plan, it is indeed beautiful.

But there is a problem stated in the same verse: "Also he has put eternity into man's mind." This is the core of the problem. It is a beautiful thing to fulfill God's purpose moment by moment, day by day. But we have eternity in our hearts. We want to do so much more—an infinity of things. Yet we are told not to be anxious even about tomorrow. Furthermore, Christ tells us that it is foolish to be anxious because "which of you by being anxious can add one cubit to his span of life?" (Matt. 6:27). Which of you, by frenetic endeavor, by worry and concern, can add one hour to the 168 that have been allotted this week?

What is the solution? There are practical suggestions which will help, but first of all, we must understand that we will never solve this problem unless we come in faith. "He who believes will not be in haste" (Isa. 28:16). So it is a matter of faith. We must have confidence in God that he has a plan, that he is going to fulfill it, and that he has given us all of the necessary resources to fulfill it, including adequate time resources.

Often there just does not seem to be enough time. I must be doing something that he did not intend me to do or I must be doing it in the wrong way. Let me suggest three practical steps to help a person sort out what God's agenda is and how to get it done: set priorities, examine for inefficiency, start at the bottom and cut.

Setting Priorities. It helps in setting priorities to list everything one *must* do, everything one *wants* to do, everything *other people* want one to do. How does one put them in order of priority?

First, there are basic responsibilities that absolutely must be cared for, such as: fellowship with God, maintenance of physical life, responsibility for personal dependents, church ministry, and vocational responsibilities.

Note the order of priority. Fellowship with God is first because this is the ultimate basis of life, the reason for our creation and redemption. This is the one area of responsibility that is the essence not only of time but of eternity. In this responsibility there is personal fellowship with God, worship with any other believing members of my family, and fellowship with other members of God's family in the church.

Next comes maintenance of physical life. It is second because if one does not have physical life, he cannot do much else! So it is essential to take care of the physical: eating, sleeping, exercise.

Then comes responsibility for others. After family comes responsibility for friends and time invested in serving one's community. "Thou shalt love thy neighbor as thyself."

Finally comes vocation. One needs to define clearly obligations and goals. They may not be the same. Goals may be very high. The time required to accomplish such goals should not be listed under "basic obligations." Only what is required to adequately meet one's responsibility should be included here.

These four responsibilities overlap and often reinforce one another, but all must be cared for, and we can count on God to enable us to do this within a twenty-four-hour day.

Next come secondary activities, those things that should be included if possible. For example, if one is an officer in the church or if he teaches a Sunday school class, that would be on the "must" list. But then the person is asked to do other things, and the load increases until he is asked to be out every night of the week. This is extra church service which must be evaluated in the light of other "must" responsibilities. Or consider vocational excellence beyond one's basic obligations. The ambitious person has goals and wants to reach them, dreams of what might be done. Those extra goals and the estimated time they would consume should be listed under "secondary activities," which are included in one's schedule only if they fit.

Next there are the extras for personal dependents, such as special occasions, which mean so much in personal relations. Finally, there is the time needed for personal improvement, improving one's mental, social, emotional, and physical well-being.

Note that there is abundant Scripture for the "must" category of basic responsibilities. But under "secondary" and "incidental" I do not find a biblical mandate. Of course, since there is no biblical mandate for these categories, they are the areas one begins to cut when he finds himself overextended. This is one approach to sorting out priorities. There are many other ways, no doubt, but assignment of priority must be based on biblical principles. One of the most difficult parts of this basic time analysis is to distinguish in each responsibility what is a Bible-given "must" and that which goes beyond what God requires. Whether on the job or in church there is always a demand for "more." It is essential to sort out the basic responsibility, list it under "must" and put the rest firmly under "secondary activities" which should be included only if "must" responsibilities are fully cared for.

Examine for Inefficiency. After all responsibilities have been recorded in order of biblical priority, it is time to examine each activity for efficiency. For example, a student who is reading 250 words a minute could easily double his reading capabilities. Almost every job has been analyzed by some efficiency expert to determine the best way to do it. Anyone who is serious about escaping the bondage of time pressure would do well to tap into such resources.

Another way to become more efficient is to combine responsibilities. A man needs exercise, so he puts in six hours a week shooting basketball at the Y. He also needs fellowship time with his wife, so they watch four TV shows a week. Every good father should spend time with the kids, so they play Monopoly two evenings a week. He might discover that all three responsibilities could be combined in one activity: backpacking, for example, or gardening or jogging. Hobbies brought into the service of the church or chosen to fulfill some other basic responsibility such as exercise or eating or fellowship combine activities and save time.

After thoroughly examining each activity for maximum efficiency, time may still be inadequate. What then?

Start at the Bottom and Cut. Although it is often possible to cut back on the time invested in a "must" responsibility, in the end it may prove that the only way out is radical surgery, elimination of whole categories in the "secondary" classification.

It is hard to say no. Some people have never learned to say no without feeling guilty. That is why we must begin with biblical priorities. Of course, the hardest "no" may be to self. We often have too little time for basic responsibilities because we are undisciplined. We do what we *want* to do.

In the final analysis, the problem is a spiritual one: Do I really believe that God has planned my life and that he has provided all the time resources needed to meet my responsibilities? If I truly believe this, am I prepared to obey him in refusing those activities that are not of him and working hard to "work smarter" in those which are?

We have looked in some detail at the problem of inadequate time because this seems to be a point of unusual tension in many lives. In spite of the fact that our society has provided more leisure than any in history, we are tempted to be discontented, a clear violation of the Tenth Commandment. We turn now to consider the cure for covetousness: contentment.

CONTENTMENT

I have learned, in whatever state I am, to be content. I know how to be abased, and I know how to abound; in any and all circumstances I have learned the secret of facing plenty and hunger, abundance and want. I can do all things in him who strengthens me. (Phil. 4:11-13)

There is great gain in godliness with contentment; for we brought nothing into the world, and we cannot take anything out of the world; but if we have food and clothing, with these we will be content. But those who desire to be rich fall into temptation, into a snare, into many senseless and hurtful desires that plunge men into ruin and destruction. For the love of money is the root of all evils; it is through this craving that some have wandered from the faith and pierced their hearts with many pangs. (1 Tim. 6:6-10)

Keep your life free from love of money, and be content with what you have; for he has said, "I will never leave you nor forsake you." (Heb. 13:5)

Do not be anxious about your life, what you shall eat or what you shall drink, nor about your body, what you shall put on. . . . For the Gentiles seek all these things; and your heavenly Father knows that you need them all. But seek first his kingdom and his righteousness, and all these things shall be yours as well. Therefore do not be anxious about tomorrow, for tomorrow will be anxious for itself. Let the day's own trouble be sufficient for the day. (Matt. 6:25-34)

It is important to recognize a distinction between being dissatisfied and being unsatisfied. To be dissatisfied is to demonstrate unbelief and ingratitude, one of the most destructive of all sins (Rom. 1:21). Contentment is a beautiful and healthful condition. On the other hand, the godly person is in a sense never satisfied with the status quo. So long as we fall short of all the fullness of God, we strive for the goal. Even in material things, the Christian may legitimately work hard to improve his condition, but always with contentment.

Covetousness is a cancer that destroys the one who covets. Unchecked, it destroys others as well. The cure is gratitude and trust. There is little room for covetousness in a heart that overflows with gratitude for all that God has given and in trust that God will keep his word. Such trust is not apprehensive that the resources of life will prove inadequate but is confident that God does not lie and that he will fulfill his promises to meet every need.

PRIDE AND HUMILITY

Pride is in a class by itself as a root sin. Whether the prophet spoke only of the wicked king of Babylon or whether he had in mind also the Enemy who controlled that king, the description of the essence and end of pride is unequaled in human literature:

How you are fallen from heaven, O Day Star, son of Dawn! How you are cut down to the ground, you who laid the nations low! You said in your heart, "I will ascend into heaven; above the stars of God I will set my throne on high; I will sit on the mount of assembly in the far north; I will ascend above the heights of the clouds, I will make myself like the Most High." But you are brought down to Sheol, to the depths of the Pit. (Isa. 14:12-15)

Notice that the essence of pride is a distorted view of self, leading to unwarranted self-confidence that, in turn, propels a dependent being into a disastrous attempt at independence.

WHAT IS PRIDE?

Is it a sin to take pride in one's country or family? Is it a sin to take pride in one's God? What of self-esteem that makes possible the response of shame when one does not measure up to his self-imposed standards?

Of the ten different Hebrew root words for the concept of pride, almost all have the idea of high, exalted, elevated, grand, whereas many of the twelve root words for humble and the twenty root words for humiliate have the basic idea of sink, bow down, depress, put down, subdue. Another root idea of some words for pride is to inflate, puff up, to swell; yet another is to broaden, make wide. The Old Testament not only employs such an astoundingly rich vocabulary, it has literally hundreds of references to pride and humility so that the two concepts are crystal clear.

In the New Testament, the concepts of pride and humility grow out of Old Testament concepts, not out of the contemporary Greek viewpoint that valued the self-sufficient, well-born aristocrat and despised the humble. In using the Greek words, New Testament authors added descriptive words to make the meaning clear. They spoke not only of being high-minded but of vain or empty glorying; appearing to be above others; thinking well of self vainly or without cause; being puffed up.

The basic idea is clear: Sinful pride is much like alcohol or drugs—the one who imbibes has a distorted view of reality. He attempts to impress others with this inflated evaluation, and even more destructive, he begins to believe it himself (Gal. 6:3). That is when self-confidence grows, and a person becomes convinced he is autonomous and should be independent. He begins to act as if he could sovereignly decide the shape of his life (1 John 2:15-17) or decide his own future (James 4:15-16). Scripture teaches that self-confidence is the fatal flaw in the godless (Ps. 52:1; 74:4; 94:3). No wonder pride comes before a fall and a haughty spirit leads to destruction (Prov. 16:18). No wonder the Bible is so full of condemnation of pride and extols humility and God-dependence.

In summary, pride is setting on self a value greater than it merits. The businessman who relies on the impregnable fortress of his wealth, the college professor who trusts his autonomous reason, the scientist who arrogantly dismisses all reality beyond the natural, the beauty queen who considers her charms invincible, the athlete who congratulates himself on his physical power and skill—all are relying on deadly illusions. And so is the preacher who believes the compliments his admirers heap on him or the saint who considers herself quite holy.

If the essence of sinful pride is the distortion, the lie of it, then feeling good about some true excellence may not be sinful pride. Certainly to be proud of God is simply another way to express a spirit of gratitude and praise. One may also legitimately exult in other blessed realities like his children or his parents (Prov. 16:31; 17:6). Paul speaks often of boasting in many things, but all are attributed to the grace of God (Gal. 6:13; 1 Cor. 3:5ff.; 4:7; 15:10).

AREAS OF PRIDE

Pride can be confidence in self across the board—every facet of one's person is well-pleasing to one's self. But more often the object of pride is concentrated in some specific area.

Pride of Position. The Pharisees loved the places of prominence and the proper titles (Matt. 23:6ff.). The scramble for prominence, controlling authority, even the pitiful scrabbling for titles is hardly confined to those ancient religious "play actors," and the temptation to lord it over God's flock is pride of position, which the church leader must constantly eject from his thinking (1 Pet. 5:3).

Pride of Ability and Achievement. Paul speaks of wrangling over the ability some had to speak well in public (1 Cor. 2:1-3), an ability he apparently lacked. How tempted we are to take full credit for any ability at all, even the ability to pray eloquently! Yet, what do we have that we did not receive?

Pride of Possessions. This is foolish because getting them is among the least of human achievements and so little able to fill the human heart; not to mention how transient and undependable a source of pride they are (Jer. 48:7). And yet they tell us that it is pride more than avarice that drives Americans in their unending quest for material goods. "As for the rich in this world, charge them not to be haughty" (1 Tim. 6:17).

Pride of Knowledge. This is what brought down our first parents. More than anything else, perhaps, knowledge "puffs up" (1 Cor. 8:1). "Let no one deceive himself. If any one among you thinks that he is wise in this age, let him become a fool that he may become wise" (1 Cor. 3:18). This was the first great problem in the church at Corinth, and Paul devoted to this theme his first three chapters in his first letter to them.

In his devastating critique of the modern temperament, one of the great thinkers of the twentieth century, Charles Malik, put his finger on the basic problem:

More serious is what happens to the scientist himself. . . . First is what I call the pride of knowledge and power. This is the subtlest failing. Because he controls his subject matter, the scientist slips into the feeling that he is a kind of god. People speak of the humility of the scientist; in truth I find very little humility among scientists. They know, it is true, but what they do not know is not only greater but far more important than what they know. The scientists are not noted for loving or sacrificing for one another. . . . They are more celebrated for their rivalries and jealousies, and for making sure that their ideas and discoveries are not plagiarized by others but are exclusively attributed to them. . . . If we are to characterize the spirit of the scientific community, we will have to say that in the final analysis it is passion for knowledge with a view to power.[4]

In response to this spirit, God replies:

Your wisdom and your knowledge led you astray, and you said in your heart, "I am, and there is no one beside me." (Isa. 47:10)

Let not the wise man glory in his wisdom, let not the mighty man glory in his might, let not the rich man glory in his riches; but let him who glories glory in this, that he understands and knows me, that I am the LORD who practice steadfast love, justice, and righteousness in the earth. (Jer. 9:23-24)

[4]Charles Malik, *A Christian Critique of the University* (Downers Grove, Ill.: InterVarsity, 1982), 42, 50.

Pride of Spiritual Attainment. Because it is so evil to judge oneself praiseworthy in godlikeness, such opinions have to go underground. So the feeling that we have attained, especially in comparison to someone else, is usually disguised even from self. But it slips out in the testimony artfully crafted to demonstrate to others how holy—yes, even how humble—we are. Even prayer can be more for the benefit of the fellow-prayers than for the God we address. The harsh judgment and spiritually phrased criticism of another may give away an inflated self-evaluation: "Let us make this a matter of prayer—you and I who are above such failure—that our sister may see the error of her ways." But God sees, God knows, and he judges hypocrisy more severely than any other sin.

The areas of temptation to pride seem unending: pride of appearance, pride of class or race, pride of family descent. But whatever the object of pride, God responds, "a proud heart is sin."

FORMS OF PRIDE

Some forms of pride are highly visible, others so subtle as to go undetected altogether. Consider the levels of visibility in the form pride takes.

Boasting. The most obvious evidence of pride is straightforward boasting. The braggart is so roundly condemned in Scripture that few serious Christians are guilty of boasting.

Seeking Praise. Each of us by nature is inclined to work hard at "public relations" so that the childhood "Watch me!" gives way to more civilized and sophisticated ways of getting center stage. We may reject allowing our name to be published with the notice of our gifts, but it is not easy to do as Christ taught and give with total anonymity.

Another way to seek the acknowledgment of my own excellencies is to compare myself or my personal performance to others, with the thought that this will put me in a better light. I will come out much better than comparing me with Jesus! But God says this is foolish:

> Not that we venture to class or compare ourselves with some of those who
> commend themselves. But when they measure themselves by one another, and
> compare themselves with one another, they are without understanding. For it
> is not the man who commends himself that is accepted, but the man whom the
> Lord commends. (2 Cor. 10:12, 18)

Accepting Honor. To be pleased with a deserved compliment
may not evidence pride, but to allow others to promote one's
excellencies can become an expression of pride. In the day of
hype and PR-produced celebrities, it is difficult to graciously
accept honor from others without promoting an image of
excellence that eclipses the honor due the Savior. Rejecting the
honor others proffer must be done in a way that does not reject
the person. Graciously acknowledge the gesture, but never allow
people whom one can control to consistently promote one's
greatness.

Self-Confidence. A less visible evidence of pride is self-
confidence and the resulting independent spirit. Why is it so
difficult to apologize, to seek forgiveness? Why are we stubborn,
insisting on our own way? Why so dogmatic? Defensive? Why
should a person choose his own way rather than God's way? All
these responses are telltale evidence of a proud heart, hard and
brittle, still relying on its own resources, unwilling to declare
bankruptcy and consistently accept God's evaluation and to rely
always on God's resources.

Invisible Pride. Various forms of pride may not look like pride.
Putting down others is often a way of attempting to lift oneself
by comparison. An argumentative stance or thin-skinned
readiness to be offended often are rooted in pride. "Why wasn't
I invited [or elected, or recognized]? Surely I'm as good as *that*
person [who *was* invited, elected, recognized]."

Pride Masquerading as Humility. Surely the timid soul, the
person with a poor self-image who denigrates himself, is the
quintessential Humble One. Not ordinarily. Fear to attempt
something may stem from pride—unwillingness to let my
weakness be seen, fear of being viewed a failure. Self put-down
can be an attempt to beat the other person to it. That may

lighten the blow or may even squeeze a boost from the other person. Self-pity is often unadulterated pride, grieving that others do not see me for what I truly am.

Pastor Harold Burchett tells us there are two varieties of pride: the turtle and the peacock. The turtle withdraws silently into its shell to protect itself, while the peacock struts its magnificent splendor to draw attention to itself.

Samuel Shoemaker is even stronger when he says, "You can never have real humility while you are preoccupied with yourself, and an inferiority complex is the most self-centered state of mind in the world."[5] How, then, does the question of self-image relate to pride and humility?

SELF-IMAGE

Two pathways for attaining success in the Christian life are charted by leading spokesmen; two paths that seem to run in the opposite direction. The dominant voices of the latter half of the twentieth century tell us: "A strong self-image is indispensable to successful Christian living; a poor self-image is the greatest cause of failure among Christians." Another line of thought was dominant in former years, but today can get onto few platforms or best-seller lists: "I have been crucified with Christ . . . it is no longer I who live . . . I am nothing . . . if anyone does not hate himself, he cannot be a disciple of Christ." How do we reconcile the current emphasis on feelings of worth and importance with teachings of biblical humility?

I was sitting in the hospital room, awaiting my wife's return from emergency surgery. It was Sunday morning, and I turned for encouragement to television. "The solution is not to look at the problem," said the well-known preacher, "but to look at . . ." He paused and lifted his hands and eyes toward heaven and concluded, "the possibilities!" I thought of the possibility that the anesthesiologist might have erred. The preacher continued to encourage me: "What I want to help you to do is have faith in . . . *you!*" I didn't really find much consolation in that thought as the projected hour-and-a-half surgery was now stretching into three hours. I must confess, however, a powerful magnetism and strong fascination in what I learned of "possibility

[5]Samuel Shoemaker, "The Nature of Humility," *Christianity Today,* 6 December 1963, 14.

thinking." More people were desperately looking for jobs than at any time since the Great Depression, so "tough times never last, but tough people do" was a constant refrain that morning. "Believe it and you can achieve it!" In fact, "nothing is impossible unless . . ." I was waiting for a biblical quote, but he concluded "unless you have negative thoughts." There were other slogans intended to build a good self-image: "It takes guts to leave the ruts." "The me I see is the me I'll be."[6] I'm sure this would have been great therapy under other circumstances, but not in a hospital room, waiting with rising anxiety.

Would I have received greater help from the older message?

This is the highest and most profitable reading, the very knowing and despising of a man's self. For a man to account nothing of himself but evermore to think well and highly of other folks is sovereign wisdom and perfection.[7]

True humility comes when, in the light of God, we have seen ourselves to be nothing, have consented to part with and cast away self, to let God be all. The soul that has done this, and can say, "So have I lost myself in finding Thee," no longer compares itself with others. It has given up forever every thought of self in God's presence; it meets its fellowmen as one who is nothing, and seeks nothing for itself; who is a servant of God, and for his sake a servant of all.[8]

Sinful pride is thinking of self more highly than one ought to think (Rom. 12:3). Paul tells us how to think of self: rationally, objectively, honestly. "Don't cherish exaggerated ideas of yourself or your importance, but try to have a sane estimate of your capabilities" (Phillips). So a "good self-image" is a *true* self-image, an image based on reality. An accurate assessment is what true humility demands. "But let each one examine his own work, and then he will have *reason* for boasting in regard to himself alone, and not in regard to another" (Gal. 6:4, NASB).

If I am the most skilled pianist in the congregation, it is not godly humility to act as if I were not. The fact that humility is required does not sanctify an attempted deception, either of self or others. On the other hand, to insist on getting what I deserve, on receiving "what I am worth" may be dangerous.

Deeper than the level of accurately assessing one's skills or achievements is the basic evaluation of the self, the essential

[6]Robert Schuller, "Hour of Power" broadcast, 17 October 1982.
[7]Thomas à Kempis, *The Imitation of Christ* (New York: Dutton, 1910), 4.
[8]Andrew Murray, *Humility* (London: Nisbet, n.d.), 47.

"me." Who am I? What am I worth? The Bible gives two basic facts that must be held in balance or, by emphasizing one or the other, we fall into a distorted view of self and consequently of life and how it is to be lived. I believe many spokesmen for the older view of self and some for the newer have erred in just this way—concentrating on one truth to the neglect of its complementary truth, they have led us astray.

Both extremes are a distortion of reality and thus are destructive. A psychologist or a strong media blitz may convince me that I am important, capable, just as good as the next guy. But when I leave the office, classroom, or TV set and meet the reality of my circumstances and the opinions of others, what happens when they do not correspond with my shining new self-image? On the other hand, if I finish the book or leave church convinced that I am in reality a big zero and the sooner I admit it and behave like it, the better, what credit does God get for working on me? The biblical reality, on the other hand, gives strength, the strength of a true self-image.

Did the psalmist have a correct view when he called himself a worm (Ps. 22:6)? How well it fits with Christ's consistent teaching that we must deny self, even hate self, if we are to be his disciples. We are viewed in Scripture as hopeless, helpless sinners, incapable of gaining acceptance with a holy God. We are so limited in time and space, having so insignificant a slice of knowledge, that all mankind combined cannot amass enough wisdom and power to merit even a flicker of attention from an infinite God. So it is quite fitting that Paul should consider himself the least of apostles (1 Cor. 15:9), the least of all saints (Eph. 3:8), even the foremost of sinners (1 Tim. 1:15). This is one aspect of reality that a person must see clearly or his self-image will be grossly distorted.

On the other hand, Paul was exuberantly confident. He often boasted (though chiefly of his own weaknesses: Rom. 5:3; 2 Cor. 4:7-11; 10:8ff.; 11:23-30; chap. 12). But whether in incredible achievement or weakness and failure, Paul gave God the credit:

But by the grace of God I am what I am, and His grace toward me did not prove vain; but I labored even more than all of them, yet not I, but the grace of God with me. (1 Cor. 15:10, NASB)

So then neither the one who plants nor the one who waters is anything, but God who causes the growth. Now he who plants and he who waters are one; but each will receive his own reward according to his own labor. (1 Cor. 3:7-8, NASB)

What is this grace of God? First, we are created in the likeness of God, not after the pattern of animals or angels. Surely that is basis enough for strong confidence and deep gratitude. No matter how others may evaluate my worth, God chose me before he started his creative work (Eph. 1:4), and he fixed his love on me so firmly that even though I was a rebel sinner, he gave his own Son in my stead. If value is judged by the price paid, how could I be invested with any greater value? Do not err as some have—I am not worthy of such a price. He is all-worthy, giving such an incomprehensibly gracious gift to one so utterly undeserving. But the price *has* been paid. That is what I cost God, and my infinite value is in the investment made.

There is further worth. God has come to live in me, bringing wonderful gifts of grace: a godlike quality of life and abilities to accomplish his purposes in the world. To deny these accomplishments of God is not humility but unbelief. To deny a true quality of life or ministry is basically a hesitancy to admit it *to my own credit*. To recognize it rightly is to give God the glory.

With these two balancing truths about self in dynamic tension, a true self-image emerges in which I, of myself, fall far short, but by the grace of God I can be all he meant me to be. Luther said that before he was a Christian he always took credit for what he did right and refused responsibility for what he did wrong. Afterwards he refused credit for what he did right and accepted responsibility for what he did wrong.

Brother Lawrence tells of finding the same secret:

When I fail in my duty, I readily acknowledge it, saying, I am used to do so: I shall never do otherwise if I am left to myself. If I fail not, then I give God thanks, acknowledging that the strength comes from him.[9]

Jacob said, "I am not worthy of the least of all the steadfast love and all the faithfulness which thou hast shown to thy servant" (Gen. 32:10). Moses responded to God's call in the same way: "Who am I?" (Exod. 3:11). David used the very

[9]*Practicing the Presence of God* (New York: Revell, 1895), 21.

same words, "Who am I?" (2 Sam. 7:18; 1 Chron. 29:14).
Solomon echoed his great father: "Who am I?" (2 Chron. 2:6).
Job cried out, "Behold, I am of small account. . . . Therefore I
despise myself" (Job 40:4; 42:6). Isaiah responded thus to a
vision of God (Isa. 6:5), and Jeremiah remonstrated, "Ah, LORD
God! Behold, I do not know how to speak, for I am only a
youth" (Jer. 1:6). Paul returned often to a similar theme: "Not
that we are sufficient of ourselves to claim anything as coming
from us; our sufficiency is from God" (2 Cor. 3:5).

The greatest "achievers" of the Old Testament and of the
New shared in common a rather low self-image. But rather than
suffering for it, that very view of self made possible the high
achievement. They knew God had created them on purpose (Ps.
139); that God had redeemed them on purpose (Phil. 3:12);
that all the necessary resources had been provided to fulfill his
every purpose (2 Pet. 1). Instead of self-centered thinking—
building self-esteem and self-worth through self-affirmation to
find self-fulfillment—they were God-centered, affirming *his*
worth and competency, seeking *his* fulfillment through their
lives.

PROTECTION OF EGO

The ego is very delicate so it erects barriers to protect itself from
damage, little knowing that if reality were only allowed to crash
through, the truth about self could lead to freedom. A proud
person is easily humiliated (offended, hurt) but not easily
humbled. To prevent that, he mounts a skillful defense.

Rationalization. When I have failed, it is painful to admit it
even to myself, so I seek for an explanation that makes the failure
appear inevitable, if not actually good: I fell again before the
temptation to lust, but with a sex-saturated society engulfing
me, I can hardly be expected to do otherwise. Don't even the
greatest preachers testify of the same failure? I do have a short
temper, but then my father did, too, and the repression I
suffered under my parents you wouldn't believe! The boss didn't
seem pleased with my performance, but that's just the kind of
guy he is. Actually, it's something of a compliment to have *him*
disapprove.

And so we survive the failure with self-image intact, but we thereby forfeit the success that might come from acknowledging the truth and being pressed to trust One who *is* capable of coping.

Our use of language is the clearest evidence of rationalization. We "goof" or "make a mistake" or "hurt" or "have an illness"— anything but "sin."

Once the Finnish Broadcasting Company offered substantial prizes to the individual who could come up with the largest number of synonyms of any word. A working man in northern Finland won the first prize by listing 747 synonyms for drunkenness. A man serving a prison term at Turku came second with 678. The same man found 170 synonyms for stealing. Another person knew 203 synonyms for lying. Many of the synonyms conveyed the meaning of such words but without connotations of evil.[10]

Gilmore comments in the same article that a person may even acknowledge certain transgressions, "but still regard himself as basically good because he keeps most of the law or meant to keep it!"

Projection. If the excuse is too weak to provide an adequate defense, we may try to find relief by ascribing to someone else our own unworthy attitudes or thoughts. Somehow it lessens the guilt of selfish behavior if we can discern that motive in the actions of others, especially in good and great people. It is said, with some measure of evidence, that we tend to see in others our own weaknesses. Those who declaim against corrupt politics most loudly have sometimes proved to be the most corrupt. The liar trusts no one, the immoral person convinces himself that "everyone is that way."

Repression. When the two more direct defenses prove inadequate, it helps to forget about it, to refuse to admit the failure. It is quite possible, they tell us, to reject from consciousness painful or disagreeable ideas, memories, feelings, or impulses. They also tell us that this is psychologically damaging. But it is also spiritually damaging, for one can hardly seek forgiveness or strength from another to overcome a weakness he doesn't admit exists.

[10]John Lewis Gilmore, "The Other Side of the Soul," *The Presbyterian Journal,* 22 July 1964, 10.

Thus in our depravity, we are not only set up for a fatal fall by a distorted view of reality, we invest enormous energies in keeping ourselves and others deceived. What results?

RESULTS OF PRIDE AND HUMILITY

Pride brings tension with others (Prov. 13:10) and the opposition of God himself (James 4:6). Pride brings many a fall (1 Cor. 10:12) and finally leads to destruction (Prov. 16:18). These are built-in results, for a break with reality always tends to brokenness in every other area. But humility—honest appraisal of one's own inadequacies and God's full adequacy—leads to benefits unending.

Pride may lead to a fall, but humility has the opposite effect, a lifting up (Ps. 147:6; Matt. 23:12)—the opposite direction one might expect in both cases! Humility brings God's approval and honor (Ps. 138:6; Prov. 15:33; 18:12; 29:23), indeed his very presence (Isa. 57:15; 66:2). God's salvation (Matt. 5:3-6) and mercy (Luke 18:13-14) are reserved for the humble. And with himself and his salvation God bestows many other graces (Prov. 3:34) on the humble: peace (Ps. 131:1-2) and rest (Matt. 11:29), guidance (Ps. 27:11), wisdom (Prov. 11:2), and joy (Isa. 29:19).

ANTIDOTE FOR PRIDE

> CURE

In all other virtues, in all righteousness and holiness, God himself is our perfect example. But can God be humble? Does he not refuse to give his glory to another? Is it appropriate to speak of God's humility? Strange as the words may ring, it must be appropriate, for we are clearly told to model our own thinking after Christ's way of thinking when he deliberately humbled himself (Phil. 2:1-8). "In the case of Jesus, humility could coexist with the most exalted claims for the reason that the claims contained no exaggeration nor were they the expression of an aspiring ambitious spirit."[11] The essence of pride is an exalted, inflated opinion of self—in other words, a lie. So the truth about one's self, whether good or bad, cannot be sinful pride. Indeed, God himself, as seen in his Son, is the model of true humility. How do we follow his example?

[11]Everett F. Harrison, "Humility," _Baker's Dictionary of Christian Ethics,_ ed. Carl F. H. Henry (Grand Rapids: Baker, 1973), 306.

Recognize and Publicly Acknowledge the Truth. As we have seen, the task is to have a true evaluation of self. This includes the reality of my sin and inadequacy as well as the wonder of all God's great grace revealed in this human "showcase" of his own glorious excellencies. But how can a person inclined by nature in the opposite direction resist the lie of pride?

Gratitude and Praise as the Greatest Antidotes to Pride. It is very difficult, while giving God the credit for some great success in my life, to take any credit to myself—if I am genuinely giving him the credit and not mouthing hypocritical spiritual passwords. The Old Testament idea of humbling oneself was often connected with fasting—deliberately "afflicting" self with denial of food for a time of worship, adoration, and celebrating the greatness of God. Paul spoke of praise as an antidote, both positively and negatively. "But far be it from me to glory except in the cross of our Lord Jesus Christ, by which the world has been crucified to me, and I to the world" (Gal. 6:14). Negatively, Paul made it clear that the great damning sin of humankind was the failure to give God credit. As a result of this ingratitude, God gave people up to the final degradation that stems inevitably from self-exaltation (Rom. 1:21ff.).

Faith comes along with praise and is, in a sense, more the opposite of pride than humility. In place of self-reliance is God-reliance. To trust God is possible only to the one who distrusts himself. Faith, fostered by a continual spirit of thanksgiving and praise, is a great antidote to pride. Central to the teachings of Jesus was the assertion that there is no way to God apart from becoming as a child, trusting him for everything, and self for nothing (Matt. 18:2-4; Mark 9:33-37; Luke 9:46-48).

Assuming the Servant Role. We are called on to stop seeking great things for ourselves lest we become incapable of believing God because we are preoccupied with courting the praise of men (John 5:44). We must actively humble ourselves (1 Pet. 5:6), even put on the clothes of humility (Col. 3:12, NIV). But the focus in New Testament teaching on humility is more on action than a frontal attack on prideful attitudes (Matt. 20:26-27; Mark 10:43-44; Luke 22:26). Assume the role of a servant, and humility will come as a by-product. The apostles, like us, were busily trying to decide who was Somebody, the Very Important Person, jockeying for position, when Christ taught them through startling example what it means to take the servant role. The task that was needed at the beginning of the meal had gone undone, refused by everyone present, no doubt because of inflated evaluations of personal importance. Finally, Jesus took the towel and basin himself, deliberately modeling the servant role for all true disciples (Luke 22:24ff.; John 13:1-17).

In even clearer and stronger language, if possible, Paul holds up the Servant as our model. We are to think the way Jesus thought when he relinquished all his rightful prerogatives as Deity in order to become one of us. He humbled himself, not to a kingly role—as great a condescension as that would have been—but to the role of a servant. And then, as a servant among men—men who actually owed him their all—he stooped to accept a criminal's death (Phil. 2:1-8).

But who can deliberately choose to serve others, to treat others as superior to self, even when truthfully they are not (Phil. 2; Rom. 12:10; Eph. 5:21)? Who can deliberately and consistently choose the menial task all others avoid, forgive the arrogant offender, pick up after the careless destroyer, give to the ungrateful? Who, that is, would deliberately choose to consistently respond as a servant is expected to respond? Only one who loves deeply.

Love as a Great Antidote to Pride.

Love is patient, love is kind, and is not jealous; love does not brag and is not arrogant, does not act unbecomingly; it does not seek its own, is not provoked, does not take into account a wrong suffered, does not rejoice in unrighteousness, but rejoices with the truth; bears all things, believes all things, hopes all things, endures all things. (1 Cor. 13:4-7, NASB)

This is a perfect description of everything pride is not. Love, as an emotion strong enough to make one a servant, may not be self-produced. But one can choose to take a servant's role whether or not he feels like it, and to this the love of Christ draws us. But if we are not drawn, God in his love may bring into our lives that which will press us to our knees, aiding us to become humble even when we neglect or refuse to humble ourselves.

Suffering as God's Gift to Produce a Meek Spirit. Paul often gloried in his infirmities (2 Cor. 11:30; 12:5, 7). Why are so many of the Hebrew words for *humble* rooted in ideas of being crushed, bruised, broken, chastened, afflicted, subjugated? For stiff-necked, arrogant sons of men this is often the only way to a humble and contrite heart. One biblical term for *gentleness* has the root concept of taming a wild animal. Meekness in Scripture is not weakness but strength harnessed. Is not a great crushing of spirit often the only route to Christlike humility? Even Jesus learned obedience in the school of suffering (Heb. 5:8).

Without tenderness of spirit the most intensely righteous, religious life is like the image of God without his beauty and attractiveness. It is possible to be very, very religious, and staunch, and persevering in all Christian duties, even to be a brave defender and preacher of holiness, to be mathematically orthodox, and blameless in outward life, and very zealous in good works, and yet to be greatly lacking in tenderness of spirit. . . . We often come across Christians who are bright and clever, and strong and righteous; in fact, a little too bright, and a little too clever . . . and there seems too much of self in their strength, and their righteousness is severe and critical. They have everything to make them saints, except the crushing weight of an unspeakable crucifixion, which would grind them into a supernatural tenderness and limitless charity for others. But if they are of the real elect, God has a winepress prepared for them, through which they will some day pass, which will turn the metallic hardness of their nature into gentle love which Christ always brings forth at the last of the feast.[12]

The ways to the great grace of humility, the means to conquer demon pride are to acknowledge reality, concentrate on God with gratitude and praise, trust him actively for the resources of life, assume the servant role, love deeply, and accept God's loving chastening. In conclusion, consider the words of the renowned yet godly English clergyman of another era, Jeremy Taylor (1613–1667), excerpted from *The Rule and Exercise of Holy Living*:

The grace of humility is exercised by these rules:
Think not thyself better for anything that happens to thee from without.
If thou callest thyself fool, be not angry if another says so of thee. He is a hypocrite who accuses himself before others with an intent not to be believed.

[12]"October Mellowness," *World Conquest*, September-October 1951.

Love to be concealed and little esteemed, never being troubled when thou art slighted or undervalued.

Never be ashamed of thy birth, thy parents, or thy present employment, or for the poverty of any of them.

Never speak anything directly tending to thy praise or glory.

When thou hast said or done anything for which thou receivest praise, take it indifferently and return it to God for making thee an instrument of His glory.

Use no stratagems and devices to get praise.

Suffer others to be praised in thy presence and think not that the advancement of thy brother is a lessening of thy worth.

Never compare thyself with others. . . .

Be not always ready to excuse every oversight or indiscretion or ill action, but if thou be guilty of it, confess it plainly.

Give God thanks for every weakness, deformity, and imperfection and accept it as a favor and grace of God and an instrument to resist pride.

Upbraid no man's weakness to him to discomfort him. Be sure never to praise thyself or to dispraise any man else, unless God's glory or some holy end do hallow it.

FEAR AND COURAGE

Though some may hold that all sin stems from the three roots of lust, covetousness, and pride, it seems apparent that some sin may result from none of these. Just as lust, covetousness, and pride are distortions of basic drives that God gave for our good, so the most basic drive of all, self-preservation, may be pursued in sinful ways. Our minds are armed with the instinct to protect self from harm or death, just as our bodies are "wired" with a defense mechanism of pain-sensors without which we would be totally vulnerable. The fear of danger is a good gift that makes survival possible. In fact, in the Old Testament the fear of the Lord is seen as the basis of all life and good.

But when the strong drive for survival becomes obsessive or overpowers other higher obligations, it becomes sinful. There is no moral law that demands preservation of my well-being or life at all costs. On the contrary, a higher loyalty to God and even love for others may well demand self-sacrifice rather than self-protection. In answer to the sin of unbelieving fear stands the strong virtue of courage.

Of course, the absence of fear may not come from faith. A fearless person may simply be ignorant of the danger that threatens. Presumption dispels fear quite as effectively as faith.

Presumption is confidence misplaced, relying on some person or something that is not reliable. Thus a person may receive advice from a godless psychiatrist, rely on it, and rush headlong to destruction. We may fearlessly trust a great leader or a dear friend, only to be hurt badly. But confidence placed in God will never be betrayed. This confidence produces fearless courage. The lack of it leads to fearful timidity.

Ordinarily we stress the gentler virtues of kindness, humility, meekness, patience, but Scripture stresses the stronger virtues as well: courage, loyalty, discipline, endurance. The champions of the Old Testament were men and women of incredible valor. Consider how even the name evokes a sense of courage: Noah against the world; Abraham leaving his homeland; Jacob and the Angel; Joseph and the temptress; Moses versus Pharaoh; blind Samson; Gideon and the three hundred; Deborah and the weak-kneed generals; David against Goliath; Elijah and the prophets of Baal; Daniel and the lions; Esther and the king. And think of Daniel's friends: "Our God whom we serve is able to deliver us from the burning fiery furnace; and he will deliver us out of your hand, O king. But if not, be it known to you, O king, that we will not serve your gods!" (Dan. 3:17-18). And consider the words of the Letter to the Hebrews.

And what more shall I say? I do not have time to tell about [those] who through faith conquered kingdoms, administered justice, and gained what was promised; who shut the mouths of lions, quenched the fury of the flames, and escaped the edge of the sword; whose weakness was turned to strength; and who became powerful in battle and routed foreign armies. Women received back their dead, raised to life again. Others were tortured and refused to be released, so that they might gain a better resurrection. Some faced jeers and flogging, while still others were chained and put in prison. They were stoned; they were sawed in two; they were put to death by the sword. They went about in sheepskins and goatskins, destitute, persecuted and mistreated—the world was not worthy of them. They wandered in deserts and mountains, and in caves and holes in the ground. These were all commended for their faith, yet none of them received what had been promised. God had planned something better. (Heb. 11:32-40, NIV)

Heroes of the faith. But were any more fearless than Paul?

I have served more prison sentences! I have been beaten times without number. I have faced death again and again. I have been beaten the regulation thirty-nine stripes by the Jews five times. I have been beaten with rods three times. I have been stoned once. I have been shipwrecked three times. I have been twenty-four hours in the open sea. In my travels I have been in constant danger from rivers, from bandits, from my own countrymen, and from pagans. I have faced danger in city streets, danger in the desert, danger on the high seas, danger among false Christians. I have known drudgery, exhaustion, many sleepless nights, hunger and thirst, fasting, cold and exposure. (2 Cor. 11:23-27, Phillips)

But who can compare with the Son of God who took on himself the guilt of mankind, alienation from his Father, and the spite of the very ones he came to rescue?

Not only do we have the example of the courageous, we are often admonished to courage:

Be strong and courageous! Do not tremble or be dismayed, for the LORD your God is with you wherever you go. (Josh. 1:9, NASB)
Then David said to Solomon his son, "Be strong and of good courage, and do it. Fear not, be not dismayed; for the LORD God, even my God, is with you. He will not fail you or forsake you." (1 Chron. 28:20)
Be on your guard; stand firm in the faith; be men of courage; be strong. (1 Cor. 16:13, NIV)
Whatever happens, conduct yourselves in a manner worthy of the gospel of Christ. .thn one spirit, contending as one man for the faith of the gospel without being frightened in any way by those who oppose you. (Phil. 1:27-28, NIV)
For God did not give us a spirit of timidity, but a spirit of power, of love and of self-discipline. (2 Tim. 1:7, NIV)

God's wrath burns against sin, but we seem to have so imbibed the spirit of the age that our primary rule of conduct is tolerance. Yet God is intolerant of every evil; if we are to be like him, we also must be angry people, yet without sin. Fearful cowardice and timidity let us put forever behind us as we march with the Conqueror, trusting him for the victory against sin and death and hell! The just shall live by faith as a way of life, faith that risks all, faith that reaches beyond the status quo, even beyond excellence, to do the impossible!

The Christian is called to fight aggressively for right, truth, justice. As Samuel Shoemaker said, "The person who sits silently by while God, faith, the church, take a beating from some loud-mouth is not humble; he is being cowardly."[13]

13"The Nature of Humility," *Christianity Today*, 6 December 1963, 14.

Valor is the active, aggressive side of courage, but there is a passive side as well: fortitude or endurance. The New Testament speaks constantly of this, but we don't recognize it, for often it is translated "patience." Patience in Scripture is not Milquetoast acquiescence but rather tough endurance.

The one who endures to the end will be saved (Matt. 10:22; 24:13; Mark 13:13). Those who overcome, who endure steadfastly to the end are the ones who receive a "welcome home" and all the rewards of the victors (Rev. 2:7, 10-11, 17, 26; 3:5, 12-21; 21:7). In contrast, the fearful and unbelieving, along with murderers and idolaters, will have their part in the lake that burns with fire and brimstone (21:8). Therefore we are enjoined to run with endurance, to stand fast, not to be weary in the battle, to put on the whole armor, to strive mightily, to wrestle, to war. In fact, through him we are more than conquerors in the face of every enemy and obstacle.

CONCLUSION

We have probed the depths of scriptural teaching about the darkness of sin in order to see more clearly righteousness in its many-splendored brilliance. The roots of sin, buried deep in the human heart, are lust, covetousness, pride, unbelief. They are not dug out by celibacy, vows of poverty, asceticism, monasticism, and self-negation. These have the appearance of godliness, but they are will-worship, not God-worship and, as Paul points out, they are of no value (Col. 2:23). No, the answer to lust is self-control; the answer to covetousness is contentment; to pride, humility, born of praise and faith; and the answers to fear and unbelief are faith and courage. Feeding these roots of righteousness is love, the subsoil (Eph. 3:17). Watered by the Word of God and nurtured by the Holy Spirit, they grow up into the fullness of the likeness of Christ to the everlasting glory of God.

Notice how each of these wonderful graces reinforces the others. Humility leads to faith, faith to contentment, and courage, in turn, reinforces self-control, and all are motivated by love. Begin with any of them, and like a giant spiral heavenward, each is a step to the other.

These graces do something else. Each reproduces a harvest of its own kind. That is, the decision to control self leads immediately to greater strength in self-control. Contentment breeds more contentment; each servant act begets greater humility and a disposition more prone to behave as a servant. Courage produces courage, faith more faith, love more love.

We have called these the roots that bear the fruit of right thinking, right words, right actions. And they are. But they have wonderful by-products as well: They bear the glorious fruits of joy and peace. Why would anyone choose sin and reap its harvest?

SUGGESTED ADDITIONAL READING

Unlike most topics in biblical ethics, the scholarly literature on sin, especially the root sins of lust, covetousness, pride, and fear, is limited. The best sources are found in standard works on theology under these specific topics. On the other hand, devotional works address these issues extensively. Here is a brief bibliography on the overall topic of sin:

BIBLICAL PERSPECTIVE

Muller, Julius. *The Christian Doctrine of Sin*. Edinburgh: T & T Clark, 1857.
Orr, James. *Sin as a Problem of Today*. New York: Hodder, 1910.
Owen, John. *Temptation and Sin*. Wilmington, Del.: Sovereign Grace, reprint, 1972.

A PSYCHOLOGICAL PERSPECTIVE

Kierkegaard, Søren. *The Sickness unto Death*. Translated by Howard V. and Edna H. Hong. Princeton: Princeton University Press, 1968.
Menninger, Karl. *Whatever Became of Sin?* New York: Hawthorn, 1973.

SITUATION ETHICS

In a study of *biblical* personal ethics, why consider an approach to morality that is frankly nonbiblical? For three reasons. First, human beings ever since Eve have practiced situation ethics. This includes Christians of all varieties. The new feature is that this approach is, for the first time, being *advocated* by some within the church, advocated as an operating *principle*, not just as exceptions to norms, and advocated as the *only* legitimate basis for morals.

Second, as we shall see, the Bible itself demonstrates a form of situationism in which normally wrong behavior becomes right under certain circumstances. It is important to understand the so-called New Morality in order to distinguish clearly how Scripture handles some of the painful moral dilemmas of our human condition.

Third, it is of vital importance to understand the philosophical undergirding of a movement that has captured the thinking of leading influencers in academia, literature, art, and the media. In a few decades this way of thinking has redirected the course of our civilization. It pervades not only magazines, novels, and television, but is also the basis for public moralizing.[1]

Not only is situationism pervasive in secular education and society at large, it is strong in the church, making inroads among evangelical theologians as well. Consider an article by Margaret

---

[1] Situationism undergirds the opinions of the exceedingly popular advice columnist, "Dear Abby," who says, in a typical response: "I wouldn't call a thirty-six-year-old virgin a 'tramp' for deciding to live a little before she died. It's wrong only if you hurt yourself, someone else, or if you feel it's wrong for any reason." *The State* (Columbia, S.C.), 14 November 1977.

E. Kuhn, coordinator of administration for the United
Presbyterian Division of Church and Race, entitled "Female and
Single—What Then?" in the March-April 1970 issue of *Church
and Society,* a magazine published at that time by the Church and
Society units of the United Presbyterian Church, USA, and the
Presbyterian Church, U.S. (two denominations which have
since merged):

> Could not the church encourage lonely retired persons to live together or
> work out whatever other relationship would provide loving companionship
> and sexual enjoyment? The church should "point the way with compassion
> and wisdom to a way of life" that enables those who are single to express their
> sexuality and to establish deep sustaining relationships with men who may or
> may not be married. . . . Such relationships between single women and
> married men might or might not involve coitus.

The United Church of Christ authorizes the ordination of
homosexuals on the basis of situationism. Evangelical
psychologists use pornography therapeutically, evangelical
anthropologists advocate polygamy for church elders in a
polygamous society, and evangelical theologians advocate
divorce for marriage gone sour.
It is important here to distinguish between secular and
religious situationism. Both flow from the philosophical stream
of existentialism, so that the method is similar. There are no
prescriptive ethical standards for either. The decision as to what
is right or wrong, good or bad, is relative to the situation at
hand. In that approach, secular and religious situationism agree.
They part ways, however, when it comes to the criteria for
judging what is good or bad or, more likely, what is preferable.
For the secularist, the criteria is self-love; for the religious
situationist it is other-love. In actual practice, there are non-
Christians who try to use other-love as the touchstone, and there
are religious people who slip into advocacy of some form of self-
love. The borders are often fuzzy and overlapping, but the
distinction is real and very important.
Daniel Yankelovich, in *The New Rules,* documents the
massive shift in social values in America during the seventies.[2] In
the book he states that, for the majority of Americans, the
highest value is self-fulfillment. This is the ethical norm, the

2New York: Random House, 1981.

"new rule." If self-interest does not take precedence over all other values, a person is dishonest, immoral. This is the ethics of the secular situationist. Every decision, every choice should be made first of all on the basis of how it affects my perceived best interests. That is how one determines what is good and what is bad—good for me, bad for me.

Secular situationism is so blatantly antibiblical we need not devote extensive attention to it in developing a biblical ethic, but it is so pervasive we cannot ignore it. We must recognize its inroads in Christian thinking, expose it, and seek to destroy its power.

Joseph Fletcher, leading spokesman for Christian situationism, clearly makes love for others the touchstone, the criterion for judging good and bad in any given situation. Our study will deal with religious situationism.

Some have called the "New Morality" the old immorality, but this is to misunderstand the position of the theologians who are behind the movement. It is certainly new, and it does make a serious attempt to establish some sort of morality. That morality can be summed up in one word: love. This is the only moral requirement, but this requirement is absolute.

DEFINITION AND HISTORICAL ROOTS

Christian ethics or moral theology is not a scheme of living according to a code but a continuous effort to relate love to a world of relativities through a casuistry obedient to love; its constant task is to work out the strategy and tactics of love, for Christ's sake.[3]

Why is this new? Where did it come from? Briefly, the old standards were under attack. Not just the ethical mores of Christendom but the Bible itself, the Ten Commandments. Away with all the old rubbish! It's nothing but legalistic puritanism, pharisaic hypocrisy.

What are good men to do in the face of such an attack? Liberal theologians could see that all morals and society itself were in danger. But they couldn't say, "Hold on! Thus saith the Lord!" They had no such assurance that what was written in the

[3]Joseph Fletcher, *Situation Ethics: The New Morality* (Philadelphia: Westminster, 1966), 158.

Bible was indeed what the Lord had said, or, for that matter, if indeed there is such a person. And even if there is a God and he did say what the Bible says he said, what has that got to do with us in the twentieth century, man come of age, man evolved to maturity? In other words, the destructive criticism of the Bible and its authority left these sincere men with no foundation to build a defense against the new onslaught.

What then should be done? Shall we throw it all out and forget morals altogether? No. The old ship may be going down, but surely we can salvage something. Diving around in the moral debris of a rapidly disintegrating society, they came up with a flag on which was inscribed "love." If the old ship of Christianity goes down, if the unseaworthy Bible sinks in twentieth-century storms, if God himself is lost, still we have love.

Fletcher traces the history this way:

Situationism . . . is the crystal precipitated in Christian ethics by our era's pragmatism and relativism. Historically, most men really have been situationists, more or less, but the difference today is that we are situationists as a matter of rational and professed method. Gone is the old legalistic sense of guilt and of cheated ideals when we tailor our ethical cloth to fit the back of each occasion. We are deliberately closing the gap between our overt professions and our covert practices. It is an age of honesty, this age of anxiety.[4]

The modern history of the arts and sciences, and of the technologies that undergird them, makes it plain that they no longer bow down . . . to authoritarian principles. Their lifeline is no more handed down in advance or dropped from above by "revelation" or majesty. Men have turned to inductive and experimental methods of approach, working by trial and error, appealing to experience to validate their tentative and loosely held generalizations. As a strategy or method of inquiry and growth, it has worked with unprecedented success. Psychology, for example, got its start and growth this way. The same is true in many other sectors of the growing edge of the human enterprise. Now, at last, ethics and moral inquiry are doing it too.[5]

Love is the be-all and end-all. But what is love? What does love do? How does it behave? The modern theologian could no longer go to the Bible for answers to such problems because he had accepted a naturalistic base. Naturalism shut out revelation and gave us the empirical approach, relativistic, pragmatic. So the only place left to look is to man, and modern man has given

[4]Ibid., 147.
[5]Ibid., 158.

the answer to his own plight in the philosophy of existentialism.
We must respond to the situation in which we find ourselves.
We are always responding to the people and things and events
around us. We may respond in resentment or hatred; we *should*
respond in love. Thus we have situation ethics, called by some
the New Morality. The ethic? Love. The situation? That varies
with each person and with each new circumstance.

For example, a situation: Your mother is dying a slow death
by cancer. What should you do? Don't say, "Thou shalt not
kill." That's legalism. What would love do in that situation?
Perhaps it would be loving to end her life. Another situation: A
spinster is frustrated to the point of emotional disintegration
because of lack of love and sexual fulfillment. You are married,
but you can provide what she needs. Don't say, "The Bible says
thou shalt not commit adultery." That's legalism. What would
love do?

So there is no set of rules. You must decide yourself as you
face each decision: what would love do?

POSITIVE ASPECTS

What can be said in favor of the New Morality from a position
loyal to biblical authority? Certainly we can be grateful for the
motivation of men who, in an age that seems bent on destroying
all standards, take a stand for some sort of morality. Furthermore, we can be grateful that these men promote love of others
as the basis of morality, rather than love of self or power.
Certainly love is important. Christ tells us that love is a summa-
tion of all the biblical teaching concerning the will of God for
man (Matt. 22:34-40). Paul affirmed that love is the fulfillment
of the law (Rom. 13:10). Furthermore, Paul seems to be telling
us something in 1 Corinthians 13 very similar to what the
situationists are saying, that nothing is as important as love.

Again, there is a type of response in the Bible that might be
called situation ethics of a sort. For example, the Bible is clear in
its teaching that Christians should obey the constituted
authority of government (Rom. 13). However, the apostles
themselves said, *in that situation,* "We must obey God rather

than men" (Acts 5:29). And they were speaking to the supreme court!

What, then, is the problem with situation ethics? Why are those loyal to Scripture so opposed to the movement and its teaching?

THE ERROR OF SITUATION ETHICS

There are <u>five</u> reasons that situation ethics is unacceptable to a biblical theology.

PHILOSOPHICAL PRESUPPOSITIONS

There is an inadequate basis for the fundamental assumptions of the situation ethicists. It is weak in its epistemology; the authority for its assumptions is missing.

What is the authority for saying that love must be the basis of our morality—that all things are relative except this one absolute? How can one say that neighbor love is an absolute? Perhaps self-love might prove more effective in personal fulfillment. Perhaps pleasure would be a better standard. At this point the situationist often appeals to Christ, to his example, and to the Bible. But if the Bible has been thrown away with the left hand, it is impossible to take back certain parts with the right hand. In choosing from the Bible selectively, the Bible loses its independent authority; the only authority left resides in the selector and his basis for selecting.

One of the presuppositions of situation ethics is religious positivism.[6] A truth is "posited" or asserted without compelling external, sensory evidence.[7] That means a person chooses this standard by faith. But this is a free-floating faith with no external authority. Ultimately it is irrational, since there is no reason for this assumption, just an invitation to accept it by faith without evidence.

Further, no basis is demonstrated for relativizing all other ethical norms. To prove that love alone is an absolute standard in a world of relativity one would need to prove not only that love is absolute but also that there are no other absolute

[6]Ibid., 46-47.
[7]Note that religious positivism is the opposite of the philosophical positivism of Comte and others.

standards or universal norms. The situationist does not attempt to do this. And it is just as well that he doesn't, for it would be an exercise in futility. If love is made absolute without adequate supporting evidence, who is to deny that many other standards share in this quality of absolute, binding authority? But more is required—proof not that some fail to be universal standards, but that *no* others qualify. This of course cannot be done, except on a positivistic basis by which we are invited to accept a whole string of assertions by faith without any supporting evidence.

A further philosophical problem is the internal contradiction that simultaneously teaches an absolute truth (love as the absolute norm) and advocates the negotiability of truth (one must not tell the truth if a loving result is endangered). Attorney-theologian John Warwick Montgomery points this out:

The insurmountable difficulty is simply this: there is no way, short of sodium pentothal, of knowing when the situationist is actually endeavoring to set forth genuine facts and true opinions, and when he is lying like a trooper. Why? Because deception is allowed on principle by the new morality, as long as the ultimate aim is love. Consider: If Professor Fletcher acts consistently with his premises, and if he should consider it an act of true love toward me or toward the audience . . . to convince us of the superiority of situation ethics, he can to this end introduce any degree of factual misinformation, rhetorical pettifogging, or direct prevarication into the discussion.

But wait! Should he assure us, by swearing on his mother's grave, etc., that he will tell us the truth no matter what, can we even then relax our vigilance? After all, that very assurance may well be a situationally justified prevarication for the sake of "doing us good in love" by convincing us of the merits of situationalism. . . . If a situation ethicist, holding to the proposition that the end justifies the means, in love tells you that he is not lying, can you believe him?

And since mutual trust is the basis not only of institutions of justice but also of economic life (money itself is little more than a symbol of mutual confidence, as every inflation and depression illustrate), community relationships, and all other societal phenomena. . . . Not a single aspect of human society—from regular garbage collection and public library book-borrowing through friendship and marriage to equal protection under the law and the search for truth in institutions of higher learning such as this one—could survive the general onset of situation ethics.[8]

The fundamental problem with situationism is, then, the complete lack of evidence, either empirical or philosophical, for its basic presupposition that love is an absolute standard and

[8]John Warwick Montgomery in dialogue with Joseph Fletcher at San Diego State College, 11 February 1971, reported in *The Christian News*, 22 March 1971, 6-7.

that there are no other unchanging and universal standards of behavior.

LOVE IN SITUATION ETHICS

The basic problem with the situationist's concept of love is that it is without content. To say that the one norm of life is love makes the meaning so broad and general as to be in practice no norm at all. "Love in all cases" is like saying, "do right in all cases." But the question remains, what is right? Those who crucified Christ did so from the motive and principle of "doing right." The Inquisition was done by men who felt they were doing right. What is right? In the same way, what does love do? How does it behave?

The situationist is right in emphasizing that the basic agent of love is the will rather than the emotions. Furthermore, the situationist is right in insisting that the reason for love should not depend on the lovableness of the object, but on the character of the one loving. Thus it is possible to act lovingly for the welfare of one's enemy. Furthermore, the situationist is altogether correct in insisting that the expression of one's love for self should be limited by his commitment to love others.

However, by divorcing love from law, the situationist empties it of concrete meaning. Each person is obligated only to do what he feels would be in the best interest of his neighbor. But the Bible will not allow us to split love and law.

The test of our love for God's family lies in this question—do we love God himself and do we obey his commands? For loving God means obeying his commands, and these commands of his are not burdensome. (1 John 5:2-4, Phillips)

"Love is the fulfilling of the law" (Rom. 13:10). Jesus also clearly ties the two together, "If you love me, you will keep my commandments" (John 14:15). Again he says, "If you keep my commandments, you will abide in my love, just as I have kept my Father's commandments and abide in his love" (John 15:10). In the Old Testament, also, to love God means to keep his commandments (Exod. 20:6).

Biblical commands to love are not the only commands. They are the most important, to be sure, but are not contradictory or preemptive of God's other commands. We are not given a choice among his commands. Love is not only the most important, it may be the most comprehensive. It is seminal, leading to many other commands, and comprehensive, summarizing the others. But by this very "umbrella" nature it is too general to guide a person in his specific choices. This characteristic of love is no doubt one reason it so appeals to the relativist with his autonomous reason. But God doesn't leave us with a single general principle; he spells out the implications of the law of love in his other laws. He does not leave us to improvise on the basis of personal perception of what action might turn out to be the most beneficial for the most people; he goes to a great deal of effort to define love, to fill it with content, to describe loving behavior in specific commandments.

In these ways, situationism, though adopting the term "love" from Scripture, actually empties the term of its biblical content.[9]

SITUATION ETHICS AND THE LAW

The situationist wages an unremitting war against the law, aggressively denouncing the law of God as a standard of life. The prophet of the New Morality might say, "Be clear that I am come to destroy the law."

For the situationist there are no laws; only maxims. Biblical laws are principles or recommendations such as the principle in football, "Punt on the fourth down." Obviously, one would not punt on the fourth down if he were within five yards of the goal. In like manner, the Bible is filled with maxims which we are to take into account. However, we must improvise on these and apply them in each case according to the dictates of love. If we do not do so, we will do the unloving thing in obeying the commandment, we are told.

The situationist insists that law is negative, a dead legalism that makes binding demands on one without adequate reason. It takes away our liberty. It deprives us of the freedom to become truly human. Law is negative, the situationist insists.

It is true that man's law and man's interpretations of God's law may become a sterile legalism, but God doesn't make that kind of law. None of God's laws were made to take away our

[9]See chapter on "Love" for an examination of the biblical concept of love.

liberty, to make us miserable, to deprive us of happiness. Rather, his laws were made to set us free.

God's laws are like the tracks on which a train may run at high speed, fulfilling its "train-ness." True, it is restricted, but the very restriction provides for freedom to move toward fulfillment. So it is with the law of God. His law is not given to restrict, but to free; not to bring evil, but to bring good; not to make miserable, but to make happy; not to repress, but to fulfill.

If no conceivable human action is per se immoral and sinful, if there is no prescriptive ethics, if no one but the person himself can decide in his own situation whether any act is right or wrong, there is no moral basis for prosecuting any man at law for any act he might commit. If *agape*, the manner in which a man ought to treat his neighbor, cannot be defined and codified into a valid and binding law, then love not only has escaped an unwarranted legalism but also has lost all its obligatory force and sense of ought.[10]

God is a God of love. Nothing he does is contrary to this characteristic. Therefore he wills that we be like him so that we may fully enjoy his love and fully participate in loving him and loving one another. His law is simply the detailed spelling out of what we will be when we are like him, how we will think when we think like him, what we will do when we behave like him. So the law gives content to the standard of love.[11] The situationist errs in misunderstanding the purpose and nature of biblical law and in failing to relate it properly to love.

SITUATION ETHICS AND THE NATURE OF MANKIND

Situation ethics not only misunderstands love in which it specializes and law which it opposes. Situation ethics misunderstands human nature. The New Morality places a burden on people which is too heavy to bear.

If humans were not finite and sinful, perhaps they could make the judgment in each situation, but human beings are finite and very sinful. A person can't make the right decisions because he doesn't have enough information, and he wouldn't make the right decisions even if he had the information because his motivation is never pure. That is why God never laid

[10]Editorial, *Christianity Today*, 8 October 1965, 33.
[11]See chapter on "Law" for an examination of the biblical concept of law.

the heavy, frustrating, and impossible burden on him that the new moralist would. Consider the words of Fletcher.

> It is a matter of intelligence, not sentiment. Nothing is as complex and difficult as ethics, even Christian love ethics, once we have cut loose from law's oversimplifying pre-tailored rules, once we become situational.[12]
>
> With the development of computers all sorts of analytical ethical possibilities open up.[13]
>
> There are four questions of basic and indispensable importance to be raised about every case, four factors at stake in every situation, all of which are to be balanced on love's scales. There are no foregone conclusions.[14]
>
> As the Christian situationist sees it, his faith answers for him three questions of the seven always to be asked. These three are his "universals." He knows the *what*; it is love. He knows the *why*; for God's sake. He knows the *who*; it is his neighbors, people. But only in and of the situation can he answer the other four questions: When? Where? Which? How? . . . is adultery wrong? One can only respond, "I don't know. Maybe. Give me a case. Describe a real situation."[15]
>
> Note that in this complex program of deciding how one should act in each case, the questions to be answered are not simple. In addition to questions about motive (love, hopefully) there is the indispensable question, "What are the foreseeable *consequences*?" Given any course of action, in the context of the problem, what are the effects directly and indirectly brought about, the immediate consequences, and the remote? This last question means, we must note, that there are more results entailed than just the end wanted, and they all have to be weighed and weighted.[16]

Here is a load too heavy for finite man to bear adequately. So the computer is called in. But certainly there is no one with this godlike level of intelligence, and even if one had that level of intelligence, the situation rarely allows enough time to figure things out in order to make the proper decision. A person is asked an embarrassing question in the presence of others. In the split second before he answers he must evaluate seven or more questions about that situation, including the question as to the immediate and long-range results of telling the truth, telling a lie, or finding some other way out. Even if a computer were nearby, only a fraction of the necessary data is available to program the computer, and even if it were available, will his questioner wait?

[12]Fletcher, *Situation Ethics*, 114.
[13]Ibid., 117.
[14]Ibid., 127.
[15]Ibid., 142.
[16]Ibid., 128.

Soon after Fletcher's first book on the subject hit the best-seller list, *Time* commented:

In the situational approach of the new morality, he said, "one enters into every decision-making moment armed with all the wisdom of the culture, but prepared in one's freedom to suspend and violate any rule except that one must as responsibly as possible seek the good of one's neighbor." Which is quite a long thought for an eighteen-year-old during a passionate moment in the back seat of a car.[17]

Where is the wisdom of this? Where is the time for this? The Bible takes man's finitude seriously and gives more than complicated advice concerning a multitude of conflicting principles; it gives commands.

Man is not only finite, he is very complicated. The editor of *Christianity Today* pointed this out.

Fletcher's book in particular forgets that life is a network of habits, dispositions, and desires, partly inherited and partly acquired, which we cannot shed as an old suit of clothes. And it overlooks the fact that acts that seem innocent to us may hurt others, even years hence.[18]

Not only does finite man find it almost impossible to judge exactly what constitutes his neighbor's highest good, he will find even greater difficulty in deciding *which* neighbor's good! The loving "surrogate husband" may decide to provide for the sexual needs of an unmarried and lonely fellow church member, but what effect may that have on other "neighbors"—his wife, his children, the church, God himself?

Life, too, is complex. How can one judge the outcome of a single act toward a single person, let alone what a series of acts involving many people might become in the future? Abraham taking Hagar could hardly imagine the impact four thousand years later as the Arab sons of Ishmael fiercely pursue their destiny.

I may decide that it is so important for a particular political candidate to win an election that a little espionage would be the act of greatest love for the most people. If my opponent should win, the whole nation would suffer through a weakness toward

[17]*Time*, 5 March 1965.
[18]Editorial, *Christianity Today,* 22 December 1967, 25.

communism; in fact, the whole world would suffer. Surely, the loving thing for the most people would be to assure that the election will turn out right. In the historic incident in which this decision was made, the election turned out "right," but who could have foretold the complicated and wholly undesired consequences of the simple little well-intentioned act of the Watergate conspirators? The most unreasonable—though highly predictable—response came from the liberal establishment which so loudly lamented this activity, though Watergate was nothing more or less than a classical case of situation ethics. The participants were doing exactly what they had been taught by that same liberal establishment. The only problem was that they had the temerity to apply the approach to an unacceptable cause! Life is, indeed, far too complex for mortal, sinful man to improvise on his own authority, setting aside moral standards in the interests of a higher "law of love."

Situationists not only underestimate the significance of man's limitations, they seem to deliberately downplay an even greater handicap man must overcome to succeed at situational ethics: sin. Even if a person could consistently figure out what was the ultimate good of each person in his life, would he choose to act in accordance with that knowledge if the cost to himself were very great? Neither experience, history, nor revelation leave us much hope that he will consistently make this choice. Man is sinful and consistently chooses to sacrifice his neighbor's welfare for his own.[19] Thus, the ideal of the situationist—to act always for the highest good of all involved in a given situation—is possible only for God. Man is too finite to know even the fringes of such a vast and complicated situation, and he is too fallen to choose consistently what he does know to be best.

GOD AND SITUATION ETHICS

This is the crux of the problem. Situation ethics is nontheistic. To be sure, some situation ethicists believe in a personal, immutable God, but many, like Fletcher, do not. However, even for those who do believe in God, he is not the foundation of the ethical system.

[19]See chapter 3, "Sin," for an explanation of the biblical concept of sin.

Properly used, the word [situation ethics] is applicable to *any* situation-sensitive decision making whether its ideology is theological or nontheological—e.g., either Christian or Marxist.[20]

My reason is that the basic challenge offered by the situationist has nothing to do in any special way with theological over against nontheological faith commitments.[21]

Lovingness is often the motive at work full force behind the decision of non-Christian and nontheological, even atheist, decision makers. Christians have no monopoly of love, i.e., of the Holy Spirit, i.e., of the power of the love of God, i.e., of God himself.[22]

The frank presuppositions of the movement are relativism, pragmatism, and personalism. Relativism: There are no absolutes but love. *Only* the end justifies the means. Pragmatism: Will this action work out for the best interests of the most people? Personalism: Man is the center and criterion. The "best interests" are defined in terms of man's evaluation of his own best interests on naturalistic presuppositions.

But the most important and basic truth about ethics in Scripture is that it is theistic or God-based, not personalistic or man-based. By his own nature God defines what is good and loving. He went to a great deal of effort to reveal this to man. To build an ethic on love divorced from the unchanging character of God and the clear and absolute requirements revealed by that God is to distort the concept of love and law from the outset. This godlessness is the ultimate flaw in situation ethics.

CONFLICTING ETHICAL REQUIREMENTS

Although the situationist has given a nonbiblical answer, he has certainly raised a very important question. Practically speaking, how does a Christian, committed to the absolute nature of the whole law of God, face a situation in which these laws seem to conflict? When Christ tells us to preach the gospel and the government tells us to be quiet, what do we do? When spies who are God's people are in my home and the police come to arrest them, do I betray them or deceive the authorities? When

[20]Fletcher, *Situation Ethics,* 14.
[21]Ibid., 15.
[22]Ibid., 155.

the same God who commands, "Thou shalt not kill" also commands to destroy a whole people, what does the soldier do?

Christ himself gives a classic example of "biblical situationism" when he tells us that David did *well*—not a bad but forgivable act—in violating the law by eating the showbread in an emergency (Matt. 12:3ff.). When the priests profane the Sabbath, he does not say they are forgiven, but rather that they are *blameless*. If the Pharisees only understood these things, they would not have condemned the *guiltless* disciples who did on the Sabbath a *lawful* thing that otherwise would have been unlawful.

How does one decide when to keep the law and when to violate it?

DEFINE THE LAW CAREFULLY

The first step in solving this dilemma is to define the particular activity precisely. Is it truly a sin on *biblical* terms? For example, many people feel that all deception is a form of sinful lying; all killing is a form of sinful murder; all civil disobedience is a form of sinful lawlessness; all work on Sunday violates the Sabbath law. However, these definitions are not only naive, they are not biblical. When a soldier kills, he is not necessarily committing murder. When the government taxes, taking some of my possessions by force, it is not stealing. We will study these particular problems later in more detail, but at this point it is important to insist that the Bible itself define what kind of deception, if any, is legitimate; what kind of killing is legitimate; what kind of taking by force is legitimate; what kind of civil disobedience is legitimate. We are not free to decide; the Bible itself, giving the command, must be allowed to define the limits of that command.

THE FAITH WAY OF ESCAPE

Normally there is a third alternative when we face a moral dilemma. Scripture promises that God will provide a way of escape (1 Cor. 10:13). Often, this is the way of faith.

Fletcher uses the example of the mother in a German concentration camp whose family desperately needed her. The only way to gain freedom was to become pregnant. Should she consort with a willing guard and gain her freedom (which she did, in the illustration), or should she remain pure and leave her family to suffer? The situationist never seems to face the alternative of trusting God. She could trust God with her family. In the final analysis, she does not have any moral demand laid upon her to avert suffering. She does have a moral demand laid on her to remain pure.

We must choose to do right and trust God with the consequences. As Brother Lawrence said, "I hope that when I have done what I can, he will do with me as he pleases."[23] Such is the utter God-confidence and childlike trust of an obedient child. God who is love, infinite in wisdom and power, can be trusted to handle the outcome of our obedience.

When we define the ethical choice in biblical terms and seek for the third alternative, the way of faith, most dilemmas are solved. I personally have never experienced a moral dilemma that was not resolved by biblical definition and choosing to trust God with the consequences. Beyond this, I am not sure of biblical authority. As a result, in counseling, I would not advise a troubled person to do more than this. However, some have been in positions in which a choice must be made between two actions, both of which they consider wrong. How should the choice be made?

CONFESS SIN

If one feels he *must* make a choice and do what the Bible describes as breaking a law, he should make the choice in line with biblical precedent and confess the sin as a sin.

√1. *Making the choice according to a biblical precedent.* There is a biblical hierarchy of both virtue and sin.[24] So, if a person concludes he must make a choice between two apparently sinful alternatives, he should certainly choose the lesser of the two evils, not the greater.

2. *Having made such a choice, however, one should confess this as sin.* Ask God's forgiveness. This does not necessarily mean that God judges it to be sin. The early disciples disobeyed the law, saying to the supreme court, "We must obey God rather than men" (Acts 5:29). Apparently, God did not consider this civil

[23]Brother Lawrence. *The Practice of the Presence of God* (New York: Revell, 1895), 36.
[24]See chapter 3, "Sin."

disobedience sinful. It was not "the lesser of two evils" but the "higher of two goods." Suicide is wrong, but is the soldier in a bunker who clutches the live grenade to his belly to save his comrades, guilty of sin? "Greater love has no man than this, that a man lay down his life for his friends" (John 15:13).

God may have a different evaluation of a given act, and in the end this "tragic moral choice" that one feels compelled to make may be judged by God as a righteous act, not the lesser of two evils. In the meanwhile, however, it is important, lacking the perspective of God, to confess as sin what one believes may be sin. Whatever is not of faith is sin. In this way, one upholds the law and refuses the situationist's policy of universalizing the procedure as the norm of ethical behavior.

DO NOT MAKE AN EXCEPTION NORMATIVE

We do not ordinarily encounter the extreme examples consistently proposed by situational ethicists. More than half the illustrations used by Fletcher are extreme, rare, and complicated, and many are from non-Christian fiction. These are used to establish an ethic for everyday behavior. Of course, deny Christ if by denying him one can save his life and live to serve another day. Of course, have illicit relations if good seems to be the result. Of course, lie for almost any good purpose. Rare and unusual cases have been transformed into the norm of moral judgment.

If one feels in conscience before God that a tragic moral choice must be made, he should do so only with the firm conviction that this is a rare exception, not to be repeated and certainly not to be made the basis of daily ethical choice. In other words, the exceptional situation cannot be used as a norm to establish an ethic, which is what the name situation ethics implies.

I would emphasize again: My personal, positive conviction concerning the affirmative biblical teaching in facing moral dilemmas does not go beyond precise definition and seeking the faith-way of escape. I offer the additional guidelines of confession and restriction for those who accept the idea of choosing the lesser of two evils.

While recognizing that there are problems to be solved, we

must stress the reasons for utterly rejecting the approach of the
New Morality as being untenable, unbiblical, and unworkable.

Situation ethics, designed for a post-Christian age and built
on the prevailing philosophies of the twentieth century, is a
meticulously crafted castle founded on sand. It will fall and
shatter those who live in it because it was not built on the rock
of God's revelation. Our task is to unmask the deception and
rescue the deceived.

SUGGESTED ADDITIONAL READING

Erickson, Millard J. *Relativism in Contemporary Christian Ethics*. Grand
Rapids: Baker, 1974. A solid response to situationism by a leading
evangelical theologian.

Fletcher, Joseph. *Situation Ethics: The New Morality*. Philadelphia:
Westminster, 1966. The most lucid popular exposition of "Christian"
situationism.

Geisler, Norman L. *Options in Contemporary Ethics*. Grand Rapids: Baker,
1982. Includes a strong evangelical critique of situational ethics. Advocates
hierarchicalism, which has some similarities to situationism in method and
outcome, but is a more biblical alternative to situationism, insisting, as it
does, on biblical norms.

Lutzer, Erwin W. *The Necessity of Moral Absolutes*. Grand Rapids: Zondervan,
1981. A strong evangelical analysis and response.

Tillich, Paul. *Morality and Beyond*. New York: Harper and Row, 1963. The
most sophisticated presentation of the situationist position.

PART II

APPLYING THE BIBLE TO LIFE

CHAPTER SIX

GOD FIRST

Thou shalt have no other gods before me.
Thou shalt not make unto thee any graven image.
Thou shalt not take the name of the LORD thy God in vain.
Remember the sabbath day, to keep it holy.

For most people in the Western world the horizontal has totally eclipsed the vertical. Man's relationship to man is all-important; his relationship to God is of secondary or no importance. Even in the church, reconciling people to people, rather than reconciling people to God, has become top priority for many. Christians find it difficult to feel that violating the first table of the law is nearly as serious as violating the second table of the law. We cannot understand the Old Testament prescription of capital punishment for working on the Sabbath, for profanity, or for worshiping another deity.

Why is the command to love God with all our being the first and great commandment? Why are the first four of the Ten Commandments prohibitions of sin against God? Why not put them last, after the important ones like murder and adultery? Obviously Scripture holds that sin against God is of greater seriousness than sin against fellowmen.

God is the ultimate reality, the fundamental fact, the integrating factor of the universe. Therefore, to be rightly aligned with him is the most important relationship in human existence. To be in alignment with reality and truth is life; to be out of alignment is destruction and death. To leave God out of the equation of life or to diminish his role is like seeking to build a skyscraper without mathematics or to bake a cake without flour.

God knows this, so his commandments simply reinforce the facts. He treats this relationship as the most important because it *is* the most important.

Yet it is not simply a matter of reality and truth. God *cares* about this relationship. God is repeatedly called a jealous God. That is, it makes a difference to him whether or not we are rightly related to him. This word for jealousy in the Old Testament is the same word used when a husband is jealous of the affection of his wife. This is not a petty envy of legitimate competition. It is a profound caring and total unwillingness to allow any other to replace the prior and ultimate love relationship.

The First Commandment has to do with our heart attitude, our thoughts, our personal relationship with God. But God is also interested in our deeds, what we do about how we feel. Furthermore, he is concerned about our words, how we use his name, what we say about him. Some tend to spiritualize the relationship with God and are careless with the external manifestations of that professed heart relationship. But that God is interested in deeds and words as well as in thoughts is clearly revealed in the first three commandments.

HAVING OTHER GODS

I am the LORD your God, who brought you out of the land of Egypt, out of the house of bondage. You shall have no other gods before me. (Exod. 20:2-3)

Idolatry is the sin most vehemently condemned in the Old Testament. In the New Testament also, it is clearly condemned (see 1 John 5:21), but not nearly so often. The reason is obvious. Through centuries of terrible suffering, Israel learned her lesson well, so that by the time of Christ, whatever the failures of God's chosen people, the worship of idols was not one of them. Yet this is a great issue in most non-Western cultures today. Because it is not an issue in most Western societies, we think little of it, if at all. But we must not look lightly on the sin which God considers the most hideous.

When I arrived in Japan it grieved me deeply to see people

call earnestly on gods who are not gods. But before long, I was among those who enjoyed photographing "quaint oriental customs." On one occasion an earnest Japanese Christian was giving us a guided tour of a famous shrine.

"What is your reaction to places like this?" I inquired.

"The same as all Japanese. I'm just sightseeing."

"But," I responded, "some of these people really worship these idols. How do you feel about that?"

"Oh, I think it's comical, an interesting custom."

Let us remind ourselves that God does not consider the worship of false gods merely an interesting custom.

> If your brother, your mother's son, or your son or daughter, or the wife you cherish, or your friend who is as your own soul, entice you secretly, saying, "Let us go and serve other gods" . . . you shall not yield to him or listen to him; and your eye shall not pity him, nor shall you spare or conceal him. But you shall surely kill him; your hand shall be first against him to put him to death. (Deut. 13:6-9, NASB)

The most obvious violation of this commandment is worshiping someone or something other than God, yet it is quite possible to violate this commandment without ever praying to another deity.

To "have" a God is to ascribe to someone or something attributes that belong only to God or to relate to someone or something as the ultimate—to seek above all else, to trust above all else, to love above all else, to serve and obey above all else is to treat as god. To make something central in life, the pivot or ultimate reference point, is to "have a god." To yield ultimate allegiance to or to consider someone or something as the ultimate happiness or most desirable object, even to fear above all else is to "have a god."

Notice that the First Commandment does not say that we should have no other gods. Actually, the rest of Scripture teaches that there are no other gods in reality; there is only one God. And yet this command prohibits having other gods *before* the true God. It is quite legitimate to have other loves, loyalties, and ambitions. But none of these loves and loyalties can come before God or we have broken the ultimate relationship and violated the supreme commandment. It is not the one who loves his father, mother, son, or daughter who is unworthy of the

Lord Jesus, but the one who loves someone else more than him (Matt. 10:37).

In the light of this, one's trust and obedience, allegiance or love may be quite legitimate and never demand a special, conscious evaluation until the loves or loyalties come into conflict. Then one's god stands revealed. At the point of choice, which love or loyalty we put before the other will determine who our true god is.

What is most valuable to me? What do I hold to be most irreplaceable? What would I be lost without? What do I think of with most intensity in the long stretches of my thoughts? What is my incentive for living? What gives my work meaning and purpose? This I worship.[1]

In Western civilization there is very little religious veneration of material objects; in fact, there is not a great deal of worship of invisible deities, such as ancestors, either. This does not mean, however, that there is no idolatry. "Having" a god before the God and Father of our Lord Jesus Christ is idolatrous. Money and things can be sought above all else. A friend, a mate, a child, or a parent can be loved above all else. One can seek pleasure or fame above all else. One's love of country, a hero or leader, a philosophy or ideology can be an idol. Even something as abstract as art, education, or service can usurp the place of God. The most common idol of all is self.

The occult, including witchcraft, astrology, and fortune-telling, has made a strong comeback in the Western world. Satan worship is obviously the most hideous of all idolatry, and all idolatry is, in a sense, the worship of demons (1 Cor. 10:20). But what of palm-reading, crystal-ball gazing, discernment of the future through tea leaves, astrology, ouija boards?

When you enter the land which the LORD your God gives you, you shall not learn to imitate the detestable things of those nations. There shall not be found among you anyone who . . . uses divination, one who practices witchcraft, or one who interprets omens, or a sorcerer, or one who casts a spell, or a medium, or a spiritist, or one who calls up the dead. For whoever does these things is detestable to the LORD. (Deut. 18:9-12, NASB)

God repeatedly forbade all varieties of the occult (Lev. 19:26, 28, 31; 20:6) and hated this kind of activity so much that he

[1]Gladys and Gordon Depree, *A Blade of Grass* (Grand Rapids: Zondervan, 1967), 9.

made death the penalty for practicing it (Lev. 20:27) and judged Israel with deportation and captivity for allowing it (2 Kings 17:17-18; 2 Chron. 33:6). That all forms of the occult are wicked and hated by God is clear enough, but are they a violation of the First Commandment against worshiping other gods?

Isaiah seemed to pinpoint the evil in consulting fortune-tellers as seeking from other sources that which should be sought only from God (Isa. 8:19). In other words, disclosing the future or supernaturally affecting the future is the prerogative of God, and when usurped by false prophets, demons, fortune-tellers, astrologers, mediums or anyone else, the person has attempted to be godlike in the immutable attributes of the Almighty. Those who consult them have given to man or Satan the confidence and obedience due God alone.

Saul experienced this. At first he eliminated all occult practice from the land, but when God refused to speak to him or guide him, he turned to a medium (1 Sam. 28). Although he was successful, it resulted in his judgment, death, and the loss of the crown for his descendants. This terrible judgment came, no doubt, as the result of his many transgressions, but consulting a medium was the crowning insult to God.

Does the growing influence of occult practices indicate some measure of success in predicting or manipulating future events? How can these activities be successful? In the case of Saul, God himself must have intervened in the mysterious appearance of the dead prophet—for judgment, to be sure! Often it is clearly the supernatural work of unclean spirits (Acts 16:16), and sometimes it is trickery and deceit (Acts 13:10). Occult activity was a constant plague not only in Israel but also in the early church as these enemies of the gospel confronted Paul wherever he went. Today also, the plague is universal and calls down the judgment of a God who will have no other gods before him.

MAKING AND WORSHIPING IMAGES

You shall not make for yourself a graven image, or any likeness of anything that is in heaven above, or that is in the earth beneath, or that is in the water under the earth; you shall not bow down to them or serve them; for I the LORD your God am a jealous God. (Exod. 20:4-5)

The prohibition of graven images does not prohibit works of art, as some hold. We know this because in the same Sinaitic commandments there are instructions for "graving" the cherubim and the pomegranates for the robe of the high priest. Later Moses was to erect the brazen serpent. The command is against creating any object for *religious veneration*.

Scripture never tires of contrasting the gods who cannot see or hear or save with the Creator God of wisdom, power, and saving grace. The prophet Jeremiah gives a stinging contrast in pointing out the utter foolishness of worshiping such idols (10:1-16), and both Isaiah (44; 45:20-22; 46:1-7) and Habakkuk (2:18-20) make the same devastating contrast. John returns to the same theme (Rev. 9:20).

The psalmist eloquently exposes the foolishness of idolatry:

Why should the nations say, "Where, now, is their God?" But our God is in the heavens; He does whatever He pleases. Their idols are silver and gold, the work of man's hands. They have mouths, but they cannot speak; they have eyes, but they cannot see; they have ears, but they cannot hear; they have noses, but they cannot smell; they have hands, but they cannot feel; they have feet, but they cannot walk; they cannot make a sound with their throat. Those who make them will become like them, everyone who trusts in them. (Ps. 115:2-8, NASB)

The foolishness of idolatry as well as the enormity of betraying the living God is a theme throughout Scripture. Also the inherent evil of idolatry is pointed out: man makes gods in his own image, but they in turn make the worshiper into the image of the idol (Ps. 115:8; 135:18)!

The Roman Catholic and Eastern Orthodox churches have held that images of God or the saints are quite legitimate as aids to worship, so long as they are not used as objects of worship, but this is specifically prohibited in the Second Commandment, which forbids the creating of objects before which people "bow down." Among Protestants it is common to have paintings of Christ or even representations of God the Father, but there is no use of these objects for worship, so they can hardly be considered in violation of the Second Commandment. I personally prefer to be without the artist's imagination of my Lord's appearance, but I find no prohibition of this in Scripture.

Those who are not accustomed to using aids in worship should be especially careful when among those who do, or among idolaters. For example, if one lives in a Protestant community in the United States, he might cause no one to stumble or take offense by having a painting depicting the face of Christ, whereas such a picture could lead others astray in a village in South America or Southeast Asia. As a new missionary I asked an older Japanese pastor if there was a problem with displaying a photograph of my deceased father. He gently advised against it. In a land where such photographs are objects of veneration in ancestor worship, a perfectly innocent custom becomes a stumbling block. It is far better to err on the side of caution than to risk promoting violation of the Second Commandment.

If a person does not actually worship an image, but simply uses it as an aid to devotion, why should it be prohibited? History teaches that the object has consistently become an object of worship. This was true when the brazen serpent was destroyed because it had become an object of worship (2 Kings 18:4). It is true in Roman Catholic countries where church theology does not hold that the image is to be worshiped, but where the common people do in fact pray to and venerate the image itself. Even if a person himself might use the image solely as an aid to prayer to the invisible God, he may well lead others into actual worship. Certainly he will give the appearance of evil to many. In any event, the making of graven images of this kind is prohibited in the Second Commandment.

What of those who go through the form of worshiping before an idol or image but in their own heart pray to the true God? In times of persecution is it better to go through the formality of idol worship to preserve one's life in order to live and serve the true God? If God does not accept us when our worship is mere form and not in truth, why should he condemn us if we go through the formality of worshiping some other god but do not do so in truth?

The Bible is very clear on this point. We are not only forbidden to make such objects of worship, we are commanded not to bow down to them. It is unacceptable to God to worship him—or claim to be worshiping him—with the use of images of other gods (Exod. 32:4-10) or in the wrong place or manner) (2 Chron. 33:17). Some missionaries have kept fetishes and idols as curios or instructional material. But God says that the idol must be destroyed (Deut. 7:5-11, 25-26). Why does God take this hard line on idols?

In the first place, to go through a form that is not true is to lie. But it is not an ordinary lie. It is a particularly pernicious lie because it is the lie of betrayal. "But whoever denies me before men, I also will deny before my Father who is in heaven" (Matt. 10:33). Peter may have denied the Lord with very good motives. He may have been attempting to save himself so that he could rescue his Master from impending execution. Whatever his motivation, it was the act of unfaithfulness that broke his heart.

A couple in Japan was at the point of divorce when God rescued them and their home by his grace through Christ Jesus. Unknown to me or to the young wife, the husband did not destroy the photographs of the other woman, but put them in the bottom of a bureau drawer. Many months later, his wife discovered these photographs and in anger cut them to pieces. This made her husband so angry that the home was on the verge of breaking again. He said that the relationship with the other woman had been broken off, that there was no continuing contact of any kind, and that the pictures meant nothing. It is very hard for an outsider, let alone a wife, to believe that the pictures meant nothing when he took scissors and shredded her clothes in retaliation. Somehow there is unfaithfulness even though it is merely an outward form. God is a jealous God and will not countenance any competition for first place in our lives or the appearance of it. Not only is making gods forbidden, the act of "bowing down to them" is strictly prohibited as well.

In many countries the entire culture is saturated with religious practices. Even cultural festivals have religious overtones. When is it legitimate for Christians to participate in such activities? It is not enough to say that a Christian is free to participate if he himself has no religious feeling in the matter. In the evolution of a culture, religious ceremonies and particularly festivals tend, like our Christmas, to become secular. In the light of the Second Commandment, a Christian may not participate simply because the activity has no religious connotation for him. He may participate only when others see in his participation no endorsement of the religious element. For example, though Christmas may have strong religious meaning for the Christian, it has become so secularized that no one would think a Jewish merchant had compromised his faith by having carols broadcast in his store in December. On the other hand, if his children defected to Christianity because of his soft line in the matter, he would probably have second thoughts. So the Christian in another religious culture must be careful not to compromise his message in the minds of others, particularly the new believer who could be stumbled in following his example.

"Little children, keep yourselves from idols" (1 John 5:21).

TAKING GOD'S NAME IN VAIN

You shall not take the name of the LORD your God in vain; for the LORD will not hold him guiltless who takes his name in vain. (Exod. 20:7)

The primary prohibition of this commandment is the prohibition of breaking contract. It is wrong to invoke the name of God to validate the truthfulness of one's statement when it is actually untrue. It is wrong to call God as witness to a contract, to make a vow before him and then to break contract or vow. This is the way the Third Commandment is used in Scripture (Lev. 19:12; Matt. 5:33-34, 37; Matt. 23:16ff.; Matt. 26:63). James 5:12 prohibits the using of an oath in any event. It seems that the Christian, by the very name he bears, has validation enough for every statement he makes. His word should be his bond. His yes or no are complete in themselves. For a Christian to break contract or to tell a lie is to break the Third Commandment, for it is to use profanely the name of God which he bears, whether or not he invokes the Name. Though breaking a contract given in God's Name is the primary focus of the Third Commandment, there are other implications.

Did Jesus and James forbid all oath-taking? Some have held that it is wrong to take an oath in court or to swear allegiance to one's nation. The first problem with this view is that the Israelites were commanded to swear by the name of their God

(Deut. 6:13; 10:20) and it was considered praiseworthy (Ps. 63:11). In line with this, Paul often said, "For God is my witness" and at least once took an oath (Rom. 1:9; 1 Thess. 2:5, 10). God himself takes oaths and swears by his own Name (e.g., Heb. 6:16ff.). Christ spoke under oath in court (Matt. 26:63). How is this apparent conflict to be resolved? Most branches of the church have held that Christ and James are reinforcing the teaching originally intended to prohibit oath-breaking, not oath-taking.

Of course the scope of prohibition was broader than just the breaking of a formal oath. In the first place, a covenant people (Exod. 19:5-6; 1 Pet. 2:5, 9) are name-bearers of God, and, by virtue of that, every word they speak must be trustworthy, every act in conformity with the covenant or oath of allegiance they have sworn to God. The employee who does not give a full measure of faithful work and the employer who does not pay a fair wage are both profaning the name of God, for stealing profanes his name (Prov. 30:8-9). In fact, every sin is the occasion for God's name to be blasphemed among the unbelievers (Rom. 2:24-25). Who has broken the solemn vow of marriage in getting a divorce? The Lord will not hold him guiltless who takes his name in vain. Who has broken the solemn pledge given at baptism? The Lord will not hold him guiltless who takes his name in vain.

But sometimes it seems impossible to live up to the promises made and every promise, even every "yes" and "no" of a Christian, is given in God's presence. He is the witness. Difficult to be sure, but God loves the kind of person who sticks to his word no matter how costly (Ps. 15:4). God loves the bankrupt businessman who spends his life attempting to repay his creditors. Integrity, rock-ribbed integrity, is the key idea in the Third Commandment and in the reinforcement given by Christ and James.

In the second place, the custom of invoking God's name to induce confidence in what one says had become so commonplace as to empty it of meaning. They were literally "taking God's name in vain." Today people use God's name without meaning it—mindlessly profaning God's holy name, often just a habit revealing an impoverished vocabulary. Even preachers use God's name flippantly, in a casual way, or in quoting a profane person. Against this both Jesus Christ and his brother James spoke stern words of warning.

Is this the only prohibition of the Third Commandment? Literally, to "take in vain" means to use in an empty way. Therefore, to use God's name without meaning it is to use it profanely. In a sense, to pray or to sing without meaning it is to use God's name in vain. The great temptation of those in full-time Christian work is to do religious activity professionally, simply to go through the routine of "performing" a church service. This is another way to profane the name of God.

Certainly any sort of irreverence violates the Third Commandment. To joke about sacred things or to joke with sacred things in such a way as to debase them is to act profanely. To use sacred things or words emptied of sacred meaning is wrong. For this reason, jokes about the Bible or sacred Bible truths such as baptism are not fitting for the Christian who holds God's name and God's things in high reverence.

Some people seem to use God's name in vain by repeating it often in prayer without thought. Others invoke God's name on almost every decision or plan they make. "God said . . ." "God told me to . . ." God's name is invoked to validate almost every activity. This may be genuine so far as a person's heart condition is concerned, but there is the danger that this become profane, invoking God's name when it is not altogether certain that God himself stands behind that particular choice or activity.

Many Christians even feel uncomfortable in putting other books on the Bible or in putting a Bible on the floor. Although this might be considered extreme and possibly leading to a magical approach to religious objects, a form of idolatry, it need not be so. Such a sensitivity may be a spirit of high reverence for that which pertains to God. Most Christians refrain from entering a room during prayer. Most people are offended when pastors or song leaders are busily looking up hymns or arranging their notes during a prayer time. These responses reflect a sensitivity to reverence for God and the things of God.

What of words which are often called profanity, such as "hell" or "damn," or scatological or sexual terms? Technically speaking, these are not a violation of the Third Commandment. The Third Commandment prohibits taking *God's* name in vain. This does not mean that a Christian is free to use such language, of course. There are other biblical injunctions concerning what we should think about, and certainly much of this language is not fit for Christian use.

What of the Christian novelist or dramatist putting profanity in the speech of his characters? This is becoming increasingly common. I consider this one of the great—and perhaps fatal—limitations on the Christian writer. I see no more justification for him to use profanity for his characters than for the minister to use similar language in his pulpit illustrations. It is difficult for me to see how a Christian novelist can say, as many do, "That is not *me*. That is my character speaking." Inasmuch as he has full control over his character and the language and thought that the character brings into my mind, I do not see how he is free of responsibility. Unlike sins such as murder, which a person can describe without committing, to use words profanely is to commit the sin—God's name is no less used in vain by putting it in quotes.

What of minced oaths? Do these violate the Third Commandment? The sensitive Christian needs to be especially careful that he does not judge others too severely in these matters. Nevertheless, a good rule might be for the Christian to refrain from using any term which a standard dictionary identifies as being a substitute for true profanity. Certainly the Christian desires to give no appearance of evil.

What of humorous language? Christ says that we must give account for every idle word that we speak (Matt. 12:36). Ephesians 5:4 seems to prohibit levity of any kind. My understanding of the passage in Ephesians is that Paul is actually speaking of what we might call dirty jokes or impure speech (Eph. 4:29). It can hardly be held a sin to speak with a humorous touch since Christ himself did so on more than one occasion. When he nicknamed James and John the "Sons of Thunder," it can hardly be understood as a dead-serious speech. A log in one's eye or a camel crawling through a needle's eye are not solemn illustrations. Actually, humor can be anything but idle. It can be very productive of good.

Yet there are other standards which must be maintained. For example, humor should not hurt another person. However, humor to relieve tension, to counteract a heavy-handed approach is certainly productive of good. Sometimes a humorous touch will get across a message where the direct approach would be unacceptable. Humor is not necessarily a sin. Does it produce good or is it idle, nonproductive foolishness? Does it violate the law of reverence or the law of love or does it spring from love in a spirit of reverence for God?

Stop

OBSERVING THE HOLY REST DAY *4/8*

Remember the sabbath day, to keep it holy. . . . The LORD blessed the sabbath day and hallowed it. (Exod. 20:8, 11)

THE REST DAY IN THE OLD TESTAMENT

The Hebrew word *Sabbath* means "rest" or "rest day." When did a special rest day begin? Who was it for? What was its purpose?

And on the seventh day God finished his work which he had made; and he rested on the seventh day from all his work which he had made. And God blessed the seventh day, and hallowed it; because that in it he rested from all his work which God had created and made. (Gen. 2:2-3, ASV)

The rest day began at the creation. The purpose stated is clear: It is for rest, and it is in a special sense holy or set apart. Note that the rest day or Sabbath is rooted in the example of God at the very beginning, long before any covenant of redemption was made with a chosen people. It was given for all mankind before man had fallen, before there was any need for redemption.

The text seems to state that God rested because of some desire or need in himself, not merely as a contrived model for humankind. Was there something in the very nature of God that desired a time to turn inward, away from outward activity, toward quiet communion among the three persons of the Trinity? The implication seems to be that something in periodic rest is of the nature of God. And this is given as a reason for his establishing the same pattern for those made in his image.

But suppose he rested merely symbolically, to serve as a model for human beings? Then the standard of behavior is, if anything, reinforced. The need of humans to have a regular day of rest is so much a part of their nature that God felt it necessary at the very beginning to deliberately model this pattern of behavior himself.

But why would God deliberately take one-seventh of a person's time and tie it up in legal bondage for some religious purpose? Because God loves us he longs to be with us—one of the most incredible revelations of Scripture. True, he purposes to have us as partners in his creative and redemptive *work*. But just as two lovers long for a time of quiet when they can stop their regular activity and spend unhurried time together, so God designed a gift of a special time with those he loves, time that is "holy," set aside for that purpose of companionship. What is our response? We can reject his gift and spend that time selfishly on our own purposes, or we can give back to him one-seventh of our time in token of the reality that all our time is his.

What a beautiful exchange of gifts, his gift of a gracious command and our gift of obedience—time to be with one who is well-loved! The gift is one we need for renewal of mind and body. But even more, the gift is one *He* desires and we desperately need to build our relationship with him and his family.

If you keep your feet from breaking the Sabbath and from doing as you please on my holy day, if you call the Sabbath a delight and the LORD's holy day honorable, and if you honor it by not going your own way and not doing as you please or speaking idle words, then you will find your joy in the LORD. (Isa. 58:13-14, NIV)

The rest day was designated as a sign for Israel of God's great redemption from Egypt (Deut. 5:15), but it did not originate then any more than animal sacrifice, which was also designated as a sign of God's redemption from Egypt, originated at the time of the Passover. The sacrificial system had been for pre-Abrahamic mankind, for all mankind. The rest day is designated as a sign of the covenant between God and Israel (Exod. 31:13), but this does not mean that the rest day was instituted then any more than that circumcision was instituted originally for Abraham. It had existed from time immemorial among mankind but was chosen as a covenant sign between God and Abraham.

When God wrote the Ten Commandments, he clearly enunciated the origin of this particular commandment.

> Remember the sabbath day, to keep it holy. . . . For in six days the LORD made heaven and earth, the sea, and all that is in them, and rested the seventh day: therefore the LORD blessed the sabbath day and hallowed it. (Exod. 20:8, 11)

Some have said that there is significance in the fact that the setting apart of the rest day in Genesis 2 is never mentioned again until Exodus 16:26-30 in connection with the giving of the manna (pre-Sinai, by the way). However, there can be no more significance in this omission than there is in the omission of the other nine commandments during the same period of time. The Fourth Commandment has this in its favor, at least, that it was enunciated at the beginning.

CHRIST'S VIEW OF THE REST DAY

Jesus Christ said both yes and no to Sabbath regulations. Christ said yes to the rest day, but a resounding no to the rabbinical additions. He contended with the scribes continuously over their interpretation of the law, with the complex hedge they built about the law to protect it.

John Wesson in the *Christian Graduate* writes to free evangelicals from the Puritan tradition of a Christian Sabbath. Nevertheless, he must admit

> Jesus' own attitude to the Ten Commandments is important here. We cannot interpret his words and actions as abrogating the Fourth Commandment—they are far more directed against its misuse and misunderstanding. He himself observed the seventh day apart from its unreasonable restrictions. (Luke 4:16; cf. Matt. 12:12).[2]

"So that the Son of Man is Lord even of the Sabbath." The rest day was made for man *so that* the Son of Man is Lord even of the Sabbath. Some interpret this to mean that all sons of men (mankind) are lords of the Sabbath and can do as they please on this day. But it is impossible to interpret the passage this way because "Son of Man" is a technical term that Christ uses in referring to himself as the Messiah. In the parallel passage in Matthew 12, immediately before he says "the Son of Man is lord of the Sabbath," he identifies the Son of Man as "greater than the temple," a clear reference to himself.

Christ is speaking of himself as being Lord of the Sabbath.

[2]John Wesson, "Sunday, Puzzling Sunday," *Christian Graduate*, September 1973, 69.

What does this mean? First, we know that Christ did not come to destroy the law, but to fulfill it (Matt. 5:17-19).

"Fulfilling the law" has several meanings, as we saw in the chapter on Law. It means that he *obeyed the law*. That is why he was in the synagogue on the Sabbath and why he obeyed the rest of the Old Testament moral law although he opposed the rabbinical interpretation.

The rest day as a special day is somewhat similar to nighttime. Man has to have several hours of rest every night. Most normal, healthy people are delighted that they can go to bed and rest at night. They don't feel it is something laid on them that is very hard to do. Even so, some things must be done at night and in an emergency a person may skip the rest time. In a similar way, Christ indicates some exceptions to the law of the rest day and some emergency situations. He said it was all right to grind grain informally and thus prepare necessary food to eat (Mark 2:23-27). He said also it was all right to water cattle on the Sabbath (Luke 13:15). In fact, he commanded a man to pick up his bed and take it home (John 5:8). So there are "works of necessity" that must continue on the rest day, and Christ was against a dry legalism that hurt people instead of helping them. Then Christ healed on the rest day (Mark 3:1-5) and was angry with the religious leaders for even thinking he should not heal the man. According to their rabbinical teaching it was wrong to heal on the Jewish Sabbath. He was angry with them because "works of mercy" are not only legitimate; they are a necessary part of the rest day: healing the sick, pulling cattle out of ditches (Matt. 12:11; Luke 14:5). These then are exceptions to the law of rest: works of necessity and mercy.

Then there is work involved in the service of God (Matt. 12:5). For spiritual leaders the rest day is the busiest day of all. But it is a special service to the Lord of the rest day and to his people, making it possible for them to worship and serve.

Finally, the Son of Man, the *Messiah,* is Lord of the Sabbath. He fulfills the law by being the fulfillment of the ceremonial laws of the Old Testament. The whole system of sacrifice was fulfilled in Christ; it was the shadow, he was the reality. The same is true of holy places. Christ taught that the day is coming when people aren't going to worship in Jerusalem (John 4:21-24). It is not the place but the relationship. Thus Christ came to fulfill the law by fulfilling the prophecies and the typology of the ceremonial system in his own life and death. He put an end to the transitory ceremonial aspects of the law while reinforcing through his own example and teaching the eternal, moral elements of the Old Testament revelation. In which category is the weekly rest day—ceremonially fulfilled in Christ or a continuing moral obligation? His life and teaching seem to favor a continuing moral obligation to obey the Fourth Commandment, but to strip it of all the scribal additions.

PAUL'S VIEW OF THE REST DAY

Paul taught his Gentile churches that the Scriptures were to be their authority and the teaching of Christ was the ultimate authority.

The only Bible these Christians had was the Old Testament, though the sayings of Christ and the early biographies of Christ were no doubt beginning to circulate. The writings of Paul are identified by Peter as Scripture and thus hold equal authority with the rest (2 Pet. 3:16). In fact, we believe that God's revelation progressed in the person, work, and the teaching of Jesus Christ and that it progressed even further in the interpretation of the person, work, and teaching of Jesus found in the apostolic letters. Nevertheless, if the authority of Scripture is to remain intact, every effort must be made to harmonize the teachings of Scripture. We cannot allow apparent contradictions to stand without seeking to reconcile them. Later revelation is authoritative in interpreting earlier revelation. However, unless later revelation (in Jesus Christ or in the apostles) clearly sets aside or annuls earlier revelation, the earlier revelation must stand.

The question then is this: Is Paul, in Romans and Colossians, deliberately annulling the teaching of Genesis 2, Exodus 20, and that of Jesus Christ?

If Paul, when consistently affirming the Ten Commandments, intends to include the Fourth Commandment as well, what does he mean when he says, "Let no one pass judgment on you . . . with regard to a festival or a new moon or a sabbath" (Col. 2:16), and "One man esteems one day as better than another, while another man esteems all days alike. Let every one be fully convinced in his own mind" (Rom. 14:5)?

The weekly Sabbath dates from Eden, but the ceremonial nonweekly Sabbaths only from Sinai. The relationship between the "moral" Sabbath and the ceremonial Sabbaths is analogous to that between the moral law and the ceremonial law or "law of ordinances." "As Thomas Boston writes of the weekly Sabbath, 'It was appointed and given of God to Adam in innocence, before there was any ceremony to be taken away by the coming of Christ,' Genesis 2:3."[3]

Paul Jewett writes in a similar vein:

It is commonly affirmed that Paul is here saying Christians are free from every distinction of days. But this can hardly be so, if the weekly division of time was accepted in the very Christian circles where he labored. The fact that he gathered with these Christians to break bread on a day designated as one of the Sabbaths (Acts 20:7) and that he designated the same day for setting aside monies toward an offering for the poor saints in Jerusalem (1 Cor. 16:2-3) shows that he not only knew that Christians distinguish that day from others by using it for religious worship, but also approved this distinction by making it himself.

If he had literally esteemed every day alike, why should he designate one day in particular on which to render a religious ministration (2 Cor. 9:12), and that a day which recurred every week (1 Cor. 16:2)? In so doing, Paul himself regarded the first day of the week above others. It is unconvincing therefore to press Paul's statement in Romans 14:5 so absolutely as to allow for no distinction in days whatever, as though he would have considered John a Judaizer for having called one day in the week the Lord's Day (Rev. 1:10), thus giving it the preeminence.

To what, then, did he have reference when he spoke of some who esteem one day above another and some who esteem every day alike? We cannot be absolutely sure. Since the context has to do with dietary restrictions, some have thought he is speaking of setting aside certain days for fasting. Recalling that the church of Rome had a large Jewish contingent, it is at least equally plausible that he had in mind the Jewish Sabbaths and other holy days, which the Jewish Christians were at liberty to esteem and the Gentile Christians to ignore, according to each man's background and personal preference. It apparently never occurred to him that anyone would construe his strictures against the legalistic observance of feast days, new moons, and Sabbaths (Col. 2:16) or his plea for liberty in the estimation of days (Rom. 14:5) as meaning he was opposed to the observance of a weekly division of time, or indifferent to the designation of the first day of the week as the day of religious worship.[4]

---

[3]Francis Nigel Lee, *The Covenantal Sabbath* (London: The Lord's Day Observance Society, 1969), 28.
[4]Paul K. Jewett, *The Lord's Day* (Grand Rapids: Eerdmans, 1971), 77-79.

What is very clear in Paul's teaching is that the old ceremonial system of sacrifices and holy days was fulfilled in Christ and was no longer binding on the believer. Does he mean more than this? Is the teaching of Christ concerning his own authority over the rest day a hint that Christ intended to abrogate one of the Ten Commandments and to set aside the original order of creation? Some would hold this. For them Paul is simply following through on what Christ hinted at and proceeding to annul this particular commandment.

But such an interpretation is far from clear. It seems to go against the rest of Pauline teaching concerning the law and the Christian's obligation to obey the moral law while being completely free from the obligations of the legal system of ceremonial requirements. Certainly it runs counter to the teaching of Christ concerning the rest day observance, and clearly such an interpretation undercuts the authority of the Decalogue and that of the origin of the rest day in the activity of God, if not in the nature of God. The more reasonable reading of Pauline intention is to see him affirming the entire Decalogue, including the Fourth Commandment, as God's eternal moral law, while setting aside the entire system of holy days, feast days, and fast days of the older dispensation as no longer binding on the follower of Christ.

THE LETTER TO THE HEBREWS ON THE REST DAY

The teaching of Hebrews (3:7–4:11) was taken by the Reformers as indicating that Christ fulfilled the Sabbath law so that we have all entered into our rest from sin and thus all days are to be treated in an equal way. Although the passage does clearly indicate the present rest we have in Christ, the even stronger teaching in the passage is clearly that a rest remains to the people of God. Heaven is the focal point of the passage. This case is like so much of typology and prophetic teaching in Scripture where there is a twofold application or fulfillment. There is a present rest and there is a final rest. Consider Jewett's words.

In this regard it is important to remember that the fulfillment of the Old Testament in Jesus Christ is a fulfillment in principle, but not yet in finality. In Christ we both have and hope for the salvation promised to ancient Israel. The whole New Testament reflects this fundamental tension between the indicative of present fulfillment and the imperative of future consummation. To this rule the law of the Sabbath is no exception. The fulfillment of the Sabbath rest which we have in Christ is not only a present reality, but also a future hope. Those who are in Christ have, indeed, found rest unto their souls, yet at the same time they must give all diligence to enter into God's rest. The principle of the Sabbath, then, is both an Old Testament ceremonialism which has been fulfilled and done away in Christ and at the same time a permanent interpretive category of redemptive history, having definite eschatological implications. Christians, therefore, are both free from the Sabbath to gather on the first day, and yet stand under the sign of the Sabbath in that they gather every seventh day.[5]

As for the Reformers, when John tells his readers that he was in the Spirit on the Lord's Day, he cannot possibly be saying that *every* day is the Lord's Day. His design was to identify the specific day on which the visions came. He is making a distinction of days; one day above others is uniquely the Lord's. (To call one day the Lord's Day is not to deny that every day belongs to him, any more than to call one meal the communion is to deny that in every meal Christians fellowship with the Lord, thankfully acknowledging his benefits as they partake). And this unique day, when Christians gather to fellowship with the risen Lord, as did the disciples on the day of his resurrection, occurs not monthly or yearly, but weekly, according to the division of time which God ordained through Moses.[6]

It might also be urged that simply because all of one's property belongs to God, there is no longer any need to give a portion for his offering. Again, to argue that to be saved is to rest in Christ and that therefore the older commandment of physical rest is abrogated would be like arguing that since our eternal and true marriage relationship is with Christ beginning now and confirmed in greater fulfillment at the marriage supper of the Lamb, therefore the physical and contemporary laws of marriage are no longer in effect. Patrick Fairbairn argues this point:

For of what nature, we ask, is the institution of marriage? . . . Does he feel himself warranted to assume, that because, after Christ's appearing, the marriage union was treated as an emblem of Christ's union to the church, the literal ordinance is thereby changed or impaired? Assuredly not. And why should another course be taken with the Sabbath? This, too, in its origin, is a positive institution, and was also, it may be, from the first designed to serve as an emblem of spiritual things—an emblem of the blessed rest which man was called to enjoy in God. But in both respects it stands most nearly on a footing with the ordinance of marriage; both alike owe their institution to the original act and appointment of God; both also took their commencement at the birth of time—in a world unfallen, when, as there was no need for the anti-types of

[5]Ibid., 82.
[6]Ibid., 81.

redemption, so no ceremonial types or shadows of these could properly have a place. And both are destined to last until the songs of the redeemed shall have ushered in the glories of a world restored.[7]

SUMMARY OF BIBLICAL EVIDENCE

We hold then, that the law of a rest day was established by God at the time of creation both by example and by ordinance. When the time came for him to reveal in permanent form a summary of his moral requirements of man, this commandment of the rest day was included. It was also incorporated in the entire ceremonial system as a special sign of redemption and covenant relationship. In subsequent years, teachers of the law, who were not authorized to write Scripture or give an authoritative revelation of the will of God, created an enormous compendium of obligations for Sabbath observance. When Jesus came he spoke with authority and cut away all the scribal additions. He faithfully observed the commandment as God originally gave it. He illustrated the kind of work that was permissible in the spirit of the day. Works of necessity, mercy, and service to God are not a violation of his intent in giving the commandment, but rather a part of his intent. This much is clear.

But what of Paul and the early church? His obedience to the command of Christ to "teach them to observe all things which I have commanded you" is clear. His affirmation of the authority of the Scripture in general and the moral law in particular is clear. His unremitting warfare against the use of the law for salvation and against the binding nature of the ceremonial system of the Old Covenant is clear. We must understand the passages in Romans and Colossians in the light of Paul's clarity in these great affirmations. Otherwise we open ourselves to a hermeneutic which, in the end, would undermine not only the authority of the Decalogue but, indeed, of the Old Testament and of the earthly life and teachings of Christ. It would undermine these because it would validate a hermeneutic based on using an obscure passage to set aside the teaching of a great many clearer passages, and it would do this with a passage that may not be so obscure after all. If Romans 14 and Colossians are

[7]Patrick Fairbairn, *The Typology of Scripture: The Divine Dispensations*, vol. 2, 4th ed. (Edinburgh: T. & T. Clark, 1864), 128-129.

taken into account, the most normal interpretation is that Paul is not speaking against the rest day but rather against the entire system of ceremonial Sabbaths.

SUNDAY IN CHURCH HISTORY

Jesus Christ was in the grave on the Jewish rest day. He rose from the dead on what was then called the first day of the week. All his post-resurrection appearances of which we know the time were also on this first day, as was the descent of the Holy Spirit at Pentecost. In this way our Lord put his seal on the first day of the week as, in a special way, the *Lord's* Day. So it was that the early church began immediately to meet for fellowship and worship on the first day of the week.

Jewish Christians continued to observe the seventh day as the rest day. Very little is known historically as to how the transition from the seventh day to the first day took place. What is certain is that early Christians honored the first day and that increasingly the Gentile churches did not feel that the Jewish rest day was binding.

The strong presumption is that a large portion of the early Christians, as slaves, really had no rest day at all as we understand the term. They met for worship at first in the evening, and after this was made illegal, they met before dawn on the Lord's Day. From the writings of the Fathers it is clear that Christians worked on Sunday until the Edict of Constantine made it an official day of rest. Until that time the Church Fathers enjoined Christians to work and not be idle on the first day of the week. Why did they emphasize this? And why should Constantine choose Sunday as a rest day if there was no precedent among the Christians with whom he sought to identify?

After Constantine's edict (A.D. 321) the Fathers began to appeal to the law of the Sabbath as applying to the first day of the week. This interpretation became common throughout Christendom until the time of the Reformers. The Reformers rejected this interpretation, holding that the Sabbath law was no longer binding for the Christian. Nevertheless, each Reformer in his own way defended the observance of the day in practice. However, their theological position combined with Roman

Catholic indifference on the issue to produce ultimately what came to be called the "continental Sabbath"—a holiday, in contrast to the English and American concept of a holy rest day.

For the first three centuries, then, the Fathers were bound by a society in which neither they nor their disciples could rest. So they "made Scripture serve Caesar"—they taught that the Bible enjoined work on Sunday. But as soon as freedom to rest was granted, the theologians returned to a theological base. It might be said that there is a parallel here to the practice of polygamy and slavery, matters far less clear in Scripture than the law of the rest day. In fact, the rest day permeates both the Old Testament and the Gospels, whereas the abolition of polygamy and slavery is not found in the Old Testament or the New Testament except by implication. Nevertheless, the seeds of change were there. In both polygamy and slavery the Christian ethic was at work in seeking change, although it took centuries in the case of polygamy and millennia in the case of slavery to return to God's original order. In each of these cases culture often inhibited the growth of God's intention, but in the end, God's original design prevailed in Western society.

Where did the English and American observance of the Lord's Day come from, an observance which was passed on through these two missionary nations to many of the younger churches around the world? Why were the convictions so strong and uniform, controlling civil law for several centuries? The high view of one day set aside as the Lord's Day in a special way, a day built theologically on the biblical commands concerning a rest day is a direct gift from the Puritans. Our Puritan forebears enunciated the theology of the rest day and applied it to public as well as private life. In one of the most remarkable social revolutions in history, the English Puritans taught and achieved total societal conformity within a single generation. Presbyterians, Congregationalists, Methodists, Baptists fell heir to this teaching and practice.

So strong was the teaching that only the modern secularized society has been able to abolish the rest day in these societies. Even after secularism moved to make changes in the "blue laws" for society at large, the church continued to hold a high view of the rest day well into the twentieth century.

APPLICATION FOR TODAY

We conclude that a rest day is a good thing, one of God's good gifts for the welfare of mankind. It is a law rather than a recommendation because a recommendation would be no blessing at all. It is the binding aspect of the rest day that releases one for rest and worship. If the rest day is merely recommended, we are not free to rest from the pressures of life and turn without hindrance to joyful fellowship with God and his people. We must still face the pressures and frustrations of mundane obligations. But a required rest day sets us free.

If the teaching of Paul does not certainly bind the Christian to observe a special rest day, even less certainly does it annul the strong teaching of the balance of Scripture in setting a special day for rest and worship. Therefore we positively choose that which certainly would please the Lord. To turn away from our daily occupation to spend a day in fellowship with him and service for him must certainly please him even more than offering to him a portion of all our possessions in token of the fact that all belongs to him. The only way the careful observance of the rest day commandment could displease our Lord would be if a person looked to that obedience as a means of earning merit or as a way of salvation.

In light of God's action in resting after work, his setting aside at that time a day of rest sacred to himself, the subsequent commands of Scripture concerning a day of rest, the example and teaching of Jesus Christ in affirming and interpreting the Old Testament standard, and the observance of the first day of the week by the New Testament church as a special day of worship, we must recognize Sunday as a special day of rest, worship, and service to the Lord.

In a thoroughly humanistic age in which man is the center, "God first!" thunders from Sinai. The first table of the Decalogue proclaims this ultimate message: "Above all else, O man, guard your relationship to your God. If this relationship is right, you will live. If this relationship is wrong, you will die."

Notice, in brief review, how every topic we have studied centers ultimately in God. We shall see as our studies continue that every standard for life is the same. Note also the outcome when God is not given first place in any standard, how quickly it disintegrates into meaningless and powerless, even destructive half-truth.

True *love* begins and ends with God. He defines it by his own character, and all other loves reach their potential only when yielding to love for God as supreme. *Law* is based on God's character—his expressed will that we be like him. Thus to violate his law is to violate his person. Even human authority derives its authority from God and must give an account to him for how that responsibility has been discharged. Those under human authority owe ultimate allegiance only to God. All *sin* is, in the final analysis, against God. This is seen in the fact that sin is falling short of God's glorious righteousness, that sins of the mind and heart are crucial, and that sin is, above all, breaking the first four commandments. *Lust* is God-given appetite gone berserk and *covetousness* is, at root, idolatry. *Pride* is the essence of sin against God for in it man attempts to usurp the credit due God and establish his own autonomy. Of all the failures of *situation ethics*, the most fatal is that it leaves God out in a horizontal-only personalism.

Thus "God first" is far more than a theoretical, appropriately courteous starting point for a system of ethics. It is intensely practical and, in fact, the only way to integrate all the other horizontal relationships. God in person is the beginning and ending point of all truly biblical ethics. *P.T.L.*

SUGGESTED ADDITIONAL READING

Carson, D. A., ed. *From Sabbath to Lord's Day*. Grand Rapids: Zondervan, 1982.

Fairbairn, Patrick. *The Typology of Scripture: The Divine Dispensations*. 4th ed. Edinburgh: T. & T. Clark, 1864.

Jewett, Paul K. *The Lord's Day*. Grand Rapids: Eerdmans, 1971.

Lee, Francis Nigel. *The Covenantal Sabbath*. London: The Lord's Day Observance Society, 1969.

Rordorf, Willy. *Sunday: The History of the Day of Rest and Worship in the Earliest Centuries of the Christian Church*. Philadelphia: Westminster, 1968.

Wilson, Daniel. *The Lord's Day*. Grand Rapids: Eerdmans, 1956.

CHAPTER SEVEN

SEX, MARRIAGE, AND THE FAMILY

Honor thy father and thy mother.
Thou shalt not commit adultery.

God's standards on human sexuality are treated in Scripture as the most important of all rules for relations among people. In the Old Testament, teaching against adultery is emphasized second only to teaching against idolatry. In the New Testament, both Christ and the apostles emphasized marital fidelity. Paul includes sexual sins in every one of his many lists of sins, and in most cases they head the list and receive the greatest emphasis. Why does the Bible view this relationship between the sexes as so important?

Sexual fidelity, more than most virtues, clearly demonstrates the purpose of law: man's welfare. Human sexuality is one of God's most delightful gifts. But the sordid record of human history and the anguish of personal experience highlight the basic reality that this joy is reserved for those who "follow the Manufacturer's instructions."

This outcome is not surprising because human nature was

designed to reflect divine nature, and God's law is simply his expressed will that people conform to the moral nature of God.

This reflection of the divine nature is many-faceted. "Image" includes the moral nature of God—and therefore fidelity and purity—but it also includes the ability to think rationally, to create, to love and be loved, and to communicate. Among these characteristics of God-similarity may be included human sexuality: "So God created man in his own image, in the image of God he created him; male and female he created them" (Gen. 1:27). The grammatical structure of this sentence does not demand a direct link between the two ideas. All that is certain is that God created human beings in some way similar to himself, and that he created humans in two different models: male and female.

Some have built an entire doctrine on the mistaken notion that this verse defines "image" as the male/female characteristic. Though Scripture does not present this as the only or even the paramount element of likeness to God, some contemporary interpreters seem to hold that this is the chief meaning of "image." Paul Jewett, Letha Scanzoni, and Nancy Hardesty are among these.[1] In fact, Jewett says that Karl Barth, the influential German theologian and father of neoorthodoxy "is the first major theologian to adopt such a position."[2] "Image," in this view, means that man is a being-in-fellowship, as in the Trinity, and that male/female fellowship is the highest and best variety of fellowship. Even though this verse does not prove such a thesis, I think we are warranted in finding here and elsewhere in Scripture the idea that the maleness and the femaleness and their relationship, in some mysterious way, reflect God's own nature.

The truth is that Scripture nowhere defines "image" nor explains the concept. But certainly, inasmuch as the Trinity is one, yet three, and the three are cemented in a relationship of loving commitment, we can see in the Godhead the ideal model for biblical marriage. The pervasive Old Testament representation of God as the Husband and Israel the wife, and the New Testament representation of Christ as the Bridegroom and the Church the bride, are more than felicitous analogies, an

[1]Paul Jewett, *Man as Male and Female* (Grand Rapids: Eerdmans, 1975); Letha Scanzoni and Nancy Hardesty, *All We're Meant to Be* (Waco: Word, 1974).
[2]Jewett, *Man as Male and Female*, 35.

effort by God to explain in human terms through a figure or "picture" what eternal spiritual relationships are designed to be. Human marriage seems designed deliberately to reflect the eternal reality of the best of all relationships—that of the Father, the Son, and the Holy Spirit and his relationship with us.

If marriage laws reflect the very nature of God and were expressly designed for man's best interests, why are these standards the most often violated? Does anything demonstrate more clearly man's independent, arrogant, foolish, perverse, blind, and demonic fallenness?

Before examining God's standards for marriage and the home, we must consider in greater detail the important subject of human sexuality.

FOUNDATIONAL CONSIDERATIONS ABOUT HUMAN SEXUALITY

INNATE DISTINCTIONS

The most obvious distinction between male and female is biological. Some say it is the only distinction and that other distinctions are made by society.

Certainly distinctions are made by society; some are biblically valid and some are not. Surely it is legitimate to have an all-male football team. Certainly it is not fair to pay a woman less than a man for identical work. But are there innate psychological characteristics unique to each sex?

Traditionally, most societies have held that there are. Is it not reasonable to assume that physical characteristics which enable a woman to bear and nurture children should be accompanied in the design of the Creator by an inner disposition to reinforce those roles? The greater size and strength of the male may indicate something of the role intended by the Maker. But these assumptions have been strongly challenged. The new folk wisdom, following the behavioral scientists, holds that all psychological distinctions between the sexes have been socialized; they are acquired characteristics, not inherent. If the early environment conditioned all girls in a society to be dominant and aggressive and to assume leadership roles, that is exactly the way women would be. Though the Bible in places seems to assume the traditional viewpoint, it nowhere gives a clear-cut answer to this question. So we may safely classify the issue as nonmoral in nature. But what is the significance of the question?

The "unisex" view of human nature recognizes no inherent distinctives apart from the basic physical distinction which all must grant, however reluctantly. Most who advocate the unisex viewpoint are strongly in favor of eliminating all role distinctions. Roles based directly on the biological functions necessary to fathering and mothering (perhaps "inseminating" and "bearing" would be more accurate descriptions) are accepted, but all other role distinctions are negotiable, dispensable, and may, in fact, be pernicious, according to this view. If the Bible is silent on the question of innate characteristics, is it equally silent on the question of role differences?

ROLE DISTINCTIONS

There is no distinction between male and female as image-bearer: each is equally designed on the divine pattern (Gen. 1:27). Each is equally a sinner, equally under judgment, equally redeemable, and equally a potential recipient of God's grace. Further, "in Christ Jesus" there is "neither male nor female" (Gal. 3:28). This verse is the cornerstone of the Christian feminist movement, and thus the meaning is greatly debated. Perhaps the expression "in Christ Jesus" means simply, "as a Christian" or "before God" or is equivalent to "joint heirs" (1 Pet. 3:7). If so, the meaning is simply that God does not discriminate along sex lines in dispensing grace. This is the interpretation of most Bible scholars. But some hold that Paul here eliminates all role distinctions for the Christian. This interpretation, however, is too heavy a superstructure to build on a verse that also says "in Christ there is no Jew or Greek, no bond or free." Paul could have added, no adult or child, no teacher or disciple, no elder or younger. But this does not keep Paul from elsewhere insisting on the distinct role responsibilities in one's position. In fact, he consistently insists on the unique responsibilities of servant and master, parent and child, teacher and disciple, elder and younger, husband and wife.

What role distinction, then, does Scripture make between the sexes? Later we shall consider the basic question of role relationships in marriage because that issue is ethical. The hotly disputed question of roles in church governance does not fall within the scope of this book. But whatever role distinction Scripture may make in the home and in the church, it is unwarranted to extend these to society at large on the basis of biblical authority. One may see a paradigm of male/female relationships in the biblical model for marriage and apply this to civic or business relationships, but he may not do this on the basis of biblical authority, for the Bible is silent on the issue of female leadership in business, industry, or government. How much more distant from scriptural teaching is the ridiculous and altogether pernicious idea that every woman must be subordinate to any man with whom she is related.

God authorized certain women to be judges, prophets, and teachers so there is nothing inherently sinful in such roles for women on some occasions: Miriam (Exod. 15:20), Deborah (Judg. 4:4), Huldah (2 Kings 22:14ff.; 2 Chron. 34:22ff.), Noadiah (Neh. 6:14), Isaiah's wife (Isa. 8:3), Anna (Luke 2:36-38), Philip's four daughters (Acts 21:9), Priscilla (Acts 18:24ff.), and many other women (1 Cor. 11:5; Acts 2:17). The issue we must address here is the question of ethics: Is it a sin for a woman ever to be cast in a role of leadership over men? The question—at least outside the realm of the home and the church—cannot be argued from Scripture on moral grounds. Those who address the issue must do so from pragmatic or other grounds. The only possible way for Scripture to be introduced would be in drawing analogies from what the Bible teaches about husband/wife relationships, but such analogies must not be pressed as having scriptural authority.

Yet there are ethical issues in the contemporary feminist movement.

EQUALITY OF THE SEXES

Treating woman as inferior—as most societies throughout history have done—is clearly sinful. From the original creation statement (Gen. 1:27) through the example of Christ in his words and actions toward women to Paul's classic affirmation

(Gal. 3:28), men and women stand on level ground before the Lord. This does not mean that men are equal to women in all tasks nor that women are as competent as men in every role. Certainly women are superior as women and men as men. But in essence, as we have seen, God views men and women as equals. And so must we if we are to be godlike.

On the other hand, to equate self-denial with subservience and self-destruction,[3] and to aggressively demand one's rights, hardly seems to fall under the blessedness of the meek or to follow the trail leading to the cross. To be sure, Scripture enjoins us to fight for justice in behalf of the downtrodden and oppressed. And so the record of inactivity on the part of Christian men who have allowed women to be oppressed, even when not participating in the oppression, is shameful. But the strident, assertive stance of some Christian women on their own behalf does not have the ring of One who taught us to turn the other cheek, to yield our own rights in deliberate self-denial, and to take up our cross daily—the way to fullness of life.

So, as is common in matters hotly disputed, sin encroaches on both sides of the issue of women's rights. Guilty are those who do not treat women as Jesus did, and who do not aggressively seek to build homes, churches, and societies in which this ideal advances. Guilty also are those who fight for true causes in unbiblical ways.

Sin mars the thinking and behavior of those in the family of God. But this is greatly magnified outside that family where women are shamelessly exploited on the one hand and where, on the other hand, unisex advocates wage ceaseless war to obliterate all role distinctions. The church must fight the enemy's advances on both fronts. It is sad that one of God's most delightful inventions—human sexuality—should be so debased by sinful men and women.

When God created the male, he pronounced an inadequacy, an incompleteness: it is not good that man should be alone. Therefore he created a partner to complement him, to complete him (Gen. 2:18). Although we cannot prove it from explicit statements of Scripture, this passage does seem to support the idea that this complementarity is primarily psychological rather than physical. The aloneness and the creation of a "help suitable

[3]Scanzoni and Hardesty, *All We're Meant to Be*, 208.

for him" do not speak primarily of physical needs. In other words, the anatomical matching of male and female is just the package of a whole delightful system of maleness and femaleness that bring to exciting completion all that God intended in creating a being modeled after his own nature. If it is true that the body has a disposition or inner structure to match it, surely God designed the total package of maleness for specific functions or roles far beyond the simple insemination necessary for the continuance of the race, and femaleness for roles not necessarily demanded by the purely physical—and not so simple—activity of bringing to birth a child. No, the original idea encompassed all of life, external and internal, with role to match: male and female he created them. Does this mean that marriage is the only way for a human being to be complete? Is there no hope for the single person?

SINGLENESS

There are two errors concerning singleness: that to be single is an unmitigated evil, and that singleness is a more holy state than marriage.

Scripture clearly teaches that for the person who is single in the will of God there is the possibility of higher fulfillment in his relationship with God (1 Cor. 7). Christ also taught that some people have the ability to remain single for the sake of God's Kingdom (Matt. 19:10-12). If a person does not have this gift, Paul's instructions are clear that he should marry (1 Cor. 7:2). If circumstances impose singleness, one should ask in faith for the ability to live happily and productively in that God-ordained state. According to Paul the advantages for those who have this gift are two: a more exclusive and wholehearted relationship with the Lord, and the potential of more unencumbered ministry for the Lord.

How does a person tell if he "has the gift"? Paul tells us an evidence of lacking this ability: burning with lust (1 Cor. 7:8-9). If desire for sexual fulfillment is so strong that a person is caused to sin because of it, he does not have the gift, at least not as yet. Paul also speaks more generally: "The man . . . who is under no compulsion but has control over his own will" (7:37, NIV). It would seem that the unmarried person who is able to live freely without consuming thoughts of marriage or distracting preoccupation with those of the opposite sex should reflect on the possibility that God may have given him or her this special gift) If one chooses to live without marriage for the higher goals Paul enunciates, such a person should ask God for this freedom of spirit and freedom from overwhelming sexual desire.

If one does not have the ability to live "at ease" without marriage, but singleness is thrust upon him or her by the circumstances of life, the "gift" should be sought in the same way.

On the other hand, it is still "not good that man should be alone," so a companion or close friend of the same sex could certainly be part of God's plan (Eccles. 4:7-12). Statistical evidence seems to confirm the hints in Scripture that this gift of celibacy is more often found in women than in men. For example, the suicide rate among single men is more than twice that of married people, whereas the rate among single women is little more than half that of married people. The gift is certainly more easily discernible in men since the sexual urge seems innately stronger, and consequently the control of it more difficult.

On the other hand, it would seem that the emotional drive for the security of an intimate relationship in marriage is often stronger in women. Thus, whether control is needed for the God-given physical, sexual desire or the God-given emotional desire for belonging, one may have another, extraordinary gift, the ability to live in contentment without the normal provision of a marriage partner.

Because of what Christ and Paul had to say about the state of singleness, and possibly because of their example as well, the teaching has arisen that marriage is somehow second best and that singleness is a better or holier way. Actually, in church history, this teaching may have come as much from Greek dualism (in which the material world is inferior and the body is the source of evil) as it did from misunderstanding Christ and Paul. Whatever its roots, the idea is firmly embedded in Christian thought as can be seen in the law of celibacy for the priesthood of the Roman Catholic church. But the Bible clearly teaches that marriage is God's way (Gen. 2:18; Prov. 18:22; 1 Tim. 3:2; 4:1-3; 5:14; Heb. 13:4), his normal plan for his children. The idea that there is anything unclean or polluted in sexual relations in the marriage relationship is wrong and will be characteristic of false teaching in the last days. Let us turn then to consider the great biblical theme of marriage.

PURPOSES OF MARRIAGE

The Bible begins with a wedding and it ends with a wedding; the greatest love song in human literature is in the center, and Christ's first miracle sanctifies a wedding.[4] And yet, a leading authority on marriage, J. Allan Petersen, says, "at least 75 percent of all marriages are failures."[5] Some pastors testify that they have never found a truly happy marriage. We are flooded with marriage seminars and books on marriage; counselors multiply and still cannot begin to meet the demand of people seeking help for ailing relationships in marriage. But the trouble seems to grow, not abate.

Eager young counselors set out to solve the problems, become successful (measured by the number of clients and income), but then turn to holding seminars or teaching in college or seminary. Why? As one leading evangelical psychologist testified, "I became weary of diving around in a cesspool all day every day with nothing more than an aerosol can of deodorant to fight the disease." Although many have found substantial help through psychological counsel, and although some counselors do more than put Band-Aids over abscesses, my conviction is that 90 percent of the problems in marriage result directly from sin, and that obedience to the plain teaching of Scripture would of itself, in most cases, produce the kind of marriage God intends. Let us consider the purposes of marriage.

WHOLENESS

Man by himself is incomplete. He needs a mate (Gen. 2:18-25; Matt. 19:3-6). So the first purpose of marriage is fellowship, oneness, wholeness—love. Consider the words of popular preacher Robert Schuller.

[4]Dennis Kinlaw, introduction to a chapel sermon, Columbia Bible College and Seminary.
[5]J. Allan Petersen, *Decision*, August 1971, 6.

Dear Abby, a columnist whose column appears in over 900 newspapers, said to me, "Dr. Schuller, loneliness, and the need for love that goes with it, is the number one problem that faces people." She told me she receives over 10,000 letters a week, and we receive that many ourselves. We both agreed that it is man's hunger for acceptance and understanding that is, of all needs, deepest. One reason our society is so infected with loneliness is that the spirit of selfish freedom has become so widespread. So we don't want to risk losing our freedom by getting involved. We don't want to lose our freedom by running the risks of making long-term commitments. We have a lot of lonely people today because the price of unwillingness to make permanent commitments is to live on a level where all relationships are temporary. . . . Unless we are willing to surrender some freedom to make permanent commitments, prepare to pay the price, loneliness. Love ends loneliness, but love has a price tag. The price of love is commitment to continuity.[6]

PROCREATION

The first man and woman were instructed to be fruitful and multiply (Gen. 1:28). Animals do this too, of course, but with a major difference. Scripture gives a pattern of the home in which parents are fully responsible to care for their children. The procreation is in the context of family, according to God's pattern. So procreation was designed by God as part of the family package, not as mere animal-like reproduction.

In spite of the purpose God had for couples to have children, many decide against parenting.

If you had it all to do over again, would you have children? When advice columnist Ann Landers asked her readers this question, 10,000 of them responded, and 70 percent said, "No." . . . Mail fell roughly into three categories: letters from older parents whose children ignore them, from younger people concerned about over-population, and from people with young children who find parenthood restricts their life-styles.[7]

Once again, it is human selfishness that derails God's plan. I do not hold that the command to "replenish the earth" (given to Adam and Eve and repeated to Noah) is binding on every couple who would obey God. Further, the application of the command may change in a world of apparent overpopulation. That is one command of God humankind has obeyed of late! Furthermore, just as some are called to forego marriage for the Kingdom of God's sake, so some couples may be called upon to forego or postpone parenting for the Kingdom's sake. But the

[6]Robert H. Schuller, "Love or Loneliness?" *The Presbyterian Journal*, 17 October 1979, 7.
[7]*The State* (Columbia, S.C.), Associated Press, 27 February 1976, 20A.

motives that keep couples deliberately childless must be examined, for having children is one purpose in God's plan for normal human marriage (Ps. 127:3-5).

The beauty of God's plan can be seen in the exuberant joy a young child brings into the home, the strength young adults and parents provide one another, and the companionship and security children provide parents in old age, not to mention the honor rendered God through yet another generation of those who love and serve him. God's plan is good.

DEMONSTRATION OF LOVE

The marriage relationship is used throughout Scripture to instruct us concerning God's desired relationship with people (e.g., Eph. 5:22-23). This is the third purpose of marriage. God is love and from the overflow of this love among Father, Son, and Spirit, came the creation of a being on the same pattern, designed to love and to be loved as in the divine model. Which is the ultimate reality, which the reflection? In a good reflection it is sometimes difficult to distinguish. However, in one sense both the divine/human and the husband/wife relationships are real and interrelated. The male-female is transient and imperfect because man is finite and sin-damaged. The divine-human is eternal. But the more we learn of one relationship the more we are able to understand the other.

Let us examine in greater detail the first purpose of marriage, the unity of husband and wife.

EXCURSUS: THE PURPOSE OF COMPLEMENTARY FULFILLMENT

God's first purpose in marriage is loving fellowship and wholeness, but the essential ingredient of that positive oneness is a negative: separation. A man must *leave* his father and mother before he can adequately *cleave* to his wife in full identity of life (Gen. 2:24). Scripture gives ample evidence that this separation was not essentially physical or geographical. To leave psychologically in the sense that primary loyalties are changed lies at the foundation of successful wholeness in marriage.

Separation also includes all other exclusive or sexually

intimate relationships as well. All the subsequent laws concerning marriage emphasize God's intention that two who are joined together must have no sexual relationships of mind or body with anyone else. This negative separation lays an indispensable foundation for the three positive elements of this unity which God intended. They are oneness of mind and heart, oneness of body, and oneness in their relationship with God.

ONENESS IN HEART AND MIND

The first positive element in oneness is not physical union (which we have come to glorify as "sex"), but the completing of another in a love relationship that embraces all of life.

Even the oneness of bodies cannot be fulfilling in its most satisfying potential, unless there is oneness to some degree in spirit as well, because sex is at root a psychological phenomenon. Heart unity provides the basis for releasing the ultimate in physical ecstasy, but it goes far beyond the momentary physical thrill to a total-life mutual satisfaction and fulfillment.

The biblical standard for oneness and wholeness is love, which includes sharing of interests, activities, purposes, and goals. Of course, partners may have interests and activities independent of the other, but their oneness of purpose and loving identity calls for open verbal sharing of all aspects of life. Communication is the channel of unity. Without it, true oneness will prove illusive.

But oneness is more than self-giving love and open communication, which can and often should characterize other human relations. These alone will not hold a marriage together for long. The romantic euphoria of the newlywed may soon be dissipated under the impact of the harsh realities of life in which two independent beings are shut up to one another, especially when the desires of one begin to impinge on the desires or rights of the other. Communication can be a weapon to destroy unity as well as a channel in which loving unity may flow. What is the essential ingredient, then, if it is not love?

The key to a successful marriage and the cement that holds two people together for a lifetime is commitment, an exclusive contract relationship that is not negotiable. This is the only basis for true oneness in marriage. Without this commitment to fidelity and loyalty, any relationship, no matter how loving at the outset, is too fragile to survive. Furthermore, without this commitment, there is a tentativeness that undermines the relationship and belies the profession of love. One who experienced this uncommitted relationship testifies:

You can't say to someone, "I love you. Let's live together to see what happens." On those terms, either of you can split at a moment's notice. As a result you never really can be yourself or feel free to disagree without fear of losing the other person. You can never have the liberty to share your deepest feelings. You have to hold back. The relationship doesn't get a chance to grow because it is based on a conditional acceptance which is the cover for the self-gratification of two people indulging themselves in what they politely term a meaningful relationship. Real commitment, on the other hand, says, "I am willing to spend my life with you to see you grow." . . . Others say, "For as long as we both shall love. . . ." Love may have some cold spots, and it alone will never be enough to hold two people together. It's commitment that carries them over difficult times. Commitment is what God intended between a man and woman. That is why he set up marriage—to express a lifelong commitment.[8]

A marriage can have the same tentativeness, of course—and the same results. The loss of integrity when marriage vows are no longer viewed as vows and when love is no longer defined as a life-long commitment is one of the greatest losses of contemporary evangelicals.

Marriage is a sign and demonstration of God's character as the great covenant maker and covenant keeper. In a covenant, the crucial element is fidelity and integrity, not emotion. In marriage, it is not romantic feelings nor compatibility nor sexual adjustment that make success possible, but the fidelity of one's covenant vow. Covenant is the crucial center of life.

Commitment, then, is the surest evidence of true marriage-eligible love, and love, in turn, is the greatest reinforcer of commitment. But oneness of spirit is not the only element of biblical unity in marriage.

ONENESS IN BODY

When God created Eve and brought her to Adam, the word was clear: The two shall be one *flesh*. This is one of the great, joyful, uninhibited themes of the Song of Songs. Furthermore,

[8]Michael Zadig, *HIS*, March 1977, 7.

Scripture in each era teaches directly that this is the good will of God (Exod. 21:10; Prov. 5:15-19; 1 Cor. 7:3-5; Heb. 13:4). In the union of the body the scriptural goal is clearly mutual satisfaction. No grounds in Scripture can be found for considering anything in this intimate sharing of body as perverted or wrong so long as there is mutual delight. If the satisfaction is not mutual, if one partner selfishly insists on his own pleasure at the expense of his mate, the law of love is violated.

Physical union takes to its most intimate and ecstatic conclusion the oneness of heart, and reinforces it as well. In fact, each unity is essential to the fullness of the other. Just as two people committed to one another in marriage vows of love are not one until the physical union is consummated, so two who unite physically without the marriage commitment, or in the bonds of marriage but without the love, are still incomplete.

UNITY IN GOD

In God's intent the relationship of husband and wife is to be completed in their oneness with God. The relationship between Adam and Eve began to deteriorate when they chose alienation from God. Perhaps their creation of clothing was the intuitive response and first evidence of this interdependence of the two relationships, horizontal between husband and wife and vertical between each and his Lord. Oneness in Christ gives depth and staying power to the human relationship.

Thus in God's marvelous design for marriage the three unities—oneness of heart and mind, oneness of body, and oneness in God—reinforce one another in a glorious spiral upward toward the fulfillment of God's purpose in marriage.

Since God planned marriage to be so good, it is no wonder that he should, in love for his people, create safeguards to keep it good. These are necessary because there are many enemies of God's good plan, many ways of abusing human sexuality that subvert and destroy the purposes he had in mind. In fact, anything that would detract from the oneness of the two God puts together, anything that would eliminate procreation, or distort the reflection in human marriage of God's own nature is the enemy of God and man.

VIOLATIONS OF GOD'S PURPOSES WITHIN MARRIAGE

MARRIAGE TO AN UNBELIEVER

The first purpose of marriage is loving companionship—the unity of two in a relationship mirroring the nature of God himself (see Eph. 5:22-23). One way to violate this unity from the outset is to marry an unbeliever. Marriage to an unbeliever reveals a very low view of marriage, of one's relationship to God, or of both. For unity to be complete, oneness in spirit is the prime requisite. If the most important relationship in life is with God, how can a couple have unity at any real depth when one is with God and the other is not?

Not only does marriage to an unbeliever diminish the potential for fulfilling the first purpose in marriage, it puts in great jeopardy the second purpose—having children in a God-fearing home environment. Finally, it completely rules out the third purpose of demonstrating the relationship God desires with his people. If the believing partner gives up his relationship with the Lord, some measure of unity can be built on a godless foundation as if both were unbelievers. But unless the unbeliever comes to Christ, no Christian marriage can be achieved, and no oneness at the deepest levels can be experienced.

At any rate, the Bible expressly prohibits such a union (Deut. 7:3-4; Neh. 13:23-27; 1 Cor. 7:39; 2 Cor. 6:14-18). Of course, one who is married to an unbeliever should remain married (1 Cor. 7:12-13). Though union will be limited, it is better than the sin of divorce, according to Paul.

How should others relate to a Christian who is planning marriage to an unbeliever, besides prayer against the consummation of the plan, and biblical counsel? Any minister of the gospel who officiates at a marriage between a believer and an unbeliever participates in the sin. Having said this, however, it should be emphasized that Christian people and pastors need so to relate to the Christian who is bent on unbiblical marriage that a trusting relationship is maintained even if the advice is rejected. Because the continuance of the marriage becomes the will of God once it has been consummated, it is important for Christian people to help the Christian partner come to repentance for disobeying God, and to assist in building as true a unity as possible in the mixed marriage. Only following the acknowledgment of sin will the believing partner be in a position to "consecrate" the children (1 Cor. 7:14), provide a Christlike model for the unbelieving spouse, and, hopefully, win that spouse to the Lord.

ROOT CAUSE OF DISUNITY

Stress and conflict in marriage are said to damage seriously 60 to 90 percent of Christian marriages. Seminars, books, and counselors devoted to treating this epidemic increase geometrically, but the infection seems to spread and deepen. The vast majority of these "combat zones" do not really need sexual or psychological adjustment. Often the cures advocated simply apply Band-Aids to cancers and drive the true illness deeper inside. The root problem in most cases is the old-fashioned sinful selfishness. "Lack of maturity is at the bottom of 90 percent of all marital problems," says widely read counselor Norman Vincent Peale.[9] Unity is impossible without self-giving as a way of life on the part of both mates. If one or both insist on personal rights and personal fulfillment rather than personal self-sacrifice in love for the other, true and lasting unity is impossible.

ADULTERY

The most serious violation of marriage is adultery, excoriated in the Old Testament second only to idolatry, and in the New Testament, second to none. Infidelity, though commonplace in most societies, has had few advocates in Western society until recently. But now adultery is promoted by popular media and behavioral scientists.

Many authorities have come to doubt our cultural belief that the majority of men and women are happiest when monogamous and faithful; it may be that many of those who do remain faithful to a single partner throughout life pay dearly in frustration, resentment of their mates and desiccation of their emotions.

The disapproved model seems better suited to the emotional capacities and requirements of many people, particularly men; it offers renewal, excitement and the continuance of experiences of personal rediscovery; it is an answer to the boredom of lifelong monogamy. We are by nature polygamous.[10]

[9]"Man, Morals, and Maturity," *Reader's Digest,* November 1965, 184.
[10]Morton Hunt, *The Affair* (New York: World, 1969), 22-23, 41.

Hunt undergirds this philosophy by appealing to the authority of leading psychiatrists and psychologists. This outlook, increasingly accepted even in some church circles, has spawned a whole family of aberrations.

For example, swinging life-styles are advocated in intellectual circles as good therapy for boring marriages. Not just an occasional "affair," but a whole life-style of continuous mate-swapping.

My wife and I came to see sex as . . . an important adult, person-to-person interrelating play activity. . . . Both my wife and I take a real delight in each other having pleasure experiences with other persons. . . . A necessary precondition for this to work well is complete trust that the precious "other" of a valued pair-relationship will not emotionally or physically desert the given partner—won't "fall in love," and so on, plus a working through of all the emotions and concept changes that are required.[11]

Adultery has thus come full circle. First engaged in as self-consciously illicit, then justified when there is true "love" between the paramours, next justified ideologically as a good thing, and finally total promiscuity, so long as "love" is *not* involved!

In such a society, even Christians ask, Why should God demand fidelity in a monogamous relationship for a lifetime? Laws of purity, built around God's wonderful gift of sexuality, are, like all his laws, designed for our good (Deut. 10, 12, 13). Violation means loss, not just because God promises punishment, though that would be reason enough for careful obedience. But God has established these standards to protect us from the loss that is inherent in one kind of behavior, and to direct us to the rewards that are the natural result of another. Violation of God's law of purity, just as violation of God's law of gravity, brings destruction. Keeping God's laws promotes one's own welfare.

In September 1975 *Redbook* startled itself and the nation with the revelation of the results of its study of 100,000 American women. The Redbook Report on Female Sexuality reported that the stronger a woman's religious convictions, the more likely she is to be satisfied with her sex life and marriage.

[11]C. Lee Hubbell, Readers' Forum on "Swinging," *The Humanist*, July-August 1974, 47-48.

Thus some theoreticians and many ordinary people are rediscovering the truth that sex God's way is best. Fidelity in marriage is good because it maximizes the potential relationship between mates; it maximizes sex itself; it protects the more vulnerable wife; it provides the atmosphere needed for children to grow up as whole people; and it safeguards a person's relationship with God.

Marriage is too good to risk diminishing its potential. People were made for a loving, permanent, exclusive, secure, intimate relationship. Sex is a delightful part of this. It enhances and brings to a periodic exquisite climax the enduring unity of spirit. But when physical intimacy is pulled out of the various elements of a marriage relationship and used separately, it fouls the whole relationship. Trust can never be quite the same again; a third party often intrudes on the intimacy, in the mind of one partner or both. True unity is fractured. In fact, so serious is the rupture that Christ indicated it could legitimately be affirmed as total and permanent (Matt. 5:32), though this is not a recommended or required response to infidelity.

Fidelity in marriage maximizes sex itself. The discipline of focusing one's mental fantasies on the marriage partner alone has the great benefit of intensifying sexual fulfillment. Furthermore, the pure in heart are safeguarded from the deception of an unreal world created by skillful photographers and makeup artists. The illusion created constantly in our society is that the world is filled with young, beautiful, available, eager, perfect bodies awaiting the conquest of the smart playboy or playgirl. One is easily seduced into thinking he is missing out on something, and by feeding his imagination on this fare he sets himself up for failure in a marriage that cannot compete with the mirage. If he had never indulged his mind in such a dream world, he might have discovered more quickly and more fully that sexual fulfillment itself is most intense, most enduring, and constantly growing only in the commitment of two who have become one flesh exclusively and permanently. The insecurity of a tentative relationship or of a defiled marriage cuts the heart out of the sexual activity itself. When one is not sure he is worthy of an ultimate, permanent love commitment or whether he is simply a desirable or available sex object, the sex-fun itself has a hollow ring, a bitter aftertaste, decreasing satisfaction.

Some have held that variety intensifies sexual pleasure. Perhaps so. Therefore the loving partner uses imagination in sex play, suspense, surprise. But variety in partners loses all the other ingredients that go to make the sex experience the climatic ecstasy it was designed to be.

Fidelity in marriage is a special protection for the most vulnerable partner, the wife. She is more vulnerable for at least three reasons. First, her deepest drive is not for physical sex so much as for belonging. When she shares her body in the secure bonds of permanent belonging, she is satisfied. But when the belonging is illusory or temporary or uncertain, she suffers loss at the deepest level, a loss that most men do not even understand, let alone experience.

Second, if the physical relationship is paramount, she can only compete for a few years. The male in our society does not suffer the same fate as the female. Advertising, the media, and cultural mores seem to dictate that a woman is physically attractive in direct proportion to her youth. Yet a true marriage focuses on oneness of heart, and in the realm of the spirit both partners have the potential of growing more and more beautiful throughout the years. When this is the basis, a woman grows in her sexual desirability through the years because that desirability is set in the context of total unity, loving giving of life, a lifetime of fully shared experience.

The third area of greater vulnerability is that the woman in our society does not have the role of aggressively seeking a partner. Though this has changed somewhat, the remarriage of men continues at a rate far surpassing that of women. For this reason, a broken marriage very often means acute loneliness for the ex-wife that the ex-husband may not experience. Finally, the woman left with children following a broken marriage becomes, statistically, the bottom rung of the financial ladder.

Fidelity is also a prerequisite for the kind of home atmosphere that grows children in wholeness to maturity. The love, the faithfulness, the integrity, the loyalty are all essential elements. Infidelity tells a child, "Your mother is not worth much and your father is a liar and a cheat. Furthermore, honor is not nearly as important as pleasure. In fact, my son, my own satisfaction is more important than you." Such a home is about the worst atmosphere in which a child could be raised. The greatest gift parents can give their children is the demonstration of faithful, loving commitment to each other.

Finally, fidelity in marriage is necessary if a person would be accepted by God. Sin separates from God, and impurity in mind and body is one way to break fellowship with God. More important, it is one way to hurt him grievously. Not only does the cheating partner harm himself, his mate, and his children, he is "crucifying the Son of God" (Heb. 6:6, NEB). Violations of one another are ultimately violations of God himself as Joseph testified (Gen. 39:9), David experienced (Ps. 51:4), and the prophet proclaimed (Amos 2:7).

ARTIFICIAL INSEMINATION

Does artificial insemination violate the marriage bond? Certainly inseminating a wife with her husband's sperm does not violate the law against adultery. But what of sperm from another donor? Or the use of a surrogate mother? Or of the implantation of a fertilized egg of another woman in the womb of an infertile wife? The Bible does not speak to these issues directly.

Is there a paradigm in the Old Testament practice of not-so-artificial insemination by the brother of a deceased spouse (Deut. 25:5-10)? Is it significant that this exception clause was strictly circumscribed? Not just anyone could perform this service. Although we may not find any direct Scripture to forbid artificial insemination, it nevertheless seems to stir deep psychological reactions in many people. Perhaps there is good reason for this.

Medical procedures for insemination certainly do not unite as "one flesh" the two participants, and the deeper unity of spirit is absent altogether. Normally the donor is not even known to the recipient, so the violation of these basic relationships of marriage does not happen. But still, most people testify of a hesitancy. Does this uneasiness about the procedure hint of a deeper level of unity—the deep mystery of partnership in creating life?

Certainly the unreasonable guilt felt by the partner who "failed" in the creative process is part of the trauma many have experienced. Surely the jealousy of one partner over a child that derives from his mate though not from him may be a source of continuing unease. But I cannot in good conscience affirm that such procedures are certainly sinful in the eyes of God.

Even should the procedure prove ethically neutral, however, it may not be the part of wisdom. If God is the one who opens the womb and shuts it (Gen. 29–30; 1 Sam. 1:5; Ps. 127:3; Isa. 66:9), if children are his heritage, perhaps we should stand back and allow him to continue to play this role, trusting him to fulfill some higher purpose in withholding children. Alternatives include adoption and the wonderful surprise of late pregnancies. Also, in the providence of God, childless couples often have made very unique contributions to the Kingdom of God because of the special resources available through their childless circumstances.[12]

INTERRACIAL MARRIAGES

Some have held that interracial marriage is prohibited in Scripture, but a careful reading of the texts will indicate that it was not Jewish-Gentile marriage as a racial mix, for many of the surrounding peoples were of the same "race," but believer-unbeliever marriage that God prohibited. It was not the foreignness of Solomon's wives but their foreign religions that led him astray.

Some have held that Paul's word about God setting "bounds of habitation" was an indication that God intended races to remain separate geographically, and thus maintain their racial purity. Therefore, by implication, God is against intermarriage. That can hardly be considered responsible exegesis, but this is the key New Testament passage for the teaching that racial intermarriage is wrong. In the first place, Paul's intent was the very opposite. He was speaking to the leaders of a people ("nation") who considered themselves different in origin and vastly superior to all others, whom they classified as barbarians. Paul tells these Greeks that God created them (no, they did not originally sprout from Grecian soil) and that God created all peoples from one. Some texts read "of one blood," but others

[12]For a detailed discussion of the ethics of artificial insemination, see Helmut Thielicke, *Theological Ethics*, vol. 3: *Sex*, trans. John Doberstein (Grand Rapids: Eerdmans, 1979), 248-268.

omit "blood," thus implying one human ancestor. Either way the point is the same: all are one. In line with this, Paul probably did not speak of "all nations" (Acts 17:26, NIV), but rather, "The whole human race." The entire text is aimed in precisely the opposite direction of this recent and strained interpretation.

But some say that Paul alludes here to Moses' hymn in which he uses similar terminology (Deut. 32:8). This is not much help to the position, however, because Moses is simply praising God for setting limits on the surrounding nations to provide a place for Israel.

If racial purity, apart from Israel as a community of faith (not a "race"), is part of God's plan, Scripture nowhere makes this evident. Learning a foreign language is hardly a sinful activity, and the same observation might be made of immigration—the only thing that could be directly implied from Paul's comment. If setting "the bounds of the peoples" were intended to imply that intermarriage is wrong, it does so only by the implication that if it is wrong to move the bounds (immigrate), then intermarriage becomes impossible. In other words, to make the implication of a prohibition on intermarriage stick, it would be necessary to forbid migration or moving outside of one's "bounds." If such an interpretation were true, all non-Indians should be deported from the United States. Perhaps the strongest evidence against such an interpretation is that the most important immigration of all time was ordered by God, not once but twice—from Ur and later from Egypt. In any event, the contention that interracial marriage is sinful has no biblical foundation.

On the pastoral side, it should probably be added as a footnote that cross-cultural marriages (as distinct from cross-racial marriages) are notoriously hazardous because of the nature of marriage. Those contemplating such a union should be made aware of the additional handicaps involved, for unity is much more difficult to achieve with one of another culture. Another major problem is the link with family each partner brings into the marriage. In some societies, children of mixed marriages may suffer. So it is that cross-cultural marriages may not be advisable, but they certainly cannot be held unethical on biblical grounds.

POLYGAMY

Monogamy is almost certainly the ideal marital arrangement for humankind. We must say "almost certainly" because the inference from Scripture is such, but, at the same time, we must admit that the Bible nowhere directly condemns polygamy and nowhere directly affirms monogamy as the only legitimate arrangement. Furthermore, polygamy is definitely not viewed in Scripture as sexual impurity. Marriage to a second partner was to be as indissoluble as to the first. Infidelity was in breaking that relationship or defrauding one of the wives, not in having the relationship and faithfully adhering to marriage vows.

The inferences of Scripture in favor of monogamy are two. To fulfill the purposes of marriage God created Adam and Eve as a monogamous couple. And in that couple, God's image was complete. We infer, therefore, that this was God's ideal.

On the other hand, unlike adulterous relationships, homosexual relationships, and other immoralities which violate one or more of the three basic purposes of marriage, polygamy does not inherently do so. Certainly the second purpose of having children and providing a home is a purpose accessible to a polygamous family. Furthermore, the purpose of reflecting God's nature could hardly be violated since God's love relationship is with many simultaneously. However, this observation leads naturally to a possible reason that monogamy clearly seems to be God's will for human beings. We are not infinite and we are fallen. Therefore, even if the first purpose of a marriage, oneness in body and spirit, could theoretically be fulfilled in a polygamous marriage, in practice it has not been done. Not being divine, the husband does not have the infinite capacity to love fully and equally all his wives (see Gen. 29:23, 28, 30), and the wife does not have the capacity to lovingly receive a rival to the husband's affection and attention (see 1 Sam. 1:6). So in practice, the primary purpose of marriage is consistently violated in polygamous households.

Although the male may be said to have, at least in his fallen state, built-in polygamous tendencies because of his powerful and nondiscriminating sex drive, the female's desire is for a caring, intimate, secure relationship. Perhaps these built-in counter-drives have had more to do with the structuring of a culture's marriage code than innate moral convictions. Social factors also have contributed. In societies where females far outnumber males (because of war, hunting, or other dangerous male activities) and the female is an economic benefit, polygamy has prevailed. But when male and female are in equal supply and the maintenance of a wife is an expense, monogamy prevails. For example, in the time of Christ, the *Pax Romana* (Roman peace), monogamy was the custom for Greek, Roman, and Hebrew.

Thus, left without direct teaching, we seek to reason philosophically and sociologically to reinforce the inference of monogamy in the original creative act. God created Adam and Eve, not Adam and Eve and Mary and Jane and Susan.

The second major basis for the inference is the teaching of Paul that a polygamous man was not eligible for holding the office of deacon or elder in the church. If the higher standard for spiritual leadership precluded polygamy, it could hardly have been viewed as an ideal. It will not do to argue that the requirement could have been nonspiritual in nature, for the context of requirements for office-holder, which includes both spiritual (e.g., "without reproach") and nonspiritual (e.g., "not a novice"), is predominantly of spiritual qualifications and seems to include this prohibition among life-style requirements.

There are five basic interpretations of the Pauline passages (1 Tim. 3:2, 12; Titus 1:6):

1. A few have held that he means an elder must be married. There is some difficulty in this since neither Paul nor Christ himself would be eligible for spiritual leadership in the church. Another problem in this passage itself is that if it is pressed that a person must be married, it would seem that he must also have children (1 Tim. 3:4), yet few hold that a married man without children should be barred from office. There seems no ready rationale for either requirement.

2. Some have held that this is merely an injunction to purity. He must be a "one-wife-sort-of-man." This has not commended itself to many both because of the grammatical construction and the lack of examples of the use of the term in this way, but also because the passage clearly seems to imply more than this.

3. The Roman Catholic view is to make the bishop the husband of the one church. This strained exegesis clearly comes

from superimposing a predetermined doctrine on this particular passage.

4. Some in our day interpret this to mean that a divorced and remarried person is no longer eligible for spiritual leadership. Some hold further—and consistently—that a person who is remarried after the death of his wife would be ineligible. Any second marriage would be out. This came to be the preferred interpretation of the ancient church. No second marriages were permitted. Since remarriage after the death of one's partner is seen by Paul as permissible (Rom. 7:2-3; 1 Cor. 7:39) or actually good (1 Tim. 5:14), this would seem to be a strange requirement.

5. The predominant interpretation is that polygamists are not permitted to hold positions of spiritual leadership in the church. Most interpreters who hold other views admit that this is included. The early commentators were unanimous in this view.

This teaching clearly makes monogamy God's ideal for spiritual leaders in the church and, by implication, a spiritual issue.

Other passages have been held to demand monogamy as the only moral standard acceptable to God, but none seem to hold up under scrutiny. Solomon clearly did wrong in violating the injunction against multiplying wives (Deut. 17:17). Adding and multiplying may not be the same, but 300 wives and 700 concubines would certainly qualify as "multiplying." Yet the condemnation of Solomon (1 Kings 11:1, 3) was almost certainly for marrying foreign idolatrous wives rather than for the number of wives.

Christ's teaching of what was intended from the beginning, that the two become one flesh, has been taken to forbid polygamy. But this is far from conclusive. If a polygamous society were assumed, Christ's teaching would be just as applicable—it is the breaking he is condemning, not the joining. My conviction is that Christ was not assuming the Old Testament polygamous context, but his own contemporary monogamous society, and that he was indeed affirming the permanence of a monogamous marriage. If he considered polygamy a good option, he could have pleased many by proposing it as at least one solution to the problem of troubled marriages. The teaching of Christ on divorce, however, simply does not address the question of polygamy.

The Old Testament law, though not condemning polygamy, did, however, control polygamous relations for the protection of the wives. "If he takes another wife to himself, he shall not diminish her food, her clothing or her marital rights" (Exod. 21:10). And the law of divorce applied equally to polygamous marriages. In other words, the overriding moral consideration was faithfulness, integrity, keeping covenant, whether to one wife or more than one. But the two evidences—the creative order and the church order—are so strong that the church is altogether correct in considering monogamy God's ideal.

What does this teaching have to do with our contemporary monogamous society? Two things. First, not all contemporary societies are monogamous. True, many of the polygamous societies of Africa, for example, are becoming monogamous because the sexes are equalizing in numbers, and extra wives have become a financial liability because of changing employment structures. But for the Christian missionary to require a polygamous seeker-after-truth to divorce all but his first wife in order to become a member of the church is clearly a violation of scriptural teaching. Certainly he is excluded from spiritual leadership as noted above, and it is quite legitimate to require monogamy as the standard for the yet-to-be married or those with only one wife at conversion, but to demand of the new believer that he put away one or more wives not only violates the pervasive teaching of Scripture on divorce, but causes great disruption in society and risks bringing the gospel into ill repute.

Second, it is significant to consider biblical teaching on polygamy since it is an integral part of the far more pressing issue of divorce and remarriage to which we now turn.

DIVORCE

It is hard to exaggerate the evil effects of divorce on the mates involved, the children, and on society, as the fabric of its basic institution rips apart. No wonder "God hates divorce" (Mal. 2:14-16). Some use statistics to show there is an unparalleled increase in the divorce rate, and others use statistics to prove there is not so great a change. When the highly unstable marriages of teens and of the previously divorced are left out, the normal pattern in American society is still permanent monogamy. But that the attitude toward divorce has changed in the church is beyond dispute. In 1965 *Christianity Today* reported:

In 95 percent of all divorce cases, either one or both partners did not attend church regularly. In regular church families, one marriage in fifty-seven fails. And in families that worship God publicly in church and privately in the home, only one marriage in five hundred breaks up.[13]

Twelve short years later a Knight-Ridder survey disclosed that one in fifteen clergy marriages ends in divorce.[14] In 1976 the United Methodist Church published a new book of rituals entitled *Ritual in a New Day,* including several services for sanctifying divorce proceedings. While conservative denominations predictably have responded more conservatively, even some of the most conservative have made concessions to the new realities.

If the increase in literature on the subject is any indication, an unprecedented ferment is in progress. *Divorce in the 70s: A Subject Bibliography* lists almost five thousand entries.[15] And the conflict on standards concerning divorce and extramarital sex is nowhere more intense than in the evangelical church. There are many contributing factors such as the shifting attitude toward the authority of Scripture. But the basic problem is still self-oriented thinking. The emerging duty-to-self ethic may prove to have been the greatest single factor contributing to the breakdown of the home. C. S. Lewis describes the problem in his inimitable way:

When I was a youngster, all the progressive people were saying, "Why all this prudery? Let us treat sex as we treat all our other impulses." I was simple-minded enough to believe they meant what they said. I have discovered that they meant exactly the opposite. They meant that sex was to be treated as no other impulse in our nature has ever been treated by civilized people. All the others, we admit, have to be bridled. Absolute obedience to your instinct for self-preservation is what we call cowardice; to your acquisitive impulse,

---

[13]Norman MacFarlane, "What Has Gone Wrong with Marriage?" (*Christianity Today,* 17 December 1965), 15.
[14]*Evangelical Newsletter,* 10 March 1978.
[15]Kenneth D. Sell, *Divorce in the 70s: A Subject Bibliography* (Phoenix: Oryx, 1981).

avarice. Even sleep must be resisted if you're a sentry. But every unkindness and breach of faith seems to be condoned provided that the object aimed at is "four bare legs in a bed."

Our sexual impulses are thus being put in a position of preposterous privilege. The sexual motive is taken to condone all sorts of behavior which, if it had any other end in view, would be condemned as merciless, treacherous and unjust.

Now though I see no good reason for giving sex this privilege, I think I see a strong cause. It is this. It is part of the nature of a strong erotic passion . . . that it makes more towering promises than any other emotion. . . . To be in love involves the almost irresistible conviction that one will go on being in love until one dies and that possession of the beloved will confer, not merely frequent ecstasies, but settled, fruitful, deep-rooted, lifelong happiness. Hence all seems to be at stake. If we miss this chance we shall have lived in vain. At the very thought of such a doom we sink into fathomless depths of self-pity.

Unfortunately these promises are found often to be quite untrue. Every experienced adult knows this to be so as regards all erotic passions (except the one he himself is feeling at the moment). . . . When two people achieve lasting happiness, this is not solely because they are great lovers but because they are also—I must put it crudely—good people: controlled, loyal, fairminded, mutually adaptable people. If we establish a "right to (sexual) happiness" which supersedes all the ordinary rules of behavior we do so not because of what our passion shows itself to be in experience but because of what it professes to be while we are in the grip of it. Hence, while the bad behavior is real and works miseries and degradations, the happiness which was the object of the behavior turns out again and again to be illusory. Everyone (except Mr. A. and Mrs. B. [two married people who are divorcing in order to marry each other]) knows that Mr. A. in a year or so may have the same reason for deserting his new wife as for deserting his old. He will see himself again as the great lover, and his pity for himself will exclude all pity for the woman.[16]

What does Scripture say about divorce? Christ taught clearly that God's original intent was permanence in marriage (Mark 10:1-12; Luke 16:18). The model is God himself (see the Book of Hosea) who, though grievously sinned against more than any human spouse, forgave and remained faithful to his covenant. Even in the Old Testament, divorce was explicitly forbidden in some cases (Deut. 22:13-21, 28-30).

At the same time, Moses, Jesus, and Paul recognized that the ideal was not always met and thus set up restrictions and safeguards to correct the failure or to limit the damage where uncorrectable.

In the key Old Testament passage (Deut. 24:1-4) Moses did not endorse divorce, but neither did he forbid it. He simply set up some guidelines to protect the wife when a husband divorced

16"Have We No Right to Happiness?" reprinted in *The Saturday Evening Post,* April 1982, 42-44.

her. Christ taught that this was a concession to "their hardness of heart" (Matt. 19:3-9), that is, to their sinfulness. The husband could not simply send her away; he had to make it official in writing so that she would be able to marry someone else and not be left as a pariah of society. Further, in some unexplained way, should she ever become free again, the first husband could not remarry her because she was "defiled." Since the rationale is not given, and since God's explicit instructions to Hosea seem to be the opposite—taking back the harlot again and again—most Protestants do not seek to apply this aspect of the law today in the church age.

But did Christ or Paul make any concessions to human failure? This is the crux of the debate. In both Matthew passages on the subject (Matt. 5:31-32 and Matt. 19:3-9) Christ forbids divorce "except on the ground of unchastity." For those who believe there is never any ground for divorce recognized by God, several approaches have been taken.

Some have disallowed the exception phrase, saying that Matthew added this as a commentary on what he felt Christ really intended, or the church or some later scribe added the exception to soften the teaching. To one committed to the independent authority of Scripture, such approaches are unacceptable. There is no textual evidence to cast serious doubt on the phrase as part of the original text, so we accept it as the authentic word of Christ.

The second line of attack on the traditional understanding is an appeal to a restricted definition of the term *unchastity* or *fornication*. This argument holds that there is indeed an exception, but that it is for the rare case of the Jewish man who in the betrothal period discovers that his espoused is not a virgin. The very serious obligation of Jewish betrothal could then be set aside and the contract broken, just as Joseph was of a mind to do with Mary (Matt. 1:19).

Others argue that *fornication* refers only to the specific sin of certain marriages forbidden in Leviticus 18. Why so limited? Because in the difficult Acts 15 teaching on what would be forbidden to Gentiles, Leviticus 17 and 18 is held to be the single Old Testament passage that refers to all four elements forbidden: eating strangled animals, (eating) blood, eating food sacrificed to idols, and fornication. The "fornication" of

Leviticus 18 is in the context of various ceremonial laws that applied only to the Jew, so that this exception made by Christ was recorded by Matthew who wrote especially for a Jewish audience who would understand and feel obligated by it. If the divorce, then, was because of a violation of one of the proscribed incestuous activities of Leviticus 18, it was legitimate. Divorce for any other kind of fornication was not intended, but in these special Jewish cases it would be demanded, the argument runs, because the marriage itself would be illegal. Of course, this argument assumes that the early church did put these ceremonial restrictions on the Gentiles and that Leviticus 18 is the reference point (interpretations that few accept). If the argument seems complicated and the exegesis torturous, that is because they are!

The problem with these arguments is that human language cannot be treated that way. The Greek word translated "fornication" is the broader term referring to all varieties of sexual sin. It includes incest, to be sure, and it also includes adultery, premarital sex, and homosexual relations. In fact if a person were looking for a word to describe every variety of sexual coital sin, this is the Greek word he would choose. If Christ had said, ". . . except for adultery," hearers would surely conclude that violating a betrothal contract and marriage to an in-law (incest in Lev. 18), for example, would be excluded, and only a married man having sexual relations with another man's wife or a married wife having relations with a person not her husband would be the exception. As it stands, the word includes the betrothal period of ancient Israel, incestuous relations, and indeed, other sins such as those recorded (curiously enough!) in the very same passage in Leviticus: adultery, bestiality, and homosexual relations. Words with a broader meaning cannot be restricted arbitrarily to a narrower meaning unless the context requires it. The context in the Matthew passages is silent on any possible restriction. Such restrictions must be imported from the outside, and that is not legitimate exegesis.

A third line of attack focuses on the grammar. It is said that the structure requires that divorce is permitted, but not remarriage following divorce. This interpretation is held by only a few grammarians; but most scholars say that the grammar used must be read to include both—that the exception is for divorce *and* remarriage.

In addition to questioning such an unusual understanding of the grammatical structure, there are two further objections to this line of reasoning. "Divorce" in the Old Testament and New Testament and in Greek and Roman society was specifically for the purpose of remarriage. This is what the term meant— dissolution of marriage, never simple separation. That was the point of Moses' teaching: A man may not simply send his wife away or abandon her. He must make it official and give her a document of divorce that will free her to marry (Deut. 24:1-4).

The second problem with the "divorce-but-not-remarry" view is that an exception for divorce without remarriage is no exception at all. He may be doing wrong, but he is not committing adultery, no matter what the reason for divorce, if he doesn't have sexual union with anyone else. This interpretation makes Christ speak nonsense: "But I tell you that anyone who divorces his wife, except for marital unfaithfulness, causes her to become an adulteress, and anyone who marries the divorced woman commits adultery" (Matt. 5:32, NIV). If Christ makes an exception to the rule only insofar as divorce is concerned and not remarriage, in what way is the divorced-but-single person committing adultery? Only the remarriage makes adultery an issue, and remarriage is exactly what divorce provided for in both the Hebrew and Greek societies.

A further disagreement has to do with the nature of the "test" the Pharisees had in mind in asking Christ if a man could divorce his wife for any reason. Some say that all the participants were well aware that the test was to see which of the Rabbinic schools Jesus would follow and thus trap him into offending those on one side or the other. Shammai held to the stricter interpretation of Deuteronomy 4 and held that divorce (and remarriage) was only permissible when there was some sexual impurity, possibly short of adultery since that was supposed to carry the death penalty (but rarely did). Hillel, on the other hand, held that anything at all was reason enough for a divorce. Which side would Christ take? If he simply reiterated Shammai, possibly tightening his exception a bit, so the argument runs, why would the disciples have been so amazed at the teaching and conclude that it would be better not to get married in the first place? Therefore, the argument goes, Christ made no exceptions at all (as in Mark and Luke) and rejected both schools of thought. Only this scenario adequately explains the disciples' shock, it is held.

To this we may respond that a heavy weight is put on speculation—rejecting the normal meaning of the key word, rejecting the normal structural analysis, rejecting the theological implications, simply to avoid an assumed contradiction between Mark and Luke on the one hand and Matthew on the other. As we shall see, the passages need not be in conflict, but the conjectural argument itself may need an answer.

In response, let me make other conjectures. Christ's exception was not nearly so broad as Shammai's. He restricted the exception to sexual immorality. He had answered, by implication, "No. I reject both interpretations" and then gave even tighter restrictions. This could easily evoke surprise from an audience hoping against hope that he would vote for Hillel. On the other hand, perhaps their response was the standard current reply to anyone who rejected the popular view of the Hillel in favor of Shammai. As long as we are speculating, maybe this wasn't the context of their thinking at all. Maybe, since Christ had just come into Herod's territory, the "test" was to trap Jesus by having him side either with the dead John the Baptist in condemning the king, or with Herod against the prophet who got killed for speaking against his marital relations.

In the final analysis, the decision must not be made on conjectural grounds, but on the text itself, or the possibilities for distorting the author's intended meaning are almost limitless.

One further argument is given in favor of "no exception" or exceptions not meaningful to any but Orthodox Jews. The early Church Fathers, it is said, all rejected the idea that there was intended any exception to the absolute rule against divorce. It surprises me to discover that evangelical writers appeal to the early Fathers on a subject like this. We are not speaking here of Apostolic Fathers, but of later writers during the time when celibacy gradually became the standard for a truly holy life. The whole context of the Fathers was of increasing capitulation to Greek dualism and the consequent view of marriage that Paul had predicted as part of apostasy: forbidding to marry. We must, with the Reformers, go back to the Scripture and find our sole authority there. But to accept the standard Protestant interpretation of Matthew 5 and 19 is said to leave Matthew in conflict with Mark and Luke.

It is difficult for me to see any contradiction between a passage that gives a law or principle and another that affirms it and adds an exception. Actually Christ said exactly the same thing in Matthew 19 as he said in Mark and Luke—no divorce. Then Matthew records that the Pharisees didn't let it go at that, but pressed him: If you are right, then Moses must be wrong, for he gave permission for divorce. Only then did Christ repeat the principle and add the exception. Did his second response contradict the first?

To give a standard in one passage of Scripture and then to give exceptions in another is common and quite legitimate. We may not improvise and add other exceptions. But if Jesus Christ, the Son of God, or Spirit-inspired authors clarified at a later time what was given at an earlier time, they have every right to do so. For example, in the Ten Commandments we find the absolute command, "Thou shalt not kill." Actually, we learn elsewhere it is wrong to kill most of the time, but killing animals, executing criminals, and killing in legitimate war are exceptions to the general rule. We may not add to this and improvise on the example of Scripture to say there are additional exceptions such as people who offend me grievously or with whom I can no longer live peacefully. If there are exceptions, Scripture alone may make them. Thus the general rule is "no divorce." Christ gave the rule himself. Then he made just one exception: When one party in the marriage cheats sexually, the other partner does not commit the sin of adultery if, following divorce, he remarries.

Are there other exceptions enunciated by later inspired authors? Probably. Paul, in 1 Corinthians 7, reaffirms the general principle: no divorce. In fact, he appeals to the words of Christ (v. 10). Furthermore, if a mate does leave (reason unspecified by Paul), he has only two options: remain unmarried or be reconciled to his mate. (Of course, if the mate remarries or commits adultery in some other way, Christ's teaching comes into play.) Then Paul deals with the problem of an unconverted mate who wants to leave. Don't coerce, says the apostle, let him go free. I assume this applies to any mate who is behaving like an unconverted person whether or not he is a church member. The majority opinion in Protestant circles has been that this is a second exception, a ground for legitimate divorce and remarriage: permanent desertion. Though recognition of the exception for adultery is all but universal, there are many who do not see this as a second exception.

The term "is not bound" (v. 15) is considered by many scholars to be a technical term often used for divorce; therefore, the one who has been permanently deserted is considered eligible for remarriage. Others hold that the freedom is simply to remain single, not feeling guilty for failing to hold on to the departing mate. Most hold that such "freedom" is hardly true freedom; one did not need apostolic approval to be deserted. But the interpretation may not be as clear-cut as Christ's exception.

Suppose someone is divorced and remarried on grounds other than adultery or permanent desertion? That person, according to Scripture, commits adultery. In contemporary Western society most people who have unwillingly been divorced will sooner or later have biblical grounds for remarriage. The unbelieving spouse, or the spouse behaving like an unbeliever, will almost certainly remarry, thus committing adultery, even if he or she does not have an illicit affair while married to the first spouse or divorced from him or her.

But what of the person who commits adultery by remarrying following a divorce which lacked biblical grounds? Is the sin forgivable? If so, on what grounds? Some have held that if by getting remarried a person commits adultery, it must mean that an adulterous relationship is entered and continues as long as the marriage continues. On this interpretation, the only sign of true repentance is to dissolve this adulterous relationship. Very few have held this view, possibly because the Scripture nowhere directly addresses the issue. Some appeal to the tenses of the verbs used in the Greek, but this is inconclusive since both continuous action and simple action verbs are used, and the nuance of tense cannot really be pressed into settling the issue anyway.

The only real help comes from the related problem of polygamy. Polygamy, like divorce, is not God's ideal. But once the commitment is made to a second wife, God required faithfulness to that commitment. He could not divorce his second wife any more than his first.[17] In a parallel way, to remarry following divorce on nonbiblical grounds is sinful, but to divorce again would simply be another sin that could not correct the first. The remarried person should remain married to his second mate. Another analogy is the person who marries an unbeliever. He sins in doing so, but once the contract is consummated, the marriage is the will of God, and breaking it becomes sinful.

In summary, then, God's will is monogamy, and divorce is wrong. If, because of either partner's "hardness of heart" (sin), divorce takes place, the believer should remain single. If adultery or permanent desertion are involved prior to or subsequent to divorce, the one who did not commit these sins does not necessarily sin by marrying another person. If he does commit the sin of adultery (as, for example, in a nonbiblical remarriage) or any other sin (as, for example, selfish behavior that drove a mate to divorce) and truly repents, God will forgive him and God's people should.

Some make a distinction between divorce prior to conversion and divorce subsequent to conversion, but the argument is not tenable. As with other ethical issues, biblical principles apply equally to the Christian and non-Christian. Repentance for sin is required of sinner and saint, and the making right of any wrong relationship as well. The same is true for wrongs that cannot be made right—upon repentance, the believer can no longer be held accountable whether or not the wrong was subsequent to conversion.

I have addressed the issue of divorce, not as a pastoral concern, but strictly in terms of the ethical issues involved. Nevertheless, there are certain additional complicated ethical issues involved in applying this basic biblical teaching. I do not offer this judgment with the same confidence as the preceding analysis of biblical data, but do seek to base it on biblical principle and not dodge the difficult issues involved.

[17]It seems clear from biblical data that fidelity in a polygamous relationship is more pleasing to God than breaking off a monogamous relationship and remarrying. A family is better able to fulfill God's three purposes in marriage with stable polygamy than with unstable monogamy. In fact, divorce and remarriage may well be viewed by God as serial polygamy, in which the greater of the sins is the breaking of commitments.

How does a Christian minister advise married people who are having problems? In the light of the preceding study, he should communicate God's standard that divorce is not an option.

The same advice would be for those separated or divorced for any reason. Remain single. Who knows but what the ex-mate's spouse may die and the opportunity be afforded to restore the original marriage? Use the state of singleness for the sake of the Kingdom. But if the person does not have the ability to remain single, and biblical grounds exist for divorce and remarriage, I would advise him or her that marriage to another is a legitimate option.

How does a minister decide concerning officiating at the wedding ceremony of one who has been previously married? Only for those who are divorced on biblical grounds or whose ex-mate subsequently provided biblical grounds (through adultery, remarriage, or, perhaps, permanent desertion) may the minister validate the marriage by participating in the ceremony "before God and his people" and in the name of the Trinity. Otherwise he will sin himself through giving official sanction to the sin of adultery when performing the ceremony.

Who should be accepted into full membership in the church? All those who give evidence of true repentance. If the person is in the process of deliberately violating God's law (for example, by continuing unbiblical divorce proceedings) he does not give evidence of repentance and should not be accepted until repentance has been demonstrated. What gross hypocrisy for a church to readily accept a repentant philanderer and to reject or ill-treat a devout Christian who has lived legally first with one mate and then with another!

What role in the church may be filled by a person who has been divorced and remarried? I am fully convinced that Paul excluded polygamists from roles of spiritual leadership. I am not certain whether he intended to exclude also those divorced but whose present marriage is the will of God. Since I am uncertain, I urge married people with a divorce in their past to play a support role rather than a leadership role. Even if Paul did not expressly exclude a technically monogamous person who has more than one living mate, the parallel to polygamy is too strong to ignore.

The more successful a person is in his public ministry and in his new marriage, the more temptation he provides for every person having marital problems. To them he is a constant reminder that divorce and remarriage may be a way out. The remarried couple can never model the permanent monogamy ideal. Far better to maintain a low profile and serve as a humble warning that there is a price to be paid, but at the same time demonstrating the glorious grace of God that one can be forgiven and useful in the Kingdom of God. I would hesitate to make this a law of the church, but thus I would counsel.

NONMARITAL VIOLATIONS OF   4/14.
GOD'S PURPOSES FOR SEXUALITY

SEXUAL COVETOUSNESS

Sexual relations not only begin in the mind, but the primary sex organ is the mind. For example, it is very difficult to have satisfying physical relationships with one who is repulsive; that is, one whom the mind does not appreciate. Christ was reinforcing this basic psychological and spiritual fact that sex at root is mental when he said:

> You have heard that it was said, "You shall not commit adultery." But I say to you that every one who looks at a woman lustfully has already committed adultery with her in his heart. (Matt. 5:27-28)

There are two common errors in interpreting Jesus' words. Some hold that to look with desire is the same as committing the act. Others hold that there is no sin in sexually desiring someone other than one's wife; there is sin only if a man fantasizes having sexual relations with that person.[18]

To hold that the thought and the act are the same in God's eyes is to ignore Scripture and to trivialize sin. Christ is not saying that they are of equal gravity, but that the desire itself is sinful and the same variety of sin as adultery, just as hatred itself is sinful and the same variety of sin as murder. It is not bad because it might lead to sin; it is bad because it *is* sin, the sin of adultery in its initial stage.

[18]Letha Scanzoni, "See No Evil?" *The Other Side,* February 1978, 22.

Definition of Lust. What exactly is the sin of lust? Obviously, for a person to imagine having sexual relations with another is "to commit adultery" in his mind. But is this all? The structure of the sentence in Greek does not settle the question, so it is necessary to examine the meaning of the word itself. The word translated "lust" could also be translated "desire" or "covet." A careful study of the New Testament teaching concerning sexual lust makes the conclusion inevitable that sexual covetousness is to desire any kind of sexual pleasure or satisfaction with anyone who may not legitimately provide that pleasure.[19] To covet is to strongly desire something that cannot be yours in the will of God. Is the imagined act not acceptable? Then neither is it right to entertain the activity in imagination.

Columnist Abigail Van Buren ("Dear Abby") regularly advises inquirers that sexual fantasy is normal and harmless—even beneficial so long as the imagined illicit relationships are not carried out. She says that the teaching of Christ on lust is one of the most damaging religious teachings ever perpetrated on the human race. Why, then, do we hold that a mental activity considered so harmless and fun is actually sinful?

If procreation were the only purpose in human sexuality, if humans were no more than animals, perhaps fantasizing would be harmless. But God had other purposes in mind, purposes that are violated mentally almost as severely as they would be by the act itself. He did not simply create male and female; he created them for one another in an intimate, permanent bond of marriage, a oneness patterned after his own nature. For this high purpose to be fulfilled, the intimacy must be exclusive and the commitment permanent or it is no oneness. Faithfulness is most importantly of the mind. Exclusive intimacy, permanent commitment, and mutual trust are violated first in the mind.

Mental infidelity, as it erodes the unity of marriage, simultaneously destroys the marriage as a demonstration of the unity of God the Father, Son, and Spirit. To imagine intimacy with anyone other than the marriage partner is to break unity and thus to distort the image of God. As Joseph and David

[19]See word study on "Covet" in Robertson McQuilkin, *Understanding and Applying the Bible* (Chicago: Moody, 1983), 99-106. Also see J. A. Motyer, "Idolatry," in *The New Bible Dictionary,* ed. J. D. Douglas et al., 2d edition (Wheaton, Ill.: Tyndale, 1982), 505.

testified, sexual sin is first and foremost sin against God (Gen. 39:9; Ps. 51:4).

Sexual covetousness is not the same for the married and unmarried. Just as there is a difference between coveting a neighbor's house and shopping for a house which is for sale, so thoughts of marriage on the part of those eligible for marriage are not the same as similar thoughts by a married person for someone other than his mate. Nevertheless, Scripture condemns fornication on the part of the unmarried in the same terms as adultery on the part of the married, and thus the teaching on lust is directed to both single and married persons.

How do we go about making a distinction when Scripture does not spell it out? Perhaps the key is in the biblical link between thought and act. Any thought that would be immoral to act out is sinful lust. For an engaged person to imagine a kiss with his betrothed would be innocent; for a married person to imagine this of a person to whom he is not married would be wrong. Just as it is wrong for unmarried people to have intercourse (fornication), so to fantasize about it would be sinful lust. Notice that Christ did not say, "He who desires to look on a woman has committed adultery." The enjoyment of a woman's beauty is not of itself lustful desire. A man is guilty of immorality not when he enjoys a woman's beauty but when he mentally uses sexually any woman who does not rightfully belong to him. Whenever he imagines an embrace and there is physiological change in preparation for copulation, he is "looking with desire."

Temptation by a sexually attractive object and yielding to sexual fantasizing must not be confused. Temptation is not sin. Sexually desiring someone not rightly yours is. Can a Christian man look at an attractive woman, enjoy her beauty, and not lustfully desire her? Certainly, but no normal man can give himself to a steady diet of appreciating female bodies, other than his wife's, and not begin to have illicit sexual desires.

Sexual desire has something in common with appetite. When a person is completely satiated with food, drink, or sex, the desire goes away. But only for a time. Then the desire begins again and, until it is fully satiated a nibble of food or a momentary sexual fantasy does not satisfy. It is not designed to do so. It stimulates the desire for more.

Therefore, when an earnest Christian finds himself tempted to lustful desire, he should cry to God for deliverance (1 Cor. 10:13). Furthermore, he should starve the appetite—give no occasion to the flesh (Rom. 13:14)—avoid the thing, the person, the place, the activity that sets the stage for sexual temptation. In fact, as necessary, flee—run from the tempting situation (Gen. 39:12; Prov. 5:8; 2 Tim. 2:22).

Tolerance for the appreciation of feminine beauty without sinful desire differs, just as tolerance for the appreciation of a desirable object without coveting it differs. If the sexual stimulation of the typical worldly magazine is too much for a person to control, he should not read it even though it might be harmless to another. If he cannot enjoy the figure of a normally dressed woman without desiring her, like the typical man of the world, he had better learn to avert his eyes. Our world is so sex-saturated that advertising, styles, entertainment—virtually every facet of life—seems devoted to the purpose of sexual seduction. Each person must determine his tolerance and deliberately set rigid limits beyond which he will not go (1 Thess. 4:3-7), limits that allow enough of a safety factor so that he is never tempted "beyond that he is able." Increasingly in Western society the same temptations and principles apply to women, though Jesus addressed only the male.

Just because a painting, photograph, film, or woman does not immediately stimulate sexually does not necessarily mean one is within his limits of tolerance. There is a cumulative effect. Moral pollution is very much like atmospheric pollution—one may not be conscious of the buildup in levels of pollution until he is damaged by it. Exposure to sexually attractive objects may be quite innocent, but the cumulative effect can make one vulnerable. It is quite possible to live constantly free of sexual imaginings, fantasies, mental scenarios. Failure in this is an immediate warning signal that exposure to temptation has been too great and must be deliberately, even painfully cut back. This is what Jesus said: "If your right eye causes you to sin, pluck it out and throw it away; it is better that you lose one of your members than that your whole body be thrown into hell" (Matt. 5:29).

Thus we are instructed to deal severely with temptation. This means not only to avoid temptation but to avoid being a temptation to others. Therefore the Bible teaches modesty in dress.

Modesty. The teaching of Christ on sexual desire which we have just considered is the strongest teaching on modesty. Lust is sin; and equal wrong is to cause another to sin (Matt. 18:6-7; see also Rom. 14:13, 15, 21; 1 Cor. 8:9-13). The Christian, therefore, will never deliberately dress to entice others to sexual desire.

The Bible does not say a great deal about nudity, but there are some clear indications of God's will (Gen. 2:25; 3:7-11; 9:22-23; Exod. 20:26; 28:42-43). It can be seen from God's encounter with Adam and Eve following the Fall that God has put his good gift of marriage under wraps to save it for the one of his choice. The human body is not shameful, but beautiful; when God created man and woman he said, "It is good." And, we are told, they were naked and not ashamed. But the human body is exclusive, sacred, and private—it belongs to the one other person God has given in marriage (1 Cor. 7:3-5). To unclothe certain parts of the human body is sexually stimulating to normal members of the opposite sex. Therefore, when one's dress induces lust in another person, it is sinful.

But that which is tempting differs from society to society and from era to era. In India, for example, the calves of a woman's legs are covered, but not necessarily the midriff. In old Japan it was the nape of the neck that enticed, and the daring geisha would arrange the collar of her kimono to expose a bit more of her neck. In certain African tribes the loose woman wears a bra and the modest girl goes topless, whereas in a South American tribe it is the opposite: modest women wear sleeves and tops, but no bottoms. The most shameful thing would be to expose the armpits. Modesty, then, has something to do with culture—how dress is viewed by a particular people. Biblical modesty is not to be controlled by the surrounding culture, of course, but it is certainly influenced by it.

To further complicate matters, styles keep changing, at least in the twentieth-century Western world. And the changes are not always neutral. A fallen society uses dress not to enhance personhood or inner beauty of spirit, but to exploit human weakness for financial profit. James Laver, the leading authority on the history of dress, attests to this:

> But, after a short time, . . . excessive concentration on an area brings its own penalty. The portion of the body in question becomes too familiar; it becomes a bore; or, as the psychologists say, it "exhausts its erotic capital." Now the emphasis changes, the zone shifts. The new zone always seems a little indecent at first. But that emotional impact is the real reason for the change.
>
> Did they not promote the lust of the eye? Of course they did. That was their object. So fashion and prudery began the fencing match that has lasted to this day.[20]

The world is constantly seeking to press the Christian into its own sinful mold, and the modest Christian, aware of this, will not adopt any new style that is ostentatious, drawing attention to self, or that increases sex appeal, until the style is no longer ostentatious or stimulating. Rather than join in the vanguard of change, the modest woman will wait until the new style has a history long enough so that spiritually mature Christian men testify the style no longer need be a temptation to lustful desire.

What of nudity or seminudity in art? Much of contemporary print and cinema, photography and TV is designed to be sexually stimulating. A Christian who participates in producing such art is violating God's standard of modesty. He is causing others to stumble. The unclothed figure in fine art is probably not sexually stimulating to many, though there are exceptions—some "fine art" is designedly erotic, and some people are more easily tempted. But whatever one's judgment on that issue, one point is beyond dispute: Modeling for such art is not the role of a Christian. The historic record of the moral failure of artists and their models attests to the incompatibility of nude modeling and purity.

Modest dress, beginning in the Garden of Eden, is God's wrapping for the wonderful gift of marriage. It is his fence around the pure mind of the sincere Christian, protecting it for the uninhibited fulfillment of erotic love in the exclusive intimacy and permanent commitment of marriage.

Pornography. Pornography, by definition, is the portrayal of sexually oriented material, in writing or in visual form,

[20]James Laver, "What Will Fashion Uncover Next?" *Reader's Digest,* September 1965, 149-150.

deliberately designed to stimulate sexually. Outside of marriage this means incitement to lust, according to biblical standards, and therefore deliberate seduction, deliberate temptation. This fact of contemporary life points up the problem with pornography—can it be demonstrated to be harmful to the individual viewing it, to society at large, and to the people who produce, model, and perform?

The controversial Presidential Commission on Pornography appointed in 1967 concluded that no personal change or adverse effects in youth or adults from viewing pornography could be demonstrated and therefore recommended that all legal restrictions on all pornography be lifted. But the claim that books and pictures have no influence on reader or viewer is patently false, as any advertising agent can testify.

Certainly, viewing pornography or anything else can be expected to influence the thinking of the viewer. But is it necessarily a bad influence? Letha Scanzoni thinks not:

What should we say to the Christian woman who, after attending with her husband an X-rated movie for the first time, said she wished they had seen it fifteen years ago? She said it would have helped them so much in their sexual relationship. Sex had been a problem throughout their marriage because she had felt so inhibited and afraid of certain techniques.[21]

Some in a panel of scholars, primarily from Calvin College and Seminary, seemed to take an even stronger pro-pornography position in the March 1974 issue of *The Reformed Journal*:

Feikens: I don't want to walk away from this part of the conversation by saying that a Christian artist may not write or make a movie that deals with sex in a prurient way, in an itching, longing way, or in a lascivious way. To achieve his artistic aims he may have to depict it in that way.

Wolterstorff: The Christian artist can do two things: one, he can depict degraded sex. . . . And, two, it's not inherently wrong for him to arouse sexual desire. He can write with a prurient intent.

Another participant emphasized that true art does not merely describe or depict emotions and activities—it causes the reader or viewer to vicariously experience them. Through genuine art the reader or viewer should experience the excitement and thrill

[21]Scanzoni, "See No Evil?" 23.

of heterosexual sex or revulsion at depraved sex. But what does Scripture say to this?

Whoever looks at a woman to desire her has committed adultery already in his mind. . . . Whatever is true, whatever is honest, whatever is just, whatever is pure, whatever is lovely, whatever is of good report, if there is any virtue, and if there is any praise, think on these things. . . . For it is a shame even to speak of those things which are done of them in secret. . . . But fornication, and uncleanness let it not be once named among you, as becomes saints; neither filthiness, nor foolish talking, nor jesting, which are not fitting. . . . Who, knowing the judgment of God, that they who commit such things are worthy of death . . . have pleasure in those that do them . . . flee youthful lusts . . . make no provision for the flesh. (KJV)

The average person will certainly be influenced to sexual lust by reading or viewing pornography. After all, that is the intent. Is there also an influence on society? From a biblical perspective, no sin is strictly private; there is always a bad effect on those associated with the sinner. This is especially true of lust. The relationship of husband and wife or with a future mate is damaged by every thought that damages the unity of the two. In fact, the thought often does lead to action, and no immoral act ever came from any place but the thought in someone's mind. There is not only the damaging effect on the marriage partner, resulting from a lessened bond and the invasion of exclusive intimacy, but on the children who must live under the leadership of an impure, cheating parent. In fact, in the case of the Christian, every one he touches will be affected by the loss of integrity as a true reflection of Christ and the consequent loss of personal spiritual power.

Beyond these personal relationships, however, many are concerned with the impact of pornography on society at large. Not all agree with the monumental study done by Joseph Daniel Unwin, but his conclusions are documented by a persuasive array of historical data.[22] Unwin, setting out to dispel the idea that any causal relationship exists between sexual morality and cultural advance, actually was forced to conclude the opposite. He found no exception in any human culture to his conclusion that "there is a strict correlation between the extent of sexual

[22]Joseph Daniel Unwin, *Sex and Culture* (Oxford: Oxford University Press, 1934).

regulation leading towards a strict monogamy and the extent of cultural achievement."[23]

A blue-ribbon panel of experts, in the Attorney General's 1986 Commission on Pornography, reversed virtually every conclusion of the earlier Commission![24] With detailed documentation the link between hard-core pornography and all kinds of crime and other social evils was established.

The law is clearly violated, with no First Amendment protection or controversy, when child pornography or violence connected with sex is depicted. The commission documented in grim detail the widespread illegal production and sale of this kind of pornography.

The Justice Department began to prosecute illegal operations on an unprecedented scale. Prior to this, federal attorneys rarely prosecuted, for fear of being unsuccessful against the common appeal to First Amendment freedoms.

In the private sector, the Religious Alliance Against Pornography (RAAP) convened what must have been the broadest representation of religious leaders in American history in November 1986 to consider the implications of the report and to map a strategy for the fight against illegal pornography. RAAP has led in successful clean-up battles in cities like Cincinnati and Atlanta. Several leaders at the Washington strategy conference stated publicly that the real cancer in American society was not the illegal pornography but the legal variety that is spreading unchecked throughout all segments of the population, changing our thinking, values, and behavior in regard to sexuality, women, and the home. But the only way so broad a representation could be enlisted, the leadership held, was to unite on the illegal brand of pornography. Pragmatically, the larger and the deeper problem was postponed until the day the easier battle has been won.

The RAAP's fears about the spread of porn bring us to another consideration. There is another victim of pornography that is not often considered: the subject of the photography or live production and the writer of pornography. Of late there is an outcry against the use of children in pornography, and in

[23]Rousas J. Rushdoony, *The Politics of Pornography* (New Rochelle, N.Y.: Arlington House, 1974), 146.
[24]*Final Report of the Attorney General's Commission on Pornography* (Nashville: Rutledge Hill Press, 1986).

Denmark the humane society decries the increasing use of animals in portraying bestiality, but adults are considered free agents and no victims at all. True, feminists decry the woman's role in pornography, but not so much the brutalizing effect on the performer as the demeaning of the woman's role. And this subjugation of women is indeed the normal fare of pornography. Little is said of the degrading effect on the performer himself. And yet the model, the performer, the writer, and all who participate in the production and distribution of pornography are sinning and causing others to sin.

One further word is needed concerning the impact on society of the pornographic industry. There is a demonstrable relationship between pornography and violence. Rushdoony documents extensively the philosophical neosadism that has erupted in Western society in recent years.[25] The Marquis de Sade (1740–1814) has given his name to our vocabulary: sadism, the inflicting of pain on another for personal pleasure. His view of every woman as being the rightful object of any act desired by any man, his homosexual preferences and advocacy of bestiality and every form of degradation, all provide the philosophical basis and, indeed, the detailed script for much contemporary pornography. Consider the words of the Marquis himself.

It becomes incontestable that we have received from Nature the right indiscriminately to express our wishes on all women. . . . It cannot be denied that we have the right to decree laws that compel women to yield to the flames of him who would have her; violence itself being one of that right's effects, we can employ it lawfully. Indeed! has Nature not proven that we have that right, by bestowing on us the strength needed to bend women to our will? . . . The issue of her well-being, I repeat, is irrelevant.[26]

Whether or not the philosophical underpinning outlined by Rushdoony can be proved conclusively, the parallels between the flood of pornography unleashed since the Supreme Court decisions of the 1950s and 1960s is remarkably faithful to the blueprint provided two centuries ago by de Sade. Small wonder, then, that " 'Organized crime,' says a Washington official,

[25]Rushdoony, *Politics of Pornography*,, 50ff.
[26]Richard Seaver and Austryn Wainhouse, eds. *The Marquis de Sade: The Complete Justine, Philosophy in the Bedroom and Other Writings* (New York: Grove Press, 1965), 318-320.

'dominates the traditional porn industry, as well as massage parlors, topless bars and strip joints.' "[27] Pornography destroys spiritually all who involve themselves in producing or using it, and its corrupting influence spills over into the entire life of the society that tolerates it.

PROVISION FOR THE FLESH

Christ indicated two sources of temptation to lust—sight and touch (Matt. 5:28-30). We considered earlier the temptations through sight, and here we must honestly include temptation through touch. Physical touch normally stimulates the desire for more intimate contact and is biologically designed to prepare for sexual relations. Therefore, care must be exercised in evaluating the potential for temptation in oneself and in others through casual physical contact with sexually attractive people. "Make no provision for the flesh."

Social dancing is an area that can raise ethical questions. Certainly many people who enjoy dancing have no erotic intention. But for most normal males social dancing that involves touching is erotic, and it is not likely that he can participate and not be stimulated to sinful sexual desire (unless, of course, he is dancing with his wife). In fact, the leading bestseller in the 1970s among the new genre of uninhibited sex manuals reinforces this common-sense evaluation: "All ballroom dancing in pairs looks toward intercourse. In this respect the Puritans were dead right."[28]

Left-wing evangelicals who advocate pornography as therapy and explicit sexual portrayal as authentic art no doubt agree that dancing can be sexually stimulating, but nevertheless hold it as harmless. But for the one who takes seriously New Testament teaching on purity of mind, to choose to dance with someone other than one's mate is to deliberately choose to "make provision for the flesh," either for oneself or for one's dance partner.

Young adults often tell me of struggles with sexual temptation. At the same time, they constantly testify to "making provision for the flesh," often innocently. One godly and attractive young leader told me that a good-night kiss with a

[27] *Time,* 5 April 1976, 61.
[28] Alex Comfort, *The Joy of Sex* (New York: Simon and Schuster, 1972), 162.

date was not sexual with him and was no temptation. I agreed that it could hardly be a sin for him if that were his mental response, though it might be a temptation to his date. Then I asked if no girl at all aroused him through a good-night kiss. He laughed. Oh, of course, with some girls it was sexually exciting. I was able to point out, but not to convince him, that this experience was the crux of the issue. Only sexually attractive people normally stimulate. He reflected on our conversation for several days and later sought me out. "I feel like I must tell you that you are right. I'm no different from any other guy. I've been kidding myself. Some girls I enjoy kissing specifically because of the sexual stimulation." I have had this kind of conversation too often to believe it is the exception. "Make no provision for the flesh."

SEX EDUCATION IN SCHOOLS

Sex education of children in the public school is definitely not designed to stimulate sexually, at least by most responsible sex educators. Rather, the purpose, even behind the clearing-house of sex education materials, Sex Information and Education Council of the U.S. (SIECUS), is to help children avoid the rampant sexual evils of our society and develop responsible and fulfilling sexual life-styles. Some, like the Planned Parenthood Federation, are deliberately out to change society and rid it of Judeo-Christian ethics. But most advocates of sex education aim to curb the results of sexual activity which all in a pluralistic society can agree on as evil: unwanted pregnancy, venereal disease, AIDS, sexual violence, and personally unfulfilling emotions, attitudes, and actions.

Perhaps the debate will never be settled scientifically as to whether biologically explicit education concerning human sexuality promotes or inhibits sexual activity or undesirable behavior. Some hold that sexual activity is promoted by public display and discussion of all types of sexual activity; others hold that society's social ills are diminished. This debate not only may be unresolvable, since the conclusions depend so much on the presuppositions of the investigator, but it actually misses the point altogether so far as the biblical Christian is concerned.

For the Christian, the proper question is, Is it possible to teach an acceptable view of human sexuality in a value-free, nonjudgmental context? A true view of human sexuality, unlike a true view of mathematics, physics, or English grammar, cannot be achieved apart from a biblical view of human sexuality. It would be like proposing to study engineering while agreeing in advance to rule out mathematics. Sex without love, without permanent commitment in a monogamous marriage, is not the same as sex with these crucial elements. In fact, to teach sex without the elements of the primary purpose of oneness is not merely an inadequate treatment of the whole subject, it is inherently subversive of the real thing.

But the public school in the United States may not teach sex (or anything else) in a biblical context. One of the most pernicious myths of the twentieth century is the notion of value-free education. To teach sex as if it were merely physical, or to teach all viewpoints about sexual behavior as if it made no difference, is a very powerful value indeed. It represents commitment to a relativistic ethic, and nothing could be more destructive of a true understanding of sex. Sex education in the public school must, if it is taught lawfully, portray a view of sex that reduces commitment. Sex as technical knowledge inevitably reduces the single most important ingredient of fulfillment in sex and marriage: commitment.

Of course, the ideal is to have the technical knowledge and the commitment, along with the biblical knowledge of what sex is all about. And the sad thing is that no more than 10 percent of Christian parents even attempt to provide this kind of education. How can this be changed? What role should the church play? The Christian school? In the interest of salvaging the rapidly deteriorating family, now under assault not only in entertainment but in legislation and education as well, the questions must be answered.

MASTURBATION

It is said that 90 percent of all males over age fifteen have experienced some form of self-induced orgasm at least once. Many masturbate regularly. Among females the estimates range from 40 percent to 60 percent who have had at least one erotic experience through self-stimulation. There is no demonstrated biological drive for release on the part of the female, but the male experiences a build-up of sperm until some form of ejaculation becomes biologically necessary in most males. This release can come consciously through sexual relations with another person, it can be self-induced, or it can come unconsciously in an emission during sleep, often accompanied by a dream. A sexually permissive and sex-promoting society may increase the incidence of masturbation, but it is common in all societies. What does the Bible say to this? Nothing—at least not by direct commendation or condemnation. What, then, do Christians say to the questions which arise so insistently?

Historically, most churches have spoken against masturbation. Many myths have spread concerning adverse physical results of masturbation, but these have all been discredited upon scientific investigation in recent decades. Nevertheless, either because it is wrong and the conscience, knowing this, brings condemnation, or because the churches or society have spoken against it as wrong, the most common response still seems to be a sense of guilt or shame about the practice. But in recent years a number of Christian marriage counselors have followed the lead of secular psychologists in condoning or advocating masturbation.

There seem to be four viewpoints among Christians who speak to this issue:

1. Masturbation is a gift of God.
2. It is probably all right if not indulged in with lustful fantasies, is not compulsive, is not performed in a group and does not produce guilt.
3. It is probably wrong because it is against nature and may be in violation of the biblical law of purity.
4. It is certainly wrong.

Until the last half of this century the church held that masturbation is certainly wrong, and, though there are no statistics to validate this judgment, it is likely that most evangelicals adhere to this position or to the position that it is probably wrong. Since both positions lean on the same arguments, let me combine the two positions.

Though the Bible does not speak directly to this issue, neither does it speak to many other issues which we hold to be moral questions: polygamy, slavery, pornography, drug abuse, abortion, sex-play by the unmarried. The Bible may not speak to this particular issue because young people were married much earlier and achieved sexual maturity much later than today. In Bible times marriage was ordinarily consummated from the twelfth birthday onward, and the first menstrual period occurred at eighteen, whereas in America today the age at marriage averages in the early twenties and the first menstrual period is at thirteen.[29] Thus in ancient Jewish society temptation to masturbation was greatly reduced. It is our early sexual maturity, coupled with a late age of marriage, that creates the pressure to find alternate sexual outlets. So it is not surprising that Scripture does not address the issue. In any event, the argument from silence is notoriously inconclusive. Rather, we should ask, does Scripture hold us to any principles that would preclude autoeroticism?

Christ indicated the beginning of sexual sin (mental sexual desire), and Moses gave the ending (sexual intercourse with a person other than one's marriage partner), so that any form of sexual activity in between would seem to be included. Since most masturbation is connected with sexual fantasy or imagination, that form of it, at least, is wrong. Even when this is not so, 1 Corinthians 7:4 gives the clear principle that one's body does not belong to oneself but to one's partner so far as sexual activity is concerned.

Furthermore, self-stimulation, at least apart from sexual play in marriage, violates two and probably all three of God's purposes in marriage. The first purpose of marriage is oneness; sex was designed to cement and promote that oneness. Masturbation runs in the opposite direction. It is sex stripped of love, stripped of commitment, stripped of all the purposes for which sex was created. Rather than uniting with another for mutual fulfillment, it is typically pure self-centeredness. The second purpose of marriage is procreation, and, needless to say, masturbation does not promote that. In fact, it is advocated by some as an excellent form of population control. The third purpose of marriage, reflecting the image of God, would also seem to be violated since the self-induced sex act is by definition isolated from one's rightful partner and self-oriented.

[29]Ronald L. Koteskey, "Growing Up Too Late, Too Soon," *Christianity Today*, 13 March 1981, 25.

I personally feel that if it is impossible from Scripture to make an absolute case for forbidding the practice, it is impossible to make a clear case for condoning it. One thing is clear, "whatever is not of faith is sin," and if one does not have a solid conviction of God's approval, based on Scripture, this behavior is wrong at least for him.

The most important means beyond prayer at the time of temptation is to starve the appetite—cut out as much sexually stimulating intake as possible. Self-discipline is God's formula for fulfillment. Certainly feeding the sexual appetite will not help the problem.

Second, the involuntary nocturnal emission is nature's (if not God's) release valve and is no grounds whatsoever for a sense of guilt. When erotic dreams accompany the emission, they *may* be related to overexposure to sexual stimulation during conscious hours.

What of female release? Let it be emphasized that in the case of the female there is no proven biological pressure, so that if there is any pressure other than the desire for pleasuring oneself, it is psychological. For this reason Herbert J. Miles says, "Frankly, I don't see how we can justify the female masturbating."[30] To which Letha Scanzoni replied, in the same article, "I can't go along with a double standard." In other words, the only justification for Charlie Shedd's position ("I think it can be a lovely release for the female") is an appeal to sexual equality. But the reason urged for the inevitability (and thus the rightness) of ejaculation in the male can reasonably apply only to the male.

Then there is another way of release for both male and female: sublimation. While deliberately choosing to stay away from people, material, places, and occasions that lead to masturbation, one devotes energy to "draining off or burning up sexual desire through physical and mental exercise, activities and projects."[31]

SEX BEFORE MARRIAGE

Though the violation of God's wonderful purposes for sex begins in the mind, it does not ordinarily end there—sex was

[30]Herbert J. Miles, "But What about Right Now?" *Campus Life,* March 1972, 42.
[31]Ibid.

never intended to be merely imaginary, but to be enacted. The greatest emphasis in biblical teaching on sexual impurity concerns behavior. Furthermore, it soon becomes clear that violation of God's purposes for marriage can take place prior to marriage. What, then, is God's standard of conduct in sexual relationships for the single person?

Premarital Relations. Sexual relationships outside marriage, including sex prior to marriage, are explicitly forbidden in Scripture. In the Old Testament this is seen in two ways.

First, the law concerning sexual relations with an unmarried woman held that the man, by possessing her sexually, was thereby taking her to wife (Exod. 22:16). "There is to be no intercourse where marriage is not intended, and once the sexual act has taken place, marriage has already been initiated: the two have become one flesh."[32]

Second, "whoredom" is excoriated throughout the Old Testament, and the term refers to relationships on the part of the unmarried. In other words, "premarital sex" either did not exist (it initiated marriage), or it was a form of prostitution. The New Testament also is very clear in condemning fornication (Acts 15:20; 1 Cor. 6:9, 13, 18; Gal. 5:19; Eph. 5:3; Col. 3:5; 1 Thess. 4:3). Why this condemnation? Because sexual relationships *before* marriage damage the fulfillment of God's purposes *in* marriage.

The primary purpose in marriage is oneness—mutual fulfillment, exclusive loyalty, and intimate identity in all of life (Gen. 2:18, 24; Eph. 5:21-32). None of this can take place outside marriage. So those who engage in only the physical are deceived about the nature of unity, and thus reduce the potential before the real, total unity even begins. The second purpose, procreation, in the setting of providing a loving family, is by definition violated. It is not even intended, and if pregnancy happens by accident, it is considered an evil. Finally, the prior infidelity to one's partner-to-be certainly distorts the reflection in the human model of a faithful God. God designed sex to be an exclusively monogamous relationship for human welfare.

[32]Richard F. Lovelace, *Homosexuality and the Church* (Old Tappan, N.J.: Revell, 1978), 109.

This means that the most exquisite of physical delights can be fully experienced only in the total commitment of marriage.

Walter Trobisch in his best-seller *I Loved a Girl* reinforces these biblical truths:

When I as a pastor am called in to counsel in a marriage crisis, I can almost always trace the origin of the problems to the kind of life which the husband and wife lived before they were married. The young man who has not learned self-control before marriage will not have it during marriage. . . . In a sense, you deprive your future wife of something, even if you do not yet know her, and you endanger your happiness together.[33]

What Trobisch testifies to from his experience, statistics consistently bear out. The incidence of unfaithfulness in marriage and divorce is much higher among those who have had premarital sexual experience than among those who have not.

From a biblical perspective, an unmarried person may relate to all those to whom he is not married as brother/sister, mother/son, father/daughter (1 Tim. 5:1-2); or he may marry. But what about the transition from brother/sister to marriage? Unfortunately, contemporary Western society has made that transition very difficult.

In a society in which couples marry soon after puberty, the need for self-control is minimal. But in our society there is a period of six to ten years in which young people experience the height of physical sexual desire but are not considered marriageable. Add to this the moral climate in which premarital sex is increasingly considered normal, and the idea of chastity is likely to be thought of as either ludicrous or an unattainable ideal.

One of the leading arbiters (or reflectors) of American mores, Abigail Van Buren, summarizes the emerging ethic: "The best rule of limitations is: Anything that goes on between consenting adults is OK as long as it's agreeable with both parties and harms no one."[34] "Harms no one" is the key—yet who but God knows that? Dr. Robert J. Collins, in the *American Medical Association Journal,* showed that at a midwestern school 80 percent of the women who had premarital intercourse hoped to marry their partner, while only 12 percent of the men had the

[33]Walter Trobisch, *I Loved a Girl* (New York: Harper and Row, 1975), 8.
[34]"Dear Abby," *The State* (Columbia, S.C.), 8 December 1983.

same expectation.[35] Consenting adults? Yes. Agreeable to both parties? Yes. Harms no one? That is another question.

What fruit does the sexual freedom tree bear? Is no one harmed? Is it true freedom?

Arnold Toynbee [dean of American historians] writes: Of 21 notable civilizations, 19 perished, not from conquest from without but from decay within." Another historian, J. D. Unwin of Cambridge University, made a study of 80 civilizations ranging over 4,000 years and concluded: "Any human society is free to choose either to display great energy, or to enjoy sexual freedom; the evidence is that they cannot do both for more than one generation."[36]

As a twentieth-century example, consider the Soviet Union. Pitirim Sorokin, distinguished sociologist and professor at Harvard, in 1956 published the influential volume, *The American Sex Revolution*. Before coming to America he was professor of sociology at the University of St. Petersburg in Russia. He wrote:

During the first stage of the Revolution, its leaders deliberately attempted to destroy marriage and the family. Free love was glorified by the official "glass of water" theory. If a person is thirsty, so went the Party line, it is immaterial what glass he uses when satisfying his thirst; it is equally unimportant how he satisfies his sex hunger.

The legal distinction between marriage and casual sexual intercourse was abolished. The Communist law spoke only of contracts between males and females for the satisfaction of their desires either for an indefinite or a definite period, a year, a month, a week, or even for a single night. One could marry and divorce as many times as desired. Husband or wife could obtain a divorce without the other being notified. It was not even necessary that marriage be registered. Bigamy and even polygamy were permissible under the new provisions. . . . Premarital relations were praised and extramarital relations were considered normal.

Within a few years, hordes of wild, homeless children became a menace to the Soviet Union. Millions of lives, especially of young girls, were wrecked; divorces skyrocketed, as did abortions. The hatreds and conflicts among polygamous and polyandrous mates rapidly mounted—and so did psychoneuroses.

The results were so appalling that the government was forced to reverse its policy. The propaganda of the "glass of water" theory was declared to be counter-revolutionary, and its place was taken by official glorification of premarital chastity and of the sanctity of marriage. . . .

Considering that the whole cycle occurred under a single regime, the

35Jim Conway, "Cheap Sex and Precious Love," *HIS*, May 1976, 34.
36Peale, "Man, Morals, and Maturity," 178.

experiment is highly informative. It clearly shows the destructive consequences of unlimited sexual freedom.[37]

Perhaps a similar swing back toward more traditional values is in progress in America. If the sexual revolution has been slowed, it is largely because of fear, not through any renewed acceptance of biblical values. "AIDS may be a voice from glory calling people back to responsibility and family values."[38] Note that this is not a quote from Jerry Falwell, but from Joseph Lowery, Executive Director of the NAACP! How soon a means to cure or at least to prevent AIDS will be discovered, no one knows. But until then the freedom and widespread promiscuity of the sexual revolution have been drastically curtailed. When Sol Gordon, a leading authority on sexuality, was given the 1982 award of the American Association of Sex Educators, Counselors, and Therapists, he said: "There has to be some disadvantage in being young. No sex is one. I can't think of any good reason for teenagers to have sex. What is going on is a national social disaster!"[39]

George Leonard, as senior editor of *Look* magazine, promoted the sex revolution, but a decade later wrote *The End of Sex* in which he says the revolution has gone sour.[40] The joys anticipated have not been found; sex has been trivialized and depersonalized and love has been lost.

Scripture and history testify that the way of sexual self-control is the way of fulfillment for the unmarried. But in a society where the customary relationship between teenage boys and girls is a socially enforced, exclusive, private, personal relationship, how does one pursue the ultimate goal intended by God?

Dating for Mating. Different societies have different ways of selecting mates, and the Bible does not authorize one way as better than another. Each must be evaluated on the basis of how well it promotes the purposes God has in marriage.

In the Western world romantic love is the basis for marriage;

[37]Pitirim Sorokin, *The American Sex Revolution* (Boston: Porter Sargent, 1956), 113-115.
[38]*World*, 14 September 1987.
[39]*The State* (Columbia, S.C.), 24 March 1982.
[40]George Leonard, *The End of Sex* (Los Angeles: J. P. Tarcher, 1983).

young persons are expected to find their mate through the dating process. However, in many cultures finding a mate is a family affair with investigations, negotiations, and contracts. There are, no doubt, advantages and disadvantages in both the romantic, companionship marriage in Western society, and the rational, pragmatic, and contractual marriage in other cultures. American young people do not act rationally. More care is used in employing a temporary unskilled laborer, often, than in seeking one who will be compatible for a lifetime of intimate life-sharing.

On the other hand, many of the family-arranged, contractual marriages ignore love altogether. Where there is little or no emphasis in the culture on developing a loving relationship, this is not usually considered part of the marriage and thus two of the three reasons for marriage are damaged or destroyed.

Neither pattern can be said to be intrinsically "right" or "wrong." In Genesis 24 Isaac and Rebekah were joined through family arrangement. In Genesis 29 Jacob and Rachel actually made a romantically-based personal choice (though the permission of Rachel's family was required). Whichever method or combination of methods is used, great care must be given to be sure all three purposes of marriage are adequately prepared for.

In the dating system there are both advantages and disadvantages for fulfilling the three basic purposes of marriage. Advantages of this system might be the screening of potential mates before entering into serious engagement; and the "steady" system's sense of security, of "belonging." There are some disadvantages, too. If steady dating is begun too early and continued too rigidly, there is a tendency to limit social development; there is a tendency to become involved prematurely without exposure to many of the opposite sex; and the greatest danger is that intimacy without commitment will constantly be a temptation. Furthermore, if entering and breaking exclusive relationships becomes a pattern during adolescence, it can be an emotionally poor preparation for marriage. Finally, the system usually leaves all the decision making to the young person who is emotionally involved and beset with peer pressure with little significant input from parents or church. However, it can hardly be said that this pattern is morally wrong, unless morally wrong attitudes or actions develop.

The dating system is not ideal in preparation for marriage because it introduces romantic feelings and sexual impulses as the context in which a person is to "discover" the other person. Friendship would be a much better context for self-discovery and other-discovery, yet friendship and dating are not very compatible. Dating is a pointing-to-marriage arrangement. Friendship, unencumbered by romantic overtones—in the "gang," in the church, in the family—is a better context for growing as a person, particularly in the social and spiritual dimensions. But dating is with us to stay. How do we make the best of it?

Since the primary purpose of marriage is the oneness of two, the opportunity for two to get acquainted before commitment to a lifelong relationship has potential for good. One can determine in advance whether there is personal compatibility, an opportunity not available in cultures where parents make the decision and the couple meets for the first time at the wedding.

In dating, however, there can be an illusion of confirmed compatibility when actually the two do not know one another. This is because there are two kinds of static in the atmosphere of dating that inhibit true and full communication. The first confusing distraction is the erroneous notion of falling in love. In truth one doesn't "fall" in love— one grows in it. One may fall into desire very precipitously or fall to a romantic feeling of excited attraction and call it "love," but such strong emotional surges are not in themselves the real thing. True love is other-oriented while what is often called romantic love is self-oriented. They run in opposite directions. One is interested in giving and the other in getting; one is preoccupied with the welfare of the other person, the other is primarily concerned with personal fulfillment. Romantic affection can be part of good, genuine, biblical relationships. In fact, I never recommend marriage to one who doesn't have that excitement. But by itself romantic feeling is not the genuine article, not very deep or very strong— not deep enough to satisfy the human spirit very long, and not strong enough to hold two people together when the going gets tough. But it gives the illusion that all the ingredients necessary for a happy marriage are present. Further, "being in love" makes it very difficult to evaluate the other person as a whole person.

A second distraction is physical attraction. Any reasonably attractive person of the opposite sex can "turn on" a person, particularly a man, given the right set of circumstances. So sexual magnetism of itself should never be read as an indication that this particular person is more suitable as a mate than any of the other millions who have the same set of physical characteristics. But it is hard to resist the illusion.

As a result of these two illusory feelings—surging affections and sensual desire—many American young people get married for the wrong reasons. They have "fallen in love" when in point of fact they may have merely fallen in love with love, or at most are caught up in romantic feeling and sensual desire. Under those circumstances, full communication or adequate exploration of the other person's inner being is rendered virtually impossible.

Another damaging problem with the contemporary dating system is that what the Bible holds to be sin—physical sexual expression between unmarried people—is considered part of the definition of "dating." Sexual covetousness and sexual activity are wrong because they damage the ultimate unity of marriage before marriage even begins. Memories of intimacy with someone else will always be there.

If a person is aware of these hazards and decides firmly in advance to resist temptation and to avoid illusion, the system can become a positive help. One can get acquainted in depth with a number of people and gain a basis of comparison for evaluating in those he or she dates the potential for a life-time commitment. But our dating system can be tough on the girl (who traditionally must always wait for an invitation) and on the guy (who must always risk rejection).

In American society the escalating relationship from casual acquaintance to marriage usually goes through the following stages: time spent together (dating) leads to emotional involvement; emotional involvement leads to a feeling of exclusiveness and possessiveness ("going steady"); this mutually shared sense of belonging exclusively to another person normally leads to intimate talk and behavior. But the sincere Christian postpones the intimate talk and behavior until lifetime commitment has been made. A sure sign of maturity is the ability to postpone present gratification for future benefit.

This escalation of relationship is normally accompanied by a rising sexual desire for the other person.

> Biologically, such a courtship pattern acts as a stimulus to sexual excitement, and is one of a series of stimuli of increasing intensity, leading naturally to physical union. . . . The biological function of such "petting" actions is not intended to satisfy our emotions and impulses, but rather to stimulate and excite them, and the progression develops. We are made that way. Holding hands at first seems a tremendous privilege and satisfies us for a while. Then it stimulates a desire for kissing. Holding hands begins to seem a bit tame! Before long kissing begins to seem a bit tame, too, and it, in turn, leads to a desire for caressing, and so on.[41]

Any attitude or action which lies in the line of rising desire from initial thought to consummation in sexual intercourse is immoral if it goes beyond the commensurate degree of mutual commitment (Matt. 5:27-30). If the commitment is not there, expressed and mutually agreed to, fantasy of sexual intimacy is a form of unfaithfulness, mental cheating. In God's plan, then, before a person indulges in erotic imaginations, a commitment to marriage is needed (engagement). Only such a commitment can validate a relationship which otherwise would be lustful, outside the bounds of God's standards. Engagement then normally leads to vows of marriage, which are consummated in sexual union.

Some hold that physical compatibility in sexual relationships must be tested before one can be sure that the prospective mate is suitable. The problem is that sex-in-marriage cannot be tried outside of marriage. The essential ingredients aren't present and so what one "tries out" is something else. The security of lifelong trust, for example, is missing. It is like taking some of the ingredients of a cake—oil and eggs, for instance—and "trying out" their compatibility for making a cake. When you have finished combining them, who knows what wholly other and exciting thing might have happened if the flour, sugar, milk, and baking powder had been in the mix? Again, sex outside of marriage is like practicing ice skating on the living room floor— not too good for the floor, though you might begin to get the hang of staying on your feet. But have you really tested the

[41]Oliver R. Barclay, *A Time to Embrace* (London: InterVarsity Fellowship, 1964), 19.

exhilaration of the real thing? For the woman, to whom the security of belonging is so crucial, even physical climax may prove illusive. Perhaps there is a degree of pleasure and excitement, but they have not experienced the real thing, sex in marriage. In fact, their "experience" may make finding the winning combination even more difficult.

A 1981 study, *Women in Sweden,* reported that couples who lived together before marrying have nearly an 80 percent higher divorce rate than those who did not.[42] American researchers are using this study of more than four thousand women because Swedes tend to precede American social trends by ten to fifteen years. "Trying it out" in advance does not enhance the potential for success of marriage.

God's pattern is for each person to save his mind and body for the one to whom he will be married. The basic question is not, "How do I feel?" nor even, "How does she (he) feel?" But rather, "What level of commitment have we made?" To engage in talk or activity that is sexually arousing to either party before commitment to lifelong responsibility in marriage is mental fornication, that is, sexually coveting that which is not one's own. A person has responsibility not only for self, but for the other person. Love, not desire, must control. The pure-in-heart and loving person will be careful not to arouse desires in the other person which he is not prepared to meet through commitment.

Only in a total relationship can one experience the highest physical ecstasy, the deepest satisfaction, the growing fulfillment. If the relationship is only partial—primarily physical—it not only erodes the wholeness emotionally and spiritually, it makes the physical itself less satisfying. The relationship God designed is a total one—intimate identity in all of life.

So the most important thing about dating is to put the physical on hold until the whole-person relationship has matured to the place of life-time commitment in marriage. The first thing in preparation for marriage is not to find the right person, but to become the right person. The more practice one gets in self-giving love in all relationships, in sacrifice to help others become whole and fulfilled, the more solid a foundation

42Associated Press, 7 December 1987.

will be laid for a successful marriage. The more character is hardened in faithfulness, integrity, and loyalty, the greater the assurance of a good marriage.

Preparation days are to build purity of mind and body into one's thought life so that when the time comes, the total giving in a wonderful, exclusive, intimate relationship will be unsoiled.

Engagement. In the American dating system, there comes a time when a couple may make a commitment to get married. For the Christian, this is a solemn commitment to a lifelong relationship. It is the first stage of the marriage vows. The purpose originally was to provide a legitimate way for a couple to get to know one another, since society prohibited the private and intimate association of a man and woman who were not committed.

The sexual mores of contemporary society have changed so that dating seems to take the role once reserved for engagement, and engagement seems to be the basis for a trial marriage. But then again, marriage is not held to be much more serious than engagement formerly was viewed. But for the Christian, engagement is a solemn commitment and may be broken only for the most weighty reasons. It is better, of course, to break an engagement than to enter a marriage that was not meant to be, but better yet not to become engaged until one is quite sure of God's direction. When an engagement is broken, the trauma for one or both parties is usually in proportion to the seriousness with which the original commitment was made.

If engagement is indeed a solemn promise, sexual desire can no longer be considered immoral. It is no longer coveting something that is not rightfully one's own. So long as both are responsible and sensitive to the other person's stage of response, there need be no feeling of guilt.

However, every physical expression of affection builds pressure for more until the desire for physical union is unbearable for some couples, and the union is consummated before vows of marriage. Some would hold that marriage takes place at that point and that the intercourse cannot technically be called fornication. But few serious Christian couples can accept this view, and the failure in self-control becomes the beginning of strain resulting from guilty feelings and undermines mutual trust before marriage ever begins. Furthermore, there is commonly a sense of shame and hypocrisy in keeping the secret from others while participating in what was designed to be the pure and joyous, sacred public vows. Therefore, it is wise for engaged couples to concentrate on knowing one another socially, intellectually, and spiritually—establishing oneness at these more basic levels. Discipline is necessary. Physical expression of affection should be simple and occasional rather than prolonged, and often. Otherwise an engagement, particularly a longer engagement, can lead to temptation, frustration, and friction. Gratification delayed builds toward ever more wonderful fulfillment and the beginning of marriage on a solid foundation with no regrets.

Restoration after Failure. In our sex-saturated society the rate of failure, even among Christians, continues to escalate. Is there no hope for those who fail? Is the glorious gift prepared by God for the pure in heart forever out of reach?

Though the wages of sin is death-dealing, and the destruction of the very things grasped for has set in, it is also true that the gift of God is life. Forgiveness and grace are the great antidotes, and for the truly repentant, healing begins immediately.

Yet experience cannot be undone. One can never have the first experience again. And if the first experience is morally distorted, the pristine glory God intended for that initial taste can never be experienced. If the first experience was sinful and *was* a happy one, the problem may be even greater, for the memories are even more difficult to efface, and the shadow stretches long into the future. "The bird with the broken wing may fly again, but never will fly so high again."

Some people resent this concept, but it is a basic biblical truth. The result of sin in eternity is fully covered by the atonement, but some of the results of sin linger on in this life. The drunkard who lost a limb in his drunken stupor will live with a stump the rest of his life. The selfish parents who alienated their children before coming to Christ may suffer a lonely old age. And so with sexual sin: the potential fulfillment has no doubt been reduced.

But forgiveness is real, and cleansing is too. So the failed person must gratefully accept this and then begin rebuilding a

254 ■ BIBLICAL ETHICS

mind that is pure and a will that is trustworthy. If time for
growth is allowed, God in his grace may erase many of the
memories and provide a very fulfilling relationship in marriage.

Does anything need to be done about the past? Does the one
who has failed have any obligation to the prospective mate?
Since openness is a prime requisite for a healthy marriage and
secrecy breeds suspicion potentially worse than reality, my
judgment is that the question of the past should be faced before
engagement. The person who has had previous sexual
experience needs to ask two questions: Would my friend want
to marry me if he/she knew of my past? Could I live openly with
a sense of security and integrity if he/she did not know? To be
sure of the answer to the first I know of no other way than to ask
frankly, "Do you want to know about my past? Would it make
any difference?" Since, in the heat of romantic desire, a person
may not even be honest with himself, let alone with the person
he may want to marry, the immediate answer may not be
sufficient evidence of his true feelings.

If the person seems to want such information (which is
rightfully his, in any event), we can recommend giving only the
most generalized facts: "Before I knew you, I sinned by having
sexual relationships with another. I am deeply sorry and hope
you will forgive me." Further detail is probably not wise, but if it
is requested, go only as far as is absolutely necessary to satisfy the
loved one that all is past, nothing of the former relationship
lingers, and that God has so delivered that there will never again
be infidelity. If the person definitely does not want to know I
would not speak of the matter further. Deal with the Lord about
any need you might feel to share. Sexual sins less than
fornication should be left undisclosed unless specifically
requested.

Though the Scripture does not speak directly to this issue, it
does speak of restitution and reconciliation. In the nature of the
case, no restitution can be made to a future spouse for a past
sexual offense, but full understanding and mutual trust could be
advanced by the approach outlined above. The danger of
ignoring the issue before marriage is that it may become an
issue. Sin always has destructive effects. But at least the couple
will be able to deal with the known rather than the unknown,
and there can be no charge of deception. If full forgiveness is not

possible, a far deeper malady than sexual offense is evidenced and must be dealt with.

HOMOSEXUALITY

Sexual desire toward one of the same sex and the expression of that desire in genital sexual activity has been known in most societies throughout recorded history. In the Western world during the Christian era, homosexual activity has been proscribed by law. This began to change when the British Parliament in 1967 decriminalized same-sex sexual relations. Following this, the gay rights movement became more public, spearheading a reversal of public attitudes toward homosexual behavior. Historically, homosexuality was considered sinful and criminal, later a psychological illness (following Freud's lead), then a normal alternative (much like left-handedness), and finally advocated by some as a preferred way of life to provide the highest form of loving relationships (lesbians) and the best means of population control (male homosexuals).

About 4 percent of American males and 2 percent of American females are thought to be exclusively homosexual in orientation. Most authorities question the idea that this proportion has changed significantly, despite changing popular and legal attitudes. Alfred Kinsey's *Sexual Behavior in the Human Male* (1948) was a watershed study in the homophile movement. Kinsey claimed that a large proportion of males (25 percent), though not exclusively homosexual, nevertheless had some same-sex sexual desires (thus being bisexual), though they may not have necessarily acted on these desires.

The idea is that, though a mere 2–4 percent of the population is exclusively homosexual, a larger proportion has sexual desire for both male and female and, indeed, has had some experience with both at some time during life. This "bisexual" characteristic is often promoted as the normal, natural human response to sexuality. Just as the ancient Greek society, following the teaching of Socrates, Plato, and Aristotle, idealized same-sex love, the gay community in the latter half of the twentieth century presses for a return to Greek "enlightenment" in sexual matters.

On the question of bisexuality, leading psychiatrist Ernest Van den Haag says,

> I have some doubts also on the existence of "bisexuals." If the word refers to more than the human condition—that we all are capable of sexual acts with either sex, and, in appropriate cases, willing—that is, if "bisexual" means an equal leaning toward either sex, I simply have never seen it. People develop a preference for one or the other. . . . It is trivial and irrelevant to say that activity with either sex is possible for all.[43]

But why are any people homosexual in preference? Throughout church history this was assumed to be the result of a willful, sinful, perverted choice. But with the rise of psychology in the last century, homosexual orientation was viewed as morally neutral, but nevertheless a pathological condition that was held to be the result of an inherited maladjustment (Freud). There would be little possibility of changing sexual orientation.

But the prevailing view of medical and psychological specialists in the 1970s and 1980s came to be that the condition is attributable to environmental conditioning. The most widely accepted view is that a dominant or overprotective mother and a hostile or distant father have skewed sex-role perceptions in the child at an early age. Poor home conditions have produced negative attitudes toward the opposite sex and caused a confused sense of sexual identity. One cannot be held responsible for one's sexual orientation, and seeking to change it is for the most part futile and, when successful, may be harmful. Not all agree.

> Mansell Pattison, chairman of the psychiatry and health behavior department at the Medical College of Georgia in Augusta, in an article in the December issue of the *American Journal of Psychiatry,* documented 11 cases of men who claimed not only to have resisted successfully their homosexual drives, but changed their basic homosexual orientation to the point where they have developed satisfactory sexual attraction to females. Eight of them no longer have homosexual dreams, fantasies, or physical arousal.
>
> In other words, these eight were cured—something gay activists often claim is impossible. The changes documented by Pattison came without psychotherapy, but by what he called "religiously mediated change." . . . All Pattison's subjects were true homosexuals.
>
> Donald Tweedie, a clinical psychologist in suburban Los Angeles, has counseled about 300 homosexuals in 25 years of practice. He is more

[43]Ernest Van den Haag, *The Humanist,* July-August 1973, 16.

optimistic than Pattison about reversing homosexuality, although he doesn't believe a "cure" necessarily implies a life free from homosexual temptation. He explained that many of his patients have gone on to satisfactory married lives.[44]

Psychologist Lars Granberg points out that successful therapy depends on whether the person really desires to change.[45] To this might be added that any kind of basic change will come only when a person believes that he can change. It is important, then, in watching the ebb and flow of theory on this controversial subject, to note that presuppositions have a great deal to do with the outcome. One who believes the condition is normal and healthy does not seek "healing"; one who believes it is not sin, but rather a gift of God, does not need conversion; one who believes that change is impossible will hardly seek to change and, should he do so, could not be expected to achieve it. For these reasons, the homosexual community is adamant in its refusal to admit that a true homosexual can change, and has been reluctant to go along with more recent theory that disallows a congenital origin of the condition, or the view that if certain conditions brought it about, other conditions might change it.

What is the result of homosexual activity? Since most practicing homosexuals are promiscuous (from the isolated and short-lived "marriages" to the typical experience of sexual contact with scores of different people per year, to the few who claim to have more than a thousand contacts a year), venereal diseases are far more common than among the heterosexual population. Then there are the diseases particularly characteristic of the homosexual population: AIDS and hepatitis A and B. Beyond this, there are illnesses resulting from damage to the anal canal and infection from disease-carrying semen, waste, or blood when ingested or absorbed through breaks in the skin. The psychic damage is probably greater than the physical.

Are homosexuals gay? Or is "gay" an attempt to mask a basic dislocation of spirit? Three-fourths of the psychiatric community believe homosexuals are not happy in their condition.[46] Statistics tend to bear out the same conclusion: "Eighteen per cent of the white homosexual males reported at

[44]Tom Minnery, *Christianity Today,* 6 February 1981, 38-39.
[45]*HIS,* October 1963, 25.
[46]Allen Young, *Gay Community News* reprint, 21 January 1978.

least one suicide attempt; the figure for white heterosexual males was 3 per cent."[47]

The changing attitude toward homosexual behavior is in the context of a society that is rapidly relativizing all moral standards and particularly all sexual standards. It should come as no surprise to discover prohomosexual literature increasingly denigrating the nuclear family, while advocating incest, bestiality, and every form of nontraditional sexual behavior as a matter of personal preference unrelated to right or wrong. Earlier the plea was for liberty for consenting adults so long as no one was harmed. Now the right to seduce children is increasingly advocated. If the child is "seducible," it proves he is homosexual in orientation, and the seducer would thus prove to be a commendable educator and liberator.

Against this background of a changing society, what does the church say? Until the mid-twentieth century, the position of the church from the earliest fathers through Aquinas, Luther, Calvin, and even modern theologians such as Karl Barth have considered homosexual behavior a violation of God's law.

But in England an informal group of Anglican clergy and physicians produced a report in 1954 which marked a turning point, leading eventually to the Wolfenden Report and the modification of centuries-old English law. One member of the group, D. Sherwin Bailey, published the book which has become the foundational study for all later innovating theological approaches, *Homosexuality and the Western Christian Tradition*.[48] Since then studies by churchmen, church commission reports, and church council actions have almost always kept pace with their secular counterparts and sometimes led the way in the "gay liberation" movement. In America, though official studies in the United Presbyterian, United Methodist, and Roman Catholic churches all favored admission of and ordination of practicing homosexuals, the respective church councils turned down these recommendations. The United Church of Christ had no such inhibitions and was the first major denomination to ordain a practicing homosexual.

This shift in values was not limited to the mainline

[47]*Homosexualities: A Study of Diversity Among Men and Women,* as quoted by Samuel McCracken, "Are Homosexuals Gay?" *Commentary,* January 1979.
[48]New York: Longmans, Green, 1955.

denominations. In 1968, Troy Perry, an ordained minister with a Pentecostal background and professed evangelical, left his family to form the Metropolitan Community Church in Los Angeles. This church has since given inspiration to the founding of scores of daughter churches.

Perry was first, but perhaps the most articulate spokesperson of the movement is Ralph Blair, prime mover and president of Evangelicals Concerned. In a pamphlet titled "What is EC?" the answer is given to the question, "What does EC believe?"

We believe that Christian gay people are a part of God's kingdom and are bona fide disciples of Christ. . . . Doctrinally, we are evangelical in the historic sense of believing the basics of Christianity as revealed in the Word of God. Some Evangelicals and Charismatics say it's un-Christian and that homosexuals should "get delivered" and if that doesn't work, they should just sit and be quiet and forget about romance and sex for the rest of their lives. People are swallowing this baloney.[49]

Before considering the passages which deal directly with the issue, it is well to recall God's purposes in making us sexual, in some mysterious way a reflection of his own nature. God ordained exclusive, permanent, monogamous marriage as the only way to achieve the full unity of two human beings, to provide children and home, and to reflect God's own relationship to humankind. Although some gay activists are bold enough to claim the first and third purposes are available to a monogamous homosexual relationship, the whole thrust of Scripture is on the union of one man and one woman as God's only way of fulfilling these purposes. When he saw it was not good for man to be alone, he did not create another man. Adam and Eve was God's arrangement. Thus, while only a few passages deal directly with homosexual conduct, the pervasive teaching of Scripture is to condemn all sexual relationships outside the heterosexual marriage bond.

Some scholars, following D. Sherwin Bailey's lead, have contended that the Scripture is silent on the subject of homosexuality, that all passages thought to refer to same-sex relationships have been misunderstood. This is the position taken by self-proclaimed homosexual and Yale University professor John Boswell in his exhaustive study of the subject

[49]A pamphlet published by the Western Regional Fellowship of EC, "Sometimes a Bunch of Baloney Can Be Very Tempting," n.d.

from a theologically liberal viewpoint.[50] Bailey's line of argument is used in whole or in part by some who declare themselves evangelical. Mollenkott and Scanzoni, for example, eliminate (with many of the same arguments) the relevance of the texts which have traditionally been understood to condemn homosexuality.[51] What are the texts?

"You shall not lie with a male as with a woman; it is an abomination" (Lev. 18:22).

"If a man lies with a male as with a woman, both of them have committed an abomination; they shall be put to death, their blood is upon them" (Lev. 20:13).

These passages seem clear enough, though with tortured exegesis they have been restricted by some to forbidding temple worship with male prostitutes.[52] The real problem with these commands is their context. Do they apply beyond their immediate audience of Jewish people under Mosaic law? The answer to this must depend on what the rest of Scripture says or refrains from saying, since there are a few commands in the same chapters which we no longer consider morally binding (restrictions on eating certain foods, using cloth with a mixture of fibers, or sexual intercourse during menstruation). We do consider the bulk of the commands in the immediate context universal moral edicts (those forbidding incest, adultery, bestiality, and child sacrifice). But how do we decide? By what the rest of Scripture teaches, particularly the New Testament. Thus, if these commands are treated as normative elsewhere, they become very clear and strong statements of the will of God for all mankind for all ages. And the results of violation predicted by Moses are terrible indeed—both for the individual and for the society which tolerates this kind of sin.

Another Old Testament passage has given us an alternate name for homosexuality, the traditional name used for many centuries: sodomy.[53] It is a mystery to me why proponents and opponents of homosexuality spend so much energy trying to

[50]John Boswell, *Christianity, Social Tolerance, and Homosexuality* (Chicago: University of Chicago Press, 1980), 91-118.

[51]Virginia Ramey Mollenkott and Letha Scanzoni, *Is the Homosexual My Neighbor?* (New York: Harper and Row, 1978).

[52]See Boswell, *Christianity, Social Tolerance, and Homosexuality,* and Fred L. Pattison, *But Leviticus Says!* (Phoenix: Cristo Press, n.d.).

[53]*Homosexual* is actually a recently invented and clumsy hybrid of Greek (*homo,* meaning "same") and Latin.

prove what the sin of Sodom's men was or was not (Gen. 19; see also Judg. 19:22-26). To say that the men simply wanted to meet and find out who Lot's guests were ("know"), as Bailey and his successors attempt to prove, appears to me to border on the ridiculous, but such an interpretation does not make the passage any more or less relevant to the question of whether some form of homosexual activity is legitimate. Even if the men of Sodom intended homosexual rape (which seems apparent), and even if this would be the ultimate show of inhospitality to guests (a terrible offense in Bible times), it tells us nothing directly about how God views voluntary homosexual relationships. That rape is abhorrent to God is all that can be deduced from this passage.

The former passages, then, are the extent of Old Testament data on the question of voluntary homosexual conduct. In the New Testament there are three basic passages around which the battle rages, and none of them are in the Gospels. Since Christ did not directly address the issue, some gay advocates hold that he was neutral or favorable.[54] But an argument from silence proves nothing. There are many things Christ did not teach about directly: bestiality, prostitution, incest, rape, idolatry, racism, to name a few. Does this prove he was not opposed to them? All were common in the Roman world. No, we look to the principles he taught and find that he reaffirmed repeatedly in the clearest and strongest terms that permanent heterosexual monogamy was the original and continuing will of God as the only legitimate context for sexual relationships.

So we come finally to Paul for definitive statements on the subject. To the Corinthians (1 Cor. 6:9-10) Paul lists the sins of the *malakoi* and *arsenokoitai* as abhorrent to God, and to Timothy he identifies *arsenokoitai* in the same way (1 Tim. 1:8-10). Although recent effort by pro-gay scholarship has attempted to prove other meanings for the terms, the bulk of scholarly opinion is solidly on the side of considering each of the terms as referring to homosexual men, probably identifying the active and passive roles in male copulation.

But the passage considered by all as the crucial text is Paul's denunciation of some kind of homosexual conduct to the

54Some, including at least one professor in an "evangelical" seminary, have tried to adduce evidence that Christ himself was homosexual.

Christians of Rome (Rom. 1:26-27). Rather than attempting to analyze all the arguments recently adduced to set aside or limit Paul's obvious condemnation of homosexual conduct, I will address what seems to be the crucial argument: that Paul intended to identify as sinful only promiscuous homosexual relations, or gay sex by lustful bisexuals who should stick to women because they are capable of it, not to the loving, faithful "monogamous" relationship of two truly homosexual persons.

For those committed to the full inspiration and authority of Scripture, there is no option to set Paul aside as in error because of ignorance. But was he speaking only of the lust of a heterosexual for one of the same sex? He could hardly have been ignorant of both varieties. He lived in a society that was thoroughly saturated with homosexual conduct of every kind. Even had he not read the Greek literature where homosexual love was touted as the ideal (especially the "love" of a man for a boy), the art and graffiti of the day made public the activities of what was done in private. He lived at a time when a steady succession of Roman emperors was notoriously homosexual and led a society in unspeakable orgies and maltreatment of slaves and boy prostitutes. Paul surely knew well the Greek homosexual ideal of loving fidelity ("marriage" was common) and Roman promiscuity, and he made no distinction—all was an abomination to God and the ultimate degraded end of rejecting the knowledge of God and his ways.

It is said that Paul speaks of that which is "against nature" and thus excludes those who act according to their own (homosexual) nature. Actually Paul here does not speak of the decline from one degree of darkness to another of an individual so much as the decline of a society; though, of course, an individual could follow the same course. As he does on other subjects, Paul here identifies the natural order of things and says that homosexual sin violates it. He does not speak of the violation of what may have become the private nature of some individual. To identify some seagulls that mate with the same sex or to document 2–4 percent of a population who are wholly sexually inverted does not prove that such is the natural order of things. It could well be evidence of the opposite. An aberration simply by virtue of its existence is not thereby constituted "natural." Paul here identifies sexual perversion as one of the

most salient evidences of human depravity, along with many
other sins which go directly against "nature" as God intended it.
One may argue that Paul was in error, but it is difficult indeed to
convince a nonpartisan observer that he thought otherwise.

The advocacy of a monogamous homosexual relationship by
Blair and others in Evangelicals Concerned is marginal to the
gay movement within the church as well as outside the church.[55]
Rather, most gay activists argue that sexual expression should
not be denied anyone, whether he or she is homosexual,
bisexual, heterosexual, married, or single. In other words, God
made us sexual, and he would not expect us to live a celibate life.
And, it is held further, very few people can and do live such a
life. Consider the words of Professor Walter Wink.

The crux of the matter, it seems to me, is simply that the Bible has no sexual
ethic. There is no biblical sex ethic. The Bible knows only a love ethic, which is
constantly being brought to bear on whatever sexual mores are dominant in
any given country, or culture, or period.
The Bible clearly considers homosexuality a sin, and whether it is stated
three times or three thousand is beside the point. Just as some of us grew up
"knowing" that homosexuality was the unutterable sin, though no one ever
spoke of it, so the whole Bible "knows" it to be wrong.
I freely grant all that. The issue is precisely whether that biblical judgment is
correct.[56]

This professor of biblical interpretation at Auburn Theological
Seminary in New York City has clearly identified the issue:
biblical authority. As far as Scripture is concerned, all varieties of
homosexual conduct are a particularly abominable form of
immorality. Every time the New Testament castigates
fornication (*porneia*) without specific application to a particular
form of immoral conduct, it is condemning all forms of
homosexual and heterosexual relations outside the married state
of a man and woman.

What, then, should be the church's attitude toward the
homosexual? First of all, we must recognize the distinction
between homosexual disposition on the one hand and
homosexual lust and behavior on the other. The Bible explicitly
forbids homosexual lust and activity but is silent on the question
of sexual preference per se.

[55]But see also *The Other Side,* June 1978.
[56]Walter Wink, "Biblical Perspectives on Homosexuality," *The Christian Century,*
  7 November 1979, 1083, 1085.

To the heterosexual the Bible says: Do not sexually desire any member of the opposite sex to whom you are not married. To the bisexual the Bible says: Do not sexually desire anyone other than the person of the opposite sex to whom you are married. To the homosexual the Bible says the same thing: Do not sexually desire anyone other than the person of the opposite sex to whom you are married. In other words, virtually all human beings have strong sex drives that the Bible holds may be properly satisfied only in heterosexual marriage. Homosexuals who are thereby frustrated are in no greater discomfort than single heterosexuals. To both God holds out the assurance of fulfillment either through marriage or by the grace to remain pure though unmarried.

What of those who fail? God offers to forgive and accept, and so must his people. The church must fully accept the homosexual sinner who does not justify his sinful behavior but confesses it and seeks God's deliverance. Furthermore, the church must compassionately work with such a person to enable him to become what God originally intended, heterosexual, or to sublimate his sexual drive into other creative channels.

But is it possible for a fallen human being to change his sexual preference or hold in check his sexual appetite? Is not the church cruel and unrealistic in demanding that a person choose between fidelity in a permanent marriage to one of the opposite sex or remaining celibate? If the salvation we offer does not include deliverance for this kind of sin, how can we expect it to provide deliverance for the many other dispositions and drives of our natural fallen state? The whole point of the gospel is that God not only forgives, but that he does indeed give deliverance from sin.

I know of no body of statistical evidence on the cure rate for the many Christian groups that work with homosexuals, nor for those who counsel in church settings. Paul apparently knew some who were cured, for he said, "And such were some of you. But you were washed, you were sanctified, you were justified in the name of the Lord Jesus Christ and in the Spirit of our God" (1 Cor. 6:11). Pastor Harold Burchett testifies of many who have come to total deliverance. Even without the aid of the Spirit, therapy has brought many back to normal. Some time ago the New York Academy of Medical Science reported a rate of cure of 50 percent in the psychiatric treatment of homosexuality.[57] The process of psychotherapy entails a very large element of helping the sufferer to understand that he is not a victim of something beyond himself, but that choices made in the past, however unconsciously, can be reviewed and new decisions taken.[58]

Some would argue that most of the reported cures, if the truth were known, were of bisexual people, not of hard-core, exclusive, "constitutional" homosexuals. Of course, from the pastoral point of view, the majority of those caught in the web of homosexual behavior, and especially the majority of those who seek deliverance, are these so-called bisexuals. They must be sought out, welcomed, and healed. But, as we have seen earlier, the true homosexual has often changed his sexual orientation when he truly desires to change. And that desire is the crux of repentance and deliverance from any sin.

One question remains: Should Christians seek legal sanctions to restrict the freedom of homosexuals in any way? If sexual preference is simply a personal matter, homosexual people should be granted full freedom as a legitimate minority. But if the behavior is immoral, it has social effects; others suffer from the fallout of any person's sin. And the social effects of homosexual conduct are not limited to the deaths of hemophiliacs infected by blood transfusions of homosexual AIDS carriers and sufferers from hepatitis who ate in a restaurant served by a homosexual cook. No, the entire fabric of society is changed when such moral aberrations are officially recognized as morally neutral.

My contention is that most civil law seeks to legislate morals, and that Christian people should without apology work for laws that enforce the biblical ideal. Nevertheless, in a democratic society, legislation that is not acceptable to the majority of the people or even to a large minority, may do a disservice to morality in general, adding impetus to lawlessness. Therefore, I conclude that Christians should work to enforce restrictions on homosexual conduct to the extent that the community can be persuaded that such restriction is in the best interest of society.

[57]Klaus Brockmuhl, "Homosexuality in Biblical Perspective," *Christianity Today*, 16 February 1973, 17.

[58]Ruth Tiffany Barnhouse, "Homosexuality," *Anglican Theological Review*, June 1976, 127.

For example, though gay organizations are currently working to abolish laws safeguarding children from adult sexual seduction by lowering the age of consent, society at large could still be persuaded to maintain present restrictions. If the community is willing to restrict the teaching profession or the military from practicing homosexuals, Christians should fight to introduce or maintain such restrictions. On the other hand, it would be difficult to enforce any law that reinstated severe punishment of homosexual activity. Rather, such a law could lead to wholesale refusal to implement it, thus promoting a lawless spirit. Therefore, Christian people may be wise to refrain from seeking such legislation in the Western world of the late twentieth century.

OTHER ISSUES

Incest. Outside the church a movement is developing to decriminalize incest. Laws against incest are considered the next frontier that must be conquered. This is the natural outcome of the prevailing notion that sex is inherently nonmoral so that if it is pleasing, do it. The goal in this new movement is to allow and even foster free sexual relations of all kinds between all family members. In speaking of incest, Rene Guyon says that such behavior should not be condemned but considered "the legitimate exercise of the sexual sense for its own ends . . . and the thing itself [as] ethically indifferent. Thus in time the community itself will cease to be interested in this out-of-date taboo, will no longer demand punishment for those who transgress it, and will eventually tend to disregard it altogether."[59] Apart from the terrible lifelong psychological damage that ensues, and apart from the ultimate loss of true sexual fulfillment itself, God promises severe judgment for those who practice such things.

Bestiality. If incest is the natural outcome of the nonjudgmental view that holds all sex to be morally neutral, bestiality is increasingly advocated and practiced under the same sanctions with the added philosophical undergirding that views sex as

[59]Rene Guyon, *Sex Life and Sex Ethics* (London: The Bodley Head, 1933), 309-310.

primarily physical. If three-dimensional sex is reduced to one, the physical, so that orgasm is the primary object of sex, why not "have fun" with an animal? When physical union is divorced from emotional and spiritual union, sex cannot deliver on its promise of unending and growing fulfillment and ecstasy. Therefore it needs to be hyped by the titillation of new physical experiences. Bestiality is just one degree on the downward spiral to ever lessening fulfillment and increasing destruction. Scripture is categorical in its condemnation of bestiality (Lev. 18:23; Deut. 27:21; Lev. 20:15-16; Exod. 22:19).

Rape. Two issues in regard to the rape of women need to be addressed: the role of the woman and the nature of the crime.

Although women often have a sense of guilt following rape, and although law enforcement officials and courtroom treatment often reinforce the sense of pollution and guilt, no victim of forced sexual intercourse should feel guilty. If she is guilty of making herself vulnerable by carelessly exposing herself to danger, she is still not guilty of anything but poor judgment. If she deliberately entices through dressing provocatively or flirting and then refuses the advances of some man to whom she gave false signals, she is guilty of deliberately tempting another to sin, but still she is not guilty of fornication or adultery. The same innocence is true also of the homosexual rape victim and children sexually abused by family members.

The church has a responsibility to help the victim of sexual assault through the terrifying crisis and the slow and painful process of healing. Often the victim is treated like the criminal, not only by police and the defense attorney but by the church family. It is almost as if she were violated again and again. These are the sins against the victim of rape which must be stopped.

A great shift in scholarly opinion and public perception about rape is taking place. The traditional notion that rape is primarily the passionate response of a sex-starved man has been challenged. A landmark book on the subject has been very influential in the thinking of those who study the subject, those who deal with the problem, and the feminist movement.

All these views share a common misconception: they all assume that the offender's behavior is primarily motivated by sexual desire and that rape is directed toward gratifying only his sexual need. Quite to the contrary, careful clinical study of offenders reveals that rape is in fact serving primarily nonsexual needs. It is the sexual expression of power and anger.

Rape is never the result simply of sexual arousal that has no other opportunity for gratification. In fact, one-third of the offenders that we worked with were married and sexually active with their wives at the time of their assaults. . . . Of those offenders who were not married (that is, single, separated, or divorced), the majority were actively involved in a variety of consenting sexual relations with other persons at the time of their offenses.[60]

Study of rape and scholarly writing on the subject has been very limited. In fact, Groth laments that the psychologists and psychiatrists have not viewed rape as the pathological illness he sees it to be. What, then, is the pathology? What kind of sick men commit sexual assaults on women, children, and other men?

Some men who ordinarily would never commit a sexual assault commit rape under very extraordinary circumstances, such as in wartime, but the likelihood of such a person's being a repetitive offender is very low. There are other men, however, who find it very difficult to meet the ordinary or usual demands of life, and the stresses that we all learn to tolerate are unendurable and overwhelming to these individuals. The extent to which they find most life demands frustrating, coupled with their inability to tolerate frustration and their reliance on sex as the way of overcoming their distress, make the likelihood of their being a repetitive offender very high.[61]

The data of Groth's thesis is based exclusively on studies of repetitive offenders. It would be very difficult to refute the impressive data assembled by Groth to prove that, among repeat offenders who have been apprehended and convicted, the sex drive is certainly not the only and rarely, if ever, the primary driving force. Although many ardent feminists insist that the crime is exclusively one of violence and not one of sex, Groth does not say that. He holds, rather, that sex is never the *primary* motive. He has done all of us a great favor by demythologizing our understanding of the complex and multifaceted sin that is involved. But the popular view seems to be shifting beyond Groth to desex that crime. What are the results?

Making sex offense exclusively the result of illness or mental aberration does for rape what the same theory has done for

[60]Nicholas Groth, *Rape: The Psychology of the Offender* (New York: Plenum Press, 1979), 5.
[61]Ibid., 7.

other crimes and for sins such as drunkenness. A sick person is less morally responsible. In fact, society is the primary offender. Furthermore, the general public can relax, assured that only a fringe of deranged among us is capable of such sick behavior and, since all sex acts are morally neutral, the sexual aspect of such offenses should not be our concern so much as the violence and the imposition of power over the woman's autonomous self-determination. Some would like us to believe that pornography in no way promotes sexual assault, and no normal man need ever fear that the fantasies lurking in his mind could ever break out, no matter what the inducement of circumstances. He can feed them, not curb them.

The new approach tends to reinforce the idea that though violence is (almost) always wrong, sex is (almost) always right. We have, because of the emerging consensus on rape, come to view sex crimes as less heinous. Perhaps as results of this, the apprehension and conviction of offenders have become more difficult and the punishment has become increasingly light. It is hard to believe that even in the 1950s men were executed for rape.

To this we must respond that pornography itself is a form of sexual assault, that every normally sexed human being is capable of taking sexual pleasure without the consent of the object of his desire, given the right set of circumstances, and that, therefore, he needs to bow before the biblical standard of purity and rely on God for deliverance. We need to recapture the horror of this terrible crime of violence and sex. In other words, the root problem is not sociological, medical, or educational, but spiritual.

The biblical viewpoint on violence, rape, and sexual sin against another is clear enough. But there is clinical evidence as well that would suggest stronger elements of sexual motivation than Groth, other rapologists, and the feminist world would allow. At Johns Hopkins, less than 5 percent of sex offenders on Depo-Provera (a drug that decreases the male libido) become repeat offenders. About 85 percent of sex offenders nationwide repeat the offense if they don't get medical treatment, according to Fred Berlin, cofounder of the Johns Hopkins Biosexual Psychohormonal Clinic.[62] Obviously there must be some strong

[62]*The State* (Columbia, S.C.), 2 July 1984, 5-A.

connection between some men's sex drive and their desire to rape a woman (or man or child) if control of *sexual* desire reduces the typical 85 percent repeat offense rate to 5 percent.

But there is even stronger evidence, perhaps conclusive. All specialists agree that the majority of rapes go unreported and that most of these are cases of "date rape" or sexual relations forced on a companion. Though some of this may be motivated by hostility or the desire to dominate, clearly most of it is passion-driven. The study of convicted criminals may not legitimately be used as the sole or even primary foundation of theories on the cause and cure of this crime of passion and violence. *The Chronicle of Higher Education* (13 January 1988) reported on two studies in the mid-eighties:

Ms. Koralewwski says that while studies of incarcerated rapists had indicated that such men have serious deficiencies in assertiveness and social perception, no such deficiencies were found in the sexually aggressive college males. . . . Another recent study on date rape has found that sexual aggression is most likely to occur when the man pays for and drives his date, when the victim or rapist is extremely intoxicated, and when the couple spends time in a secluded location, especially in a parked car . . . not on their first date with the person who raped them, but on their fourth or fifth.

In other words, in the majority of cases of forced intercourse (companion rape), the offense appears to be primarily a crime of sexual passion.

How terribly we humans have debased the good gift of God! It has been necessary to review all the ways in which God's plan for the expression of human sexuality is violated, but our purpose in this overview has been to highlight more clearly the beauty of the ideal against this dark background and to clearly articulate the safeguards God himself has built around marriage, that firstborn and most basic human institution. Marriage is just too good to be reduced even slightly from the full purposes God intended. But we have done so much more than merely reduce it. Its debasement must surely rank among the most obvious evidences of man's terrible fall and of the derangement of his sin-darkened mind. We turn now to consider the responsibilities of members of a Christian home to one another.

E

RESPONSIBILITIES IN THE CHRISTIAN HOME

ROLES IN MARRIAGE

We considered earlier the basic distinctions between male and female in the biblical view. This viewpoint, when adopted, has proved liberating for women in most societies, but in recent years it has come under fire as demeaning women. The feminist movement in America first targeted civil rights (the vote), then economic rights (equal pay for equal work), then employment rights (equal access to any position), marital rights (egalitarian marriage), and finally, ecclesiastical rights (ordination).

Few today would argue against civil and economic rights for women, though some still hold that leadership roles in government and the workplace should be restricted to men. Because every person sees through the lens of his own culture, it is probably hypocritical to condemn our ancestors for blindness to biblical truth. (In what respects do *we* remain blind?) Yet it is difficult from today's vantage point to see how the oppression and subjugation of women could have been so universal for so long, often justified on the basis of (misunderstood) Scripture. Because of our past record of molding Scripture to culture's shape, we must pursue biblical truth for contemporary issues with courage.

When it comes to male/female role distinction in marriage and the church, controversy rages. George Gilder points out that each marriage partner *can* do what the other does. Throughout history each *has* done the work of the other, when necessary. What is novel today is the idea that the members of each sex *ought* to do the other's work, or that it makes no difference for society who does what. Gilder marshals impressive evidence from the spheres of biology, anthropology, history, and psychology to reinforce the biblical viewpoint.[63] Whatever may be said of empirical evidence, there is little dissent from the view that the Bible speaks directly to the issue and that it is not altogether on the side of contemporary feminist viewpoints.

Historically, the Bible has been viewed by all interpreters as patriarchal. At least in the home, the husband was viewed as the responsible leader. Most feminists, both within the church and outside the church, accept this understanding of the biblical data

[63]George Gilder, *Men and Marriage* (Gretna, La.: Pelican, 1986).

and, consequently, reject the authority of Scripture. This viewpoint is forcefully articulated by Sister Ann Patrick Ware, associate director of the National Council of Churches' Commission on Faith and Order:

> The Scriptures are unredeemably sexist. . . . To say that this portrayal reflects the cultural condition of the age in which the books were written in no way solves the problem. In my view, the explanation ignores the claim made by both Synagogue and church: that the books purport to contain God's Word. If the Word of God can be so corrupted by the mores of the culture in which it is received and on a matter of such centrality, it is in need of correction.[64]

The understanding of Scripture as making the husband head of the home has been challenged on three grounds by people who consider themselves evangelical: traditional interpretations are wrong, application to the contemporary situation is faulty, and some authors of Scripture are not reliable guides when addressing cultural issues.

Interpretation. The magna charta of the Bible-based branch of feminism is Galatians 3:28: "There is neither Jew nor Greek, there is neither slave nor free, there is neither male nor female; for you are all one in Christ Jesus."

This declaration is divorced from its theological context and applied to the sociological entities cited by Paul in an absolutist sense. No differentiation is permitted when it comes to race, sex, or the possession of one person by another. To view the text in this way it is necessary to reinterpret other themes of Scripture.

1. *Creation order.* It is held that male and female were created coequal and that the subordinate role of the wife was a result of the Fall. The curse stated, "Your desire shall be for your husband, and he shall rule over you." Just as it is legitimate for people to work against the other results of the Fall (pain in childbirth, hard ground and thorns) those who live under grace should reject this pattern and return to the original design of an egalitarian marriage.[65] To this George Knight responds:

> We should carefully recognize that the Bible never builds its case for the role relationship of men and women in marriage or in the home upon the effects of

[64]*Evangelical Newsletter*, 4 April 1980.
[65]Scanzoni and Hardesty, *All We're Meant to Be*, 34-35, 69, 109; Jewett, *Man as Male and Female*, 114.

sin manifested in Genesis 3:16. The Apostle Paul appeals to the pre-fall creation order as normative—as he does in Ephesians 5, 1 Corinthians 11 and 14, 1 Timothy 2. (The closest he comes to the other is in 1 Timothy 2, and there not as the grounds for the relationship but to show the dire consequences of what happened when the relationship was reversed.) It is God's creation order for the man-woman relation as evidenced in Genesis 2 (and also Genesis 1) that is normative in the New Testament, not the effects of sin as evidenced in Genesis 3.[66]

2. *Old Testament*. The Old Testament view of marriage is conceded by all varieties of feminists to be "hopelessly sexist" in its clear assumption and strong reinforcement of patriarchal relationships.

3. *Headship*. Paul speaks of the leadership of the husband. A few feminists have held that he merely referred to the historical fact that man was created first and thus was the source ("head") of the woman. Each mate, in turn, becomes the source of life to the other.[67] The interpretation is strained, but an even greater objection is that whatever *head* means, it describes the relationship between Christ and the church (1 Cor. 11:3; Eph. 5:23). And that is all the most ardent traditionalist would claim as a model for relationships in the home. Not many have championed this interpretation of *head*.

4. *Submission*. The key battleground between feminists and traditionalists is the extensive passage on husband/wife relationships in Ephesians 5. What does *subject* mean?

The word "subject" is a translation of the Greek *hupotasso*. *Hupo* means "under" and *tasso* means "arrange." It was originally a military term referring to the relations of a soldier to his commanding officer. Paul uses it in this passage (Ephesians 5) to explain the relationship between Christians. It is best translated *relate yourselves to*, *respond to*, or *adjust yourselves* to one another out of reverence for Christ. . . . There is nothing in the fifth chapter of Ephesians that would even remotely indicate (that wives are to submit to their husbands).[68]

Once again, the traditionalist has not felt compelled by the argument because whatever *submission* means, Paul says it is

[66]George Knight, "Male and Female Related He Them," *Christianity Today*, 9 April 1976. See also his book, *The New Testament Teaching on the Role Relationship of Men and Women* (Grand Rapids: Baker, 1977). This was republished by Moody Press (1985) under the title *The Role Relationship of Men and Women* and contains an extensive appendix by Wayne Grudenson on the meaning of the Greek word translated "head." It is the most exhaustive study on the subject currently available.

[67]Scanzoni and Hardesty, *All We're Meant to Be*, 30-31, 100.

[68]Herbert and Fern Miles, *Husband-Wife Equality* (Old Tappan, N.J.: Revell, 1978), 31.

similar in marriage to the appropriate response of the believer to Christ. Or, to use the Mileses' own analogy, between a soldier and his commanding officer.

Of more force is the emphasis that the key idea in the passage is the twenty-first verse, "Be subject to one another." This is taken by feminists to apply equally to husband and wife with no role distinction. The difficulty with such an interpretation is that the following section on parent/child relationships must be treated in a parallel fashion. And that, even for the most committed feminist, is difficult. To this idea of making verse 21 cancel the apparent meaning of the following verses, Paul Jewett, staunch advocate of a biblical feminism, responds:

When he exhorts his converts to subject themselves to one another (5:21), he does not mean simply that in Christ everyone should be mutually submissive to his neighbor as an expression of humility. There is, in the Christian household, a certain order, and our subjection to one another in Christ is determined by this order: Wives are to be subject to their husbands as the church is subject to Christ (5:22-23); children are to be obedient to their parents as the fifth commandment enjoins (6:1-3); and slaves are to be subject to their masters with fear and trembling, in singleness of heart as to Christ (6:5ff.).[69]

The pervasive teaching of Paul that the husband should be the responsible leader in the home is so clear and strong that most feminists concur. But feminists have other ways of dealing with Paul.

Application. Paul's meaning seems clear enough, but did God intend this approach to marriage for today or was it the cultural application of eternal truth to the transient culture of that day?

There are several biblical texts which suggest that men should rule over women. But there are also several texts that indicate that hereditary monarchs should rule over commoners and that masters should rule over slaves. . . . All those texts reinforced the existing social order of Paul's first-century Roman world. . . . It may have seemed prudent to Paul to avoid relatively less crucial challenges to the status quo.[70]

Biblical feminists contend that this teaching is no longer binding in the form Paul gave it because Paul in the same

[69]Jewett, *Man as Male and Female*, 137.
[70]John Scanzoni, "Pornography: A Symposium," *The Reformed Journal,* November 1974, 21.

context taught about slavery, and all agree that the institution of slavery is not universal and permanent.

Thus the parallel to slavery is crucial to the argument. Scripture does reveal that slavery is not the ideal, both in Old Testament laws forbidding the enslavement of fellow Israelites, the law of Jubilee, and other indications. Perhaps the clearest indication is what Paul himself said in his letter to Philemon concerning Onesimus. Most agree that the institution of slavery was not established by God, was never commanded by God, was never approved by God, and was only regulated by God to ameliorate the fallen human condition. Therefore, the abolition of slavery is not only permissible by biblical standards but demanded by biblical principles.

But the parallel between husband/wife relations and slave/master relations will not hold. It would be necessary to advocate the abolition of both institutions, not the abolition of one and the abolition of submission in the other. Actually the instruction on relationships within both institutions is normative. In a society where slavery exists, the Pauline instructions for slave and master would be as fully authoritative now as the day he gave them. But the institutions are not parallel. Marriage, unlike slavery, was God's own idea, the fundamental human relationship in his design. The institution of marriage is normative for all peoples of all time, and therefore the instructions for how that marriage is to be conducted are as normative as the institution itself. The parallel is being drawn by feminists between the *system* of slavery and the *conduct* of marriage and thus is fallacious. The institutions are not parallel: one God-ordained, the other man-initiated; one permanent, one crying out for abolition.

Even if the parallel were valid, what of the relationship Paul deals with in Ephesians 6 (between the marital and slavery passages): parent/child? Some secular human rights activists are calling for the abolition of parental authority as well. Biblical feminists have not suggested that the submission of child to parent be abridged, but if one parallel is mandatory, why not the other?

Error. Because the arguments from interpretation (meaning) and application (significance) are not compelling, feminists who accept the Bible as normative in most instances are increasingly following the lead of Jewett in his precedent-shattering contention that Paul simply erred.[71] Scripture with error in it introduces a problem far more basic and beyond the scope of this treatment of husband/wife relationships. But for those who accept the Scripture as fully authoritative, this approach is ruled out from the start.

Where does the intensity of the assault on biblical teaching concerning role relationships in marriage come from? All agree that the initiative has not come from an objective reexamination of biblical data, but from the impetus of radical feminism, and that movement is thoroughly based on the concept of personal autonomy. Feminist leadership in the twentieth century has commonly advocated the abolition of the family and has consistently viewed religion, especially Christianity, as the greatest barrier to feminine liberation. This does not mean that such a movement has nothing valid in it nor that it should be rejected without a hearing. But the movement as a whole is no friend of Scripture nor of biblical values. Therefore, we must have caution while we listen attentively. Evangelical feminists have erred by hearing valid questions and then accepting nonbiblical answers. Feminists like Scanzoni and Hardesty, for example, not only advocate egalitarian marriage, but defend divorce, abortion, and homosexual relations. The contemporary feminist movement is firmly rooted in commitment to full personal autonomy and grows in whatever direction that may lead.

When Paul speaks of the husband as head of the home, of the wife as submissive in her relationship, he is advocating what today we might call responsible leadership. God's instruction concerning the home, the church, government, and the world of work all speak of God's own authority delegated to human authorities. These human authorities are not established to provide unconditional acceptance with a nonjudgmental attitude, to preside over a democratic vote, nor merely to give good advice. They are charged with responsibility to legislate, administer, adjudicate. Apparently God knows that two fully autonomous heads will produce institutional schizophrenia. Thus, the organization of human beings reflects the

[71]Jewett, *Man as Male and Female*, 112ff., 138.

organization of the divine: a trinity of persons, each with his own role, but with a Father to whom the Son submits (John 5:18-23, 30; 14:28; 1 Cor. 15:24-38).

The unfounded assumption of feminist thinking is that subordination means inferiority;[72] that self-denial means subservience and results in self-destruction.[73] But how can this be applied to the relationships in the Godhead? Is Christ inferior or self-destructive because he freely chooses to acknowledge the authority of the Father? Is the Christian, by yielding to the lordship of Jesus Christ, in danger of self-destruction? Or in human relationships, who is superior, an unknown college president or a world-renowned professor who serves under him? Marriage calls for role distinction, but not for an inferior/ superior relationship. The husband is superior in his role and only in his role, and so with the wife. Interchangeability of role may not bring freedom so much as confusion and marriage failure.

Which is more important in holding a car together—the nuts or the bolts? And what if all the nuts went on strike because they were discriminated against and refused to serve if they couldn't function as bolts? They would be unfulfilled, the bolts also would be useless, but worst of all the whole organization would come to pieces and its purpose go unfulfilled. Differing roles do not mean less value or inferiority unless one role is, indeed, less important. But Jesus and Paul claimed that each person is of infinite value, in whatever role God may put him. Freedom and fulfillment come from fitting one's role, not demanding someone else's.

The Bible assigns the husband a role of loving leader and the wife the role of loyal completer. The root problem in marriage is the unwillingness of each to accept the role for which he was designed. Columnist Abigail Van Buren testifies that the number one complaint of wives is, "My husband doesn't appreciate me," and the number one complaint of husbands is, "She nags me." Each has failed *specifically* in his own responsibility.

The roles are clear in principle, but these will certainly be expressed differently in different cultures. A loyal support role

72Ibid., 8, 14.
73Hardesty and Scanzoni, *All We're Meant to Be*, 208.

for a Japanese wife might seem like demeaning subservience for a Swedish wife; leadership in an Italian home might seem like unloving arrogance in an American. But success in marriage is the magnificent gift of God to those who accept, in whatever culture, the role designed by God.

Every fallen human culture stands under the judgment of God for its distortion of marriage roles ordained of God. The task of the church is to listen carefully to the cries of the oppressed and look more deeply to see what God would say.

What is the result of the pursuit of personal autonomy through the obliteration of sex-role distinctions in marriage? After documenting the major shift in values during the seventies toward an ethic of self-fulfillment above all other values, a distinguished research professor of sociology at New York University concludes:

> By concentrating day and night on your feelings, potentials, needs, wants and desires, and by learning to assert them more freely, you do not become a freer, more spontaneous, more creative self; you become a narrower, more self-centered, more isolated one. You do not grow, you shrink.[74]

The fractured marriages experienced by many of the leaders in the feminist movement—including many in the evangelical camp—seem to fulfill Yankelovich's prediction all too tragically.

There is a legitimate alternative to accepting biblical marriage roles: stay out of marriage! There are many things worse than singleness and one of them is a marriage filled with tension because of role confusion. The single person is not bound by husbandly or wifely roles and responsibilities. *But if one chooses to marry in the Lord, he is choosing a specific role.* What, then, are the roles of each as taught in Scripture?

RESPONSIBILITY OF THE HUSBAND

Loving. First and predominantly, the husband is to love his wife, and the standard in that relationship is the way Christ loved the church (Eph. 5:22-23). He loved the church through total sacrifice. Although no mere mortal can attain this goal

[74]Daniel Yankelovich, *New Rules: Searching for Self-Fulfillment in a World Turned Upside Down* (New York: Random House, 1981), 242.

fully, this is the standard by which a man must ever evaluate his performance as a husband.

How does Christ love the church? There are many ways to consider this, but think of what Paul alludes to, the dark hours on the cross when he gave his life. Five of the seven sayings were in behalf of others.

"Father, forgive them." Forgiveness is the standard—and he forgave even when they did not ask for it. Longsuffering, forbearance. Even when she usurps my role? Yes, even when she crucifies you—that is God's kind of loving.

"This day you will be with me in Paradise." He accepted the sinner as he was, the ultimate failure, hanging on a cross. So with one's wife, fastidious or sloppy, disorganized or computer-perfect, young and beautiful or aging and overweight—acceptance. By grace, introduce her to paradise.

"Mother, here is your son; Son, here is your mother." Incredibly selfless, kind, and gentle. He makes provision for all her needs, all her weaknesses, even while he himself is in mortal agony.

"Why have you forsaken me?" The ultimate sacrifice—his most precious right, union with his Father. But what of my right to time for my own fun or my important ministry? God's kind of love is to forsake all rights necessary to love her well, to choose and act in her best interests as a way of life.

"It is finished." Faithful to the end. To the end of the argument, to the end of the day, to the end of life.

Leading. The husband is responsible for his wife, and this involves leadership. But leadership is not arrogant machismo—he must never have a bullying or domineering spirit (1 Pet. 3:7). Rather, he must gently lead, modeling the standard of loving well. In Christian American marriage, characterized by open communication and loving sacrifice of personal prerogatives, consensus is the normal way for decision making, and "pulling of rank" rarely if ever necessary. Nevertheless, the husband is leader and responsible to God for the direction the marriage goes.

Providing. The first provision is for the wife's spiritual welfare, which is encouraged by means of daily Bible study and prayer together. Closely associated with this is provision for full development of a wife's intellectual potential. For the husband to live on the sacrifice of his young wife while he goes to school and then shut her up at home with no opportunity for growth is to fail in loving provision. Her emotional health is his responsibility as well. Provision physically means protection, but increasingly the greatest need for protection is from the husband himself. Physical abuse should be unthinkable, and the standard must be never to touch her in anger. Ever.

Of course there are other, more deadly, ways of harming— verbal abuse, psychological wounds—and from all these his responsibility is to protect her. If any home is caught up in un- Christlike behavior, outside help should be sought by the wife if the husband is not man enough and Christian enough to seek it.

Another physical provision is for sexual fulfillment (1 Cor. 7:3-5). The husband who is consistently gratified sexually but does not take the time and care to provide fulfillment for his wife wrongs her grievously.

Material provision is a husband's responsibility (1 Tim. 5:8). This does not mean that the wife may not earn income nor that it is wrong for her to earn more than he or provide more for the family from her estate. But these blessings do not relieve him of ultimate responsibility. Finally, provision includes social relationships. A husband's desire in relationships with those outside the home may not dictate the extent of social involvement.

Limits of Responsibility. Although loyalty to one's wife takes precedence over loyalty to parents, to children, or to anyone else, loyalty to God takes highest precedence. When and how is one to "hate his wife" (Luke 14:26) or behave as if he were unmarried (1 Cor. 7:29)?

A new idolatry has crept into evangelical thinking, the idolatry of family. All resources of time and money are reserved for family above church, family above service to God, family above work, family above national security. This attitude has come as a reaction to earlier attitudes that put wife and children last. Correction was desperately needed. But there are times when the interests of the Kingdom of God demand that a husband "hate" his wife and children— that is, that he choose to sacrifice some potential benefit of theirs for the sake of fulfilling God's purposes in the world. Thus the husband (and/or wife) has chosen for a particular time in a particular way to behave "as if he were not married." The order of Scripture is clear: self-sacrifice as needed for the welfare of wife and children, family sacrifice as needed for the welfare of the Kingdom of God.

RESPONSIBILITY OF THE WIFE

Loving. The first responsibility of the wife, as of the husband, is to live in love (Titus 2:4-5). In biblical terms this means to consistently choose to act for the welfare of the other at whatever personal sacrifice. When both partners are committed to this way of life, the vast majority of marital problems are solved.

Homemaking. Though it is in conflict with much contemporary Western world thinking, Paul clearly states that the wife is responsible to maintain the home (Titus 2:4-5; 1 Tim. 5:14; see also Prov. 31, which is not in the form of a command but of a description of an ideal wife). This principle does not imply that a loving husband will refuse to participate in household responsibilities, but that the primary responsibility is the wife's.

Loyal Completing. Her role is to be a "help complementary" to her man. She is the accompanist providing for a successful team performance through reinforcing her husband. "Submission" includes honor and obedience (Eph. 5:22-33; Titus 2:5; 1 Pet. 3:1-7).

In a modern, liberated society, this often is a cross a wife is unwilling to bear. By rejecting it, however, she does not find freedom and fulfillment, but diminishing fulfillment, if not destruction, of that which might have been her most precious possession. The sacrificial love demanded of the husband is precisely the response a "natural-born" leader does not want, and the submission demanded of the wife is exactly what the proud, autonomous person does not want. Actually, the standard is higher for the husband, if anything. Christ's kind of loving is far more demanding of sacrifice than Sarah's kind of submission.

There are exceptions to the law of submission. No Christian woman may obey a husband who would cause her to sin. Leadership in any such direction may be rejected. On the other hand, if she is forced to do wrong, it seems that God holds the husband responsible, not the wife (Num. 30:15). Furthermore, if conditions obtain that would make a divorce legitimate on biblical terms, a wife is not bound. Finally, on the basis of the Bible authorization of self-defense I hold that a woman who is in physical danger or whose children are in physical danger may remove herself and her children from such danger. Here I advocate separation (temporary, it is hoped), not divorce, since this is not a reason enunciated in Scripture as grounds for a divorce.

Sex. The wife, like the husband, is to provide fully for the husband's sexual needs. If she for any reason finds it impossible to participate wholeheartedly, she may need to get professional counseling, since halfhearted or passive participation does "deprive" a husband of his "due." Creative partners will find ever growing ways to pleasure the other. Paul did not want Christians tempted outside the home by lack of sexual fulfillment inside the home.

RESPONSIBILITIES OF THE PARENTS

Reproduction. The original command to multiply (Gen. 1:28; 9:1, 7) seems to win the approval of the psalmist (127:3, 5; 128:3) and Paul the Apostle (1 Tim. 2:15; 5:14). This is certainly God's ordinary plan, but is it sinful to avoid pregnancy?

Birth control. Perhaps there is a parallel between the first Great Commission and the last. Just as the Great Commission to evangelize the earth (replenish God's family) was for the whole church, yet not intended to make a pioneer missionary of every believer, so the first "great commission" to replenish the earth may be for humankind as a whole rather than for every married couple. Some say that the earth cannot bear the population that is in the making, while others hold that the specter of overpopulation is a hobgoblin with no adequate scientific base. At any rate, I can find nothing in Scripture either in direct command or in principle that prohibits the use of contraceptives. Genesis 38:8-10 is held by some to indicate God's displeasure with birth control, but the plain meaning of the passage is that Onan's sin was one of selfishness and unbelief, disobeying the law (Deut. 25:5-6) by refusing to raise up seed to his brother.

The Roman Catholic church continues to take a very strong stand against any form of birth control by artificial means (as distinct from abstinence and the "rhythm" method). In 1930 the famous papal encyclical *Casti Conubii* declared that artificial contraception is an unspeakable crime, shameful, and intrinsically immoral. This opposition to artificial birth control has been reaffirmed by Popes Pius XI, Pius XII, Paul VI, and John Paul II.

Many Protestants until World War II held similar positions. What is the rationale?

Marriage is of value not as an end in itself but as a means to an end. What end? As the *Corpus Iuris Canonici* makes clear (1013, Par. 1) and as the Holy Office reasserted in 1944 (Denzinger, 2295), the primary purpose of marriage is the generation and raising of children; other aspects of the marriage relationship must be viewed as contributory to the procreative purpose.[75]

This opposition to the use of contraceptives is based on natural law, however, not on Scripture. Scripture may not back this view, but refusal to have a child may be wrong. It may be the sin of unbelief, the sin of disobedience to God's will, or the sin of selfishness in desiring a more affluent way of life. Some modern Christians are afraid to have children because they may not be adequate parents and "the children may not turn out right." This may come from belief in environmental determinism, a major contemporary heresy we will consider shortly. Others wonder if they can make it financially when astronomical sums are projected as necessary for raising even one child to maturity. All of these reasons stem from unbelief.

But if the couple plans the family with biblical values and Christ-centered rationale, I find nothing in Scripture to prohibit

[75]John W. Montgomery, "How to Decide the Birth-Control Question," *Christianity Today*, 4 March 1966, 8.

the use of contraceptives that prevent impregnation. Methods that induce abortion are another matter, which we shall consider in detail later.

What of permanent birth control—sterilization? Sterilization is the same kind of ethical issue as contraception, and similar guidelines should be followed. In the nature of the case, since none of us is infallible in knowing the will of God or even in knowing our own future circumstances or disposition, a decision to be sterilized should be taken with great care.

Perhaps there is a parallel with what Paul taught concerning the desirability of remaining single because of "the present stress." Perhaps God would call some special people to remain childless for a shorter or longer period of time to enable them to do some special task for him. I know of nothing in Scripture to preclude this possibility.

Adoption. Adoption is a wonderful solution for the couple who feel called of God to such a ministry, whether they have their own children by birth or not. Just as there is no biblical ground for hesitancy in this, there is no mandate to adopt. There is a mandate for the godly to care for the fatherless, however, taught throughout the Old and New Testaments.

Sex Selection. Perhaps because sex selection was unknown until recent scientific advance, Scripture does not address the issue. Abortion of a child of the unwanted sex, like the abortion of any other child, is wrong. But what of choosing in advance which sex to conceive, an option that will soon be available? The end result of these two procedures—identifying the sex of the unborn and aborting the unwanted—is hardly more terrifying than the depravity of people who apparently would choose the virtual genocide of the race through decimation of the female population. Assuming that enlightened governments will intervene with restrictions and incentives before long, still I find the thought of sex selection distressing. Perhaps with high motives, sex selection before impregnation would be ethically justifiable in particular cases. I have no problem with many of the scientific advances that critics claim "play God." I believe we were created to "play God," to participate in his creative activity. But somehow, choosing a child's sex seems to be encroaching a little on God's prerogatives, at least as a general practice or for trivial reasons.

Loving. Parents are to love the children they beget (Titus 2:4; Eph. 6:4; Col. 3:21). The model of what our heavenly Father does in love for us is the standard of total self-giving.

Love for children must be spoken and demonstrated. If it is acted but not spoken, a child may miss the point and languish in the fear that love is not really there. But far worse is to talk it without consistently doing it.

The ultimate unlove is divorce. Divorce is such a terrifying and destructive force in the life of a child because, no matter what the explanation, he knows that at least one—and maybe both—of his parents do not love him enough to make the home work.

Perhaps the best gift parents give their children is to love one another well. When this is visible and strongly felt, an atmosphere of security is created and the parents become role models for all of life's relationships.

Modeling. Every Christian is expected to model the image of God in the process of restoration, so that people may see and give glory to God (Matt. 5:16). In a special way, parents are responsible to live authentic Christian lives before their children (Prov. 23:26). They provide the strongest human influence in the life of the child.

Providing. Parents are responsible to provide materially, physically, socially, spiritually, and mentally (education in contemporary American society) for dependent children. In this way children will grow in wisdom and stature, in favor with God and man (Luke 2:52).

Providing for the family in our society takes money, and earning money almost always takes time away from home. The Christian parent thus faces one of the most critical factors in the current crisis in family stability. At a deeper level, the care for children requires time spent with them. How can this double demand on parental time be reconciled? Though the feminist drive for equal pay is understandable, the end result may well be a leveling down rather than the hoped-for leveling up, and increasingly both parents will have to work to maintain financial viability. In most societies of the past mothers worked outside the home, just as the ideal mother of Proverbs 31. But until the

Industrial Revolution (a terrible time for mothers and children), that work was in the field or forest, with the whole family participating so that the caring and nurturing continued on unabated. How do we solve the dilemma?

The attitude of parents toward one another and toward the children and the quality of time spent together have more to do with the creation of a health-giving atmosphere than does the amount of time together. Nevertheless, the amount of time is part of the equation.

To begin with, children need both parents as a vital part of life. True, the mother seems to have been assigned by nature and Scripture the primary role in nurturing, at least the younger children. But both parents are essential. The solution may be connected with motive—why does the father work such long hours? Why does the mother seek outside employment?

The father may work long hours because of unbiblical values or a misperception of how love is best expressed. Many a sincere father is genuinely surprised to find children alienated when he has "proved his love" unstintingly by such tireless work for many years, never dreaming that his son or daughter really wanted *him* all along, not his lavish gifts. Others are simply materialistic and put the acquisition of things above the development of quality relationship. Still others are proud and drive to prove their worth through outdistancing others in achievement or wealth. Still others are selfish and enjoy work or hobbies or recreation or fun with "the boys" more than time with the family. All these motives are wholly inadequate and if followed may well lead to the crippling or destruction of the family or of some member of the family.

Christian workers sometimes neglect family responsibility for a higher motive—advancing the Kingdom of God. There are times when such a motive is legitimate. Motives must be clear, however. Many a traveling minister travels because he enjoys it. He may even be afraid to face the reality of failure at home and thus seek to escape. If a man is truly called to an itinerant ministry, he may well be called to a life of celibacy, like Paul. If he is already married, he has part of his ministry call already settled—his home—and he will neglect that responsibility only at the risk of everything, for church ministry is reserved for those who succeed in the responsibilities of the home (1 Tim. 3:2-5; Titus 1:6-9).

And why does the mother seek outside employment during the hours a child is at home—or ought to be? If economic survival is the question, the choice is right, but "economic survival" and a better standard of living are not synonymous. Some mothers have a compulsion to work outside the home because only in such work do they find self-worth; otherwise, they're "just a housewife." Instead of glorying in what must surely be the highest of all callings—making a home—she is deceived into thinking that success in the marketplace is the only way to prove one's value. Others work as an escape from the drudgery of diapers and dishes, only to find the drudgery of a nine-to-five routine. And in our society at least, 95 percent return home to play catch-up and do the housework anyway. If material goals or self-image or competing on "an even footing" with men are more important than nurturing children, perhaps the choice not to have children is more reasonable—a choice increasing numbers of "liberated" women make. But that choice, though honest, does not redeem a distorted system of values.

Instructing. Scripture places a premium on teaching one's children.

Fix these words of mine in your hearts and minds; . . . Teach them to your children, talking about them when you sit at home and when you walk along the road, when you lie down and when you get up. Write them on the doorframes of your houses and on your gates, so that your days and the days of your children may be many in the land that the LORD swore to give your forefathers. (Deut. 11:18-21, NIV)

Train up a child in the way he should go, and when he is old he will not depart from it. (Prov. 22:6)

Instruction in the ways of God is the responsibility of both parents, but the father is responsible to be sure it takes place. This includes full participation in the life of a Bible-teaching church, but it is also to be on a daily basis as part of the family life. A daily time when the family gathers to hear and discuss a portion of Scripture, pray and sing together should be the cornerstone of family life.

Disciplining. Solomon, who had more sons than the average modern father, had a very straightforward view of how they should be raised:

He who spares the rod hates his son, but he who loves him is diligent to discipline him. (Prov. 13:24)
Discipline your son while there is hope; do not set your heart on his destruction. (19:18)
Folly is bound up in the heart of a child, but the rod of discipline drives it far from him. (22:15)
Do not withhold discipline from a child; if you beat him with a rod, he will not die. If you beat him with the rod you will save his life from Sheol. (23:13-14)
The rod and reproof give wisdom, but a child left to himself brings shame to his mother. (29:15)
Discipline your son, and he will give you rest; he will give delight to your heart. (29:17)

Does this mean that corporal punishment is the only valid means of discipline? At least these passages mean that corporal punishment cannot be considered wrong. I take it that Paul intended to enunciate the basic principle when he taught parents, and especially fathers, to nurture children in the chastening and admonition of the Lord (Eph. 6:4). Here the chastening is part of the overall nurturing and includes the instruction we have just considered. Perhaps the form of discipline will vary from culture to culture, but the necessity of it is clear.

But Paul warns us: "Fathers, do not provoke your children, lest they become discouraged" (Col. 3:21). What is a biblical balance among love, instruction, and discipline? Child abuse is rampant. It is not confined to drug users and drunks, though the incidence is much higher in such environments, nor is it confined to non-Christian homes. A minister proudly showed me his instrument of justice—a baseball bat split in half. He called it his "rod," but it was actually a club. Had he used it? Only once, he said. When he made it, he called all his six children together and demonstrated the use of his "rod" on his eldest son. "What had he done?" I asked. "Nothing. I just wanted all to see what would be in store for any who disobey."

In reaction to child abuse many are advocating child rights. Certainly a child has every right to be free from physical, verbal, or psychological abuse, but the child liberation movement does not have merely such objectives in mind. In 1979 the Swedish Parliament passed a law by a vote of 259 to 6 prohibiting parents from striking their children or treating them in any other humiliating way. "Humiliating treatment" was construed to mean sending a child to bed without supper, cutting TV rights, bedroom confinement—any of the normal ways in which a child might be punished. Children may have parents prosecuted for such behavior and even may sue for "divorce" from parents with whom they prove incompatible.

What is the biblical middle way between child abuse and domestic anarchy? The first guideline is *consistency*. When discipline is erratic and unpredictable—whether on the part of one parent or when one parent specializes in "love" and the other in "justice"—the child will become discouraged.

The second guideline is *balance*. The results of undisciplined permissiveness on the one hand or unloving discipline on the other are equally damaging.

A final guideline is to *use discipline only when a moral principle is at stake*—deliberate, repeated lying, for example. Of course any issue can become "moral" if the parent issues a direct command. Some parents seek for such confrontations. It is, with them, always, "Pick up the socks!" never, "Would you mind picking up your socks?" Constant confrontation on nonmoral issues will surely cause a child to become discouraged or rebellious. Rules should be appropriate, clear, and as few as possible.

Many earnest young Christian parents try too hard. They are determined that this firstborn will bring glory to God—and credit to his parents. Therefore, the tendency is to drive the child to perfection beyond his years and capacity. At any rate, it is humanly easier to go to one extreme or the other—to become permissive or severe—than to stay at the center of biblical tension, balancing a loving, affirming atmosphere with instruction and guidance in the ways of God. As in God's dealing with his children, rewards are more effective than punishment.

"Daddy, do you 'member?" he chirped in his squeaky little voice. Five-year-old Kent was running after me in the rain to meet the school bus, clutching three umbrellas on his arm for his sisters and brothers, and trying to keep his own new umbrella overhead. "Long legs and short legs."

"Long legs and short legs?"

"Yes, you know. Long legs go faster 'n short legs . . . like big wheels and little wheels."

Then I remembered. A few days earlier he had struggled to keep up on his hand-me-down little rattletrap bike and had asked why my bike coasted downhill faster than his.

And that is a parable of our lives with little people. No parents are good enough or smart enough to create a perfect environment. Why create confrontation by constantly demanding obedience as a parental right? Why not invite participation, counsel, instruct, and slow down in the rain for short legs? Discipline may become virtually unnecessary in a partner relationship custom-designed for each little person.

Limits of Responsibility. Environmental determinism has so triumphed in our thinking that many young couples are afraid to have children and are nervous about them when they come, older parents are burdened with guilt, and young people find themselves locked in a box with no exits. For if it is possible to determine the outcome of a person's life by the environment in which he grows, what parents can carry such a load or bear such a burden of guilt when things do not turn out as they had hoped? And if early environment determines what one will forever be, what hope is there to become something else, to be free from the results of parental failure?

And yet most evangelical counselors and preachers assume the contemporary view that early environment determines what a person will be. I heard a preacher and educator known nationally for his opposition to secular humanism give a series of talks on the family. He proved a total captive of one of the basic tenets of secular humanism. His presentations were unrelieved environmental determinism: If you do the following things, your children will be godly, successful people; if they are not, it is because you failed in the following ways. But Scripture teaches several factors in the outcome of a person's life, not just one.

1. *Heredity.* The Bible takes heredity much more seriously than we have been schooled to do. Family solidarity from

generation to generation is assumed in Scripture, but is difficult for us to understand, committed as we are to individual autonomy. Still, the sins of the fathers, for example, are visited upon the children unto the third and fourth generation (Exod. 20:5). We are all bound to our first father in the most important and most terrible of all acquired characteristics: sin. Generation after generation is infected with the virus of sin, and that one characteristic is more determinative than any other, save for the grace of God. There may be other characteristics that come from one's genetic makeup. Intelligence, for example, is influenced by heredity.[76] Some seem to be independent rebels from birth, whereas others seem to have always been sweet and pliable.

2. *Environment.* The Bible takes environment very seriously: "Train a child in the way he should go, and when he is old he will not depart from it" (Prov. 22:6). Note that this is a proverb, not a promise. It points out the importance of environment, but it does not *guarantee* the outcome of parental endeavor. The parental responsibilities we outlined earlier are of utmost importance for the outcomes in the lives of our children. Environmental influence, yes. Environmental determinism, no. Environment is not the only factor, nor the chief factor. If it were, God himself would be the greatest failure, for the perfect environment he created (with his own presence a chief element of the environment), did not prevent his only two children from rebellion and destruction.

3. *Choices.* Adam and Eve had the perfect Father, perfect "genes," a perfect environment, but the outcome of their lives hinged on their choices. Whether or not human choices are free in the absolute sense, I leave for the theologians to debate. But that God holds us fully responsible for our choices is one of the main themes of the Bible.

Scripture rejects environmental determinism out of hand:

The word of the LORD came to me: "What do you people mean by quoting this proverb about the land of Israel: 'The fathers eat sour grapes, and the children's teeth are set on edge?' As surely as I live, declares the Sovereign LORD, you will no longer quote this proverb in Israel. For every living soul belongs to me, the father as well as the son—both alike belong to me. The soul who sins is the one who will die. Suppose . . . a righteous man . . . has a violent son. . . . Will such a man live? He will not! . . . But suppose this son has a son

[76]Cheryl Fields, "Heredity and Environment, But Not Race, Found to Influence Intelligence," *The Chronicle of Higher Education,* 12 September 1977, 5.

who sees all the sins his father commits, and though he sees them, he does not do such things. . . . He will not die for his father's sin; he will surely live." (Ezekiel 18:1-17, NIV)

This greatly abridged version of God's own detailed exposition of personal responsibility for human choices and his affirmation that they are crucial for the outcome of life, appears in the specific context of parental influence.

4. *Providence*. God's intervention with forgiveness, cleansing, strength to change, and hope is the most important factor in the outcome of a life. He is in the business of reversing all that my heredity, early environment, and wrong choices have done to me. Here is relief from fear that I will be an inadequate parent. Of course I will be. But God is not. His sovereign plan will be accomplished no matter what my failure or that of others. Here is my relief from guilt when my children fail. They are ultimately responsible, and the same God who is changing me is available to them. Here is relief from hopelessness. No matter how others have failed me or how I have failed myself, God can set me free! And here is the corrective for sinful arrogance—assuming full credit for children who turn out well.

RESPONSIBILITY OF THE CHILD

"Honor your father and your mother" (Exodus 20:12) is the comprehensive statement of the child's responsibility. Such honor is due, not on the basis that a parent has earned it or is worthy of it, but on the basis of an eternal relationship. No one will ever have any other parents from whom he derives life. Honor is due because of this permanent relationship. It expresses itself in several ways.

Loving. "My son, give me your heart" (Prov. 23:26) is the cry of every parent worthy of the name. But there are some parents who shamefully abuse their children. Those children can hardly respect their parents or follow them. But they can choose to act in a loving way. They may not be able to control their affections to feel warm or close, but they can choose to act for the eternal best interests of those parents.

Obeying. Children are to obey their parents (Eph. 6:1; Col. 3:20). Are there circumstances in which this law does not apply? The command is that the child obey his parents in the Lord. This seems to imply some condition in the relationship, though precisely what is not stated.

If a child feels that the parent is requiring moral wrong of him, he is justified in refusing obedience. However, if he does obey, there is a principle of Scripture that would indicate he is guiltless and the guilt rests with the parent who forced him to sin. Numbers 30:15 states this in the relationship of husband and wife. When the husband countermands the wife, he bears the guilt, not she. This seems to indicate a principle of releasing from guilt one who feels he has no option but to obey his God-given authority. In such a case he is judged by God, apparently, as being no more than an instrument of the other person's action.

On the other hand, there is the basic principle enunciated repeatedly in Ezekiel 18 that there is personal responsibility on the part of each person. As an adult, at least, one cannot assign responsibility to the parent. Personal responsibility for one's choices and behavior are clearly enunciated throughout this passage.

Another principle (Gen. 2:24) has to do with the question of when a man is to leave his father and mother. As we have seen, this is not simply or even primarily a physical leaving, but an emotional leaving. The honor for parents is to continue a lifetime, but this priority-relationship is not to overbear when the adult is married. Much grief and marriage failure come from the sinful interference of in-laws and the sinful acceptance of that interference on the part of the married son or daughter.

In some way, then, the child should obey until he reaches the age of independent responsibility to God. What is the age of direct responsibility to the Lord for the son or daughter who is not married? The Bible does not address this question directly, but by analogy with the law concerning marriage, it would seem that a person should obey his parents in all nonmoral matters so long as he is dependent on them for his livelihood. This does not mean he may not seek to persuade them while he is still dependent, nor that he will reject their counsel when he is independent. But he will assume personal responsibility for his choices of marriage partner, vocation, investment of life. He cannot delegate this responsibility to others. In honoring his parents at this stage he respects their counsel, carefully weighs their judgment, follows their advice if at all possible. And he is patient, praying for and wisely working toward a consensus with them. But in the final analysis he must make his own choices, particularly in life-determining decisions.

Many sincere Christian adults have missed God's way because ungodly or selfish parents stood in the way. But this is thoroughly unbiblical.

> Do not think that I have come to bring peace on earth; I have not come to bring peace, but a sword. For I have come to set a man against his father, and a daughter against her mother, and a daughter-in-law against her mother-in-law; and a man's foes will be those of his own household. He who loves father or mother more than me is not worthy of me. (Matt. 10:34-37; see also Luke 12:51-53)

> If any one comes to me and does not hate his own father and mother and wife and children and brothers and sisters, yes, and even his own life, he cannot be my disciple. Whoever does not bear his own cross and come after me, cannot be my disciple. (Luke 14:26-27)

These sayings are difficult to understand and more difficult to apply, but Christ clearly means to distinguish a priority of obligation. To fulfill God's will, it may be necessary to violate the will of the very one we would most desire to please. There are times when one must take a position that parents may consider a hateful response, but which is, in fact, rejecting the desire of a human being for the higher responsibility to please God. But the son or daughter who truly honors his parents will never make such a choice lightly, nor will he ever use it as an excuse to cover his own stubborn self-will (Mark 7:11).

Furthermore, the honor continues throughout life. Even if the parent is dishonorable, cruel, an alcoholic, or has sexually violated the child, it is the responsibility of the Christian son or daughter to keep his end of the obligation. It does not mean that the behavior of the parent is to be approved or even accepted. I lived for many years with a man who honored his father by not saying much about him. What he did say was positive. Only after the son's death did I learn that his father was alcoholic and, as a result, that the responsibility for a large family fell on his teenage shoulders. He rejected his father's ways, but he honored him always.

Caring for in Old Age. The Lord arranged a beautiful solidarity of generations: the parents have the privilege of caring for their children for the first decades of life and the children may have the privilege of caring for their parents for the last decades. Sometimes there is a child who is dependent for a lifetime, and sometimes a parent becomes dependent for what seems a lifetime; but the average responsibility of child for a parent is less than a decade in contemporary America. No child should feel any sense of guilt for putting a parent in an institution if that is truly the only place the parent can be adequately cared for. But the multitudes of children who put away their parents for selfish reasons—often neglecting even to keep in touch—violate the Fifth Commandment in a despicable way. "If any one does not provide for his relatives, and especially for his own family, he has disowned the faith and is worse than an unbeliever" (1 Tim. 5:8).

Should not the parents fully provide for their own old age and possible infirmity? In fact, does not Paul teach that parents should lay up in store for their children (2 Cor. 12:14)? Indeed, Paul quotes a proverb to make an analogy to what he intends to do for his spiritual children, not burdening them. But the parent who cannot provide for his old age, or the parent who has not done so, becomes a wonderful opportunity for his children to demonstrate their love and loyalty and gratitude for life itself and for all the sacrifice those parents have invested in them.

There is some tension between this isolated proverb quoted by Paul (to make another point) and the overwhelming New Testament teaching about seeking first the Kingdom of God as the primary investment of one's resources. I resolve the tension in two ways: A parent should provide for his children as fully as he is able until they are independent. To provide more for them often has the very opposite effect of that intended: continued dependence on the efforts of others, lack of initiative, ingratitude, greedy sibling conflict, and a host of other evils spawned by one's inborn love of money (1 Tim. 6:10). Rather, the parent who has prepared his child well for life and demonstrated the New Testament mandate to invest above all in the Kingdom of God, will do the best for his children.

On the other hand, a parent should not hesitate to provide prudently for his own old age. The average person cannot provide for every possible eventuality and, in honest stewardship of the Lord's possessions entrusted to him, probably should not try to. Certainly if such effort is based on fearful unbelief or is an excuse to justify a materialistic outlook, it is clearly wrong.

One biblically authentic approach, then, would be full provision for his children to reach independence, prudent provision for his own retirement if he is able and free of conscience to do so, and joyful trust in the Lord and in his children for any further provision that may become necessary.[77]

Such are the responsibilities of children for their parents: honor, love, obey, and provide.

We have devoted more attention to the topic of sex, marriage, and the home for several reasons. In the first place, we have combined the consideration of two of the Ten Commandments (the fifth and seventh). Furthermore, this topic is emphasized more than any other ethical issue in Scripture. Finally, this is the area of life which seems to be most under assault by the powers of evil. We seem most vulnerable here, and we must do all within our power to mobilize the forces of our biblical understanding, of our combined Christian commitment, and of the concerted action of right-thinking people to defend this basic building block of personal and social well-being.

God's invention of human sexuality is wonderful. It is his good gift of love to his children for their delight and welfare. It is fully worthy of defense against all exploitation and distortion, and this we have attempted to do with the strong Word of the living God.

SUGGESTED ADDITIONAL READINGS

SEX

Chapman, Gary. *Toward a Growing Marriage*. Chicago: Moody, 1979.

LaHaye, Tim and Beverly. *The Act of Marriage*. Grand Rapids: Zondervan, 1976.

Small, Dwight H. *Christian, Celebrate Your Sexuality*. Old Tappan, N.J.: Revell, 1974.

Thielicke, Helmut. *Theological Ethics*. Vol. 3, *Sex*. Translated by John

[77]These principles will be considered in greater detail in the chapter on "Integrity."

Doberstein. Grand Rapids: Eerdmans, 1979.

Trobisch, Walter, and others. *Essays on Love: A HIS Reader*. Madison, Wis.: InterVarsity, 1968.

Tournier, Paul. *To Understand Each Other*. Translated by John S. Gilmour. Richmond: John Knox, 1967.

Wheat, Ed and Gaye. *Intended for Pleasure*. Old Tappan, N.J.: Revell, 1981.

CHRISTIAN HOME

Adams, Jay. *Christian Living in the Home*. Grand Rapids: Baker, 1974.

Christiansen, Larry. *The Christian Family*. Minneapolis: Bethany Fellowship. 1970.

Hendricks, H. G. *Heaven Help the Home*. Wheaton, Ill.: Victor, 1973.

SINGLENESS

Collins, Gary R., ed. *It's OK to Be Single*. Waco, Tex.: Word, 1976.

CHILDREN

Campbell, Ross. *How to Really Love Your Child*. Wheaton, Ill.: Victor, 1977.

Dobson, James. *Dare to Discipline*. Wheaton, Ill.: Tyndale, 1973.

Meier, Paul. *Christian Child Rearing and Personality Development*. Grand Rapids: Baker, 1977.

White, John. *Parents in Pain*. Madison: InterVarsity, 1979.

DIVORCE

Laney, Carl J. *The Divorce Myth: A Biblical Examination of Divorce and Remarriage*. Minneapolis: Bethany House, 1981. Perhaps the best defense of the "no-divorce-or-remarriage" position.

Murray, John. *Divorce*. Philadelphia: Presbyterian and Reformed, 1961. Considered by many the standard work on the traditional view of the Protestant church.

WIFE ABUSE

An annotated bibliography may be found in *Christianity Today*, 25 November 1983.

ROLE OF WOMEN

Boldrey, Richard and Joyce. *Chauvinist or Feminist? Paul's View of Women*. Grand Rapids: Baker, 1976. A scholarly defense of biblical feminism and an annotated bibliography by Donald Dayton.

Johnson, Robert K. *The Role of Women in the Church and Home: An Evangelical Test Case in Hermeneutics, Scripture, Tradition, and Interpretation*. Edited by W. Ward Gasque and William Sanford LaSor. Grand Rapids: Eerdmans, 1978. An excellent overview of opposing views on the role of women in the church, primarily, and also in the home.

HOMOSEXUALITY

Bailey, D. Sherwin. *Homosexuality and the Western Christian Tradition*. New York: Longmans, Green, 1955. The sourcebook for much of the rationale for the new, more open view toward homosexuality within the church.

Lovelace, Richard F. *Homosexuality and the Church*. Old Tappan, N.J.: Revell, 1978. The most comprehensive and scholarly presentation of the history, theology, and biblical teaching on homosexuality by an evangelical.

McNeill, John J. *The Church and the Homosexual*. 3d ed. Boston: Beacon, 1988. According to Lovelace, the most complete survey of the theological literature on homosexuality available.

CHAPTER EIGHT

LIFE ISSUES

Thou shalt not kill.

Murder is considered the worst of all crimes more universally than any other, and at the same time is the sin most universally practiced. Most practiced, because Christ would not let us get away with restricting the law to those who slit throats or blow off heads. Jesus said, "You have heard that it was said to the men of old, '. . . whoever kills shall be liable to judgment.' But I say to you that every one who is angry with his brother shall be liable to judgment" (Matt. 5:21-22). Even anger violates the Sixth Commandment.

FORMS OF KILLING

By including anger and verbal abuse in the category of murder, Jesus did not say nor mean that they were as evil as murder. But they are the same variety of sin and may not be excused as mere human weakness. In fact, all sin, including murder, is rather like an onion. Beneath the final act are lesser acts, and beneath all the acts is a corrupt heart. Murder is highly visible, the full-grown sin, but when the outer layer is peeled away, various levels of violence are seen as part of the same "onion," and beneath the physical and verbal abuse is the heart of anger, hatred, or failing love. If the core of inadequate love is planted and allowed to grow, the hateful activity will follow. And all of it falls under the judgment of God.

MURDER

Some vegetarians have held that when God inscribed "You shall not kill" (Exod. 20:13) in stone at Sinai, he forbade the taking of any life for any cause. Some pacifists have held that he forbade the taking of any human life for any cause. But the commandment cannot be taken that way, for Moses, who received the Law, commanded the taking of animal life for sacrifices and food and the taking of human life in war and capital punishment. "Thou shalt not kill," in the context of Old Testament law, meant to deliberately take a human life which the Bible gives no authority to take. The questions of war and capital punishment are so important and complex we shall consider them later in greater detail. But there is one other biblical exception to the law against taking human life: killing in self-defense.

SELF-DEFENSE

Physical resistance in self-defense seems to be validated in Scripture (Num. 35:22ff.; Exod. 21:13; 22:2) but not commanded. There is a higher way—the law of love. Christ did not resist evil, but gave himself to evil men to provide for their salvation.

Not all actions called self-defense are legitimate, and there is a hierarchy among those which are. Defense of others or even of one's self is certainly of higher priority than the defense of material possessions. Bu when there is danger of physical harm, a key question is whether or not life is in jeopardy. That is the clearest validation of self-defense.

Another basic question for the Christian is whether the impending harm is crime-oriented or whether it is persecution for Christ's sake. One might choose nonresistance when suffering for Christ, but choose to resist in a crime-oriented aggression for the sake of others or even for the sake of the aggressor himself. If the choice is made to resist physical violence, the Christian should ask whether or not physical resistance is the only action available or whether there are other options such as talk or deception. If there seems to be no other option but to resist with physical force, the Christian should discern whether killing is the only alternative or whether lesser violence would accomplish adequate restraint.

Though there are exceptions in which God authorizes the taking of human life, the sin of murder is the ultimate sin against a human being (Lev. 24:17; Num. 35:16-21). Life may not be the supreme value, but it is certainly a critical one for the continued pursuit of other values! And the value of life is probably the watershed issue for any society.

VIOLENCE

In a decaying society murder may still be abhorred, but violence short of murder often becomes acceptable. Studies have repeatedly shown that violence in the entertainment media fosters such acceptance. But the ugly end result is a sick society where spouse abuse and child abuse is said to touch one of four people.

Christ's commentary on the Sixth Commandment emphasized *verbal* abuse. James (1:26; 3:1-12) and Solomon (Prov. 13:3; 15:1, 4, 23; 17:28; 18:8, 13; 21:23; 29:20) had a great deal to say about sins of the tongue, but the rest of Scripture is strong on the subject as well. James says the tongue is like wildfire and poison. It not only poisons relationships and burns up the lives of others, it consumes the one himself whose tongue is not disciplined by the Spirit (James 3).

A direct attack on a person with carping criticism or biting depreciation, sarcastic humor, or subtle insinuation can destroy something in that person. But just as deadly is the criticism spoken about a person to others. The law of love seals the lips. Any word that harms another is murder, unless spoken in love to that person or spoken only to another who is responsible to correct the wrong (Matt. 18:15-18). The absent person is just as safe with the Spirit-directed child of God as the one who is present with him.

NEGLECT

Another way to harm is by doing and saying nothing when a word or an action would keep from harm. Failure to put a balustrade around a flat rooftop brought bloodguiltiness if someone fell from the roof (Deut. 22:8). Failure to do good, when in one's power to do so, is sin (Prov. 3:27-28). So the poor, the helpless, and the starving are my responsibility to the extent I have ability to help. To be silent when another is falsely accused, whether in a court of law or in the presence of private gossip, is to participate in the harm. Neglect, then, is another form of murder (see also Exod. 21:29-31).

ANGER

Incredibly, Christ's commentary on the Sixth Commandment includes a person's inner state. Anger is subject to God's judgment (Matt. 5:22). This was not original with Jesus. Moses had already recorded God's will, "You shall not hate your brother in your heart . . . or bear any grudge against the sons of your own people, but you shall love your neighbor as yourself" (Lev. 19:17-18). Lack of love, as well as positive hatred, is a form of murder.

Anger is not always wrong. If it were, God would be the chief sinner, for he is angry every day (Ps. 7:11). And note that David does not say God is angry merely at sin. He is angry with wicked people.[1] The wrath of God is seen throughout the Old and New Testaments and is the inevitable result of his holy character exposed to unholy attitudes and behavior.

But is it possible for a sinful mortal to be godlike in his anger? It must not be easy, for the Bible is filled with teaching against anger. Anger is to be put away (Eph. 4:31; Col. 3:8); whoever is angry is in danger of judgment (Matt. 5:22); anger is one of the works of the flesh (Gal. 5:19-20); does not work the righteousness of God (James 1:20); and is the prerogative of God, not man (Rom. 12:19). Proverbs condemns anger repeatedly.

But Jesus was angry (Mark 3:5), and we are commanded in our anger to refrain from sin (Ps. 4:4; Eph. 4:26), to be slow about it (Titus 1:7; James 1:19), and to get over it quickly (Eph. 4:26). There seems to be approval of being angry under some circumstances, but the major biblical emphasis is on anger as evil; exceptions seem very limited.

Anger at sin, even anger at the sinner, can be a good thing (2 Cor. 7:11). Jeremiah was full of the fury of the Lord (6:11),

[1]For a full exposition of this theme, see Leon Morris, *The Apostolic Preaching of the Cross* (Grand Rapids: Eerdmans, 1955).

and Paul was angry over the idolatry of the Athenians (Acts 17:16). Yet Christ himself refrained from anger when the offense was against him personally (1 Pet. 2:23-24) and "like a sheep that before its shearers is dumb, so he opened not his mouth" (Isa. 53:7).

Righteous and unrighteous anger can be distinguished by the cause of anger. One should be angry over sin that offends God, harms others or harms the person sinning. The difficulty with being righteously indignant is that our motives are mixed. Am I distressed over a sin that offends God and harms people, or am I angry over the way I am affected? Since motives are mixed, the safe thing may be to eschew anger altogether when the sin of another directly affects me, as when my child does wrong but the wrong embarrasses me. Better to wait till the anger subsides to be sure the resulting action does not come from a mixture of righteous and unrighteous indignation. Anger is sinful when it is for the wrong reason or results in the wrong action.

Some say that God's anger is merely judicial—he takes a position of judgment against sin. The theory is that God's wrath is impersonal and objective and without any emotion of indignation on his part. But this is not the biblical picture of a God who burns with fury. Judging by the reaction of Jesus to sin against himself, this fury is over what sin does to the sinner and those he sins against rather than over what sin does to God himself. But God's example does imply that some people, if they were filled with the Spirit, would become angry, possibly for the first time. In an age when "there is no sin but the sin of intolerance," some of us need to be stirred to participate with an angry God against the wickedness, oppression, and evil of this world.

To keep this emotion from igniting for the wrong reason or from burning out of control, Scripture gives two ways of control: Take it easy—don't get angry suddenly (James 1:19) and don't let it keep burning—don't let it last till the next day (Eph. 4:26). Either a "low flashpoint," a quick response without reflection, or a "slow burn," continuing on with the emotion, seem to risk causing even righteous indignation to go astray.

Against the clear teaching of Scripture that most (not all) human anger is wrong and that the proper response is to control it (Prov. 16:32), many Christian psychologists hold that anger is morally neutral and must be expressed.[2] To this we respond that anger is neutral in the same way that hatred and killing are neutral: sometimes they are right, mostly they are wrong. Anger in itself is a wrong emotion to have if it is directed against the wrong object (God, an innocent person, a thing); for the wrong cause (personal offense); or leads on to wrong behavior (retaliation, vengeance, physical violence).

Anger under these circumstances should not be denied *or* expressed. It should rather be confessed as sin and the resources of God appropriated to control the emotion itself.

Lloyd H. Steffen, writing in "On Anger," indicates that anger is not always bad: "Sometimes only anger will make us act to address a grievance or change a situation." But, addressing the position common among psychologists that anger must be ventilated, he responds:

Ventilating anger is like ventilating a fire. The environment will only become more heated and smoky, the damage will only increase. Ventilating anger postpones investigation of its causes and the beginning of repairs. . . . Our anger is usually a response to things that we perceive as somehow injuring us, or that keep us from having our own way.[3]

To encourage a person who feels guilty about his anger by assuring him that there is nothing wrong with this perfectly human reaction, and that the only healthful thing is to express the anger and not feel guilty, will simply drive the sensitive Christian's real guilt "underground" and put off the day of biblical resolution. Rather, the person needs to be encouraged to evaluate in the light of Scripture whether his anger is godly, and if it is not, to confess his sin, thus removing all guilt. Then he should trust God for his resources in overcoming the temptation.

RACISM

Racism technically refers to the idea that certain nonracial characteristics, especially cultural patterns, are the result of race. An example would be to generalize from the behavior of some

[2]For a helpful exchange on the matter, see Charles Cerling, Jr., J. Pedersen, and John Hower, *Journal of Psychology and Theology,* 1974, vol. 2, numbers 1, 2, and 4.
[3]Lloyd H. Steffen, *The Christian Century,* 16 January 1985, 47.

people of a given race, assigning that kind of behavior to all belonging to the same race. The result is often hatred, intolerance, or unjust discrimination. Since this attitude is often expressed more freely and forcefully by the majority race in a given community, the label "racist" is often assigned to those who consider their own race superior and oppress others. But racist attitudes and actions are quite possible among an oppressed minority, even when the assumption of their own inferiority is accepted. No people is immune to the virus of racism, ungodly attitudes based on racial differences. Of course, the same kind of sinful attitudes and behavior can be based on differences of culture, language, tribe, socially defined class or caste, as well as on race.

CORPORATE RESPONSIBILITY

Unjust and unloving behavior can become characteristic of a group and become corporate or even institutionalized injustice or oppression. Laws themselves or the way a legal system operates may discriminate against a class of people. Again, there may be no law, but society may function in unjust and unmerciful ways.

BIBLICAL VIEW OF DISCRIMINATION

Class discrimination that works to the harm of some in a society is virtually a universal phenomenon. For the Christian even to have *feelings* of superiority is sin (Phil. 2:1-8). To base such feelings on class distinction is both sinful and foolish (James 2:1-9). Racial discrimination is widespread but not so universal as class discrimination. The Bible has very little to say about race, possibly because the contemporary distinction based on physical characteristics was not the same issue in the ancient world.

Ironically, modern racism received its greatest impetus from scientists of the last century. The subtitle of Charles Darwin's *Origin of Species* was "The Preservation of Favored Races in the Struggle for Life." Virtually all nineteenth-century evolutionists held to the theory of superior and inferior races.

Some have held that the Bible affirms both racial segregation and unjust discrimination (slavery, for example), but it does not do so.[4] God did require segregation and discrimination among people, but always based on religious distinctions, never on race or class distinctives.

Though slavery was not forbidden in Scripture, God's attitude can clearly be seen in the restrictions set on an existing system of slavery (Deut. 15:12-18; 23:15-16 compared with 22:1-4; Philemon). His view of discrimination against the poor, the weak, the minority person, the oppressed is clear and strong. The alien was to be fully incorporated in the law of love and into the social community (Lev. 19:33-34; Exod. 23:9; Deut. 10:18); treated equally before the law (Lev. 24:22; Exod. 12:49); included in the religious life (Exod. 12:48-49; Ezek. 44:9; Isa. 56:3); and would participate fully in God's plan for the future (Isa. 49:6; 52:14-15; Ezek. 47:22-23; Zech. 2:11). God's terrible judgment on Israel was in part because of their treatment of foreigners (Jer. 7:5-7; 22:2-5; Ezek. 22:7-15; Zech. 7:10-14; Mal. 3:1-5). God himself is set to protect the alien (Num. 15:15-16).

When God so strongly opposes all injustice, including the injustice resulting from class and racial discrimination, why do Christians almost universally participate in their own cultural patterns of discrimination rather than joining with other believers to provide a radically biblical counter-culture of justice, mercy, and unity?

CAUSES OF RACISM

Pride is a root cause. And it is such a foolish pride, based on physical characteristics for which one has no responsibility. Probably pride of race, however, is based on cultural differences more than on the purely physical differences. We generalize from the very real, profound, and wide-ranging differences in culture to assume that the highly visible physical differences are an indispensable part of the group's distinctives. Since people naturally prefer to associate with those whom they understand and with whom they agree, segregation in one form or another seems inevitable. Which natural affinity grouping may be legitimate and which is sinful thus becomes an abiding dilemma. It is the task of the Christian and the church to work at solving this

[4]See chapter on "Marriage." James O. Buswell III has written in detail in *Slavery, Segregation, and Scripture* (Grand Rapids: Eerdmans, 1964).

dilemma with wisdom, compassion, and courage. Pride says, "Our way is the best way," and then concludes that all other ways are inferior.

Ignorance extends this judgment to identify cultural patterns with skin color, and the observed behavior of some is generalized to characterize all in the group. "All Indians march in single file . . . at least the one I saw did." So pride and the ignorance of faulty logic combine to divide and hurt.

In addition to pride and ignorant generalizing, fear is a major cause of racial and class strife, fear of the unknown. Patterns of segregation increase the ignorance of what the other group is really like, and the prior decision to view whatever it *is* like as inferior to "our way" creates an atmosphere of fear in which imagination has more influence than reality. Another fear is that of being hurt by "the enemy," either through his deliberate antagonism or through being deprived of some real or potential benefit because of him. When one's person, possessions, or position is put in jeopardy by someone else, fear, whether reasonable or not, begins to determine behavior. Fear can cause a member of a powerless minority to be just as racist in attitudes and actions as those who have the power to impose injustice. Thus pride and fear often combine with ignorance to produce the full range of attitudes and actions of racism, from inadequate love, through hatred and violence, to structured injustice and killing.

Who is correct, the blacks or the whites? Consider the following standoff:

If there are niggers in heaven, I don't want to go there. [leading church layman in private conversation]

We have begun to draw pictures that will make people go out and kill pigs [police] . . . we will not hesitate to either kill or die for our freedom.[5]

Whatever the perceptions and misperceptions, how did we get into the terrible impasse of blacks locked into ghettos of poverty, crime, unemployment, and disintegrating families, while white Christians don't consider it a major problem? White Americans rated racism thirty-first among the problems facing the nation. . . . Yet blacks, in the same survey, said racism was the number one problem facing America.[6]

[5]*The Black Panther*, 31 October 1970, 4.
[6]Mark Olson, "White Follies, Black Shackles," *The Other Side*, June 1979, 16.

THE AMERICAN BLACK

Some, like Tom Skinner, leading black evangelical spokesman, say American racial problems are a white problem. There are at least two differing emphases among those who hold this view. (Some hold that black and white are today reaping the whirlwind from the winds generated by America's slaveholding forefathers. White attitudes and black behavior patterns, both destructive to the black, were created during 250 years of American slavery.)

Later studies discount this and point to present social structures and personal attitudes as the problem.[7] This view sees high potential in black Americans, but a potential from which most blacks are permanently barred by a tightly woven social fabric that begins with poverty and poor education leading to unemployment, low-paying jobs, and crime.

Others say that the problem is basically black. The older view was that blacks were, as a race, inferior; therefore, it was appropriate for others to treat them so and for black people to accept inferior roles. The nineteenth-century evolutionists reinforced that position, and to this day a few religious people advocate it, some even defending the institution of slavery. Perhaps this viewpoint has gotten a new lease on life through the studies of Berkeley professor Arthur Jensen, Stanford University Nobel Prize winner William Shockley, and a handful of others who suggest the possibility of genetically derived mental characteristics.[8] These views have been rejected with a sense of outrage by the vast majority of behavioral scientists who refuse even to make the question a matter of scientific investigation. The conclusion reached by most American academic, media, and political leaders is that society, particularly white majority society, is responsible to change the environment (as noted above).

But another conclusion from the same theory of social conditioning holds the black person primarily responsible for his own deliverance; at least deliverance cannot be won without his participation. Charles Silberman, a strong advocate of black causes, holds this position:

[7]See Herbert G. Gutman, *The Black Family in Slavery and Freedom, 1750 to 1925* (New York: Pantheon, 1979) and Alex Haley, *Roots: The Saga of an American Family* (New York: Doubleday, 1979).
[8]See *Chronicle of Higher Education,* 12 September 1977.

The Negro will be unable to compete on equal terms until he has been able to purge from his mind all sense of white superiority and black inferiority—until he really believes, with all his being, that he is a free man, and acts accordingly. In this sense, therefore, only the Negro can solve the Negro problem. . . . If all discrimination were to end immediately, that alone would not materially improve the Negro's position. The unpleasant fact is that too many Negroes are unable—and unwilling—to compete in an integrated society.[9]

These grave black problems will not be fully solved by human wisdom and political actions, not only because of their vast complexity but because the root problem is sin. Therefore, the church alone holds the solution, but the church has failed. We turn next to consider that failure.

Note that we have dealt with America's most severe racial problem, but that the principles involved apply equally to Jewish, Hispanic, and all other ethnic groups who have been wrongly discriminated against.

RACISM IN THE CHURCH

Political action is necessary, but only a cure of the spirit can bring about a lasting solution. Only the transforming work of Christ in the human heart is adequate to the sin problem. But the problem remains: racism has infected the church with the same virus. In fact, sometimes the strain within the church seems more virulent and less subject to cure than outside. How can the church cleanse and heal its own members and then become God's instrument to cleanse and heal society?

The New Birth. New people alone can build a new society. But church membership does not bring this about automatically. The most severe racial problems have been in the southern states and in South Africa where the incidence of born-again church members is high. Historically, black Christians, under far greater provocation, have overcome racial prejudice more than white, though this seems to be changing. How does one get Christians to behave like Christians?

Teaching. The church has the responsibility to teach the truth that we are all one in Christ Jesus (Gal. 3:26-28; Eph. 2:11-14;

[9]Charles E. Silberman, *Crisis in Black and White* (New York: Random House, 1964), 12, 70.

4:3-4; Col. 3:10-11). But since attitudes are so enculturated as to be unconscious, the church must apply this truth rigorously, pointing out the insidious outcroppings of racial prejudice and God's hatred of this sin against the unity of his body.

Personal Relations. Teaching must be activated in the personal relationship of blacks and whites on the job, in the community, in the home, and in the church. The loving fellowship intended by the Father among members of his family must be lived out. "Teaching" includes spiritual supervision, of course, so that members of the church are disciplined in living what is taught.

Truly new people who are taught and disciplined in Scripture, sensitive to the Holy Spirit, and obedient to the Lord of the church can make a difference. Black and white people of this kind can build godly personal relations and wake a culture-bound church. The awakened, free church can influence its community to build a more just and merciful society.

Structure and Program. The church must not only teach and help individuals find the right way, it must eliminate every direct or indirect church policy of racial discrimination.

Affirmative Action. It would be absurd to insist that all who speak different languages must belong to the same local congregation when more than one language group has a church. There are other "languages" as well—cultural and theological. Ways of worship differ radically, and doctrinal issues are important to people. Must all be forced into the same local congregation when more than one type of fellowship is available? Does "affirmative action" mean that Scripture requires every black church, for example, to aggressively recruit whites until there is a racial balance equivalent to society at large? I believe this goes beyond any biblical mandate. On the other hand, though churches and other groups tend to develop along lines of cultural compatibility, this does not give license for any church to put formal or informal impediments to full participation by anyone, regardless of race, social status or any other nonmoral characteristic.[10]

[10]For further discussion of this controversial issue, see *The Pasadena Consultation* on the homogeneous unit principle, (Pasadena: LCWE, 1977; also printed in *Missiology,* October 1977); Donald McGavran, "The Priority of Ethnicity," *Evangelical Missions Quarterly,* January 1983.

We must, however, work aggressively for unity in the body of
Christ and labor together for the advance of Christ's Kingdom
in which there is no barrier between white and black, high-class
and low-class, male and female, rich and poor.

Another evidence of racism in the church were the
paternalistic, if not colonialistic, attitudes and relationships of
many missionaries in the past. This has been replaced, in some
instances, by a new racism, a nationalism that has given birth to
anti-white attitudes among some church leaders in non-Western
nations. Either type of racism is unworthy of those who are
called Christian.

The principles enunciated for racism in the American church
apply just as much to the far more common worldwide problem
of classism, or making un-Christian discrimination on the basis
of a person's social status. Tribal warfare across the continent of
Africa, for example, and the caste system which holds hundreds
of millions of Indians in abject bondage make the evil of racism
in North America pale by comparison. Yet we are responsible
not for the sins of others, but for our own. And measured by the
pain inflicted, racism in the United States is a grievous personal
and social ill.

ABORTION AND INFANTICIDE

Unwanted infants and unwanted fetuses have been killed from
time immemorial, both when the killing was legal and when it
was illegal. Until recently the church never seriously debated the
morality of killing an infant for any reason. But because of the
recent introduction into the abortion controversy of new
concepts about "personhood" and "quality of life," the debate
has begun to encompass the newborn as well. Even so, for those
ethicists who acknowledge the full authority of Scripture, there
is no room for any view that would justify the killing of infants,
no matter how handicapped or unwanted. To deliberately take
the life of an infant is, in orthodox Christian belief, murder.

Since many of the arguments used to vindicate the
widespread fatal neglect or actual killing of infants are the same
as those used in the abortion issue and since Bible-committed
Christians do not debate the morality of killing an innocent

person, we leave the question of infanticide and turn immediately to the abortion issue.

To set the context, consider the stages of human development:

1. Sperm. There are between 250 and 300 million spermatozoa in a single ejaculation.

2. Zygote. One sperm and the ovum unite (conception) within forty-eight hours of intercourse, and the fertilized ovum makes its four-to-six-day journey down the fallopian tube, seeking implantation in the uterus (womb). Up to one half of zygotes do not make it to implantation.

3. Embryo. The fertilized ovum or "egg" is implanted, and the embryo is established in its own individual life, though 4 percent of twins divide *after* implantation.

4. Fetus. The embryo has developed all human physical characteristics by about eight weeks and is called a fetus from then till birth.

5. Infant. Birth into physical independence of the mother, though, unlike most animals, still wholly dependent on others for survival.

6. Child

7. Youth

8. Adult

Killing of a human being at stages 5 (infant) through 8 (adult) has been considered a violation of the Sixth Commandment throughout church history. Killing sperm (stage 1) or preventing conception has been opposed by the Roman Catholic church as sinful, but has not been opposed by most Protestant churches.[11] Controversy rages concerning stage 2 (zygote) through stage 4 (fetus) of human development.

BEGINNING OF LIFE

The crux of the issue is the question: at which stage does an immortal person begin?

Perhaps "soul" is the theological equivalent of the secular "person." Historically the church has debated the issue of ensoulment—when does the physical body possess a soul? Is it

[11]See chapter on "Sex, Marriage and the Family."

passed on through biological generation from one's parents? Or is there such an entity called "soul" with an existence separate from a body? Does God create a soul and "implant" it in a human body? If so, at what stage does he do this? At conception? At "quickening"? At birth? Theologians do not agree because Scripture does not say.)

The question of the beginning of "soul" is the key issue for the Christian, for he wants to know when a merely potential human being becomes an immortal soul. *That* is when truly human life begins. Will all failed spermatozoa live as human beings through eternity? What will become of spontaneously aborted zygotes and embryos? Will only fetuses who reach live birth prove immortal? Even the concept of what the term *soul* means is difficult to determine from scriptural data, let alone when the soul begins. Since Scripture does not speak directly to the issue of when "ensoulment" takes place, if we are to discover when immortal human life begins, we are shut up to rational deduction from what Scripture says concerning the unborn and to the data of science and philosophical ethics.

Because of recent advances in our knowledge of prenatal life, virtually all agree that the zygote (fertilized egg) is alive and that it is human. The contention of some pro-choice advocates that the embryo is merely a tissue or organ of the mother, like her appendix, gave way in the seventies before the weight of scientific evidence. Virtually all agree that zygotes, embryos, and fetuses are individuals of the human species. The zygote's unique DNA code is already determining its independent existence, including the processes of the pregnancy itself. So the debate has shifted from the question of when human life begins to the question of the value of various forms of life.

VALUE OF LIFE

Since the unborn are already a form of human life, many in the pro-life movement hold that abortion of zygote, embryo, or fetus is a form of murder and must be outlawed by any moral society. At the other extreme are those who hold that there are differences of value among human lives and that not all human beings are "persons." In the landmark 1973 *Roe v. Wade* decision of the Supreme Court, Justice Harry Blackmun introduced the concept of "useful life." To end a life that is not useful may not only be permissible but actually mandatory for the ethically sensitive person. The key issue is said to be the "quality of life," not the "sanctity of life." Between these two opposite viewpoints range the majority of specialists and ordinary people in America.

THE RIGHT TO CHOOSE

Pro-abortion forces say that abortion was common in nineteenth-century America until the medical associations campaigned to bring it under their jurisdiction for reasons of professional self-interest, and that the contemporary more lenient view of abortion was triggered by a British Act of Parliament in 1967, which merely returned us to "normal." This reading of history is questionable. In the first place, the action of the medical associations was moral in nature and based on fresh scientific evidence that human life began prior to "quickening." Second, the contemporary movement for liberalizing abortion laws did not just happen spontaneously.

Humanist Manifesto I, the Magna Carta of the liberal establishment, strongly promoted abortion and euthanasia in the 1930s. Furthermore, the women's liberation movement early on made abortion a key issue. In fact, the great tides of contemporary history moved society inexorably in the direction of abortion liberalization.

First came naturalism, which viewed man as a mere animal, then humanism, which made man's autonomous reason the sole basis for value judgments, and finally the duty-to-self ethic, which put an individual's self-interest at the center of all values. Abortion in the self-interest of the mother seemed the only reasonable choice. The direction was so clear that in 1970, three years before the bombshell Supreme Court decision, I predicted on public radio that abortion would soon be legalized and that euthanasia would then follow quickly. How did I know? I read *The Humanist* quarterly and knew what the agenda was.

A whole new vocabulary has developed: an unwanted pregnancy is "violence against a woman's body," "invasion of a woman's bodily space." There must be no "coercion in childbearing," and each woman must maintain her right to "optimal procreation choice." After all, the fetus is not a full member of the human class of beings and the woman is. Pro-abortion author Beverly Harrison puts it this way:

> The question "When does human life begin?" or . . . the more precise moral question "When shall we predicate full human value to developing fetal life?" has become pivotal to the debate about the morality of abortion for reasons having to do with moral consensus. The moral status of fetal life simply is not the obvious fact that many "pro-life" proponents contend. . . . To conclude that fetal life, admittedly a *form* of human life, is already full human life does not follow. . . . Because predicating the intrinsic value of human life and opposing killing are the *least* controversial aspects of the moral debate, the question of the value of fetal life has become the core issue on which everything else appears to hinge.[12]
>
> Reproductive choice for women is requisite to any adequate notion of what constitutes a good society. Transformed social conditions of reproduction are absolutely critical to all women's well-being. No society that coerces women at the level of reproduction may lay claim to moral adequacy.[13]

Each woman, on this view, has an inviolable right to privacy (to make her own choice independent of anyone else), which was the basis of the *Roe v. Wade* decision. She also has the right to economic, emotional, and physical well-being and to have only a child that is wanted.

PERSONHOOD

If both sides are agreed that a fully human person should have her or his right to continue living protected against the demands of some lesser right of someone else, how does one define "fully human" or "personhood"?

Many qualifications have been suggested, all of them psychological or sociological, not biological. A person is one who is self-conscious, who has the capacity to look to the future and to understand what continued existence means, to be aware of others and to be "socialized," it is said. "A person is one who has the capacity to make self-determined conscious choices and to survive without dependence on others." The problem with psychological and social criteria for defining personhood is that infants, severely handicapped people, and many aged would fail to meet those criteria and thus would become expendable if they become burdensome or impinge on the rights of true "persons."

12Beverly W. Harrison, *Our Right to Choose* (Boston: Beacon, 1983), 193.
13Ibid., 199.

Even the commonly accepted marks of the image of God—conceptual thought, articulate speech, loving relationships, moral consciousness—would disqualify infants, the aged, and many handicapped people. And that is precisely the reason euthanasia, infanticide, and abortion have all been linked in the minds of "value-of-life" proponents. In fact, it was a political decision that split the campaign for abortion rights from the combined abortion/euthanasia campaign. The leadership concluded that abortion legislation could be more easily achieved, so temporarily dropped the euthanasia campaign. In this they proved correct.

A "useful life" definition as the basis for establishing the legal right to life is not a new concept. Leo Alexander, director, Neurobiologic Unit, Division of Psychiatric Research, Boston State Hospital and formerly serving with the Office of the Chief of Counsel for War Crimes, Nuremberg, documents the astonishing development of medical thought in Germany between the Great Wars:

The guiding philosophic principle . . . of the Nazis, was Hegelian in that what was considered "rational utility" (what is useful?) and corresponding doctrine and planning had replaced moral, ethical, and religious values. Medical science in Nazi Germany collaborated with this Hegelian trend particularly in the following enterprises: the mass extermination of the chronically sick in the interest of saving "useless" expenses to the community as a whole; the mass extermination of those considered socially disturbing or racially and ideologically unwanted; the individual, inconspicuous extermination of those considered disloyal to the ruling group; and the ruthless use of "human experimental material" in medico-military research. Remember, physicians took part in this planning. . . . This was all before Hitler. And it was all in the hands of the medical profession.[14]

Malcolm Muggeridge, commenting on the same phenomenon, points out that the process began with the concept of the "value of life" and at first was applied only to severely, chronically ill, but was gradually expanded until, under Hitler, it became the Holocaust.

Such elitist definitions of true personhood or "worthy life" led eventually not only to the attempted extermination of the Jewish race, but in an earlier era, led to the enslavement of vast numbers of black "nonpersons." The definition of some as

[14]Leo Alexander, *The New England Journal of Medicine*, 14 July 1949.

subhuman or less worthy was the implication of the Dred Scott decision by our Supreme Court (1857) and lay at the root of American justification of the slave system. Today it is used to justify abortion of unborn children.

Psychological and social definitions of what constitutes a true, full, worthy, useful human being have not been accepted by Bible-committed ethicists because Scripture nowhere evaluates human life in this way and also because such attempts have proven hopelessly elastic. No consensus in defining *person* has been achieved by the ethicists, and no limits to ever-expanding categories of expendable human life have proved possible in societies that begin to move in this direction. Thus pro-life ethicists have tended to seek for definitions of human life in terms of biology, rather than in psychology or sociology: At what point does science indicate an independent human existence has begun?

BIOLOGICAL EVIDENCE

Some have said that when God breathes the breath of life into an infant (presumably at birth) it becomes a living soul. But actually the unborn child has its own way of "breathing" or receiving life-sustaining oxygen, and few now hold that there is a significant biological distinction between the late-term fetus and the newborn. Neither one can survive without the assistance of others, and either one can survive with that help. Medical science keeps pushing back the time of "viability," when a child can survive outside its mother's womb. In fact, with the development of an artificial uterus, there seems almost no limit to what will be considered a viable fetus or even a viable embryo.

Therefore, pro-life people usually hold that fully human life begins at conception, that a zygote has the right to life over all rights of the mother, except, perhaps, her own right to life. This belief may present a problem, since the zygote may divide and become twins. Some answer that perhaps the soul divides, too. Even the embryo may divide, so others hold that just as death is defined as the cessation of heart and brain activity, so life begins with heart and brain activity. Brain waves have been measured as early as six weeks after conception.

Bernard Nathanson, an atheist and formerly a leading

abortion advocate and practitioner, suffered such revulsion at the ugly violence involved that he became a leading pro-life advocate. He produced the film *Silent Scream*, in which he demonstrated that neurological beginnings take place by the sixth week and that the embryo-fetus already experiences pain by that time. Though this has been disputed, all agree that all biological human functions are present by the second trimester (twelve weeks). The small person at that stage can change his position, respond to pain, suck his thumb, and have an attack of hiccups.

From this brief overview of the biological data presently known, it seems obvious that there is no clear-cut logical demarcation in the development of human life from conception to adulthood. If it is argued that an embryo still lacks essential human characteristics such as brain activity, it cannot be argued that the life of the fetus (from two or three months till birth) is biologically different from the life he will experience following birth.

So from a biological point of view there is little difference between aborting a fetus and killing an infant. An embryo, and especially a zygote, is qualitatively different, and it may not be possible to prove categorically that fully human biological life exists at that stage. But it would be impossible to prove that the zygote or embryo does not possess a fully human existence. The burden of proof lies with those who deny that the life is fully human and thus authorize the taking of that life. This point was made by Ronald Reagan in his book *Abortion and the Conscience of the Nation*.

Anyone who doesn't feel sure whether we are talking about a second human life should clearly give life the benefit of the doubt. If you don't know whether a body is alive or dead, you would never bury it.[15]

With eloquent simplicity he outlines the issue:

The real question today is not when human life begins, but *What is the value of human life?* The abortionist who reassembles the arms and legs of a tiny baby to make sure all its parts have been torn from its mother's body can hardly doubt whether it is a human being.[16]

[15]Ronald Reagan, *Abortion and the Conscience of the Nation*. (Nashville: Thomas Nelson, 1984), 21.
[16]Ibid., 22.

Every legislator, every doctor, and every citizen needs to recognize that the real issue is whether to affirm and protect the sanctity of all human life, or to embrace a social ethic where some human lives are valued and others are not. As a nation, we must choose between the sanctity of life ethic and the "quality of life" ethic.[17]

The president felt that the damage done was not alone to the millions of unborn who were denied continued life, not alone to the morally deadening effect on the abortion mothers and abortionist doctors, but to the whole society. As Malcolm Muggeridge said in the introduction, "The abortion issue is far and away the most important one now facing what we continue to call Western Civilization."[18]

The weight of evidence seems to lie with the biological arguments of those who advocate the sanctity of life rather than with the psychological and sociological arguments of those who advocate the quality-of-life position. But what does Scripture say to the issue? After all, the abortion question is ultimately theological and moral.

BIBLICAL EVIDENCE

Scripture does not directly address the issue of abortion. This does not mean that God is indifferent to the issue, however, any more than the Bible's lack of direct teaching on genocide, suicide, or euthanasia indicates that those actions are morally neutral. "Thou shalt not kill" is the overarching principle and covers all varieties of taking innocent human life. Since every moral principle of Scripture is universally normative unless the Bible itself limits its application, what exceptions to the Sixth Commandment are indicated in Scripture? Only justifiable warfare, capital punishment, and self-defense, as we shall see later. All other homicide falls under the ban. The only question about abortion, then, is whether or not the unborn human life is an immortal soul, bearing the image of God.

Most serious discussions of the biblical evidence for or against abortion wrestle with Exodus 21:22-25. When two men fight and a pregnant woman is injured so that the fetus "departs," punishment is due for any harm that follows. Is the harm to the mother, to the premature infant, or to both? The question has

17Ibid., 25.
18Ibid., 11.

been hotly debated.[19] The majority of scholarly opinion holds that the mother's injury is in view, but Luther and Calvin in their day and the great Jewish scholars today hold that harm to the fetus also demanded the *lex talionis,* eye-for-an-eye punishment, including capital punishment in the event of death. Such an unclear and hotly disputed passage could hardly be used to establish the status of the unborn with unassailable biblical authority. So we are restricted to passages which speak of God's view of life before birth. Perhaps the clearest in Psalm 139:13-16:

> For you created my inmost being; you knit me together in my mother's womb. I praise you because I am fearfully and wonderfully made; your works are wonderful, I know that full well. My frame was not hidden from you when I was made in the secret place. When I was woven together in the depths of the earth, your eyes saw my unformed body. All the days ordained for me were written in your book before one of them came to be. (NIV)

An interesting account of fetal life is recorded in Luke 1. John the Baptist, a fetus of six months, leaps for joy (1:44) at the arrival of his cousin Jesus, in all probability a zygote and certainly no more than an embryo. Elizabeth addresses Mary as "the mother of my Lord" (1:43), not as "the future mother of my potential Lord." With the dramatic account of four people interacting, two mothers and their two unborn children, it is hard to suppress the question, Had Mary sought an abortion as a pregnant, unmarried young woman, what would have been aborted—a potential human being or the eternal Son of God?

The common references in Scripture to God's interest and call to people while still in their mothers' wombs would be conclusive evidence that God considers these "fully human" before birth except for the fact that Scripture uses similar terminology of people before *conception*: "Before I formed you in the womb I knew you, and before you were born I consecrated you" (Jer. 1:5). Indeed, in God's purposes, his own were chosen before the foundation of the world (Eph. 1:4). Nevertheless, the preponderance of evidence is that Scripture views the unborn as having individual personhood.

One further line of evidence suggests the identity of prenatal

[19]See, for example, *Christianity Today,* 8 November 1968; 16 March 1973, and the *Journal of the Evangelical Theological Society,* Spring 1976, for the remarkable intellectual pilgrimage of one Old Testament scholar, Bruce K. Waltke.

and postnatal life. In both Hebrew and Greek, a single word is used of both the fetus and the child.

The Hebrew word *yeled,* used of children generally, is also used of children in the womb in Exodus 21:22. The Greek word *brephos* is used in Acts 7:19 to refer to the young Hebrew children slaughtered at Pharaoh's command, and in Luke 1:41, 44 to refer to John the Baptist while still in his mother's womb. This usage suggests that the biblical writers saw a continuity between the prenatal and postnatal states.[20]

The Bible does not directly answer the question, Is the fetus an immortal soul? But the evidence of deduction from the many passages which speak of the unborn is clearly on the side of yes, the very weak argument from silence is all that can be mustered in favor of no. Therefore the moral issue is whether it is acceptable to take the life of a being that is almost certainly an immortal soul made in the image of God. Just as we must act on the presumption that an unconscious person is alive and not treat him as dead till proof is certain, so with the unborn child. The evidence of modern biology strongly reinforces the evidence of Scripture, that fetal life should be treated as sacred as infant life.

ABORTION AS MURDER

Should a person who performs an abortion or who requests one be subject to the same penalties as one who kills a child or an adult? Why do we not name a miscarried embryo and hold a funeral service for it? Why do parents not grieve in the same way, especially when the spontaneous abortion is early?[21] We may not use mere human judgment to determine the relative value of various lives, but Scripture does indicate, under the Mosaic economy, differing values among humans. This is not to say that God so values each life, for we have the New Testament teaching that in Christ there is no distinction between rich and poor, bond or free, Jew or non-Jew. Nevertheless, the punishment for injury or death was not the same for a Jewish

[20]John Jefferson Davis, *Abortion and the Christian* (New Jersey: Presbyterian and Reformed, 1984), 17. See also John Warwick Montgomery, "The Fetus and Personhood," *The Human Life Review,* Spring 1975, 41ff.; and Harold O. J. Brown, *Death Before Birth* (Nashville: Thomas Nelson, 1977).

[21]R. F. R. Gardner, *Abortion: The Personal Dilemma* (Grand Rapids: Eerdmans, 1972), 126.

freeman and a slave (Lev. 19:20), or, for that matter, for women and children.

Although the New Testament does not permit us to make such distinctions, this Mosaic distinction may serve as a paradigm for us to refrain from considering abortion as the full equivalent of murder. Should the teenager, who, seduced and distraught, takes a "morning-after pill" be executed for a capital crime? After painstaking research I have concluded that abortion of a zygote or embryo is morally wrong because there is no substantial evidence to prove that it is anything less than an immortal soul, but that one who commits such an abortion should not be treated as one who commits premeditated murder. It is impossible to prove conclusively from Scripture that the zygote or embryo *is* an immortal soul.

What, then, is the sin? Both ancient Jewish law and contemporary law hold a person responsible for criminal neglect or reckless behavior that is not aimed deliberately at any person but results in harm or death. It is morally wrong, a violation of the Sixth Commandment, but is not judged with the same severity as deliberate violence against a person. For example, to shoot at the shadow moving silently across one's bedroom in the dark of night might end in the death of a family member, but the distraught and fear-stricken person would not be prosecuted for murder, though he might be for involuntary manslaughter. Similarly, to destroy a zygote or embryo is at least such a crime, since no one can be certain that the object of violence is not an immortal soul.

Should capital punishment be sought for those who deliberately abort a fetus? Since Scripture does not prescribe such a punishment, we might be presumptuous to do so, especially since we do not seek capital punishment for a variety of sins and crimes for which the Mosaic law *did* prescribe death.

I conclude that preventing conception before, during, or after intercourse, is not of itself wrong; but abortion of a zygote or embryo is a sin of reckless violence, a possible homicide; and that abortion of a fetus is a crime, almost certainly a homicide, deserving severe punishment, though not necessarily deserving capital punishment.

How should such a position be applied to the many difficult

problems and issues which arise in this great contemporary moral issue?

APPLICATION

Right to Choose. It is said that each woman alone has the right to choose what is done to and in her body. But rights to self-determination are limited by the rights of others. A man has the right to choose how he will dispose of his income, but if he chooses to get married and divorced, the courts may hold him to the results of those prior choices, limiting his free choice about the use of his money.

A wife who chooses to give birth to a baby is no longer free to behave as a nonmother, and if she does is rightly condemned for child abuse. The pregnant woman has made a prior choice to have intercourse, a choice which brought another party into her life, a separate individual whose rights now limit her own freedom of choice. Choices often lead to conditions that are physically or morally irreversible. Her choice as to what happens to and in her body should have been made earlier. It is too late to choose for or against motherhood. The pregnant woman is already a mother. Theologian Helmut Thielicke makes this point: "For once impregnation has taken place it is no longer a question of whether the persons concerned have responsibility for a *possible* parenthood; they have *become* parents."[22]

Another way to put the question of the "right to choose" is this: Whose choice? Who gives the unborn child a choice? Who is his advocate? Who stands with him against a threat of violence far more serious than any threat he poses to his host body?

Economic and Social Well-being. This is probably the most trivial reason for violating the right to life of another human, but it is also probably the most common motivation for abortion. Kristin Luker gives us a profile of the pro-choice activist. She is well-educated, well-off financially, nonreligious, white, and works outside the home. In fact, "94 percent of all pro-choice women work."[23] It appears that, second only to the drive for

22Helmut Thielicke, *Sex,* vol 3, trans. John Doberstein in *Theological Ethics* (Grand Rapids: Eerdmans, 1979), 227.
23Kristin Luker, *Abortion and the Politics of Motherhood* (Berkeley: University of California, 1984), 195.

personal autonomy, the desire for freedom from the limitations of parenting and for an affluent life-style are primary driving forces behind the pro-choice movement. Of course, for those—especially in the third world—where the desire is not for affluence but for escape from grinding poverty, the motivation may be somewhat higher. But the irony is that poor people are not the chief abortion advocates. In fact, Mother Teresa of Calcutta, chief advocate of the poor, holds abortion to be the greatest crime. Says Teresa, "It is a very, very great poverty to decide that a child must die that you may live as you wish."

Mental Health of the Mother. Of higher value than her material welfare is the mental welfare of the mother. But is the potential of psychological damage to be compared with the certain loss of life and the possible agony of a violent, painful, and protracted dying? Furthermore, studies indicate a far higher incidence of psychological damage to those who choose abortion than to those who choose to give birth. John Jefferson Davis speaks to the issue of psychological suffering because of an unwanted pregnancy.

Threats of suicide are frequently presented as psychiatric indications for abortion. But . . . the suicide rate among pregnant women in fact appears to be one-sixth the rate among nonpregnant women of the same age.[24]

Life of the Mother. Protestants historically have justified taking the life of the unborn when a continued pregnancy would put the life of the mother in jeopardy. This has been justified on the basis of self-defense and also on the basis of choosing the lesser of two evils—the loss of a wife, and, possibly, mother, being a greater loss to the family and society. Roman Catholic teaching, on the other hand, does not permit this "tragic moral choice." Unless both lives are in jeopardy, to take deliberately the life of one merely to avert the danger of loss to the other is not deemed ethically justifiable.[25] Whatever the outcome of the debate over fetus-life versus mother-life, the practical truth is that, due to the rapid advances of medical science, this dilemma is extraordinarily rare.

[24]Davis, *Abortion and the Christian*, 30-31.
[25]See Fred M. Frohock, *Abortion: A Case Study in Laws and Morals* (Westport, Conn.: Greenwood, 1983), 31-32.

Unwanted Children. "No one should be forced to bring an unwanted child into the world." This argument is possibly the least worthy. In the first place, many unwanted children, upon birth, become very much wanted. Babies have a way with people. Furthermore, it can hardly be said that any child is unwanted in the present day United States where the desire to adopt seems almost limitless. This is a clear, practical answer for unmarried mothers, who account for 80 percent of abortions. If the fetus is not a human being, the question of his wantedness may have some validity, but if he is human, the claim of unwantedness has no more merit than it would have in the case of the unwanted child who has already been born. Do we say, "No parent should be forced to *raise* an unwanted child"?

This question raises another: What happens to unwanted children? Do not unwanted children become abused children? Is it fair to bring a child into the world who must face such a future? This argument is not used for children and adults who may face possibly unpleasant futures, or the entire race would be in jeopardy. True, many now advocate suicide as preferable to continued intolerable suffering, but suicide is self-chosen; abortion is not. Before the 1973 Supreme Court decision it was said that abortion on demand would reduce child abuse, but during the first decade following that decision, even though 15 million unwanted children were aborted, child abuse climbed nearly 400 percent. One study showed that 90 percent of battered children were from *planned* pregnancies. But the truth is, abortion is the ultimate child abuse, and violence against the unborn seems to create an atmosphere—both personal and social—in which violence to the already born proves to be less abhorrent.

To say that one does not "want" a being one has brought into existence is gross betrayal of a life compact already entered into, and quite hypocritical. Why not rather face the consequences of one's past choices and make sure that the child *is* wanted, either by the natural parent(s) or by others who stand in line waiting the opportunity to adopt? That seems a more honorable, civilized, and moral way than killing.

One further word concerning wantedness. In every place where the prenatal determination of sex has become commonplace, female fetuses have been aborted far out of proportion to the male. How ironic that women, seeking to assert their rights at the expense of their own children's right to life, actually open the way to a perverse form of genocide, with womankind as the initial victims.

Those who oppose the right to an abortion should take responsibility to assist mothers with unwanted pregnancies. If we fight to take away the right to have an abortion, we have a moral obligation to work toward providing alternatives. The pro-life community must work to provide counseling, shelters for unwed mothers, adoption options, even assistance to parents who cannot cope with special medical or financial needs. We must demonstrate our love for mothers as we seek to protect their unborn children. Compassion with tears would seem more appropriate weapons in the battle for life than bitter words and bombs.

Rape, Incest, and the Handicapped. In the case of rape and incest, the new life did not originate through any choice of the mother, so the responsibility of the mother is of a different kind. What to do now is her *first* choice, not her second.

It is not easy to justify making an exception to a rule against abortion. Because of physical and emotional factors, pregnancy following rape is rare. A study of 20,000 rapes in Yugoslavia recorded no pregnancy, and a ten-year study in Minneapolis and St. Paul revealed no pregnancies in 3,500 cases of rape. Dr. Helen Roseveare reports that during the Congo rebellion she and her many nurses were raped repeatedly months on end and not one got pregnant. In the second place, there is readily available medical treatment to prevent pregnancy following such an attack. Admittedly a woman victim of rape is more likely to seek such assistance than a child who has been seduced or forced by a family member.

Ultimately, however, the answer to the terrible dilemma faced by a girl or woman who finds herself pregnant under such circumstances depends on whether the fetus is a human being. If it is, no matter what the source, to destroy it is wrong. A second act of violence cannot correct the first. The mother's lack of responsibility for the conception does not remove the child's inalienable right to life. The unborn child is not the attacker but is, in fact, a second victim who should not receive capital punishment for his father's crime.

There is a further problem concerning legislation which permits abortion in cases of rape or incest. Such laws invite trivialization of the crime of rape since women with unwanted pregnancies often have used this exception as a loophole, claiming to be victims of rape when in fact no rape occurred. If the rape is reported immediately, no legal exception would be needed, as the procedure would normally be contraceptive rather than abortive. Abortion of the handicapped or potentially handicapped accounted for fewer than one percent of abortions in America in the mid-eighties, so this cause can hardly be urged as a major reason for abortion. Furthermore, arguments for aborting handicapped fetuses are compelling only if the fetus is not a human being. If it is human, the handicapped fetus, like the handicapped child or adult, has the right to life. Terrible tragedies will occur, but the frontiers of medicine are moving dramatically into health care of the fetus. Furthermore, in all but the few extreme cases, physical handicap does not need to mean a life not worth living. On the contrary, "The suicide rate among handicapped people is virtually zero."[26] It is often the parents and society that feel burdened, and it is the parents and society that can experience the joy and moral freedom that come from accepting the handicapped into full membership in the family of "worthy," "useful," "fully human," and valuable persons.

Abortion Law. If abortion is wrong, it should be made illegal. But some say that laws enforcing the private religious convictions of some citizens should not be imposed on all. There is an element of truth in this. If laws are made that a community has no intention of enforcing, it is bad law as it promotes a lawless society. But to call abortion a private matter is far off the mark. Abortion immediately involves the unborn child, quickly involves others, such as the father, and soon has an impact on all society. Furthermore, to say that morals should not be legislated is foolish. Most of what is legislated is in the realm of morals. If one's private religious convictions demanded that he hold slaves, have many wives, discriminate against blacks, or mutilate Orientals, these same liberal defenders of personal rights and

[26]*MacNeil-Lehrer Report,* 22 April 1980.

328 ■ BIBLICAL ETHICS

freedoms would seek for legislation to stop him. The key
questions are, *Whose* rights? (the mother's or the unborn
infant's?) and, *What* rights? (the right to life of the infant or
some lesser rights of the mother?)

So we work to enforce moral standards, and above all to
protect innocent human life. But if a society is ready only to
prohibit abortion of the fetus (second and third term) and to
leave options open for abortion of zygotes and embryos under
limited circumstances, I would work toward that end. It would
be a better law than no law and would create an atmosphere for
further education and advance toward the ideal, while averting
wholesale violation of a law that could or would not be
enforced. Unless strict conditions were placed on first-term
abortions, however, the number of abortions would not be
substantially decreased because 90 percent of American
abortions are first term.

But would restrictions not lead to the "bad old days" when
abortions were done illegally and women were slaughtered in
back-alley abortion mills? In the first place, the number of
abortions that took place before liberalization has been highly
inflated and, at least in Scandinavia and Britain where we have
records, liberalization has not decreased those numbers
substantially. Apparently many people still want the anonymity
that can be secured only in an illegal facility. Furthermore, the
number of deaths of mothers under the old system has been
greatly inflated. In 1971, two years before the *Roe v. Wade*
decision, there were only sixty-eight deaths from illegal
abortions and abortion attempts in the entire United States.
Compare that with 15 million deaths of the unborn in the
decade following liberalization.

Lewis Smedes summarizes the issues cogently:

A *pluralist* society does not allow people to follow their consciences if their
consciences lead them to kill an innocent human being. A *free* society will
invade a person's privacy if it is certain that she is privately about to kill an
innocent human being. A *just* society may well pass laws whose execution leads
to unfairness to some people if not to pass them causes a greater unfairness, the
killing of innocent human beings. A *merciful* society may well make laws that
burden parents if not to make them encourages the killing of innocent, unborn
children. A *wise* society may well make laws it does not have the will to enforce
if not to pass them makes killing human beings legal. In sum, all of the

arguments that are based on what a good society will or will not do fail at the frontier of the rights of a fetus to live.[27]

Believing that the Word of God clearly teaches that no one may shed another person's innocent blood because God created humankind in his own image, and believing that unborn children are fashioned in the image of God, and believing that it is the duty of the state to protect the innocent, we, as Christians, should exhort one another and our fellow citizens to reject abortion as an answer to the dilemma of an unwanted pregnancy, to provide compassionate alternatives within a biblical framework, and to require that our laws respect the sanctity of human life which is a continuum from conception until natural death.

SUICIDE AND EUTHANASIA 4/20

Suicide and euthanasia, like abortion and infanticide, have generated intense controversy because of new attitudes developing in Western civilization. As with abortion and infanticide, Scripture does not address the issues directly. Until recently, the major church bodies have always condemned all four activities as violations of the Sixth Commandment, "Thou shalt not kill."

Not all societies have condemned suicide and euthanasia. In Japan, for example, suicide to expiate one's lost or threatened honor is heroic. Even as an escape from intolerable circumstances, suicide is quite acceptable. Japanese Christians have told me of the ecstatic feeling of freedom they experienced in their pre-Christian days as they journeyed to some special scenic spot, hallowed as the trysting place with death by countless suicides, and of their disappointment when their plan for suicide was thwarted.

Now, increasing numbers in the West espouse similar views. Societies that endorse suicide produce detailed handbooks on how it may best be committed. Scholars in heavy tomes and pragmatic lobbyists in state legislatures promote new ways for family and others to find a "good death" for the sufferer.

[27]Lewis Smedes, "The Arguments in Favor of Abortion Are Strong . . . ," *Christianity Today*, 15 July 1962, 62.

Why the new, more lenient attitudes? Do they well up from long-suppressed reservoirs of compassion, or do they come from an overall depreciation of the value of life? If a person is no more than a time-bound animal with no responsibility to Deity and no hope beyond the grave, why should human life be viewed as "sacred"?

The Christian view of physical life is both higher and lower than the view of the secularist. It is higher because man is created in the image of God, indwelt by God, belongs to God, and will exist forever; the secularist views man as an animal facing extinction. On the other hand, to the Christian, physical life is temporary and not the ultimate value; it is the supreme value of the nonbeliever since it is all he has.

Thus, in the paradox, to the believer life and death are simultaneously more significant and less significant than to the unbeliever. The true believer does not cling to life because he cannot lose it and because it does not belong to him anyway. In fact, by losing it, as Christ taught us, by treating it as expendable, we find it in its full, true meaning. On the other hand, because life is a gift of God, reflects his own likeness in some mysterious way, and belongs ultimately to him, we hold it in sacred trust as one of the highest values. One's own life is not higher in value than truth, honor, justice, and love, for example. But certainly the life of another is a far higher value than one's own higher comfort, ease, material prosperity or a host of other self-oriented rights and privileges. Indeed, Scripture treats human life as so sacred that a society's view of the value of human life is a sure test of its moral integrity and social durability.

SUICIDE

Suicide as Sin. Suicide is wrong, in the Christian view, because it violates the prohibition of taking innocent human life. It is nowhere condoned in Scripture either directly or by implication. Nevertheless, difficult problems inhere in this prohibition and seem to cluster around two opposite poles. At one pole, is suicide so light a sin, so unlike murder, that attempted suicide should go unpunished? At the other extreme, is successful suicide an unpardonable sin?

The question for the Bible-committed believer is not, Is suicide wrong? but rather, How wrong is suicide? There is tension between two biblical principles. The believer is not owner of his body, and, furthermore, it is the home of God himself, so suicide is very serious. On the other hand, it does belong to him in a sense that others do not, so that violence to his own body would seem to be less a sin than violence to others.

How bad a sin is suicide? No matter how we may seek to excuse suicide, it is a sin needing repentance and God's forgiveness. The act of suicide is not against one's self alone. Others are affected, often tragically. Many times this is the deliberate intent.

On the other hand, no matter how serious, it is certainly forgivable, as any other sin. The difference between this sin and most others is that for other sins there is normally a period of grace following the sin to permit repentance. Though repentance is necessary to restore fellowship broken through sin (1 John 1:8), those who believe one's salvation can never be lost as well as those who believe it can be lost hold that a single sin would not forfeit salvation. Would a Christian, suddenly enraged and suffering a heart attack, go to meet God unforgiven? Is anger, in such circumstances, an unpardonable sin? No, the redeemed suicide, crashing uninvited into God's presence, is acceptable to the Father because of One who deliberately gave his own life a sacrifice.

Suicide as Crime. Suicide is clearly a sin, violating God's law. But is it a crime? Are there ameliorating circumstances? For example, does ignorance make a difference? Christ prayed for his murderers, "Father, forgive them for *they know not what they do*." Does illness make a difference? Is one who is depressed and not rational at the time less responsible? If the one committing suicide served as his own prosecutor, judge, and jury and condemned himself to death for some sin, did he have that right? Why do we not prosecute attempted suicide in the same way we do attempted murder?

Self-Sacrifice. Self-sacrifice is not sinful suicide. If it were, God himself would be the most guilty. No one took Christ's life from him. He laid it down of himself (John 10:18). In fact, "Greater love has no man than this, that a man lay down his life for his friends" (John 15:13). Far from being the worst of crimes, it is the greatest of virtues. The mother starving herself to feed her children, the friend leaving another with the life jacket and swimming off into the night—these are heroes, not sinners.

Refusing Medical Care. Another form of self-chosen death that can hardly be considered sinful or criminal is refusing medical attention—foolish, perhaps, but not sinful. Though I do not agree with those who feel that using medicine is wrong (a sign of unbelief), it would be very difficult, in the light of scriptural teaching, to condemn as sinful or criminal those who choose the way of "faith alone." The Bible is full of promises about God's healing power, and there are even a few passages that seem to hold medical procedures in low esteem. This is not the place to adduce the evidence in Scripture that medical help is not only legitimate but a gift of God; however, I must grant liberty to those who interpret Scripture to mean that the way of faith precludes medical help.

If those who, believing in faith healing reject medical treatment, are not guilty, neither are those who refuse it for other biblically valid motivations. How can it be sinful for a person at the threshold of death to refuse further treatment that would only prolong the dismal process? He longs to be with Jesus, and Jesus is calling him home. Why should he not cast himself on Jesus to dispose of his case according to the divine will? Why should he desperately fight off the enemy of death, as a hopeless pagan might, when that enemy is the very one who, betraying himself at last, ushers the believer into the wholeness and freedom of real, eternal life? As poet Arthur Hugh Clough put it, "Thou shalt not kill; but need not strive / Officiously to keep alive." If, in addition, he is motivated by love for his family, shielding them from crushing financial loads, is he a worse person for so choosing? No, let us have done with pagan ideas of the ultimate value of physical life and learn to live by faith, especially at the end.

One final word concerning the ethics of suicide. Often in the life of the victim of suicide there are those who deliberately or through insensitivity helped create an environment which the suicide eventually judged to be intolerable. In the final analysis, though, a person is responsible for his own choices; the family and friends of the victim cannot bear the guilt of his choice. Repentance may be needed for whatever real or imagined complicity may exist, but to continue to bear a burden of guilt is to deny the grace of God.

EUTHANASIA

Killing others deliberately, whatever the motive, violates God's law and should be condemned by human law. But in the twentieth century a new element has been introduced into the agony of seeing a loved one suffer. The triumph of man's creativity in medical science, bringing vast blessings, has also brought problems: the prolongation of the process of dying and the astronomical cost of such care. The brief postponement of death, often in the form of agonizing pain or vegetable-like existence, may be purchased at the price of financial ruin for the family, and increasingly threatens even the resources of the state.

Active and Passive. To help solve the dilemma, ethicists distinguish between active and passive euthanasia. Actively promoting death has been universally condemned in the Western world under the Hippocratic Oath taken by all medical practitioners until recently. But passively permitting a patient to die has become the center of controversy. In this view, it is always wrong to cause death, but it may be ethical to withdraw treatment that might postpone death. In fact, in this view, it may be ethical to give medication that will hasten death, if that is not the purpose of the treatment. This is often called the principle of double effect. For example, if the medicine is to relieve pain, but as a side effect may hasten the dying process, this would be considered passive, not active, euthanasia.

Ordinary and Heroic. Another distinction divides medical techniques into ordinary and heroic. The distinction, particularly at the borderline between the two, is difficult to draw. But the reasoning is clear that when a person faces certain, imminent death in the judgment of the physicians, it may be ethical to withdraw the kind of extraordinary (and expensive) treatment that would be mandatory when the dying process can be reversed. The real-life situation is always complex, but the distinction is legitimate and may prove helpful on occasion.

Note that this argument applies only to those who are clearly in the irreversible process of dying and is not legitimate in the treatment of infants, for example, who could, with medical assistance, live. Extraordinary measures are justified to buy time for additional treatment or for the patient's normal organ functions again to take over. If the organs can no longer function, such means are no longer justified.

Responsibility for the Decision. A further crucial distinction must be made between those decisions made by a person for himself and those made for him by others. The Christian may, as an act of faith, refuse medical treatment. The nonbeliever should have the same liberty, in my judgment, since he is responsible for his own life. The individual should be free to refuse medical treatment but must not request or take action to actively cause his own death.

Those who counsel the sufferer, whether pastor, family, physician, or friends, have the ethical responsibility to assist him in making his own free, informed choice and to refrain from any subtle influence, not to speak of psychological coercion or social manipulation.

What of those who cannot make a decision because of mental incompetence, such as those in a comatose state? If the condition is judged by several reliable physicians to be irreversible, those responsible for the dying person should feel no guilt if extraordinary life-sustaining efforts are withdrawn.

The chief ethical problem with these arguments and with laws designed to relieve unnecessary physical and financial suffering is that others often cannot be trusted to make decisions that are in the best interest of the one who suffers. Their own self-interests intrude, whether materialistic desires for an estate or to avert financial burdens, or, on the other hand, guilty feelings that would drive one to postpone death at any cost. Because honesty and objectivity are so difficult to have under such stressful circumstances, I advocate that the responsible people be restricted to decisions concerning the use of extraordinary means and that decisions on the part of others be permitted only where there is no hope of the person's return to mental competence to make his own decision. After all, many a "terminal patient" has recovered to an extended, useful life.

Serious talk of doing away with those who do not have a "useful life," who suffer greatly, or who are a burden to themselves, their families, or society is a sure indication of moral decadence and may be the warning sign of the demise of a civilization that no longer holds human life to be inviolable.

WAR

Violence was introduced into human experience by the archviolent being Satan. It erupted first in Cain and has been the common experience of man ever since. *Time* magazine notes that in the last thirty-five centuries of recorded history, only one year out of fifteen has been without war.[28] In the 5,560 years of recorded human history there have been 14,531 wars, or 2.6 a year. Of 185 generations only ten have known unsullied peace. And it is getting worse: "Since 1900 almost 100 million men have died in 100 wars—compared with 3,845,000 in the 19th century."[29]

Is war an unmitigated moral evil, the ultimate expression of human sinfulness? Or is war sometimes good, and peace sometimes a moral evil? Or is war always wrong, but sometimes the lesser of two evils? There are pagans who glorify war and hold it to be the ultimate way to prove and develop true manliness and extend civilization. Famed American general George Patton sometimes spoke that way. The opportunistic wage war simply because of potential gain that, as James says, they may spend it on their passions (4:1-3). Those who take the Bible seriously and see war and violence as the evil result of our fallenness have a wide range of viewpoints. Let us consider them under two broad categories: "nonresistance" and "justifiable force."

[28]*Time*, 9 March 1970, 46.
[29]Ibid., 47.

NONRESISTANCE

There are several varieties of nonresistance, or pacifism. The secular humanitarian and the liberal churchman hold that war is immoral because of ethical principles derived in part, perhaps, from Scripture, but primarily from philosophical reasoning. Among the various biblically based peace churches there are two main lines of approach. There are those who hold that it is wrong for the Christian to participate in war because war is wrong, and there are those who hold that nonparticipation is part of the Christian's special vocation as an elite spiritual "priesthood" and "aristocracy," but that some war by the secular state prosecuted by unbelievers is justifiable.

History of Christian Attitudes. The church from the second century till the time of Constantine was uniformly nonmilitary. Christians were not to serve in the Roman army, and from the Apostolic Era until A.D. 170 there is no record of one doing so. It should be noted that the early church rationale for not serving in the Roman army was not only the "peace" issue but especially the impossibility of being in the army without participating in various idolatrous practices. Outside the army a young man might survive the ruthless persecution, but in the army he could not, except by apostatizing. Following Constantine (fourth century), the church espoused the just war doctrine (see below).

In the Middle Ages the Anabaptists took a nonresistance position, and some of their spiritual descendants form the bulk of biblically based peace churches today. Again, the peace aspect was not uniformly a major issue at first. More than non-resistance, the foundational doctrine was total noninvolvement in the citizenships of this world.

Nonparticipation in military force was, in both the early church and among the early Anabaptists, the outcome of a life-style developed as a result of being cruelly persecuted, helpless minorities. Nevertheless, pacifism gradually emerged with clarity as a central doctrine for many Anabaptists, even where persecution was no longer an issue. The early church, on the other hand, quickly gave up the noninvolvement stance when persecution ceased and Christians were accepted by the establishment.

Catholic and mainline Protestant churches uniformly held to some form of the "just war" position until this century, when many liberal Protestants became ardent pacifists, not from the force of biblical teaching but from an optimistic view of the goodness of man and the perfectibility of society. This viewpoint was shattered by the events of the first half century, went into retreat during World War II, and reemerged with a different rationale upon the gradual realization of what nuclear warfare would mean. In this latter era, many Roman Catholic leaders also entered the ranks of selective (nuclear) or full pacifism.

Example of Christ. The nonresistance view is founded on the teaching and example of Jesus Christ. Some pacifists believe that Christ's teaching, "Resist not him that is evil," applies to nations as well as to individuals. Other pacifists hold that the teaching applies only to believers. Love will never harm another person. Even if my nation is at war, I am guilty if I participate, especially in killing. I must turn the other cheek, no matter what others may do. What if the Christians are not a mere insignificant minority but of such number or in such places of influence that their nonparticipation means the nation is conquered and loses its freedom? This is the cross we must bear. We do not have to be free. We do not even have to live. We *do* have to do what is right; we *do* have to love people no matter if we are crucified. Can you imagine Christ throwing a hand grenade or bayoneting an enemy?

This teaching of nonresistance is seen as pervasive in the New Testament. A Dunker tract from about 1900 outlines a biblical basis for the position:

> Christ is the "Prince of Peace" (Isa. 9:6). His kingdom is "not of this world" (John 18:36). His servants do not fight (John 18:36). "The weapons of our warfare are not worldly" (2 Cor. 10:4). We are to "love our enemies" (Matt. 5:44). We are to "overcome evil with good" (Rom. 12:21). We are to "pray for those who persecute you" (Matt. 5:44).[30]

Those who oppose the pacifist position do so on the basis of hermeneutics (the biblical data is not adequately handled) and of

[30] Robert Culver, "Between War and Peace: Old Debate in a New Age," *Christianity Today*, 24 October 1980, 51.

theology (the world/life view undergirding pacifism is nonbiblical).

THEORY OF THE JUST WAR

Although it is called the "just war" position, not many in this century have held that any war in the Christian era is just in the sense of being a holy war in which one side is wholly righteous and the other wholly unrighteous. Rather, the idea is that though most war is unjustifiable, there are wars that are. Many "just war" theorists base their position on philosophical ethics, but here we deal with those who seek a foundation in biblical teaching.

The majority today holds that the only legitimate or "just" war is defensive, since God no longer has a chosen people whom he sends into war by direct revelation. A minority holds the earlier viewpoint that preemptive strikes or ideological crusades can be justified under some conditions.

Augustine (early 400s) created the first great synthesis of Christian faith and the practice of war. Drawing heavily from the ancient pre-Christian philosophers, he argued for the necessity of just wars. With rare exceptions Augustine's defense of war became the standard position of all major branches of the church from that day to this. He argued that any justifiable war must have peace as its goal. Its purpose must be to secure justice, including ordinarily the preservation of the state. It must be waged in love. The decision must be made not by private citizens but by rulers responsible for the conduct of government, and the war itself must be conducted with a minimum of cruelty.[31]

This thesis was developed further by the Roman Catholic church, especially by Thomas Aquinas (1225–1274):

To be just, a war must: (a) Have been declared by a legitimate authority. (b) Have a just and grave cause, proportioned to the evils it brings about. (c) Only be undertaken after all means of peaceful solution of the conflict have been exhausted without success. (d) Have serious chances of success. (e) Be carried out with a right intention.[32]

The just war approach culminated in Grotius's massive study *The Law of War and Peace,* which effectively introduced the theory into international law.

[31]Ibid., 32.

[32]J. H. Ryan and F. J. Boland, *Catholic Principles of Politics* (New York: Macmillan, 1943), 254-255.

The earlier statements have been further developed by a contemporary advocate:

1. *Just cause*. All aggression is condemned; only defensive war is legitimate.

2. *Just intention*. The only legitimate intention is to secure a just peace for all involved. Neither revenge nor conquest nor economic gain nor ideological supremacy are justified.

3. *Last resort*. War may only be entered upon when all negotiations and compromise have been tried and failed.

4. *Formal declaration*. Since the use of military force is the prerogative of governments, not of private individuals, a state of war must be officially declared by the highest authorities.

5. *Limited objectives*. If the purpose is peace, then unconditional surrender or the destruction of a nation's economic or political institutions is an unwarranted objective.

6. *Proportionate means*. The weaponry and the force used should be limited to what is needed to repel the aggression and deter future attacks, that is to say, to secure a just peace. Total or unlimited war is ruled out.

7. *Noncombatant immunity*. Since war is an official act of government, only those who are officially agents of government may fight, and individuals not actively contributing to the conflict (including POWs and casualties as well as civilian nonparticipants) should be immune from attack.[33]

Some just war theorists hold that this is too restrictive and that sometimes justice calls for preventive aggression or even a crusade:

If self-defense is legitimate at all, then it must be legitimate to anticipate a deadly or crippling first blow. No one would expect to wait until a gun-brandishing pursuer had fired the first shot and perhaps scored a hit before shooting at him. Severely menacing behavior, depending on its circumstances and extent, is generally accepted as a legitimate basis for initiating an act of self-defense.[34]

A crusade . . . is a war fought to undo something that no one had a right to do in the first place. Although the term *crusade* is usually attached to a conflict with some affinity to Christian ideals or ethics, it might also logically be applied to what we generally call a "revolution" or a "war of national liberation." Revolutions and wars of liberation, too, are fought to undo past injustice and are supposedly motivated by a concern for an ethical principle

[33]Arthur F. Holmes, "The Just War," in *War: Four Christian Views*, ed. Robert G. Clouse (Downers Grove, Ill.: InterVarsity, 1981), 120-121.
[34]Harold O. J. Brown, "The Crusade or Preventive War," Ibid., 161-162.

(such as freedom, equality or the right to self-government) rather than for territory, power or treasure.[35]

Most contemporary Christian advocates of the just war position reject this broader definition as uncontrollable and unjustifiable. Issues of international scope are so complicated, motives are so mixed, and it is so easy to control what information the general populace receives that almost any war can be justified as a crusade. The majority position is that no government can know enough and no nation is good enough to wage a justifiable crusade.

Opinions split on the preemptive strike, with most holding that if the anticipated attack is certain and imminent, preventive action may be justified as self-defense and thus is not actually broadening the definition of a just war. This simple logic on prevention has been vastly complicated by the introduction of nuclear weapons.

To all of this, the pacifist replies that neither the teaching and example of Christ, nor the evidence of history permit us to believe that any war is justifiable. So let us turn to the biblical and theological data.

A THEOLOGY OF PEACE

War in the Old Testament. When war and peace are evaluated in the light of Scripture, it is important to distinguish between Old Testament and New Testament teaching. In the Old Testament God's people constituted a nation gathered out from among the rest of the nations, whereas in the New Testament God's people constituted a spiritual kingdom dispersed among the peoples of the world. For this reason, the commands concerning war for the people of God in the Old Testament and the people of God in the New Testament are different. In the Old Testament war was not only sanctioned but was actually commanded by God. (See Num. 1–4; 26; 32:20-22; Deut. 1:6-8; 3:3; Josh. 6:2-3; Judg. 5; 1 Sam. 15:2-3; 17; 2 Sam. 5:19-20; 2 Chron. 14:11-13; Pss. 68; 83; 108; 124; 136.)

Possible reasons war is sanctioned in the Old Testament:

1(The primary purpose of judgment is salvation)(Ps. 83:16-18).

[35]Ibid., 158.

2. The enemies of Israel were God's enemies as well (Ps. 139:19-22).

3. War seems to have been necessary in a world of incredible depravity to separate a people sufficiently to receive the revelation of God and create an atmosphere for the coming of a Redeemer. The Israelites were always polluted by contact with pagan peoples (see Ps. 106:34-39) when they compromised God's command to destroy the enemy.

4. The people against whom war was made had time to repent. Some, like Rahab, did so. God's original and comprehensive plan was to displace, not annihilate (Exod. 23:27-33).

5. Judgment for sin *always* comes, in some cases sooner than others. The death of all men is part of this judgment. God uses various instruments in this judgment, and in the Old Testament he used the nation Israel.

6. We do not really understand the *wrath* of God. He has a deep, unremitting hatred of sin which is the chief, though not the only, object of his wrath (Ps. 5:5). If we do not understand his wrath against sin, we will never understand the depth of his love in providing redemption from that sin.

7. The physical life of man is not nearly as important as the spiritual or eternal, not nearly as important as truth and righteousness. For those who will not repent, the shorter the life, the less accumulation of judgment. This is especially so in the case of children.

8. War in the Old Testament was waged by special revelation, something that cannot be claimed for war in this era.

God is called a God of War, the Lord of (military) Hosts. Though theological systems may differ on the unity of Old and New Testaments, no one can dispute that not only were certain wars sanctioned in the Old Testament, but the final, great wars, according to New Testament prophecy, are to be waged by God himself. Thus it cannot be said on biblical authority that waging war is always immoral. The only debate is whether man-initiated violence is ever justifiable in this church age.

War in the New Testament. Those who hold to a position of nonresistance often ask, What would Jesus do? Since he is our supreme example, the question is valid, but not the assumption that his every activity becomes a mandate for his followers. Jesus had a special mission. He came specifically to die, so that any attempt to divert him was considered satanic. We, on the other hand, are called upon to remain in the world as citizens, and though we should live sacrificially, even "becoming conformed to his death," our vocation is not his and may or may not be like his in a death for others. Even where one is called upon to lay down his life for others, some might be called to meekly submit to martyrdom and others to die valiantly defending the life of another. In any event, the appeal to Jesus' example cannot be a rationale for nonresistance under all circumstances.

Furthermore, if we consider Jesus as the model, what do we do with the fact that at the end of the era Christ himself will become the greatest military conqueror of all time, according to biblical prophecy? His special roles of sacrifice for sin and conqueror of all certainly demonstrate eternal principles, but neither may be used legitimately as a direct calling for anyone else.

Another common assumption is that Christians constitute a powerless minority in society, thus making pacifism a viable option—let the general citizenry care for the affairs of state. But the tiny minority of apostolic times, living under the heel of totalitarian Rome, is not necessarily a model for Christians in a democracy where they share governmental authority and, in fact, are sometimes so numerous or in such roles that they determine the course of the government.

A third assumption is that war is always evil and should be eliminated. Certainly war is the megaphone of sin. But should it be eliminated in a sin-filled world? Is not force necessary to justice in such a world? If love does not include retributive justice, God himself is unloving.

Yet Christ clearly taught us not to resist evil people. In the New Testament Christians are forbidden to use force in the interest of the Kingdom of God. Christ clearly taught that his kingdom is not of this world and that it is not to be extended with force (John 18:36). This would rule out the medieval crusades or any other religious war waged in the name of God. Jesus is the Prince of Peace, and the peacemakers have his blessing (Matt. 5:9). He must have referred to physical nonresistance, for he constantly waged spiritual warfare and commanded his followers to do the same.

The crux of the question is whether his command not to resist evil was an absolute interdiction of any use of force by any Christian authority or whether it was a general principle limited to physical resistance in private interpersonal relationships. Jesus said, in the same context, to turn the other cheek, but when he was slapped he did not do so (John 18:23). He also said to pluck out the eye and cut off the hand of those engaged in sexual sin, but he did not prescribe these actions or the capital punishment due the woman taken in adultery and the woman at the well. In the Sermon on the Mount he gave principles; not all the commandments there are literal. Is there other New Testament evidence to suggest that the command not to resist evil is absolute and universal? I cannot find it. Rather, governments are established by God, specifically authorized to use force in discharging that responsibility (Rom. 13:1-7; 1 Pet. 2:13-14).

Furthermore, if the hermeneutical principle of the unity of Scripture is applied, Christ's teaching concerning personal sacrificial love fits with all the rest of biblical teaching and his own example, while Paul's and Peter's teaching on human governmental authority also fits with the rest of biblical teaching and God's own example. The two principles are not in conflict.

The New Testament, in addressing the issue of war and peace, does not go beyond the principle of governmental authority, which includes the use of force. After all, it was written during the longest period of universal peace in recorded history, the great Pax Romana. But the New Testament does speak of military officers on four occasions, and all of them appear in a favorable light (Matt. 8:5ff.; Acts 10:1ff.; 21:31-40ff.; 27:1-6). To say that the lack of condemnation means approval would be an illegitimate argument from silence. On at least two occasions (Luke 3:14; Acts 10), however, instructions were given on how to do right, how to be acceptable to God, and on neither occasion does this include leaving military service. Neither Jesus nor Peter said, "Go and sin no more." Yet we would have every right to expect this if military service were viewed as wrong. Would Christ have instructed a prostitute simply not to charge too much?

So we have in the New Testament the combined affirmation of government force and the lack of condemnation of those exercising that authority, supporting the overall biblical distinction between government and the private individual and the legitimate response of each to evil. Government has a responsibility for restraining evil, protecting its citizens, and maintaining their welfare. If it has a responsibility to protect its citizens from criminals, does it not also have the responsibility to protect them from criminal nations? Christ's teaching of nonresistance, if it is to be harmonized with the rest of biblical teaching on human authority, was not given to nations, police, or parents in their official capacities.

Though the data of the New Testament on the issue of the Christian's participation in war are not direct nor abundant, the basic principles are clear: To be godlike is to make a sacrificial, loving response to maintain a nonvindictive, nonresistant attitude in all personal relationships when one's own rights are at stake; and human government is responsible, with accountability to God, to use force when necessary to assure righteous behavior.

Based on this foundation, what theology of war and peace can be deduced from other biblical principles? Consider three areas of concern: values, man's responsibility, and God's sovereignty.

Values

War vs. Peace. Peace is preferable to war, ordinarily. God is on the side of peace, ordinarily. We know this because peace will be the final state of those who have made peace with God. So, "blessed are the peacemakers." Always. But sometimes war is to be preferred to peace and may be the only route to righteous peace. When people speak of war as the lesser of two evils, as when war is said to be preferable to bondage, it cannot mean that God-initiated, God-approved, or God-executed war is a lesser moral evil. If war is ever waged in the will of God, it is a moral good. It may, of course, be a lesser (or greater) human grief than some other value. But peace is not the ultimate value to which all other values should be sacrificed.

Justice vs. Love. The dichotomy is often made in favor of justice or love, but never is it made biblically; true love is tough, and true justice is tempered with mercy. Sometimes punishment is the truest expression of love for the person receiving it as well as for others who need protection from him. God holds both as ultimate values.

Physical vs. Spiritual. Though the claim is often made that even a single human (physical) life has infinite worth, this is not the biblical view. Continued physical life is not the supreme value. Many things are of greater value, such as loving relationships, loyalty, truth, justice. Perhaps even freedom, though only the lonely hero has ever acted on such a premise. He who inordinately clings to earthbound life, Jesus told us, will lose it in the end. Spiritual life is infinitely more important than the physical. Furthermore, spiritual warfare is more significant and more deadly than physical war ever could be.

Time vs. Eternity. The human life span is brief enough, whether cut short by illness, accident, or violence, or lived out to the painful weakness of old age. It is nothing compared to the eternal existence which lies before each human being. To pay too high a price for time is foolish in the light of eternity.

Individual vs. Group. If one individual means so much to God and to the person himself, surely the more people, the greater the value. And so war escalates the cost of human loss immeasurably.

Church vs. State. Church and state both are of value, though neither is of supreme value. Christ and the martyrs laid down their lives for the church, and soldiers lay down their lives for the state. But the modern nation-state is an artificial contrivance at best and certainly has no biblical basis to claim ultimate allegiance. It cannot legitimately control the church nor demand sinful behavior of the Christian. On the other hand, the church, though speaking prophetically to the state, should not use the force of the state to accomplish its spiritual goals. Furthermore, the church is a brotherhood that knows no national boundary, and citizens of heaven have stronger ties with Christians of other lands than with non-Christians in their transient citizenship here on earth. The church is eternal and God's own, so its value must be far greater.

Human Rights and Freedom vs. Order. Rights and freedom are valuable, but none of absolute value. Every person's rights are limited, if by nothing else, by the freedom of others. Order, then, adjudicates among the rights and freedoms of those whose lives are associated. Tyranny is order gone mad, and anarchy is freedom gone mad. And yet, Scripture has very little to say about civil rights and freedoms and a great deal to say about order. To overthrow order for the sake of rights and freedoms may be too high a price to pay. Note that a biblical resolution of the tension in each value seems to lean more toward a "just war" position, but note also that the issue of values is very complex.

Man's Responsibility for War. Humankind may not lay the blame for war on God or Satan, for man is responsible for war, one of the most grievous results of his sinfulness. Because of this sinful, selfish disposition, conflict is inevitable, and for this sinful behavior he is accountable to God.

A second aspect of man's responsibility is that humans have been chosen as instruments both of God's judgment and grace. God has chosen civil governments as the primary agents of his judgment, and the church as the primary agent of his grace. If he waited for perfectly good and wise people to mediate his purposes on earth, his purposes would go unaccomplished. So human government—whether family or state or employer—is hobbled by its own finitude and fallenness. Nevertheless, it is God's own instrument. Human responsibility, then, depends somewhat on the role one plays—whether ruled or ruler—and also on the type of government under which one finds himself. In a free society, for example, especially in a representative form of government, the ordinary citizen has a great deal more responsibility for the righteousness, justice, and mercy of the society than he would under a totalitarian state. Still, the person under the most repressive regime is not absolved from "obeying God rather than man." Coerced sin is certainly less culpable than freely chosen sin. But coercion does not relieve guilt if any choice—even the choice to submit to death—is available. At the same time, since the citizen of a free nation has far more responsibility than the citizen of a totalitarian state, he should hold himself to a higher standard than he holds his less fortunate brother.

God's Sovereignty. The sovereign God is judge of each person in time and eternity. Among all other elements of that judgment, the time and manner of his death are in God's control. Not even the most cruel and unjust tyrant can take away a person's life without God's permission. This should not make anyone careless about human life or cavalier about war, but it should be reassuring to the child of God.

The sovereign Lord also controls the destiny of the nations. He will judge the evil, and he ordinarily uses human instrumentality.

Finally, God is the Judge over all and will bring his purposes to a successful conclusion. He will not shuffle off the stage of time in red-faced defeat. Justice and righteousness will triumph at last, and in this confidence his people can rest, whether oppressed or free.

NUCLEAR WAR

Conventional vs. Nuclear. Is nuclear warfare qualitatively different from conventional warfare, or only different in scale? In an article significantly titled, "The 'End' of Just War Theory," Donald Heinz states unequivocally that nuclear warfare is not only qualitatively different, but that a consensus is developing toward what has been called "nuclear pacifism": "Thinking Christians will need to come to terms with the powerful consensus in Protestant and Roman Catholic ethics that all or nearly all nuclear war is impossible on just war grounds."[36]

In explaining his own radical change of attitude toward the use of nuclear weapons, John C. Bennett writes:

In 1950 there had been little discussion concerning the chances of keeping a nuclear war limited, once it has started. Now, after years of reflection and debate, there remains little confidence that any planned limitations would be realized, whether in targets, weapons used, or the geographical areas affected. Also, in 1950 we had no knowledge of the probable long-term effects of many

[36]*Theology, News and Notes*, March 1981, 5.

nuclear explosions on the earthly or atmospheric environment and on the support systems of most or all of humanity. Today we realize that the very existence of the human race would be at risk. . . . If we put together those last two changes since 1950, it seems clear that it would be utterly irresponsible for any nation to initiate a nuclear war or the nuclear stage of war. No conceivable issue at stake could justify the risking of human existence or the continuities of civilized life. . . . The Roman Catholic bishops spoke for many of us when they said: "The danger of escalation is so great that it would be morally unjustifiable to initiate nuclear war in any form."[37]

Scale of Destruction. Certainly, nuclear war differs radically in scale of destruction, but is it a greater escalation than from the sword to gunpowder? Hamburg under conventional saturation bombing during World War II suffered four times more casualties than Hiroshima under the A-bomb. In either case, though, is the scale of destruction really greater than the destruction of Canaan under Joshua, when every living being was put to death in city after city?

Civilian Population. Some say nuclear war is qualitatively different because civilian populations are the object of warfare. Others counter that strategic warheads can be used against military objectives alone. But the issue is fuzzy on two counts. First, though just war theory in the middle ages developed the idea of the protection of civilian populations, historically this has rarely taken place. Franklin Roosevelt spoke against the Japanese when they bombed Nanking in 1937:

This Government holds the view that any general bombing of an extensive area wherein there resides a large populace engaged in peaceful pursuits is unwarranted and contrary to the principles of law and humanity.[38]

But short years later America under Franklin Roosevelt engaged in obliteration bombing in both Germany and Japan. The purpose was to break the will of a people to fight, and in this the approach was successful. A Japanese pastor once told me the bombing of Hiroshima and Nagasaki saved multitudes— perhaps millions—who would have died in the struggle of conventional war.

[37]"Nuclear Deterrence Is Itself Vulnerable," *Christianity and Crisis*, 13 August 1984, 297.

[38]*New York Times*, 23 September 1937, 19. For an extensive discussion on the evolution of mass bombing, see Robert C. Batchelder, *The Irreversible Decision* (Boston: Houghton Mifflin, 1962), 170-189.

Second, protection of the civilian population may be difficult to defend logically. Perhaps as Reinhold Niebuhr suggests, the concept of protecting the civilian population arose more from knightly chivalry than from carefully reasoned ethical distinctions. It is difficult to see how a soldier drafted to serve his country in the army is any more or any less "innocent" than his brother left to work on the farm, producing grain to feed the army. The whole nation participates—either all adults are guilty or none except those in power. One thing is certain, if any nation publicly committed itself to refrain from touching civilian population centers, the enemy could have instant immunity for military preparation by making sure that military installations were in close proximity to civilian populations. Though the idea of protecting "innocent" civilians may be difficult to defend logically, impossible to perfectly follow, and rarely implemented, most ethicists and ethically sensitive civilized people recoil from the idea of deliberately attacking civilians.

End Result. There is one element in nuclear warfare that does seem distinctly different. Just war theory holds that war is legitimate only if the end result in view is of greater value than the potential loss in securing that end. In an all-out nuclear exchange, what would be left of any possible value compared to the total loss of people and property? Even so, some hold that the freedom from oppression gained by the survivors would be worth it and that even the prospect of losing everything should not deter a people from defending justice or liberty, even if it means national self-sacrifice. Though the ethics of the distinction between conventional and nuclear war may be debated, that there can be a qualitative difference in outcome seems clear.

Nuclear Peace. The potential fearful outcome is what has led to what may be called the nuclear peace. As a direct result of the "balance of terror," the historic average time of twenty years between general wars has been more than doubled since World War II. Some applaud this stand-off as a beneficial result of nuclear stockpiling, but who believes that such a stalemate can indefinitely prevent nuclear hostilities?

God's Judgment. So we live in the dread of nuclear apocalypse. Will it come as the tragic miscalculation of a computer or the calculated act of a madman? Will it be God's way of bringing just judgment on a rebel race? Can it be averted?

God still blesses the peacemakers, and since we have not been made privy to the secret counsels of God, all men certainly must work to avert a holocaust of self-annihilation. Even while so laboring, the Christian can rest in the assurance that no chance or malicious act of man will thwart God's sovereign purpose and plan. Prophetic Scripture seems to indicate that the final firestorm of destruction will be God's direct action, not man's. Either way, however, the final word is God's.

Options for Response. Do we urge leaders of the free world to engage in unilateral disarmament? But unilateral disarmament removes all deterrence. If the potential enemy is a nation of proven peaceful intent and behavior, the risk might be justifiable, but if there is evidence of expansionist intent, unilateral disarmament is almost equivalent to national self-sacrifice.

Do we work toward bilateral nuclear disarmament? Given the radical sinfulness of humankind, is this a reasonable expectancy? Can one nation be sure that the other will not cheat? And what of the many nations with nuclear weapons that are not part of the bilateral agreement?

Do we keep silent and watch the irrational escalation of nuclear armament? Even if we pursue the arms race unabated, do we need "superiority"? Will not adequacy of retaliation do? If we have the arsenal that can destroy every man, woman, and child five times over, do we really need enough to destroy them all a hundred times over?

Do we publicly renounce first-strike use of nuclear weapons no matter what the provocation? The deterrent value of any weapon depends on the possession of it and the will to use it. Bluffs do not deter, especially on the part of a free nation. If an enemy really believed you would never strike first, he would have an open invitation to do so unless, of course, the result of his strike would be certain and unacceptable retaliation.

In this new kind of warfare, the arms race seems to be a race toward mutually assured destruction (MAD), so every effort to keep talking and working toward mutual control, limitation, reduction, and ultimately, nuclear disarmament is surely worth the effort. At least, such effort may postpone a man-made doomsday. We no longer have the option of living in a nuclear-free world; that option died in 1945. But we can and must work toward peace with justice in a nuclear age, no matter how frustrating and hopeless the efforts may seem.

Another element of reality: Personal hope and inner peace cannot depend on the prior assurance of immunity from the ravages of war. Our hope is in God. The ultimate violence I may suffer is death, and that is the beginning of real life and true, eternal peace. Furthermore, I *will* die. The time and manner of death are all that is in question. And that is true for all of us.

The new dilemma humans face in the nuclear age was forcefully enunciated some years ago in an exchange between author Philip Toynbee and the archbishop of Canterbury, Geoffrey Fisher. Toynbee argued that nuclear destruction was so terrible that the only solution was immediate disarmament and peace with the Russians on any terms, even surrender. Fisher responded:

I am convinced that it is never right to settle any policy simply out of fear of the consequences. . . . For all I know it is within the providence of God that the human race should destroy itself in this manner (nuclear war). There is no evidence that the human race is to last forever and plenty in Scripture to the contrary effect. Though, as you say, the suffering entailed by nuclear war would be ghastly in its scale, one must remember that each person can only suffer so much; and I do not know that the men and women affected would suffer more than those do who day by day are involved in some appalling disaster. There is no aggregate measure of pain. Anyhow, policy must not be based simply on fear of pain. I am not being unfeeling. Christ in his crucifixion showed us how to suffer creatively. He did not claim to *end* suffering, nor did he bid his disciples to *avoid* suffering. So I repeat, I cannot establish any policy merely on whether or not it will save the human race from a period of suffering or from extinction.[39]

 Summary. In summary, nuclear war is substantively different from conventional warfare, at least in the scale of potential destruction. This difference arguably makes general nuclear war unacceptable by at least two canons of historic "just war" theory: the end must justify the means, and one should choose the lesser of two evils. Therefore, in this terrifying dilemma, I conclude

[39]Philip Toynbee, *The Fearful Choice* (London: V. Gollancz, 1958).

that nuclear warfare should not be accepted as a normal way for
settling international differences; all ethically sensitive people
should work toward the ideal of, first, control; then, limitation;
next, reduction; and finally, elimination of nuclear weapons.

CRIME AND PUNISHMENT

A crime is some activity or negligence that a human authority
has decided should be punished, usually because it is deemed
injurious to others. *Crime* and *sin* are not synonymous. Not all
sin is criminal: no human society can punish lust, covetousness,
and pride. Sin is Godward—it violates his standards. And not all
crime is sinful. It may be a crime in a given society to speak of
Christ, but it is no sin to do so. Crime and its punishment are
determined by a society, presumably for the welfare of its
members, and hopefully based on moral principles. Since crime
is against others, it normally violates the biblical law of love and
often harms another person. Thus, it fits under the Sixth
Commandment in its broad and deep implication. The
punishment of crime is certainly a life issue—depriving the
criminal of part or all of his life as a free citizen. But controversy
rages as to the cause of crime, the nature of crime, the purpose
of punishment, and the kind of punishment a just and merciful
society may employ. On these issues the Bible sheds great light.

PHILOSOPHICAL ISSUES

The Cause of Crime. Until the last century, crime generally
was considered the outworking of a sinful disposition, and even
where moral implications were disallowed it was universally
considered an act for which the criminal himself was
responsible. That began to change in the last century when
people proposed other explanations—physiological,
psychological, sociological. For example,

A Frenchman by the name of Charcot, a neurologist, began to focus his work
upon disorders which simulated organic neurological conditions. . . . These
pronouncements on the part of Charcot, as well as their eventual acceptance,
mark the beginning of the modern study of so-called "mental illness." With
Freud, a disciple of Charcot, and psychoanalysis, a new system of classification

came into being. . . . Mentally sick persons did not "will" their pathological behavior and thus were not considered "responsible" for it.[40]

The end result of the general acceptance of this approach was to distinguish between criminals who were normal and thus responsible for their crime and those who were abnormal and needed treatment, not punishment. To prosecute a person for being crippled, for example, would make as much sense as prosecuting a mentally ill person who has committed a crime. He needs caring compassion, not discrimination and persecution. A legal definition of insanity, determined by the Supreme Court in the M'Naughten Rule (1843), was gradually refined until most courts in the United States came to rely on the American Law Institute Rule which states that

a person is not responsible for criminal conduct if at the time of such conduct as a result of mental disease or defect he lacks *substantial capacity to appreciate* the wrongfulness of his conduct or to conform his conduct to the requirements of the law.[41]

With the advent of sociology, the line of reason initiated earlier by psychology has been taken much farther. Not just the mentally ill, but all people are the product of their environment, so that the person who commits a crime is not guilty but the society (environment) that produced such a person. Famed psychiatrist Karl Menninger wrote a book whose title says it all: *The Crime of Punishment*.[42] His main thesis is that the crimes committed against criminals are greater than the crimes they commit. In fact, many leaders in psychology now strongly oppose the whole concept of mental illness.

Who is to judge which person is abnormal or "ill"? Each person's behavior is normal to him. Thus cultural relativism leads inexorably to personal autonomy and the rejection of all absolute norms of behavior. We have not witnessed the end of the process. Gratefully, society as a whole has not accepted the final logic of this reasoning, but it has generally accepted environmental determinism, so that people are viewed as the inevitable product of family and social conditioning.

[40]G. Roy Sumpter, "Crime, Individual Culpability, and Punishment," *Journal of the Evangelical Theological Society*, Fall 1973, 224.
[41]Ibid.
[42]New York: Viking, 1968.

This viewpoint increasingly prevails in one form or another and has profound effects on a society's view of crime and punishment. Scripture teaches that environment has a very powerful influence on a person. Criminals have been strongly influenced by their environments, and, hopefully, a change of environment might assist them toward making better choices. But determining what elements in a person's environment were most influential and trying to create an environment that will help a person change for the better seem very elusive.

For example, why is the crime rate in the Jewish population so low and in the black population so very high? The most widely accepted theory is that poverty and all that goes along with it are the root causes. But Charles Silberman, though solidly on the side of the black, exploded that theory in his definitive and widely acclaimed study *Criminal Violence, Criminal Justice*.[43] He demonstrates in his book on the criminal that the crime rate among blacks is dramatically higher than that of other ethnic groups mired in the same poverty. He holds that the elements of black culture that have repressed violence heretofore now seem to encourage it. Poverty alone cannot be demonstrated to produce criminal behavior, but the prevailing wisdom is that a combination of environmental factors do so.

The Other Side interviewed a group of prison inmates, asking the question: Who is responsible for your being here?

Ezzo: The state is responsible for my being here. I was originally sent to reform school for the terrible crime of playing hookey. . . . I wasn't a criminal then, but I was by the time I got out.

Jones: If you want to know who is responsible, look who is in the prison: blacks, Indians, Puerto Ricans, Chicanos, and poor whites. You don't see any rich people here. In a sense the system condemned us to poverty and a life of crime. To be any one of these people is a political, social, economic condition. We are systematically deprived of justice. We couldn't get jobs because of our color or education. Why don't we have education? Because when we were in school the teachers were teaching only one thing, and it didn't correspond to what we had to know. So we had to steal to feed our families.[44]

The thesis could not have been more clearly stated by a learned psychologist, sociologist, or criminologist. Shifting responsibility from the criminal to society may masquerade as

[43]New York: Random House, 1978.
[44]*The Other Side*, November-December 1972, 39.

compassionate humanitarianism, but it is really a destructive cruelty, for the psychological cost of shifting one's responsibility to someone else is to lose control of one's own destiny. The spiritual cost is even greater; it shuts one off from the only ultimate solution: the grace of God made available only to those who accept responsibility for their own behavior.

The Bible is much more realistic. It recognizes the influence of environment and thus the responsibility of people to create as good an environment as possible for others as well as for themselves. It also recognizes the role of responsible choice. The Bible locates the cause of crime where it must ever rest if we are to find true solutions: the responsibility of each person to make his own choices for the right. The root of crime is sin, and the final responsibility for crime rests with the sinner. Lack of discipline or love in the home, failure of justice in society, evil companions, and poor education all may contribute, but in the final analysis, we sin because we are sinners and choose to sin.

And every choice to sin accumulates to form a character that is capable of committing crime. Given adequate provocation and real or imagined immunity from punishment, only the grace of God would keep any person from crime.

Some contend that crime itself is not increasing, but that law enforcement has improved; more criminals are apprehended, more crime is reported. Most, however, agree that crime is increasing in America. Some blame prison administration and environment, and virtually all agree that the prison system has utterly failed if rehabilitation is the purpose. About 68 percent of those released return again. Others blame the courts and the process of criminal justice. Still others blame the schools, the violence and sex of television, narcotics, racial discrimination, unemployment, poverty.

I believe the breakdown of the family is the leading negative environmental influence. Public education and the media share major responsibility in eroding the family and moral values through their deliberate commitment to moral relativism, however. Thus, these negative factors tend to reinforce one another.

Since environment is a major influence in the formation of human personality and character, we must work to make it as just and merciful as humanly possible. At the same time, we must insist that each person is responsible for his own moral destiny and is held accountable for any conduct that is injurious to others.

Nature of Crime. We have distinguished between sin and crime. God punishes sin; man punishes crime. Since man is not authorized to punish sin, society must determine which sins are criminal and therefore punishable. When people say that no morals should be legislated, they speak out of ignorance or prejudice. Most law has to do with questions of morality. By making a matter law, even if it were not inherently a moral matter, it becomes a moral issue. But when a person says *private* morality should not be legislated, most people would agree. Private sin should not be punishable by human courts of justice. But other than sins of the heart, what is "private"?

In the final analysis, no sin is truly private, since every sin has an adverse affect on others in the life of the sinner. Even so, moral perfection is beyond human achievement and cannot be coerced by law. Therefore, all that can be done by law is to hold a person accountable for unwarranted injury to another's property or person or for behavior that might jeopardize another. Because of this legitimate distinction between sin and crime, a strong movement has emerged toward decriminalizing victimless crimes in which there is no complainant. Chief among these are said to be the use of drugs, adult consenting sexual behavior, drunkenness, gambling, vagrancy, prostitution, and pornography. As can be seen, if all these were decriminalized, a large portion of the current law enforcement overload would be eliminated.

But are these activities victimless? Drinking is a "private matter," but half the homicides and traffic fatalities in the United States are alcohol-related. Is this victimless crime? A society that condones pornography and homosexual conduct creates an atmosphere (environment, if you please) that strongly influences the rising generation's view of human sexuality. Is this a purely private matter?

Any behavior that a society believes is directly or potentially injurious to others may be legitimately outlawed. Of course, a society is responsible to enact only laws which it intends to enforce and can enforce. Any behavior, private or public, victimless or not, which a society declares criminal and then does not enforce, undermines the rule of law, promoting a lawless society.

So the crucial element in law making is not whether an act is private or whether there is a direct victim who complains, but whether that society judges the behavior to be potentially or actually injurious to others and whether society has the will to enforce the legislation.

Purpose of Punishment

Rehabilitation. Whether in the judgment of Israel in the Old Testament or the discipline of church members in the New, God's primary purpose in punishment has always been the restoration of the sinner. "Have I any pleasure in the death of the wicked, says the Lord God, and not rather that he should turn from his way, and live?"[45]

So the position of humanitarian criminologists that rehabilitation is the purpose of punishment has strong biblical precedent. But contemporary theory makes rehabilitation virtually the only valid reason for punishment. Furthermore, led by psychology and psychotherapy, we come to have unrealistic expectations of our ability to rehabilitate. The *New York Times* reported that rehabilitation efforts for criminals have been abandoned by most governments in the West.[46] Most interesting is the example of Sweden, where prisons are held to be the most progressive and humane. The rate of conviction for crime subsequent to release (recidivism) is over 70 percent, as high as anywhere in the world. Silberman's central finding is that very little can be done about the crime problem.[47] We must lower our expectations. He concludes that no one knows what "rehabilitates" criminals. He is not discouraged, however. He argues that most criminals are in fact caught and punished with some deserved severity. How can this be with a 12 percent average apprehension rate for serious crime? Because criminals keep on committing crimes and, in fact, expect to be caught and spend time in prison as a cost of doing business. A Rand

[45]Ezek. 18:23. See also 2 Thess. 3:13-15; 1 Tim. 1:19-20; and 1 Cor. 5:5 compared with 2 Cor. 2:6-8.
[46]5 September 1977.
[47]Silberman, *Criminal Violence, Criminal Justice.*

Corporation in-depth study of forty-nine adult armed robbers reported that among them they admitted committing a total of 10,500 serious crimes even though they had spent half their adult lives, on an average, behind bars![48] In fact, the only thing known to improve the behavior of criminals, apart from regeneration, is age. "Criminal activity diminished with age, even among the pros. The average was thirty-eight serious offenses per year as juveniles, eighteen as young adults, and seven in the mature adult years."[49]

Deterrence. A second biblical reason for punishment is to deter others from doing wrong. "As for those who persist in sin, rebuke them in the presence of all, so that the rest may stand in fear" (1 Tim. 5:20). This was seen most clearly in capital punishment in both Old and New Testaments (Deut. 17:12-13; Acts 5; Rom. 13:1-7). Punishment is a warning to all other potential law-breakers. This purpose is assailed by those who admit only the rationale of rehabilitation. They say that punishment or the fear of it does not deter. Professor Norval Morris disagrees, though he admits that "surprisingly little is known about what deters criminals."[50]

But the question really is not whether criminal law deters. It seems to be manifestly clear that it does deter. You can test this in a police-strike situation. You can test it in situations where there is no enforcement of a wide range of criminal law. In those situations, differentially for different crimes and taking account of all difficulties in counting, crime increases. Crimes against property, particularly the smaller crimes against property, increase quite startlingly and sharply.[51]

Ernest Van den Haag is one of a new wave of conservative penologists who emphasize the deterrent and quarantine value of imprisonment as over against elusive rehabilitation. This is the main thesis of his book *Punishing Criminals.*[52] By way of example, he tells of an experiment in which students were asked to calculate their own grades by checking to see if they had given the correct answers. Thirty-four percent cheated by changing

[48]*The State* (Columbia, S.C.), 8 September 1977, 18-A.
[49]Ibid.
[50]*The Center Magazine,* May-June 1971, 33.
[51]Ibid., 33-34.
[52]New York: Basic Books, 1976.

their answers. Next they were exhorted to be honest, but the rate of cheating rose to 41 percent! But when a threat was made to punish all cheaters and was made credible, the cheating was reduced to 12 percent. Later, Van den Haag, testifying before a congressional hearing on crime and punishment, said:

I am suggesting that the law mandate courts to impose a much more severe sentence on second offenders than on first offenders who commit serious crimes. . . . Whatever mitigates a first offense does not mitigate the second. Anyone who commits a third offense must be considered a career criminal (and) if his crime was violent, or if, like burglary, it involves physical exertion, he should not be released before he reaches the age of 40. Few people commit violent crimes after 35. Age rehabilitates.[53]

Though there is no consensus as to what actually deters a person from criminal behavior, there is something of a consensus that the certainty and swiftness of apprehension and punishment do deter. But if sure and swift punishment are the greatest deterrents, our system can hardly be expected to deter.

The Eisenhower Commission offered the proposition . . . that of a hundred indexed crimes, major serious felonies, fifty are reported to the police. For the fifty incidents reported, twelve people are arrested. Of the twelve arrested, only six are convicted of anything—not necessarily of the offense reported. Of the six who are convicted, 1.5 go to prison or jail.[54]

Protection of the Innocent. A third legitimate purpose of two forms of punishment—imprisonment and execution—is to protect others from one who has proved himself capable of crime. Because of increasing frustration over achieving rehabilitation, Western society seems to increasingly emphasize the quarantine purpose of imprisonment. Yet 95 to 98 percent of present American inmates will be returned to society, and 68 percent of them will commit further crime.

Scripture is filled with admonitions to protect the innocent and helpless—the widow, the fatherless, the alien, the weak. Government is established that citizens may lead a "quiet and peaceable life" (1 Tim. 2:2). Therefore, any just society must create structures to protect its citizens. But the Bible says little

[53]William Rasberry, *The State* (Columbia, S.C.), 23 June 1977.
[54]Norval Morris, "Crime and Punishment in America," *The Center Magazine,* May-June 1971, 10.

positive about imprisonment. It was not the normally prescribed mode of punishment. Furthermore, though the prescription of the death penalty for a wide variety of sins certainly protected society from repeated offenses, the protection of the innocent is not given as the rationale for capital punishment. We have already seen how society is not protected very well under the present arrangement. Prison sentences are short, early parole the rule, and subsequent crime all but certain. So, on this purpose also, the contemporary American system has failed. One form of protecting the rights of crime victims and the state has gained some attention of late: restitution. Under this theory, the offender would be given sentences for the purpose of restoring both the loss suffered by the victim and the loss of the government in apprehending, convicting, and incarcerating the criminal. Restitution is certainly a biblical principle and was the idea behind the Old Testament punishment by fine (Lev. 6:2-5; Num. 5:7).

Punitive. Retribution (punishment due in vindication of justice) is the one purpose disallowed almost universally by self-styled humanitarians inside and outside the church. It is held to be abhorrent to a civilized people who should have long since abandoned vindictive vengeance. Yet, though this is not the sole or even the paramount reason given in Scripture, it is clearly one purpose of punishment, inherent in the meaning of the word *punish* itself. The New Testament also clearly identifies the vindication of justice as one basic purpose of criminal punishment: government officials are established to mete out vengeance on evildoers (1 Pet. 2:14). All four purposes of punishment for crime are biblically valid and should be emphasized in law and criminal justice. The biblical order of priority in emphasis is probably (1) rehabilitation, (2) justice, (3) protection of the innocent, and (4) deterrence.

VARIETIES OF PUNISHMENT

Bad Law vs. Good Law. In general, good law reinforces moral standards, and bad law weakens moral standards. There are many ways to create bad law or systems of justice.

Unenforceable law (or laws which society does not choose to enforce, such as America's prohibition) is bad because nonenforcement undermines respect for the law and promotes corruption among the citizenry and law enforcement officials.

Unjust law comes in many forms. It is unjust to accept hearsay evidence or to convict without adequate evidence. It is unjust to subject a victim of sexual assault or child abuse to repeated emotional and mental assault, shame, and intimidation in the courtroom. One pervasive form of injustice in our present system is that the poor, friendless, and uneducated are convicted far out of proportion to those who can afford expert legal representation, have friends in high places, and know how to "work the system." It is unjust to give a prison sentence to one who shoplifts ten dollars' worth of merchandise, yet have no law to keep the owner of the chain store from unjustly depriving the government of hundreds of thousands of dollars in income tax.

Inappropriate or unequal punishment is another kind of bad law. In October 1964 in Sicily, Gaetano Furnari killed a college professor who had seduced his daughter; in Manila a Chinese businessman was apprehended for kissing his Filipino secretary five years earlier. The murderer and the kisser were both given four years in prison. At about the same time, I read in a Tokyo newspaper the story of some young men who got drunk, captured a swan from the imperial palace moat, roasted the swan, and were given four years in prison. Buried in an inside column of the same paper was the brief report of a young mother who deliberately drowned her infant in a cesspool; she was given a two-year sentence, suspended. Somehow, one's sense of justice is offended. Good law and good law enforcement must be equitable and appropriate to the crime. In protecting the innocent, good law does not make an unwarranted infringement on the rights and freedoms of others. This delicate balance is difficult but is the object of good law.

Nonpunishment. Is it always wrong for society not to punish a crime? Apparently not, for many criminals went unpunished in the annals of Scripture. Not only wife-stealing kings like David, but a powerless woman taken in the act of adultery and a thirsty adulteress at the Samaritan well were not executed according to law. This does not mean that crime should be overlooked or that criminal justice should be subverted; Scripture is abundantly clear on that. But it does mean that mercy and forgiveness may sometimes be legitimate without violating justice.

Alternatives to Imprisonment. The American system of imprisonment is the primary sanction against crime, whereas in Scripture it was not mandated for that purpose. The prison system has utterly failed in three of the four purposes of punishment. It only functions well as a just form of punishment; retributive justice is served.

Frequent outbursts of prison violence give the public brief glimpses of the appalling situation behind the walls. Most prisons were constructed before 1920, many more than a hundred years ago, and for populations a fraction of the size now incarcerated. Violence is endemic, corruption a way of life, drugs and homosexuality rampant. It is estimated that up to 80 percent of inmates are homosexual or have had homosexual experiences, voluntary or involuntary. "Prison reform" is evident primarily in reports by investigative commissions, rarely in action taken. Are there any viable alternatives?

Deprivation of privilege is a common form of punishment, whether a relatively light deprivation such as a driver's license or a severe deprivation like one's license to practice medicine or law. Perhaps there are other creative ways to match the crime with appropriate deprivation of something of value other than freedom to live in normal society.

Corporal punishment is unlikely to be acceptable any time soon in Western society. Banishment or exile, formerly common, also has fallen out of favor except in the deportation of criminal aliens. It would seem less cruel than the typical prison environment, but that would depend largely on the place of exile. Military service is used in some societies as a form of punishment. None of these could be ruled out on biblical grounds, but none is likely to be acceptable in America today.

There is one present form of punishment that could be greatly expanded—the monetary fine or expropriation of property. The convicted criminal could be required to pay a stipulated amount to the victim and to the government (for costs of apprehension and prosecution) in monthly installments if necessary. This could be restricted to the 75 percent of the prison population who are not guilty of crimes of violence. Supervising such a program would be a fraction of the cost of incarceration, and the victim would have some hope of restitution for the loss suffered. A by-product would be to keep first offenders from the prison "schoolhouse in crime" and the brutalizing effect of prison.

Other alternatives would be a community service assignment or an assignment to serve or care for the victim in some way. These might be especially appropriate for juvenile offenders, many of whom are guilty of truancy, incorrigibility and other offenses that would not be punishable as a crime in an adult. These juveniles crowd the system and are society's greatest loss. Surely a society with creativity sufficient to put a man on the moon need not settle for a failed system of punishment here on earth.

Capital Punishment. There are two prevailing views on what Scripture teaches about executing convicted capital offenders: Those who advocate abolition of capital punishment and those who advocate capital punishment for premeditated homicide.

Abolition of Capital Punishment. England abolished the death penalty in December 1969, and a number of other nations have followed, bringing the total to eighteen. Most American major religious bodies have officially called for abolition. Not only does taking a human life offend liberal sensibilities (except in the case of the unborn and those who do not have a "truly human" existence), it offends New Testament ethics, according to many evangelicals. First of all, the Old Testament commandments are held not to be applicable any longer because they were part of the Mosaic system that was set aside. Furthermore, no one today holds that the capital punishment outlined in the Old Testament should be prosecuted today.

The Mosaic code prescribes the death penalty for eighteen crimes: (1) Murders—Exod. 21:12-14, 20; 22:2-3; Lev. 20:2; 24:17, 21; Num. 35:11-21, 30; Deut. 19:11-13. (2) Accidentally causing the death of a pregnant woman or her baby (?) if injured in the course of a fight—Exod. 21:22-25. (3) Killing of a person by a dangerous animal that had killed before, yet was not kept caged (both the animal and the owner to be killed)—

Exod. 21:28-30. (4) Kidnapping—Exod. 21:16; Deut. 24:7.
(5) Rape of a married woman (but not rape of a virgin)—Deut.
22:25-29. (6) Fornication—Deut. 22:13-21; Lev. 21:9;
exception, Lev. 19:20-22. (7) Adultery—Lev. 20:10; Num.
5:12-30; Deut. 22:22-24. (8) Incest—Lev. 20:11-12, 14.
(9) Homosexuality—Lev. 20:13. (10) Sexual intercourse with
an animal—Lev. 20:15-16; Exod. 22:19. (11) Striking a
parent—Exod. 21:15. (12) Cursing a parent—Exod. 21:17;
Lev. 20:9. (13) Rebelling against parents—Deut. 21:18-21.
(14) Sorcery, witchcraft—Exod. 22:18; Lev. 20:27.
(15) Cursing God—Lev. 24:10-16. (16) Attempting to lead
people to worship other gods—Deut. 13:1-16; 18:20; cf. Exod.
22:20. (17) Avenging a death despite acquittal by the law—
Deut. 17:12. (18) Intentionally testifying falsely against
someone in jeopardy of the death penalty—Deut. 19:16-19.[55]

More important than the problem of using Old Testament
standards today, biblical advocates of abolition hold that the
teaching of Christ deliberately set aside capital punishment. The
story of the woman taken in adultery (John 8) figures in most
discussions. Why did Christ not uphold the law when that is
precisely what the accusers were testing him on? Not only did he
protect her from execution, he did not even turn her over to the
authorities for a lesser punishment. But more important than his
example, in his explicit teaching Christ set aside the Old
Testament *lex talionis* (Exod. 21:23-25), the eye-for-an-eye
demand for equivalent retribution (Matt. 5:38-42). Christ's
allowance of divorce (Matt. 5:31-32; 19:9), rather than
advocating execution for adultery, is seen as an example of what
he intended concerning all other laws requiring the death
penalty, it is held by some. Nor, according to opponents of the
death penalty, did the apostles advocate the use of capital
punishment. The sword of Romans 13 is understood as the
symbol of authority, much as a badge would be today. The
officer wore it as a symbol of authority, but could use it as a
weapon much as a policeman carries a gun, not as an instrument
of execution, but for defense and for enforcement of his
authority. Could a badge and pistol prove that a state practices
and demands capital punishment? Besides, swords were not the

[55]Dave Llewellyn, "Restoring the Death Penalty: Proceed with Caution," *Christianity Today*, 23 May 1975, 11.

normal instrument for execution in capital cases, the argument runs.

Beyond this, the New Testament law of love is said to rule out capital punishment: "The idea that we could kill his body while loving his soul is excluded."[56] The loving thing is not to deprive a person of his highest value—his own life. How can a person claim to be pro-life and then deliberately take the life of another? Finally, the death of Christ is said to do away with all expiatory suffering, so that all of us, deserving the death penalty as we do, stand on level ground at the foot of the cross.

Death Penalty for Premeditated Homicide. Though some advocates of capital punishment hold that the death penalty should be applied in cases of rape and treason, most who write on the subject speak primarily of murder as the one capital offense. They point out that though the Mosaic civil law may have been set aside by Christ and the apostles, the command to execute those guilty of murder predates Moses and, indeed, is in the original order of creation: "Whoever sheds the blood of man, by man shall his blood be shed" (Gen. 9:6). The reason given by Moses is based on the very dignity of man that abolitionists say is violated: because humankind is made in the likeness of God, only capital punishment is an adequate retribution. Though the structure of the Hebrew could either be a statement of fact or a command, no serious Bible scholar to my knowledge holds that a command was not intended. The overwhelming evidence of Scripture is that Moses intended to convey God's view that such a person shall *surely* be executed (example Lev. 24:17; Num. 35:16-21). The Old Testament teaching is clear, whether or not the practice is.

Advocates hold that the New Testament also is clear. Christ, though setting aside some Old Testament law, specifically did not set aside the law of capital punishment. Furthermore, they say, Paul's instruction on civil authority (Rom. 13) speaks of the sword not merely as a symbol of authority, but as a symbol of the specific authority to execute. Though beheading was not the only method of capital punishment, it was one method.

56John Howard Yoder, "Capital Punishment and the Bible," *Christianity Today,* 1 February 1960, 5.

Furthermore, a sword could hardly symbolize imprisonment or flogging, it is argued.

Other abolitionist arguments are answered as follows: If a person cannot be executed in love, how can God execute the sinner? Certainly, those with the heavy responsibility to take a human life should do so reluctantly with sorrow, not lightly or with some distorted pleasure in vengeance. Again, how many people are privileged to know in advance the time of death and so to prepare? The criminal on death row has an uncommon opportunity to repent and prepare for his eternal dwelling place. But more important, justice is love distributed, and love for the guilty individual cannot override love for all those in a society put in jeopardy if the violent go unchecked while justice languishes.

Does capital punishment deter more than other punishment? The question is hotly debated. The underworld certainly thinks it deters and so applies the principle ruthlessly. The deterrent value, if any, is greatly reduced because few expect to meet such a fate. Even when capital punishment was in full force in the United States, less than one percent of murderers were executed. Furthermore, 75 percent of murders are crimes of passion— family members or close acquaintances. Many of these murderers would be blind to the threat of any penalty. Of course, the person who forfeits his life will not kill again, so there is that much deterrence. Isaac Ehrlich, a University of Chicago economic theoretician, employing a sophisticated statistical technique, published a study indicating that each execution may prevent as many as eight murders.[57] Arguments based on comparing the rates of executions and murders between states or different societies are valueless because there are so many variants that contribute to rates of homicide.

In the final analysis the question of deterrence is probably unanswerable because we can never know who did *not* commit an intended murder and for what reason he refrained. We know this much: the Bible holds that capital punishment deters (Deut. 17:12-13). But, as we have seen earlier, the deterrent value is the least important among the biblical purposes given for punishment.

[57]Isaac Ehrlich, *The Presbyterian Journal*, 26 May 1976, 11.

Conclusion. My personal conclusion is a mediating one. Capital punishment cannot be inherently immoral because God commanded it. On the other hand, God himself did not insist on it, either for the first murderer, Cain, nor for the most prominent, David. Therefore, it cannot be wrong to show mercy.

Two arguments pull me in opposite directions. First, the command was pre-Mosaic, which means that God must have intended it for universal application. On the other hand, the New Testament introduced a new approach to civil law, and any affirmation of capital punishment is indirect and tenuous at best. In the light of this biblical tension it seems to me that the death penalty should be viewed more as a prerogative of human government than as a mandate.

Therefore, capital punishment is legitimate, but should be operative only if gross injustices have been eliminated. By injustices I mean the former pattern in America in which 50 percent of those executed between 1930 and 1967 were black. Black killing of a white brought almost certain death, white killing of a black almost never. Furthermore, executions were reserved primarily for the poor and ignorant who could not afford adequate representation or did not understand how to seek assistance. Often they were mentally retarded, almost always poorly educated.

Another form of injustice, mistaken execution of the innocent, has been overemphasized. The most liberal estimates of all varieties of crime in which innocent persons have been convicted is up to 5 percent. In capital cases, where no expense is spared and no avenue of defense is unprobed, such error is highly unlikely, but in the rare instance when it may occur, one is faced with the alternative of what the lack of this sanction may do in a society. As much as the naturalistic humanitarian might protest, extension of physical life is not the ultimate value.

In summary, if capital punishment is part of a reasonably just system and is used only in cases of premeditated murder with no mitigating factors and certain proof, it would probably enhance the value of life and the fabric of justice in a society. But if it is invoked capriciously or in unjust ways, it would be better to set aside this God-given prerogative of human government.

CHRISTIAN RESPONSIBILITY FOR CRIMINAL JUSTICE

What can the individual Christian and the church do toward promoting a just and merciful society, other than by being just and merciful and teaching God's standards?

Rehabilitation. Since this is the primary purpose of punishment and since there is a growing consensus that our present system works directly opposite, the church and individual Christian must do all within their power to promote the one thing that can rehabilitate: regeneration. To persuade the individual to take responsibility for his own failure is the first step. But personal guilt and responsibility is a cruel message if it stops there and leaves him helpless to change. He needs to know of forgiveness and the way to be transformed into a new and different person. He needs the caring family of God, especially after his release. But these things the average prisoner never receives from the Christian community.

Probably the most notable example of what God can do and of what Christians must do is Charles Colson, convicted Watergate criminal, and his Prison Fellowship. Perhaps Colson is showing us the way to obey Christ's injunction to visit those in prison (Matt. 25:36, 39, 43-45). It is dreadful to note what Christ promised those who fail to visit the prisoners.

Christians actually hold the only proven key to transforming a criminal and making him a good citizen—of earth *and* heaven!

Punishment. If we insist that retributive justice must be restored as a primary purpose in criminal punishment, we must work hard toward a more just system of criminal justice. As citizens in a democracy we cannot sit by and shout "law and order." We must listen carefully to those who feel oppressed, examine carefully what is actually taking place, and insist on laws and law enforcement that are just and humane. Although our *prisons* do fulfill this one purpose of punishment, our *system* does not, in that most crime goes unpunished. We must work toward the justice of consistent apprehension as well as justice in sentencing and punishment.

Protection of the Innocent. Fewer and fewer Americans are willing to take the risk of personal involvement in reporting crime. The Christian must act in love for the innocent by stopping crime through direct action, at least by reporting all crime or suspicious activity. It may prove costly, but that is what love is all about. This action is the loving response toward the criminal as well. He needs to be protected from accumulating ever greater guilt and to have opportunity for enforced reflection on his wicked ways and their certain end.

More stringent pretrial qualifications of bail/bond release, longer prison terms, and less parole may protect society in about 25 percent of the cases. But upwards of 75 percent of convicted criminals could be punished in alternative ways at no risk of violence. We may need to redirect some of our very limited resources in criminal justice.

Deterrence. Deterrence depends, we are told, not on the severity of the threatened punishment so much as on the certainty and swiftness of apprehension and punishment. Solomon agreed (Eccles. 8:11, NIV). Private citizens can assist in making apprehension more swift and certain by reporting crime or suspicious activity, but they can also contribute through advocating legal and fiscal reform. For example, more tax revenues could be allotted to criminal justice efforts, such as the development of alternative systems of punishment. This would not only reduce the overcrowded condition of prisons (which contributes to their failure), but also would make room for the enormous backlog of pending cases which, as much as anything else, works toward long delays in prosecution and a tendency toward a light sentence and early release.

But the greatest contribution the Christian and the church can make toward deterrence is to faithfully teach God's holy standards and God's holy judgment.

MISCELLANEOUS LIFE ISSUES

NEGLIGENCE

Not all legally liable negligence is moral negligence, and very little that constitutes moral culpability has been legislated against. For example, an automobile defect or medical malpractice which is unintentional could well be subject to civil prosecution but not be sinful negligence from a biblical point of view. If adequate precautions were not taken, the moral element is introduced. For example, extensive correspondence by leading asbestos manufacturers indicates that they knew very well the hazardous nature of manufacture and use of the product, but deliberately decided to continue manufacture. Since the results are not fully manifest for several decades, the general public was not aware of this negligence, which was certainly a moral failure.

As another example, a student told me of a part-time job on which he was required to use hazardous chemicals. When state inspection time came, the chemicals were hidden and the inspection passed. He and others continued in the employment of such an unscrupulous employer because of economic necessity. Marginal laborers, such as illegal aliens and people with little or no education, are often victims of this kind of negligence, which is both criminal and moral in nature.

On the other hand, there are matters of negligence on which governments do not ordinarily make laws. In Matthew 25, where the final judgment is previewed, we are taught that neglect to feed the hungry, clothe the naked, and care for the oppressed is subject to the most severe judgment. So to respond to natural disaster that threatens the life or health of people is the responsibility of believers to the extent of their ability. At least, to ignore human problems which I could help is moral negligence, even though I may never be prosecuted in a human court.

The potential for failure in negligence is virtually limitless. For this reason, we are called upon to be sensitive, compassionate people of integrity, recognizing our own great limitations in wisdom and resources to meet human need, and pleading the grace of God to cover our shortcomings.

ETHICS IN BIOMEDICAL ISSUES

Recent advance in medical science constantly raises new problems for the morally sensitive person. So fraught with potential for evil are some of these scientific advances that even committed humanists, whose central doctrine is freedom, have begun to use terms they considered unacceptable, like "normative ethics" and "public morality." What do we do with genetic manipulation, cloning, organ transplants, psycho-surgery, mind-altering chemicals, fetal—or even human—experimentation? How does a society maintain the delicate balance of individual rights and obligations on one hand and social benefits and harms on the other?

Some hold that much of the recent advance is wrong because men are playing God. I take exception to this position, holding that man was created specifically to "play God" in the sense of bearing his likeness and participating with him in creativity. The advances of science, far from being unwarranted meddling in the affairs of God, can actually be to the glory of God. This is not to justify the arrogance of a scientist who does not acknowledge God, nor the sinfulness of those who use scientific advance for selfish or malicious purposes.

In any event, we do not have any teaching in Scripture that would cast doubt on man's potential for creativity and God's intention that he "subdue . . . and have dominion over . . . the earth" (Gen. 1:28). I believe this approach should be applied to questions of organ transplants and artificial organs. It is hard to see how this process can be ethically different from creating an artificial limb. Of course, there are many ethical questions involved, such as when the prospective donor is dead, but there can hardly be moral objections to the process itself.

The questions of *in vitro* fertilization and genetic manipulation are similar. More than fifteen hundred diseases have been identified as being genetically transmitted. Can it be morally wrong to seek the elimination of these when it can be done without bad side effects? On the other hand, who is wise enough to orchestrate the "evolution of humanity," to create a super-race through governmental control? Human experimentation has opened the door to many medical advances. It has also been terribly abused, as in Nazi Germany. Again, people may be manipulated into participating in an experiment without full knowledge of the consequences. There are many other possible abuses, but the concept itself can hardly be faulted.

I confess a deep hesitancy, not to say revulsion, to the use of psychosurgery, mind-altering drugs, and the cloning of a whole individual, or genetically producing a post-human species. The misgiving arises because I cannot determine from Scripture the relationship between brain, mind, and spirit. It seems indecent, if not irreverent and immoral, to manipulate the soul. Not all share my concern. Fuller Theological Seminary psychologist Paul Clement, at the 1984 Conference on Human Engineering and the Future of Man, celebrated the prospects of a "technology of the spirit" that could presumably produce by behavior modification such virtues as the fruit of the Spirit. To me this is the area of scientific development which must be examined most carefully for ethical validity and monitored diligently in its development.

Human sins of pride, self-interest, and malice constantly pollute the stream of scientific advance. Often the ethical issue does not come at the point of theoretical scientific investigation but in the technological application. Even more often does it come at the point of using the technology. And it is not the scientist or physician alone who must be monitored. Paul Kurtz, editor of *The Humanist,* states:

Regrettably, it is not the scientist who is apt to misuse the fruits of his work, but the military man, politician, industrialist, commissar, or theologian.[58]

Ethically sensitive Christians and the church must monitor this entire process, identifying wrong applications of scientific inventions or procedures and working for their correction. But we should not fear human creativity as such.

Having said this, however, I do not mean that everything which can be done should be done. At the same time, knowing human nature, it would be safe to conclude that everything which can be done, will be done. So it is surely the responsibility of the Christian scientist to make himself biblically and theologically capable and to work with others, who, though not scientists, are learned in biblical ethics, to monitor the process.

When Jesus Christ probed the command forbidding murder all the way to the depths of the human selfish heart, he encompassed all the harmful activities and attitudes in between the least thought and the most terrible act. In this long and

[58]Paul Kurtz, "The Uses and Abuses of Science," *The Humanist,* September-October 1972, 8.

complex chapter, we have probed the most prominent ways in which human beings harm their fellows and deny the law of love. Perhaps it is not too much to say that whatever is not of love is sin.

SUGGESTED ADDITIONAL READING

RACISM

Cone, James H. *Black Theology and Black Power.* New York: Seabury, 1969.
_____. *A Black Theology of Liberation.* New York: Lippincott, 1970.
_____. *God of the Oppressed.* New York: Seabury, 1975. Cone is probably the most prolific black religious thinker and writer on these issues, and these books give a clear understanding of black theology.
Franklin, John Hope. *From Slavery to Freedom: A History of Black Americans.* New York: Random House, 1974. Perhaps the most comprehensive history of black Americans.
Malcolm X. *The Autobiography of Malcolm X.* New York: Grove, 1966. Helpful for understanding the reasons behind black rage.
Scherer, Lester B. *Slavery and the American Churches in Early America, 1619–1819.* Grand Rapids: Eerdmans, 1975.
In addition to Tom Skinner's work already cited, two blacks give alternative views of the issues from an evangelical perspective. John Perkins tells of his unspeakable personal experience of the worst kind of southern racism and the answers God has given in his best-selling book *Let Justice Roll Down,* (Ventura, Calif.: Gospel Light, 1976). Howard Jones, associate evangelist with Billy Graham, speaks to the black church itself in *Shall We Overcome?* (Westwood, N.J.: Revell, 1966).

ABORTION

Brown, Harold O. J. *Death before Birth.* Nashville: Nelson, 1977. A carefully reasoned and comprehensive look at the abortion issue by a distinguished scholar who was instrumental in the founding of the Christian Action Council, a leading prolife group, and the *Human Life Review,* the leading scholarly journal on life issues.
Burtchaell, James T. *Rachel Weeping: The Case Against Abortion.* New York: Harper, 1982. A powerful and well-reasoned statement from a Roman Catholic viewpoint.
Fowler, Paul B. *Abortion: Toward an Evangelical Consensus.* Portland: Multnomah, 1987. An excellent overview.
Gardner, R. F. R. *Abortion: The Personal Dilemma.* Grand Rapids: Eerdmans, 1972. A thorough study made before the *Roe v. Wade* decision, but still useful. Does not take a rigid prolife position, but does view Scripture from an evangelical viewpoint.
Gartan, Jean. *Who Broke the Baby.* Minneapolis: Bethany Fellowship, 1979. Brings to light the true nature of the main cliches of the abortion movement.
Harrison, Beverly Wildung. *Our Right to Choose.* Boston: Beacon, 1983. An irenic, well-reasoned, thorough presentation of the pro-choice position.
Hensley, Jeff, ed. *The Zero People.* Ann Arbor: Servant, 1983. Articles by

twenty-five leaders in the field cover all aspects of abortion, euthanasia, and infanticide.

Koop, C. Everett. *The Right to Live: The Right to Die*. Wheaton, Ill.: Tyndale, 1976. A popular, authoritative, brief polemic for life, treating both abortion and euthanasia, by the best known pro-life medical authority, who has since become U.S. Surgeon General.

Montgomery, John Warwick. *Slaughter of the Innocents*. Westchester, Ill.: Crossway, 1981. In his usual cogent style, theologian-lawyer Montgomery makes a telling case for life in this brief book.

Nathanson, Bernard N. *Aborting America*. New York: Doubleday, 1979. This book has had a profound effect on the abortion debate because the author was at first a leading exponent of abortion rights who "presided personally over 60,000 deaths," as he puts it. An atheist, Nathanson argues from a humanitarian point of view for the right to life.

Reagan, Ronald. *Abortion and the Conscience of the Nation*. Nashville: Nelson, 1984. A powerful appeal argued with simplicity and fervency. Strong supplementary chapters by C. Everett Koop and Malcolm Muggeridge.

Schaeffer, Francis A., and C. Everett Koop. *Whatever Happened to the Human Race?* Old Tappan, N.J.: Revell, 1979. Widely influential as Schaeffer's last great effort, accompanying the films which presented similar material.

Young, Curtis. *The Least of These*. Chicago: Moody, 1983. An up-to-date popular overview of abortion issues by the former executive director of the Christian Action Council in D.C.

The Human Life Review. Published by The Human Life Foundation, Inc. New York; the leading and indispensable journal on the subject.

EUTHANASIA: PRO-LIFE ORIENTATION

Gould, Jonathan, and Lord Craigmyle, *Your Death Warrant? The Implications of Euthanasia*. New York: Arlington House, 1973.

Grisez, Germain, and Joseph Boyle. "An Alternative to Death with Dignity" in *The Human Life Review*, Winter 1978. Explains history and significance of "right to life" legislation and offers a carefully crafted prolife alternative to other euthanasia-oriented legislation.

Horan, Dennis J., and David Mall. *Death, Dying and Euthanasia*. Washington: University Publications of America, 1977.

McCarthy DeMere, M.D., in *Legal Aspects of Medical Practice*, March 1978, says of this volume: "This reviewer has researched the subject in an official capacity for many years and can say, without fear of contradiction, that this treatise is the most comprehensive, well presented, and useful work on the subject in contemporary literature."

Marx, Paul. *Death without Dignity, Killing for Mercy*. Minneapolis: For LIFE, 1975. An excellent booklet providing a thorough introductory overview of the issues.

EUTHANASIA: PROCHOICE ORIENTATION

Fletcher, Joseph. *Morals and Medicine*. Princeton: Princeton University Press, 1954.

Maguire, Daniel C. *Death by Choice*. New York: Doubleday, 1974.

Russell, O. Ruth. *Freedom to Die*. New York: Human Sciences, 1975.

WAR

Bainton, Roland H. *Christian Attitudes toward War and Peace*. Nashville: Abingdon, 1960. A useful survey of views of war and peace throughout church history, also critical evaluations.

Buzzard, Lynn, and Paula Campbell. *Holy Disobedience: When Must Christians Resist the State?* Ann Arbor: Servant, 1984. Historical and biblical overview by two attorneys.

Clouse, Robert G., ed. *War: Four Christian Views.* Downers Grove, Ill.: InterVarsity, 1981. Includes a useful annotated bibliography.

Fortas, Abe. *Concerning Dissent and Civil Disobedience.* New York: New American Library, 1968. A succinct philosophical statement from the viewpoint of an associate justice of the Supreme Court.

Holmes, Arthur F., ed. *War and Christian Ethics.* Grand Rapids: Baker, 1975. An extremely useful anthology of definitive statements by leading spokesmen on the various views of war from Plato and Cicero through the church fathers, the Reformation leaders, down to the present.

Ramsey, Paul. *The Just War: Force and Political Responsibility.* New York: Scribner's, 1968. A leading spokesman for the new liberal realism advocated by Reinhold Niebuhr.

Sider, Ronald. *Christ and Violence.* Scottdale, Penn.: Herald, 1979. A leading spokesman for the new evangelical peace advocacy.

Yoder, John Howard. *When War Is Unjust.* Minneapolis: Augsburg, 1985. The author of *The Politics of Jesus* gives a forceful, clear, and simple presentation of the peace position against just war theory.

On a related subject that is often perplexing to the sensitive Christian who accepts the inspiration and authority of the Old Testament, *The Problem of War in the Old Testament,* by Peter C. Craigie (Grand Rapids: Eerdmans, 1978) is helpful.

CRIME AND PUNISHMENT

Menninger, Karl. *The Crime of Punishment.* New York: Viking, 1969. An articulate statement of the "soft" position on punishment by a leading psychiatrist.

Silberman, Charles E. *Criminal Violence, Criminal Justice.* New York: Random House, 1978. Norval Morris, former dean of the University of Chicago Law School, evaluated Silberman's book as "clearly the best general study on crime and the response to crime in this country."

Van den Haag, Ernest. *Punishing Criminals: Concerning a Very Old and Painful Question.* New York: Basic Books, 1976. The most influential statement of the new "hard-line" position on criminal justice.

MEDICAL ETHICS

Periodicals may be more useful than books in keeping pace, though books do stream from the press on the entire subject and on each issue. One widely used textbook was revised and updated in 1985: *Human Medicine* by James B. Nelson and Jo Anne Smith Rohricht (Minneapolis: Augsburg). See also *Biblical Medical Ethics* by Franklin E. Payne, Jr. (Milford, Michigan: Mott Media, 1985).

CHAPTER NINE

INTEGRITY: PROPERTY AND TRUTH

Thou shalt not steal. Thou shalt not bear false witness.

Integrity may be the most precious possession I have, its violation my greatest loss. Can I be trusted? If not, all other virtues become uncertain. Lack of integrity is a fault-line in the character that jeopardizes all other values and undermines all relationships. Even communication ultimately depends on the confidence that what the other person says is reliable, what he does is trustworthy. No wonder Satan is called the father of lies, the ultimate cheat. And God is the Trustworthy One. Although integrity touches every aspect of Christian behavior, the Eighth and Ninth Commandments focus our attention on two aspects: property and truth.

The prohibition of stealing (Exod. 20:15) recognizes the right of private property. Virtually all societies have recognized the right to possess and have safeguarded that right. Even communism does not do away completely with the right, since only the means of production and other specified properties are reserved to the state.

Some have held that taxation violates the Eighth Commandment, especially heavy taxation such as is necessary to a welfare state:

Using the civil authority as an intermediary does not change an immoral act into a moral act. If it is wrong for an individual to forcibly take from others to provide for his needs, then it is also wrong for him to use the power of the government to do so.[1]

Thus a professor of economics and political science seems to make the commandment mean "Thou shalt not take by force the possessions of another." But we should not be more ethical than the Bible! "Thou shalt not kill," to be sure, but Scripture itself gives exceptions. Thou shalt not take by force, but the government is authorized to tax. This was seen throughout the Old Testament, and both Christ and the apostles affirmed it in the New. Christ was accused of teaching against paying taxes (Luke 23:2), but when he himself was asked, he affirmed the right of the government to tax and the obligation of God's child to pay it (Matt. 22:17, 21; Mark 12:14, 17; Luke 20:22, 25). Paul affirmed this obligation (Rom. 13:7). Thus we conclude that one violates the Eighth Commandment only when he takes from another that which Scripture gives him no right to take.

The relationship between stealing and its root in covetousness was explored in some detail in the chapter on "Sin." So we turn now to specific areas in which this commandment is commonly broken: labor/management; work/leisure; economic systems; private integrity; social responsibility; and robbery of things other than property.

LABOR AND MANAGEMENT

Although the social context of Bible times was radically different from contemporary democratic society, the principles enunciated for slave/owner relationships are so humanitarian in their protection of the oppressed that they are easily transferable to labor/management relationships in the post-slavery era in

[1]Tom Rose, *The Presbyterian Journal*, 7 April 1976, 13.

which we live, an era brought about through the influence of New Testament teaching.

In his letters to the churches at Ephesus (6:5-9) and Colossae (3:22–4:1), Paul gives principles for both employer and employee.

RESPONSIBILITIES OF BOTH LABOR AND MANAGEMENT

Both are to work for God. Work is to be treated as service to Christ because there is both reward and punishment from God himself. Payday someday, yes, but benefits and losses now as well, from the Master of both. This sanctifies the whole relationship for the Christian and provides guidelines for behavior.

The employee is to be subject "from the heart," humble in his attitude, fearful before God of wronging his employer. The employer is to be humbly fearful of wronging his employee.

Furthermore, both are to relate honestly, without hypocrisy. They may not appear one way in the presence of the other and elsewhere behave in a contrary way. Everything is straightforward, open, and each can trust the other not only to stand by public agreements but to work for the welfare of the other.

Finally, the attitude is to be wholehearted, cordial, even cheerful. This may be the most difficult requirement, particularly when the other party does not behave Christlike, but it is nevertheless the standard that is required by the Master whom both serve. Paul says that this means the worker will work diligently and faithfully. And he says of the owner, "in like manner."

RESPONSIBILITIES OF MANAGEMENT

The manager must not threaten. He has power over the welfare and livelihood of his employee; he must not use it to coerce. When an employer demands something unethical or illegal from an employee, such as offering a bribe to a prospective customer or demanding sexual favors, the sins of cheating and immorality are compounded by the use of economic coercion.

Furthermore, all working arrangements, including pay, must be just. Unsafe working conditions in a coal mine or chemical plant are certainly unjust, but so are subminimum wages for immigrant grape pickers.

Finally, this justice includes equal or fair treatment. Justice does not permit an employer to give one person greater or less benefit for unfair reasons—discrimination for family (nepotism), friendship, race, or sex. Is it fair for the pay of executives to rise from twenty-nine times the average worker's pay in 1979 to forty times his pay in 1985? During this time when the U.S. automobile industry was threatened by imports, workers accepted reduction in pay to keep their product competitive in the marketplace, while executive income skyrocketed. Paul says management must be fair.

In addition to Paul's teaching, Old Testament teaching concerning the owner's responsibilities throws light on the responsibilities of management. God is totally against slavery and always has been (Deut. 24:14; Jer. 34:8-20). He did make laws governing the system, not by way of approval but to protect the slave. The master was not to harm the slave (Exod. 21:20ff.). There was to be a time limit for holding a fellow Israelite in slavery (Exod. 21:2-6), so that "slavery" was actually indentured servanthood for a limited time (Lev. 25:39ff.). When the slave was released, he was to be given assets so that he could start his new life of freedom (Deut. 15:12ff.). Not all these laws are applicable, of course, but principles embedded in the regulations should prove instructive.

Most of the admonitions were for the master, and this is certainly appropriate for any relationship in which one party is strong, the other weak. Management must not defraud, oppress, or harm, and must pay fair wages on time (Lev. 19:13; 25:43; Deut. 24:14ff.; Prov. 22:16; Mal. 3:5; Matt. 10:10; Luke 10:7; Rom. 4:4; 1 Tim. 5:18; James 5:4). The established rest day must be given (Deut. 5:14; 15:18; Exod. 20:9-11; 23:12; 34:21). Management must not despise the cause of the employee (Job 31:13), should reward and pay him well (Prov. 17:2; 27:18; Jer. 22:13; Matt. 24:45, 47; Luke 12:35ff.). In fact, the master was to treat his servant as a son (Prov. 29:21) or brother (Philem. 16).

RESPONSIBILITIES OF LABOR

The employee, for his part, is not to deceive or be violent (Zeph. 1:9; Luke 16:10-11); is to honor his employer (Mal. 1:6;

1 Tim. 6:1); be faithful (Matt. 24:45ff.; Luke 12:35ff.; 16:10; 1 Cor. 4:2; Titus 2:9-10); be patient and follow orders (Tit. 2:9; Eph. 6:5; Col. 3:22; 1 Pet. 2:18) even when the employer doesn't deserve it (1 Pet. 2:18-20). He is to work hard and not be lazy (1 Thess. 4:11ff.; 2 Thess. 3:7).

Let me speak plainly about the implications of this teaching. The employer who pays less than a fair wage (in terms of what others are paid, or compared to company profits) is stealing from the worker. The worker who carelessly arrives late, wastes time with small talk, inattentive work, long breaks, or daydreaming is a thief. And both sin against God, their true employer.

COLLECTIVE BARGAINING

Suppose labor does not live up to its responsibilities? Management has almost limitless economic power to enforce compliance. But suppose management does not live up to its responsibilities? Labor has only two possible recourses: protection by a higher authority or collective bargaining.

God is the ultimate higher authority, and one day he will settle all accounts. But in the meantime government is the only higher power, and government is often less powerful than management. Many multinational corporations are far more powerful than some of the nations in which they operate. Some can close down the economic life of a nation. In powerful states, the government can control private corporations but often chooses not to because of blatant or sophisticated corruption. Yet in enlightened and powerful governments, the rights of the laborer are normally protected in minimum ways and broad categories. Safety standards, minimum wages, and nondiscrimination have been legislated.

But for the specifics of how justice is worked out on the shop floor and in the office, or in the case of reluctant government initiative, management cannot always be counted on consistently to pursue "fairness and justice in humility, from the heart." The remaining option is collective bargaining. But is collective bargaining, with the threat of strike, right for the Christian?

Some, such as those who led in establishing the Christian

Labor Association, would hold membership in a non-Christian union as being "yoked together with unbelievers" and thus wrong. Others hold that collective bargaining is just as much a threat of force as management's economic pressure, and hence wrong for the Christian.

When resisting established corporate injustice, at least passive resistance may be justified. I hold, therefore, that since injustice on the part of employers rarely puts life in imminent danger, violence is not ethical for labor, but the threat of a strike to force negotiation may be justified in the face of unredressed grievances.

To be united with unbelievers is inevitable in a fallen world (John 17:15-18), whether as citizens, employees, or union members. Paul's unequal yoke had to do with separation from religious and spiritual defilement (2 Cor. 6:14–7:1, NIV), not with breaking contact with unbelievers or association with them in the ordinary this-worldly affairs of life. The risk, of course, is that one may become partner to wrong action. This is part of the risk of remaining "in the world." The Christian must not permit himself to be coerced into sinful behavior and must be prepared to pay the consequences for his refusal if that demand should be made. For example, he would not use violence against police or strikebreakers even if the union boss said to.

It is true that some "big labor" often has become just as corrupt as some "big management." Perhaps it is only the balance of such corrupted power that produces any modicum of justice. History has proven repeatedly that fallen man does not often yield his rights and privileges except to force. Without unionization in America, the lot of the laborer, no doubt, would be still one of unbearable oppression. By the same token, once labor achieved power it, too, has proved corrupt. Thus the Christian, whether in management or labor, is under obligation to the Master he serves to work tirelessly to purge the corruption.

Even if unionization is held to be biblically legitimate, what of the ethics of a closed shop? For a union to insist that it alone must represent all laborers in the company and that no one may be employed without belonging to the union goes against my sense of freedom and fair play. And yet, all the power a union has derives from the "union"; management will only be compelled to negotiate with a united front. Therefore, the nonunion employee will reap the benefits of collective bargaining only if he is one of a very small minority of nonmembers. If many refused to join, the "union" would be powerless. It seems unfair that the nonmember should enjoy the benefits without paying the dues. I fail to find a strong ethical base either for demanding or prohibiting "closed shop." I might prefer an open shop on grounds of personal freedom of choice, but would probably not continue to do so if I belonged to a union which was rendered powerless by my refusal—and by that of others—to join, and thus forfeited the potential or actual rights and privileges available only to united action.

Q3

Unions may be justified in a fallen world in which laborers are being treated unjustly. On the other hand, should management behave in just and merciful ways, I can see little biblical justification for unionization.

BEYOND JUSTICE

Beyond basic justice and fairness, what are legitimate demands on management? Must management provide for job satisfaction, personal improvement, pleasant working conditions, job security, retirement benefits? Is democracy in the workplace the only valid humanitarian goal? That is, must the workers fully participate in management decisions for those decisions to be just and fair?

United Auto Workers vice-president Irving Bluestone says yes:

> A society anchored in democratic principles should insure each individual the dignity, respect, and liberty worthy of free people. . . . The ferment of union activity in the 1930s and 1940s . . . was the first stage toward accomplishment of a larger goal: industrial democracy. . . . The next step is to provide the worker a more meaningful measure of control over his job through participation in decisions affecting his job.[2]

However, there has been an overwhelming lack of response from rank-and-file union members to this new cause.

Furthermore, even union leaders seem unwilling to promote "meaningful work" notions. Labor seems interested in basic

[2]Irving Bluestone, "Worker Participation in Decision-Making," *The Humanist*, September-October 1973, 11, 13-14.

justice and fair play, higher pay and longer vacations, security in
the job and upon retirement. But not much else. Polls consistently show that 80 to 90 percent of American workers are
satisfied with their work.

Behaviorists and humanists find it difficult to understand how workers can
possibly say they like their work when it appears so barren to intellectuals. This
view was recently expressed by the behavioral scientist David Sirota, when he
made a study in a garment plant. He was surprised to find that most sewing
machine operators found their work interesting. . . . These workers' views are
supported in a study by Weintraub of 2,535 female sewing machine operators
in 17 plants from Massachusetts to Texas. He found that "most of the
operators like the nature of their work." . . . What the behaviorists find so
difficult to comprehend is really quite simply explained: workers have similar
attitudes toward their work because *they are not a cross section of the population,
but rather a select group.*[3]

Industrial engineer Fein says that people don't continue in a
job they do not like and that many people really do like
repetitive work. So workers by and large fit jobs.

I conclude that Scripture demands justice and fairness from
management, and the law of love would nudge a manager/
owner toward providing all the benefits possible while making
the business succeed for the sake of both the employees and
owners. Profits for stockholders or management must be in line
with benefits for employees. Labor, in like manner, may demand
justice and fairness but should not coerce other benefits, especially when it might jeopardize the company's welfare.

WORK AND LEISURE

We considered the biblical teaching concerning work in the
section on "Sloth." Two aspects of the question need additional
attention: What is overwork? What accountability does one
have for the use of leisure time?

THE "PROTESTANT WORK ETHIC"

Work is a gift of God; the faithful worker is following the
example of the worker God. But many have recently taken issue
with the so-called "Protestant work ethic," that man is made to

[3]Mitchell Fein, "The Myth of Job Enrichment," *The Humanist*, September-October
1973, 31.

work and finds his fulfillment in his work. The contention is that man really was made to play, that work is a necessary evil to provide resources for finding personal fulfillment in fun activities and in the family.

Robert K. Johnston holds that play is seen as legitimate by Old Testament standards with its Sabbath, festival, dance, and music, that the New Testament is silent on the subject but very serious toward life, and that the Greek ideal was leisure devoted to creative play.[4] The modern American, with Greek and Judeo-Christian roots, is caught in the middle.

Is the work ethic rightly called "Protestant"? At the beginning of the century, German social historian Max Weber made a major study entitled "The Protestant Ethic and Spirit of Capitalism."

Weber looked for the background to the ideas of this new generation and found it in the Protestant conception of "calling," a conception unknown among either Catholic peoples or in classical antiquity. The idea of calling is a product of the Reformation and one thing was unquestionably new: the valuation of the fulfillment of duty in worldly affairs as the highest form of moral activity.[5]

Some have held that the Reformers were the source of the Protestant work ethic, though some have held that it was John Wesley. Others point out that Augustine, living in the pre-Reformation world and thus not a Protestant, rejected the concept of play as unworthy for the Christian, and that his dominant influence has molded Christian thought on the subject. Whatever the source, northern Europeans and American Protestants have tended to hold to a serious work ethic. All this is now challenged.

Rarely, if ever, has a society questioned the morality of hard work or debated the ethics of leisure until the recent affluence of a few nations made it possible for the masses to face such dilemmas. A century ago in America the average worker put in a sixty-six hour week; today such people are designated "workaholics."

First of all, work must be done as service to God. This makes the Christian's work "relevant to every social structure in every

4Robert K. Johnston, *The Christian at Play* (Grand Rapids: Eerdmans, 1983), 85.
5Henry Catherwood, *The Christian in Industrial Society* (London: Tyndale, 1964), 115.

age of history, precisely because it is 'irrelevant' to all of them."[6] So the Christian can fulfill his vocation under any political or economic system so long as it brings glory to God. To bring glory to God means to bring benefit to humankind: "Work is to be done for the benefit of humanity in Jesus' name."[7] The rationale for this statement is simply that if work does not benefit either God or man, how can it be said to honor God?

Work also should not be damaging to the worker, whether physically, morally, psychologically, or spiritually. Among other implications of this principle, Karl Barth points out the evil of working under tension:

To work tensely is to do so in self-exaltation and forgetfulness of God. . . . Tension makes work a drudgery, a mad race, an affliction, not only for the worker himself but also for those around.[8]

By tension, Barth does not mean the healthy internal pressure to achieve high goals with limited resources, which draws from the worker his best, but rather the stress-filled and fretful tension of unbelief. Research has consistently demonstrated that the amount of work is less the culprit in work-related health problems than one's attitude about his work. To work intensely, to work long hours, to enjoy one's work, to find in it life's meaning cannot, on biblical grounds, be wrong. If such an approach to work is denigrated as "workaholism," perhaps Jesus himself is the most guilty (Mark 3:20-21).

One's occupation may not give him a sense of divine calling, (vocation) which is perceived as one's very purpose for living, but if one does have such a vocation and lives accordingly, he does well, not wrong. Paul's meaning in life was not defined by his trade of making tents, but it certainly was by his call to evangelize the Gentiles. For that he was born and redeemed. Ultimately one's purpose is to fellowship with God, but he may be called to love and glorify God best by the work he does. This view of vocation has been contested by those who put worship or relationships with family and friends as the paramount purposes of life and relegate work to a lesser rank. But this

[6]Alan Richardson, *The Bible's Doctrine of Work* (London: SCM Press, 1952), 50.
[7]Alfred A. Glenn, *Taking Your Faith to Work* (Grand Rapids: Baker, 1980), 57.
[8]Karl Barth, *Church Dogmatics,* trans. Geoffrey W. Bromiley, vol. 3 (Edinburgh: T & T Clark, 1961), 553.

ranking of purposes is artificial and unbiblical (see "Root Sins
and Virtues" chapter, the section on "Coveting Time"). We
rightly recognize Moses, David, Daniel, Jesus, and Paul as
significant in God's purposes for the work they accomplished.
So, if God gives a sense of mission, one should pursue it with
vigor. And if he has not, it is no sin to ask for it.

On the other hand, to work compulsively as an escape from
other responsibilities; to work hard for wrong motives such as
avarice or pride; to neglect responsibilities to family, church, or
community; to work in ways that damage spiritual health, or
even physical health for some unjustifiable reason—all these are
sinful and call for repentance.

LEISURE

Leisure time, granted to the privileged few in our world, also
should be spent to God's glory. It is not legitimized merely by
being morally innocent. Leisure is a trust to be invested in
nurture of family, service to the church, ministry to the needs of
others, and re-creating one's own physical, psychic, and spiritual
resources.

Robert K. Johnston holds that true play must have no end or
benefit in view. But since he does not prove this position from
biblical data, I conclude that play with no end in view cannot be
proved on biblical grounds as either desirable or undesirable.
But if play results in benefit to someone, it does seem more
compatible with the scriptural injunction to do everything to the
glory of God. For example, a time of sheer idleness can be
restorative to a harried spirit, but extended idleness could hardly
be justified on biblical grounds when Scripture so strongly
condemns sloth. The American average of six hours of television
daily can hardly be a responsible use of leisure to bring glory to
God and benefit to humankind.

As any involuntarily unemployed person can testify, work is
God's good gift to humankind. Though few have attempted to
develop a "doctrine of leisure" from the very limited data in
Scripture, discretionary time also should be viewed as a precious
gift and special trust from God.

ECONOMIC SYSTEMS

Though there are many economic systems, two vie for dominance in the latter half of the twentieth century: capitalism and socialism. Because any economic system is intertwined with some political system, the two are easily confused. But for our present consideration of integrity in the use of money, it is important to separate the two, dealing with the economic rather than the political system. The ethics of political systems will be considered in the chapter on "The Christian and Society."

In the meantime, note that a socialistic economic system need not be a communistic political system or even communistic in philosophy. For example, Sweden is socialistic but not communistic. On the other hand, capitalism is the preferred economics of many dictatorships, so it should not be equated with democracy. A free market economy is quite compatible with a repressive regime. So let us consider the economic systems independent of the political structure in which they may operate.

CAPITALISM VS. SOCIALISM

Some propose a biblical mandate for capitalism, while others view Scripture as on the side of socialism. Capitalism is an economic system in which investment in and ownership of the means of production, distribution, and exchange of wealth is made and maintained by private individuals or corporations, and socialism is an economic system in which the ownership and control is by the community as a whole. Advocates of capitalism seem to dominate American evangelical thought; advocates of socialism dominate evangelical thought in most of the rest of the world. Yet there are those in America also who advocate a socialistic approach to economics.

The system which creates and sustains much of the hunger, underdevelopment, unemployment, and other social ills in the world today is capitalism. Capitalism is by its very nature a system which promotes individualism, competition, and profit-making with little or no regard for social costs. It puts profits and private gain before social services and human needs. As such, it is an unjust system which should be replaced.[9]

[9]Eugene Tolan, et al, "World Justice and Peace: A Radical Analysis for American Christians," *The Other Side,* January-February 1976, 50.

Orlando Costas, an articulate Latin American evangelical who taught for a number of years in Eastern Baptist Seminary, speaks with fire:

> The Spirit will lead us to recognize Christ in the poor and the really oppressed, because Christ stands alongside of them. . . . Once you stand by them, I see no other option but socialism. These people are where they are because of . . . a "civilized" process which has excelled in domination, controlling people, exploiting their resources, and using their cheap labor. Capitalism is not something that can be transformed and reformed. The very root of capitalism is the process of enslaving people, exploiting their resources. . . . The only alternative I know to capitalism is to reverse the whole thing and begin a proper distribution of the wealth.[10]

George Gilder, author of *Wealth and Poverty* (New York: Basic Books, 1978), responding to questions by *Christianity Today,* sees things somewhat differently:

> *Christianity Today:* You've noted, "the poor know their condition is to a great degree their own fault or choice" and that "in order to succeed, the poor need most of all the spur of poverty." One critic wrote that Gilder's theology of capitalism is long on faith and hope and short on charity. How do you respond to that?
>
> *Gilder:* These social programs that are allegedly charitable are in fact profoundly destructive. . . . The central truth in capitalism is that its progress is unpredictable. The attempt to predetermine returns, to arrogate to the human mind the capacity to know the future, to calculate carefully its precise outlines and exploit this knowledge in some prescriptive way, leads to catastrophe. Capitalism, because it is based on the unknowability of the future and the conduct of continual experiments that reveal facets of the truth, can in fact partake of providence. . . . It's [the] desire to have a master plan based on secular analysis that underlies socialism and makes it an evil system. . . . Capitalism is the economic system that is consonant with Christianity.[11]

What do we say to these fervently held and mutually exclusive viewpoints? Perhaps brilliant French philosopher Jacques Ellul comes closest to the truth in pronouncing a pox on both their houses:

[10]Orlando Costas, *The Other Side,* January-February 1976, 29-30, 39. (For strong advocacy of this position from many viewpoints, along with a good basic bibliography, see *The Other Side,* January-February and March-April 1976).

[11]*Christianity Today,* 4 February 1983, 23ff. (For a succinct and powerful statement of biblical capitalism, along with a basic bibliography, see Ronald Nash, professor at Western Kentucky University, in *Christianity Today,* 23 March 1979.)

Capitalism has progressively subordinated all of life—individual and collective—to money. Money has become the criterion for judging man and his activity. One by one the state, the legal system, art, and the churches have submitted to the power of money. . . . We must recognize the truth in Karl Marx's observation that money, in the capitalist system, leads to alienation.[12]

Does socialism, then, look more attractive? Socialism rightly attacks capitalism for subordinating man to money, for its unjust economic structures. Socialism takes for its motto "To each according to his work," which in communism becomes "To each according to his needs."

But how does socialism plan to achieve its goals? First, by strictly limiting human life to work, to economic activity. . . . This is precisely the source of real alienation—not the subservience of *being* to *personal having*, but the subservience of *being* to *doing* and to *collective having*. . . . . The differences between systems look small next to such similarity.[13]

In fact, neither theology nor Scripture gives us any criteria for evaluating one system against another. Since no economic mechanism corresponds to Christian truth, if we wish to choose we will have to do so for purely natural reasons, knowing that our choice will in no way express our Christian faith.[14]

I concur with Ellul that the data of Scripture cannot be bent to validate any known economic system. On the other hand, the principles of Scripture can and must be constantly applied by thoughtful Christians to correct the wrongs of the system under which they live. Actually this may have happened in the middle years of the century in which almost all capitalistic nations yielded to the pressure of human need and legislated social welfare. At the same time almost all socialistic regimes yielded to the pressures of human nature to make room for some private enterprise and marketplace economics.

The advocate of a free market economic system emphasizes freedom and the right to private property, while those who promote a controlled market economy for the welfare of all citizens emphasize justice, fairness, and equality. Capitalism is for freedom, socialism is for equality; neither economic freedom nor equality is very pronounced in Scripture!

True, "freedom" is important in Scripture, but the freedom advocated, especially in the New Testament, is primarily spiritual and only minimally political. Economic freedom to

[12]Jacques Ellul, *Money and Power*, trans. LaVonne Neff (Downers Grove, Ill.: InterVarsity, 1984), 20.
[13]Ibid., 21.
[14]Ibid., 24.

make unlimited amounts of money is not presented in Scripture at all; the only *economic* freedom addressed is freedom from poverty and oppression. Legislation can make citizens free to accumulate, but freedom to do so does not make it happen. "Economic freedom" can mean freedom to get (capitalism) or freedom to subsist (socialism). Since freedom to get always works to the advantage of the smart, ruthless, or economically powerful, it is only proper that the biblical emphasis should be on protecting the weak and less fortunate.

Whose freedom is more violated, a wealthy person prohibited from becoming more wealthy (or compelled to become less wealthy), or a poor person who is trapped in poverty? Who is in greater bondage, the one who has and is prohibited from getting more, or the one who has not and is prohibited by his circumstances from getting at all? On which kind of freedom does the Bible lay emphasis?

Since Scripture is strong on setting free those oppressed economically, the crucial question becomes whether the right of private property in Scripture is the right to unlimited accumulation and possession. The law of Jubilee (Lev. 25) clearly presents strict limitations to permanent accumulation on the part of the strong at the expense of the weak or unfortunate. The concept of taxation also clearly sets limits. So it would seem impossible, on biblical grounds, to make the right of private property an unlimited right.

Though it is difficult to prove from Scripture that civil government must guarantee the right to accumulate unlimited wealth, it is replete with strong teaching on the obligation of a society to protect and provide for the poor.

Give justice to the weak and the fatherless; maintain the right of the afflicted and the destitute. Rescue the weak and the needy; deliver them from the hand of the wicked. (Ps. 82:3-4)

Is not this the fast that I choose: to loose the bonds of wickedness, to undo the thongs of the yoke, to let the oppressed go free, and to break every yoke? Is it not to share your bread with the hungry, and bring the homeless poor into your house; when you see the naked, to cover him? . . . If you take away from the midst of you the yoke . . . pour yourself out for the hungry and satisfy the desire of the afflicted; then shall your light rise in the darkness. (Isa. 58:6-11)

For three sins of Israel, even for four, I will not turn back my wrath. They sell the righteous for silver, and the needy for a pair of sandals. They trample on the heads of the poor as upon the dust of the ground and deny justice to the oppressed. (Amos 2:6-7, NIV)

> Depart from me, you cursed, into the eternal fire prepared for the devil and his angels; for I was hungry and you gave me no food, I was thirsty and you gave me no drink, I was a stranger and you did not welcome me; naked and you did not clothe me, sick and in prison and you did not visit me. (Matt. 25:41-43)[15]

The Bible has a great deal more to say to the capitalist about how his behavior must be modified than it does to the socialist. But since an economic *system* cannot be imposed without political sanctions, and since human beings are radically self-oriented, thus subverting any economic system, I conclude that neither system has a biblical mandate for imposition. Either will founder on the shoals of human nature.

Therefore, the Christian in either system should work toward change to bring it increasingly into conformity with the great biblical principles of justice and mercy. If freedom can be combined with these far more basic concepts, all the better. Perhaps, in a fallen society, the freedom won through the painful balancing of the rights of one group against those of another is the only hope for some measure of justice.

PROFITS AND INTEREST IN CAPITALISM

Though profit through trade is more basic to capitalism, Scripture speaks more directly to the question of interest on loans. So let us consider first the question of capital accumulated through lending and borrowing money at interest, an indispensable element of modern capitalism.

Large sums of money are needed for major manufacturing or marketing efforts. In the socialistic system these funds may be accumulated through taxation, but in a private enterprise system it is normally necessary to borrow funds to "capitalize" an enterprise. Even wealthy people cannot normally afford such investment, so money is accumulated by borrowing from many people through the medium of giving them part ownership (stock) in the corporation, or through the intermediary of a bank or insurance company that has already accumulated large sums of money through borrowing. People will not ordinarily

[15]See also Lev. 19:9-10; 27:30, 33; Num. 18:23-32; Deut. 12:5-8; 14:22-29; 15:7ff.; Ezek. 22:7, 29.

invest in an enterprise without hope of gain, so the corporation must return, in the form of profits or interest, benefits to the lender. Yet the Bible consistently speaks against lending money at interest (Ps. 15:5; Prov. 28:8; Ezek. 18:8-9, 13, 17; 22:12). Although the *Theological Wordbook of the Old Testament* argues that what is prohibited, at least in Leviticus 25:35ff., is only *excessive* interest, most scholars believe that the Hebrew words refer to interest of any kind.[16] Nor can we argue that the Old Testament agrarian economy meant that borrowing and lending money was only an emergency situation and thus those laws do not apply to a capitalistic society. Cultural relativism cannot be allowed to do away with biblical norms. But is this teaching a universal biblical norm, or is it merely part of the civil code for ordering the life of the ancient state of Israel?

The commandments against taking interest are consistently given in the context of injustice, extortion, and oppression. One is not to take interest when lending to the poor (Exod. 22:25), take reward against the innocent (Ps. 15:5), or make unjust gain (Prov. 28:8). Ezekiel, who speaks so strongly against taking interest, decries greed and extortion in the same context. For this reason, even the church of the Middle Ages, while looking down on merchandising of any kind, nevertheless permitted borrowing and lending at moderate interest rates (often 5 percent). Today, most church ethicists in capitalistic economies have justified interest rates that are not deemed oppressive.

It is interesting to note that an Israelite could not take interest from a fellow Israelite, but could from others (Deut. 23:19-20). Thus some have concluded that a Christian is free to lend money at interest to a non-Christian (or to an impersonal institution) but not to a Christian. Principles often may be legitimately derived from Old Testament commands for Israelites, but it is hard to derive a permanent and universal principle from a command that permits taking interest from a non-Jew, but not from a Jew. Yet either taking interest is not *inherently* evil and thus may in some cases be legitimate for Christians; or taking interest *is* inherently evil and was only permitted for the

16Milton C. Fisher, *Nashak* in *Theological Wordbook of the Old Testament*, ed. R. Laird Harris, Gleason L. Archer, Jr., and Bruce K. Waltke, vol. 2 (Chicago: Moody, 1980), 605.

Israelites as a temporary expedient. In that case it would be wrong for an enlightened believer in any age.

Since the New Testament does not directly address the issue of taking interest, <u>I conclude that taking a just interest is not</u> <u>*inherently*</u> evil. Yet to follow the Old Testament model and refuse to take interest when assisting the poor or aiding a fellow Christian would be commendable under any ethical system.

Though the New Testament does not address the issue of lending money at interest, it does have a few words on the subject of indebtedness. "Owe no one anything, except to love one another" (Rom. 13:8) is taken by some to prohibit any debt whatsoever, but this is probably not a legitimate use of this isolated reference to debt, since the point of the whole passage is the command to love. Paul stresses the fact that love is an obligation, not an option. We *owe* love because of who we are and what we have received.

That it is best not to go into personal debt is clear from common sense, underscored by biblical proverbs (Prov. 11:15; 22:7, 26). But it can hardly be held sinful to lend, since Christ himself commanded it: "Give to him who begs from you, and do not refuse him who would borrow from you" (Matt. 5:42). An even better way, Jesus implies in the same verse, is to *give* to him who asks!

It is hermeneutically unacceptable to use parables that refer to loaning money at interest as biblical authorization of capitalism. Parables are true-to-life stories that are making a particular point. The details are merely part of the story and may not be pressed to yield ethical principles.

Though I am not convinced of any clear-cut biblical teaching outlawing any and all debt, perhaps the following definition from the analysis of conservative financial adviser Larry Burkett, will help:

The scriptural definition of debt is the inability to meet obligations agreed upon. In other words, when a person buys something on credit terms, that is not necessarily a debt, it is a contract. But, when the terms of that contract are violated, scriptural debt occurs.[17]

A Christian must get out of debt altogether. . . . Debt exists when any of the following conditions are true:

[17]Larry Burkett, *Your Finances in Changing Times: God's Principles for Managing Money* (Glendale, Calif.: Campus Crusade for Christ, 1975), 64.

—Payment is past due for money, goods or services. . . .

—The total value of unsecured liabilities exceeds total assets. In other words, if you had to cash out at any time, there would be a negative balance on your account.

—Anxiety is produced in the area of financial responsibility, and the family's basic needs are not being met either because of past or present buying practices.[18]

From this brief overview of the very limited biblical data on the subject, I conclude that it is prudent to avoid borrowing and lending when possible, that it is permissible to borrow or lend at interest so long as the rate is not exorbitant or oppressive, and that generous giving to those in need is a better way.

Many of the same Old Testament passages that speak against taking interest couple the prohibition with injunctions against any kind of profit-making. I assume that the abiding principle is the same: a profit rate that is comparable to a modest and fair rate of interest may be justified, but a higher profit is unjustified in that it is making gain at the expense of others, whether or not those others agree to it.

PERSONAL INTEGRITY

Personal integrity in any economic system demands honesty, complete freedom from any form of cheating, stealing, or taking advantage of others. But in a relatively free economy several special temptations should be mentioned.

BANKRUPTCY

Especially with the advent of more liberal bankruptcy laws (notably the Bankruptcy Reform Act, October 1979), it is possible to declare bankruptcy to avoid obligations, maintain one's personal resources (even wealth, with a clever lawyer), and build a fortune that cannot be touched by former creditors. Declaring bankruptcy may be legal, but that does not make it moral. A formal bankruptcy status may be necessary to make the transition to a better basis of relating to one's creditors, but the moral person will not use it as a means of avoiding liability. Of course, if a creditor agrees to forgive a debt or a part of it,

[18]Ibid., 83.

whether from altruism or for his own benefit, that is another matter.

God is on the side of the person whose word is his bond, who swears to his own hurt (e.g., assumes a financial obligation) and does not change (Ps. 15:4). The wicked borrow and pay not again (Ps. 37:21), but the righteous person assumes responsibility for any debt he has incurred and remains responsible until the debt is paid or until death.

LITIGATION

> When one of you has a grievance against a brother, does he dare go to law before the unrighteous instead of the saints? . . . But brother goes to law against brother, and that before unbelievers. . . . Why not rather suffer wrong? Why not rather be defrauded? (1 Cor. 6:1, 6-7)

In light of this clear passage, few sincere believers instigate lawsuits against a fellow believer without qualms. The question arises, But what if this person who *says* he is a believer does not behave like one? Paul seems to be addressing that specific question when he gives the alternative: Why not permit yourself to be defrauded rather than to bring disrepute on Jesus' name?

On the other hand, since Paul makes a distinction between believers and unbelievers, litigation against an unbeliever or impersonal corporation may be legitimate so long as the law of love for neighbor (Christian *or* non-Christian) is not violated and so long as justice is served with integrity.

To demand money that is not justly one's own is a form of stealing that is not made moral through the instrumentality of a court. If every church member in the United States refused to go to court to demand "whatever I can get" when suffering some real or imagined wrong, the insurance rates for accidents and malpractice would tumble. Anything beyond reasonable and just compensation is an attempt to defraud; it is an assault on the whole society, driving up the cost of products, services, and insurance for everyone. Our litigious society seems headed for economic disaster if the greed and dishonesty of consumers, clients, and attorneys is not somehow held in check. It is not always wrong to demand punitive damages beyond compensation, but such cases should be clearly established as malicious or willful neglect.

On the other hand, corporate lawyers, insurance companies, and corporations must be fair in awarding legitimate claims, or they, in turn, will be guilty of defrauding and oppressing the weaker party.

An avaricious and corrupt society is drowning in the quagmire of litigation which its own sin has created. Unwarranted litigation is stealing.

POVERTY AND WEALTH

Both Testaments have much to say about poverty and wealth, but what is poverty? What is wealth? We shall never agree.

The first reason is that each society and culture determines how material possessions are secured, used, and viewed. Suppose we agree that poverty is a state in which resources are chronically insufficient to meet one's necessities and that absolute poverty means less than adequate food, housing, or clothing. Immediately our agreement will founder on the definition of "necessity" and "adequate." Suppose we define wealth as material resources more than necessary for basic livelihood. What is a necessity? What is a basic livelihood? The answers depend, to some extent, on what is considered poverty or wealth in a given community or society.

The second problem is that these questions are very personal and charged with intense emotion. It is difficult to be detached and objective because any definition may threaten my own status. Since Scripture has so much to say on the subject, let us assume the definitions given above and grant in advance that agreement on specific applications of these definitions may not be possible. Also, let us assume that the vast majority of Americans are wealthy if wealth is considered anything more than basic necessities. Let us also assume that the primary emphasis in Scripture on this subject is the loving response of those who have to those who do not. Still, grave problems remain.

A basic problem is the apparently radical difference between what the Old and New Testaments say about wealth. Jacques Ellul says:

Incontestably, in the New Testament wealth is condemned. To my knowledge there is not one text that justifies it. The Old Testament, on the other hand, presents wealth as a blessing, willed by God and pleasing to him. There is no more apparent radical opposition between the two covenants than the one concerning wealth.[19]

How the Old and New are to be reconciled is a matter of continuing debate. Is the Old Testament view of wealth part of the overall this-worldly structure of a (transient) earthly kingdom, to be superseded by the spiritual kingdom, the church? Whether or not this is the correct explanation, it must be conceded that the New Testament nowhere teaches that wealth is the evidence of God's blessing but is often stark in its condemnation of the rich.

It is easier for a camel to go through the eye of a needle than for a rich man to enter the kingdom of God. (Matt. 19:24; Luke 18:24-25)
Blessed are you poor, for yours is the kingdom of God. (Luke 6:20)
But woe to you that are rich, for you have received your consolation. (Luke 6:24)
Sell your possessions, and give alms; provide yourselves with purses that do not grow old, with a treasure in the heavens that does not fail, where no thief approaches and no moth destroys. For where your treasure is, there will your heart be also. (Luke 12:33-34)
"No servant can serve two masters. . . . You cannot serve God and mammon." The Pharisees, who were lovers of money, heard all this, and they scoffed at him. (Luke 16:13-14)

These passages are merely a sample: *Nave's Topical Bible* lists seven double-column pages of biblical statements about the poor and five pages about the rich with these same themes. I wish the Bible consistently and clearly condemned only the wicked rich, but often it fails to make the distinction. Is that because it is impossible to be both wealthy and godly, or because it is uncommon? Taking all the biblical evidence into account, it seems that the generalized condemnations result from the fact that the temptations of wealth are so strong few handle them successfully, and therefore rich people as a class are sometimes grouped together in condemnation. But this should not be taken as evidence that there are no exceptions, for the Bible never says that possession of wealth in itself is sinful.

[19]Ellul, *Money and Power*, 35.

Wealth is, in any event, a temptation—not an evil in itself, but a temptation . . . because it urges us to put our confidence in money rather than in God. . . . It is almost impossible to have many possessions and remain righteous. Righteousness is total dependence on God's action.[20]

How do we fight such strong temptation? The biblical antidote to the virus of avarice or the fatal illness of relying on the phantom of wealth is the act of giving it away.

We have very clear indications that money, in the Christian life, is made *in order* to be given away. Note especially Paul's lovely text (2 Cor. 8:1-15). . . . If among fellow Christians we study Paul's law of equality, we see that money must be used to meet our needs, and that everything left over must be given away.[21]

The Bible does not advocate appropriating the wealth of the rich. And though there are passages that instruct us to sell and give, when the rich are directly addressed, they are not instructed to divest themselves totally, but rather to be rich toward God and toward those in need.

Perhaps rather than taking Abraham as our all-American model and the Old Testament as our instruction in this matter, we would be safer in taking Jesus Christ as our model and New Testament teaching as the norm. If we follow the example of One who, having everything, became poor for our sakes, and if we submit to his sometimes painful teaching, will we not voluntarily divest ourselves of all excess wealth in order to provide for those in spiritual and physical need?

But what is "excess"? Each man is accountable to his own master. "Who are you to pass judgment on the servant of another?" (Rom. 14:4). But it must mean *something*, and something that consumer-oriented Americans apparently find difficult to comprehend.

SIMPLE LIFE-STYLE

As the wealthy are growing more wealthy and the poor more poor, the response of many Christians around the world has been to assume some form of a simple life-style. Several thousand church leaders committed themselves to this at the great Lausanne Congress on Evangelism:

[20]Ibid., 47.
[21]Ibid., 110-111.

We cannot hope to attain this goal without sacrifice. All of us are shocked by the poverty of millions and disturbed by the injustices which cause it. Those of us who live in affluent circumstances accept our duty to develop a simple life-style in order to contribute more generously to both relief and evangelism.[22]

But what is a simple life-style? The debate is never-ending. For practical purposes, let us make an attempt. If "absolute poverty" is defined as existence below subsistence level, and "poverty" is defined as subsistence-level living without things others in the society consider necessities, then perhaps a "simple life-style" would be all the basic necessities.

Absolute Poverty	Poverty	Simple Life-style	Wealth	Riches
Below subsistence; lack of food and housing	Subsistence, but lack of other necessities	Basic necessities as defined by a given society	Possessions beyond necessities	Abundant wealth, hoarding for protection or used for extravagant living

If this comes anywhere near indicating a biblical view, every believer who lives above a simple life-style should sacrifice to the limits of his faith and love in an effort to bring those who live below that level up to the provision of basic necessities. Whatever, he can hardly rest at ease so long as there are those who lack basic necessities.

And what are necessities? At least it is safe to say that the salespeople of our consumer-driven economy should not decide.

How does one define *need* in a society where standards of living are constantly rising? . . . how do the generals of the sales army in their carpeted offices on Madison Avenue plot their strategy for meeting our "needs"? What angles do they play on besides our greed? Our anxieties? (Is your family protected?) Our sexual preoccupations? (Does your breath rob you of kisses?) Our guilt? Our snobbery? (You deserve the best.)[23]

[22]The Lausanne Covenant, paragraph 9, in *Let the Earth Hear His Voice*, ed. J. D. Douglas (Minneapolis: Worldwide, 1975), 6.
[23]John White, *The Golden Cow: Materialism in the Twentieth-Century Church* (Downers Grove, Ill.: InterVarsity, 1979), 73.

Does "need" include savings and insurance? Ellul seems to take an absolutist stand on the issue:

We must first consider what it means when a person puts money aside or insures himself (for the problem of insurance is included with the problem of savings; the two acts have the same meaning). Both these measures express the wish to take possession of the future, to guarantee oneself against whatever might happen—accidents, changes in job or financial standing. Sometimes a person is thinking of old age, sometimes of getting children established—in any case, it is a way to control the future. Facing the uncertainty of tomorrow, the risks of life, people put a stash aside to serve as a screen between themselves and reality. . . . But starting with this search for security, savings lead very quickly to a will for autonomy. Those who possess much claim to be independent and say they are free. . . . It assumes either that God is incapable of correctly directing our lives, or that he has bad intentions toward us.[24]

Ellul makes room for savings toward a specific objective (to give a gift, to buy a house to live in) or in businesses which have a very irregular income, such as farming. He also says that the judgment of unbelief applies equally to those who do not have enough to save, when they are enslaved to worry about the future. Few Americans would be willing to accept Ellul's uncompromising position, but surely we must come to terms with the underlying principle of faith.

A more moderate position is advocated by Larry Burkett, who holds, like Ellul, that savings for protection against possible future adversity is acting in unbelief, but that saving as a provision for future known needs is acceptable. Savings or insurance for what might prove crippling loss through common accidents or fire can be made in faith, but any attempt to protect against all potential hazards in life is futile as well as unbelieving. He sees the greatest failure in this regard to be in inheritances.

If I had to identify the area of Christian finances that is least understood, I would have to vote for inheritance. Not only do many people wreck their lives by hoarding, but they also wreck the lives of their children and children's children with an abundant inheritance. . . . Large amounts of money given to children will usually be squandered to their disservice, and large amounts of money stored up for children in trust can be used to buffer them from God's will. . . . Allow your children the joy of earning their own way.[25]

[24]Ellul, *Money and Power,* 104-105.
[25]Larry Burkett, *Your Finances in Changing Times: God's Principles for Managing Money,* 130-131.

My conclusion after evaluating the competing viewpoints in the light of Scripture comes down to a revision of John Wesley's dictum: "Get all you can, save all you can, give all you can." Perhaps it will serve as a summary statement of the individual's responsibility if we qualify this carefully: earn all you can with integrity, save all you can toward meeting known future obligations, give all you can in sacrificial love and faith in the God who provides.

One further note on personal integrity: "Finders keepers, losers weepers" is not a biblical text! To keep an article that has been found or comes to one by error, such as when the store clerk returns more change than is due, is to steal (Lev. 6:2-7).

SOCIAL RESPONSIBILITY

STATE

As we have seen, it is the primary responsibility of the state to create and maintain a just society. Power exercised for the benefit of king or dictator or for the ruling few is clearly against all the proclamations of the prophets and the teachings of Christ and the apostles.

Furthermore, enlightened governments of all time, but particularly in the twentieth century, have done well to promote mercy as well as justice. Sheer, cold justice is not enough when there are weak ones who need the care of a strong government, oppressed people who need relief, and poor who need uplifting. So the state is right in assuming social responsibility for all its citizens and, indeed, for the poor and oppressed of other lands as well.

CHURCH

Care for Its Own. Corporate responsibility in the church begins with the obligation to fully care for its own. This care is not merely "spiritual." In guaranteeing the livelihood of members we have, first of all, the example of the early church (Acts 2:44-45; 4:32-37; 6:1; 11:29-30; 2 Cor. 8–9). The local congregation not only assumed responsibility for the poor and the widows among its own, but it also assumed responsibility for those in need in other congregations.

We have not only the New Testament example, we have Paul's instruction concerning care for widows (1 Tim. 5:1-16), and, by implication, his instruction against idleness (2 Thess. 3:6-15). Widows and others in need were so fully cared for there was a temptation for some to take advantage of this, whether younger widows or able-bodied men. Paul strongly rejected any form of "freeloading" and instructed such to get to work. That exhortation sheds light on a system of welfare in the church so well established that many, apparently, were tempted to abuse it. Paul tells us to care for those among us who are truly in need.

Care for Others. The church has primary responsibility for its own, but is instructed to care also, to the extent of its ability, for others in need. We should be generous with "all men, and especially to those who are of the household of faith" (Gal. 6:10).

Addressing the Government. Furthermore, in matters of righteousness, justice, and mercy, the church is to speak prophetically to the state. It may lose its head for the effort (as John the Baptist did when he rebuked the king) or be discriminated against and immobilized (as Jeremiah was). Much of the suffering of prophets and apostles resulted from confronting state authority. Sometimes they were indeed subversive (as in Jeremiah's case), and sometimes the charge of illegality was merely a pretext of the officials (as in the cases of Christ and Paul), but it is always dangerous to cross governmental authority. Yet this is the risk a faithful church must take when the state does wrong.

Using Money and Getting Money. Finally, the church must act in integrity in getting and using money. Not only is there the obligation to be sure no one misuses, or even appears to misuse money, as Paul instructed the church in Corinth, but also the church must act in integrity in the way it gets money. Paul coveted no man's possessions, something many successors to Paul cannot say! Christ drove out the merchants from the temple at least in part because they were using God's business to advance their own. Peter cursed Simon for seeking to use the gospel as a means of gain (Acts 8:18ff.).

Consider first the use of money. All present-day profit-makers, whether the pastor with an unjustifiably large salary or the TV personality living in luxury, risk the same condemnation. Churches and Christian ministries can build programs and buildings that are unjustifiable or extravagant. But perhaps more than misappropriation or misuse of money, the temptation seems especially great to use questionable or dishonest ways of getting it.

Paul unabashedly commanded believers to give, but George Muller with his orphans and Hudson Taylor of the China Inland Mission told no one but God about their needs. A third method is to share information about the financial need with those who are partners in ministry but to ask only God for money. "Full information, no solicitation," they say. Who is right?

At the outset, let us agree that no method pleases God if it is not pursued in faith. Perhaps in our human weakness we find it easier to rely on what is visible than on what is invisible. Less faith is needed for success in the "direct" approach, asking visible people for money they visibly have. The converse would also be true, that telling only God of one's needs, or eschewing all promotional methods of fund-raising, could promote an attitude of faith. On the other hand, any method can be pursued in unbelief, whether blatant unbelief in trusting man rather than God or the unbelief of worry that God may not come through.

No method of securing funds can be demonstrated from Scripture as the method most approved of God. Unbelief evidenced in or promoted by any method is clearly not of God. Therefore, methods that safeguard the money-seeker from unbelief and methods that promote faith—and not merely successful fund-raising—should be favored. Clearly, many current methods, though highly successful, do not evidence faith in God nor elementary obedience to him.

Unscrupulous methods are the most blatant offense in fund-raising. Deception is common. One leading African evangelistic mission introduced a starving child, Kori, to faithful supporters, with a heart-rending plea for funds in November 1982. The fatal error was in using the same photograph a few months later and calling her Sera in July 1983. "Sera" lived in a different place from "Kori"; neither story really happened exactly the way it was told. They were composites, put together from the realities of suffering Uganda. At the end of the letter were endorsements by well-known leaders who had no idea, I am confident, of what was going on: Billy Graham, David Hubbard, Leighton Ford, all of whom are impeccably honest in their own fund-raising.

Another form of deception is to "bait and switch." The money is solicited for one cause but diverted to another, even to the personal benefit of the luxury-loving leader. In 1980 I saw a well-known TV personality plead for $100,000 for Cambodian relief—a generous project when he had so many needs in his own ministry. The average viewer did not consider that his expectancy in regular income that week was a million dollars. Everything over $100,000, of course, went to something else, and the suffering Cambodians helped make it considerably more.

Another unscrupulous method is psychological manipulation—inducing people to do things they wouldn't do if you approached them in a straightforward, honest way. One of the basic rules of the fund-raising game is that there must be a crisis once a month to produce maximum income. A friend of mine in a prominent mission organization engaged the services of one of the leading fund-raisers and was presented immediately with this approach. "But we don't have that many crises," he lamely replied. "Oh, but we can create them," responded the expert. And he did. When a missionary in Southeast Asia was slightly injured in a local uprising, treated at the local clinic, and released, an irate emergency call from the fund-raiser instructed the mission leader to send the missionary back to the hospital immediately and get the press there with cameras. "Don't you know you're missing a very profitable crisis?"

Another way to manipulate is to make the letter highly personal as well as crisis-filled and poignant. Many naive people, often desperately poor, who make an average contribution of less than $20, really believe that the TV personality is a personal friend. Through the magic of word processors and computerized mailing lists, "personal" letters now solicit on a seemingly individual level.

Not all methods are unscrupulous, patently dishonest. Some

are simply unworthy. What does the general public think of a newspaper advertisement that announces: "Contributor's name will be beautifully engraved on permanent plaques attached to each opera seat in this timeless building—a lasting remembrance of a once-in-history event. Contributions $1,500 per seat. For reservations call (714) 971-4087"? About the same time I received a personalized letter from someone of whom I had never heard who announced, "Today I learned of an evangelism strategy that has the capability of exposing at least 200 million people to the saving knowledge of Jesus Christ by Christmas of this year at an unbelievably low cost of 2.5 cents per exposure." He went on to explain that this was truly a bargain, for one-third of the viewers would respond positively to the gospel, meaning a soul would be saved for each 7.5 cents in contributions. Are these things worthy of the Lord of heaven?

Another unworthy method is the contract demanded by many stars of TV, music, pulpit, or literature. Guarantees of an astronomical sum for a single appearance, superlative accommodations, protection from people contacts or responsibilities other than the time on stage—the list can be pages long. Somehow the star system that has evolved seems incongruous with the Name of One who freely gave everything.

Unbiblical teaching *about* money is often a problem, too. Many TV personalities and song writers promulgate the pros-perity gospel—if you love Jesus (and especially if you send us cash), you will prosper financially, be healthy in body, and successful in all things. An interviewer said to Richard DeVos, founder and chief executive of Amway, "The Bible says the Son of Man had nowhere to lay his head. . . . Lay not up treasures on earth, but lay up treasures in heaven. . . . The meek shall inherit the earth. . . . God loves the poor. . . ." DeVos replied,

You've got it all in nice quotes. Now, the Bible also says that those who work shall be rewarded, that you should not covet what your neighbor has—it's none of your business. And God says, "I will heap upon you riches if you glorify me, far greater than you can ever imagine."[26]

One of the most tragic aspects of the whole evangelical materialistic business is that God's ordinary people keep supporting so faithfully, and so generously, the unworthy

[26]"Success According to Richard DeVos," *Eternity*, February 1981, 24.

"stars" along with the worthy. I agree with Don Bjork of Worldteam:

Troubled is the only word to describe our deep concern over the "star system." . . . We've been increasingly disturbed over the falling "stars"—the moral defection of so many evangelical celebrities and their continued acceptance by the general Christian public, even when their adultery, broken homes, avarice, or crookedness are plain to see.[27]

In response, let us join Paul who said, "Unlike so many, we do not peddle the word of God for profit" (2 Cor. 2:17, NIV).

CORPORATE INTEGRITY omit

Ways to Lose It. There are many ways a business can steal besides abusing its employees or lying in its advertising. Over-pricing, inordinate profits, inferior products, even planned obsolescence are common ways of stealing from the consumer. In an effort to keep a consumption-driven economy rolling, advertising manipulates consumers into buying what is not needed or what is not long wanted. The ways of misusing fellow humans for financial gain seem endless.

But there are those who do business the other way. The owner of a successful Atlanta-based corporation told me that he had recently adopted a new corporate motto: "A good name is to be chosen rather than great riches" (Prov. 22:1). As I reflected on this bold decision to restructure a business on a biblical principle, it gradually dawned on me that this proverb sets on its head standard business practice, especially the advertising business. The bottom line is supposed to be "great riches"—profit—not a good name built on solid character. In fact, the purpose of creating a "good" name through advertising is to build profits. Whoever heard of using resources to demonstrate trustworthiness, to benefit the consumer so consistently that reputation is established in a good name? And yet what could be more clearly in the interest of glorifying God in a business?

The Multinationals. If it is true that power tends to corrupt and that absolute power corrupts absolutely (Lord Acton), the

[27]Don Bjork, *Harvest Today,* Winter 1980, 2.

larger the business operation, the greater the temptation to succeed at the expense of others. Though multinational corporations are hardly the source of all social ills in underdeveloped countries, there are clearly structural injustices of which they are a part. It would be difficult to prove that the people of Haiti or the Kotoko tribe of Chad would be that much better off economically or physically if there had never been any contact with Western colonialism. On the other hand, it is true that every nation, especially a powerful nation, consistently exploits resources, even human resources, for its own benefit. And the very willing agent of the exploitation is business enterprise.

For example, if minimum wages, let alone comparable wages, were paid to every laborer participating in producing an automobile, all the way back to the tin mines of Bolivia and the rubber plantations of Malaysia, few Americans could own an automobile. As it is, though the poor may not purposely be made poor by the rich, the system does lock the poor into poverty and protects the riches of the rich. In fact, the gap between rich and poor nations is not constant with increased production advancing both poor and rich. Rather, the gap is steadily widening. Indeed, a leading spokesman for conservative causes, Michael Novak, maintains that the widening gap is not only inevitable but actually desirable, since it demonstrates the superiority of a free economy over a controlled economy.[28]

Wages and prices are not the only things working against economically weaker people. Many corporations seem to implement safety standards only to the extent compelled by local law. The highly visible occasional tragedy is only the tip of the iceberg of human suffering inflicted through careless or deliberately inferior standards of safety. Better than local standards, perhaps, but hardly thus justifiable.

Automation. One further way of corporate injustice has been alleged: automation. I have been unable to identify any biblical principle that could be used to oppose transfer of labor from people to labor-saving devices. It is quite possible, of course, to

[28]Michael Novak, "The Grand Inquisitor, Born Again," *National Review,* 14 September 1979, 1158.

make the transition in unjust or unmerciful ways, but guilt for this failure should not be assigned to the machine.

The optimistic viewpoint of Aristotle, more than twenty centuries ago, has proved true thus far: "When looms weave by themselves, man's slavery will end!"

Begin

POVERTY, FAMINE, POPULATION EXPLOSION

Poverty. There are three main types of poverty in the world. *Collective* poverty (which includes *class* and *regional* poverty) is the semipermanent insufficiency of the material means of life for an entire population and can be applied to nations such as India. *Cyclical* poverty is the widespread but temporary deprivation caused by disease, crop failure, or economic breakdown such as occurred in this country in the 1930s. *Individual* poverty is a condition of want that results from an individual's misfortune or inability to work, including the widows, orphans, physically handicapped, outcasts, aged, mentally deficient, and alcoholics.[29]

We tend to think of poverty as a personal matter, and we feel better about it when we are convinced that it stems from laziness or lack of discipline. Scripture recognizes that there is such poverty but says very little about it. Rather, the constant emphasis in Scripture is on poverty due to oppression. This oppression can be individual or corporate—a whole people can come under God's condemnation for oppression and injustice. This corporate injustice seems to be a central theme in the great pivotal events in history: violence was the only specific sin mentioned as a reason for the Flood (Gen. 6:11, 13); oppression and injustice brought judgment on Egypt (Exod. 1–12); Israel and Judah were sent into exile for injustice as well as idolatry as the prophets consistently emphasized in their denunciations. Even the Incarnation had something to do with this theme. Mary sang of it:

He has put down the mighty from their thrones, and exalted those of low degree; he has filled the hungry with good things, and the rich he has sent empty away. (Luke 1:52-53)

[29]*Encyclopedia Britannica*, 14th ed., s.v. "poverty."

Christ himself announced his calling:

The Spirit of the Lord is upon me, because he anointed me to preach good news to the poor. He has sent me to proclaim release to the captives and recovering of sight to the blind, to set at liberty those who are oppressed, to proclaim the acceptable year of the Lord. (Luke 4:18-19)

This proclamation of Christ is normally spiritualized, but Christ's own description of the next pivotal event—the Second Coming (Matt. 25)—makes abundantly clear that he will judge people, at least in part, on the basis of what was done to relieve physical need and oppression.

Is there something in societies' structures that is unjust and is the *cause* of suffering? *Something* in the system itself must contribute toward the problem World Bank President and successful capitalist Robert McNamara graphically identified:

Two-thirds of mankind . . . remain entrapped in a cruel web of circumstances that severely limits their right to the necessities of life. They . . . are caught in the grip of hunger and malnutrition, high illiteracy, inadequate education, shrinking opportunity, and corrosive poverty.[30]

I do not present these comments in an attempt to define any specific systemic cause for the present human tragedy; that lies in the province of specialists. But both Scripture and human history do point toward corporate responsibility as well as individual responsibility and call for corporate action as well as private charity. The solution must begin with the private individual. But each individual is responsible to involve those in his sphere of influence to find corporate solutions, whether a mother with her children, a pastor with his church, a businessman with his policies, or a public servant with his power to change and use the structures of society to promote justice and mercy.

Starvation and Population Explosion. The most terrifying aspect of poverty is hunger and starvation. That half the world's population subsists on below-minimum requirements for a healthful diet, that one-third are malnourished, and that

[30]Robert McNamara, *One Hundred Countries, Two Billion People* (New York: Praeger, 1973), 30.

thousands die daily from starvation, none can deny. But there the consensus ends. Is the scale of suffering greater than in the past? What are the causes and cures? The answers of experts differ radically.

Some hold that every age has been racked with famine and starvation—that the last century, for example, witnessed far more starvation than this century. There just weren't television crews to show it to us. But no one denies the dreadful condition that now exists in a world that could feed everyone.

There are two basic views as to cause and cure: some say the problem is overpopulation, others the distribution of available resources. Wealthy Western nations opt for the former theory; most "two-thirds" world leaders have held to the latter.

No one denies that human population "exploded" in the twentieth century, but is it true that there will soon be *Standing Room Only* as Karl Sax announced in his influential volume of that title?[31] This viewpoint began with Thomas Malthus, a British clergyman and economist who enunciated an economic theory in 1798 that has been the dominant theory of population ever since. In his *Essay on the Principle of Population* he said that population unchecked increased in a geometrical ratio—2, 4, 8, 16, 32, 64, 128, and so on—while sustenance increases in an arithmetical ratio—1, 2, 3, 4, 5, 6, and so on. That started a long line of the prophets of doom, who saw immediately that a finite earth cannot sustain infinite growth. With the advent of medical care, which drastically reduced the death rate, the population of the world has indeed grown geometrically. A consensus began to develop on the connection between this fact and the increase of hunger and famine (or at least the increased awareness of it).

Dr. Albert Szent-Gyorgyi, a Nobel Prize laureate, quoted Sir Howard Florey, one of the developers of penicillin, as having said that if the present population explosion continues, there will be only one square yard available on the earth's surface for each human being in 600 years. "If the acceleration of increase goes on," Szent-Gyorgyi testified, "this stage will be reached much sooner, and men will have to kill and eat one another."[32]

So the majority Western opinion is that the primary reason for poverty and hunger is overpopulation. Yet, even on the

[31]Boston: Beacon, 1955.
[32]Associated Press, 19 January 1966.

surface, it would seem reasonable to assume that there might be a third factor that could cause both poverty *and* an increase in population. More likely, there is no doubt a whole complex of reinforcing factors. Still, most Western leaders of thought and government assume Malthusian economics as the basic explanation of cause (population growth) and effect (poverty and hunger). But some scientists have undertaken to prove that there are no reasonable limits to the population our world could support, and that therefore the cause for our problems must be sought elsewhere.

Their first contention is that the projections of population growth are mathematical and therefore incorrect because they do not take into account other factors such as scientific advance and, most important, the human equation. Jean Mayer, professor at Harvard, makes a closely-reasoned analysis in his article "Toward a Non-Malthusian Population Policy." He claims that starvation itself would decimate the population and make all straight-line mathematical projections meaningless.[33]

Herman Kahn may be the most outspoken "optimist" in arguing that, in actual human existence, there are no known limits to healthy growth. He is decidedly in the minority, but in 1981 he received strong reinforcement from a professor at the University of Illinois at Urbana-Champaign, Julian L. Simon, who argued in his *The Ultimate Resource*, "We worry a lot about overpopulation, without cause."[34] The real problem, he says, is an "oversupply of bad news" based on flimsy or contradictory evidence disseminated by neo-Malthusians, or "doomsayers." Their predictions, he says, have become the conventional wisdom and have influenced public policy making and spending over the last decade to the detriment of society.[35]

The contention of these people is that there are far more resources than Malthusians recognize, that science keeps inventing ways of producing more and alternate energy and food resources, and that population will not continue to grow at present rates anyway. Population will be self-limited as poverty *decreases*, or limited by catastrophe if poverty *increases*. Science, education, and enlightened governmental policies lift people economically, and then they stop having as many children. Even

[33]Jean Mayer, "Toward a Non-Malthusian Population Policy," *Columbia Forum*, Summer 1969, 10.
[34]Princeton: Princeton University Press.
[35]*The Chronicle of Higher Education*, 30 September 1981, 19.

if this didn't happen, growth would eventually be stopped by
disease, famine, or war resulting from poverty itself.

Overpopulation cannot be the cause of underdevelopment and poverty in the
third world, since the highest densities of population occur not in the poor
countries but in the rich, developed countries. England has a population
density of 586 persons per square mile; West Germany, 606; Japan, 708;
Belgium, 814; and the Netherlands, 938. The poor countries, by comparison,
have relatively low population densities. India has 415 persons per square
mile; the Philippines, 310; China, 197; Mexico, 62; Panama, 47; Brazil, 26;
Tanzania, 25; Peru, 25; Paraguay, 12; and Gabon, 4."[36]

In the light of the mixed evidence concerning the relationship
between population growth and human welfare, I cannot
conscientiously advocate some biblical basis for demanding a
limit to population growth. Since limitation does seem
reasonable to most informed people, including now the
leadership of the largest nation on earth, we must speak to the
ethics of how population is to be limited. Abortion and coercive
family limitation are not acceptable, but persuasion and
provision are ethical ways of limiting population growth.
Education as to the benefits of having fewer children, and
provision for the poor to participate are ethically sound
approaches.

Though there may be no demonstrable causal link between
size of population and poverty, there is a clearly demonstrable
link between hunger and one other factor: poverty. No rich
people are hungry. Even in a population in which starvation is
rampant, those who have money have food. The same may be
said of general populations. Though there may be hungry
people in an affluent society like the United States, in a poor
country many are hungry, in a wealthy country, few. The
solution to this problem? Charity. Those who have resources
should share with those who do not—personally, through the
church, through business, and by national policy. This is the
way of justice and mercy, and Scripture clearly denounces not
only those who oppress the poor, but those who neglect them.

ECOLOGY

In the early 1970s a national furor developed over ecological
concerns. The general public became aware of the fact that

[36]Eugene Tolan, et al, "World Justice and Peace: A Radical Analysis for American
Christians," *The Other Side*, January-February 1976, 52-53.

environmental pollution and the depletion of natural resources were more than nuisances, more than a menace to quality of life. Scientists with one voice rose up to testify that they were a menace to life itself.

Lake Erie is dead. The beaches at Santa Barbara are deserted. The air in New York is dangerous to breathe. We are drowning in a sea of swill; in a normal year the United States "produces" 142 million tons of smoke and fumes, 7 million junked cars, 20 million tons of waste paper, 48 billion used cans, and 50 trillion gallons of industrial sewage.[37]

The most serious depredation is air pollution, the second, water pollution. Scientists say that both resources are in imminent danger. A further concern is the rapid depletion of unrenewable resources like oil and coal. Although no threat to human life, a particularly poignant loss is the gradual extinction of many species of animals.

Are science and technology to blame? Man himself is the ultimate polluter and disturber of the delicate balance of nature's varied elements. Ralph Nader, indefatigable champion of the consumer's welfare, pointed to industry as the chief culprit. But can industry alone bear the blame? Hendrik Aay digs deeper:

Yet, it is the structure of corporate industry that fouls our air and water, and treats the biosphere as a commodity. Yet, it is government, at all levels, which allows wastes to become a public menace. Yet, it is American society which is wedded to the idea of material progress.[38]

The cause of the crisis is clearly human sinfulness, though not always deliberate. Sometimes there is deliberate ethical misbehavior for personal or corporate gain, but more often the cause is blind pursuit of affluence. Growth in consumption is the deliberate governmental policy and corporate practice of America, a nation composing 6 percent of earth's population but consuming 40 percent of earth's resources.

An essay by Lynn White became famous for its attack on Christianity as the ultimate reason for the destruction of nature.[39] White, professor at UCLA, maintained that the root

[37]Robert Heilbroner, quoted in *The Progressive*, April 1970, 4.
[38]"Confronting the Ecological Crisis," *Vanguard*, November 1972, 13.
[39]The essay first appeared in *Science*, 10 March 1967, and was reprinted in "The Environmental Handbook," 1970.

problem was religious and that the solution must be religious—
the overthrow of "Christian" views of nature in favor of others,
perhaps some Eastern religion. Even animism, he said, is better
than Christianity.

It is true that Roman Catholic natural theology has been
strongly influenced by Greek dualism, which views matter as
evil. It is also true that many in the Reformation tradition
interpreted the command of Genesis 1:28, "fill the earth and
subdue it; and have dominion over . . . every living thing," as
permission, if not mandate, to exploit natural resources.

But the passage need not mean that; it could well establish a
responsible stewardship. For example, it clearly did not imply
killing animals, for that was not part of the Edenic ecological
system in which the command was given, nor will it be part of
the millennial system (Isa. 2:4; 11:6-9; see also Ezek. 34:25-27;
Isa. 35; Joel 3:18; Hos. 2:18-23).

Of late, many evangelical spokesmen have disassociated themselves from the early misperceptions of scriptural teaching. Most
notable, perhaps, was Francis Schaeffer in his *Pollution and the
Death of Man: The Christian View of Ecology*.[40] Noted scientist
and social philosopher Rene Dubois has argued persuasively
that "Judeo-Christian civilization has been no worse and no
better than others in its relation to nature."[41]

No, it is not Christianity, either true or false to its biblical
heritage. The ideological culprit is a consumer economy aimed
at material affluence, which deliberately sacrifices long-range
benefit for short-range economic profit. True, churches have not
spoken out against this and thus share the blame. But what does
the Bible itself say? There are at least two major biblical
doctrines that should control our thinking in the matter.

The second great command, to love one's neighbor as one's
self, prohibits the Christian from depriving others of benefit for
the sake of his own gain. Since the current "rape" of nature is
clearly depriving succeeding generations of benefit, if not of life,
and is often built on the exploitation of the natural resources of
poverty-bound people today, we have no choice but to work for
a restoration of ecological balance and a halt to environmental

40Wheaton: Tyndale, 1970.
41Carl H. Reidel, "Christianity and the Environmental Crisis," *Christianity Today*, 23
    April 1971, 6.

pollution and resource depletion. That is surely true neighbor-love. But there is an even higher mandate.

The *first* great command is God-centered, not man-centered, and certainly is not nature-centered. We are commanded, above all else, to love God. It is not merely that God likes the world the way he made it, though he does—he saw that it was very good (Gen. 1:12, 18, 21, 25, 31). It is not merely that he is glorified through his creation (Isa. 6:1-3; Ps. 19:1; 29:3; Rom. 1:20), that he himself goes to the trouble of holding it together (John 1:3-4; 1 Cor. 8:6; Eph. 1:9-10; Col. 1:17; Heb. 1:3) and that after we get through messing things up he intends to restore it to its pristine beauty (Rom. 8:19-23; Rev. 21:5). The truth is, he *owns* it (Ps. 24:1). It is *his*. We are just tenants. Just as we are stewards of our bodies, which are his, and thus must care for them; just as we are stewards of our finances, which are his and must be used responsibly for the advancement of his Kingdom; so with our physical environment. We can be good stewards, caring well for his world, using it for human welfare and the glory of God, or we can wantonly abuse and destroy it as the Israelites did (Exod. 23:10-11; Lev. 19:9; 25:1-7; Ps. 107:33ff.; Isa. 24:4-6; Zeph. 2:9). We also may be evicted! So we have a heavy responsibility for personal stewardship.

GAMBLING

Should not the subject of gambling be under the heading of "Private Integrity" rather than "Social Responsibility"? I chose the social context for considering the ethics of gambling because it is very difficult—if not impossible—to make a convincing case from Scripture against gambling as inherently sinful, but it is no difficult task at all to marshal biblical evidence against gambling as a social evil.

History of Gambling. Even though games of chance and other forms of gambling predate the writing of Scripture, the Bible is silent on the subject. Perhaps that is why the church has vacillated in its teaching. Kenneth Kantzer provides some insights into gambling in our own country.

America began as a gambling nation. Columbus' sailors whiled their time away crossing the Atlantic by playing cards. In 1612 the British government ran a

lottery to assist the new settlement at Jamestown, Virginia. . . . George Washington declared, "Gambling is the child of avarice, the brother of iniquity, and
the father of mischief"—but he kept a full diary of his own winnings and losses
at the card table. In 1776 the First Continental Congress sold lottery tickets to
finance the Revolution. From 1790 to 1860, 24 of the 36 states sponsored
government-run lotteries. Many schools and hundreds of churches conducted
their own lotteries to raise funds.[42]

Cotton Mather and other Puritans preached against
gambling. Gradually Methodists and Baptists began to support
the Puritans and Quakers until state after state rejected
government lotteries and declared gambling illegal. The last
state was Louisiana, whose lottery proved a disaster before the
end of the nineteenth century. But in this century it might be
said that the churches themselves, especially the Roman Catholic
church, opened the door for gambling, so that by 1985 most
states had legalized gambling, and by 1988 twenty-nine states
had followed the lead of New Hampshire (1964) in establishing
a public lottery.

Biblical Basis for Opposition. When the church has opposed
gambling as inherently sinful, what has been the rationale?
Although some have held it to be a form of stealing, this charge
seems ill-founded, since stealing is taking by force that which
one has no right to take. In the case of gambling, the loser has
agreed in advance, and the risk of loss is freely undertaken in the
hope of making a gain or having fun.

It is said to violate the law against covetousness. This is
certainly true for the serious gambler, but it can hardly be
alleged against the person who gambles for recreation.
Furthermore, though most gamblers may violate the law of love
by seeking personal gain through another's loss, a motive of
malice or lack of love can hardly be demonstrated as inherent in
the act of gambling itself.

Kantzer defines gambling as "an artificially contrived risk,
taken for selfish gain at another's expense, with no constructive
product or social good as its goal."[43] It seems to me that such a
definition would apply to virtually any game at all, certainly
games of chance. They are artificial, someone wins, someone

[42]Kenneth S. Kantzer. "Gambling: Everyone's a Loser," *Christianity Today,* 25
   November 1983, 12.
[43]Ibid., 13.

loses, and there is no visibly constructive product, though there
may be the social good of relaxation. I do not deny that the sins
of covetousness and selfishness are present in most gambling
and therefore that gambling of any kind may be inappropriate
for the Christian. But are these sinful attitudes inherent in the
act?

The most common argument against gambling is the sovereignty of God—to deliberately take a risk on an uncertain
outcome is to call in question God's sovereign control of our
affairs or actually to invoke God's involvement in our attempt to
gain at another's expense. The same argument was used in
earlier centuries against insurance. It will not do, this position
holds, to say that all of life is a risk and that we constantly take
chances—the farmer on the weather, the insured on his
longevity, the businessman on the market. But these are not
deliberately taking risk with the intent of avoiding exchange of
value. These are people who make every attempt to reduce risk,
who intend to pay an honest return on investment and who
have every right to humbly ask the Almighty to intervene should
they err.

The argument against gambling based on God's sovereignty
carries more weight than the others but is not compelling for
two reasons. In the first place, it is really only applicable to the
serious gambler. In the second place, even for the serious
gambler, the argument could be turned the other way. In
Scripture gambling was specifically used in making decisions
because man is finite, and God alone knows and can intervene in
behalf of one party or the other: "The lot is cast into the lap, but
the decision is wholly from the LORD" (Prov. 16:33; see also
18:18). In fact, "casting the lot" was standard practice in settling
disputes, dividing the Promised Land, choosing people for a
position—all things that could well be of greater value than
money. Even an apostle was so chosen (Acts 1:26). Contemporary gambling differs from the biblical examples of making
decisions on the basis of a "chance" outcome in that two or
more people were not offering something of value with the
hope of gain and the risk of loss. Nevertheless, subjecting the
outcome of a decision of great moment to the chance toss of the
dice was seen as deliberately invoking the intervention of the
Sovereign One, not flaunting his will or authority, much less

making light of it. I suppose the same motive could be in the mind of the contemporary gambler, though I grant it is not likely. The point is, if one deliberately trusts God with the outcome of a chance event—either planned ("artificially contrived") or unplanned—it can hardly be said that he is resisting God.

In summary, I find it difficult to make a strong case from Scripture to categorically affirm that all games of chance are inherently evil. A person could conceivably be generous, not covet, love his neighbor more than himself, and explicitly trust the sovereignty of God while betting a Coke on the outcome of a game. But that most gamblers violate one or more of these principles is beyond dispute.

Still, human experience indicates that even recreational gambling promotes covetousness and leads away from giving as a way of life. It often nurtures the fantasy that luck rather than hard work is a way to prosperity. All too often it sucks the gambler into a life of dishonesty. Even if one should escape the common evil results, is it right for the strong to validate gambling by personal example and help create an atmosphere in which others will fall? Seeing the practice in real life outcomes leads to the conclusion that gambling is not a legitimate part of a God-pleasing way of life. This proposed conclusion leads immediately to the question of the social impact of gambling.

Social Effects of Gambling. What are the social effects of gambling? Gambling addicts (compulsive gamblers) now constitute a higher percentage of the American population than alcoholics. And the results in poverty-destroyed families are hardly less tragic. *Look* senior editor Frank Trippett extensively researched what he called "The Suckers."

My gambler is a compulsive, of which there may be some 6 million, or a chronic, of which there are probably more—all those in whom the act of gambling triggers substantial emotions, a compelling thing that tends to shape the life of the one who knows it and needs it. If you casually bet, and occasionally, you are not my gambler, nor if you bet only what you can afford. "If the loss won't hurt, it's not gambling," my gambler says . . . . My gamblers seemed to get their special feeling, the compelling thing, not at the resolution of a bet, not at the winning or losing, but while the bet was pending. While the gamble was pending resolution they knew those special sensations, almost indescribable. The feelings vanish when the gamble is resolved, but they want them again, and so they bet again, and again. Inevitably they lose because the system is rigged that way.[44]

Psychologists are far from agreement as to what the basic drive is, but the results are commonly known: total obsession, so that nothing else and no other people really matter, a fantasy dream world of riches, inability to feel for others, a cloistered inner life, lying to guard their secret inner world and, commonly, poverty. Trippett quotes a testimony given at a Gambler's Anonymous meeting:

We talk about those awful years that are behind us, of borrowing money and stealing and embezzling, of living day by day behind a facade. But what we really think about is this—we think of the love we lost, and the love we were unable to find, and the love we were unable to give.[45]

The gambling business is dominated by the major crime syndicates. One organized crime boss said that the syndicates could get along very well on gambling alone even without their other mainstays: narcotics and prostitution. Estimates of the total take are little more than wild guesses, ranging up to a half trillion dollars annually.

State Lotteries. Why would state governments want to get into such a sordid business?

State governments are gambling that lotteries will provide a painless way to increase revenues. But to Roy Kaplan (a sociologist writing in the July 1984 issue of *The Annals of the American Academy of Political Science*) lotteries are a poor substitute for "dependable, equitable, and responsible methods of revenue generation." The lotteries provide only 3 percent of the total revenues of the states that sponsor them. Boosting state income taxes by as little as one quarter of one percent would raise the same amount. Lotteries are not only less efficient than taxes, they are less fair. The poor spend a larger proportion of their income on such games of chance than do the well off. Finally, the hope that legalized gambling would hurt organized crime has proved to be an illusion.[46]

Those who promote state lotteries claim that the state can get enormous income through this "painless taxation" and at the

[44]Frank Trippett, "The Suckers," *Look,* 19 May 1970, 37-38.
[45]Ibid., 37.
[46]Review of "The Social and Economic Impact of State Lotteries," by Roy Kaplan, *Annals of the American Academy of Political and Social Science,* reviewed in *The Wilson Quarterly,* January 1985, 25.

same time preempt the illegal gamblers' profits. What actually happens is the enhancement of the professional gambler's take and the increased involvement of syndicated crime because the state develops a whole new crop of gamblers. It has to, since the novelty of a state lottery normally wears off in about one year, and the state must begin major marketing to enlist new gamblers. The state cannot compete with professional gamblers in the odds offered, so every new gambler enlisted is a potential recruit for the professionals. Thus, the state finds itself an ally of organized crime, an exploiter of the poor, a promoter of social blight, and a loser in the gamble to make a bundle with little effort and little cost. No lottery has begun to measure up to optimistic projections, and many, within a decade, have failed financially. And who can calculate the cost to the state in the fight against organized crime and the accompanying corruption in law enforcement, not to mention the increase in welfare costs for increasing numbers of gambling losers?

In the light of the way gambling has worked out in the life of the nation, it seems the most responsible position for the Christian is total abstinence, opposition to any form of church-sponsored gambling, and cooperation with all people of good sense in opposing state-operated lotteries and pari-mutuel betting.

End

NONPROPERTY ROBBERY

VARIETIES OF THEFT

"Thou shalt not steal" applies not only to property; many other things can be stolen—reputation, for example. We considered the evil of gossip, slander, and other sins of the tongue in the chapter on Life Issues, but these are forms of stealing as well, often depriving the owner of a most precious possession, his name. Talk is constantly used to steal a person's position, his job, a friendship, or even a marriage. All of these thefts are far more serious in effect than the theft of property, yet rarely can be prosecuted and never compensated.

Idea Theft. Idea theft is often combined with deception to cover the theft, thus violating the Ninth Commandment as well.

Researchers claim that a majority of American students cheat, and an increasing number of teachers accept the practice. At least one judge has ruled in favor of the cheater and against the "honor system" that requires students to report cheating. Plagiarism, "the appropriation or imitation of the language, ideas, and thoughts of another author, and representation of them as one's original work,"[47] is commonly practiced by students, but also by teachers who sometimes steal not only the grand ideas of other scholars but the work of their own students!

It may be difficult at times to know when the ideas of others have been so assimilated as to be one's own, but the use of quotations from others, giving the impression that they are one's own words, or the use of a concept that is unique to its originator, clearly violates the commandments against lying and stealing.

Idea theft is not confined to schools, however, since the practice is rife in industry as well. How many technicians or junior executives have been hired away from their company in order to get at its secrets? So the theft is no longer merely private, but corporate.

A related way of stealing is to preempt the benefit due someone else. Copyright law is supposed to protect authors and artists from this kind of robbery, but all too often it is the church that steals the benefit due an author by duplicating musical scores for the choir or a "Peanuts" cartoon for the church bulletin.

There is no clear-cut principle to establish when an idea or piece of literature or art, published for the general public, becomes public domain. The limits of how long an author or artist deserves protection for additional benefit he or his descendants might get is a matter of judgment as to what is a fair return. In civilized society this judgment is corporate and established by law, though legitimately subject to change.

Laws do change, but the Christian is obligated to abide by the law as it stands, and copyright law is an honest effort to protect people from violations of the Eighth Commandment, "Thou shalt not steal."

[47]*The Random House Dictionary of the English Language,* 1968.

Time and Culture Theft. Finally, it is possible, at least in the Western world, to steal time. The employee who comes late or fritters away time on the job is not, technically, stealing time, but the benefit contracted for and due his employer. But to carelessly or deliberately keep a person waiting for an appointment is felt by most people in Protestant nations to be a form of stealing. "Time is money," we say, and to steal my time is to steal my money. This would apply equally to the teacher who is careless about the time of students, or the physician the time of his clients, just as much as to the guest who holds up a dinner party.

But people in other cultures do not always share this view. In Latin and Eastern lands, for example, people are said to be event-oriented rather than time-oriented. People are not expected to be "on time" in starting or closing a meeting or engagement, nor even in getting the bus to the terminal on schedule. In such a culture, is tardiness an ethical matter? Or, instructed by others who are more casual about life, should Americans stop being so "hyper" about promptness?

If it is accepted that stealing is taking from another that which one has no biblical grounds for taking, the precise boundaries of what is "private property" and what "one's right to take" may be somewhat conditioned by the views of a particular society. In ancient Israel it was ethical to glean the leftovers of harvest and illegal for the owner to harvest the entire crop, but in many societies this "gleaning" would be viewed as stealing. In America one certainly does not "glean" in Sears after a major sale! In Joseph's Egypt it may have been all right to expropriate people's land in exchange for a welfare handout, but the mayor of New York City had better not try that! In some tribes any property left outside one's hut is available for anyone to take, but don't try that with your neighbor's lawn mower. When people-groups following two different definitions of ownership meet, there can be a clash. To the American Indian who did not recognize private land ownership, the white man, coming with a different set of rules, was the ultimate thief.

These differences do not necessarily undermine the commandment not to steal, for all societies recognize the right of personal ownership and consider robbery a crime. This understanding does not relativize biblical standards because the difference is not in the definition of *stealing* but in the definition of *ownership,* and when taking what by whom is considered legitimate. Along the borders of definition of personal ownership there is some latitude for a society to establish its own norms, and it is wrong for the Christian in that society, even if he is the citizen of another society, to violate those norms. Whether the violation is inherently sinful or simply sinful by being declared illegal or unacceptable, the Christian should prove blameless.

Perhaps the question of stealing time falls in this category. If the person who loses time is offended, that is, considers it an unwarranted personal loss, then the sensitive Christian should not carelessly or deliberately "take that which is another's," for the Scripture gives him no right to do so.

Stealing and lying are often intertwined and feed one another. Furthermore, they have a single underlying principle: they violate integrity. So we turn now to the question of deception.

TRUTH AND DECEPTION

You shall not bear false witness against your neighbor. (Exod. 20:16)

PERJURY AND LYING

Strictly speaking, the Ninth Commandment prohibits only perjury, deliberately making a false statement in a court of law. Perjury is especially serious since it threatens the integrity of the courts by which justice is secured for a people. Yet, as in each of the Ten Commandments, there is a deeper implication. "Do not lie to one another" (Col. 3:9; see also Lev. 19:11) is a pervasive command in Scripture, and the law itself links perjury with all varieties of lying: dealing falsely, gossip, breaking contract, and, above all, swearing falsely in God's name (Lev. 19:11-12, 16). Keep your lips from speaking any kind of guile, we are taught in both Old and New Testaments (Ps. 34:13; 1 Pet. 3:10). Lying or falsehood of all varieties is a major theme of Solomon in the Proverbs, and the psalmist (Ps. 119:163) is not the only one who hates lying. God hates lying so much that no lie will enter heaven (Rev. 21:27), and indeed all liars will have a part in the lake of fire (21:8).

What is a lie? "To say words that do not conform to reality" is not a useful definition, for though we constantly say things that do not conform to reality, we do not necessarily thereby lie. We may err. Is it to say words deliberately that do not conform to reality? This also is inadequate, for it is quite possible to deceive without using false words. So we must broaden the definition of the sin of violating the truth to include the idea of a conscious purpose to deceive and to any form of deception. To lie, then, is one way of deliberately attempting to deceive.

THE NATURE OF DECEPTION

How bad a sin is deception? For the Christian, every word and act either affirms the truth of God or denies God. In other words, to the extent we conform to reality in what we do and say, to that extent we conform to the ultimate reality, God. To the extent we do not conform, to that extent we tell lies about God, we profane his reputation. When we do this knowingly or deliberately, we sin the more grievously. So the basic evil of deception is that it denies the character of God who is truth (Heb. 6:18). Jesus said, "I am the truth" (John 14:6). He also said the word of God is the embodiment of truth (John 17:17). God is utterly reliable. This is the foundation of a coherent universe.

If God may be described as "the truth," Satan may be described as "the father of lies" (John 8:44). He is the original lie incarnate, the father of lies, and his use of deceit is for the purpose of destruction. It is ideally designed to achieve that end, for every break with reality is inherently destructive. Destruction is what every liar achieves and finally experiences, first in himself, then in his relationships, and finally in the judgment he receives from a holy God.

There is no more sure method to destroy character than to deceive. Any other sin may be recognized and dealt with, but deception by its nature leads away from reality, so that ultimately truth is not even recognized. How, then, can repentance and restoration be pursued? Falsehood is the basic fault line in the foundation of the soul, putting all the superstructure in jeopardy. All the believability a person has, his very integrity, totters on the shifting sand of one lie. Deceit holds hostage all other virtues.

Not only does deceit quickly erode the character, it does not solve problems. It complicates them. The wise man put it poetically: "Bread gained by deceit is sweet to a man, but afterward his mouth will be full of gravel" (Prov. 20:17). Deceit fouls all relationships. Once a person has deceived another and is known to have done so, it is difficult ever to restore full confidence. One may think to counterbalance his lies with a greater number of truths, but it doesn't work that way. No amount of truth can quickly erase the indelible imprint of a lie, for the person who has been deceived may rightly ask himself, "When will it happen again?" Deceit is the ultimate destroyer of good relationships because good human relationships are built on mutual confidence.

Finally, we know lying is so evil because of the judgment that awaits the liar in this life (Prov. 21:6) and in the life to come (Rev. 21:8). God demonstrated at the beginning of Israel's formation as a nation in the Promised Land (Josh. 7:11ff.) and at the beginning of the church (Acts 5:1-11) how he feels about lies. Achan and Ananias are but graphic demonstrations of how severely God judges lies.

VARIETIES OF DECEPTION

Lying without Words. An averted glance, a "cool" attitude, a show of outrage can all be designed to mask the truth, to deceive by an expression, a demeanor, or an act, with no recourse to words at all. One can deceive by silence. When another is falsely accused in the easy comradery of a gossipy circle of friends, is silence a less guilty offense against the truth?

Lying with True Words. One can deceive using true words. For example, a person may quote another out of context and thus deceive as to the meaning of the original statement or tell only part of the truth, as did Satan in the Garden and Abraham concerning his wife.

A more contemporary example of deception with true words:

In a 1984 meeting of evangelical students from several seminaries, the speaker explained how the statements attributed to Christ by the Gospel writers were not always his own statements but were added later to make a point. Asked by the students if that approach would be accepted by people in the pew, he replied: "You have to be very careful. For example, you can say, 'The author, in Mark's Gospel, tells us that Jesus said . . .'"

In this way, the faith of the layman is not shaken and the speaker has not affirmed, in words, either the authorship of Mark or the authenticity of what was attributed to Jesus. But he has deliberately deceived his hearers into believing that the speaker believes the same things the hearer believes. And he is encouraged by an "evangelical" scholar to do this as a way of ministry.

Pretense and Exaggeration. Pretending to have knowledge when one only thinks or feels or guesses is deception. This temptation is especially strong for the recognized expert—the teacher or physician, for example. Exaggeration is another form of lying that is a great temptation for Christian workers as they seek to make even more glorious what God is doing, even when they subdue the temptation to exaggerate for a less worthy motive, such as the purpose of enhancing their own reputation.

Culture and Lying. We were striving to achieve accreditation for our Christian theological school in Japan, surely a good end pursued for the glory of God. But the professor in charge of the project constantly brought for my signature documents that were not factual. Finally in exasperation, he exclaimed, "A lie may become the cross you must bear!" It fit well with the Japanese proverb, "A lie also is a useful thing." When I still declined to sign, the professor gave up in disgust: "Your problem is that you haven't become accustomed to the Japanese way of doing things." Was this a mere clash of culture? Was God to be served best by deception in this cultural format? (I should add that he was the only Japanese colleague who held this position.)

But though the temptation is present in every culture, it also must be acknowledged that the ethics of truth are complicated in cross-cultural relationships. The Incas, who had capital

punishment for three crimes—murder, adultery, and lying—
were easy prey to the Spaniards, who lied "for the glory of
God." Cross-cultural communication of the truth is complicated
by cultural differences, no doubt, but I am unaware of any
biblical reason to modify the basic understanding of truth
outlined above. The Japanese professor and the Spanish invaders
were guilty of violating the truth.

Motivation: Self-Interest. "For the glory of God" is not the
primary reason people lie; usually it is pure self-interest. At a
men's retreat a young businessman sought me out. He and his
wife had been deeply in debt when his father-in-law invited him
to join the family business. It seemed God's own provision since
his father-in-law had been a leader in a strong evangelical church
for more than a quarter-century. But now his conscience was
troubling him. The only way a small business could survive in
the American economic jungle, he was told, was to keep two
sets of books, one for public inspection by government agents,
and another set of true financial records at home. Was this all
right? He was troubled but not ready to risk a stand for the
truth. When I returned to the church some years later, he and
his father-in-law were still leaders in the same church and still in
the same business, run in the same way.

Hypocrisy. The mature form of deceit is evidenced by a life of
deceit, commonly called hypocrisy: seeking to appear something
one is not. God hates hypocrisy. Why did the gentle Jesus blaze
out in excoriation of the religious leaders (Matt. 23)? It was
because they "preach, but do not practice" (v. 3). We can easily
see hypocrisy in the Pharisees, or in the correspondent who
writes "Dear Abby," furious because the "A" student he solicited
for help on his exam fed him the wrong answers. But in
ourselves? Our Sunday school men's class had been discussing
the cheating ways of politicians and the injustice of the courts.
Then the most spiritual man in the class said he had a chance to
catch fish over the legal quota, so he took along some extra
money just in case he was caught. This story was then matched
by the class president, who hooked some of his buddy's excess
catch on his own line, so that both would appear under quota. I
innocently asked, "If a man would cheat for a fish, would he

cheat for a million dollars?" An occasional attender observed that every man has his price. This comment stirred no little debate. After all, a ten-inch fish isn't a very high price.

But it isn't easy to let people in on what I really am. Msgr. Ronald Knox exposes the root of our hypocrisies:

The "folly of the cross" . . . means being ready to let the world see you as the fool whom God sees, whenever a suitable occasion arises. And it is humiliating to think how much of our unpublished thought process is devoted to doing just the opposite—trying to put ourselves in the right, to mask our ignorances, to explain away our failures, to pretend that the gaffe meant something else. Oh, we laugh at ourselves in private, that costs us nothing. We even amuse our friends and cultivate a reputation for modesty by dwelling on the record of our own discomfitures—afterwards, when we are in safe company. But really to put aside our self-esteem and follow, stripped, in the footsteps of a stripped Master—that is a rarer gift.[48]

Of all hypocrisies, religious hypocrisy is the worst. When a wicked person engages in religious activity, it is not merely that God rejects such falsehood. God hates hypocrisy so intensely that the religious activity itself, instead of improving the situation of the unrepentant sinner, is actually an abomination to God (Prov. 15:8). Far better to have had no religious activity at all.

Self-Deception. Hypocrisy is an attempt to deceive others, but it often stems from or is intertwined with a deeper malady: self-deception. We can be deceived about reality, convincing ourselves that we are better or worse than we really are. Both are equally dangerous and destructive. Lack of self-honesty can be profoundly damaging. Failures in self-honesty are at the root of almost every emotional and mental disturbance.

A particularly virulent strain of self-deception is the contemporary notion of what it means to be honest. A senior Bible student once came to me for counsel about an earlier immoral relationship with an unconverted man. We seemed to be getting nowhere, so I inquired, "Have you ever decided to finally break off all relations with him and have nothing to do with him ever again?" Her response revealed clearly the new concept of what integrity is: "That wouldn't be honest, would it?" One must be honest to or act in harmony with his feelings. If one must act

[48]Sheed and Ward, *Stimuli*.

contrary to what is wise or right, that is the price one must pay to maintain his "integrity." Abiding commitments, future relationships, and all other values are negotiable if the integrity of one's feelings is at stake.

A certain man has what he considers an attractive wife who has stood by him for thirty-five years and raised "five marvelous sons," but is no longer as sexually exciting to him as is a certain divorcée. What should he do? He concludes: "I have too much character to live a lie any longer." Thus runs the contemporary redefinition of honesty. But to be honest to oneself means to be honest to one's *whole* self, to one's commitments, to one's sacred relationships, to God, to right, to reason, as well as to one's feelings. The most honest thing this man could do would be to reject his desires and feelings and act with true integrity to his marriage vows.

Hypocrisy is despicable, self-deception is malignant, and if they are not dealt with, a habitual liar may come to the place where he does not even recognize the truth: "The heart is deceitful above all things, and desperately corrupt; who can understand it?" (Jer. 17:9).

EXCEPTIONS

Incomplete Truth. The command of God to tell the truth does not mean that a person must tell all that he knows in every situation. Christ did not tell his brothers all the truth concerning his intention to go to Jerusalem (John 7:8-10). God instructed Samuel to tell part of the truth (1 Sam. 16:1-5). Jeremiah deceived through a similar method (Jer. 38:24-27). In Christ there was no guile (1 Pet. 2:22), and it is impossible for God to lie (Heb. 6:18). Yet God himself does not tell the whole truth. He tells us only that portion of the truth which is necessary for our good. Jesus tells us explicitly concerning his use of parables: "That seeing they might not see." A mother may not tell her small child everything she knows in answer to the question, "Where do babies come from?"

One does not have to tell all he knows to speak the truth, but does this mean that deliberate deception is ever approved in Scripture? Just as killing does not equal murder and taking by

force does not equal stealing, could it be said that deception is
not always sinful?

The Lesser of Two Evils. In an interesting exchange on this
perplexing problem in the May 1964 *Eternity,* Peter Wagner
argued that sometimes it is necessary to lie as the lesser of two
evils. The Gentiles who harbored Jews in Nazi Germany, for
example, had to choose between lying to the SS troops or
turning over the Jews to certain death. Both options are, strictly
speaking, evil, so they should choose according to the mandate
of love, the lesser of the two evils. Several well-known
theologians responded: Bernard Ramm, Edward John Carnell
of Fuller, Henry Stobb of Calvin, Lloyd Kalland of Gordon, and
a Catholic theologian, Arthur Koestler. Though each took
exception to one or another of Wagner's points, all in essence
agreed that lying under some circumstances was the right
choice. Some, however, felt it was a good, not the lesser of two
evils.

   The doctrine of the tragic moral choice (the idea that we may
sometimes need to sin by choosing the lesser of two
unacceptable choices) was argued by the editor of *Christianity
Today*:

If and when a Christian does have to choose one evil over another, he is not
free from the guilt of the evil he chooses. If he lies, he is guilty of having told a
lie, no matter what his motives. In calling for truth the Bible mentions no
exceptions. The commandment of Sabbath-keeping had exceptions: works of
mercy and necessity were permitted. The law against killing allowed for
exceptions; at certain points in the Old Testament, war and capital punishment
were commanded by God. But the commandment of truth-telling had no
exceptions.[49]

John Mitchell took exception, responding in *The Presbyterian
Guardian,* May 1976:

We do agree that lying is not permitted by the law of God. We agree, too, that
there are no exceptions. I would go on to point out that those biblical
instances sometimes cited as exceptions are not that at all. When Rahab lied to
protect the Israelite spies, the fact is recorded. The Bible commends her faith,
but it nowhere approves the lie as such. . . . We are to approach such situations
in full confidence that our sovereign God will provide a way of escape—and

[49]23 April 1976, 33.

we are not responsible to develop it for him by choosing to lie. God controls every event of the Christian's life, and he is fully able to order it for our good.

And so the controversy rages. But are there in fact no biblical exceptions to the law against deception? Before examining the biblical texts, let us review two important facts.

The basic sin is deception, not merely the deliberate verbal expression of falsehood. Words can be in conformity to facts and still be designed to deceive. Words can be apparently out of conformity with the facts and be true. My young son was to drop a letter in a mail slot for me and asked, "To America or Japan?" Although the destination was Tachikawa, Japan, I replied, "America." No amount of explaining would have conveyed the truth that an APO address had to go in the "America" slot to reach a destination in Japan. I answered (truthfully) his question, not his words. I did not deceive him.

The other ground rule we follow is to recognize that Scripture alone must be our guide, and that cuts both ways. If Scripture truly allows no exceptions, then we must allow none, no matter how poignant the circumstances. But if Scripture justifies exceptions to any law or principle, then we must not try to be "more spiritual" than Scripture.

My contention is that the Bible does justify deception in three categories: inconsequential social arrangements, war, and in opposing criminal activity. If these exceptions are valid biblically, then to deceive in these circumstances in any way, including verbally, is no evil to be confessed, but legitimate moral behavior.

Inconsequential Social Arrangements. When Christ acted as if he would go on, but did not intend to (Luke 24:28ff.), or when he instructed his disciples to use a little "makeup," so as not to appear as if they had been fasting (Matt. 6:17-18), he apparently did not consider these sinful deception. Though the Bible does not tell jokes as such or instruct in ancient games, these would seem to fall in the same category of mutually agreed upon social arrangements. The unexpected ending is what makes a joke funny, so the more the audience is led astray (deceived), the better the punch line. The better his ability to deceive, the better the quarterback or chess player.

Many of our greetings and social expressions are of this nature. Those who lay heavy burdens of explicit veracity on casual social exchange do not help the cause of truth.

One should adapt even common salutations to conform as much as possible with reality. When the other person asks, "How are you?" unless he stops and makes a point of it, no one really thinks he wants a medical description of body or psyche. I feel more comfortable with an evasion such as, "I'm sure I'll survive," but that is no more moral and filled with content than the more common and meaningless response, "Fine." To impose on humor, games, or casual social greetings the requirements of the Ninth Commandment is not to serve the cause of truth; actually it trivializes the weighty demands of biblical integrity.

If the biblical evidence for legitimate deception in inconsequential social arrangements is not abundant, either for or against (possibly for the very reason that it *is* inconsequential), this lack cannot be alleged against the case for deception in war.

Deception in War. War by its very nature is waged with all available weapons, including psychology and deception. God himself wages war this way. He not only told Joshua to set an ambush (Josh. 8:2), a very deadly deception, he himself set an ambush on at least one occasion (2 Chron. 20:22). Elisha and God worked together on a project in which the prophet told the enemy troops, "This is not the way and this is not the city," when in fact it was the city. When it was time to launch an attack on the enemy, God instructed Israel to set up the most professional and quintessential form of deception: send spies into the land. These spies were hidden, in good spy-thriller fashion, by an ancestor of Jesus, Rahab. At that point she began the act of deception, not when she uttered words that further deceived the home troops. For this act she was commended and rewarded by God (Heb. 11:31).

Some have argued that Rahab was commended for her faith, not for her activity. Apart from the fact that all three of these passages say explicitly that it was *because* of what she did, how is it possible so to divorce faith and works? In fact, James, who emphasized not divorcing faith and works, said explicitly of Rahab that she was justified for what she did (as evidence of her faith) (James 2:25). A dangerous theological notion with unending potential for mischief is introduced if one may deliberately do a sinful act for a good cause and be rewarded for his faith. If a person sins, should he not be reprimanded rather than rewarded? Especially when the act is designed to save one's own skin? No, Rahab acted in the faith that the God who was with Israel was mightier than the gods of Jericho, and she did the right thing—she sided with God's people and deceived through actions and words in what may properly be called an act of war. Others have argued that the hiding of the spies was acceptable but that she sinned when she spoke untrue words. But this is an inadmissible definition of the sin of deception and opens the door to all kinds of theological vagaries in which words are sacrosanct but actions are not.

If war is legitimate (see the section earlier on war), then ambushes, camouflage, spying, deceptive strategy, communicating in code, as integral parts of war, are also legitimate.

Deception in Opposing Criminals. Deception is apparently one form of resistance which, like physical resistance, is ordinarily wrong, but not wrong in resisting a criminal or an enemy in war.

The Egyptian midwives resisted an ungodly and oppressive regime by disobedience and lying. For this "God dealt well with the midwives" (Exod. 1:15-21). How can it be said that their faith was good and their subversive activity bad? Or how can it be said that their disobedience was good and their lie bad? The Bible does not make such distinctions. It just says that God approved.

If a homeowner, away on a trip, leaves a timer on his light system to deceive potential robbers into believing a lie (that he is home), surely he does not sin. Deceptive police activity is a good thing when needed to apprehend a criminal. When a robber demands entrance to a home, or access to possessions or people within, and he can be deflected by deception (with true words or false words), the deceiver has not chosen the lesser of two evils but has done right.

Note that we are not justifying these deceptions on the grounds of situationism, deciding for ourselves which course of action is the more loving for the most people. Nor are we saying that both courses of action are sinful and that one must sometimes make a tragic moral choice (and lie rather than kill, for example). No, we are saying that any form of deception is a very bad sin, except those situations in which Scripture itself permits or advocates deception: inconsequential social arrangements, war, and criminal resistance. In the instances cited, either God himself took the deceptive action, commanded it, or is said to have approved of those who did.

One does not make exception to any biblical law on the basis of what may appear reasonable or loving. If exceptions are made, they are made on the basis of exceptions sanctioned by Scripture. In this way any exception is guaranteed by Scripture and cannot spill out and contaminate the rest of life with deception whenever it seems to the deceiver to be reasonable, loving, worthy, or necessary to achieve some good end.

The Second Commandment cannot be taken to mean that no art may picture any object in nature because there are clear biblical exceptions to the command against making "images." Certainly the Fourth Commandment (on the rest day) and the Sixth Commandment (against killing) have exceptions enunciated in Scripture. If the Fifth Commandment is taken to mean that children must obey parents as part of the "honor," there are exceptions. If the Seventh is taken to identify all sex outside marriage as morally wrong, then the victim of rape is an exception, and if the Eighth Commandment against stealing were defined as "taking by force," exceptions are clear. In the same way, if the Ninth Commandment against perjury is taken to include all forms of deception under all circumstances, what do we do with the clear biblical exceptions? I will readily grant that the evidence for exceptions to the law against killing is far more abundant than the evidence for exceptions to the laws against deception. At the same time, I must urge that the evidence for exceptions to the law against deception is more abundant than that for the Second, Fourth, Fifth, and Seventh Commandments, which exceptions most scholars and laypeople freely grant.

I conclude, then, that it is a sin, a violation of the Ninth Commandment, to deliberately deceive someone whom Scripture gives no right to deceive. And though I am not under obligation to enlighten everyone on every subject on which I may have knowledge, I have no right deliberately to attempt to deceive in any manner anyone except in mutually agreed upon social arrangements, an enemy in war, and in resisting criminal activity.

We have dealt in some detail with possible exceptions to the law of truth because these matters are of such crucial importance to our daily lives and are so hotly debated among equally learned and committed believers. But let us return to the main burden of this chapter.

God is the ultimate reality, and his reliability is what enables the world to hold together and make sense. If he were unstable and random, let alone deliberately deceptive and capricious, the world would be not simply an erratic rogue world—it would not cohere at all. It could not exist.

And so it is with our lives. To the extent we conform to reality, to that extent we live. To the extent we split from reality, especially when we consciously choose the untrue, to that extent we destroy and are destroyed. That is why God demands integrity and hates every form of dishonesty. To love the truth is to hate the lie. So we have considered dishonesty in relationship to property and truth, sought to trace it through all the intricate labyrinth of its evil in an effort to help us find our way out into the bright light and pure beauty of God, the trustworthy One, that we may be recreated by his Spirit into his own likeness, into people who are trustworthy.

SUGGESTED ADDITIONAL READING

In this chapter we have dealt with more than thirty major topics on which books have been written—from a handful (such as "The Christian and Leisure") to thousands (such as "Economic Systems"). A number of key authors and sources have been cited in the text and footnotes. A full bibliography on each topic is beyond the scope of this text, but I list here a useful title for several of the major topics.

LABOR AND MANAGEMENT
Catherwood, Henry F. R. *The Christian in Industrial Society*. London: Tyndale, 1964.

ECONOMIC SYSTEMS
Ellul, Jacques. *Money and Power*. Translated by LaVonne Neff. Downers Grove, Ill.: InterVarsity, 1984. Controversial, but stimulating.

PERSONAL FINANCES

Burkett, Larry. *How to Manage Your Money*. Chicago: Moody, 1982. A helpful presentation of practical biblical guidelines for personal finance.

SOCIAL RESPONSIBILITY

Mooneyham, W. Stanley. *What Do You Say to a Hungry World?* Waco, Tex.: Word, 1975. Motivational, widely read, and less controversial than Ronald Sider's better-known work *Rich Christians in a Hungry World*.

LYING

Bok, Sissela. *Lying: Moral Choice in Public and Private Life*. New York: Vintage, 1979. Interesting survey of historical attitudes toward different types of lies.

CHRISTIANS AND SOCIETY

We have considered biblical moral mandates which we must follow, biblical principles which we must apply to our own context, and biblical "permissibles"—areas of freedom which may not be taken away on biblical authority. We have used the framework of the Ten Commandments, but now we come to areas which are more problematical, matters which are not the visible themes of Scripture and about which swirl storms of controversy: the Christian and society, matters of conscience, and personal guidance.

What responsibility does the Christian have beyond modeling and teaching ethical behavior? Does he have a mandate from Scripture to attempt to control the conduct of others? Is he *permitted* by Scripture to do so? Are there biblical principles to guide us through the complexities of the puzzling problems of private vs. public, the individual Christian's relationship to the institutions of society? And what role is the organized church to play?

CHURCH AND STATE

Throughout the history of the church, people have debated the question of whether it is legitimate to work toward

Christianizing society. In the Reagan era the debate heated up again. Some decried "politicizing religion" or "religionizing politics." Others wedded church and state with enthusiasm.

Contrary to what some protagonists say, no one position is the exclusive domain of a given theological persuasion. Liberals and conservatives alike range through all positions, and, most disconcerting, an individual may demand separation of "religion and politics" on some issues while demanding they mix in others. In other words, it is the agenda that seems to divide.

If the issue is race, equitable distribution of wealth, a guaranteed livelihood, feminism, armament control, or human rights (in democracies), you can usually count on liberal involvement and fundamentalist uninvolvement; but if the issues are abortion, law and order, pornography, the traditional family, a large defense budget, or human rights (in communist lands), the roles are reversed. It is not exactly that one is for big government and the other wants government to shrink to minimal roles; each wants lots of government involvement to achieve what it thinks important to the public welfare and no government presence at all in what it considers its own private business. Just a different agenda. But in seeking to win, the cry is raised, "Politics and religion must not be mixed!" What we fail to add is, "by our opponents." This (unconscious, we hope) hypocrisy adds a great deal of confusion to the already complex controversy. But the church never has agreed on these issues.

THE STREAM OF HISTORY

For the first three centuries of its existence the church was heavily involved in social action, but not through government agency. In fact, Christians were excluded from public life by intense persecution. Nevertheless, they were widely recognized for almsgiving (even the poor gave generously through stinting and fasting), support of widows and orphans (pagan Emperor Julian said, "These godless Galileans feed not only their own poor but ours"), care for the sick and disabled (establishing the first hospitals), care for prisoners and slaves (some Christians sold themselves into bondage to buy the freedom of others), providing work for the unemployed, caring for those suffering calamity (in times of plague only Christians continued to care for the dying), and providing hospitality to those on journeys.

Then came Emperor Constantine (312), and the outcast minority gradually became the establishment. At first the state controlled the church, but over the centuries the church came to control—or at least to excessively manipulate—the state. It was Pope Gregory VII (reigned 1073–1085) who said, "The pope alone may use the imperial insignia; all princes should kiss his feet and his alone; he may depose emperors; he may absolve the subjects of wicked rulers from their allegiance." Pope Innocent III (reigned 1198–1216) was probably the most powerful pope, constantly maneuvering the monarchs of Europe as he wished. The popes claimed that in a (theoretically) Christian Europe they, as heads of the church, had every right to allegiance from every secular ruler. But while Gregory and Innocent were basically fair, wise rulers, many popes led scandalous lives and proved that power does tend to corrupt.

Though differing in philosophy of government, all the Reformers held to the separation of civil and religious government. The Anabaptists went even further, insisting that civil government is only for non-Christians and that Christians should remain outside these worldly systems. This position is maintained today by some of their spiritual descendants, such as the Amish and some Mennonites. It influences others strongly, so that Baptists of all varieties strongly emphasize the separation of church and state.

Nevertheless, the dominant Reformation-Protestant teaching was not for separation of *influence,* but for separation of the *powers* of each so that neither controlled the other. Church and state were viewed as partners in separate but overlapping spheres of responsibility for achieving God's purposes in the world. This view prevailed in northern, Protestant Europe, while the legacy of Roman Catholic church-state intermingling dominated southern Europe. The New World fell heir to the Protestant approach in the northern hemisphere and the Roman Catholic approach in the southern, where these approaches continue to this day.

Perhaps the most successful and long-lasting experiment with the "Protestant model" was introduced by John Knox (1505–1572) in Scotland, where for a century the prisons were said to be empty and capital crime unheard of. The Scriptures, seen through the theology of John Calvin, were accepted by a whole people as the standard of life. This robust Presbyterian godliness did not seem to influence their southern neighbor, which slipped further and further into moral decadence so that England was ripe for revival under the preaching of George Whitefield and John Wesley.

This led to the "Evangelical Awakening," which is often held up as a model of how Christian people (not the corporate church, as in Scotland) can change the course of government and national destiny.

British politics between 1750 and 1850 was dominated by Anglican evangelicals, many of whom came out of the Wesleyan revival. The "saints" or "Clapham Sect," met in the home of Henry Thornton and hammered out the most formidable pressure group Britain has ever seen. William Wilberforce, Grenville Sharp, Thomas Clarkson, Zachary Macaulay, and Lord Shaftesbury determined to cure the moral evils of their land. They brought about the abolition of slavery, fought for humanization of factories and prisons, the relief of debtors, and opposed all discrimination against minorities. Sunday was firmly established as a day of rest, and the national lottery was abolished. Bear- and bull-baiting and cock-fighting were stopped. Even profanity and adultery were legislated against.

How did they do it? They sought to mobilize every possible force. They used political action. Some who were not authorities in certain fields made themselves authorities in order to be effective. By 1815 half the peerage had given up their old amusements of the hunt and ball and devoted themselves to setting up Bible study groups.

The Clapham Sect used money. The African colony of Sierra Leone was founded in 1787 as a home for freed slaves and was privately sustained for twenty years. Agnew, a Scottish evangelical member of Parliament, bought up thousands of railway shares so that he could press for Sunday closure of the railroads. The Clapham Christians were not only concerned about the black slave traffic (which they stopped) but also the lost souls of unevangelized areas of the world. For example, distressed that the giant East India Company banned missionary activity in India, they bought up stock and took over the entire directorate of the company for the purpose of opening India to the gospel.

They used boycott. Hannah More, called "the high priestess of the Evangelical Revival," persuaded "ladies of gentility" to abstain from using West Indies sugar in their tea as part of the overall antislavery campaign. In fact, the evangelicals' greatest weapon was the influencing of public opinion. They held public campaigns that succeeded in reversing the value system of an entire people in less than a generation. They intended to rid the land of all wickedness: slaveholding, the oppression of women and children, Sabbath-breaking, injustice, adultery, profanity— whatever violated the law of God.

CHURCH AND STATE IN AMERICA

The colonies in North America fell heir to the Protestant heritage of England and Scotland. There is little evidence to support some contemporary views that the Founding Fathers had anything radically different in mind than the benevolent reinforcing of the state by the church and the church by the state while determining that neither should dominate or control the other. Consider the words of Julius Poppinga, a trial attorney and former president of the Christian Legal Society:

The meaning of the First Amendment language on religion has long been beclouded and distorted by the unfortunate metaphor contributed by Thomas Jefferson in 1802 in a letter to the Danbury Baptist Association of Connecticut. There he described the First Amendment as "building a wall of separation between church and state." Jefferson was not writing as a jurist, and surely he was not suggesting that religious life in America would best be served by walling it off. But his language took hold. . . .

We discover that the Founding Fathers expressed two fundamental, but competing, concerns: first, that government should not sponsor religion, and second, that government should not impede its expression. The precise constitutional language reads, "Congress shall make no law respecting an establishment of religion, or prohibiting the free exercise thereof."[1]

In the elections of 1984, the implications of the First Amendment for the relationship between religion and politics became a central issue, generating a great deal of emotional rhetoric. In the midst of this, religious liberalism's chief voice in the arena of church and society, *Christianity and Crisis*, devoted

[1]Julius Poppinga, "Religion and the First Amendment: Choosing Sword or Shield," *Theology News and Notes*, December 1980, 3.

an issue to analyzing the subject.[2] In addition to the expected far-left contributors to the symposium, two of the leading mainline authorities on religion and society, Robert N. Bellah and John C. Bennett, wrote perceptively on what the separation of church and state does *not* mean.

Bennett: When President Reagan said at the famous prayer breakfast in Houston that "politics and religion are necessarily related," he said the obvious. The separation of church and state has never meant the separation of religion from the community or of the church from public life with its political choices.[3]

Bellah: The liberal state does not concern itself with ultimate things. It is only a means that individuals use to pursue their private ends. Religion is a purely private matter whose concern for ends applies only to individuals and in no way involves the state. That, in the liberal view, is the very meaning of the separation of church and state.

I would argue that the liberal theory never has described American reality. . . .

The liberal theory does not work because it describes no real state and no real religion. No state, and certainly not the contemporary behemoth state, can fail to have an influence on the ends of life: on war and peace, on wealth and poverty, on racial and sexual equality or the lack thereof, on relationships in family, work, and local community. The notion of the neutral night watchman state was fiction when invented and is even more of a fiction today. What, in turn, would the religion of liberal theory look like? It would be a purely private matter of individuals and "the church or synagogue of their choice." It would concern itself with the feelings of individuals and the warmth and friendliness to be found within the religious group, but that is all. It could not speak to the nation and the world about matters of moral and spiritual concern. . . .

The liberal theory is dangerous not only because it is a fiction. It is dangerous because the society it envisions would not be humanly bearable. Such a society would be composed of abstract atomized individuals, sharing nothing in common, and having individual rights to do whatever they pleased and no standards whatever except the thinnest consensus about not harming others. While such abstract freedom is appealing to Americans, usually in particular realms such as economics or sex, they do not really wish to live in a world of vacuous, formally free individuals sustained by no common culture or group commitments.[4]

The clear intent of the First Amendment was to keep the federal government from creating a state church on the European model, which would have forced the individual states to relinquish their respective established churches then in place. Many of the colonies had state churches, but of different denominations. The founding fathers did not oppose that, for

[2]29 October 1984.
[3]*Christianity and Crisis,* 29 October 1984, 397.
[4]Ibid., 391-392.

those churches continued in the new republic for some decades. But they did not look benevolently on the potential power of a monolithic national church.

Whatever the attitude or intention toward "church" may have been, it is clear that the prevailing consensus of a religiously-based Protestant ethic was viewed as essential to the success of the fledgling experiment in democracy. Thus a moral consensus dominated the making and interpreting of the law well into the twentieth century.

The problem of the First Amendment is that it appears to attempt the impossible. Depending on the way it is read, it seems to guarantee two conflicting rights—freedom *of* religion and freedom *from* religion.)People should not be coerced by religion, so the government may not sponsor religion, but people should be free to practice their religion, so the government should not interfere.

But suppose that in protecting one citizen from unwanted religion it is necessary to deprive another of his freedom to practice his religion? Whose rights prevail? In an earlier day the government seemed to favor the rights of the religious person to freely practice his religion, whereas recently the courts, at least, have favored the rights of citizens to be protected *from* religion. But in seeking to disentangle itself from favoring religion, it has backed into just as great an entanglement. The entanglement of the state with the churches is just as prevalent as before, and probably inevitably so. The difference is that the entanglement now tends toward inhibiting the church, whereas earlier it tended to favor and promote religion. Not only are churches increasingly denied previously granted privileges, the direction seems to be toward isolation of religion from public space altogether.

Perhaps the change was inevitable, with the constant infusion through immigration of many other value systems and religious traditions.

Certainly secularization has been hastened by the unrelenting assault of liberal secularists since the 1930s. In the social upheaval in the 1960s and 1970s the church began to grope for a cohesive rationale for relating religious moral convictions to public policy development. Though strong groupings, left and right, began to emerge in the late 1970s and 1980s, the process of developing a clearly articulated cohesive rationale that could lead to consensus is far from complete. What are the dominant lines of thinking?

CONTEMPORARY VIEWS

It is possible to arrange the relationship between church and state in various ways: state controls church; church controls state; church and state assigned mutually exclusive roles; or church and state have distinct spheres of responsibility but with mutual respect and negotiated authority and influence.

In historic fact, no arrangement seems to have been "pure"; there has always been some spillover in the outworking of whatever arrangement was officially prescribed. The Bible gives no mandate but does give instruction on the purpose of the church and the purpose of human government. So we conclude that the best arrangement is that which provides maximum freedom for each to do best what it is designed to do. But discovering the ideal arrangement is not easy. There seems to be only so much space in which social institutions may operate. And as a result, when the authority (or freedom or "rights") of one expands, that of the other must contract. As the sphere of government control expands over the lives of its people, for example, the freedom of other social institutions to speak or act with independent authority diminishes. How does each of the four arrangements meet the requirement for maximum freedom to accomplish the God-given roles of both the church and the state?

State Controls Church. When human government, as in many communist lands, aims to control the religious life of the people, the result has rarely been to the benefit of religious life. If the record of secular or anti-Christian government has been poor in this regard, that of Christian men in totalitarian or comprehensive governmental authority has not been much better. The will of the authority, no matter how well-intentioned, when extended to the religious life of the people, inevitably binds the free conscience. Our Puritan forefathers understood that well enough.

In the theocracy of Old Testament Israel, where God himself

was directly behind the government, it may have been an effective arrangement, but rarely have God's people been free to do God's will in freedom of conscience when fallen human beings are in charge of the total life of the subjects.

Church Dominates State. The church dominated the state for a few centuries in medieval Europe, and though a few people advocate it today, it is not likely to happen in democratic or communistic lands of the twentieth century. Islam controls the state in some Muslim lands, and there has been almost full church control in a few Catholic countries during the twentieth century, but a return to such a relationship in the Western world seems highly unlikely.

The professed fears of liberals that some conservative Christians intend to impose a rightist totalitarian regime with coercive moral requirements is not even a remote possibility. No person or group of people in a modern pluralistic democracy can impose its will on an unwilling majority—or even on an unwilling minority, for that matter. Every interest group executes whatever pressure it can to have laws made and interpreted in the way that best furthers its own interests, but this can hardly be called "imposing."

It is just that many long-silent conservative people have discovered their voices, and the liberal establishment finds it hard to accept. At first the roar to the right was dismissed as an illusion created by media hype; next, curiously, it was decried as unfair, and then it was frantically opposed as an attempt at a takeover by mindless, un-American, rightist moralists who would soon impose all the worst kinds of Puritan and Victorian private moralities on freedom-loving, benevolent, intelligent, and morally relativistic true Americans. More of that later, but what can be said of the emotional reaction of the erstwhile sober *New York Times* to charge that "there are certain similarities in the theses advanced by the Red Guards who rampaged through China, the Ayatollah Khomeini's wild-eyed Islamic principles . . . and the Americans who call themselves the Moral Majority "?[5]

It must be noted, however, that there are some evangelicals

[5]*The Moral Majority Report,* August 1984, 6.

who do advocate church control of the state. One group clearly states this in its constitution:

> The Christian Government Movement is an association of United States citizens who are united in the effort to promote through education the concept of Christian government and to achieve its realization thereby in the United States.[6]

Similar in goals, but with a greater emphasis on the Old Testament and without political organization, is the movement among Reformed people called "Theonomy." Though the primary emphasis is on the conformity of believers to all the standards of the Old Testament, it is held that these standards are not merely for ancient Israel nor for merely private observance. They are universal in God's intent and should be imposed on any society in which such imposition is possible.

But such movements are minuscule, and the likelihood of the viewpoint prevailing seems nil.

Even if the church or church people could control government, it would not be a good thing. A religious totalitarianism is no better than a secular totalitarianism. Inquisitions are not the exclusive domain of one particular brand of religion. But even if we are persuaded that it might turn out for the common welfare, we may have no part of it because Christ himself forbade it: "My Kingdom is not of this world." Because of the unacceptability of church dominance in the affairs of state, the recent intellectual and political history of America, at least, has tended toward assigning church and state mutually exclusive roles—a totally secular state in which religion is hermetically sealed off into total privatization.

Church and State Assigned Mutually Exclusive Roles. Two opposite ideologies espouse this position: Christians (who range all the way from total disengagement in the political process through those who merely stand for "separation of church and state") and secularists of all varieties who would like to wall off from public life all religious influence.

Christian Isolation. Here we speak not of the private Christian citizen's involvement in politics, but of church participation in the development of public policy.

[6]*The Christian Patriot*, vol. 30, January 1974, no. 6.

Leighton Ford, socially active evangelist and leader of the Lausanne movement, summarizes the conflict succinctly:

Social responsibility is variously seen as a distraction from evangelism ("Why shift furniture when the house is burning"?); as the result of evangelism ("Changed people will change the world"); as a preparation for evangelism ("Hungry people can't listen to sermons"); as a partner of evangelism; or as an essential element of evangelism. Some [nonevangelicals] might even see social responsibility as the equivalent of evangelism.[7]

Many hold that the church's only legitimate mission is spiritual—evangelizing non-Christians and nurturing Christians. It is held that Old Testament teaching is irrelevant because it was given to a God-ordained civil government, Israel, and Christ, explicitly set this aside for the church, stating that his Kingdom is not of this world. He was reinforced by the apostles, who taught that our warfare is spiritual and the weapons we use are not of this world.

The position that the church should stick to spiritual and moral issues has a long and illustrious list of advocates. The Westminster Confession of Faith, which had such strong influence not only on Presbyterian churches but on the formation of the American republic, seemed clear on the issue:

Synods and councils are to handle or conclude nothing but that which is ecclesiastical; and are not to intermeddle with civil affairs, which concern the commonwealth, unless by way of humble petition, in cases extraordinary; or by way of advice for satisfaction of conscience, if they be thereunto required by the civil magistrate. (Chapter XXXI, Section IV)

The position is put in even bolder terms by David Lutzweiler in the pages of *The Alliance Witness,* official organ of the Christian and Missionary Alliance:

Jesus Christ viewed society as a sinking ship damaged beyond repair, and he taught that all attempts to bail it out and keep it permanently afloat were doomed to failure at last. He taught his followers to try only to save as many of the passengers as possible, and even this effort, he predicted, would salvage only a small minority. . . . For the Christian, victory is always a matter of the spirit. It is an individual victory, not the triumph of an earthly movement. . . . The whole world can disappear in a nuclear cloud around him, and he can still come out of it spiritually victorious, his character eternally conformed to the

[7]Leighton Ford, *Evangelical Newsletter,* 13 November 1981.

image of Christ; and as far as God is concerned that is the only victory that matters.[8]

Although I will shortly argue against this position, I must admit that were I part of a small Christian minority in a Muslim land, I might prefer absolute isolation of the majority "church" influence from the political process. I would probably prefer a secular state, especially if it were benevolently neutral toward all religion. But as I live in a nation with strong Protestant roots, I cannot be certain what position I might espouse under other circumstances. This inner tension highlights the fact that the entire issue of church-state relationships is impossible of final resolution because God has not revealed the preferred arrangement. Possibly he has not done so because there is no ideal arrangement for fallen humankind.

In any event, some Christians are not the only ones who hold that church and state have mutually exclusive roles. Many secularists are militant in this position and their viewpoint seems increasingly to prevail.

The Secular State. In a "secular state" the government and all political processes are kept separate from religion and even from religious influence. This is a separation not known in the earlier days of the republic in which government was favorable toward religion and open to religious influence but was benevolently neutral toward any specific Christian denomination. Later this neutrality came to include all religions. But the emerging "secular" state is no longer merely nonreligious but increasingly irreligious and even antireligious.

We seem to be moving toward the awkward position that the government cannot support values in the framework of any traditional religion (either Protestant, Catholic, or Jewish), but it will support them in a humanistic framework. The practical effect, thus, is to make humanism an established religion.[9]

Increasing numbers of the intellectual "elite" espouse the theory that government has no business legislating any moral standards except to prevent a person from harming others.

[8]David Lutzweiler, *The Alliance Witness*, 22 July 1964, 2.
[9]Kenneth Kantzer, "The Christian as Citizen," *Christianity Today Institute*, 1985, 31.

John Stuart Mill's words still offer the classic statement of the modern democratic notion of government's role in morality: "The sole end for which mankind is warranted individually or collectively, in interfering with the liberty of action of any of their number, is self-protection. The only purpose for which power can be rightfully exercised over any member of a civilized community, against his will, is to prevent harm to others."[10]

The government is made up of human beings whose values (or sense of "ought" and "ought not") determine the laws of that people. This sense of "what ought to be" comes from the entire cultural milieu, but most of all from the religious convictions of the people. Therefore, on the face of it, though the church and the state can be completely separated organizationally so that the church is prohibited from doing anything officially in the public domain, the so-called private religious or irreligious convictions of the people will still determine the final outcome of the rules people live by. Richard John Neuhaus argues this position persuasively in his highly influential volume *The Naked Public Square*:

The idea of public religion is the subject of great public confusion. The idea is widely accepted that religion is something between an individual and his God. . . . Religion is the business of church and home and has no place in public space. These and other axioms are, it is commonly said, part of the American way. Legally and politically, they are supported by a notion of the "separation of church and state" that is understood to mean the separation of religion and religiously based morality from the public realm. . . . Again, the democratic reality, even, if you will, the raw demographic reality, is that most Americans derive their values and visions from the biblical tradition.[11]

The truth of what Neuhaus says is reinforced by the polls which consistently show that more than 90 percent of Americans subscribe to the Ten Commandments whether or not they know what they are, and, more important, almost the same proportion believes our laws are and should be grounded in them. Yet the direction of our public life ignores this basic reality.

Comments Neuhaus,

[10]Lewis B. Smedes, "On Cleaning Up America," *Theology News and Notes,* December 1980, 8.

[11]Richard John Neuhaus, *The Naked Public Square* (Grand Rapids: Eerdmans, 1984), 20-21, 139.

Deinstitutionalizing of religious truth claims . . . sounds like a fine and liberating thing, until we recognize that it really means the reduction of all moral claims to individualistic passion. Then indeed every question of value is dissolved into a question of power.[12]

What is the end result of the new pluralism?

Often [pluralism] is used to argue that no normative ethic, even of the vaguest and most tentative sort, can be "imposed" in our public life. In practice this means that public policy decisions reflect a surrender of the normal to the abnormal, of the dominant to the deviant. Indeed, it is of more than passing interest that terms such as *abnormal* or *deviant* have been largely exorcised from polite vocabulary among the elites in American life.

[The teacher] may publicly espouse atheism and be quite public about having sexual relations with the girls, or boys, in his class. These are matters of constitutionally protected belief and life-style. But he may not pray or evangelize. Is this absurd? Of course it is, but it is not very far from the logic that has moved us incrementally from government encouragement of religion (although not of any one religion), to government neutrality toward religion, to government hostility to religion. We are arriving at the point where the privileged status of religion, which was clearly the intention of the First Amendment, is becoming the most particular handicap of religion.[13]

Our efforts then, in shutting up religion to the realm of the private life of citizens has had bad results not only in relativizing the ethics of public life, but has begun to do the same thing in a kind of moral sewage back-flow into the private lives of our people. In the end, our experiment seems to be proving that public policy and private moral convictions cannot be split. They can't be split because each inevitably affects the other— whether the composite religious convictions of the people influencing law-making, or the structure of government in turn influencing the private behavior of citizens. Since an integral relationship exists between public and private, what arrangements best make that relationship productive of common good? I hold that the fourth option is best.

Church and State Distinct But Mutually Influential. Church and state have distinct spheres of responsibility but will best discharge those responsibilities with mutual respect and negotiated authority and influence.

Before presenting the case for this position, it is necessary to

12Ibid., 142.
13Ibid., 146, 148.

pause and answer the objection that if we follow the example of
Christ and the apostles, we will not be active politically nor seek
to influence public policy.

We may be quite sure that Christ and the early church were
not social activists because a leading social activist magazine says
so with graphic force:

The catch is that it's not obvious that Jesus bought *The Other Side's* program or
strategies. . . . Jesus suffered under a gross dictator, propped up by a foreign
military power. Around him he saw a few people who were very wealthy and
many who were hideously poor. Yet Jesus didn't join the local guerrillas. Nor
did he mount a nationwide, nonviolent campaign. He didn't organize workers
into unions, start a food co-op, or paint "Yanqui, go home" on walls. . . . What
Jesus said about changing structures is pretty scarce. And the same is true of
the early church and "The Economics of Jesus."[14]

Jacques Ellul, professor of the history and sociology of
institutions at the University of Bordeaux and brilliant, prolific
advocate of controversial positions, holds that Jesus did have the
option of political action (the militant Zealots) and that he
deliberately chose to go the opposite direction.[15] This reinforces
the idea that Jesus' own role was definitely apolitical, but it may
not do what Ellul avers—give additional evidence concerning
what his followers, called to other roles, should do.

First we must seek to establish *why* Jesus was uninvolved
politically. Because Jesus and the apostles did not do something
is no reason in itself that others should not do it. Whether we
are to follow their example in this depends on the reasons for
their abstinence. If those reasons apply to us today, we also
should refrain from involvement. If they do not apply, we are
free to implement the principles of Scripture in our
contemporary situation as best we can. Scripture does not tell us
why, unlike the Old Testament, there was no social action, so
we must deduce what answer we may from the evidence
available.

*Vertical relationships and the eternal dimension take priority over
horizontal relations and the temporal dimension.* To reconcile man
to man and to heal man's environment are only temporary. Even
the reconciliation of man to man on a wide scale or a permanent

[14]*The Other Side,* October 1978, 15.
[15]Jacques Ellul, *The Ethics of Freedom,* trans. Geoffrey W. Bromiley (Grand Rapids:
Eerdmans, 1976), 371ff.

basis would be less important than reconciling man to God and preparing him for his eternal home. The New Testament gave priority to this reality.

Principles are more powerful than specific corrective action. Principles are permanent and universal, applying in any culture, age, or society. If specific action had been taught, it might not apply in other situations. For example, the principles of justice and of love are major themes of Scripture; they apply in any generation in any society. Richard N. Longenecker makes the point that the principles taught in the New Testament were subversive to prevailing unjust social arrangements and ultimately brought them down.

When first-century Christians spoke of being "sons of God," "baptized into Christ," and having "put on Christ" (Gal. 3:26-27), they also spoke of their faith in terms of a new relationship socially in which there is "neither Jew nor Greek, there is neither slave nor free, there is neither male nor female" (3:28)—three pairings which cover in embryonic fashion all the essential relationships of humanity.[16]

A new human raw material is necessary to build a new society. Man will never get to the moon on a bicycle, and he will never build a skyscraper with wooden beams and pegs. A new mode of transportation, a new building material is necessary. Of course, a new kind of human being will not *guarantee* a new society. It will only make it possible. The invention of steel and concrete will not guarantee that someone will build a skyscraper, but it will make it possible.

Christ and Paul had specific vocations. Christ was sent to provide redemption and not, at his first coming, to work out all the social implications of that redemption. Satan tempted him to address the political issue first, but this would have subverted the mission. In the same way, Paul had the specific commission to evangelize the Gentiles, not to reform the Roman Empire. Christ did not evangelize the Roman Empire—the attempt to evangelize prior to his provision of the evangel would have subverted the whole plan. In the same way, Paul had a unique commission, but it did not include evangelizing China. Nor ruling the Roman Empire. Those tasks would be assigned other

[16]Richard Longenecker, *New Testament Social Ethics for Today* (Grand Rapids: Eerdmans, 1984), 33-34.

people in other times. But merely because these other roles were not theirs does not mean they are illegitimate for others.

The condition of state and church differed from today. Even if the specific roles of Jesus and Paul were not for political action, it is conceivable that others in the early church might have participated in public life except for the fact that believers formed a very small minority in a strong dictatorship. Successful political action had already proved impossible through the various Jewish militant sects. Of course, God could intervene and make it possible, but Jesus deliberately said no to that option. The time for celestial military intervention and establishing an earthly government had not yet come. The situation today in free nations is radically different from the apostolic era. In fact, in a democracy, the citizens are responsible for the affairs of state; to neglect this public responsibility would be equivalent, in a lesser way, to the neglect of justice and mercy on the part of a Christian king or government official.

For these reasons, and perhaps others, most evangelicals have not accepted the New Testament example as a mandated model for Christians of all time to follow, but they have concluded that both the Christian citizen and the church officially should actively exercise a moral influence on public life.

Let us outline the broad parameters of a mutually influential relationship between state and church. The state is responsible to protect all its citizens, by force if necessary, and to promote the common good. The church also is responsible to promote the common good, but only through spiritual means such as evangelism, teaching, and benevolence. It has a primary responsibility for the behavior of its own members and only through its powers of persuasion for the behavior of others. Therefore the state (1) should not use its power to restrict the church from fulfilling its mission and (2) should listen carefully to the voice of the church when it speaks to moral issues. The church for its part (1) should not demand special privileges that encroach on the rights of others and (2) should carefully refrain from compromise in order to secure benefits from the state, or idolizing the state by treating the prevailing culture as some form of "civil religion."

The term "civil religion" seems to have acquired its present nuance through the classic article by Robert N. Bellah on "Civil Religion in America,"[17] but there is little common agreement on what it means and what kind of "civil religion" is good or bad. For example, Bellah and a number of other authorities wrote chapters in *American Civil Religion* with at least five different categories of definitions identified by the editors: (1) folk religion, (2) the transcendent universal religion of the nation, (3) religious nationalism, (4) the democratic faith, and (5) Protestant civic piety.[18] These do not exhaust all the potential uses!

The former editor of *Christianity Today,* Kenneth Kantzer, speaks in favor of one type of "civil religion:"

It is the style to decry American civil religion as blatant idolatry—American Shinto. For my part, I thank God for it. But since that phrase now has so many definitions, we should clarify our meaning: When I speak of "civil religion," I mean "political and social convictions," or "political value systems," or "political philosophy," or Walter Lippmann's "public philosophy."

More technically, I follow many sociologists who accept Emile Durkheim's definition of civil religion as those convictions and practices that determine the consciences and conduct of a people in terms of politics and general social structures. Some do not call that "civil religion."

In this sense, civil religion is the cement that holds a nation together. It is indispensable for the nation's existence, and its nature determines the nation's character. . . .

American civil religion is, of course, amorphous. Its tenets and practices are constantly changing. However, certain basic convictions have characterized it since its founding days: government exists for the good of the citizens. Its duty is to seek their welfare, protect them, reward the innocent, and punish the guilty. Its ethical code is roughly comparable to the second table of the Decalogue, prohibiting stealing, adultery, murder, and false witness.[19]

This viewpoint has generally characterized the post-World War II evangelical movement. In fact, that was a major distinguishing mark that set "evangelicals" apart from "fundamentalists." "Fundamentalists" in the 1950s and 1960s often advocated noninvolvement in "politics" in reaction to the social and political activism of mainline churchmen and the National Council of Churches. Many "evangelicals" during those decades sought to distance themselves from fundamentalists on this issue, advocating social involvement and

[17]*Daedalus,* Winter 1967.
[18]Russell E. Richey and Donald G. Jones, eds. (New York: Harper and Row, 1974).
[19]Kenneth Kantzer, *Christianity Today,* 13 July 1984, 14.

political action. But toward the end of the 1970s, with the general political climate shifting to the right, many fundamentalists like Jerry Falwell and his Moral Majority (later Liberty Federation) became socially and politically active. The agenda of causes engaged was radically different from that of the older liberal establishment and from many of the new evangelicals whose agenda was virtually identical with the older mainline church interests. But the desire to change society as a whole and the political instrument to effect that change were identical for mainline liberals, evangelicals, and some fundamentalists.

An early leader in the evangelical movement toward social activism, Vernon Grounds, states why political action is necessary:

(1) regenerate people are often lazy; (2) a bad social structure can keep good people from doing good; (3) a good social structure can keep bad people from doing bad; and (4) today's social problems are so large and confusing that private charity is often ineffective.[20]

The chief spokesman of evangelical activism for many years, Carl F. H. Henry, summarizes a moderate position on the role of the church:

Evangelicals face the social predicament today with four controlling convictions:

1. The Christian church's distinctive dynamic for social transformation is personal regeneration by the Holy Spirit, and the proclamation of this divine offer of redemption is the church's prime task. . . .
2. While the corporate or institutional church has no divine mandate, jurisdiction, or special competence for approving legislative proposals or political parties and persons, the pulpit is responsible for proclaiming divinely revealed principles of social justice as a part of the whole counsel of God.
3. The most natural transition from private to social action occurs in the world of daily work, in view of the Christian's need to consecrate his labor to the glory of God and to the service of mankind.
4. As citizens of two worlds, individual church members have the sacred duty to extend God's purpose of redemption through the church, and also to extend God's purpose of justice and order through civil government. Christians are to distinguish themselves by civil obedience, except where this conflicts with the commandments of God, and are to use every political

[20]Vernon Grounds, *Evangelicalism and Social Responsibility* (Scottdale, Pa.: Herald, 1969), 28-30.

opportunity to support and promote just laws, to protest social injustice, and to serve their fellowmen. [21]

This general approach was officially endorsed by more than three thousand evangelical church leaders who signed the Lausanne Covenant in July 1974:

We affirm that God is both the Creator and the Judge of all men. We therefore should share his concern for justice and reconciliation throughout human society and for the liberation of men from every kind of oppression. Because mankind is made in the image of God, every person, regardless of race, religion, color, culture, class, sex, or age, has an intrinsic dignity because of which he should be respected and served, not exploited. Here too we express penitence both for our neglect and for having sometimes regarded evangelism and social concern as mutually exclusive. Although reconciliation with man is not reconciliation with God, nor is social action evangelism, nor is political liberation salvation, nevertheless we affirm that evangelism and sociopolitical involvement are both part of our Christian duty. For both are necessary expressions of our doctrines of God and man, our love for our neighbor and our obedience to Jesus Christ.[22]

Though there is a certain appeal in the third option (a clean-cut division and isolation of the two spheres), the evidence so far seems to be that such a relationship is neither possible nor desirable. Two traditions advocate this position, but from opposite viewpoints. The Anabaptist separation of church and state might prove workable and could have some benefits, especially where Christians are a persecuted minority; but the pervasive drive of the antireligious secularists to reject every vestige of religious influence in public life was seen for what it is—the substitution of one set of values for another.

The coloration of public policy by the values of the citizenry, whether religiously inspired or antireligiously inspired, is inevitable. Therefore, to establish secular humanistic values as if the state could thus be neutral or religiously aseptic is a fundamental hypocrisy. Public policy is inevitably influenced by some ethical ideology. And the faith commitment to a relativistic, nonjudgmental approach to ethics is at least pseudo-religious in nature and has already fed back into the private lives of citizens the virus of a self-serving, individual autonomy that

[21]Carl F. H. Henry, "Evangelicals and the Social Struggle," *Christianity Today,* 8 October 1965, 11.

[22]J. D. Douglas, ed., *Let the Earth Hear His Voice* (Minneapolis: World Wide Publications, 1975), 4-5.

has in it the seeds of destruction. In a world free of any moral "ought" each person becomes his own standard for what is good (for him), and both public and private life tend increasingly toward might-makes-right relationships.

Therefore, we conclude that the best arrangement is a benevolent cooperation between church and state in which the state is frankly open to religiously-inspired moral influences and the church does not seek special privileges and confines its moral pronouncements to moral issues.

THE ROLE OF THE CHURCH

All would agree that the church as the church must clearly proclaim the principles of justice and mercy. Furthermore, most would agree that it is imperative for the church either directly or through its representatives to organize medical care, social care, financial care, involvement in education, correcting poverty, and all other "works of mercy." Thus the church influences society. But what of political action?

Primary Spiritual Role. The church must ever keep its primary responsibility toward the world as one of evangelism, bringing men out of the kingdom of darkness into the kingdom of light. Furthermore, its primary responsibility toward its own is building new men. For this reason, social action must be secondary. If the church does not evangelize and disciple, no amount of political activity will improve society very much and, more important, the basic business of populating heaven for eternity will go undone.

In seeking justice and mercy, the primary responsibility of the church is creating a climate, making new citizens and new leaders. To do this, the church must speak to its own. It must build Christians who are *committed, courageous, filled by the Spirit, and informed,* both of biblical truth and of the issues that harass the sinful, troubled community in which they live.

If the church does not follow Christ's example, concentrating on saving men, spiritual nurture, teaching eternal principles, and directly alleviating the suffering of men, it will run the risk of missing its basic purpose for existence. Furthermore, it will undermine its authority for proclaiming the eternal message, especially if it gives social or political answers that prove wrong. A credibility gap develops and the lack of confidence in the church shifts back to lack of confidence in the Bible and ultimately to God. As C. S. Lewis has said,

This raises the question of theology in politics. The nearest I can get to a settlement of the frontier problem between them is this: that theology teaches us what ends are desirable and what means are lawful, while politics teaches what means are effective. Thus theology tells us that every man ought to have a decent wage. Politics tells us by what means this is likely to be obtained. Theology tells us which of these means are consistent with justice and charity. On the political question, guidance comes not from revelation, but from natural prudence, knowledge of complicated facts, and ripe experience. If we have these qualifications we may, of course, state our opinions: but then we must make it quite clear that we are giving our personal judgment and have no command from the Lord. Not many priests have these qualifications. Most political sermons teach the congregation nothing except what newspapers are taken at the Rectory.[23]

Not only does the church lack biblical authority and thus special competence to speak to the pragmatics of implementation, it is not certain that the church will advocate the right cause when questions of justice and morality are camouflaged in the complexities of political realities.

The German church of the 1930s is sometimes cited as an example of the dire results of political inaction. "If only the German church had opposed Hitler instead of remaining quiet," the argument runs, "how much better the world would have been." It is a compelling argument, but it has two flaws. First, it assumes that if the German church had been politically active, it would have opposed the Nazi movement. That is an enormous assumption. Churches have often in good conscience supported evil political movements. The czars were supported by a church. Their Communist successors receive the same support from the successors to that church.[24]

In the light of these many serious and abiding ambiguities I conclude that the church should concentrate on its primary mission modeled by Jesus and the apostles and clearly taught in the New Testament. But, as we have earlier argued, the church does have an obligation to its community as "salt" and "light." How should it discharge that responsibility?

[23]C. S. Lewis, *God in the Dock,* ed. Walter Hooper (Grand Rapids: Eerdmans, 1970), 94.
[24]Malcolm T. Nygren, "The Church and Political Action," *Christianity Today,* 14 March 1969, 10.

Prophetic Ministry to Society

Address Specific Issues. Should the church speak to such issues *only in generalities* or should it speak *specifically?* It certainly has the right to speak specifically. John the Baptist did not address Herod with the general principle that "adultery is wrong." He said, "It is not lawful for *you* to have *her*."

Address Means as Well as Ends. May the church address its message to *goals* only, or may it speak of *means* also? The church should speak of ultimate goals (e.g., the abolition of slavery) and also to means, political implementation (do not free slaves by shooting slaveholders). The church should not speak to the pragmatics of the means in which it has no special competence, but it does have the responsibility to judge the justice and mercy of means as well as ends.

When the Church Errs. What if the church says the wrong thing? It has certainly done so in theology, and we do not solve the problem by saying the church should not interpret the Bible. The church often errs in evangelistic practices, but we do not cease engaging in evangelism. We simply say, "That interpretation is wrong, and the churchmen who make it do not represent me."

For example, I would speak out in favor of Sunday closing laws, while other churchmen would speak out against them. And the mystery of it is that I might be right morally and wrong politically. But this is the risk one runs.

For maximum effectiveness the church should limit its social action agenda to causes that are clearly biblical mandates. The problem with so much of both the religious left and the religious right agendas is that they are often a carbon-copy of non-Christian society, whether the change-agent elite on the left or the traditional culture-captive on the right. This means that nonbiblical items are included on both agendas, and thus the moral force of whatever biblical mandates may be on the agendas is greatly reduced. Does defense build-up or the ownership of the Panama Canal really have the same clear biblical mandate as the sanctity of the home or the right to life? Far better to limit our agenda so that we establish battle lines on clear biblical mandates.

This will not only give us God's own authority in the battle for truth, it will go far toward bringing believers together for a united impact. A graphic illustration of this truth was seen in the experience of Evangelicals for Social Action. The Thanksgiving meeting in 1973 brought together a broad spectrum of evangelical leaders who united in writing "The Chicago Declaration of Evangelical Concern." But the unity was soon dissipated and the promising movement quickly failed of its potential because the agenda got too long with too many disputed specifics so that the hoped-for powerful, united voice for justice and mercy faded to the weak, if strident, voice of a band of loyalists who insisted on an extensive leftward-leaning agenda dealing with political means as well as moral ends.

Official Voice of the Church. May the church make *official pronouncements,* or is this prophetic ministry limited to the preacher speaking in private as a citizen? If Billy Graham speaks on a social issue, such as nuclear disarmament, it will have more of an impact as "the voice of the church" than almost any major church council resolution. When any Christian speaks, he is the voice of the church to the people who accept him as a responsible spokesman of Christianity. The clergyman in the pulpit, the layman on the street, the church body in council or the mother with her children—they are "the voice of the church" to those who look to them for spiritual guidance.

The Christian *citizen* should provide the primary fighting force for justice and mercy, and the *church,* through its leaders, should avoid partisan politics and work hard at creating truly Christian citizens and speaking prophetically to clearly biblical moral issues.

Legislated Morals. Can morals be legislated? The idea that morals cannot be legislated is usually based on a cultural or ethical relativism which teaches that moral behavior depends entirely on the culture and that nothing is right or wrong for all cultures at all times. This is a difficult position to follow consistently because the culture of the Mafia must be granted legitimacy just as much as the Supreme Court.

The truth of the matter is that "it is no more possible to define a sphere of private morality than it is to define one of private subversive activities."[25] Consequently, there are no theoretical limits to the extent to which the law may move against immorality. The truth is that most legislation is based on morality. If morality cannot be legislated, nothing can be.

Most sensible people would agree with this in general, though there would be sharp disagreement as to which are private morals and which are public. Drinking alcoholic beverages has been considered private for some decades. But is it truly private? Who pays the bills for the results of drinking alcohol? Who loses life in an automobile accident? Who lives in a society that condones and fosters consumption? Who raises children in such a society? The same might be said of any moral issue.

If the government is representative or democratic, it cannot but reflect the judgment of the society as to what moral standards should be required of all its citizens. If such a society legislates morals that are not acceptable to the majority, or even to a large minority of its citizens, the law becomes unenforceable. It is a bad law because it promotes lawlessness. Therefore, if a Christian is interested in having morals legislated, he must not only ask what is right and what is good for society, he must also ask, What will this society accept? Of course, he may fight for a losing cause on principle. But if he actually intends to impose a minority standard on the majority, he should understand that the legal fabric would be weakened, and in the end much more than the specific moral issue would be lost.

THE ROLE OF THE INDIVIDUAL CHRISTIAN

Order of Priorities in Social Responsibilities. Following the example of Christ, the Christian should order his priorities with primary concern for the reconciling of people with God and the eternal dimensions of life while at the same time maintaining a deep concern and involvement in relationships among people and their physical and material needs.

[25]Sir Patrick Devlin, quoted by Burton M. Leiser in *Liberty, Justice, and Morals: Contemporary Value Conflicts* (New York: Macmillan, 1973), 13.

Responsibility for Self. As a foundation for social good, the Christian is responsible to provide for himself (1 Thess. 4:11-12; 2 Thess. 3:10).

Responsibility for Family. Furthermore, he has a primary responsibility for his own family (1 Tim. 5:8). The entire fifth chapter of 1 Timothy deals with one's responsibility to provide for his family. In connection with this the Bible clearly outlines the responsibility of parents in the training of their children (Deut. 4:9-10; 11:18-19; Prov. 13:24; 22:15; 23:13-14; Eph. 6:1-4). Here is the foundation for a society under the reign of God.

Responsibility for Fellow Christians. The believer's next responsibility is for fellow believers. "As we have opportunity, let us do good to all men, and especially to those who are of the household of faith" (Gal. 6:10). Large portions of 1 John emphasize the loving responsibility a Christian has for his fellow believers' physical welfare.

Responsibility for Neighbors. Finally, the Christian has responsibility for his neighbor—all those outside the immediate responsibility of human and divine family who, in some way, bring responsibility through relationship as "neighbor."

Responsibility toward Society. The Christian's responsibilities for his society are especially clear in a democratic society in which the Christian citizen is part of the governing body—the people.

1. The Christian is responsible to honor those in authority and to *pray* for them (Rom. 13; 1 Tim. 2:2).

2. The Christian is responsible to *obey* the civil laws and authority (Rom. 13:1-10).

3. The Christian is responsible to *pay taxes* (Rom. 13:6).

4. The Christian is responsible to *practice justice and mercy,* dealing justly with employees, working to relieve the poor, the minorities (aliens), the oppressed, the weak (widows, orphans). Perhaps the strongest passage of all is Matthew 25:31-46, where we are told in advance the basis of judgment on the Last Day: we shall be judged on the basis of whether we have fed the

hungry, given drink to the thirsty, lodged the homeless, clothed the naked, and cared for the sick and imprisoned.

There are other guidelines that seem consonant with the principles of Scripture, though they cannot be held to be the clearly revealed will of God.

5. In order to fulfill our responsibility in seeking justice and mercy, the Christian should *study the Scriptures* to determine God's view on any specific issue that arises. The Word of God must be our controlling authority.

6. The Christian must *study the needs* of the community—drugs, crime, slums, poverty, migrants, pornography, racism, family life, unemployment, housing, disease, unfair tax policy, discrimination, political corruption. What are the specific facts? What should we do about these problems? When do we begin, and how? Since I cannot personally bear all the burdens of the world, to what specific areas of need would God be pleased for me to give my attention?

7. *Vote.* The Christian in a democracy abdicates his responsibility for seeking a just and merciful society when he deliberately fails to vote. But does a single vote make any difference? Whether or not it makes a difference, a Christian ought to be involved. However, the truth is that it does make a difference.

In the fall of 1842, Madison Marsh was elected to the State Legislature of Indiana by a margin of one vote. One who voted for him was Henry Shoemacher who rode horseback twelve miles to the voting place. This legislator had the responsibility of choosing a United States senator. Edward A. Hannegan was chosen by a majority of one, and Marsh was one who voted for him. In 1846, trouble erupted between the United States and Mexico. War was declared by a majority of one, the vote of Senator Hannegan. The American forces won the war which resulted in bringing into the Union the Southwest Territory which was to become Texas, California, Idaho, and Oregon. One vote makes a difference![26]

8. The Christian should *voice what he believes* in personal conversation, letters, articles, sermons and letters to the editor as opportunity affords.

9. The Christian may *work in behalf of candidates* in whom he has confidence, working for the election of candidates or to

[26]*The Presbyterian Journal*, 27 January 1971, 11.

influence legislation through correspondence, petitions, and in every way possible.

10. Sometimes it may be appropriate for the Christian to engage in *nonviolent dissent* such as in sit-ins and marches.

11. *Legal action* in behalf of a just cause is one of the most potent instruments for social change in a society whose public and private values are increasingly being set by judicial order rather than legislative or executive action.

12. *Special Vocation*. Some Christians may be called to professional service in correcting physical and temporal ills. Those engaged in medicine, social work, or politics may be sent of God just as surely as those called to carpentry or the pastorate. It is certainly appropriate for a Christian to run for office.

Furthermore, vocational choice and financial investment have historically been means by which Christians have influenced society. For example, the architect for most of the buildings at Columbia Bible College and Seminary eventually left the field of general architecture and chose to devote the balance of his life to hospital work. He did this deliberately with the vision of combating the high cost of medicine by implementing creative and innovative ideas in lowering the cost of building hospitals. He felt that the high cost of medicine was oppressive to the poor and to society in general.

The Christian who sits by in silence as evil prevails, excusing himself as responsible only for more important "spiritual" matters, must give an account for his disobedience to the words of King Lemuel:

Speak up for those who cannot speak for themselves, for the rights of all who are destitute. Speak up and judge fairly; defend the rights of the poor and needy. (Prov. 31:8-9, NIV)

THE ROLE OF GOVERNMENT

The strongest evidence for human government being an institution ordained of God is found in the New Testament rather than in the Old. To be sure, Israel was established as a human government, and the prophets certainly hold all human governments accountable to God's Law, but it takes some strong imagination to make Genesis 9:1-6, for example, evidence of God's establishing human government in the abstract or in some particular form. But human government as a divine ordinance is clearly affirmed in Scripture:

> Let every person be subject to the governing authorities. For there is no authority except from God, and those that exist have been instituted by God. (Rom. 13:1)

PURPOSES OF GOVERNMENT

Restraining Evil. According to the most extensive passage on government (Rom. 13), the purpose of human government is to restrain evil, especially in protecting the citizens. Human sin created the acute need for coercive civil government.

Most people have preferred human government to none, but since rulers have seldom been content with the minimum authority necessary to protect the rights of the citizenry, government has tended to expand to increasingly control the lives of citizens. For this reason some have held that no government was preferable. Those who oppose the idea of human government on ideological grounds are concerned with liberty. But desirable as total liberty may seem to be, in a society made up of sin-prone, selfish people, coercion seems the only way to keep some people from harming others.

Promoting Human Welfare. A minimal amount of government could conceivably achieve that protection, but when the purpose of "promoting the welfare" is introduced, the potential for expanding government seems limitless. For this reason some hold that the only legitimate role of government is to protect citizens from injustice, especially since this is the only role ascribed to government in the classic passages, Romans 13 and 1 Peter 2. But the only government superintended directly by God—ancient Israel—certainly established law for the promotion of the welfare of the citizens.

Furthermore, the biblical principle of neighbor-love would seem to demand such activity, especially in the twentieth century with states too large and complex for private charity adequately to meet human need. Nevertheless, the primary purpose remains the role of guaranteeing justice, protecting people from malicious harm. Most contemporaries value freedom of personal choice so highly that any governmental restrictions beyond the minimal needed for protection of human rights is resisted in situations where resistance is a viable option.

When government expands, either to control evil or to promote human welfare, it does so at the expense of human freedom.

Providing Freedom. The Bible has much to say about freedom, but not about *political* freedom. It speaks of freedom from sin (Rom. 6:14-23); from the power of darkness (Col. 1:13); from bondage to Satan (John 12:30-33); from the Mosaic law (Rom. 7:6; Gal. 2:4; 4:5, 21; 5:1); and from bondage to death (Rom. 8:21-23). There is a glorious freedom in Christ (John 8:32, 36); for where the Spirit of the Lord is, there is freedom (2 Cor. 3:17). Biblical freedom is spiritual, not a general, absolute, abstract, philosophical concept, but freedom from something very specific: freedom from sin.

No one is free in any ultimate sense, then. He may be free, for the time being, from the authority of God's Law, but this means he is a slave of sin. On the other hand, if Christ has set him free from the penalty and authority of sin, this is only because he has chosen to put himself completely under the authority of Christ. Every person's freedom to do what he pleases is drastically limited by his finitude, his sin, and the circumstances of life that are beyond his control. So freedom is relative. When we speak of freedom or liberty we should always define it, qualify it: what sort of freedom? Freedom from what?

Spiritual freedom, for example, is not license to do what I please, but ability to do what I ought. In the political realm, also, liberty is not an absolute, God-ordained right. Freedom cannot be absolute, for my freedom to do as I please will sooner or later run into your freedom to do as you please. No two people could possibly have absolute freedom simultaneously unless they perfectly willed the other's good, and that, in a fallen world, is not a possibility.

If by "freedom of choice" we mean that people should be allowed to use their free will to make either an ethical or an unethical decision, without suffering for choosing unethically, we are engaged in an absurdity that, if carried to its logical conclusion, would put an end to public law.[27]

Nevertheless, we advocate personal freedom of choice to the extent possible in a just society. Though the Bible is not strong in emphasizing it, when God himself intervenes in human affairs, it is to set the captives free from Egyptian bondage, and, indeed, through the Messiah to break the bonds of all injustice and set the captives free (Isa. 61:1; Luke 4:18).

If the case for political freedom is not strong in explicit biblical teaching, it certainly can be strongly advocated on the basis of the principles of Scripture. For example, the Bible teaches clearly that a person's first responsibility is to God, yet in feudalistic or totalitarian society one's freedom is restricted to such an extent that he cannot follow his conscience in fulfilling that responsibility. Furthermore, God created each individual on purpose and a measure of freedom is necessary to fulfill that purpose. Political freedom enables a citizen to discharge his primary responsibility in life, which is to God, not the state.

Another principle has to do with the worth of the individual made in the image of the infinitely free God. When human freedom is needlessly diminished by governmental controls, not merely the individual but the very image of God in humankind is demeaned. The state has no divine right of ownership.

Perhaps the strongest reason for advocating maximum political freedom is the nature of man. Man is a sinner and this includes all human authorities. In such a sin-filled society a check is needed so that human authorities do not misuse that authority for personal or partisan benefit or begin to arrogate to themselves godlike prerogatives of unbounded authority. Therefore, governmental authority must have limits.

FORMS OF GOVERNMENT

There are two basic ways to organize people: (1) autocratic (monarchy—rule by one, and oligarchy—rule by a few) and (2) democratic (including representative forms of government by the people, such as a republic). Though the Christian can live under any form of government, and though the ideal form

[27]Harold O. J. Brown, "The Passivity of American Christians," *Christianity Today,* 16 January 1976, 8.

would be a monarchy with an infinitely wise and loving God as the monarch, it would be difficult to demonstrate from Scripture that any particular form of human government is absolutely and always right.

It is said that, toward the close of the twentieth century, there are not more than a dozen truly free democracies and that more than two hundred nation-states are autocracies, whether a dictatorship, a feudalistic regime, or the oligarchy of communist party leadership. The estimate may be exaggerated, but the ineluctable fact is that the vast majority of people in this "enlightened" era, like those of all past eras, live under governments that severely restrict personal freedom. Therefore, most Christians must come to terms with this reality. How helpful that the biblical authors lived under just such circumstances!

Because of man's sinfulness, when power is concentrated in the hands of one person or small group, the potential for evil is incalculable. Thus totalitarian regimes—whether to the right in capitalistic dictatorships or to the left in communistic oligarchies—have consistently proved evil for their unhappy subjects. Therefore, I advocate the concept of a constitutional democracy or a republic in which private rights and the limits of freedom are not subject to the will of those in authority. This seems to hold the best set of checks and balances for the vexing problem of the relationship between liberty and authority. Both government and citizens are subject to constitutional law. The liberty of the people is thus limited by governmental authority, and government is limited by the free consent of those governed.

This does not mean democracy is flawless. It must be admitted that the same sinfulness may well mean that democracy in the long term is doomed to self-destruction. Alexander Fraser Tytler, historian, jurist, and Judge Advocate of Scotland, said as much in critiquing the ancient Greek experiment in democracy:

A democracy cannot exist as a permanent form of government. It can exist only until the voters discover they can vote themselves out of the public treasury with the result that democracy always collapses over a loose fiscal policy, always to be followed by a dictatorship.[28]

[28]*The State* (Columbia, S.C.), 1 June 1974.

Judge Tytler spoke just prior to the founding of the American experiment in democracy. Did he speak prophetically? In the interest of freedom, I am prepared to run the risk. If the leaven of biblical impulses toward justice, fairness, and mercy can continue to influence public policy debate, perhaps the sinful selfishness of the people who vote can be held in check. And if those same people will awaken from an apathy induced by security (a stronger human desire, by the way, than the desire for freedom), perhaps the inherent drive toward the expansion of governmental power also can be held in check, at least for a time.

GOVERNMENTAL SOCIAL ACTION IN A FREE SOCIETY

There is probably a universal consensus that government ought to protect its citizens from injustice, but that unanimity dissolves when the power of government is expanded to guarantee the welfare of all its citizens. All true Christians would agree that both they as individuals and the church should actively participate in alleviating human suffering. We would even agree, in theory at least, that the church should guarantee the welfare of its members, though, sad to say, for the most part, the church has abdicated this responsibility to the government. But will private initiative ever prove adequate to meeting human need commensurate with the total resources available?

Most modern societies have concluded that private initiative cannot or will not suffice to meet human needs, that government alone can adequately meet the needs of all its people and should attempt to do so. This is the official stance of virtually all governments, whether autocratic or democratic. A vocal minority of the affluent object to this philosophy, some on the grounds that the Bible does not mandate this role for government, others that it is not working and cannot work. But, for the time being at least, opposition to government involvement in welfare schemes appears to be a futile rear-guard action attempting to protect the advantages of the privileged. Be that as it may, if one accepts any government role in promoting human welfare, what are the legitimate means of accomplishing this in a free society?

The means for bringing about social change through

government action in a democracy are available through all three branches of government.

Executive Branch. The chief means of influencing government through the administrative branches at the federal, state, and local levels is through the elective process. Lobbying for a candidate committed to the action one feels important has a direct effect through the elected executives themselves and an indirect effect on the agencies under their administration.

Some object when the lobbyist concentrates on a single issue, but this is usually a hypocritical objection, since bringing to bear the force of everyone interested in a particular issue is what lobbying is all about. Single-issue politics is what brought about emancipation in the last century and civil rights legislation in this.

Some issues are doubtless more worthy of such concentration than others. Whether one issue is important enough to blot out consideration of all others must be left to the judgment of the advocate of that position. It may be unwise to vote for a candidate because of the single issue, since the person elected may pursue all manner of undesirable objectives along with the single desirable objective one is concerned about. But it can hardly be held morally evil or undemocratic to make one's choice based on a single, paramount consideration. Fortunately, most issues tend to cluster, so the electorate is usually satisfied with the "package."

Legislative Branch. A second means of influencing government is through the legislative branch. The same electoral process indicated in the case of the executive branch of government is the first line of attack on the status quo or the first bulwark for the status quo. But the lobbying effort only begins with the election. Those same efforts must be maintained to influence those in office to enact particular laws because electing the "right" legislator may not assure that he will vote "right"!

Judicial Branch. The third recourse is to take legal initiative through the courts. The objective should be to pursue legal justice, not moral justice. The pursuit of moral justice should be through legislation.

Though the courts may deliberately induce social change through reinterpretation of the law, it does not seem to me worthy of the Christian to seek such legal action. Not all Christian attorneys agree with this position. For example, the *Quarterly* of the Christian Legal Society eulogizes Lord Denning as an example of the ideal Christian advocate and judge.

> Denning's refusal to apply laws which he regards as outmoded and unjust has been unremitting and relentless. . . ."We do not now in this court stick to the letter of the statute. We go by its true intent. We *fill in the gaps.*"[29]

Historically, the judiciary was never intended to function in such a law-making role. By functioning in this way, socially activistic courts usurp the authority of the legislative branch and destabilize the balance of powers among the three branches of government.

Since the entire structure of government is man-made, perhaps it is not possible to settle the matter on biblical grounds, except to insist that public officials act honestly and within the bounds of constitutional authority.

Take a practical example. If a government agency promulgates a policy that takes away the liberty of a Christian school to employ only people with certain beliefs and life-style (insisting, for example, that a lesbian agnostic be employed as secretary to the dean), the school and all other defenders of liberty should appeal first to the government executives responsible. If this is not successful, legal action can be taken to seek protection from the courts. Should the courts concur with the regulations of the agency, the only recourse left is to seek legislation to restore the specific freedom that should have been guaranteed by the general principles of the Constitution.

Although it is not appropriate for government officials to transfer biblical standards wholesale into the prosecution of their responsibilities in a pluralistic society, the Christian executive, legislator, judge, or other government official can certainly gain insight from Scripture on the thinking of the chief Law-giver and Judge.

[29]Spring 1981, 6-7.

OPPOSITION TO GOVERNMENT

How does a Christian relate to authority in his dual role as citizen of heaven and of some nation-state here on earth? Some have held that he is a true citizen only of heaven and that he should separate himself as much as possible from involvement in the earthly state. On the other hand, most church traditions have held that the better one practices his heavenly citizenship, the better citizen he will be on earth. Both those who believe in isolation and those who believe in involvement teach that the normal response of the Christian toward civil authority is obedience.

SUBMISSION

Everyone must submit himself to the governing authorities, for there is no authority except that which God has established. The authorities that exist have been established by God. Consequently, he who rebels against the authority is rebelling against what God has instituted, and those who do so will bring judgment on themselves. For rulers hold no terror for those who do right, but for those who do wrong. Do you want to be free from fear of the one in authority? Then do what is right and he will commend you. For he is God's servant to do you good. But if you do wrong, be afraid, for he does not bear the sword for nothing. He is God's servant, an agent of wrath to bring punishment on the wrongdoer. Therefore, it is necessary to submit to the authorities, not only because of possible punishment but also because of conscience. (Rom. 13:1-5, NIV)

Submit yourselves for the Lord's sake to every authority instituted among men: whether to the king, as the supreme authority, or to governors, who are sent by him to punish those who do wrong and to commend those who do right. (1 Pet. 2:13-14, NIV)

MANDATED DISOBEDIENCE

The commands to obey civil authority are clear, but is it ever right to resist civil authority? Not only *may* a Christian resist, he *must* resist when any authority demands disobedience to God. "We must obey God rather than men" (Acts 5:28-29; see also Acts 4:17-20). The Supreme Court said not to speak in this Name. Christ told his disciples to proclaim the good news to every person. The issue was clearly drawn. The German government said to apprehend and execute innocent Jews. The Christian SS guard or common citizen must obey God rather than men and protect the innocent. These actions are not choosing the lesser of two evils. Obedience to the state when commanded to sin is in itself sinful; disobedience to the state in this case is a moral good. Daniel did well to defy the king's orders to stop praying and his friends to refuse to worship the image. Jochebed and the Egyptian midwives are commended for disobeying an evil law.

But what if the forbidden activity is good and under other circumstances might be justified as the will of God, but there is no biblical mandate? Japanese law gives almost total freedom for propagating the gospel. But distributing literature on public conveyances is against the law. Must the Christian missionary insist on this particular form of evangelism? Can he claim a mandate from God to do so? Does God command the believer to smuggle Bibles into countries where there is restriction on Bible production or distribution? My conclusion is that good activity, when not mandated by Scripture, may sometimes be justifiable but is not required. Personal guidance may be claimed, but such guidance does not have clear biblical authority and should be resorted to with caution. Prudence must be used since the activity may not be necessary for obedience to God and may jeopardize other more important values, such as freedom to witness in other ways. Furthermore, the lawbreaker must be prepared to suffer the consequences. Paul said, "If then I am a wrongdoer, and have committed anything for which I deserve to die, I do not seek to escape death" (Acts 25:11).

Thus, when commanded to disobey the revealed will of God, the Christian *must* disobey the human command; when forbidden to do something good that is not mandated by Scripture, the Christian *may*, under some circumstances, disobey the human command.

CIVIL DISOBEDIENCE

But what of resistance when the government does not make demands on the believer concerning his religion or moral behavior, but itself does wrong? It should be remembered that when Paul instructed the believers in Rome to obey the government, he was not speaking of a just and benevolent government. Caligula and Nero were two of the most depraved madmen ever to exercise despotic rule over people. And the Christians themselves were the object of their vitriolic hatred.

Yet Paul said, "Submit." These evil Roman emperors and their depraved system were the authorities "ordained by God." Jeremiah instructed the captives living in Nebuchadnezzar's Babylon, the epitome of merciless totalitarian regimes, to "seek the welfare of the city where I have sent you into exile, and pray to the LORD on its behalf, for in its welfare you will find your welfare" (Jer. 29:7). This teaching reflects general principles but does not tell us whether there are biblical exceptions. At least they indicate that it is no sin for a believer to submit to an unjust government. Certainly it leaves no room for those in a free society to sit in judgment on a brother or sister living submissively under totalitarian rule.

At the same time, we must note that Rahab of Jericho and the Egyptian midwives, for example, were not submissive—they resisted their own governments. For this resistance they were rewarded by God and enshrined among the biblical heroes of faith. Thus we conclude that sometimes it was not wrong to resist unjust authority.

How do we put the two apparently contradictory concepts together? Ordinarily the believer should be an obedient subject when not required to disobey God, but sometimes it may be God's will to resist an unjust or merciless ordinance or regime. When?

After World War II and the rise of the civil rights and antiwar movements, it seemed that liberal church people advocated civil disobedience in the tradition of Rahab, while conservatives stuck with Jeremiah in advocating law and order.

The increasing advocacy of civil disobedience led to or climaxed in liberation theology on the part of many liberal churchmen.

The theology of liberation came into prominence with the World Conference on Salvation Today held by the World Council of Churches in Bangkok early in 1973. Its message is very simple: salvation is liberation . . . from injustice, from every form of oppression and exploitation, from everything that prevents man from being "truly human." Although the theologians of liberation acknowledge personal sin, they ascribe its existence to oppressive political and social structures; these alone produce and perpetuate it, they say. Guilt is fundamentally social; consequently no liberation from individual sin is possible except through the overthrow of these oppressive structures that make it inevitable.[30]

[30]Rene de visme Williamson, "The Theology of Liberation," *Christianity Today*, 8 August 1975, 7.

At about the same time, a new mood began to develop among fundamentalists and evangelicals. Though the majority continued to advocate law and order as the absolute requirement of Christian citizens, increasing numbers began to be politically involved and to resist governmental authority in various legal and illegal ways. Perhaps the precipitating event was the 1973 Supreme Court decision making abortions legal. By the 1980s the chief difference between liberal and conservative advocates of civil disobedience in the United States was merely which laws should be disobeyed. The most articulate and widely read conservative advocate of civil disobedience was Francis Schaeffer.

> God has ordained the state as a *delegated* authority; it is not autonomous. The state is to be an agent of justice, to restrain evil by punishing the wrongdoer, and to protect the good in society. When it does the reverse, *it has no proper authority*. It is then a usurped authority, and as such, it becomes lawless and is tyranny. . . . It follows from Rutherford's thesis that citizens have a *moral* obligation to resist unjust and tyrannical government. . . . If there is no final place for civil disobedience, then the government has been made autonomous, and as such, it has been put in the place of the Living God.[31]

So advocates of force in resisting unjust or oppressive civil authority range across the entire theological spectrum. The problem is not whether to disobey the government when it demands disobedience to God, but whether the Christian citizen is obligated to force the government itself to stop disobeying God. The question is not whether I must refuse to abort my unborn child, as might be required of a Christian in China, but whether I must force the government to stop subsidizing the abortion of fetuses, and even whether I must force the government to stop everyone from aborting. When do I take up arms against the government—or bombs against abortion clinics?

I do not believe the full range of civil disobedience advocated by Francis Schaeffer can be justified from Scripture. The Apostles Paul and Peter are too clear on the central thesis that subjection to civil authority is normative Christian behavior. Civil disobedience when the citizen is required to sin? Yes.

[31]Francis A. Schaeffer, *A Christian Manifesto* (Westchester, Ill.: Crossway, 1981), 91, 101, 130.

Resistance to human law that violates God's Law? On occasion, yes, in the tradition of the Egyptian midwives. But *required* of the believer as normative behavior? Hardly. And I do not believe Schaeffer means that, though he seems to say so.

RESISTANCE BY FORCE

The next and perhaps most important question is, What method of resistance is biblically acceptable? The case of violating one's conscience when commanded to do wrong is fairly simple: do right. And accept the consequences. But how does one go about correcting the evils in government when *it* does wrong or requires/permits others to do wrong? Is force permissible?

The greatest modern prophet of civil disobedience, Gandhi, said, "Not to cooperate with evil is my duty. And the British rule is evil." But he adamantly refused to use force in his resistance. Against cruel repressive measures by the British, unrelenting pressure from his own colleagues, and in the face of mob violence that he himself had part in igniting, he stood firm, admonishing us that if we follow the doctrine of an eye for an eye, we will make the whole world blind. He repeatedly staked his life on the principle that civil disobedience to injustice is a moral imperative, but violence in its prosecution is wrong. For this stand he gave his life. Resistance, yes, but only passive resistance. Francis Schaeffer disagrees:

Force, as used in this book, means "compulsion" or "constraint" exerted upon a person (or persons) or on an entity such as the state.[32]

The proper use of force is not only the province of the state. Such an assumption is born of naivete. It leaves us without sufficient remedy when and if the state takes on totalitarian dimensions.[33]

Although Schaeffer justifies armed revolution under some circumstances, he advocates strict limitations:

In *Lex Rex* [author Samuel Rutherford] does not propose armed revolution as an automatic solution. Instead, he sets forth the appropriate response to interference by the state in the liberties of the citizenry. Specifically, he stated

[32]Ibid, 106.
[33]Ibid., 107.

that if the state deliberately is committed to destroying its ethical commitment to God, then resistance is appropriate.

In such an instance, *for the private person*, the individual, Rutherford suggested that there are three appropriate levels of resistance: *First*, he must defend himself by protest (in contemporary society this would most often be by legal action); *second*, he must flee if at all possible; and, *third*, he may use force, if necessary, to defend himself. One should not employ force if he may save himself by flight; nor should one employ flight if he can save himself and defend himself by protest and the employment of constitutional means of redress.[34]

He then indicates that corporate resistance would be similar, except that flight is often not practical for a group. Furthermore, if the group itself constitutes a legitimate government, such as a state in a federation or a local community or church, it has the right and obligation to stand against the higher governing body. Schaeffer justifies the American Revolution by attempting to prove that it was initiated as a legitimate government (the colonies) in self-defense against the aggression of an outside power.

Note that Moses followed these three steps in order when leading Israel in its protest against oppression and bondage.

Stages One (protest) and Two (flight) are clearly biblical, but Stage Three introduces physical force (normally called "violence"). To use such force in the cause of the church is clearly unbiblical. In the case of defending the oppressed, passive resistance is more in keeping with the example of our Savior and is less open to abuse. But it should be noted that the successes of Gandhi were possible because his followers protested in the context of humanitarian governments. They would serve as misleading models for those under unscrupulous totalitarian regimes. There the example of the early church would be more realistic: three hundred years of martyrdom as lion fodder and human torches to light the orgies of depraved Roman emperors.

But the question remains, When all nonviolent means have been exhausted in an attempt to seek redress of wrongs, is military force to overthrow an evil regime a channel open to believers? If war itself is ever justifiable, when two governments exist and are in conflict, the Christian may choose the side he feels most just. But in the absence of a second government, such as a revolutionary government, the private citizen, or the

[34]Ibid, 103-104.

church, or any other group of private citizens violate Scripture
in resorting to force.

THE SCHOOLS

STATE SCHOOLS AND VALUES

Though Scripture assigns the responsibility of nurturing
children to parents, society as a whole may have a legitimate
interest in assuring that the rising generation is adequately
equipped for a useful role in the community. There is also the
self-interest of a society in the literacy, skills, and socialization of
its citizens. If the state does not guarantee education for all
children, history would seem to indicate that only the privileged
few will benefit from formal education. So there is also a
humanitarian element in providing free public education for all.

When a society is homogeneous—as, for example, American
society of a century ago and Japanese society today—public
education can easily incorporate commonly held values. But
when a society becomes culturally and religiously diverse, a
common education becomes increasingly fraught with
problems.

Pluralism in the society would seem to demand pluralism in
education. But in post-World War II America the confrontation
of ideologies has given way to the secular state, which purports
to be not only religiously neutral but value-neutral as well.
Perhaps there is no greater educational myth—and none with
greater potential for harm—than the notion of value-free
education. One of America's most influential educators, Earl J.
McGrath, quotes approvingly a leading intellectual, Max Lerner,
on this crucial issue:

At times a debate has raged about whether education should be concerned
with values. It is an idiot debate in that form, on a hopelessly archaic question.
As well ask whether religion should be concerned with the problem of
Godhead. Every actor in the educational drama—teacher, student, family,
administrator, media, peer group—is up to its neck in values. Like it or not,
education is values drenched.[35]

[35]"Relating Faith and Learning," *Private Higher Education: The Job Ahead*, vol. 12,
American Association of Presidents of Independent Colleges and Universities,
1983, 25.

Secularism. What has actually resulted from the increasingly dominant viewpoint that education can and must be value-neutral is, by definition, the establishment of a very powerful and all-pervasive value: secularism. It is not merely that the state (in this case, the state school or teacher) says, "It is inappropriate for me to publicly affirm any specific moral standard." This would be bad enough and, if carried to its logical conclusion, would destroy civilized society. More than that, cultural relativism and, thus, moral relativism, is what is intended by many advocates of this secularism. A secular state could conceivably be religiously neutral and not value-neutral. But contemporary secularism is neither. It is antireligious and against any specific absolute values as well.

"Values Clarification." In the ethical vacuum created when religion was dismissed from the public schools by Supreme Court action, educators have tried to introduce an alternative: "Values Clarification." Courses designed on this model have only one clear absolute: tolerance of all viewpoints.

Here is a typical problem posed to junior high classes: Mary, a sixteen-year-old, got pregnant and is now faced with the dilemma of whether to get an abortion. Her parents don't know of her plight. What should she have done? What should she do now? As the eighth-graders wrestle with the problem, the teacher gives them only one rule: They mustn't be judgmental because no answers are universally right for everyone.

The process of thinking about behavior is the goal, and each student is judge, expected to decide what course of action is best for him. His conclusion may fly in the face of community standards and certainly will reject any final authority for parental values. The objective is to learn how to make responsible, independent choices based on—what? If nonjudgmental acceptance of any viewpoint is the process, there can, by definition, be no objective or universal standard. That approach is an ethical, moral, yes, "religious" doctrine of fundamental importance to individual and social outcomes.

Dogmatic Relativism. But is the descent we have experienced inevitable and irreversible? At first public schools were *denomination*-neutral, but Protestant values dominated and, though Roman Catholics started their own schools, Jews and atheists had to put up with it. As society changed the schools changed, becoming increasingly *religiously* pluralistic but still teaching values informed by religion: "Judeo-Christian" values, the term primarily referring to the last half of the Ten Commandments. Still, agnostics and atheists felt discriminated against and became increasingly vocal about it. No matter that they constituted, as indicated repeatedly in the polls, no more than 2 percent of the population.

They had an influence far out of proportion to their numbers because a much larger group, though affirming the existence of God and the validity of the Ten Commandments, had already accepted moral relativism. This was the basic tenet of an emerging secular consensus which was a curious development—religious absolutes affirmed by (almost) all, along with ethical relativism as an operating dogma for the majority. This development led to *ideological* pluralism.

Assuming that the descent was inevitable, is it also inevitable that *ethical* pluralism be established as the official position of public education? Are there to be no residual values, only dogmatic relativism? Though many secular humanists in elitist positions in education, the media, and public life press for this relativism, the Supreme Court has not so ruled.

I contend that value-neutral education is impossible; the attempt to impose total relativity in values is not inevitable in secular or religion-neutral society; and pressures in that direction should be resisted.

Religious Pluralism. Some seek to roll back the times to a day when religion and general religious values could be inculcated in public schools. For example, widely read evangelical attorney John W. Whitehead argues this position with massive documentation concerning the meaning of the First Amendment in his volume *The Separation Illusion*.[36] The movement to reintroduce prayer and devotional Bible reading into the public schools was preferred by 80 percent of the populace in 1985.

I have two problems with this. Given the present diverse ideological makeup of American society, public prayer has

[36]Milford, Ore.: Mott Media, 1977.

retreated into a parody of true prayer. The first casualty was the idea of prayer in the name of the Lord Jesus Christ. But that was only the first casualty. The final outcome is often a "prayer" expressing a selfish hope for general well-being (conceived in physical, material, and secular terms) addressed to an unnamed being or unseen force. Is a poor prayer better than none? Is it not at least educating people in bad prayer and at worst insulting the Almighty?

My second objection is more basic. I can't get away from the Golden Rule. If I would not want my children subjected to religious rites and values in a public school in, say, Saudi Arabia, is it "doing to others what I would have done to me" to subject Jewish, Muslim, or atheist children to my religion? The argument that participation in group worship is voluntary may well apply to adults, but can hardly be argued in the case of children.

I grant that overtly religious values and even activity may be legitimately required in a homogeneous society; the small minority of dissenters would then have to endure as best they could. But such is no longer true of America—ideological diversity is a major fact of life. On the other hand, though a religious consensus no longer exists, a moral consensus does exist, and this is what should be advocated for the public schools of our time. These values may or may not be religiously motivated. Why and how we go about seeking a consensus—through education or legislation, for religious or secular reasons—is irrelevant. If the consensus on a given value is present or can be established, that is what public schools should inculcate. And there is certainly no consensus today to reject all standards in favor of some deceptively named "value-neutral" ideology.

In the past, this consensus varied widely from community to community, and it may have been legitimate to leave to local school districts decisions on the values to be inculcated. But such a local consensus, though operating fairly smoothly where it still exists, is becoming increasingly less possible. The mass media, nationally distributed textbooks, and our incredible mobility are bringing about a least-common-denominator cultural consensus that is making a local option approach less and less viable. There are, however, at least two ways to teach specific values in a pluralistic public school.

Establish Consensus Values. The Supreme Court has ruled that "public policy"—or the general consensus—takes precedence even over some Constitutional rights, such as the freedom to practice one's religious tenets. Public policy, it ruled, makes it mandatory for the state to promote black-white integration even if this is against the convictions of a religious body (*IRS v. Bob Jones University,* 1983). In this way, the general consensus about a value is sufficient to establish public policy, even when, as in this case, the judgment is reached, not through any electoral referendum or scientific poll to determine consensus, but by the intuition of the court. Could not the same approach be used for other values as well, even if they happen to be traditional?

State or, less likely, federal laws could be enacted permitting, if not mandating, the teaching of majority-sanctioned values. The last six of the Ten Commandments might be a good starting place for Christians who would promote such legislation. Not all of these commandments would be equally acceptable, but a majority consensus now exists and could surely be enhanced if advocated not on a religious basis, but on the demonstrated evidence that such standards are essential to the common good.

The easiest commandments to "establish," and which would need no legislation at this point, would be the Sixth and Eighth Commandments against murder and stealing. Opposition to personal violence and the inviolability of private property may not be universally taught, especially in all their implications, but they could be and should be. Though integrity in truth-telling is being undermined by current emphases on personal-autonomy, duty-to-self, and moral-relativity ethical concepts, the Ninth Commandment against deception also could be vigorously taught under present limitations.

The big problems are in the Fifth and Seventh Commandments dealing with the home and human sexuality. It will take enormous effort on all fronts to reclaim lost ground in these areas, but we should surely make the attempt. The Tenth Commandment against covetousness is, I suppose, hopeless.

Local Option Values Education. In a second approach, a true pluralism could be established by allowing any person or group to provide education in values for his child from any perspective he desires by any qualified person of his choice as part of the program of public school education.[37]

Since values are so widely divergent and strongly held, that would be an accommodation to the reality of our pluralistic society. It would not lead toward a greater community consensus in values, but if the only allowable value is tolerance of all values as equally worthy, certainly even reinforcement of diverse values is preferable to that anti-value. At least we would communicate that values are important!

There is another alternative: the private school.

PRIVATE CHRISTIAN SCHOOLS

A Constitutional Right. Though earlier Supreme Court decisions granted the right to states to mandate public school education for all children, recently it has consistently ruled in favor of parents who wish to provide alternatives. The state has the right to require standards, but not to bar privately operated equivalent education. Constitutional law expert William Bentley Ball makes the distinction clear:

> There is a vast difference between saying that "education is a function of the State" and saying that "education belongs to the State." To say that the State has a legitimate interest in educating some of the people is far from saying that it may control the education of all of the people.[38]

Although the High Court is clear on this, not all local administrators are. So vigilance is necessary to protect the rights of parents who want their children to have an education which conforms to their conscience as well as to the educational standards of the state.

[37]An excellent presentation of the legal basis for this approach may be found in *Religious Released Time Education: The Overlooked Open Door in Public Schools,* Samuel E. Ericsson, Kimberlee Colby, and Robert Payne, Center for Law and Religious Freedom of the Christian Legal Society, 1982.

[38]William Bentley Ball, "Law and the Educational Mission of Christianity," *Theology, News and Notes,* December 1980, 9.

Validity. Private Christian education may be legitimate in a pluralistic society, but is it desirable, is it valid? There are several reasons that seem almost to demand private education as the public schools move farther into secular humanism as the underlying assumption.

Ultimately, the only true way to get at reality is to keep all data in the context of the fundamental truth—God. Thus it can be argued that the only true education is God-oriented. It must be granted that the implications of this truth vary with the subject matter. As I have argued elsewhere, the more the subject-matter of the discipline overlaps the subject-matter of divine revelation, the greater the conflict and, in a secular school, the greater divergence from biblical truth.[39] Thus, for example, a statistically documented great conflict exists between behavioral science disciplines, which deal with the nature of man and society, and Scripture. The conflict lessens somewhat in the humanities and is even less in the sciences, except for those which deal with human origins. In medicine and agriculture, on the other hand, matters to which Scripture has little to say, any divergence in religious faith on the part of college professors and the general public is virtually nonexistent.

Thus when it comes to certain subjects, a secular approach need not be that divergent from a "Christian" approach, but there are other subjects in which the religious faith of the child will be under direct assault.

Far more significant than this direct subject-matter divergence from ultimate reality, however, are the assumptions of a secular humanism which infiltrate the whole educational process. This is not the place to enumerate and explicate them, but it should be noted that underlying the cultural relativism noted above is the naturalistic assumption that significant reality—and perhaps all reality—is limited to what is material, and that autonomous human reason is the sole basis for understanding reality. When revelation and the realm of the spirit are ruled out and man himself is the measure of good, for education to go astray it is not even necessary to introduce all the other ideologies such as the duty-to-self ethic and environmental determinism.

[39]"The Behavioral Sciences under the Authority of Scripture," *Journal of Evangelical Theological Society*, March 1977.

No longer is the acquisition of truth the goal of education, nor even the search for truth. Truth in any objective, absolute sense does not exist, so the teacher joins the student in an unending quest among the relativities of the material universe for personal self-fulfillment. Christian schools offer an alternative; truth and spiritual values are recognized and honored. Furthermore, at another level, parents who believe in an ordered, disciplined approach to life and value the verbal and mathematical fundamentals of traditional education find reinforcement in Christian schools.

But there are problems with the Christian school movement. Some schools are definitely substandard educationally, and more would be held substandard if rote memory were considered less than the ideal basis of education.

Many schools are academically superior, however. But even in those cases critics hold that students are isolated from "real life." Christian educators counter that public school education is the truly "unreal" or artificial education, isolated as it is from ultimate reality. True, the Christian critic may grant, but the student in a Christian school is isolated from hurly-burly interaction with majority opinions and life-styles and is consequently less able to function effectively in a secular world upon graduation. This is accentuated when a child has all his education—from elementary school through college—in a Christian setting. It is even more accentuated in what is now the most dramatic growth area in Christian education: home education.

Available data about "coping ability" does not bear out those fears of the critics. But the decision for most people will probably be made on a philosophical rather than a statistical basis. With the direction public education in America is going, increasing numbers of conscientious parents can be expected to join the exodus to Christian education.

The dilemma is not easily solved. In more conservative communities the need for separate education is less pressing, and where there are many Christian schools, the isolation from main-stream American culture may not be so apparent. Perhaps there is no ideal solution of universal validity. But two God-ordained institutions can be affirmed with confidence as the primary antidote to the problems generated by man-made educational systems, public or private: the Christian home and the church.

Values derive from many sources. Paul tells us that the Law is written in a man's innate moral consciousness (Rom. 2:14-15), and most contemporaries agree with the ancient Israeli proverb that the chief formative influence is the home—"Train up a child in the way he should go, and when he is old he will not depart from it" (Prov. 22:6).

The church also is very influential. It has been estimated that in the United States more people attend church on a given Sunday morning than attend all athletic events in a year, though one would never suspect this from the relative newspaper coverage. *The Connecticut Mutual Report on American Values in the 80s: The Impact of Belief* startled the researchers and the wide audience it quickly gained by its documentation that the ordinary American citizen is still committed to traditional values, across the board.[40] Those who are widely divergent from the American general public are educators, editors, politicians, and media people. In other words, the elite molders of society represent a different set of values. The influence of the church is not directly proved by such data but a connection may reasonably be theorized.

THE MEDIA

TELEVISION

Newspapers, magazines, and movies all participate in value formation, but the strongest of all influences is television. Compared with school, "By the time the typical American school child graduates from high school he or she will have spent 11,000 hours in school and 15,000 in front of the television tube."[41] Compared with the church, during an average life-span, the typical American will have spent twelve years watching television and the equivalent of four months of Sunday school.[42] Compared with other influences in the home,

[40] Conducted by Research and Forecasts, Inc. Commissioned by Connecticut Mutual Life Insurance Co., Hartford, 1981.
[41] *New York Times,* 20 April 1980.
[42] Malcolm Muggeridge, "Christ and Media," *Journal of Evangelical Theological Society,* September 1978, 195.

the average American spends, according to one study, slightly more than seven hours daily in the solitude of "fellowship" with television personalities.[43] To what extent this influences the values of people is hotly debated, but it does seem strange that industry would spend billions in advertising on a medium that does not influence behavior.

Some hold that the media mirror society rather than mold it, and certainly it is true that the media are going to produce only what people will pay for. Money still has the strongest voice. On the other hand, media people for the most part see themselves as change agents and deliberately attempt to foster a value-neutral if not an anti-religious, anti-traditional-value perspective.

Two obvious evils of television, and the most often attacked, are the constant violence and exploitation of sex. These are not to be underestimated, for television is certainly at the forefront of the cultural revolution in these matters. But the attack on traditional values is far more thorough and widespread than these two paramount concerns. Consider the observations of James Hitchcock, a history professor at St. Louis University.

Here [the mass media] the reigning pieties of twenty years ago—religion, capitalism, patriotism, the family—find themselves subject to relentless attack. "News" coverage emphasizes obsessively the problems associated with all these traditional institutions. They are habitually represented as dying, and as dying because they are rigid, sclerotic, and atavistic, their only hope for survival based upon their ability to change beyond all recognition. In those areas of the media which purport to be merely entertainment the powerful weapon of ridicule is constantly directed at traditional values and those who espouse them. Such people are routinely depicted as insecure, stupid, neurotic, and ridiculous. In television fiction, for example, religion is often shown as a deforming influence, rarely as a positive and supportive element in people's lives. Religious believers are either hypocrites or fanatics.[44]

POPULAR MUSIC

Music is the most influential value-former for American youth today, according to Allan Bloom, influential professor of philosophy at the University of Chicago:

This is the age of music . . . a very large proportion of young people between the ages of ten and twenty live for music. It is their passion; nothing else excites them as it does; they cannot take seriously anything alien to music. . . .

43A. C. Nielsen report, January 1984.
44James Hitchcock, "Competing Ethical Systems," *Faculty Dialogue*, Winter 1984-85, 35.

Rock music is as unquestioned and unproblematic as the air the students breathe.[45]

But rock music has one appeal only, a barbaric appeal, to sexual desire—not love, not *eros,* but sexual desire undeveloped and untutored. . . . Young people know that rock has the beat of sexual intercourse.[46]

Though the central thesis of Bloom's best-selling volume is that higher education has failed democracy and impoverished the souls of today's students, the chapter on music holds that the entertainment industry has bypassed the parents and schools and captured the minds of the young with a revolutionary view of sex that has transformed all of life. Most young people are constantly plugged into their music—while studying, jogging, driving, dating. And the message throbs incessantly with overpowering volume: experience sexual relations. All of them. Now. It is your right, what you were made for, and any members of the establishment who would keep such pleasuring from you must be rejected.

NEWS MEDIA

The *Statement of Principles* of the American Society of Newspaper Editors, Article V states: "Sound practice, however, demands a clear distinction for the readers between news reports and opinion. Articles that contain opinion or personal interpretation should be clearly identified." This traditional commitment to objectivity in news reporting is impossible to achieve since news reporters and historians must be selective in what is reported, and their personal biases will inevitably condition their selections. But the honest reporter used to seek diligently to compensate for his biases by recognizing them and striving to be objective. No longer. "Advocacy journalism" is increasingly becoming the common approach. The reporter frankly admits his bias and uses his craft to forward the ideas he feels worthy.

For years I have followed *The State,* a Columbia, South Carolina, newspaper whose editorship is still committed in theory to objectivity. Nevertheless, one need not read the editorial page to learn quickly that *The State* is in favor of

[45]Allan Bloom, *The Closing of the American Mind* (New York: Simon and Schuster, 1987), 68.
[46]Ibid, 73.

abortion, liquor, pari-mutuel betting, unrestricted Sunday commerce, and freedom for pornography. The subjects chosen for a big play and those that are ignored or buried in Section D, page 12, soon prove what is important to the editors. Who is interviewed and how it is reported are part of the total campaign when the legislature is considering any of those matters. Even the phrasing of the headline is often an advocacy statement. Sometimes the slant of the report itself is biased, including the choice of terminology to demean the unwanted and enhance the desirable. For example, in the long battle in the Southern Baptist Convention, the more conservative were labeled "fundamentalists" whereas the more liberal were called "moderate." Instead of calling both parties by the name each preferred (conservative and moderate) or both by the label of its opponents (fundamentalist and liberal), the media used the opponents' label only of the party least acceptable to the press. And yet *The State* is a conservative newspaper as media standards go.

But a deeper problem than the direct confrontation over traditional values in the media is the subtle and pervasive infiltration of basic anti-Christian philosophies mentioned earlier: naturalism, materialism, humanism, determinism, relativism. These influences are visible only to the most critical observer but are nonetheless subtly transforming the values of our society.

ANTIDOTES

Scripture and Critical Vigilance. The primary response to media influence is personal, and the antidote is the Word of God. We must have our minds renewed by the values of Scripture and our discernment sharpened to read and view critically, evaluating constantly, and, when necessary, screening out the evil input altogether. A deliberate choice must be made to study Scripture seriously so that a person's mind is renewed, his ethical and spiritual judgment sharpened. The amount of exposure to God's truth must match exposure to non-Christian values. Creeping ethical insensitivity often becomes a fatal illness before a person knows he is a patient. The primary defense, then, is the Word of God.

Christian Media. Purchase of TV time for Christian broadcasts and the increasing influence of Christian publications and Christian radio and television stations are part of the answer. For Christian broadcasting and publishing to be the antidote they could be, serious self-reflection in the light of Scripture, repentance, and radical reformation may be necessary.

Christians in Media. At a more basic, systemic level, the media will change only as media people change; thus many see a call for Christians of talent to gain the training and experience necessary to infiltrate the secular media in greater numbers, transforming them from within. Creative evangelistic approaches to media leaders have proved successful as well.

Pressure. But what of the direct assault of lobbying against manifest evils in television and other media? Is it legitimate for Christians to move beyond organized letter writing to economic boycott? I see no biblical principle barring anyone from organizing to bring economic pressure to bear on advertisers and thus, indirectly, on networks. Threats that cannot be fulfilled are worse than useless, but if the National Federation of Decency or others can actually reduce revenues by a significant percentage, the approach will prove useful.

Whether a Christian should be conscience-bound to personally boycott every product made by a company that has sponsored any undesirable program is another matter. In the complex economic system in which we live one would have to leave this world, it would seem, to be totally "clean," certain that not a cent of his expenditures would ever benefit any evil person or cause. But when an advertiser, media company, or particular program becomes blatantly antibiblical in the values it propagates, a personal boycott may be demanded as the only worthy response.

We have briefly surveyed the major institutions of society, seeking to determine at what points Scripture gives light on how a Christian and the church itself should relate to government, education, and the media. The issues are complex and the light often only dim and oblique, but still we have the promise of the Spirit to guide us through the Word. So let us not despair, but press forward to more perfectly understand the world in which our lives are set and the Word God has given to illumine our pathway through it.

SUGGESTED ADDITIONAL READING

Culver, Robert. *Toward a Biblical View of Civil Government*. Chicago: Moody, 1974. Culver's treatment is uneven in quality but invaluable in the exhaustive manner in which all biblical data is identified and thoroughly exegeted.

Mander, Jerry. *Four Arguments for the Elimination of Television*. New York: Morrow, 1978. An excellent critique from the secular point of view. Mander does not attack TV's morals so much as its effect on rational thought processes.

Muggeridge, Malcolm. *Christ and the Media*. Grand Rapids: Eerdmans, 1977. A scathing critique of the media, especially news reporting, by a veteran media man who is now a Christian.

Neuhaus, Richard John. *The Naked Public Square*. Grand Rapids: Eerdmans, 1984. An influential, scholarly work demonstrating the impossibility of a totally secular state and the negative results of an attempt to establish one.

Nichols, J. J. *Democracy and the Churches*. Philadelphia: Westminster, 1941. A respectable treatment with guide to the literature since 1911 on to 1941.

Niebuhr, H. Richard. *Christ and Culture*. New York: Harper & Row, 1951. Considered by many the classic presentation on the Christian and society.

Niebuhr, Reinhold. *Christianity and Power Politics*. Hamden, Conn.: Archon, 1969; reprint of Niebuhr's 1940 classic. Probably the most influential volume in countering the optimism of liberalism on what government can and should do.

Ramsey, Paul. *Who Speaks for the Church?* Nashville: Abingdon, 1967. A liberal churchman and leading ethicist gives a brilliant, hard-hitting critique of ecumenical ethics.

Thielicke, Helmut. *Theological Ethics*. vol. 2, *Politics*. Edited by William H. Lazareth. Grand Rapids: Eerdmans, 1979. A major theological treatise on the subject by one of the most prolific ethicists of the twentieth century.

Troeltsch, Ernst. *The Social Teaching of the Christian Churches*. Translated by Olive Wyon. 2 vols. Chicago: University of Chicago Press, 1981. Much of the current second-time-over study of Christian response to the challenge of civil government in particular and society in general would be greatly simplified by attention to Troeltsch. He is practically exhaustive down to 1911.

CHAPTER ELEVEN

FALLIBLE CHOICES

Although our standard for the Christian life—the Word of God—is infallible, our understanding and practical application of that standard are subject to error. In this final chapter we turn to two crucial areas about which God does not even give a direct revelation to start us off.

First, the divisive issue of what to do when we believe there is no ethical issue at stake, but other Christians feel that there is. Do we stand by our Christian liberty, bow to our brothers' scruples, or take some other course of action?

Second, does God have a preference about the choices in our lives that are apparently neutral—vocation, marriage partner, employment? If he does, the choice becomes an ethical issue, since it is morally wrong to neglect or reject the will of God. But our discovery of his will must be considered fallible, since it is not like the infallible revelation experienced by the Bible's authors. Yet, fallible or not, how do we go about being as certain as possible of God's will?

First, to set these matters of fallible choice in the context of our previous study, note that we have sought to determine God's will as revealed in Scripture from two distinct but thoroughly integrated sources: clear universal *mandates* and clear universal *principles*. When a teaching of Scripture is not clear or is not clearly universal, we may use it, but not with the authority of "thus saith the Lord." Examples of clear universal mandates would be the Ten Commandments, which have formed the outline of our study in the middle section of this book. Examples of clear universal principles might be love, self-control, contentment, humility—topics in the earlier chapters, in addition to principles derived from the direct mandates. A chief problem with direct commands or mandates is determining what audience God intended, and a chief problem with general principles is applying them to the present with authority.[1]

We have attempted to deal with the scriptural data with integrity, settling those issues with certainty which seem to be the clearly revealed will of God and acknowledging lesser degrees of certainty in other important matters. We now turn to issues on which the Bible does not give direct revelation, but on which it does shed the light of principles that assist in making choices in the will of God.

ETHICAL QUESTIONS ON WHICH CHRISTIANS DIFFER

Life would certainly be simpler and the church much more tranquil if Christians were all agreed on what is right and wrong. Why cannot Christians agree? Why is there such disparity of belief and action? Why are Christians so divided on ethical questions? There are several reasons.

REASONS FOR DIFFERENCE AMONG CHRISTIANS

Authority of Scripture. Many Christians are at odds with other Christians as to what is right and wrong because they are at odds with what the Bible clearly teaches on the subject. The first and most important source of division, then, is a division over the authority of Scripture. For those who do not accept the authority of Scripture, any clear command of Scripture which does not seem reasonable can be rejected on the basis of appeal to the authority which *is* accepted—personal judgment, cultural consensus, religious authority, or whatever. Very naturally, there will often be disagreement between these people and those who accept Scripture as the final authority.

On the other hand, there are those who believe in Scripture as the final authority but on a particular subject may find that obedience is very difficult or very costly. There are several ways

[1]For a hermeneutical approach to determining the audience God intended and the response he desires, see chapters 18 and 19 in my *Understanding and Applying the Bible* (Chicago: Moody, 1983).

such difficult commands can be handled. They can be recognized as legitimate, but violated on an appeal to the frailty of human nature and the impossibility of fulfilling the requirements of the Law. As Mark Twain put it, his problem was not with the Scripture he couldn't understand, but with the part he could!

Again, there are those who would "interpret" the plain teaching of Scripture to invalidate the command for application to life today. For example, it is often held that a particularly offensive biblical norm is simply a cultural application for the time and place in which it was originally given. Thus the command is useful only to illustrate how the principle which lies behind it might be applied today. In this approach, the interpreter has become the authority. Conflict over ethical norms then becomes inevitable because each interpreter becomes his own standard of evaluation as to which commands apply and which do not. This is another way of disallowing the authority of Scripture and results in direct conflict with those who accept the plain teaching of Scripture as final authority.

For example, one leading evangelical theologian-anthropologist holds that in certain African tribes where the qualifications for leadership include the economic strength to support two or more wives, the churches should require polygamy as a condition of church leadership. Paul was not really speaking against polygamy, it is held; he was listing the qualifications for human leadership *in his own culture*. So the faithful interpreter will not insist on the cultural form of the instruction but apply the principle to the present culture. Instead of a prohibition against a polygamous eldership, Paul's teaching becomes a mandate for it.

These examples derive from a single cause: for various reasons there is a refusal to bow to the clear teaching of Scripture on some particular ethical command.

Ignorance. Another source of conflict is ignorance. Some people differ on ethical questions because they do not know what the Bible teaches. This is common among new Christians who simply have not read Scripture, but also it can be true of those who, through tradition or a particular theological or ecclesiastical system, have been programmed to see Scripture in a particular way.

For example, slavery was justified by many Christians who, though committed to the authority of Scripture, were blinded by tradition.

Disputed Meanings. Among those who understand Scripture and are fully committed to obedience there are often differences as to what Scripture actually teaches on a given issue. How to approach those disputed issues will be the focus of our attention. Often when a matter is not clearly, directly commanded in Scripture, people who are apparently equally godly and biblically learned differ as to what is pleasing to God.

It is very difficult to see any issue from the perspective of an opponent, and this complicates the problem of disputed ethical issues. If I have convictions on an issue, those who differ must be ignorant or spiritually rebellious. If they have convictions and I do not, on the other hand, then I conclude they are ignorant or spiritually arrogant. Conflict is inevitable.

One way to assure conflict is to rule out the opposition in advance by the way terms are defined. For example, in his otherwise very helpful workbook on the subject entitled *Disputed Practices,* Bobby Clinton writes, "A *disputed practice* is a practice which has *no* inherent moral value *but* about which some people have religious convictions."[2]

The author has decided that an issue has no moral significance, even though some people are distressed about the matter precisely because they think it *is* a moral issue. He has defined the issue in terms of the person who is free in conscience: it is "amoral." But there will never be a resolution of conflict until the person who is without scruples recognizes that the dispute is not over an "inherently amoral" issue but over whether a particular issue is moral or not.

Another source of confusion is misunderstanding Paul's use of "strong" and "weak." Who is the "weaker brother"? In Paul's terms, it is the one who has scruples. Is he weaker in convictions? Certainly not. On this issue at least he has the stronger convictions. Is he weaker spiritually? Not necessarily, though if one differs with Paul on a specific issue (as distinct

[2]Coral Gables, Fla.: West Indies Mission [now WorldTeam], 1975, 13.

from differing with, say, a contemporary churchman), he surely runs the risk of being weak spiritually as well.

But that is not the point of Paul's discourse in Romans 14. The strong person is one who is strong in faith. He is strong in the confidence that God does not condemn him, particularly that eating meat offered to idols and violating certain Jewish holy days are not of themselves sinful. He is strong enough in that confidence to be free in conscience, whereas his brother is weak in faith, lacking faith that the disputed practice is actually morally neutral. Obviously most earnest Christians are "strong" on some issues and "weak" on others; they consider certain disputed practices wrong and others innocent. What one considers amoral or immoral is likely to differ even among those in the same fellowship.

The chief point Paul makes in both Romans 14 and 2 Corinthians 8 and 10 is that we must accept those with whom we differ without, on the one hand, belittling those whom we may consider unbiblically narrow or, on the other hand, belittling those whom we may consider unbiblically compromising. The free-of-conscience tend to view the conscience-bound as intellectually inferior, while the conscience-bound tend to view the free-of-conscience as spiritually inferior. Paul condemns both attitudes. "Receive one another" as authentic, worthy Christians, he says. But practically speaking, how does one decide the issue itself? Does a standoff of this kind indicate that each person is free to choose the course of action which pleases him most?

RESPONSE TO DIFFERING OPINIONS

Attitude. The goal of the Christian is not to please himself but to please his Lord. He does not wish to settle for that which is least harmful, but to reach for that which is highest and best. He is not seeking to avoid punishment but to bring joy to his heavenly Father. He is not testing himself to see how much darkness he can stand, but striving to see how near he can get to the Light.

His is not a negative obedience demanded of him but a positive eagerness to please God in every possible way. If this is his orientation, he will not choose between two interpreters on the basis of personal preference. Rather, he will soon recognize that not all learned people are godly, and not all godly people are learned. One of the greatest sources of confusion in ethical matters is that so few of those highly acclaimed as theologians are equally highly acclaimed as devout, and few of those who are noted for personal godliness seem to be masters of biblical interpretation. Each Christian must assume responsibility to work at both thorough understanding of the Bible and making godlikeness the goal of life. Only one who has high achievement in both areas simultaneously is a reliable guide concerning ethical questions on which Christians differ.

Study. Once a person's attitude on the disputed issue is settled, and he eagerly desires God's will alone, the next step is to discover whether it is truly a moral issue. When Scripture does not speak plainly on a question of conduct, the Christian must seek for biblical principle to guide him. Scripture is much more a book of principles than of precepts; any issue will have biblical principles bearing on it—either to direct the Christian or to free him to do as he pleases.

Often these will be specific principles. For example, the biblical principle of purity applies to a whole range of activity not directly dealt with in biblical precept, such as publishing or selling pornography. "Freedom of the press" may make it legal in some societies, but the biblical principle of purity makes it sinful before God.

General Principles. There are general principles which apply to a whole range of subjects and which seem especially helpful in making choices concerning disputed or uncertain practices. Many have set these principles in the form of various questions to be asked when facing such choices. Here is a sample derived from many sources.

Thirteen Questions to Ask about Questionable Matters 1. Is it for the Lord? Does it bring praise to him? "So, whether you eat or drink, or whatever you do, do all to the glory of God" (1 Cor. 10:31). (See also Rom. 14:6-8.) 2. Can I do it in his name (on his authority, implicating him)? Can I thank him for it? "And whatever you do, in word or deed, do everything in the name of the Lord Jesus, giving thanks to God the Father through him" (Col. 3:17). 3. Can

I take Jesus with me? Would Jesus do it? "Whither shall I go from thy Spirit? Or whither shall I flee from thy presence?" (Ps. 139:7). "Christ . . . lives in me" (Gal. 2:20). "Christ . . . leaving us an example that ye should follow his steps" (1 Pet. 2:21). (See also Matt. 28:19-20; John 14:16-17, 23.) 4. Does it belong in the home of the Holy Spirit? "Do you not know that your body is a temple of the Holy Spirit within you, which you have from God? You are not your own; you were bought with a price. So glorify God in your body" (1 Cor. 6:19-20). (See also Eph. 4:30.) 5. Is it of faith? Do I have misgivings? "But he who has doubts is condemned, if he eats, because he does not act from faith; for whatever does not proceed from faith is sin" (Rom. 14:23). "Beloved, if our hearts do not condemn us, we have confidence before God" (1 John 3:21). 6. Does it positively benefit, build up (not simply, "Is it harmless?")? "Let us then pursue what makes for peace and for mutual upbuilding" (Rom. 14:19). "Let all things be done for edification" (1 Cor. 14:26). (See also Rom. 15:2; 1 Cor. 10:8; Eph. 4:12-16.) 7. Does it spring from, or lead to, love of this world and its value system? "Do not love the world or the things in the world. If any one loves the world, love for the Father is not in him" (1 John 2:15). (See also Mark 9:47; 11:14-15.) 8. Does it involve union with an unbeliever? "Do not be mismated with unbelievers. For what partnership have righteousness and iniquity? Or what fellowship has light with darkness?" (2 Cor. 6:14). 9. Does it come from or have the potential of leading to bondage? " 'All things are lawful,' but not all things are helpful. 'All things are lawful,' but not all things build up" (1 Cor. 10:23). 10. Is the motive pride, or love? "We know that 'all of us possess knowledge.' 'Knowledge' puffs up, but love builds up. If any one imagines that he knows something, he does not yet know as he ought to know" (1 Cor. 8:1-2). 11. Is a godly mind-set the context of my decision on the matter? "Finally, brethren, whatever is true, whatever is honorable, whatever is just, whatever is pure, whatever is lovely, whatever is gracious; if there is any excellence, if there is anything worthy of praise, think about these things" (Phil. 4:8). (See also Rom. 12:1-2.) 12. What does the church say about it? "He who thus serves Christ is acceptable to God and approved by men" (Rom. 14:18). "For it has seemed good to the Holy Spirit and to us to lay upon you no greater burden than these necessary things" (Acts 15:28). (See also Rom. 14:16.) 13. Would I like to be doing this when Jesus comes? "And now, little children, abide in him, so that when he appears we may have confidence and not shrink from him in shame at his coming. . . . We know that when he appears we shall be like him, for we shall see him as he is. And every one who thus hopes in him purifies himself as he is pure" (1 John 2:28; 3:2-3). (See also 1 Thess. 5:2-4; Matt. 24:44-51; Luke 23:34-35.)

This is not a list to memorize, but a few examples of general principles that help decide disputed issues. Furthermore, many have found it a useful checklist to consult.

Christians who believe that certain conduct is wrong because principles of Scripture are violated must take a stand against the position of those who do not see a question of right or wrong involved. But what does one do when he himself is convinced that there is *not* an ethical issue? He has wholeheartedly committed himself to the will of God alone, thoroughly studied the Scripture, considered what Bible scholars have said on all sides of a given issue, and concludes that the Scripture teaches nothing either directly or indirectly and that he is free in the matter. He has strong faith that he is doing right, but his brother or sister is convinced that he is doing wrong. Does he have any obligation to his brother?

Response of the Free Person to One with Scruples. Scripture teaches that he has several obligations to the one who has a conscientious scruple about a matter.

He must *receive this brother* who differs from him (Rom. 14:1; 15:7), recognizing him as a brother of equal standing before the Lord. Any tendency to put him down as ignorant, any show of friendliness in order to set him straight, violates this biblical principle.

He must choose that which would *build up his brother* and not that which would hurt or destroy him (Rom. 14:13, 15-16, 19, 21; 1 Cor. 8:1, 9-13; 10:23). If I believe beverage alcohol is legitimate, but my drinking could in any way become a stumbling block to others, a hazard to their growth and success as Christians, then I am no longer free to exercise my rights in the matter. Freedom for me is not license to do what I please but strength to sacrifice my rights for the welfare of others. Some hold that the binding of conscience by another is limited to this: If my freedom actually leads someone else to sin (stumble), I must give up my freedom for his sake, but if it merely offends him, I am under no obligation. *The Other Side* journal was called to task by a number of readers for using what they considered an unworthy, if not an obscene, term. Co-editor John Alexander responded:

Once and for all it is time to realize that the passage in 1 Corinthians 8 does not refer to annoying those who disagree. Causing weaker people to stumble means tempting them to do something they think is sinful. We doubt that our joke tempted people to use words in a way they believed was wrong.[3]

Certainly "cause to stumble" means "cause to sin," and a "free" person is not free to exercise that freedom if it will lead another to follow that example, either to actually sin or to

[3]John Alexander, *The Other Side*, June 1979, 4.

503 ■ FALLIBLE CHOICES

violate his conscience in doing what he feels is sin. Of course, causing a person to sin by violating his conscience is not the only way to cause him to sin. If by needlessly insisting on my rights I cause him to fall into the sin of anger or resentment, this also would be causing him to sin. But is "cause to sin" the only meaning of the term *stumble?* I hold that Paul used the term in its normal sense including both "causing to sin" and "being offensive." The Pharisees were "offended" when Christ set aside their tradition (Matt. 15:12). They were unhappy and angry but were far from following his example. So in the Corinthian passages both meanings must be intended, for Paul expands on both principles. If my freedom causes another to sin, or if it merely offends him, I am called to give up my freedom for his sake.

The person who sees no ethical issue involved must nevertheless choose to do that which *pleases his brother* (1 Cor. 10:24, 28-33; Rom. 14:15, 18; 15:2; Matt. 7:12; 22:39). This is the law of love. It says that I am responsible for my brother's happiness and thus must let his conscience be my guide. Love is prepared to sacrifice its own preference, happiness, and rights to satisfy a brother. This sacrificial love does, however, have biblical limitations.

The "free" person is not the only one bound by the law of love. The "bound" person must also act in love. He must not needlessly lay his scruples on others. He must not make demands on others or even permit them to bind themselves by his conscientious scruples, unless he believes the matter so serious that he must forbid others as well as himself.

The "free" person, however, cannot demand this kind of loving response from the "bound" person. His only option is to continue lovingly and joyfully to yield until his brother lovingly chooses to release him. The reason is easily understood. For the person who has convictions on a matter, to compromise would be to violate his conscience, and that, according to Scripture, is sin. The person who does not have convictions on the matter is free to yield his freedom without violating his conscience. For one, right is at stake; for the other, only rights. Thus, the motto for the truly free person is: "Let *his* conscience be *my* guide."

Of course, if there is a conviction that his compromise with the "bound" brother's position would actually be sin, then we have a confrontation of consciences, and that is a different matter, as we shall see.

No Christian should feel bound by the conscience of every other Christian. This voluntary binding of one's own conduct by the conscience of another only applies when the person who might be offended is close enough to be offended. There is no obligation for me to dispose of all my neckties and remove all my buttons because some brothers in Pennsylvania think such are worldly. I live in South Carolina and do not belong to an Amish church. If the person with a "bound" conscience is distant geographically or organizationally, he has no legitimate reason to be personally offended, and the "free" person, who sees no ethical issue involved, should not consider himself bound.

This principle of loving concern is, in the nature of the case, limited to those with a close relationship. Examples of a responsible relationship would be, in descending order, members of the same family, the same church, the same institution, friends, near neighbors.

A person is wrong to be bound by the scruples of another if those scruples are damaging the actual welfare of others.

The clearest example of this relates to the salvation of the lost. If someone is inhibited from coming to Christ because of a matter judged nonethical by the "free" Christian, the issue of that person's salvation becomes a matter of conscience. There is a confrontation of consciences: the "free" is compelled to maintain that freedom in order to clear all unnecessary blocks from the path of one who needs Christ. This principle is stated very strongly in 1 Corinthians 9:12, 18-23, where Paul emphasizes repeatedly that he adapts his personal preferences and activities toward the goal of winning men to Christ.

Furthermore, this principle of adapting for the sake of the salvation of "the many" need not be limited to an immediate individual matter. It may be necessary to teach freedom when there is an issue that may cause the whole fellowship to be an unnecessary block to unbelievers considering the claims of Christ.

Paul was not two-faced when he bound himself by the scruples of others under one set of circumstances and behaved in freedom on the same issue in other circumstances. He did that which was pleasing to those he was near. He was truly free. He could go either way. But top priority went to winning people to Christ. If that were involved, the scruples of his Christian brother did not bind him.

The couple sitting on the floor with me in our Tokyo home had recently professed faith in Christ and were preparing for baptism. They looked a little nervous and giggled as each said the other should broach the next question. Finally it came out: Would she have to give up wearing makeup to be an authentic Christian? It seemed a ridiculous question; she, of all people, should wear makeup. Their home had almost broken up over his affair with a woman he found more attractive than she, and it was the entrance of Jesus Christ that saved them and their home.

But then, on second thought, it wasn't so ridiculous. My wife did not wear makeup; some of the sisters in the missionary community thought makeup worldly. But from the time of this encounter with the worried Japanese couple, my wife began to wear makeup. But never on Monday. At least on the first Monday of the month—prayer day for missionaries. She could not sacrifice her freedom to wear makeup, which she did not consider a moral issue, in a context where the lack of makeup became a hindrance to the gospel. The unhindered growth of newborn believers was a higher priority than easing the sensitivities of the veteran Christians. But she did not need to flaunt her freedom and wear makeup when in the company of those who might be offended.

In this confrontation of consciences, the person who is free to go either way must maintain that freedom for the sake of the lost, even though it may be an offense to the brother who is bound.

By extension, it might be said that any scruples which inhibit the growth of Christians also would become a matter of conscience for the "free" person to oppose the bondage. For example, when a church drives away young people by denying fellowship on the basis of standards not clearly taught in Scripture (such as a particular musical form), the leaders should seriously study the Scriptures and determine whether the standard is biblically mandated.

In specific relationships, it may be the responsibility of the person who is strong in faith and knows that there is no ethical issue involved to instruct the person who is bound by the scruple. Instruction can be verbal, or through actions. This depends on the importance of the issue and the level of his responsibility.

If it is a minor issue that does not affect the proclamation of the gospel or spiritual growth, it would hardly seem necessary or even loving to challenge it. For example, if the older folks in the congregation feel that the proper attire for a pastor is a three-piece suit, why wear casual clothes in the pulpit or when visiting these parishioners?

If the "free" person does not have a responsibility for the spiritual development of the person, he should simply respond in love, giving up his rights for the sake of the other person.

As a guest speaker I have no pastoral responsibility to enlighten the congregation on the benefit of some translation other than the King James Version. Though I feel free to use other translations, why create static that may hinder my communication? But when there is personal responsibility such as the parent of a minor child, the pastor of a church, or the teacher in school, the person who is strong in faith must work to free those with scruples on any important issue. As a theological educator, for example, I must teach students what constitutes a valid translation, which translations are stronger than others, and why.

Both the "free" person and the "bound" person need to decide in favor of *that which makes for peace* (Rom. 14:16-17, 19, 20; 15:5-6). Peace in the family of God is of extremely high value. However, it is not the highest value, and a person may not compromise truth in order to achieve it. Rights, yes. Right, no. The key to the problem of controversy lies with the free person more than with the bound person. To compromise for the sake of peace will require, on the part of the free person, sacrifice of some of his rights. But compromise on the part of the bound person would violate his conscience, and this he cannot do.

Response of the Person with a Conscience on the Disputed Issue. What of the person who is bound in conscience on a certain matter but finds that others do not consider the matter an ethical issue? Perhaps he begins to suspect that he has a nonbiblical inhibition. What should he do? The first thing he should do is decide to obey God at any cost. "For whatever does not proceed from faith is sin" (Rom. 14:23).

He cannot behave as a free person on the issue until his conscience is wholly free with no shadow of a doubt. So the next step is to study the Word. Many Christians are bound by scruples that are not scriptural. Conscience is simply moral judgment, conditioned by past input. His mind needs to be constantly reprogrammed by the Word of God. It is the truth, God's Word, that will set a person free.

His first responsibility is, like the "free" person, to receive the person who differs. He must receive him without judging him as inferior—to his own Master he stands or falls (Rom. 14). He must also act in love, not needlessly hassle his brother, and work for peace.

His responsibility to help his brother understand the issue depends on the relationship. For himself, the standard is absolute obedience to what he believes to be the right. But for others, the responsibility ranges from that of parent to hold the child to biblical standards as he understands them, through lesser responsibility as a pastor to teach the truth as he sees it without insisting on obedience, to no responsibility at all for those who are unrelated to him.

In summary, the biblical goal for those on both sides of a disputed issue should be twofold. First, to understand Scripture with ever greater clarity, and second, to obey God's will wholly. Thus, learning should not be considered the province of the free-of-conscience and godliness the specialty of the conscientious. Learning and godliness must be the goal of both. Or, it might be better said, learning *unto* godliness.

KNOWING GOD'S WILL IN MATTERS NOT REVEALED IN SCRIPTURE

Scripture is given to reveal God's will to us. This revealed will is the same for all men: moral godlikeness. But beyond this revealed general will does God have an individual will for each believer? Or does he simply will that we obey him, be like him, and for the rest of it do as we please? If God has a custom-designed plan for each believer, does it extend beyond the major directions of life such as one's vocation? Does it extend also to the incidental activities of a single day?

INTRODUCING THE ISSUE

First of all, we must recognize that the great emphasis of Scripture concerning the will of God deals with what is clearly revealed. Even in those passages that speak of God guiding his children, guidance in right behavior and right thinking is usually the focus (Ps. 25:8-15; 32:8; 73:23-26). "For this is the will of God, your sanctification" (1 Thess. 4:3). "The Lord is my shepherd," to be sure, but he is primarily interested in leading us in "paths of righteousness" (Ps. 23).

This clearly revealed will that we be transformed into his likeness is certainly sufficient to occupy a person for a lifetime. What one is and becomes is of far greater importance than what he does for a job (see 1 Cor. 12:31–13:3), yet even the main thrust of what a Christian should do is also clearly revealed in Scripture. "As the Father has sent me, even so I send you" (John 20:21). We are assigned to partnership with God in his great purpose of world evangelization. As his witnesses, we have a full-time vocation of bringing all of life's activities into alignment with his purposes in the world.

But what of the specifics—vocation, marriage, education, location, healing, finances—does God have a specific purpose for each person? If he does, is it possible to know God's will in such matters and consciously follow it?

✳ Gary Friesen, in his influential book *Decision Making and the Will of God,* devotes more than four hundred pages to prove the thesis that <u>God does not have an individual will or plan for each believer.</u>

The major point is this: God does not have an ideal, detailed life-plan uniquely designed for each believer that must be discovered in order to make correct decisions. The concept of an "individual will of God" cannot be established by reason, experience, biblical example, or biblical teaching.[4]

Freedom and responsibility to make all decisions by means of godly wisdom is his thesis:

[4]Gary Friesen with J. Robin Maxson, *Decision Making and the Will of God: A Biblical Alternative to the Traditional View* (Portland: Multnomah, 1980), 145.

In those areas where the Bible gives no command or principle (nonmoral decisions), the believer is free and responsible to choose his own course of action. Any decision made within the moral will of God is acceptable to God.[5]

At the outset, let us agree that two of the major emphases of this view are true and that they are much needed correctives to popular abuses of the traditional view.

The first important corrective is the recognition that most of the teaching about guidance in Scripture is concerned with moral guidance.

A second important contention of Friesen is that there are many abuses of the traditional concept of guidance. So true is this contention that we will deal with the more common of these abuses in some detail. But a swing of the pendulum to the opposite extreme is not the only corrective. We need not replace dogmatic subjectivism with objective rationalism, though it is, indeed, much easier to go to a consistent extreme than to stay at the center of biblical tension.

I speak of the abuses as "popular" because I have not been able to discover a single reputable Bible scholar who advocates any of the abuses Friesen cites. The abuses are rampant and of great evil consequence in the life of the church and of individual Christians, but it is a caricature to treat them as "the traditional view."

Is Friesen alone in this position? No, not quite. A. W. Tozer, the author on themes of holiness, wrote along similar lines decades before:

Except for those things that are specifically commanded or forbidden, it is God's will that we be free to exercise our own intelligent choice. . . . In almost everything touching our common life on earth God is pleased when we are pleased. . . . God's choice for us may not be *one* but *any one* of a score of possible choices.[6]

Part of Friesen's popularity may stem from the rising tide of dissatisfaction with such rampant abuses as intuitionalism and attitudes of infallibility about knowing God's "plan" in advance, even in the minute details of daily living, not to mention the

[5]Ibid., 151-152.
[6]A. W. Tozer, "How the Lord Leads" (Harrisburg, Pa.: Christian Publications, pamphlet, n.d.).

strange ways of finding his will. But I suspect there is a deeper cause.

There has been a shift in interest from the clear commands of Scripture and the great principles of Scripture (such as God's revealed purpose for world evangelism) to an individualized goal of personal fulfillment. There is a concurrent drive for freedom, for personal autonomy in achieving that fulfillment. In a way, Friesen's effort would seem to drive this generation back to the moral law of God and obedience to the principles of Scripture, but the primary effect of his message for many is a sense of liberation from the old bondage to some difficult-to-determine but absolutely binding will of God for every choice in life. This exhilarating freedom fits well with the dominant contemporary mood.

On the other hand, the responsibility is heavy; loneliness and insecurity may prove to be a high price to pay for the freedom. A sense that God doesn't really care about a decision that seems all-important to me and the realization that I am on my own and fully responsible for the outcome of each choice are heavy loads to bear. But the psychological results of either position are not conclusive for the believer. What is the *truth* on the subject? Does Scripture tell us?

I propose five lines of argument from Scripture which reinforce the traditional view that God does indeed have a plan for each of his children, a preference about many of the choices we make, and a commitment to bring about his special purpose in each life.

THE CASE FOR DIVINE GUIDANCE

Divine guidance, according to the traditional view, is one of the Christian's deepest needs and highest privileges. What is the biblical evidence?

The general tenor of Scripture, both Old and New Testaments, would lead even the casual observer to believe that God has an interest in the nonmoral choices of his people and that he goes to great lengths to see that his own will is carried out. What difference did it make where Israel encamped? And yet God gave both supernatural guidance through the pillar of cloud and fire and also the very natural wisdom of an expert human guide. How could it matter whom Isaac married, so long as it was one of the same faith? Yet God went to extraordinary lengths to guide Abraham's servant to a particular girl (Gen. 24). These are not isolated instances; Scripture is replete with reports of God's guidance in nonmoral matters.

Christ's life was so planned out that even inevitable events had to wait their time. Often it was said, "The time is not yet come." In other words, it made a difference what was done and when it was done. There was a plan. His very sustenance was to do the will of the Father (John 4:34); he did nothing, in fact, that was not taught him by the Father (John 5:19-20, 30; 8:28). This will of God does not refer to moral standards but to God's individual will for Jesus' own life. He was constantly guided by the Spirit (e.g., Matt. 4:1) and was sensitive to God's timing for each phase of his life as it unfolded. Was such planning only for the divine Son of God, or does he in this, as in so many other things, serve as our model, demonstrating by his responses that God put him here on purpose and that his whole life was devoted to fulfilling that purpose?

The Bible gives the unbiased observer the strong impression that the examples are chosen, not only (or even always) for their special significance in the plan of redemption, but also as windows on God's way of doing things.

Possibly the most often recorded prayer in Scripture is for guidance. It was only natural for Saul to cry out, "What shall I do, Lord?" (Acts 22:10). God responded with the beginning of his revelation concerning Paul's vocational call, not with some reference to the moral laws Paul was so violently breaking.

Was this kind of experience restricted to the elite?[7] No one denies that many biblical characters, like Paul, were created and redeemed for a purpose. God had a special design, a plan, a destiny for them, and he said so, often in advance. But those who contend that this is true only for a few special people have many biblical teachings to reckon with.

God's sovereignty and man's responsibility are crucial doctrines for understanding guidance. This incomprehensible mystery helps explain why it is so difficult to settle all questions surrounding the important theme of divine guidance in human affairs. Scripture is clear that God is in charge and knows where

[7]Friesen, *Decision Making and the Will of God,* 90.

he is going, for Paul states that "according to the purpose of him who accomplishes all things according to the counsel of his will, we who first hoped in Christ have been destined and appointed to live for the praise of his glory" (Eph. 1:11).

This is no incidental or isolated teaching, nor does it carry with it any restrictions. *All* things are not only known to God but are determined by him. On the other hand, though Scripture nowhere speaks of human "free will," it is full of admonitions concerning full responsibility for the choices humans make. How may the two themes be reconciled? Not easily.

Many have sought reconciliation by siding with one aspect of the truth and neglecting the other. But whatever the solution, it has crucial implications for the question of God's plans and guidance for humans. However the two are related, the integrity of God's sovereign will on the one hand and human responsibility on the other must be maintained simultaneously.

For our own salvation we identify with God's sovereign plan through seeking him and, by the prayer of faith, ratify that plan, while simultaneously God is seeking us, revealing himself to us, ordering our circumstances, and giving us faith. In evangelism the process is repeated as we become part of God's sovereign purpose for another person. In fact, intercessory prayer concerning anything is seeking to identify with some purpose of God for a hoped-for future. Why should we suppose that guidance would be any different?

I do not pretend to solve in a paragraph what the sages of all ages have not solved in multiple volumes on the subject, but the theory that appeals most to my understanding is that God is not subject to our human dimension of time sequence. He exists outside the limitations of time and space so that it may not be accurate to speak of *fore*knowledge or *pre*ordination. Rather we should, from the viewpoint of God's time, speak of "knowledge" and "ordination." All events are in his eternal now, by this understanding, and though we legitimately speak from our own human perspective in terms of past, present, and future, in ultimate reality it is not so.

If this approach even hints at the infinite mystery involved, God's purposes are exercised in the eternal now, and he incorporates my responses in his activity. Whether or not I pray or evangelize or choose wisely is already (to use a timebound expression) a part of his divine design. On this view it would not be altogether accurate to speak of a plan, for that implies a time sequence. This view, then, would mean that when I err through ignorance or rebellion—marry an unbeliever, for example—God doesn't have to go back to the drawing board and redesign. He has a purpose for the *now,* and what I do really does make a difference to him and to what Scripture calls, in accommodation to our finite time categories, his "plan."

If this proposed solution to the dilemma approximates reality, it would not be accurate to say that God knows in advance all potential events or all possible choices and their outcomes. No event other than actuality could be called "potential" in any real sense other than from the limited (and thus artificial, "two-dimensional" as it were) human perspective. Therefore, there are no "what ifs"—what if I had taken the other path?—only the "is."

But perhaps this theory does not conform to the mysterious reality of God's inscrutable, unchanging, sovereign purpose. What then? Whatever the ultimate reality, the solution put into practical operation in all varieties of human responsibility—to believe for salvation, to pray, to evangelize—must also apply to the question of guidance. God's sovereign purpose may be hidden, but we are called on to relate responsibly to it by faith.

The fundamental responsibility of the finite human is faith, faith that God does have a will, that as we obey, he will direct our participation in that plan, and that when we err, he will even then work all things together for our good and his glory (Rom. 8:28).

Faith includes obedience to his will revealed in the Bible, humble acceptance of his accomplished will in the circumstances of life, and active participation through prayer in identifying with that part of his will yet to be unfolded in our time/space existence.

In this way, faith is in *God,* not in our own judgment about his hidden purposes. So we recognize that we are not infallible in determining what his desire is in a given instance, and that neither our error nor even our sin can thwart his eternal purposes. He will accomplish all he intends.

Perhaps the strong biblical teaching on God's sovereign

purpose is the key to understanding guidance. He knows exactly where he is going, and he is going to get there. Furthermore, we are called to participate with him in the accomplishment of his purposes.

Some say that God is interested in or has a "will" only in important matters; the insignificant matters are of no concern to him. But this can be a loose cannon on deck. While I grant that there is a legitimate and important distinction, often what appears the least significant can prove in the end to have been the most significant. How less consequential can a decision be than when and where to take a bath? Yet the whole career of the greatest human leader of all time was decided by that choice of Pharaoh's daughter. For an Eastern potentate to take a slave girl for a night (and with a good purpose in mind, yet, and in response to his wife's urging) was not considered a moral issue and would not have seemed a very significant event. But, in point of fact, Abraham's liaison with Hagar resulted in a conflict that rages four thousand years later with greater intensity than ever in the confrontation between Arabs and all others, especially the descendants of Sarah. "Little" choices have a way of becoming "big"!

In any event, biblical teaching on God's sovereignty is clear that he does have a plan for human affairs and that our primary link with that plan is prayer.

Prayer is a primary means for us to receive from God his promised wisdom, power, and all resources necessary to accomplish his purposes in the world. Why should we have such unlimited promises of answered prayer in Scripture if we are not supposed to ask God for what is often our most felt need? The request for guidance was often on the lips of God's people.

Elizabeth Elliot holds that guidance is "the single kind of help most frequently prayed for in the Bible."[8] Why did the saints of Bible times pray and expect events to turn out differently as a result, if God was indifferent to the choices they made? No, guidance also is a promise of God, as we shall see, and prayer is one of God's appointed means of securing the promise.

The role of the Holy Spirit includes, possibly above all else, the task of guidance. In the Old Testament, so intent is God on

[8]Elisabeth Elliot, *A Slow and Certain Light* (Nashville: Abingdon, 1982), 43.

revealing his will, that "surely the Sovereign Lord does nothing without revealing his plan to his servants the prophets" (Amos 3:7, NIV). How did God do it? Often we are not told how the guidance was given though sometimes we are: visions, miraculous events, ordinary events, the inner impulses of inspiration—in many and various ways (Heb. 1:1). But in the New Testament God had an entirely new way of communication—God himself takes up residence in every believer and decision making (John 14:16-26).

The Holy Spirit was given to lead us into all truth (John 16:13). Perhaps, as some say, this promise is for the apostles to write infallible Scripture, but most interpreters see a broader meaning. God within us is not a silent God. He is there to communicate, to fellowship. In other words, God does not merely send us an ancient package of general directions for a moral life; the Guide himself has taken up residence within. The mystery is Christ *in* us (Col. 1:27). And he is present on purpose. Furthermore, that purpose is fulfilled through communication, not abandoning us to our own devices with no concern about our decisions and decision making.

Part of the Holy Spirit's responsibility is to illuminate what he inspired Bible authors to write, but he has other roles as well. He gives each believer an ability to serve God in the church (1 Cor. 12:7, 31; 14:1, 39). Spiritual gifts have to do with nonmoral activity and are something he distributes "as he wills." God has a will in the matter, a different plan for each believer. What kind of work I do in the church is planned and initiated by him, not by me. It makes a difference to him whether I do what he planned. The Holy Spirit will guide the obedient, seeking believer into knowing and doing God's will in the matter of spiritual vocation and decision making.

How does one teach "in the Spirit" or preach "in the Spirit"? What sort of conscious or unconscious transaction takes place that enables me to respond to the Father, "Abba," through his Spirit witnessing with my own? Must Scripture describe the mystery as to its mechanics, explicitly stating that it is an internal activity in which one's mind is influenced by another personality? Are we not to assume that it is the impression of spiritual communication within, a mystery which parallels what we know of human communication but that is not fully explained by it? We do not have to claim infallibility for this mode of communication any more than for ordinary human communication, but lack of infallibility does not deny the validity of either.

The Bible promises guidance in all matters and instructs us to seek it. The major emphasis in Scripture in regard to guidance is on moral guidance, whether promises of guidance, exhortations to seek it, or testimonies of having found it. That is why this textbook is devoted to the subject! But many of the biblical passages could refer to nonmoral personal guidance and to moral guidance as well, and some clearly refer to personal guidance. Here is a sampling to reflect the tone of Scripture: "Who, then, is the man that fears the LORD? He will instruct him in the way chosen for him" (Ps. 25:12, NIV).

This entire psalm is a beautiful exposition of guidance, including ethical guidance, deliverance from enemies (nonmoral) and, in verse 12, personal guidance. This is almost certainly the case because the following verse speaks of prosperity and the inheritance of the author's descendants, not ethical issues.

Psalm 48 is not at all ethically oriented. The psalmist extols God for his victories in behalf of Jerusalem. He closes with a climactic exaltation of God the Guide: "For this God is our God for ever and ever; he will be our guide even to the end" (v. 14, NIV). The guidance may be corporate rather than personal, but it is clearly not moral guidance.

In Psalm 139 David expresses wonder that God knows him exhaustively (vv. 1-6) and that God is ever with him (vv. 7-12). In none of this does David speak of ethical matters, but simply of ordinary daily life. Then he says, no matter where in the universe he may go, "even there thy hand shall lead me" (v. 10). Next he gives the key biblical passage relating God's sovereign purpose to the individual's daily life:

For you created my inmost being; you knit me together in my mother's womb. I praise you because I am fearfully and wonderfully made. . . . All the days ordained for me were written in your book before one of them came to be. How precious to me are your thoughts, O God! How vast is the sum of them! Were I to count them, they would outnumber the grains of sand. (Ps. 139:13-14, 16-18, NIV)

Clearly David states that God is interested in every aspect of his life and that God ordained a plan for him even before he was born.

Perhaps the clearest exposition of personal guidance was given by the wisest of men, David's son, Solomon:

Trust in the LORD with all your heart, and do not rely on your own insight. In all your ways acknowledge him, and he will make straight your paths. (Prov. 3:5-6)

Not only were poets and kings sure of God's intent to guide: the prophets also insist on it.

Isaiah warns that people should not seek guidance from mediums and spiritists but from their God (Isa. 8:19). People would hardly consult a medium for ethical guidance! The same prophet gives a very beautiful promise of guidance to all those who meet the conditions (trust and obey) which, as usual, precede the promise: "The LORD will guide you continually" (Isa. 58:11). This is clearly general guidance since it is set in the context of many nonethical promises to those who cease wickedness and aid the oppressed.

One of the most instructive teachings concerning guidance is the beautiful analogy, common to both Testaments, of the shepherd with his sheep. The shepherd protects the sheep and provides for them, but he also guides each sheep to experience an abundant life in his daily walk (e.g., Ps. 23; John 10).

James makes a straightforward promise of wisdom to any who recognize they lack it and ask for it in faith (James 1:5-6). This wisdom, in the context, is for the very practical question of how to respond to difficult circumstances.

Perhaps the most complete New Testament word on guidance is found in the familiar words of Paul:

I appeal to you therefore, brethren, by the mercies of God, to present your bodies as a living sacrifice, holy and acceptable to God, which is your spiritual worship. Do not be conformed to this world but be transformed by the renewal of your mind, that you may prove what is good and acceptable and perfect. (Rom. 12:12)

If one yields his life to God, constantly resists the conforming influences of a sinful environment, and keeps on renewing his mind to think like God thinks, the result will be the personal experience of all the beautiful plan God has for him. This "will of God" is described as good (or beautiful), pleasing, and the perfection of all God intends for the person, or ideally suited to him.

These five lines of biblical teaching reinforce the conviction that God does have a plan for each of his children: the general tenor of Scripture as seen in the lives of biblical characters, the pervasive teaching that God has a sovereign purpose in all things, the nature of prayer, the role of the Holy Spirit, and the direct teaching of Scripture.

No matter how one views the question of divine guidance, if he is committed to the authority of Scripture he will recognize biblical and nonbiblical approaches either to "making wise choices" or to "discovering the will of God." Let us consider these principles.

PRINCIPLES FOR PLEASING GOD IN THE CHOICES OF LIFE

The Directed Life. How does one come to know God's will in matters that are not revealed? Perhaps Proverbs 3:5-6 is the clearest passage in Scripture concerning guidance. Not just anyone, but certain people will have direction. Actually, the promise here is not that God will send directions. He promises to *direct* our paths (see also Prov. 16:9). In other words, if we meet the conditions, we will indeed be doing the will of God. Guidance is *God's* responsibility!

The supreme qualification for experiencing God's direction is faith: "Trust in the LORD with all your heart, and do not rely on your own insight." This does not say that we should not use our own understanding, but that we should not "put our whole weight" on it, that we should not rely on it as people of the world do. Rather, we should rely on the Lord wholly.

The second phrase, "In all thy ways acknowledge him," is not an additional condition, but reinforces the initial condition of trust. The word translated "acknowledge" is normally translated "know" in the Old Testament. It is that profound Hebrew word which goes far beyond intellectual comprehension; it means to experience personally. When used of man's relationship to God, like a man's relationship to his wife, it encompasses a life of intimate belonging, sharing, and love. In other words, the promise of guidance is for the one who loves God and walks with him daily, maintaining a relationship of being wholly one with him in intimate, mutual possession and unqualified confidence.

This relationship is the basis for experiencing God's purpose in life. It would almost seem from this key passage that one can consistently experience God's will without necessarily having it revealed in terms of conscious understanding. But for those who do not meet the qualifications, there is no such promise.

Why is our vision blurred? Why is reality out of focus? Why is there confusion even concerning important matters like standards for Christian living? Why is there uncertainty about God's purposes in the world, doubt about his provision of resources for us to live and accomplish his purposes? Simply because we have not met the qualifications: "He who has my commandments and keeps them . . . I will love and manifest myself to him" (John 14:21). Only those who demonstrate biblical faith through obedience will have a manifestation of God in his fullness.

To trust God is not merely to yield our lives to him and believe that he will guide. Faith is not merely passive; it is active obedience, actively seeking his will. The first step, then, in knowing what God has in mind is unconditional commitment to do his will and aggressive action to find it. God does not guide the uncommitted, unconcerned, or uninformed. In other words, as in all our relationships with God, attitude is paramount. And in this case, if the attitude is right, the promise is more than an assurance that correct instructions are on the way. If that were all, I might be stupid and misunderstand, or confused and misconstrue the directions. But if my heart is right, God will actually *direct* my life.

The promise is not merely for the "biggies" or obviously crucial decisions in life, like marriage and vocation. He deliberately specifies both the major thoroughfares ("ways") and the incidental footpaths as well, for only God knows what insignificant decision may lead on inexorably to life-determining events.

Of course, he does not normally give us a marked road map

for the long trip; usually he leads step by step, giving just enough light to see the next step. This arrangement keeps us dependent on the Guide so that ours is the walk of faith rather than the walk of sight. Furthermore, step-by-step guidance has the benefit of leaving the future difficulty in obscurity until we have grown in wisdom and strength sufficient to handle it.

God will certainly direct us. Does this mean we are to move only when he has given a clear, personal revelation of his will? Not at all. If we are walking with God, saturating our minds in the will of God as revealed in Scripture, we may simply decide, and whatever we do will be the will of God for us. If it is not, he has assumed the responsibility to (re)direct us. Does he manipulate circumstances to force us into the right course, or does he take whatever course we choose and work it together for his purposes? I do not believe this difficult question can be authoritatively answered from Scripture. Perhaps both elements are included. Nevertheless, we can act with the certainty that God is keeping his promise to direct our paths.

But does he not also *send* directions? Since our minds constitute the major avenue of our relationship with God, can we not expect God to show his will to us so that we can understand it and make an intelligent choice of action? Apart from the question, then, of *how* he "directs our paths" (which may well remain in large part inscrutable to us) how does he "send directions"?

Receiving Directions: Understanding the Will of God

Scripture. The first step is actively to seek to understand the will of God through Scripture. The biblical "way of wisdom" is synonymous with moral uprightness, alignment with the revealed moral Law of God. And that wisdom is found in the Word of God, the first and *most* important part of divine guidance. But divine wisdom through Scripture is not only through the direct commandments. The principles of Scripture concerning life and what God is up to in the world are even more wide-ranging in their implications for guidance in godly wisdom.

Prayer. The second principle is to actively seek God's will in prayer. "If any of you lacks wisdom, let him ask God, who gives to all men generously" (James 1:5). To ask God for his will in any choice (wisdom) does not mean that we ask him once and then let it drop. The clear teaching of Scripture is that we are to keep on asking (Matt. 7:7) if we really expect to receive an answer. This is what Paul did when he sought the Lord for healing on three occasions. In this case the will of God, which was finally revealed to him, was that he should not be healed (2 Cor. 12:8-9).

Prayer is not only for wisdom to make the best decision; it is especially necessary to ask for strength to *do* God's will. Often our problem is not so much in knowing what he wants but in willingness to do it. Until we are willing, he is not likely to give further light. In any event, we could not fully understand it if he did. Christ in the Garden of Gethsemane knew the Father's will, but his great agony of prayer brought him to final subjection to the known will of God through repeated requests for God's deliverance (Matt. 26:37-44).

Most think of prayer as necessary simply to petition God to make his will known. Prayer is important in this respect, but often a more important purpose in prayer for guidance should be to gain the willingness to do God's will. Thus, prayer for guidance is focused on the following requests:

1. For *faith* that God will keep his promise and direct the affairs of my life to the full accomplishment of his purposes.

2. For strength to *obey* his will no matter what the personal cost.

3. For *wisdom* to understand scriptural teaching and the circumstances that impinge on the decision.

If there are mysteries in guidance, there are even greater mysteries in prayer and, as we have seen, the two are intimately related. Elisabeth Elliot, missionary author who has been called on to experience the mysteries of divine guidance more than most of us, speaks to this point:

> When Jesus taught his disciples to pray, he did not explain the mysteries we glimpse there—why, for example, a disciple needs to pray for the holiness of God's name or the coming of God's kingdom (is his name not holy, is his kingdom not coming unless we pray for it?), or how the prayer may affect the daily provision of bread, or the leading of God. He did not explain the whys.

He simply told them what to say. This is not the place to study all the petitions he taught them, but it is worth noting that two, "Thy will be done," and "Lead us not into temptation," concern specifically the matter we are discussing. The fact that the short prayer Jesus gave the disciples includes the matter of guidance assures us that it is an entirely proper request.[9]

The Church. A most important factor in finding God's will, and the most neglected in twentieth-century American life, is the word of the church. Especially in those decisions which involve service to the Lord, this is one of the most important elements of guidance. The idea of a solo flight in which we consider guidance to be primarily an individual matter does not seem to be wholly biblical.

The biblical way of finding the mind of the Spirit is to seek it unitedly (Acts 13:2-3; 15:22, 28; 16:10). Of course, we may not abdicate responsibility to the group because each will ultimately be held responsible for his own choices. Paul indicates clearly in his letter to the Christians in Galatia that the decision of the church council recorded in Acts 15 was obeyed by him only because he felt it was right. But even the great Apostle Paul consistently moved as God spoke to the group.

Seeking advice from individual Christians may be part of the process of "consulting the church," but it is not really the same thing and should not be given the same weight. The "voice of the church" is heard when those who are responsible unitedly pray and seek the will of God together.

Nevertheless, "with many advisors they succeed" (Prov. 15:22; see also 11:14; 12:15; 19:20; 20:5, 18; 24:6). When asking the advice of others, there are principles to follow. A spiritually mature Christian is the only one who could give reliable advice concerning spiritual matters. If advice is needed concerning technical matters, the one with the greatest expertise should be consulted, whether or not he is a Christian. Just because a person has been a Christian a long time or is famous does not necessarily mean that his advice will be sound. He should be a person with knowledge of the Word and human affairs, and of demonstrated wisdom in making sound judgments.

For an objective evaluation the counselor should not be one who is already committed on the issue being faced or one who is

[9]Elisabeth Elliot, *A Slow and Certain Light*, 44.

involved or related to the problem. Such a person can give valuable input but should not ordinarily be relied on for objectivity. Especially, we should not seek one who is considered "soft" and who might be expected to concur with us in the easy solution we may want. Some people keep "counseling around" until they find the answer they want.

After a person has studied the Scripture for principles which bear on the issue, prayed earnestly, and consulted the church (in matters appropriate for church consultation), and he still does not have a clear indication of the will of God, what next?

Reason. If it is a decision that cannot wait, make an intelligent choice and act. Act in faith. Act in the faith that God who has promised to direct will do so. "Direction" is promised whether "directions" have come through clearly or not. God will incorporate this in his purpose for us, or he will certainly deflect us into another course of action.

So, if the time has come to make a decision, grasp that God-given responsibility and make it! Don't demand supernatural manifestations, because the supernatural Person resides within. In the Old Testament when the Word of God was incomplete and the Spirit of God came only sporadically on certain people, it was appropriate to have visible, miraculous interventions when some great issue was at stake. But now Scripture is complete and the Holy Spirit is a constant companion, so that what was the extraordinary has become the ordinary daily experience of the trusting and obedient child of God.

The longer a believer has saturated his mind in the teaching of Scripture, and the longer he has intimately companioned with the Guide himself, the more trustworthy becomes his spiritual judgment. Parents must physically guide every step of the infant, but guidance gradually changes till the teenager is led more by principles instilled and counsel requested; only in emergencies does the parent intervene. So in an earlier era or to rescue an immature believer in our day from gross error in judgment, or to preserve some great purpose of his, God may coerce through a miraculous display of power or compel through unremitting circumstances. He may still "seize" a twentieth-century Lot and drag him to safety in spite of his error or rebellion (Gen. 19:16). And, of course, God may give a special experience to the most mature saint as well. But ordinarily we are responsible to make the choices of life according to our best judgment. That judgment might be called, in biblical terms, wisdom.

The human mind should not be treated as suspect in the matter of guidance. It is God's good gift for making wise judgments. I have listed this as fourth in order of importance, but in truth the use of Scripture, prayer, and evaluating input from the church are all mental activities. None of these is used apart from the others. One's mind is the arena in which all the factors come together and choices are made.

In addition to using our minds in study of Scripture, we also rely on mental judgment to evaluate our circumstances. These circumstances include what others say, especially the authorities in life and among them, especially the church. But "circumstances" also include our proven spiritual gifts and natural talents, our past experiences and present opportunities, our personalities, even our interests and preferences. Various tests, inventories, and specialists are available to help in evaluating these "circumstances," and their use, though optional, is fully compatible with a biblical approach to making choices in the will of God.

In the light of this common New Testament approach of relying on sanctified judgment, perhaps it would ordinarily be more appropriate to speak of "a good choice" or "the best option" rather than "the right way." Then if the decision proves to have been less than wise, no one is embarrassed—what did you expect from a finite sinner?—and, more important, God is not blamed. Plans made in the ordinary events of life without a clear indication of divine guidance should be made in pencil! Nevertheless, we can decide with confidence because God has promised to guide and also to "direct."

Inner Conviction. After the decision has been made in the light of scriptural teaching, prayerful contemplation, consultation with the responsible spiritual leaders, and careful consideration of the circumstances, in matters that matter to God we can count on him to give a quiet conviction that he is pleased. Some say that this inner intuition is not part of guidance.

This reasoning seems strange to me. Can we find anywhere in the Bible an explanation of how authors were inspired to write

Scripture? We are told that biblical writers were "moved by the Holy Spirit" (2 Pet. 1:21), and perhaps that is a good clue as to how the Holy Spirit works within us to accomplish his purposes. How does he activate the conscience (John 16:8-11)? Is not his call to the sinner an inner impulse? We are not told *how* God works in the believer, but we are certain from Scripture that he dwells within, comforts, quickens our conscience, and enlightens our minds concerning scriptural truth. Is it unreasonable to assume that the process is similar in the guidance he promises?

We have more evidence, however, than the strong analogy with the unexplained mystery of inspiration and the parallels with many other types of divine inner influence. Often in the Old and New Testaments God promises inner peace to those who please him (e.g., John 14:27, where peace is promised in this same passage as Holy Spirit guidance). Paul describes this on at least one occasion as his basis for decision making.

Now when I went to Troas to preach the gospel of Christ and found that the Lord had opened a door for me, I still had no peace of mind, because I did not find my brother Titus there. So I said good-by to them and went on to Macedonia. (2 Cor. 2:12-13, NIV)

Even the circumstance of God-given response was not enough to put Paul's mind at ease. He may have erred in his judgment, but he treats his own inner response without any apology as the normal, right thing to do. In many of the unexplained statements in the New Testament about the Spirit's leading there may have been just such an inner impulse, a sense of peace (or lack of it), and a settled conviction about the will of God.

Thus, one of God's methods of direct communication with a beloved companion is the divine superintendence of one's emotions. This must not operate independently of the more objective means of divine guidance; peace, or a lack of it, should not be treated as the sole or ultimate method of guidance. And it certainly should not be viewed as the infallible "voice of God," for the inner impulse is more often evidence of our own preferences than of God's will. But, consulted along with the more substantial methods of guidance, inner convictions are certainly a valid part of determining the course of action that most pleases the Lord.

Ordinarily, peace will follow when we have made the right choice. This does not mean that we will feel good about it; we may feel very bad if the choice goes against our natural desires. It does not mean that we will immediately have an overwhelming confidence about the decision. Ordinarily the conviction that we have made the right choice is a growing, settling conviction that is "confirmed by the signs which follow." That is, the circumstances themselves will ordinarily give evidence that one has made his choice in the will of God.

If assurance does not follow or if the circumstances challenge the initial decision, one must reconsider, as Paul and his team twice did when traveling through Asia Minor (Acts 16:6-10). No one is infallible at discovering the will of God; one aspect of faith is humility. Faith includes (1) honest recognition that we may have missed the best choice and (2) a quiet confidence that if we have, God will keep us unsettled in spirit until we make the best choice; or (3) that he will engineer the circumstances so as to channel us into right action.

How can one distinguish between the intimations of the Holy Spirit and one's own feelings? Since Scripture does not answer this question, I assume that it is not important to do so. When the time comes to act, simply act in faith in the light of one's understanding of the circumstances and leave the results to God.

For many of the ordinary choices of life, we simply should go ahead and do what we are disposed to do (1 Cor. 10:27). In other words, God expects us to do what we prefer on most occasions.

In summary, perhaps a personal testimonial would be appropriate. In the ordinary choices that must be made constantly throughout each day, I just "do what comes next." When the decision is obviously important for the future course of my life, of others, or of God's work, I usually pause to pray or, when others are involved, invite them to pray with me. Often in a deadlocked committee meeting, when we pause to pray, things come clear. But for the most part I simply use my judgment, trying to take into account any biblical principles that might inform the issue, make a decision, and act.

In the major decisions of life or when my circumstances become baffling in their complexity, I usually go away for several days of fasting and prayer. The primary objective is companionship with God, and the time has never failed to prove an unforgettable experience. I can vividly recall those mountain top experiences, even decades later. But the time is also very practical, not merely some ineffable mystical experience. I read extensively in Scripture, prayerfully meditating on its implications for me, and affirming my eagerness to obey. All the while I am evaluating the circumstances of my life, including a fresh look at strengths and weaknesses, past failures and successes, future hopes and dreams, opportunities and limitations. I write out my "stream of consciousness," my judgment concerning each aspect of my circumstances and how they fit together or fail to fit, especially with what God is saying in his Book. Gradually, things begin to come together, a light begins to suffuse the dimness and confusion of my thinking, and a clear judgment concerning the next step begins to emerge. Finally I am able to step out with a sense of confidence that God has done it again. He is indeed opening the way before me and will keep his promise to direct me in the way that pleases him.

DANGERS TO AVOID

Intuitionalism. We saw from Scripture that the inner superintendence of our thoughts and emotions is part of God's provision in guiding us to right decisions. The difficulty is in distinguishing between the impulse of the Spirit and the response of our emotions, which may reflect conscious preferences, fatigue, illness, or any number of other influences. One's inner impulse is not of itself a valid basis for decision making.

As G. Allen Fleece, former president of Columbia Bible College and Seminary, once said, "Even gamblers have hunches. When you come to me and say, 'I feel led . . . ,' I respond, 'So does that gambler.'" A friend of mine associated with the Brethren Assemblies, where visiting elders are often asked to speak, reports that an assembly in Daytona Beach, Florida, received eighteen letters from brethren in the frigid north indicating that "the Lord has given me a message for you," all for the same Sunday in the month of February!

A young man who had come to faith in Christ after leaving his wife and child came to me for counsel. He had stopped attending church because the Lord gave him all the wisdom he needed through the Holy Spirit and fellowship with a friend. He took up with a non-Christian girl, and, after living with her for some time, asked the Lord what his will was. He learned through prophecy that he was to stay with her, that they were to be life partners. The girl got pregnant but so far had not accepted his invitation to "believe in Jesus." Living in direct violation of several clear biblical directives, he "knew" God's will with no church, no Bible, not much prayer—just "revelation."

Another young man came to me about the second most common problem of guidance among young adults: marriage. He was the most disciplined ex-Marine I have known, always making the tough decisions—like his decision never to buy clothes, a watch, or any other "unnecessaries"; not to give to his parents when they desperately needed it because he was led to give it to a mission project; not to go home for their rare family reunion because of guidance to do some Christian outreach. Over a period of thirteen years he had come to the point of marriage with a succession of seven girls, only to break up because he "had no peace about it." His problem: he had become interested again in one of the seven. Should he ask her to marry him? He consistently violated the plain teaching of Scripture and his own promises all because of subjective guidance.

This subjectivism or intuitionalism is wrong. Feelings and intuition are not wrong, but it is wrong to give them ultimate authority in one's life. Subjective confirming evidence is just that—confirming, not independently decisive.

A pilot friend told me that when he is in a cloud and cannot see, the worst thing is for him to trust his own instincts. He can be flying in a vertical bank and feel like he is flying level. It is absolutely essential that he trust his instruments and fly by them alone although he may feel very uncomfortable about it. So in the dark, uncertain times of life we must rely on our instrument, the Word of God. In the darkness and in the storm, we must not rely on our feelings or we may spin out and crash.

Rationalism. The opposite danger to total reliance (or even over-reliance) on feeling is total reliance (or over-reliance) on our own understanding. Those who reject any legitimacy to an inner impression by the Holy Spirit often insist that decisions are to be made solely on the basis of objective rational choice in the light of Scripture and the circumstances.

But to rely wholly on one's reason, even when that reason is redeemed and biblically informed, is to approach decision making with the same equipment as the morally upright unbeliever. The result will likely be more pleasing to God than if one relied wholly on his feelings, but Scripture directly forbids this approach, as we have seen.

Magic. I use "magic" to describe the view of guidance where a person moves only if there is some supernatural manifestation to indicate God's will. Certainly God does intervene supernaturally, but this is not the primary means of guidance nor should such guidance ordinarily stand without other confirmation.

Many people use Scripture itself in this way. Though few open the Bible and choose a verse at random to indicate divine revelation, some still follow this magical method, which is hardly different from reading tea leaves.

People who use the "random approach" may be diminishing in number, but many look for indications of God's will in their daily reading of Scripture. In fact, some refuse to make a major decision without "scriptural confirmation," by which they mean a verse that speaks directly to the situation about which they are praying. "You have compassed this mountain long enough" is taken as God's command to leave one's present ministry in the mountains. This "word from God" bears no relationship to the intent of the Bible author. God may occasionally accommodate human frailty and allow an immature believer to find his direction in this way, but this is not what the Bible was given for.

If there is a supernatural element of guidance in the remarkable matching of one's present circumstances and the words of a Scripture passage (unrelated to the meaning intended by the biblical author), one could claim the same intervention of God if he discovered a similar parallel in some novel or newspaper report. In other words, the miracle (if it is one) is in the unexpected and unusual circumstance, not in the fact that the Book used is holy. Its holiness is unrelated to any oracular use to which it may be put.

Other forms of remarkable events may be sought or accepted as divine in origin and a clear indication of God's will. That God works through circumstances is abundantly clear in Scripture, and an unexplainable circumstance may indeed be evidence of God's own intervention. But "fleecing"—asking God to work some specific miracle to indicate his will—may actually be testing God, as Christ told Satan when that enemy proposed a "fleece."

A young couple, each from a tragic home situation, was having an exceedingly stormy courtship. Their immaturity and emotional instability boiled over in my presence as they came for counsel as to whether they should be married. He expected unequivocal obedience even then in their semiengaged state, and she was still in love with another man with whom she had periodically cohabited. I counseled caution, but a week later they came with the announcement that God had revealed they should be married. "We asked God to show us in the Bible reasons why we should not be married by the end of the week, and if he didn't, we would know it was his will for us to be married."

There is no limit to the tests one can put to God in ingenious ways to achieve what one wants, with apparent divine approval. If God's miraculous intervention is achieved, one no longer has to assume the responsibility for the outcome of the decision.

Others assume that an "open door"—an opportunity or manifest success in the present undertaking—is a clear indication of God's will. But entering an open door takes no more discernment than an animal probing a maze. Who opened it? Where does it lead? And, most perplexing, what if there is more than one "open door"?

Divine intervention may sometimes be part of God's guidance, but one should not insist on this as the normative way for understanding the way he should take, nor assume that such an unusual event is in itself sufficient to establish God's will in the matter.

Though most circumstances are inconclusive of God's will,

some *are* conclusive. Lack of opportunity is a sure sign that a particular option is not of God, at least for now. If the girl turns you down, the boss fires you, the church doesn't issue a call, these are clear indications of whom not to marry or where not to work. Positive circumstances may indicate the will of God: a miraculous healing or deliverance from accidental death certainly indicates that God still has something in mind for you to do. But for the most part, circumstances alone, either "miraculous" or ordinary, should not *determine* a choice, though, as we have seen, they do properly figure in the choice.

Infallibility. When one believes he can consistently achieve absolute certainty in his judgment about the course of action he should take, he subjects himself to great frustrations. He is caught whether the choice proves right or wrong. If the choice proves to have been good, he will be reinforced in the arrogance of his own infallibility, and if he makes the wrong choice, he must bear the guilt of having failed God.

But God never intended his children to partake of his attribute of infallibility. Even the Apostle Paul, though so influenced by the Spirit that he could write infallible Scripture, did not claim to be infallible in the ordinary decisions of life.

A side benefit of realizing that my judgment and my decisions are fallible is not only the release from arrogance on the one hand or guilt on the other, but freedom to make corrective decisions. My father spoke to this:

God's will for me is always in the present. Not only does God guide according to my powers and limitations, but he guides me where I am now. He does not guide according to what I might be had I acted differently in the past. His will for me is a present will, in view of all that has happened in the past. Oh that we might learn this secret of turning over the past to him, and not handicapping his glorious present will for us by worse than vain regrets over past failures. Here is a man who believes he made a terrible mistake in his marriage. He is a Christian and wants only God's will, but he has no hope of any peace or victory because of that past mistake. But he *is* married, and God's perfect will for him now is in the place where he is. Just there he may find the peace that passes all understanding, whatever the problems may be. If he does not find that peace, the reason is not that past wrong decision but his present wrong attitude. God's will for me is good. . . . God has no "second best will" for me. His will in this present moment is his only will, and it is good.[10]

[10]Robert C. McQuilkin, *Good News about Guidance*, pamphlet published by Columbia Bible College, n.d., 5-6.

Trivialization. Another way to misuse the wonderful gift of guidance is to trivialize it. This can run in two directions. Every little choice in life can be exalted to a will-of-God class decision, or in the opposite direction, no choices may be considered the single will of God in the matter. We have considered the second way of trivializing God's sovereign purposes at some length, but here we should note that it does not honor God, in recognizing that he orders all things after the counsel of his will, to insist on discovering "God's one-and-only will" in every incidental choice of life.

Pastor Peter Letchford tells of a youth meeting for which the speaker failed to appear. At the end of the meeting the scheduled speaker arrived, and Peter Letchford asked him if he had missed the bus.

"No," replied the young man.

"Some other trouble?"

"No . . . you wouldn't understand. I was praying."

"What about?"

"About whether to wear a blue suit or a brown suit."

Many of God's earnest children are virtually immobilized by this terrible distortion of God's way of guidance. I wish they could all listen to Elisabeth Elliot.

"If a pagan asks you to dinner," wrote that severely disciplined saint, Paul, "and you want to go, feel free to eat whatever is set before you." Imagine! "If you want to, if you feel like going, go." That shocked me at first. An invitation to a pagan feast would be the sort of thing I would not have dreamed of accepting without praying long and earnestly. God might want me to go, all right, but not—heaven forbid—because it would be fun. He might want me to go for some exalted reason such as to "witness" to those present (which—heaven help me—would not be fun). So I would have had to inquire very carefully in order to separate my own desires from his. Paul took the whole thing very casually. It could happen any day, and, like crossing the street, it might be dangerous. But Paul was writing to Christians, and he assumes that if they went, they went with God. It was nothing to pray and fast over.[11]

To treat every choice as one which must have positive direction may have the appearance of magnifying God's role, but it actually trivializes it and is not in conformity with the instruction of Scripture nor with the behavior of any biblical character.

[11]Elisabeth Elliot, *A Slow and Certain Light*, 100.

Irresponsible Deferring to Others. It is possible to seek guidance in an attempt to avoid responsibility for my own choices. Though talented people may be tempted to rush ahead of God's revealed plan, risking the sin of presumption or even arrogant self-confidence, less confident people may be tempted to assign the responsibility of choice to others or, in unbelief, to lag behind God's advancing purposes. Unbelief will lock the treasure chest of divine guidance just as surely as disobedience.

In certain church circles during the 1960s and 1970s it became so popular to stress the role of the elders or pastor that all significant choices were made by the "shepherd." This unbiblical "lording it over the flock" may have a show of spiritual discipline, but it is actually the usurpation of authority that belongs to God alone. Though the believer may abdicate his responsibility to choose his own vocation, his place of work, even his life partner, God holds him responsible for those choices. One day he will give account for the product of his life investment (1 Cor. 3:10-15).

Privatization. The opposite abuse, fitting with the twentieth-century emphasis on personal autonomy and individualism, is the more common total privatization of decision making—my decisions are my own private business.

We have already considered the necessary role of the church and the counsel of others in decision making. At this point it might be well to add one additional principle on the corporate aspect of divine guidance. Proverbs, the book that lays greatest stress on the corporate element of decision making, strongly emphasizes the role of parents. If we neglect this aspect of guidance, we do so to our own loss in wisdom and good choices. How many tragic marriages might have been averted if this simple advice of Solomon were more often heeded! Of course, balance is needed. The adult may not abdicate personal responsibility to his father or mother.

Those are seven hazards for decision making in the will of God, each stemming primarily from emphasizing one legitimate element of guidance while neglecting others. In closing we must emphasize again one of the most precious truths of the Christian life—God does have a specific purpose for each of his children, and he has guaranteed that purpose to those whose hearts are obedient and trusting.

As I researched what the scholars and saints have said about divine guidance, the summary of one saint of a by-gone era surfaced more often than any other. George Müller is justly famed for discovering God's will consistently and most remarkably over a period of many years in his unusual ministry at the orphanage in Bristol and in his worldwide missionary involvement. Perhaps these words of his will still prove helpful.

How I Ascertain the Will of God
1. Surrender your own will. I seek at the beginning to get my heart into such a state that it has no will of its own in regard to a given matter. Nine-tenths of the trouble with people is just here. Nine-tenths of the difficulties are overcome when our hearts are ready to do the Lord's will, whatever it may be. When one is truly in this state, it is usually but a little way to the knowledge of what his will is.
2. Do not depend on feelings. Having done this, I do not leave the result to feeling or simple impression. If I do so, I make myself liable to great delusions.
3. Seek the Spirit's will through God's Word. I seek the will of the Spirit of God through, or in connection with, the Word of God. The Spirit and the Word must be combined. If I look to the Spirit alone without the Word, I lay myself open to great delusions also. If the Holy Ghost guides us at all, he will do it according to the Scriptures and never contrary to them.
4. Note providential circumstances. Next, I take into account providential circumstances. These often plainly indicate God's will in connection with his Word and Spirit
5. Pray. I ask God in prayer to reveal his will to me aright.
6. Wait. Thus, through prayer to God, the study of the Word, and reflection, I come to a deliberate judgment according to the best of my ability and knowledge, and if my mind is thus at peace, and continues so after two or three more petitions, I proceed accordingly.

In trivial matters, and in transactions involving most important issues, I have found this method always effective.

In this final chapter we have turned from the wonderful subject of God's revealed will for his children to be like him, to the mysterious and difficult subject of "fallible choices." But even though these choices are subject to error, here also we have found good news. It is possible to live at peace with those who differ from us, and it is possible to walk through life making choices confident that "this God is our God, and he will be our guide even unto death."

SUGGESTED ADDITIONAL READING

Books on the subject of personal guidance seem almost without number, and most of them offer sound biblical advice. One I have found particularly biblical, balanced, and brief: *Knowing God's Will: Biblical Principles of Guidance,* by M. Blaine Smith, foreword by Richard C. Halverson (Downers Grove, Ill.: InterVarsity, 1979).

AFTERWORD

We have attempted an impossible task—to examine all the major themes of God's revealed standards for human conduct. We proposed to examine these biblically more than philosophically, and to do so at an introductory level rather than to attempt any kind of exhaustive treatment, aiming at broad coverage of all aspects of divine revelation on ethical issues. Finally, we attempted to make authentic application of biblical teaching to our own situations today.

Though we began with the certainties of broad biblical principles, we moved on to sometimes controversial particulars and concluded with the problems of fallible choices. I have not avoided discussing controversial matters; that would not be fair to Scripture nor to the reader. But such discussions can be frustrating, especially when we discover no clear biblical resolution to a problem. Yet I have tried to be objective and not claim "thus saith the Lord" when I could not conscientiously discover such certainty in the biblical data. This is frustrating for those who want an authoritative answer to every question. On the other hand, when I see in Scripture a clear word on some controversial issue, no matter how unpopular, I must affirm it or violate my conscience. This has no doubt been frustrating for those who differ. But let me ask of them what I seek to give them, space for an unfettered conscience.

Have the implications for personal living proved overwhelming at times? For many they have. A graduate student once told me, "It is as if I entered the hospital to have a toenail removed only to discover I had a terminal malignancy." Not quite. Malignancy, yes, but not terminal! During these studies many have wept at the depth of human perversity discovered within, and the seemingly hopeless task of achieving any recognizable degree of godlike holiness. Always there is the lurking awareness that there is a "holiness without which no one will see the Lord" (Heb. 12:14). "Wretched man that I am! Who will deliver me . . . ? Thanks be to God through Jesus Christ our Lord!" (Rom. 7:24).

This text does not extend to discovering God's great resources for spiritual growth and transformation into the image of Christ. But lest we miss the way by preoccupation with God's standard for holy living, the subject of this text, let me summarize briefly God's plan for the Christian to grow toward meeting that standard.

God himself is our resource for holy living. The indwelling Holy Spirit not only companions with us personally, he provides wonderful means for growth and victory that we can see and touch and utilize—Scripture, prayer, the church.

But these resources do not work automatically. We must have a particular response to release their effectiveness in our lives. That response is not difficult to understand, not reserved for some elite, saintly minority. It is the same uncomplicated response that brings salvation—faith.

Of course, biblical faith has both positive and negative terminals. If either is unconnected, the life-giving current will not flow. Negatively, faith means unconditional yieldedness to the known will of God, and positively it means to trust him and his resources rather than our own. "Trust and obey for there's no other way" to success in the Christian life.

So the secret to living a life pleasing to a holy God is not achievement based on personal intelligence or disciplined behavior, but attitude. Of course, the attitude of faith is not passive. True faith is very active, seeking holiness with aggressive determination. But successful growth toward the goal of Christ-likeness depends on a personal relationship, and just as one must enter that saving relationship through faith, so the relationship is maintained by an attitude of biblical faith.

Let us close, then, on this high note of confidence in the One who has transformed us, who is transforming us, and who will transform us into the image of his dear Son. He is the One who will enable us to bring him honor on that Great Day when we stand before him: "Everything is uncovered and laid bare before the eyes of him to whom we must give account" (Heb. 4:13, NIV).